THE
FARMERS'
MOVEMENT
1620-1920

CARL C. TAYLOR

GREENWOOD PRESS, PUBLISHERS
WESTPORT, CONNECTICUT

PREFACE

This study, as is explained in considerable detail in Chapter 20, was started approximately thirty-five years ago and was pursued with increasing intensity between 1920 and 1931 when the author was teaching a course entitled The Farmers' Movement at North Carolina State College. All during that period, and since, opportunities have been grasped to work in many libraries, interview numerous leaders of farmers' organizations, past and present, to rummage secondhand and rare-book stores in search of fugitive literature, and to pursue contemporary studies being made in this field. The analysis presented would have been impossible without the contributions of the numerous articles, monographs and books which have appeared since this study was begun. By the great number of citations to these detailed studies in the text, the author hopes he gives adequate credit to some of the persons to whom he owes an immeasurable debt.

It is not possible to name all those—in the Library of Congress; the North Carolina, Nebraska, Kansas, Iowa, Minnesota, Wisconsin, Indiana, Arkansas, and Texas State Libraries; the Masonic Library at Fargo, North Dakota; the Crerar and City Libraries in Chicago; the St. Louis and Omaha Public Libraries—who helped me to locate fugitive literature and run down newspaper accounts which reported events transpiring in the areas where these libraries are located. The libraries just named were storehouses of pertinent information in this field.

For outstanding financial assistance the author owes long-delayed thanks to Mr. and Mrs. Leonard Elmherst, who through the solicitation of my long-time personal and professional friend, Professor Eduard C. Lindeman, made a grant of $2,000 from the Whitney Foundation which enabled me in 1932 to work intensively for about six months consolidating the ground I had covered over previous years of work. Because Mr. and Mrs. Elmherst must have felt during the last twenty years that their grant to this project was wasted, I am especially delighted to show them the research product from that grant and thank them for the only financial assistance I have had in this task.

It is impossible for me to list all those to whom I am indebted for the assistance they have given me in writing this book, although there are two persons to whom my debt is so great that I desire to mention their contributions in some detail and to confess that it is a little less than fair not to list them as joint authors of this study.

Mrs. Helen Wheeler Johnson, who copied this manuscript and read the proof of this book, and who at one time was my colleague in the Bureau of Agricultural Economics, did detailed research in many of the fields which constitute whole chapters of this book, notably the two chapters on the Nonpartisan League. She for years did detailed bibliographic work, not only in locating but in briefing volumes of the diverse information which had to be studied and analyzed in this broad field.

Mrs. Pauline Schloesser Taylor, also at one time a colleague in the Bureau of Agricultural Economics, is co-author of an unpublished bibliography and syllabus on the Farmers' Movement from 1620 to 1940. This bibliography contains hundreds of citations many of which are cited here in footnotes. Her work not only contributed directly to a great many sections of this book but uncovered sources which the author would not have studied had not her meticulous search for them and analysis of them brought them to his attention.

The author of course takes full responsibility for the use he has made of the contributions of others. Neither they nor any of the institutions or agencies with which the author was associated during the course of preparing this manuscript are in any way responsible for its contents.

To a number of professional colleagues, among them Dr. Kimball Young, editor of this series, I owe thanks for urging that I publish this segment of my study of the American Farmers' Movement, rather than waiting until I could complete and offer for publication the analysis of that movement over the last three decades.

The reader should understand that this book is not primarily a history; it is a sociological analysis of a movement. It therefore makes no attempt to cite all sources which were read in its preparation. In hundreds of cases it utilizes the much more detailed researches of other scholars, most of them historians, who have cited thousands of sources which the author has not studied. He took the products of their work as well validated and used their works as his original sources. Only in this way could any one in a lifetime cover a field so broad. This practice, it would seem, is necessary in a task the purpose of which is to run a specific conceptual thread through an elaborate and diverse body of recorded history.

CONTENTS

.1.

THERE IS AN AMERICAN

FARMERS' MOVEMENT

Those who know only about such episodes as Shays' Rebellion, the Populist party, and the Nonpartisan League wonder why otherwise conservative farmers now and then stage radical upheavals. Political scientists have made few analyses of these upheavals, and historians have, until recently, analyzed each farmers' revolt chiefly in terms of its immediate economic climate. Economists have given little attention to the economic issues involved in farmers' upheavals, and sociologists have not analyzed the common patterns of these types of behavior. Notwithstanding this fact, there have been few decades during the last three hundred years in which American farmers in one or more broad areas of the country have not felt impelled to make stern protests against the economic and social conditions under which they lived and worked. They have at times manifested their discontent in crowds and even mobs, at times in organized political parties, and at times in violent revolts. These protests have all been part of a farmers' movement which consists of more than a series of "green risings."

A movement is a type of collective behavior by means of which some large segment of a society attempts to accomplish adjustment of conditions in its economy or culture which it thinks are in maladjustment. If

· 1 ·

the society is so structured that public manifestations of discontent are forbidden, then either revolutions are staged or the maladjustments continue. In a society which permits and believes in democratically initiated change, movements are to be expected. It is the thesis of this book that the tide of American farmers' discontent has ebbed and flowed with economic conditions, and that the various farmer revolts have been only the high tides of a Farmers' Movement which is as persistent as the Labor Movement. The Labor Movement evolved out of and still revolves around the issues of wages, hours, and work conditions. The Farmers' Movement evolved out of and still revolves around the issues of prices, markets, and credits. It is as old as commercial agriculture in the United States. Like most movements, it has been composed of loose and fluctuating relationships which are not easy to analyze. Because this is so, the writer deems it necessary to present the story of a number of episodes in the American Farmers' Movement before attempting to analyze their common economic and social patterns.

The reader will not find it easy to see common patterns of social behavior in the numerous episodes to be described in the following chapters. These patterns will be discussed in some detail in Chapter 20, but it is probably well to state in the beginning that the most easily identified is a pattern of core issues which constitute the basis of all upheavals as well as the thesis of the economic, social and political philosophies sustaining the movement between episodes. Each upheaval has developed a marked farmer public and thus a chain of recurrent publics has constituted the chief social structure of the movement.

EPISODES IN THE AMERICAN FARMERS' MOVEMENT

The following is a word picture of a scene that occurred in the 1870's:

At an early hour the roads centering at Independence were thronged with wagons ladened with living freight, and the air was filled with music and with dust. From the North, South, East, and West the Grangers came, on horseback and in every conceivable style of vehicle. Several miles from the grove chosen for the celebration, at the intersection of the various roads, the organizations from different parts of the county met and formed in line. The delegation from the West consisted of two hundred and thirty wagons filled with merry-hearted youths and gray-haired veterans, of Tipton county, and seventy-five wagons brought the delegations from the North. All preliminaries being perfected, the line of march was taken up, headed by the Cicero band, seated in a wagon gaily decorated with flags, banners, and various devices. Then came the Grange Lodges, according to number. The Cicero Grange banner bore on one side the following motto: "If any party stands between us, let it die," and on the other side, "Build up and foster home industry." Bennett's Grange mottoes: "In union there is strength" and "Farmers' rights." Dixon Grange mottoes: "The voice of the people shall be heard" and "Conquer we must—our cause is just." Union Grange had but one motto: "Farmers, you are the strength of the nation." Plum Grange mottoes: "Justice, peace, and union" and "God and our country." Clay Grange motto: "The hand that holds the bread—the farmer," and also, "Who would be free must himself strike the blow." The banner of the Union Grange from Hamilton county bore the following motto: "We'll support no Congressman who supported the salary grab." The banner of the Centre Grange, from the same county, had the following inscription: "Corn must go up—monopolies must come down." The other Lodges, having but recently organized, had not yet adopted their banners, but unfurled the flag of our country as an excellent substitute.[1]

The above is the description of a Granger holiday in 1873. It could be duplicated in the Alliance days of the late eighties or in the Farmers' Union days of twenty years later.

The following description of an episode in Shays' Rebellion in 1786 might, if it were not for a few descriptive words which betray its period, be thought to be an Associated Press dispatch from Iowa or Wisconsin in 1933:

On the 29th of August, four days after the rising of the Convention—the day appointed by law for the sitting of the Court of Common Pleas and the General Sessions of the Peace of Northampton—there assembled in the town, from different parts of the county, a large mob, some of them armed with swords and muskets, and some with bludgeons, with the professed intention of stopping the

---

[1] Stephe Smith, *Grains for the grangers*, pp. 237-238. San Francisco: Union Publishing Company, 1873.

session of the Courts, and preventing the transaction of business. The newspapers ... estimated their numbers at 400 or 500, while Minot,[2] who probably was guided by the representations of the judges themselves, estimates the number to have been nearly 1,500. The mob took possession of the ground adjoining the Court House, and dispatched a messenger to the justices, and the other gentlemen of the Court who had already assembled, with the not overimpolite statement that, as the people labored under divers grievances, it was "inconvenient" that the Court should sit for the dispatch of business, until there was an opportunity for redress. The Court, of course, saw the whole drift and meaning of the message. If they had any doubts, based on the smoothness of the language used, the bludgeons and muskets displayed without, the threats of violence openly uttered, and the shrieking of fifes and the beating of drums left nothing to be understood. The answer of the justices was necessarily what the rioters would have it. No Court was held, and the mob, after holding possession of the Court House until 12 o'clock at night retired and dispersed, having conducted from first to last with less insolence and violence, and with more sobriety and good order than is commonly to be expected in such a large and promiscuous assembly, collected in so illegal a manner, and for so unwarrantable a purpose.[3]

The purpose of the mob action described above was to stop the collection of debts and taxes which to the farmers of that time were unbearable because of rapidly falling farm prices. An equally vivid word picture of another violent revolt of distressed farmers, which occurred one hundred and twenty years after Shays' Rebellion, is furnished in the following:

Toward midnight, Friday, December 6th, three hundred masked men, heavily armed, rode into the town of Hopkinsville, Ky.... There [in that town] is much and varied business, but the backbone of it is tobacco. There are possibly a dozen big warehouses and factories concerned in the handling of that staple.

The masked men had come to burn these tobacco houses—at least some part of them. They did the work thoroly, setting guard over

---

[2] George R. Minot, who wrote *The history of the insurrections, in Massachusetts, in the year 1786.*

[3] Josiah Holland, *History of western Massachusetts*, Vol. I, p. 239. Springfield, Massachusetts: Samuel Bowles and Company, 1855.

the fire company so there should be no interference. Only a windless night saved the whole town from burning. The night-riders had driven out the telephone operators to prevent calling help from the outside. They encountered some resistance. One citizen was killed, and two night-riders so sorely wounded that they have since died. Another man, an independent tobacco buyer, was severely whipt, after he had refused to obey orders to leave town and never come back to it. By way of finish the night-riders shot out windows.[4]

This farm revolt occurred in 1907, spread over the dark-fired tobacco belt, and, by imitation, into two states of the cotton belt. It was a fight of the members of a Tobacco Planters Protective Association against the middlemen in the tobacco business and against other tobacco farmers who the pool members claimed were scabbing on the cooperative.

How like the two rebellions or revolts just described were the Farmers' Holiday Association activities of 1932-1933 can be seen from the following two excerpts from newspaper accounts:

MILWAUKEE, WIS., May 18, 1933 (AP). Half of Wisconsin's national guard was mobilized Wednesday night as state authorities prepared for a finished fight against milk strike pickets.

Officials sought to bring the disorderly strike to a climax today and were bent on stamping out the outbursts of violence which authorities charge begin to assume the proportions of organized rebellion. . . .

Near Milwaukee city police and deputy sheriffs, assailed by an overwhelming number of pickets south of the city, fought it out with clubs, and police scored an impressive victory.

About 50 pickets surrounded four milk trucks being convoyed by a dozen officers in squad cars. Pickets clambered into the squad cars and officers came out with clubs swinging. Four wounded pickets were left when strikers retreated and three were taken to a hospital.

At Racine authorities disclosed Wednesday afternoon that Russell Helding had been shot and critically injured Tuesday night when strikers surrounded the home of W. H. Gifford, whose son, Allen, is president of the Progressive Dairy Co. Surgeons Wednesday took a

---

[4] Martha McCulloch-Williams, "The Night-Rider's Reason of Being," *The Independent*, Vol. LXIII, No. 3081 (December 19, 1907), pp. 1478-1488.

.38 caliber bullet from Helding's spine. Helding, a farm youth, denied he was a picket....

Gov. A. G. Schmedeman's last word to the pool, spoken Tuesday, was "surrender unconditionally."

The pool spurned the suggestion, whereupon the governor, adjutant general and sheriffs started their stern measures to suppress violence....

At Shawano, where about 130 farmers were nominal prisoners, two men were in the municipal hospital, their heads injured when they were clubbed with riot sticks.

Abraham LeFevre of Oconto, 37, was suffering from a possible skull fracture. Valentine Gonering, 55, of Green Leaf, Brown county, has numerous gashes about the scalp....[5]

DENISON, IOWA, Friday, April 28, 1933. More than a dozen officers were injured near here Friday afternoon when some 50 officers engaged in a pitched battle with more than 500 farmers as Sheriff Hugo Willy attempted to hold a foreclosure sale at the J. F. Shields farm....

Many farmers were reported to have been injured.

The battle started shortly after 1:30 P.M. The sheriff, surrounded by his officers, six of whom were state agents and the rest special deputies, had sold two cribs of corn when several truckloads of farmers rolled into the farmyard.

The farmers jumped from their trucks and rushed the officers, who were armed with clubs and axe handles. Men went down but more farmers arrived and entered the fray.

Clubs and fists thudded.

Men shouted.

The area between two large barns soon was filled with a swirling, swinging mass of men.

The battle lasted for fifteen or twenty minutes. It ended when the sheriff and his deputies retreated, climbed into their cars and returned to Denison, where the sheriff announced the sale had been postponed until 10 A.M. Saturday.

Several of the officers were taken to doctors for medical treatment, among them William Zelinski, state agent, who was cut over the eye.

By 3:15 P.M. scores of farmers had gathered in knots about the

[5] Des Moines *Register* (Iowa), May 18, 1933.

Crawford County courthouse. There were reports that an attempt would be made to rush the building.[6]

The next day after the Denison incident, martial law was declared in Crawford County, as it had been in one other county in Iowa two days before.

Not all farmers' revolts have been marked by violence. In fact, the three from which episodes have just been described are the chief ones in American history in which blood has been shed. More often, the revolts have been marked by demands for legislative action by Congress and by state legislatures; often, they have been marked by attempts at cooperative buying and selling; and a number of times, by direct political action. They are, and have been since 1870, best and most truly represented by the programs of general farmers' organizations such as the Grange, the Farmers' Alliance, the American Society of Equity, the Farmers' Union, and the Farm Bureau. Only the high tides in farmer discontent have been marked by violent revolts and rebellion; even the direct-action farmers' groups have been only the left wing of a more stable and consistent farmers' movement which over the years has attempted to make necessary adjustments to a price and market economy into which American farming has gradually entered.

General farmers' organizations have not openly participated in political party action since the days of the Populist party. They have regularly passed resolutions on issues currently before state legislatures and Congress, have made demands and backed them with pressure groups, and, a number of times, have organized nonpartisan legislative farm blocs. Equally important is the fact that they conduct discussions and debates on practically all economic, social, and political issues in their hundreds of thousands of local organizations. They discuss these same issues in their house organs. By these means, they create or at least cement opinion on the issues about which the Farmers' Movement revolves.

---

[6] Des Moines *Tribune* (Iowa), April 28, 1933. Reprinted by permission of *The Register and Tribune*.

THE ECONOMIC AND SOCIAL PATTERNS OF THE
FARMERS' MOVEMENT

Most persons who know something about the American Farmers' Movement assume that it started in the early 1870's when the Grange temporarily turned from its fraternal and educational objectives and became deeply involved in cooperative and political ventures. This would be approximately correct if a movement were to be measured and understood solely by its institutional membership structure. But such is not the case. It must first be understood by the issues out of which it arose and around which it revolves. One will not read far in the history of the Farmers' Movement before he learns that farmers' organizations joined the movement rather than originated it. Once having joined it, they quite generally became its official mouthpiece and its most specific vehicle for action. For that reason, the history of the Farmers' Movement since 1870 has to a great extent been also the history of general farmers' organizations. A mere detailed description of these organizations, however, would be far from an adequate analysis of the Farmers' Movement, even since 1870, for it always has included and still does include in its patterns of organization and behavior more than those who are constitutionally organized farmers.

The American Farmers' Movement developed, so to speak, on a two-dimensional scale. The agricultural economy involved an ever-increasing number of farmers in the issues of prices and markets, and the development of the price and market economy created additional issues in which farmers became involved. The colonial farmer engaged very little in either buying or selling. He lacked capital with which to purchase tools, implements, or livestock sufficient to make it possible to produce more than enough for his family's needs. He therefore had little to sell except naval stores, pitch and tar, which he obtained from the forest, and furs and deer hides which he obtained by trapping and hunting. Edwards records that the Plymouth colony had no plows for twelve years, and the Swedish colony in Delaware had none until 1655. Plymouth had no cattle for three years and no horses or sheep for seven years. Wheat, the first cash crop of the northern colonies, did not become an important crop until about 1640, and its first use beyond that of home consumption was in the payment of taxes.[7] This is another way of saying that much of early American agriculture was not a commercial enterprise. The same was largely true of pioneering farming as population moved westward. Prior to 1850, most American farmers, particularly those in the West, raised produce to be consumed on their farms or to be exchanged at local stores for sugar, salt, spices, and minor items of clothing. There could be no Farmers' Movement based on price and market issues until farmers were engaged in marketing in terms of prices. As we shall see later in the case of tobacco farmers, when they became commercial farmers these issues did arise, and the farmers organized to meet them.

[At first gradually, and then with increasing acceleration, agriculture was transformed from a simple, largely self-sufficient occupation into a business enterprise on a capitalistic, commercial basis.] Farmers sold an ever-increasing proportion of what they produced and purchased an ever-increasing amount of goods to carry on their agricultural production and improve their levels of living. Their markets were no longer only local stores and shops but became national and international. Middlemen— assemblers, processors, packagers, storers, transporters, salesmen, and financiers—handled the economic processes which were carried on beyond the farms, not only for the things the farmer sold, but for the things he bought. More and more government control and more taxes, especially state and federal, became necessary. As the whole economy of the nation became greater in magnitude, the system became more complex. The farmers, like others involved in this increasingly complex, capitalistic-commercial economy, were involved in new issues. Taxes, credits (and thus banking), railroad regulation, cost of manufactured goods, middle-men costs, as well as prices, became issues about which the Farmers' Movement revolved. They were all a part of a price and market economy as contrasted with the self-sufficient economy out of which farming was emerging.

A clear identification of the issues about which a movement continuously revolves and the historical-cultural origin and evolution of these issues is the necessary first step in the analysis of that movement. So long

---

[7] E. E. Edwards, "American Agriculture the First 300 Years," *Yearbook of the United States Department of Agriculture, 1940,* pp. 171-276. Washington, D. C.: Government Printing Office, 1941.

· 10 ·

as American agriculture was largely a self-sufficient family economic enterprise and was represented largely by home-owning farmers, there was little occasion for a Farmers' Movement beyond general farmer protests against quitrents in colonial days. The self-sufficient farmer theoretically had no market or price problems. His sole task was to produce his own food, clothing, and shelter year after year, go without those things which he could not produce, and, so to speak, let the outside world go by. American farmers, of course, never were fully self-sufficient. Wheat, livestock, corn, and other products were grown for sale in earliest colonial times. Tobacco was a cash crop almost from the beginning, and on the basis of its production, certain areas in Maryland and Virginia were converted into commercialized agriculture at the very beginning of their settlement. Interestingly enough, the first farmers' revolt was staged by these highly commercialized farmers.

The American Farmers' Movement originated with the awareness of farmers that they had become a part of the price and market economy. It evolved as more and more of them entered this economy and as this type of economy became more and more dominant in American rural culture. By none of its identifiable characteristics can the Farmers' Movement be recognized as prevalent in the predominantly noncommercial farming areas of the country until recent times.

The high tides in the Farmers' Movement in the United States have come during periods when farmers found themselves at comparative disadvantage in relation to prices, markets, and credits (that is, debts). If, a curve be drawn to represent the high and low tides in the Farmers' Movement, the crests of this curve will be seen to coincide quite regularly with the troughs of the farm commodity price curve. This correlation has gradually diminished, probably because the ideological pattern of the movement has become sufficiently fixed to sustain itself without the superstimulus of farm depressions.

It is doubtful that any movement would develop without a great deal of evangelism. Insofar as records are available, it appears that all stages of the Farmers' Movement have had their share of flamboyant oratory. The following illustration is selected from Alliance-Wheel days:

> The walls of prejudice are being battered down. The North and South will join hands against a common foe. The New England

farmer will grasp the hand of his sun-tanned brother of the South and West. The cry of universal brotherhood shall pierce the pine-clad hills of Maine. Its reverberations will be heard among the mountains of Vermont and New Hampshire. It shall float out upon the soft sea breezes, until encircling the Atlantic and Gulf coasts it reaches the maritime metropolis of the Lone Star State. It will rebound over the rock-ribbed hills and through the forests of Arkansas, Tennessee, Mississippi, Kentucky, and Missouri. Its welcome sound will float over the prairies of the rich and fertile states of the great Northwest, and be wafted across the continent, where ocean's proud wave kisses the shores of the Golden State. The independent manhood of the country is rising up in defense of its liberties. An army of oppressed producers are organizing for victory. They are marshalling their hosts on the hilltops of freedom. Upon their banner they have inscribed: "Liberty, Justice and Equality." A million hearts are beating in response to this sentiment, and millions of arms are ready to defend it. The march of this mighty army is already felt by the enemy, intrenched behind the fortresses of King Mammon. With flying banners and an irresistible force, they are moving, inspired with a confidence that says the victory is already won. The Wheel and Alliance stand today like a young army flushed with victory, without regret for the past, or fear for the future. Let us fondly hope that their mission may be accomplished, and peace, prosperity and happiness may be the inheritance which they bequeath to future generations.[8]

Such speeches are seldom made in the early stages of a movement because no audiences, either listening or reading, are ready for them. Quieter techniques of developing public sentiment—across-the-fence conversations, discussions in the homes of neighbors and in local meetings, most often called for other purposes—precede audience meetings. It is only after a movement is rolling that parades, grandiose claims, and propaganda come into play. These then give confidence to those in the movement and undoubtedly stimulate organization for more specific action.

Few leaders of the most militant episodes in the American Farmers' Movement seem to have been thoroughly aware of the long-time adjust-

---

[8] W. Scott Morgan, *History of the Wheel and Alliance and the impending revolution,* pp. 17-18. Hardy, Arkansas: published by the author, 1889.

ments in which their followers were involved. They often helped to clarify the issues only to the extent that they pointed out other segments of the economy and other economic groups which they believed to be in opposition to the farmers' interests. Thus they helped to create publics which have been one of the means by which movements evolve and operate. Early agrarian intellectuals such as Thomas Jefferson and John Taylor saw the issues very clearly as industrialism and merchant capitalism developed, but frontier farming was still largely self-sufficient and farmers so culturally isolated that no precise conjunction was made between their ideologies and the felt need of the great mass of farmers. By the time of Andrew Jackson, however, the financial structure of the country's total economy was sufficiently developed to make possible the arrayment of borrowing farmers against lending merchants and banking capitalists into clear-cut publics representing opposing economic interests. For the last few decades, the leaders of general farmers' organizations and agricultural cooperatives have seemed to have a fairly clear understanding of the basic issues involved. They have also had at their command powerful organizations through which to promote their demands for action.

In the chapters that follow, the reader will be interested in watching the patterns of behavior and organization which farmers have used in wrestling with these issues. He will read about crowds, even mobs, parades, propaganda pamphlets and books, crusading leaders, farm pressure groups, farmers' cooperatives, reform and antimonopoly political parties, and farmer publics. All these, with variations, and others have been techniques and tactics of some other social movements. More detailed consideration will be given to the patterns of these activities in the final chapter of this book.

THE DESIGN AND PURPOSE OF THIS BOOK

This book does not so much present a general theory of social movements as a detailed record of a movement which concerned one important segment of our population, the farmers. It is the author's considered judgment that no adequate conceptualization of social movements has yet been formulated and cannot be formulated until what may be called laboratory studies of a number of movements have been made. His purpose here is to attempt a laboratory study of the American Farmers'

Movement. The laboratory is, of course, immense, reaching in time over three hundred years. Most of the observations have had to be made through the eyes of other persons, chiefly historians, newspaper reporters and editors, and the farmers themselves. The accounts of historians have been accepted as valid interpretations of facts. Newspaper accounts have been used for descriptions and, of course, for interpretations of events currently reported. Opinions and attitudes of farmers and their leaders, however, furnished most of the raw materials out of which understanding of the movement has been gained. The historians and other intellectuals did not create and do not perpetuate the Farmers' Movement. Newspaper reporters and editors have often been parties to it and helped it to spread. Its validation, however, has been mainly what farmers and their leaders have thought, said, and done. Much of what they have said is recorded in fugitive literature, a great deal of it not available to the average reader. Therefore many quotations are presented from that literature, not merely because they are picturesque and interesting, but because they document farmer ideology and animus. This chapter is concluded with an excerpt which states the farmers' case as vividly and powerfully as any which can be found:

> The American farmer of today is altogether a different sort of a man from his ancestor of fifty or a hundred years ago. A great many men and women now living remember when farmers were largely manufacturers; that is to say, they made a great many implements for their own use. Every farmer had an assortment of tools with which he made wooden implements, as forks and rakes, handles for his hoes and plows, spokes for his wagon, and various other implements made wholly out of wood. Then the farmer produced flax and hemp and wool and cotton. These fibers were prepared upon the farm; they were spun into yarn, woven into cloth, made into garments, and worn at home. Every farm had upon it a little shop for wood and iron work, and in the dwelling were cards and looms; carpets were woven, bed-clothing of different sorts was prepared; upon every farm geese were kept, their feathers used for supplying the home demand with beds and pillows, the surplus being disposed of at the nearest market town. During the winter season wheat and flour and corn meal were carried in large wagons drawn by teams of six to eight horses a hundred or two hundred miles to market, and traded for farm supplies for the next year—groceries and dry goods.

Besides this, mechanics were scattered among the farmers. The farm wagon was in process of building a year or two; the material was found near the shop; the character of the timber to be used was stated in the contract; it had to be procured in a certain season and kept in the drying process a length of time specified, so that when the material was brought together in proper form and the wagon made, both parties to the contract knew where every stick of it came from, and how long it had been in seasoning. During winter time the neighborhood carpenter prepared sashes and blinds and doors and molding and cornices for the next season's building. When the frosts of autumn came the shoemaker repaired to the dwellings of the farmers, and there, in a corner set apart to him, he made up shoes for the family during the winter. All these things were done among the farmers, and a large part of the expense was paid with products of the farm. When winter approached the butchering season was at hand; meat for family use during the next year was prepared and preserved in the smoke house. The orchards supplied fruit for cider, for apple butter, and for preserves of different kinds, amply sufficient to supply the wants of the family during the year, with some to spare. Wheat was thrashed, a little at a time, just enough to supply the needs of the family for ready money, and not enough to make it necessary to waste one stalk of straw. Everything was saved and put to use.

One of the results of that sort of economy was that comparatively a very small amount of money was required to conduct the business of farming. A hundred dollars average probably was as much as the largest farmers of that day needed in the way of cash to meet the demands of their farm work, paying for hired help, repairs of tools, and all other incidental expenses, because so much was paid for in produce.

Coming from that time to the present, we find that everything nearly has been changed. All over the West particularly the farmer thrashes his wheat all at one time, he disposes of it all at one time, and in a great many instances the straw is wasted. He sells his hogs, and buys bacon and pork; he sells his cattle, and buys fresh beef and canned beef or corned beef, as the case may be; he sells his fruit, and buys it back in cans. If he raises flax at all, instead of putting it into yarn and making gowns for his children, as he did fifty years or more ago, he thrashes his flax, sells the seed, and burns the straw. Not more than one farmer in fifty now keeps sheep at all; he relies upon the large sheep farmer for the wool, which is put into cloth or clothing ready for his use. Instead of having clothing made up on the farm in his own house or by a neighbor woman or country tailor a mile away, he either purchases his clothing ready made at the nearest town, or he buys the cloth and has a city tailor make it up for him. Instead of making implements which he uses about the farm—forks, rakes, etc.—he goes to town to purchase even a handle for his axe or his mallet; he purchases twine and rope and all sorts of needed material made of fibers; he buys his cloth and his clothing; he buys his canned fruit and preserved fruit; he buys hams and shoulders and mess pork and mess beef; indeed, he buys nearly everything now that he produced at one time himself, and these things all cost money.

Besides all this, and what seems stranger than anything else, whereas in the earlier time the American home was a free home, unincumbered, not one case in a thousand where a home was mortgaged to secure the payment of borrowed money, and whereas but a small amount of money was then needed for actual use in conducting the business of farming, there was always enough of it among the farmers to supply the demand, now, when at least ten times as much is needed, there is little or none to be obtained, nearly half the farms are mortgaged for as much as they are worth, and interest rates are exorbitant.

As to the cause of such wonderful changes in the condition of farmers, nothing more need be said in this place than that the railroad builder, the banker, the money changer, and the manufacturer undermined the farmer. The matter will be further discussed as we proceed. The manufacturer came with his woolen mill, his carding mill, his broom factory, his rope factory, his wooden-ware factory, his cotton factory, his pork-packing establishment, his canning factory and fruit-preserving houses; the little shop on the farm has given place to the large shop in town; the wagon-maker's shop in the neighborhood has given way to the large establishment in the city where men by the thousand work and where a hundred or two hundred wagons are made in a week; the shoemaker's shop has given way to large establishments in the cities where most of the work is done by machines; the old smoke house has given way to the packing house, and the fruit cellars have been displaced by preserving factories. The farmer now is compelled to go to town for nearly everything that he wants; even a hand rake to clean up the dooryard must be purchased at the city store. And what is worse than all, if he needs a little more money than he has about him, he is compelled to go to town to borrow it; but he does not find the money there; in place of it he finds an agent who will "negotiate" a loan for him. The money is in the East, a thousand or three thousand or five thousand miles away. He pays the agent his commission, pays all the expenses of looking through the records and furnishing abstracts, pays for every postage stamp used in the transaction, and finally receives a draft for the amount of money required, minus these expenses. In this way the farmers of the country today are maintaining an army of middlemen, loan agents, bankers, and others, who are absolutely worthless for all good purposes in the community, whose services ought to be, and very easily could be, dispensed with, but who, by reason of the changed condition of things, have placed themselves between the farmer and the money owner, and in this way absorb a livelihood out of the substance of the people.

The farmer is not extravagant in his habits of life. He has in many cases provided himself with comforts, even luxuries; but the average farmer is a frugal man, trying hard to live within his means. He has no more on his table now than had his ancestor a hundred years ago. He lives plainly. The argument often used against farmers in this respect is answered sufficiently by the critics themselves; for, as soon as they have concluded an attack on that line, they at once proceed to show that the depression of agriculture not only does not come from waste and extravagance, but from overproduction. Farmers are not wasting, these people say; on the contrary, they are raising too much wheat, corn, cotton, and cattle, and that is what ails them.

In the beginning of our history nearly all the people were farmers, and they made our laws; but as the national wealth increased they gradually dropped out and became hewers of wood and drawers of water to those that own or control large aggregations of wealth. They toiled while others took the increase; they sowed, but others reaped the harvest. It is avarice that despoiled the farmer. Usury absorbed his substance. He sweat gold, and the money changers coined it. And now, when misfortunes gather about and calamity overtakes him, he appeals to those he has enriched only to learn how poor and helpless he is alone.[9]

---

[9] W. A. Peffer, *The farmers' side*, pp. 56-60, 74. New York: Appleton-Century-Crofts, Inc., 1891. Peffer was a Populist United States Senator from Kansas.

Senator Peffer was not the most powerful orator of Alliance and Populist days, but he was one of the most highly honored and probably the most influential Populist of his day. He spoke as a member of the United States Senate whose members respected him and for the farmers of the Middle West who elected him to office to represent their views.

· 2 ·

THE FARMERS'

MOVEMENT BEFORE 1790

THE MARKET SURPLUS OF COLONIAL TOBACCO

Early American colonists, like pioneer settlers in all countries and at all times, were by necessity highly self-sufficient farmers. There were literally no markets for farm products in this country, and England, following a mercantilistic policy,[1] refused to purchase products which competed with those produced by her own citizens. Tobacco was about the only colonial marketable farm crop not produced in abundance in England and was therefore readily accepted in exchange for manufactured products. It is historically significant that the first farmers' revolt arose out of the economic issues involved in the marketing of this first American cash crop.

Tobacco was planted in Virginia as early as 1610-1611, the colonists having learned its culture from the Indians. England was not at that time a large purchaser of tobacco, although she had purchased some tobacco

---

[1] To those who are not familiar with the term "mercantilistic policy," it may be explained that it is a governmental policy which dictates that home markets shall be reserved for home producers, and that a favorable balance of trade shall be maintained at all times. The American protective tariff policy is a typical mercantilistic policy.

from Spain and the West Indies. To purchase her supplies from her own colonies, however, fitted well into her mercantilistic policy and she therefore gave preference to American colonial tobacco. In 1621, Parliament enacted a law which practically prohibited the importation of foreign tobacco, colonial tobacco, of course, being excepted. Prices of American tobacco were therefore very high, Jacobstein listing them at 3 shillings per pound in 1619.[2] Naturally, high prices, plus the virtual monopoly which the colonial farmers now had in the English market, gave great stimulus to the expansion of tobacco in those sections where the soil and the climate were suited to its production. Colonial exportation, most of it from Virginia and Maryland, increased from 20,000 pounds in 1619 to 40,000 pounds in 1620, and to 1,500,000 pounds in 1639. "In Virginia," Jacobstein says, "the tobacco crop and its value were the barometer that measured the material prosperity of the colony."

Under the conditions of rapidly increasing production, prices fell precipitately from 3 shillings per pound in 1619 to 3 pence in 1628 and to 1½ pence in 1645.[3] Holmes, giving prices in terms of the United States currency, states the drop in prices as being from 54.75 cents per pound in 1618-1620 to 6.08 cents in 1639.[4] The fact that all colonial tobacco entering international trade was, by English law, forced into English ports and had to be shipped in English boats focused the issue of low farm prices for tobacco directly on England's commercial policy and especially on her monopoly of the purchase and shipment of tobacco.

There was no provision made for regular shipment, with the result that planters had to depend on the chance appearance of English boats in American ports. Buyers from these boats traveled from plantation to plantation collecting cargo, and the planters felt impelled to sell their tobacco at any price offered for fear it might spoil before another ship appeared. They, of course, knew little or nothing about foreign market

---

2 Meyer Jacobstein, "The Tobacco Industry in the United States," *Studies in history, economics and public law,* Vol. XXVI, No. 3, p. 12. New York: Columbia University, 1907. See also George Chalmers, *Political annals of the present united colonies, from their settlement to the peace of 1763,* Book I, pp. 50-51. London: printed by J. Bowen, 1780.

3 *Ibid.,* pp. 20-23.

4 George K. Holmes, "Three Centuries of Tobacco," *Yearbook of the United States Department of Agriculture, 1919,* p. 154. Washington, D. C.: Government Printing Office, 1920.

conditions and were suspicious of the buyers, who had every advantage over them. Furthermore, they were often required to take merchandise in return for their crops. Being almost constantly in need of credit, they depended upon foreign shippers and tobacco merchants for accommodations, which further compromised their position as bargainers. They felt that they were slaves of a price, market, and credit system which they had no power to influence.

In the meantime, King James I, being somewhat opposed on moral grounds to the consumption of tobacco and yet interested in obtaining as much revenue as possible, had sold a chartered monopoly in the trading of tobacco. The monopoly automatically eliminated competition in buying, and created a wide margin between what the colonial producer received and what the English consumer paid for tobacco. The Virginia Company promptly protested the action of the King; and, while the monopoly charter was shortly withdrawn, for a time it imposed a charge of as much as a shilling a pound on colonial tobacco entering English ports. It was during this period of restricted markets and falling prices that there developed the first organized American farmer protest against price and market conditions.

Prices fell so low that farmers, many of whom were producing tobacco almost to the complete exclusion of all other crops, were in dire distress. Governor Harvey of Virginia complained that merchants were buying tobacco for less than a pence per pound in 1630.[5] Farmers protested against practices of local tobacco buyers and against English shipping companies and English manufacturers. They demanded and accomplished legislative price-fixing and acreage control, and at times practiced violence in the destruction of growing fields of tobacco. Tobacco producers organized clubs, attempted to organize collective bargaining groups, and tried to curtail production by voluntary agreement among themselves.

Production, however, continued to increase, reaching 18,157,000 pounds in 1688. Prices fluctuated with varying crop conditions, with foreign wars, and with changing English import and excise taxes, all of which were beyond the control of the producers. Price fluctuations on the whole tended downward, again reaching 1 pence a pound in English money

[5] W. Noel Sainsbury, ed., *Calendar of state papers, colonial series, 1574-1660* (America and West Indies). London: Longman, Green, Longman, and Roberts, 1860.

in 1665 and remaining around that figure for a number of years. A large amount of tobacco was diverted from the English market by being smuggled into Dutch and Spanish boats. Yet continually increasing production, which was said in 1677 to be in Virginia as large as the total of three normal years and in Maryland the largest "that ever I heard of," caused Governor Culpepper of Virginia to write British authorities that the low price of tobacco "staggered" him. Says Gray, "For several years the depression continued, leading in 1682 to plant-cutting riots in New Kent, Gloucester, and Middlesex counties, Virginia. As a result of the destruction of about 10,000 hogsheads of tobacco by the rioters, the price of tobacco was improved in 1683." [6]

These acts of violence neither solved nor ended the problems of the colonial tobacco growers. The problem of a surplus in the market continued for almost another hundred years before even a marked beginning at stabilization was accomplished. Listing the different "Attempted Solutions of the Problem," Gray names chartered fiscal monopolies from 1619 to 1638, a proposal in 1690 to organize an American monopoly under royal charter; an organization of London merchants in 1728 which dealt directly with Maryland and Virginia planters' clubs and agreed upon minimum prices; legislative price-fixing, two acts being passed in 1632, followed by two other acts the following year and still others later on; restrictions of volume of production or of export in 1639-1640, followed by a great number of like attempts between that time and 1732; and finally by attempts at standardization and improvement of marketability, begin-

---

[6] L. C. Gray, "The Market Surplus Problems of Colonial Tobacco," *Agricultural history*, Vol. II, No. 1 (January, 1928), pp. 2-4, 7-10, 13-18, 23-24, 26, 29. See also: William W. Hening, ed., *The statutes at large; being a collection of all the laws of Virginia from the first session of the legislature, in the year 1619*, Vol. I, pp. 141-142, 152, 162, 164, 188. New York: printed by R. and W. and B. Bartow, 1823. Chalmers, Book I, pp. 48-49, 51-53, 57, 67, 128. Jacobstein, pp. 14, 21-24. Sainsbury, pp. 56, 63, 65-66, 71, 73-74, 76, 84, 89, 171, 239, 250-251. Ebenezer Hazard, *Historical collections: consisting of state papers, and other authentic documents*, Vol. I, pp. 224-225. Philadelphia: printed by T. Dobson, 1792. *The case of the planters of tobacco in Virginia, as represented by themselves; signed by the President of the Council, and Speaker of the House of Burgesses*. London: printed by J. Roberts, 1733. *Maryland Gazette* (Annapolis), issues of 1729 and July 4, 1765. *Virginia Magazine of History and Biography*, Vol. III, No. 3, p. 235. Richmond, Virginia: Virginia Historical Society, January, 1896. W. Noel Sainsbury and J. W. Fortescue, eds., *Calendar of state papers, colonial series, America and West Indies, 1677-1680*, p. 568. London: Eyre and Spottiswoode, 1869. *Calvert papers*, "Fund Publication No. 28," No. 1, p. 319. Baltimore: 1889.

ning about 1690 and resulting in 1747 in uniform regulations providing for inspection at public warehouses, classing and grading of products, and the issuance of negotiable warehouse receipts.[7] During this long-drawn-out tobacco war, for war it was at times, there were further riotings of farmers and destruction of growing crops. In one instance, at least, the government of Virginia, failing to limit production by law, "was forced to buy up and burn an extra heavy crop in order that the surplus might not depress prices unduly."[8]

It is interesting to note the elements in this colonial farmers' movement which are similar to, or identical with, those of relatively recent times in the United States. First and foremost, the whole movement revolved about the price and market problems of a cash crop, upon which a large body of farmers had come to depend. Second, price-fixing and acreage reduction enforced by law were demanded by farmers and attempted by the government of Virginia. Third, farmers organized into clubs and tried to place themselves in a position to bargain collectively with merchants and buyers. Fourth, before they received governmental aid, the farmers indulged in rioting and sabotage by destroying growing crops. Fifth, the government of Virginia, in order to reduce the surplus and control the price of tobacco, destroyed large quantities of tobacco that had already been processed and prepared for market, and offered financial inducements to farmers who would plant home-consumable and soil-improvement crops. Sixth, debts were made payable in tobacco and the prices of other products were fixed in terms of tobacco. Thus tobacco became the basis of currency for a time. In 1722, attempts to relieve the tobacco farmers' economic distress went so far as to make tobacco a standard of currency in the colony of Maryland. For instance, "the clergy and all other public officials received their pay in tobacco."[9] The farmers of that day,

---

[7] *Ibid.*, pp. 2-7, 23-24. Gray has provided an elaborate, carefully documented account of the first one hundred and fifty years of the history of the tobacco enterprise, recounting in detail all the acts, both voluntary and legal, which occurred from 1620 to 1750. Holmes carries the story forward, although in less detail, to 1919 in his "Three Centuries of Tobacco." Jacobstein also gives an excellent account of the tobacco enterprise from colonial times to the turn of the present century in his "The Tobacco Industry in the United States."

[8] Katharine Coman, *The industrial history of the United States*, p. 47. Rev. ed. New York: The Macmillan Company, 1911.

[9] Joseph R. Smith, *Industrial and commercial geography*, Part I, p. 341. New York: Henry Holt and Company, Inc. 1913.

finding themselves in a price and market economy and yet not fully adjusted to it, were in considerable economic chaos and sometimes in open revolt. Some of the adjustments which they attempted were combinations of the barter of a simpler economy and the price and market techniques of the more complex economy into which they had entered.

SHAYS' REBELLION—A FARMERS' UPRISING

The relation between Shays' Rebellion and the Farmers' Movement was not in the least remote. Credits are as universal and necessary a part of commercial agriculture as are markets and prices. There was need for some money in even the most self-sufficient farming colonies, and that need expanded greatly as agricultural products entered more and more into markets. What little coined money that came into the colonies filtered into the trade centers and quickly found its way back to England to help liquidate the colonies' unfavorable balance of trade. After many trial-and-error attempts with currency makeshifts, using almost every type of commodity as money, first the English merchants and then the colonial merchants became the arbiters of money and credits. According to Nettles, "In the northern towns, the growth of merchant capitalism had produced, by 1700, the nucleus of an upper class." He adds, ". . . an especially fruitful source of income to the merchants was the loan business. An interest charge always accompanied the advance of goods on credit to farmers and country traders—a charge compounded semiannually. As the bankers of the time, the merchants also made long-term loans on real estate or short-term loans on personal security." [10]

Under the Articles of Confederation, Congress was given no control over currency and banking, such as the government of Great Britain had exercised before the Revolutionary War. Instead, each state controlled its own banking and currency. [11] Coins of various kinds were in circulation in a greater or less degree and many persons, even the states themselves, were clipping or debasing coins. [12] Inflation had been a corollary of the

---

[10] Curtis P. Nettles, *The roots of American civilization*, pp. 309-311. New York: Appleton-Century-Crofts, Inc., 1938.

[11] A. C. McLaughlin, *The Confederation and the Constitution, 1783-89*, p. 138. New York: Harper & Brothers, 1905.

[12] John B. McMaster, *A history of the people of the United States, from the Revolution to the Civil War*, Vol. I, pp. 189-193. New York: Appleton-Century-Crofts, Inc., 1883.

Revolutionary War just as it has been of all major American wars. Continental money, after the war, became worth literally nothing. Much of the specie had left the country and what remained was kept in close confinement or actually hoarded. The wholesale price index levels, which stood at 225 in 1780, had fallen to 90 by 1786.[13] Debts contracted during the period of high prices could not be paid during the period of low prices, and debtors who did not and could not pay were imprisoned for nonpayment. It is estimated that private debts in the state of Massachusetts alone amounted to about $7,000,000 at that time, and that the state was in arrears to the federal government to the amount of some $7,000,000.

There thus existed an intolerable state of affairs in Massachusetts. As Fiske says, "adding to these sums the arrears of bounties due to soldiers, and the annual cost of the state, county, and town governments, there was reached an aggregate equivalent to a tax of more than $50 on every man, woman, and child in this population of 379,000 souls. Upon every head of a family the average burden was some $200, at a time when most farmers would have thought such a sum yearly a princely income. In those days of scarcity most of them did not set eyes on so much as $50 in the course of a year." [14]. With homesteads being sold for the payment of mortgages, farm animals sold to pay lawyers' fees, and farmers themselves often cast into jail, things were as ripe for trouble in New England in 1785-1786 as they were in the midwestern states in 1932-1933.

To the farmers, the obvious need was inflation of the currency. Failing to obtain this, or its failure to help when they did obtain it, caused them

---

[13] G. F. Warren and F. A. Pearson, Wholesale prices for 213 years, 1720 to 1932, Cornell University Agr. Exp. Sta. Memoir 142, Part I, Table 1, p. 7. Ithaca, New York: November, 1932.

[14] John Fiske, The critical period of American history, 1783-1789, pp. 210-211. Boston: Houghton Mifflin Company, 1916. For an excellent account of the unfortunate plight and the grievances of the people of Massachusetts, see George R. Minot, The history of the insurrections, in Massachusetts, in the year 1786, pp. 5-23, 32-33, 55-56, 83-87, 173-174. Worcester, Massachusetts: Isaac Thomas, 1708. Noah Brooks, Henry Knox, pp. 193, 194-195. New York: G. P. Putnam's Sons, 1900. William Lincoln, History of Worcester, Massachusetts, pp. 115-116. Worcester: printed by Charles Hersey, 1862. Boston Gazette and the Country Journal, October 16, 1786. Massachusetts Centinel (Boston), October 25 and December 9, 1786; January 6, 1787. Fitch E. Oliver, ed., The diary of William Pynchon of Salem, p. 231. Boston: Houghton Mifflin Company, 1890. Andrew M. Davis, The Shays' Rebellion a political aftermath, pp. 10-12. Worcester, Massachusetts: American Antiquarian Society, 1911.

to criticize lawyers who drew the foreclosure papers and the courts which executed them. Especially did the Massachusetts farmers object to the higher courts being located in Boston in what they thought was the midst of luxury-living merchants and politicians, and being operated, as they thought, almost wholly for the benefit of creditors.[15]

It is not to be forgotten that thousands of these men now in revolt had fought in the Revolutionary War for independence, liberty, and equality. Now to be classed as criminals and outlaws because they could not pay their debts was a humiliation which they refused to suffer. To begin with, however, they expressed their protests in a perfectly legal way. They brought pressure to bear on state legislatures to create banks chartered to issue paper money, held conventions in cities where legislatures were in session, circulated petitions asking for relief by way of inflation (script or paper money), asked that debts be scaled to the basis of present land values, and suggested that as ex-soldiers they be paid for their war services rather than taxed "for raising New Soldiers." [16] Their demands

———

[15] See McMaster, Vol. I, pp. 302-303. McLaughlin, pp. 157-158. Fiske, pp. 205, 211-212, 213. Minot, pp. 29-32. Chas. F. Adams, *History of Braintree, Massachusetts* (*1639-1708*), *the north precinct of Braintree* (*1708-1792*), *and the town of Quincy* (*1792-1889*), pp. 264-265. Cambridge, Massachusetts: Riverside Press, 1891. Lincoln, pp. 116-117. Josiah Holland, Vol. I, p. 238. *Boston Gazette and the Country Journal*, March 27 and May 1, 1786; October 16 and 30, 1786; February 19, 1787. *Worcester Magazine* (Massachusetts), June, 1787, pp. 132-134. *Massachusetts Centinel*, November 18, 1786.

[16] See the letter of Joseph Hawley to Ephraim Wright written April 16, 1782, published in the *American Historical Review*, Vol. XXXVI, No. 4 (July, 1931), pp. 776-778. For accounts of such pressure in Massachusetts, see McMaster, Vol. I, pp. 304-306, 309, 311, 312. McLaughlin, pp. 158-160. Fiske, pp. 212-213. Minot, pp. 23-28, 32, 42, 44-45, 53-55, 72-73, 97-98. Adams, pp. 264-266. Lincoln, pp. 116-117, 118, 120, 121, 122. *Worcester Magazine*, November, 1786, pp. 404-405, 406-410, 412-413.

For such activities in Rhode Island, see McMaster, Vol. I, pp. 331-332, 333, 335-337, 339-340. Samuel Greene Arnold, *History of the state of Rhode Island*, Vol. II, pp. 511, 517, 519, 522-523, 524, 527. New York: Appleton-Century-Crofts, Inc., 1860. Fiske, p. 206.

For New Hampshire, see McMaster, Vol. I, pp. 341-342, 344. Jeremy Belknap, *The history of New Hampshire*, Vol. I, pp. 398-399. Dover, New Hampshire: printed by S. C. Stevens and Ela and Wadleigh, 1831.

For Vermont, see McMaster, Vol. I, pp. 348-349, 351-353. Benjamin H. Hall, *History of eastern Vermont*, p. 79. New York: Appleton-Century-Crofts, Inc., 1858. *Records of the Governor and Council of the state of Vermont*, Vol. III, pp. 362-363. Edited and published by the authority of the State by E. P. Walton, Montpelier, Vermont, 1875.

were in many ways similar to those made in the early 1890's and the early 1930's.

The debates in the various state legislatures over paper money became heated in 1785 and 1786. In Rhode Island the inflationists lost the battle in 1785, but the people of the state, with the assistance of strong newspaper support, returned a legislature the following year that voted to issue a half million dollars in script, which was loaned for the most part to farmers on farm mortgages. Fiske says that "the farmers from the inland towns were unanimous in supporting the measure"; and McMaster says, "In the course of the debate which preceded the passage of the bill it was noticed that the speakers on the affirmative were invariably from the country districts, and the debaters on the negative as invariably from the rich seaboard towns." [17]

The debtors' pleas for relief were responded to in varying degrees by the different state legislatures, Rhode Island furnishing the most outstanding example of a farmer-debtor-controlled legislature. In Vermont, the people were told by Governor Chittenden, through the medium of an address published in the *Vermont Gazette* in August, 1786, that proposed relief measures were but temporary cures, and that "if they would attend to their own business, be frugal, be diligent, practice agriculture, stop importing English linens, and set their wives to spinning, their troubles would soon end." [18] Farmers were given similar advice in the later periods of the Farmers' Alliance and Nonpartisan League.

Almost immediately various disturbances broke out in Vermont. Town meetings were held, petitions were sent to the legislature bearing the usual demands for redress of grievances, and mobs were formed. They annoyed and in some cases stopped the sitting of the courts. But most of the people of Vermont evidently felt their governor's advice to be wise. The following January when, upon the request of their legislature, they were called upon to decide by vote whether "a small bank of paper money on loans or otherwise" should be emitted, the various tender acts already in existence should be continued, and a general tender act passed, the vote was rather overwhelmingly in the negative. Nevertheless, the

---

[17] Fiske, p. 206. McMaster, Vol. I, pp. 331-332. See also John R. Bartlett, ed., *Records of the State of Rhode Island,* Vol. X (May, 1786), pp. 197-200. Providence, Rhode Island: A. C. Greene and Brothers, 1865.

[18] McMaster, Vol. I, p. 350. Fiske, p. 204.

state legislature in the early spring of 1787 did succeed in passing a law which evidently served to relieve the dire circumstances of the people of Vermont. It was an act making "meat, cattle, beef, pork, sheep, wheat, rye, and Indian corn a lawful tender, if turned out by the debtors on any execution, which must be received by the creditors at the value of their appraisal of men under oath." [19]

In Massachusetts, where the farmers complained "that their wheat and their corn were of no more use to them than so many bushels of stones," [20] money became scarcer and scarcer, and the jails were becoming filled with hundreds of honest men, among others, who could not pay their debts. Governor Bowdoin urged as a remedy "that farmers in the interior towns where there was much wood to be cleared away, should devote themselves to the production of pot and pearl ashes," and that "the ashes . . . be deposited with an agent of the State . . . be sold by him, and the money used to pay the taxes of the men who brought them." [21] Instead of following this advice, good or poor as it may have been, the farmers chose to carry on their fight through the newspapers and present their demands to the legislature. In the Massachusetts legislature of 1786 the paper-money bill was voted down, 99 to 19, and a bill providing that horses and cows be made legal tender for payment suffered the same fate. However, a most unpopular bill granting Congress "supplementary funds" was passed, the action automatically increasing the already burdensome taxes. [22] This started a rebellion which marks one of the most violent revolts of American farmers ever to have occurred.

Neither the passage of legislation in some states which stimulated inflation nor the refusal to pass such legislation in others served to quiet farmer discontent. Upon the passage of the paper-money bill in Rhode

---

[19] For a detailed account of the activities of the Vermont farmers during this period, see McMaster, Vol. I, pp. 347-355. Zadock Thompson, *History of Vermont, civil,* Part II, pp. 78-81. Burlington, Vermont: printed by Chauncey Goodrich, 1842. Hall, pp. 547-552. A. M. Caverly, *History of the town of Pittsford, Vermont,* pp. 246-261. Rutland, Vermont: Tuttle and Co., 1872. *Records of the Governor and Council of the state of Vermont,* Vol. III, Appendix F, pp. 357-380. *Worcester Magazine,* April, 1787, p. 49.

[20] McMaster, Vol. I, p. 299.

[21] *Ibid.,* p. 300. Pearl ash is crude potassium carbonate and is valuable in the manufacture of soft soap and glass.

[22] *Ibid.,* pp. 302-304.

Island, not only farm prices but all others began immediately to rise; and the farmers, unable to understand why, accused the merchants of being extortionists. An additional act was rushed through the legislature commanding everyone to accept paper money as an equivalent of gold. Because this act provided as a penalty for its violation both a fine and loss of the right of suffrage, many merchants closed their shops rather than to try to operate under such provisions. The farmers responded with a market strike. They entered into an agreement not to deliver any produce to the markets until the merchants opened their shops and began to sell their goods for paper money at its face value. This the merchants refused to do and a deadlock occurred, which in the summer of 1786 had all business "at a standstill in Newport and Providence, except in the bar-rooms." [23] A similar situation developed in the Middle West in the early 1930's during the period of the Farmers' Holiday Association.

The farmers attempted to dispose of their products at more distant towns, but were blocked by merchants in those places who knew of the conflict and sided with the local merchants. The farmers stood by their agreements, threw away their milk, burned their corn for fuel, and let their apples and vegetables rot in the orchards and fields. Violence against them was forestalled only by a court decision declaring the enforcing act of the paper-money law unconstitutional. This did not stop the aroused farmers. They forced a special session of the legislature, and four judges were replaced and a new enforcing act prepared which provided that no man could vote at election or hold any office without taking a "test oath" promising to receive paper money at par. The unwillingness of some paper-money men, however, to go to this extreme, the threat of some of the rich merchants to leave the towns, and the unwillingness of some of the farmers to see their products rot in the fields caused the new act to fail of passage. Moreover, the enforcing act was called void by the courts and repealed. Thus the Rhode Island farmers lost their strike and their attempt to obtain relief by means of enforced inflation.[24]

---

[23] Fiske, p. 207. See also McMaster, Vol. I, pp. 332-334.

[24] For a detailed account of the activities of the Rhode Island farmers during this period, see McMaster, Vol. I, pp. 330-341. Fiske, pp. 206-210. Arnold, Vol. II, pp. 511, 517-530. *Boston Gazette and the Country Journal*, October 2, 1786, March 26, 1787. *Pennsylvania Packet, and Daily Advertiser* (Philadelphia), September 23, 1786. *United States Chronicle* (Providence, Rhode Island), October 5 and 12, 1786, February 22 and March 1, 1787. Minot, p. 152.

In New Hampshire a debtor-relief law was passed which provided, "When any debtor shall tender to his creditor, in satisfaction of an execution for debt, either real or personal estate sufficient, the body of the debtor shall be exempt from imprisonment, and the debt shall carry an interest of 6 per cent; the creditor being at liberty either to receive the estate, so tendered, at a value established by three appraisers, or to keep alive the demand by taking out an alias, within one year after the return of any former execution, and levying it on any estate of the debtor which he can find."[25] Thus while the debtor could no longer be imprisoned if he offered to surrender personal or real property to his creditors, the creditors were not required to accept the property but could instead refuse to push for settlement and thereby keep the debt alive, collect interest on it at the rate of 6 per cent, and exercise their rights of execution whenever they desired. McMaster says, however, that "the benefit was all with the debtors. When an execution was about to be taken out, the farmer made haste to evade it. His good clothes and his good furniture were concealed. His cattle were driven to a neighbor's pasture. His rich lands, his house and chattels were made over to a relative, and when the sheriff came he was found to possess meadows which grew nothing but iron-weed, thistles, and mulleins, cattle too weak to stand up, hens too old to lay, a few dilapidated wagons, and a barn just ready to tumble about his ear. The result was that those to whom debts were due ceased to press for payment, and those who owed were slower than ever to pay."[26]

Despite the response to the debtors' demands for relief, violence was not forestalled in New Hampshire. Town meetings were bitter and demanding; mobs assembled, annoyed the courts and even the state legislature, and were dispelled only at the persuasion of the militia.[27] As the clamor for paper money became greater, the New Hampshire state legislature, as in Vermont, decided late in 1786 to let the people give their own opinion regarding the issuance of paper money. The returns of the

---

[25] Belknap, Vol. I, p. 397.

[26] McMaster, Vol. I, p. 343. See also Belknap, Vol. I, p. 398.

[27] For a detailed account of the farmers' activities in New Hampshire at this time, see McMaster, Vol. I, pp. 341-347. Belknap, Vol. I, pp. 395-404. *Boston Gazette and the Country Journal*, September 25 and November 13, 1786, January 22, 1787. *The Historical Magazine*, Vol. V, 2d Series, No. 1 (January, 1869), pp. 37-38. *New Jersey Journal and Political Intelligencer* (Elizabeth, N. J.), October 4, 1786.

various towns were against it, and accordingly at the next session of the legislature the question was dropped by a substantial vote in the negative.

Concerning further legislative action in Massachusetts, Minot says, "While the Supreme Executive was employed in making the necessary military arrangements for supporting the administration of justice, the House of Representatives remained in the same pacific disposition toward the insurgents. Nothing of consequence was suffered to pass them, but what was connected with the grievances of the people." [28] The *Massachusetts Centinel* of November 22, 1786, lists the title of the eighteen acts passed by the General Court (the state legislature) of Massachusetts, just adjourned, the following six having to do directly with "the grievances of the people":

> *An Act* to prevent routs, riots and tumultuous assemblies, and the civil consequences thereof.

> *An Act* providing for the more easy payment of the specie taxes, assessed previous to the year one thousand seven hundred and eighty-four.

> *An Act* for suspending the privilege of the writ of Habeas Corpus.

> *An Act* for rendering processes in law less expensive.

> *An Act* granting indemnity to sundry offenders on certain conditions, and providing for the trial of such who shall neglect or refuse to comply with said conditions, and of those who shall be guilty of like offences.

> *An Act* for suspending the laws for the collection of private debts, under certain limitations.

The same issue of this newspaper carried a letter from Worcester concerning the meeting of the legislature. It said in part:

> Yesterday our great prototype. of Legislature, the Convention, adjourned to February—they sat 100 days, and fully exemplified the old adage, of the mountain in labour. However, they finally agreed on an Address to the people—its apparent object is to quiet the

---

[28] Minot, p. 60.

minds of their constituents, and that, they, the Convention, notwithstanding the evil report of their enemies, are determined to persevere in their endeavour to obtain a redress of grievances, Etc. There were members in the Convention from Hampshire and Bristol.

Hampshire and Bristol counties were in the hotbed of the "risings," and the implication is that their representatives were anything but satisfied. Minot makes it clear that the house, as is generally the case in legislative bodies, was considerably more responsive to the demand for "redress of grievances" than the senate. It fought bitterly against the act which suspended "the privilege of the writ of Habeas Corpus." [29] McMaster says the legislature "might as well have never assembled for the malcontents were more angry than ever." [30] This is easily understandable, for while there was apparently an attempt to appease the malcontents, there were almost as many acts passed which were unfavorable as were favorable to them. The act "to prevent routs, riots and tumultuous assemblies," and the act "for suspending the privilege of the writ of Habeas Corpus" served in the minds of the aggrieved to offset the acts "providing for the more easy payment of the specie taxes," "rendering processes in law less expensive," "granting indemnity to sundry offenders," and "suspending the laws for the collection of private debts."

Acts granting relief of one kind or another were in some cases prefaced by such a statement as, "Whereas many deluded persons, from a pretense of redressing publick grievances, have forcibly interrupted the regular administration of law and justice in several counties in this commonwealth, and have committed outrages..." [31] The most important relief measure, "an act for suspending the laws for the collection of private debts, under certain limitations," after providing for the "discharge" of debts by offering "real or personal estate, or both," was diluted by the following provision: "...for want of estate sufficient to satisfy such execution, it shall and may be lawful, by virtue of the same execution, to take the body of such debtor, and him commit to the common gaol of the county, there to remain until he shall pay and satisfy the remainder of the

---

[29] *Ibid.*, pp. 54-56.

[30] McMaster, Vol. I, p. 312.

[31] Quoted from "An Act Granting Indemnity..." See *Massachusetts Centinel*, November 22, 1786.

said execution, or be discharged by the creditor, or otherwise, in due course of law." [32]

Shays' Rebellion brought the creditor-debtor problem to issue on a wide front. It was not solely a farmers' rebellion, but the distressed farmers of Massachusetts and other states undoubtedly contributed at least their full quota to Shays', Day's, Shattuck's, Parsons', and Wheeler's armies. [33] The participants in Shays' Rebellion, like the Rhode Island farmers and other debtors, tried first to obtain relief by means of legislating inflation. This failing, they adopted more direct and violent methods.

The issues which had been brewing for several months came to a head at a convention held at Hatfield, Massachusetts, on August 22, 1786. The convention began by voting itself as constitutional; and, in the process of its proceedings—after a great deal of deliberation—agreed upon and listed the sources of the people's discontent. The most typical of these were the following:

1. The existence of the Senate.

5. The existence of the Courts of common pleas and general sessions of the peace.

6. The fee table as it now stands.

7. The present mode of appropriating the impost and excise.

8. The unreasonable grants made to some of the officers of government.

9. The supplementary aid.

10. The present mode of paying the governmental securities.

11. The present mode adopted for the payment and speedy collection of the last tax.

12. The present mode of taxation as it operates unequally between the polls and estates, and between the landed and mercantile interests.

---

[32] Quoted from "An Act for Suspending the Laws ..." See *Boston Gazette and the Country Journal*, December 11, 1786.

[33] McMaster, Vol. I, pp. 309-321, 355. McMaster's account of this whole period clearly reveals that while all sorts of malcontents participated in the uprisings, the backbone of the rebellions and revolts was furnished by the farmers. He often referred to them as "the farmers and ploughboys," "the terrified ploughmen," and the like, and speaks about persuading the "Regulators," as the revolters were sometimes called, "to go back to their farms."

The newspapers of the day also indicated the large participation of farmers in the revolt. See, for example, an address written by "A Poor Farmer" in *Vermont Gazette* (Bennington, Vermont), January 31, 1786.

13. The present method of practice of the attornies at law.

14. The want of a sufficient medium of trade, to remedy the mischiefs arising from the scarcity of money.

15. The General Court sitting in the town of Boston.

16. The present embarrassments on the press.

17. The neglect of the settlement of important matters depending between the Commonwealth and Congress, relating to monies and averages.

The remainder of their memorial was presented in the form of resolutions rather than grievances. Three examples follow:

18. Voted that this convention recommend to the several towns in this county, that they instruct their representatives, to use their influence in the next General Court, to have emitted a bank of paper money, subject to a depreciation; making it a tender in all payments, equal to silver and gold; to be issued in order to call in the commonwealth's securities.

20. Voted, that it be recommended by this convention to the several towns in this county, that they petition the Governor to call the General Court immediately together, in order that the other grievances complained of, may by the Legislature, be redressed.

21. Voted, that this convention recommend it to the inhabitants of this county, that they abstain from all mobs and unlawful assemblies, until a constitutional method of redress can be obtained.[34]

A month before the Hatfield convention a paper had been circulated throughout Worcester County which bound those who signed it "to prevent, to the utmost of their power, the sitting of the Inferior Court of Common Pleas for the county, or of any other court that should attempt to take property by distress." They furthermore bound themselves "to prevent all public sale of goods seized by distress, even at the risk of their lives and fortunes, till the grievances were legally redressed." McMaster adds that "they kept this engagement most faithfully." [35] He then presents

---

[34] See the *Boston Gazette and the Country Journal,* September 11, 1786. Josiah Holland, Vol. I, pp. 237-239; Minot, pp. 34-38.

[35] Quoted from McMaster, Vol. I, p. 306, who cites the New York *Packet,* August 11, 1786.

the following description of the stoppage of the court at Worcester, Massachusetts:

On the fifth of September the court was to be holden at Worcester, and early on the morning of that day a hundred men armed with old swords and muskets, and as many more carrying sticks and bludgeons, drew up on courthouse hill. After some delay, the judge, accompanied by the sheriff and the crier, came out of the house of a Mr. Allen and started for the court. As he went on the crowd divided to let him pass; nor was any opposition made to him till he reached the steps of the courthouse. There five men with muskets, and one with a sword, were drawn up. The judge, General Artemas Ward, a noted revolutionary soldier, called on the sheriff to clear the way. But the guards instantly drew back and opposed him. Meanwhile, the crier broke through them and opened the door. The judge then advanced, but was quickly covered by the muskets of the five sentries at the door. He turned to Wheeler, who commanded the men, and demanded to know who their leader was. But he was not answered. He said that he would speak of their grievances to the proper authorities. But he was told that he must put whatever he had to say in writing. This he stoutly refused to do; yet said, if they would take away their bayonets, and let him stand on some eminence where all the people could see him, he would talk to them. This was refused; and, forgetting himself, he began to curse and to swear. "He did not give a damn," he said, for their bayonets. They might, if they liked, plunge them into his heart. Then, becoming still more angry, he stamped his foot and cried out that he would do his duty, and held his life of small consequence when opposed. Wheeler then ordered his men to put up their muskets and let him stand upon the steps. He harangued the crowd for two hours, though they constantly interrupted him with jeers, and cries of "Adjourn without day." When he had finished speaking, he went on to the United States Arms tavern, and there opened court. Next day, however, finding that the militia were taking sides with the malcontents, the court was adjourned without day. The mob then demanded this decision in writing, and he gave it.[36]

---

[36] *Ibid.*, Vol. I, pp. 306-307, from a letter which appeared in the New York *Packet*, September 18, 1786. See also *Boston Gazette and the Country Journal*, September 11 and December 11, 1786. Minot, pp. 39-40. Josiah Holland, Vol. I, pp. 241-242. Lincoln, pp. 118-121.

Similar episodes occurred in other parts of Massachusetts, New Hampshire, Vermont, and Rhode Island during 1786. Paper-money parties arose also in Virginia, Maryland, Pennsylvania, North Carolina, South Carolina, Georgia, New York, and New Jersey,[37] just as they did a century later during the "Green Back" and "Free Silver" days. Seven states passed one or another kind of paper-money laws.[38]

For almost five years the discontented farmers of New England were in open revolt against economic circumstances and even against the various state governments.[39] At the height of the revolt, in the late fall and winter of 1786, there were probably 5,000 malcontents, most of them farmers, in open rebellion in Massachusetts, assembled at various points where courts were to convene.[40] Many courts in western Massachusetts were temporarily stopped by crowds and mobs, and judges were, at times, made to promise that they would not act until grievances were redressed.[41]

---

[37] For an account of paper-money activities in these states, see McMaster, Vol. I, pp. 281-294, and Fiske, pp. 200-204. For Georgia, also see *Boston Gazette and the Country Journal*, October 9 and 23, 1786. For New Jersey, December 11, 1786.

[38] The seven states passing paper-money legislation were Rhode Island, Pennsylvania, New Jersey, New York, North Carolina, South Carolina, and Georgia.

[39] Josiah Holland, Vol. I, pp. 231-232. Holland records that the first riot occurred at Northampton as early as April, 1782, when the Supreme Judicial Court and the Court of Common Pleas were disturbed by a mob. Shays' Rebellion came to an end in February, 1787.

[40] Estimates vary considerably upon the number of men in revolt in Massachusetts. For example, the *Worcester Magazine* (April, 1787) estimated the number of insurgents from one to three thousand. McMaster and Josiah Holland agree that there were about 1,900 men in Shays', Day's, and Parsons' contingents about Springfield in January, 1787, at the height of the rebellion; while Fiske estimates the number at 2,000. Park Holland, however, who was a contemporary observer of the rebellion, writes that it was said that Shays had collected from 8,000-10,000 men, a part of whom were in the vicinity of Springfield. Secretary of War Knox, in a letter to Washington, gives us a somewhat broader view of the revolt: "The numbers of these people [in rebellion] may amount, in Massachusetts, to one-fifth part of several populous counties; and to them may be added the people of similar sentiments from the states of Rhode Island, Connecticut, and New Hampshire, so as to constitute a body of twelve or fifteen desperate and unprincipled men."

[41] See McLaughlin, p. 161. For a comprehensive account of the various mobs and riots and interferences with court proceedings, see McMaster, Vol. I, pp. 306-311, 313. Minot, pp. 38-39, 42-44, 45, 48-50, 74. Josiah Holland, Vol. I, pp. 242-243, 244, 247, 251-252. *Boston Gazette and the Country Journal*, September 4 and 11, October 2 and 9, 1786. New York *Packet*, September 28, 1786. *Pennsylvania Packet, and Daily Advertiser*, September 23, 1786. *Massachusetts Centinel*, October 28, November 15, 1786. Lincoln, pp. 122-123. *The diary of William Pynchon of Salem*, p. 249.

The outcome of Shays' Rebellion was defeat after a number of actual clashes of arms between the rebels and the militia.[42] In March, 1787, the leaders were tried and fourteen of them convicted of treason and sentenced to death. Governor Bowdoin granted them a reprieve for a few weeks, and Governor Hancock, his successor, pardoned all of them.[43] Thus ended the first formidable insurrection ever to occur in the history of the new nation. Although debtors of all kinds were among Shays' troops, it was primarily a farmers' revolt against debts, taxes, and low prices.

Park Holland, who served in Shays' company during the Revolutionary War, commanded a company of the militia against him during the rebellion, and later sat as a grand juryman at the trial of the leaders, probably presented a typical view of the revolt when he said:

> Let me observe that there are many things to be considered before we condemn the mistaken followers of Daniel Shays. Their leaders were ignorant, and many of them deceived. Moreover, our government was a new and untried ship, and we had no chart of experience for our guidance. We who had stood by the side of these men in severe battles with a powerful enemy, and witnessed their hardships and sufferings, borne without a complaint, would much rather remember the good service they rendered their country than dwell upon what historians have pronounced a blot on the nation's annals.[44]

---

[42] For a detailed account of the preparations for the encounters, and the various encounters, between the insurgents and the government forces, see the *Boston Gazette and the Country Journal,* November 27, 1786, and the issues of January and February, 1787, March 12 and April 9, 1787. New York *Packet,* February 2, 1787. *Pennsylvania Packet, and Daily Advertiser,* December 27, 1786. New York *Gazetteer, and Public Advertiser,* January 22, 1787. Providence *Gazette, and Country Journal* (Rhode Island), October 7, 1786. *United States Chronicle,* October 5, 1786; March 1, 1787. *Massachusetts Centinel,* issues of November and December, 1786; January and February, 1787. Albert B. Hart, ed., *American history, told by contemporaries,* Vol. III, pp. 188-194. New York: The Macmillan Company, 1901. Minot, pp. 47-51, 74-82, 87-95, 99-102, 106-136, 141-151. Josiah Holland, Vol. I, pp. 251-275. Lincoln, pp. 126-130. McMaster, Vol. I, pp. 315-326.

[43] For a detailed picture of the trial and terms of pardon of the insurgents, see Josiah Holland, Vol. I, pp. 284-291. *Boston Gazette and the Country Journal,* February 26, 1787, and the issues of March, April, May, June, and July 30, 1787. *Worcester Magazine,* April, 1787, pp. 37, 51; May, 1787, pp. 40, 70-72; June, 1787, pp. 166-167. New York *Gazetteer, and Public Advertiser,* April 5, 1787. Minot, pp. 136-141, 161-165, 171-172, 175, 178-192. Lincoln, p. 131.

[44] Park Holland, "Reminiscences of Shays's Rebellion," edited by H. G. Mitchell. *New England Magazine,* Vol. XXIII, No. 5 (January, 1901), p. 542.

Samuel Adams, at that time president of the Massachusetts senate, expressed quite a different view when he said:

> In monarchies the crime of treason and rebellion may admit of being pardoned or lightly punished; but the man who dares to rebel against the laws of a republic ought to suffer death.[45]

Had his opinion prevailed, the State of Massachusetts would have been compelled to execute thousands of debt-ridden farmers, and adjacent states would have had to do the same. As it was, the revolts and rebellions of that time were looked upon by many newspapers and officers of state as a not altogether unnatural protest against economic circumstances over which debtors had no control and against economic arrangements which needed to be changed. Jefferson felt that the revolt was of comparative insignificance.

George Rivers, in the preface to his novel *Captain Shays: A Populist of 1786,* written in 1896, says of the revolt:

> We have but to turn to the pages of the histories of the United States dealing with the period directly succeeding the Revolution to learn that the first troubles that confronted government were much the same as those that confront it now. From the close of the Revolution until 1787-1788 the agricultural classes, especially in New England, were in very much the same frame of mind as that in which we find the farmers of the Western States today. Their farms were heavily mortgaged; they were deeply in debt; and they had the same real and imaginary grievances that we hear about now.[46]

This whole episode was indeed a populist revolt. Its orientation was naturally the economic condition and issues of that day, but its components and whole pattern of behavior were typically those of a populist movement. Persons discussed the issues across the fences, so to speak; mass meetings were called and were addressed by the more radical exponents of the movement; articles and letters were published in both the local and urban press; candidates for office were supported on the basis of promises for relief legislation; legislatures were petitioned and visited

---

[45] Fiske, pp. 218-219.
[46] G. R. R. Rivers, *Captain Shays: a populist of 1786,* pp. v and vi. Boston: Little, Brown & Company, 1897.

by delegations; and public men were impelled to take definite stands on the issues at stake. McMaster says the newspapers "called on their readers to assert their rights, and published long tirades, the burden of which was that the governor and the representatives were public servants, and that public servants must be made to do the public will." [47] But some publications were against the revolt. Josiah Holland says the newspapers of western Massachusetts, the area in which farmer discontent was greatest, "were, without an exception, on the side of law and order although their proprietors had more cause of complaint than any of their neighbors. So great was the pressure upon them, in consequence of the duties upon paper and advertisements, that they were with great difficulty kept in existence." [48] An article printed in the *Worcester Magazine* entitled "To the Honourable General Court on the Tender Law" attempted to show that the contract theory of society, upon which our free American commonwealths were founded, was violated in the provision of the law granting relief from debts. The article quoted liberally from John Locke and was signed "Aristobulus." [49]

Judge Cushing's Charge to the Middlesex Grand Jury, Delivered at the opening of the Supreme Judicial Court at Concord, on the 9th inst. (May, 1787) was published *in toto* in the *Worcester Magazine* and was apparently prepared as much for public circulation as for delivery to the court. It was a treatise on government and the courts, but was also in essence a public utterance given wide circulation during the time when the trials of the leaders of Shays' Rebellion were in progress in Middlesex and adjacent counties. He referred to "high crimes," "treason," "rebellion," "feuds, bloodshed and devastation in every town, with such a train of evils to men, women, and children, as generations yet unborn, might have cause bitterly to lament, but not be able to get rid of." He accused debtors of "want of those essential republican virtues of frugality and economy," and said they refused to pay taxes when money was plentiful. He described relief measures passed by the legislature as "unparalleled condescension and clemency of government" and decried the fact that despite such leniency they had been to no avail. He described the leader of the rebel-

---

[47] McMaster, Vol. I, p. 342.
[48] Josiah Holland, Vol. I, p. 240.
[49] *Worcester Magazine*, April, 1787, pp. 28-30.

lion, too. He said he considered the leader as one "who, by wicked and indirect means, had raised himself to the head of an army, powerful enough to control the State." [50]

Daniel Gray, chairman of the committee writing in behalf of the revolters, argued that "The present expensive mode of collecting debts ... by the reason of the great scarcity of cash, will of necessity fill our gaols with unhappy debtors" and cried out against "The unlimited power granted to Justices of the Peace, Sheriffs, Deputy Sheriffs and Constables by the Riot Act." [51] An article appearing in the *Boston Gazette and the Country Journal* entitled "Woe unto you lawyers! For you lode men with burdens grievous to be borne" argued that lawyers, "whose only God is gain," were employed to "pervert Justice, and ruin their fellow creatures," and pleaded most earnestly, "My Christian friends and fellow Countrymen, let us resolve we will put a stop to this worse than Egyptian plague." [52] General farmers' organizations until quite recent times have specified that lawyers could not be members unless they were also farmers.

How neatly we might add a comparison of the farmer uprisings of 1932-1933. Indeed the similarity in both causes and results is striking. Let us attempt to summarize those similarities:

First was the debt situation. In both uprisings, debts, accumulated during a period of inflated currency and high prices, could not be paid when deflation of currency and falling prices came. The result was first a demand for debt adjustment by arbitration and then a demand for paper-money inflation.

Second, taxes were high in the 1780's because of the costs of the Revolutionary War and the expansion of government, especially the courts. The farmers argued that as they "never used the courts and never expected to, why should they pay taxes to support them." This general attitude toward government, plus the fact that courts were enforcing the "imprisonment for debt laws," caused them to direct their chief attack against the courts. The Farmers' Holiday Association in Iowa in 1933 made their chief legislative drive against what they called "mandatory legislation," and in one county stopped a court and manhandled a judge.

———

[50] *Ibid.*, May, 1787, pp. 106-111.
[51] *Massachusetts Centinel*, January 6, 1787.
[52] *Boston Gazette and the Country Journal*, March 27, 1786.

Third, the farmers of Rhode Island in 1786 staged a market strike, just as the farmers of Iowa and Wisconsin did in 1932 and 1933.

Fourth, farmers in 1786 pledged themselves "to prevent all public sale of goods seized by distress . . . till the grievances were legally redressed," just as farmers stopped land and chattel mortgage sales in the Middle West in 1932 and 1933.

Fifth, a recognition of the reality of causes for the grievances of the farmers in both the 1780's and 1930's caused the authorities to deal leniently with the leaders who were arrested and convicted.

Sixth, apparently there were some attempts to coerce disapproving or reticent neighbors to join the revolt in both cases. McMaster says, "scarce a week went by but the sky was reddened by burning barns or blazing hay-stacks" in 1786. It is claimed by many that some farmers of the Middle West joined the Holiday Association only because they feared vengeance on the part of their neighbors who had joined.

Seventh, a study of price curves for the periods of 1787, 1893, and 1932 reveals much by way of understanding the common causes of farmer uprisings and the necessity, from the farmers' point of view, for a persistent long-time Farmers' Movement.

Beard heads his chapter dealing with this period of Shays' Rebellion, "Populism and Reaction," and makes it quite clear that Shays' Rebellion was primarily a farmer revolt. He says:

> In that commonwealth [Massachusetts] a conservative party of merchants, shippers, and moneylenders had managed by a hard-won battle to secure in 1780 a local constitution which gave their property special defenses in the suffrage, in the composition of the Senate, and in the qualifications of officeholders administering the law. Heavy taxes were then levied to pay the revolutionary debt of the state, a large part of which had passed into the hands of speculators. And just when this burden fell on the people, private creditors in their haste to collect outstanding accounts deluged the local courts with lawsuits and foreclosures of farm mortgages.
>
> The answer to this economic pressure was a populist movement led by a former soldier of the Revolution, Daniel Shays. Inflamed by new revolutionary appeals, resurgent agrarians now proposed to scale down the state debt, strike from the constitution the special privileges enjoyed by property, issue paper money, and generally

ease the position of debtors and the laboring poor in town and country.[53]

It should again be emphasized that Shays' Rebellion was not solely a farmer upheaval. It was a debtor upheaval, and farmers, being the chief owners of the real estate and chattels and constituting the majority of the population, undoubtedly constituted the majority of the debtors. The merchants and bankers, then as now, were the chief creditors. The courts, many of them newly established, and the lawyers who prosecuted cases before the courts were despised by debtors because they seemed not only to be parasites but promoters of "iniquitous practices." Politicians who argued that industry and agriculture must both prosper if there was to be a healthy economic condition were ready with advice that farmers diversify production and be more self-sufficient, but seldom if ever offered any other suggestions for alleviating the distressing conditions. Farmers, therefore, followed the typical behavior pattern of the farmers' upheavals —first pled for equity, then political redress, and finally indulged in direct action.

A person writing under a caption "The Spirit of the Times" in the *Massachusetts Centinel,* October 25, 1786, said he had mingled with the people in the "late rising" and talked with practically every person present. He wrote:

> I inquired of an old plough-jogger the cause and aim of the people of that assembly? He said to get redress of grievances. I asked what grievances? He said we have all grievances enough, I can tell you mine; I have laboured hard all my days, and fared hard; I have been greatly abused; been obliged to do more than my part in the war; been loaded with class-rates, town-rates, province-rates, continental-rates, and all rates, lawsuits, and have been pulled and haulled by sheriffs, constables and collectors, and had my cattle sold for less than they were worth; I have been obliged to pay and nobody will pay me; I have lost a great deal by this man, and that man, and t'other man; and the great men are to get all we have; and I think it is time for us to rise and put a stop to it, and have no more courts, nor sheriffs, nor collectors, nor lawyers; I design to pay no more; and I know we have the biggest party, let them say what they will.

[53] Charles A. and Mary R. Beard, *The rise of American civilization,* Vol. I, p. 307. New York: The Macmillan Company, 1931.

· 3 ·

COMMERCIAL FARMERS
ENTER POLITICS

AGRICULTURAL-COMMERCIAL CONFLICTS IN
FOUNDING THE NATIONAL GOVERNMENT

Among the evidences that rural life has been a chief conservator of custom and tradition is the struggle farmers have made to keep from coming fully into the price and market regime which came as an inevitable concomitant of the Industrial Revolution. Between the Revolutionary War and the Civil War (or the War between the States), American farming passed from a high degree of self-sufficiency to a high degree of commercialization. During a large portion of this period, American farmers were not self-organized to meet the issues involved in that transition. They welcomed and sought opportunities to produce for the market, but they did not seem to understand that a price and market economy requires finance and credit institutions, transportation and other shipping agencies, manufacturers, middlemen, and even additional government services, and thus more taxes. They therefore protested against these and supported public men who were, so to speak, anti-industry, antibank, and anti-government regulation.

In order to trace the Farmers' Movement, which was evolving during this period, it is necessary to identify the current public issues farmers were facing. This can be done by considering the events of the period in which the farmers played a part, and by considering the convictions of the public men they supported with their votes. The framing and ratification of the Federal Constitution served to raise many of these issues, which in turn resulted in two major events, the Whiskey Rebellion and Fries' Rebellion. Both rebellions were primarily farmers' protests against federal taxes. The elections of Jefferson and Jackson to the Presidency were events in which the farmers played a large part, for these candidates were heroes of the farmers because of their anti-industrial and antibank convictions. The depression of 1819 and the panics of 1837 and 1839 roused farmers against what they thought were commercial injustices. Through all of these events it is possible to trace the thread of the evolving Farmers' Movement.

THE ADOPTION AND RATIFICATION OF THE CONSTITUTION

In 1786, the year before Shays' Rebellion, a call issued for an assembly of delegates from the various states to revise the Articles of Confederation was responded to by only five of them. However, in February, 1787, the month in which Shays' Rebellion was subdued, Congress issued a second call, and the response was almost unanimous. The convention met in Philadelphia in May and was made up of sixty-two delegates, representing twelve of the thirteen states. Although the stated purpose of the assembly was to revise the Articles of Confederation, it is interesting to note the relation of certain provisions of the resulting Constitution to the sentiments of the farmers of that time about taxes, credit, banks, courts, and federal interference in local affairs.

First, and most important, was the right of Congress to levy taxes, duties, imposts, and excises directly upon the people as individuals, a provision that was bound to be objectionable to all of the debt-ridden farmers.

Second was the establishment of a federal judiciary, with a Supreme Court, which could review all legal decisions, and a system of United States marshals and attorneys to help enforce the laws. Farmers had disliked even the state courts and local lawyers. Their reaction to the new judiciary was bound to be adverse.

Third, it provided that no state should emit bills of credit or make anything but gold and silver coin legal tender in the payment of debt. This was a direct slap at farmer-controlled legislatures that had passed paper-money laws.

Fourth, the President could, on call of state authorities, send troops to suppress domestic insurrections. The passage of this provision undoubtedly was stimulated by Shays' Rebellion.

It is thus seen that the farmers had been badly beaten, without for the most part knowing it, in the struggle which brought forth the Federal Constitution. To the localist farmers and their spokesmen it simply appeared that a highly centralized federal government with great powers had been set up and was likely to be tyrannous in its regulations of credit and taxes and in its administration of the courts.

According to Beard, "It is established upon a statistical basis that the Constitution of the United States was a product of a conflict between capitalistic and agrarian interests. The support for the adoption of the Constitution came principally from the cities and regions where commercial, financial, manufacturing, and speculative interests were concentrated and the bulk of the opposition came from farming and debtor classes, particularly those back from the seaboard." [1] He made a detailed analysis of the delegates to the Constitutional Convention and concluded that "not one member represented in his immediate personal economic interest the farming or mechanic class." [2] Beard cites Libby's analysis of the votes for ratification to the effect that those sections of states which had little money out on interest were against ratification and that these were the areas from which had come a large part of Shays' support in 1886. [3]

The Judiciary Act of 1789 provided for a Supreme Court composed of a chief justice and five associates, and a federal district court for each state with its own attorney, marshal, and a number of deputies; provided for a system of appeals for carrying cases up to the federal courts; and made it possible for the Supreme Court to declare any act of either Congress or

---

[1] Charles A. Beard, *Economic origins of Jeffersonian democracy,* pp. 464-465. New York: The Macmillan Company, 1927.

[2] Charles A. Beard, *An economic interpretation of the Constitution of the United States,* p. 149. New York: The Macmillan Company, 1936.

[3] *Ibid.,* p. 253. See also A. G. Libby, *Geographical distribution of the vote of the thirteen states on the Federal Constitution, 1887-1888.* Economic, Political Science and History Series, Vol. I, No. 1. University of Wisconsin, 1894.

a state legislature unconstitutional. Another law provided for the funding of the entire national debt, domestic and foreign, principal and interest, at face value. After one defeat, a bill was also passed providing that the national government assume, at face value, the revolutionary obligations of the states and add them to the debts carried by the general treasury. These were followed, in 1791, by the establishing of a national bank, to the stock of which the government subscribed $2,000,000. The representatives of the farmers not only fought against all of these bills while they were being passed, but continued to attack them for years after they became laws.

The most onerous and least understood of the powers exercised by the federal government were the taxing powers. It was, therefore, not surprising that some farmers revolted, just as they did in Bacon's Rebellion in 1677, and in the Regulators' insurrection in North Carolina one hundred years later.[4]

THE WHISKEY REBELLION

The first actual revolt of farmers against federal taxation was staged in western Pennsylvania over a tax on distilled spirits and one on stills. The motivation for the revolt was double-barreled, a dislike for federal taxes and a conviction that their chief farm market product was marked for discrimination. Western Pennsylvania was a fertile region, but one of the most isolated colonial settlements. Wheat, rye, corn, and other cereals grew abundantly. They were ground for human and animal consumption, but, as Carnahan says:

> Rye, corn and barley would bring no price as food for man or beast. The only way left for these people to obtain a little money to purchase salt, iron and other articles necessary in carrying on their farming operations was by distilling their grain and reducing it into a more portable form, and sending the whiskey over the mountains or down the Ohio to Kentucky, then rapidly filling up and affording a market for that article.[5]

---

[4] These and similar early uprisings were as much against inefficient and corrupt government as against taxes. They, therefore, did not so truly represent the Farmers' Movement as did the Whiskey Rebellion.

[5] James Carnahan, "The Pennsylvania Insurrection of 1794," *Proceedings of the New Jersey Historical Society,* Vol. VI (1851-1853), p. 119. See also H. H. Brackenridge, *History of the insurrection in western Pennsylvania,* pp. 18-21. Pittsburgh, Pennsyl-

Albert says:

There was a time in the early history of southwestern Pennsylvania when whiskey was the one commodity that had a standard
value and all the mediums of barter and exchange, such as corn,
salt, tobacco, etc., were valued in accordance with the amount of
whiskey they would fetch. When coin was almost unknown and
paper money valueless, as it was for some years after the close of the
Revolution, a whiskey still was as necessary as a grist mill. . . . Nearly
every fifth or sixth farm had a copper still. The farmer who had one
manufactured the whiskey for his neighbors who had none, on
shares. . . . It bought farms as now it frequently loses them; and the
consideration which passed for many a tract of land was chiefly
whiskey and whiskey stills.[6]

The federal excise tax levied on whiskey was 10 cents per gallon. In
addition, there was a tax on stills. The law was drafted by Alexander
Hamilton and was opposed at the time of its passage by representatives
of western Pennsylvania. Similar taxes had been passed by the assembly of
the Province of Pennsylvania in 1684, 1738, 1744, and 1772, but each was
repealed because of popular protest against it.[7] That the new federal government should insist on enforcing compliance seemed totally unreasonable to the farmers, whose bread and butter depended on this, their main
market product. According to the Constitution of the United States "all
duties, imposts, and excises shall be uniform throughout the United
States." This provision was not technically violated by the law of 1791,
but the application of the tax was sharply discriminatory against those
farmers whose chief and almost sole cash crop was whiskey, made from
grains which, because of the condition of roads, could not be profitably
marketed in any other form.[8]

vania: printed by W. S. Haven, 1859. William H. Egle, *An illustrated history
of the commonwealth of Pennsylvania*, p. 218. Rev. 2d ed. Philadelphia: printed by
E. M. Gardner, 1880.

[6] George D. Albert, *History of the county of Westmoreland*, pp. 171-172. Philadelphia:
1882. Quoted from *Pennsylvania agriculture and county life, 1640-1840*. Pennsylvania Historical Society.

[7] Egle, p. 218.

[8] For a good condensed account of the insurrection, see *The speech of Albert Gallatin
. . . on the important question touching the validity of the elections held in four
western counties of the state, on the 14th day of October, 1794*. Philadelphia: printed

From July 27, 1791, when the first public protest meeting was held at Redstone Old Fort, Pennsylvania, sentiment against paying the tax steadily developed.[9] It was with difficulty that anyone could be found to accept the office of inspector in the western district of the state because of the unpopularity of the tax. On August 23, a set of resolutions was passed in Washington County to the effect that "any person, who has accepted, or may accept an office under Congress, in order to carry it [the law] into effect, shall be considered inimical to the interest of the country; and it is recommended to the citizens of Washington County to treat every person who has accepted or who may accept hereafter, any such office, with contempt, and absolutely to refuse all kind of communication or intercourse with the officers, and to withhold from them all aid, support, or comfort." [10]

On September 7, delegates from the four western counties met at Pittsburgh and passed resolutions severely denouncing the law. Two days before this, Robert Johnson, collector for Allegheny and Washington counties, had been waylaid, tarred and feathered, his hair cut off, his horse taken from him, and left to find his way home. When a special deputy sent by the marshal, who did not himself dare go, attempted to serve warrants against the perpetrators of this act, he, too, was whipped, tarred and feathered, his money and horse taken, and left blindfolded, tied to a tree, for five hours.[11] Collectors throughout the western counties of Pennsylvania received like treatment.

Congress, taking cognizance of the protest in western Pennsylvania, attempted to compromise by a law passed on May 8, 1792, lightening the duty and providing for payments of the tax in monthly installments. This, however, had no effect. The revolt continued, and President Washington issued a proclamation on the fifteenth of September enjoining "all persons

---

by William W. Woodward, 1795. James Gallatin, "A Memoir on the Insurrection," *Memoirs of the Historical Society of Pennsylvania*, Vol. VI (1858), pp. 188-200.

[9] Hugh H. Brackenridge, *Incidents of the insurrection in the western parts of Pennsylvania, in the year 1794*, Vol. III, pp. 16-17, 22. Philadelphia: printed by John M'Culloch, 1795.

[10] Egle, p. 221.

[11] William Findley, *History of the insurrection, in the four western counties of Pennsylvania: in the year 1794*, pp. 58, 68-69. Philadelphia: printed by Samuel Harrison Smith, 1796. Egle, p. 221. Brackenridge, *Incidents of the insurrection*, pp. 28, 36-37. Dunlap's *American Daily Advertiser* (Philadelphia), September 30, 1791.

... to refrain and desist from all unlawful ... proceedings." [12] The federal government determined to prosecute the delinquents, seize unexcised liquor on the way to market, and make no purchase for the army except of spirits on which the duty had been paid. Each act by the central government served only to add fuel to the fire.

In April, 1793, the house of the collector in Fayette County was broken into; and when warrants were sworn out against the offenders, the sheriff refused to serve them. The collector was later compelled by a mob to surrender his commission and books and publish his resignation in the newspaper. In June, 1794, an attack was made on the home of Philip Reagan, who had rented office space to the Westmoreland County collector. Some shooting took place, but Reagan capitulated after his barn had been burned. Later, a crowd of 150 men burned the Fayette collector's house. These were the first among a great number of similar acts of violence which were to follow.

On June 5, 1794, Congress again amended the law, but since repeal was the demand of the farmers, they were only more deeply infuriated by such temporizing.[13] The revolt continued, and in July, in an exchange of shots between John Holcroft and his men and an inspector and his Negro servants, five or six insurgents were wounded, one of them mortally. The report quickly spread "that the blood of citizens had been shed, and a call was made on all who valued liberty or life to assemble at Mingo Creek meeting-house, prepared to avenge the outrage." [14] They did assemble in great numbers, organized an expedition to wait upon the inspector, General Neville, and compel him to resign his commission.

---

[12] President Washington's Proclamation said in part, "I ... most earnestly admonish and exhort all persons whom it may concern, to refrain and desist from all unlawful combinations and proceedings whatsoever, having for object or tending to obstruct the operation of the laws aforesaid. ... thereby also enjoining and requiring all persons whomsoever, as they tender the welfare of their country, the just and due authority of government and the preservation of the public peace, to be aiding and assisting therein according to law." See also John B. Linn and William H. Egle, eds., "Papers relating to what is known as the Whiskey Insurrection in Western Pennsylvania, 1794," *Pennsylvania archives*, Second Series, Vol. IV, pp. 23-29, 32-33. Harrisburg, Pennsylvania: 1876.

[13] Townsend Ward, "The Insurrection of the Year 1794, in the Western Counties of Pennsylvania," *Memoirs of the Historical Society of Pennsylvania*, Vol. VI (1858), pp. 155-156. Egle, pp. 223-224.

[14] *Pennsylvania archives*, Vol. IV, pp. 10-11, 69, 73-75. See also Brackenridge, *Incidents of the insurrection*, Vol. I, pp. 6, 10, 11, 18-21, and Appendix, pp. 131-134.

Neville's home was guarded by about a dozen United States soldiers under the direction of Major Kirkpatrick. In a clash of arms Major M'Farlane, leader of the expedition, was killed. The rebels, undaunted, set fire to the barn which soon spread to the outbuildings and then to the house. With the spread of the fire to the house, Major Kirkpatrick surrendered. The "murder of M'Farlane," as it came to be known among the insurgents, not only served to rally many others to the revolt, but enlisted some very prominent men, among them David Bradford, Colonel John Marshall, Messrs. Parkinson, Cook, and Brackenridge.

Open warfare seemed now to be in progress. By intercepting the United States mail, the insurgents spotted those who were making reports to the authorities and compelled them to leave the section or go into hiding. Brackenridge describes the general state of mind of the people in western Pennsylvania as follows:

> A breath in favour of the law, was sufficient to ruin any man. It was considered as a badge of toryism. A clergyman was not thought orthodox in the pulpit, unless against the law; a physician was not capable of administering medicine, unless his principles were right in this respect; a lawyer could have got no practice without at least concealing his sentiments, if for the law; a merchant, at a country store, could not get custom. On the contrary, to talk against the law was the way to office and emolument. . . . To go to the Assembly, you must make a noise against it; and in order to go to Congress, or to keep in it, you must contrive, by some means, to be thought staunch in this respect. It was the *shibboleth* of safety, and the ladder of ambition.[15]

The insurgents were now organized into an army, with colonels over regiments in the counties. As the conflict came to a head, some half-dozen leaders issued circular letters ordering the colonels to assemble their commands at the usual place, with full equipment of arms and ammunition and four days' supply of provisions; from there to march to Braddock's field, to be there August 1. The officers for the most part obeyed the summons, and in some instances their men heard about it and went, their

---

[15] Brackenridge, *Incidents of the insurrection*, Vol. III., p. 22. Brackenridge was one of the leaders of the insurgents after M'Farlane's death and was the one to urge an orderly march through Pittsburgh.

officers following after. ". . . as they proceeded in squads to the place of rendezvous, they carried everyone with them, willing or unwilling. . . . The number assembled on Braddock's field is variously estimated at from five to seven thousand. During the day, men were assembling, some in regiments, some in companies, some in squads of eight or ten; and as they arrived, guns were fired, drums beat, and the hills rang with shouts." [16]

Governor Mifflin, on August 6, appointed an official state commission to go into the western counties "to ascertain the facts relative to the late riots, and, if practicable, to bring the rioters to a sense of their duty." [17] On August 7, President Washington issued a proclamation of warning commanding "all persons, being Insurgents . . . on or before the first day of September next, to disperse and retire peaceably to their respective abodes." At the same time he ordered the raising of 12,950 troops from Pennsylvania, New Jersey, Maryland, and Virginia, and commanded that they "be held in readiness to march at a moment's warning." [18] Governor Mifflin on that same day issued two proclamations—one for a special session of the state legislature in order that the Pennsylvania troops might be equipped and mobilized, the other expressing the determination of the governments to bring the rioters to justice. On the eighth, Washington appointed a commission to go to the western counties of Pennsylvania "in order to quiet and extinguish" the insurrection. [19]

Because of poor communication, these acts of the state and national executives, of August 6, 7, and 8, were not known in the insurgent counties on August 14 when a meeting of 260 delegates and a much larger number of spectators from the five Pennsylvania counties and Ohio County, Virginia (now West Virginia), was held at Parkinson's Ferry. At this

---

[16] Carnahan, p. 126. See also Carnahan, pp. 125-129. Brackenridge, *Incidents of the insurrection*, pp. 79-126. "General Wilkins's Account of the Gathering on Braddock Field," *Memoirs of the Historical Society of Pennsylvania*, Vol. VI (1858), pp. 183-187.

[17] Dunlap and Claypoole's *American Daily Advertiser* (Philadelphia), August 9, 1794.

[18] *The proceedings of the executive of the United States respecting the insurgents, 1794*, pp. 6-10. Philadelphia: printed by John Fenno, 1795. See also Dunlap and Claypoole's *American Daily Advertiser*, August 9, 1794. *Pennsylvania archives*, pp. 122-127.

[19] Dunlap and Claypoole's *American Daily Advertiser*, August 8 and 9, 1794. *American state papers*, Class X, Miscellaneous, Vol. I, pp. 86-87. Washington, D. C.: Gales and Seaton, 1834.

meeting, to which some of the cooler heads had gone to advise restraint, a committee of sixty, often referred to as the committee of safety and composed of two from each township, was appointed. This committee in turn appointed from its members a standing committee of twelve. The standing committee was delegated to meet with the commissioners of the United States, whose arrival at Pittsburgh had been announced during the meeting. On the twentieth, the state and the federal commissioners and the standing committee of the insurgents met at Pittsburgh, where they held a conference that lasted for a number of days. In describing the conference, Egle says:

> The committee presented their grievances, dwelling principally ...on their being sued in the courts of the United States, and compelled to attend trials at the distance of three hundred miles from their places of abode, before judges and jurors who were strangers to them. Every argument against an excise was urged, but it was clearly evidenced that there was an apprehension in the gentlemen of the committee themselves respecting the safety of their own persons and property, if they should even recommend what they conceived best for the people in the deplorable situation to which they had brought themselves.[20]

The state and federal commissioners had made it clear that prosecutions would be suspended and pardon granted only provided "full and satisfactory assurances of a sincere determination in the people to obey the laws of the United States" was given in a referendum.[21]

The standing committee of twelve reported to the committee of sixty at a meeting on the twenty-eighth, and after a heated two-day debate, a ballot was taken. Egle describes the balloting thus:

> No one would vote by standing up. None would write a yea or nay, lest his handwriting should be recognized. At last it was determined that yea and nay should be written by the secretary on the same

---

[20] Egle, p. 228. For an account of the meeting at Parkinson's Ferry, see Brackenridge, *Incidents of the insurrection*, pp. 152-189. Carnahan, pp. 132-134. For a description of the meeting between the commissioners and the insurgent committee, see Brackenridge, *Incidents of the insurrection*, pp. 100-127. Findley, pp. 117-120. Carnahan, p. 135.

[21] *Proceedings of the executive*, pp. 29-32.

pieces of paper, and be distributed, leaving each member to chew up or destroy one of the words, while he put the other in the box.[22]

The vote was 34 to 23 for acceptance of the recommendations of the standing committee. However, another committee was immediately appointed to confer with the official commissioners to see if better terms could be obtained. Instead, the commissioners decided to submit a referendum to the people. This was to be done by September 11, although the committee representing the insurgents strongly felt that insufficient time had been granted. The signing of the referendum would pledge the people to submit to the laws of the United States upon the terms proposed by the commissioners of the United States. Meetings were to be held and each citizen was to designate his willingness to submit by signing personally. No one knows what the result of the referendum would have been had this been done. There were only six days remaining until September 11, however, when the ballots were finally prepared. The people were not well instructed concerning what was to be done, and in many places no meetings were held. Consequently, the commissioners returned an unfavorable report to President Washington.[23]

The President forthwith prepared to quell the insurrection. Governor Henry Lee of Virginia was placed in chief command, and the governors of the other states which were to furnish troops, together with General Morgan of Virginia, were to command the volunteers of their respective states. President Washington, accompanied by Secretary of War Knox, Secretary of Treasury Hamilton, and Judge Peters of the United States District Court, started for western Pennsylvania on October 1. The main body of the army had preceded them.[24]

In the meantime, however, meetings had been held in the rural districts and strong resolutions passed expressing willingness to "submit to the laws of the United States." On October 2, a meeting of the committee

---

[22] Egle, p. 228. For a detailed account of the meeting between these two committees, see Carnahan, pp. 136-140. Brackenridge, *Incidents of the insurrection*, pp. 108-120. Dunlap and Claypoole's *American Daily Advertiser*, September 10, 1794.

[23] Carnahan, pp. 140-141. Egle, pp. 228-229. Findley, pp. 129-136. *Pennsylvania archives*, pp. 211-212, 296-299. Brackenridge, pp. 230-252. *Proceedings of the executive*, pp. 16-29. Dunlap and Claypoole's *American Daily Advertiser*, September 10, 20, 22, 1794.

[24] *Proceedings of the executive*, pp. 55-57, 125-130.

of safety was held at Parkinson's Ferry and two men appointed to wait upon the President and assure him that order could be restored without the aid of military force. The President's reply was to the effect that the army was already on its way, the orders would not be countermanded, but that no violence would be done if the people gave assurance of returning to their allegiance.[25] President Washington moved from place to place, reviewed various divisions of his army, and returned to the Capital on October 28, having been absent for just four weeks. General Lee remained in the area until November 17, at which time all troops were withdrawn, except a small detachment under General Morgan, which remained at Pittsburgh "for the winter defense." [26] In the meantime, and while troops were still in the area, General Neville had gone forward with his work of listing the stills at which the liquor was made.[27]

The aftermath of the rebellion resulted in the release of many who had been arrested, the sending of others to Philadelphia for trial, and the flight to the Spanish dominons of David Bradford who, because of his attempt to influence the people against submission, had been excepted from the amnesty. Several insurgents were finally tried and one or two convicted, but subsequently pardoned. Thus the protesting farmers of western Pennsylvania suffered humiliation and defeat at the hands of the federal government, just as seven years before those of Massachusetts under Shays had been compelled to submit to state authorities.[28]

FRIES' REBELLION

The suppression of the Whiskey Rebellion did not end discontent in Pennsylvania, although the location of the next farmer uprising, in 1799, was in the eastern part of the state rather than the western. Fries' Rebel-

---

[25] *Pennsylvania archives,* pp. 319-320, 389. Findley, pp. 137-139, 169-189.

[26] George M. Dallas, *Life and writings of Alexander James Dallas,* pp. 33-45. Philadelphia: J. B. Lippincott Company, 1871. *Pennsylvania archives,* pp. 428-434. Egle, p. 230.

[27] *Pennsylvania archives,* pp. 449-450, 481.

[28] The story of the Whiskey Rebellion has been documented by so many scholars and others that many incidents occurring during its progress have not been included here. Brackenridge, so often quoted, was undoubtedly biased, but he was biased in behalf of the farmers, and is, therefore, a good source for interpreting the farmers' attitudes and beliefs.

lion, taking its name from John Fries, a farmer's son and a traveling auctioneer,[29] was also a protest against federal taxes. An additional direct-tax law was passed by Congress in 1798. These taxes had been made necessary by preparation for war with France, which made them doubly obnoxious to many farmers because they, as followers of Jefferson, felt friendly toward France.[30] The southern planters had objected strongly to the Jay Treaty with England in 1794 because it had appeared to them to favor mercantile interests at the expense of agricultural interests and certainly to favor England as against France, both of whose navies and privateers were interfering with American shipping.[31] The chief leaders of agrarian interests, Jefferson and others, had always been friendly to France, had objected to Jay's Treaty; and now for farmers to be called upon to pay heavier taxes because of preparation for war with France constituted the last straw. ·

The amount of revenue to be raised by new taxes was $2,000,000. The taxes were to be direct levies on three kinds of property—lands, dwelling houses, and slaves. Slaves were chiefly the property of southern planters, and it therefore appeared to them that the tax was discriminatory. In Pennsylvania, there were few slaves, and that state was therefore called upon to raise its quota of $237,000 almost wholly from taxes on houses and lands. The amount of the appraisal was to be obtained by calculating the number and size of windows of a dwelling, an old English system of appraisal.

Eastern Pennsylvania was an area in which the *Aurora*, a newspaper

---

[29] John B. McMaster, *A history of the people of the United States*, Vol. II, pp. 435-436. New York: Appleton-Century-Crofts, Inc., 1936.

[30] Beard, *Economic origins of Jeffersonian democracy*, pp. 354-355.

[31] Jay's Treaty provided that debts contracted by citizens of the United States with British merchants prior to the Revolutionary War peace treaty of 1783 should be paid. It also provided that British trade in America be placed on the most-favored-nation basis. Thus, it made necessary the paying of old prewar debts, most of which were owed by southern planters—Jefferson calculating those of Virginia citizens at two million dollars. The planters had considered that their obligations were annulled by the outcome of the war. Parts of the treaty were negotiated as a trade to keep the English from interfering with American shipping and were thus of chief value to mercantile interests. For a copy of Jay's Treaty, see *American state papers*, Class I, Foreign Relations, Vol. I, pp. 520-525. Washington, D. C.: Gales and Seaton, 1832. See also Beard, *Economic origins of Jeffersonian democracy*, pp. 268-298, 354-355.

published at Philadelphia, circulated widely. The editor of this paper was William Duane, one of the bitterest enemies of Jay's Treaty and, in fact, of the whole system of centralized government under which federal taxes were levied. The people of this particular area, and especially the readers of this paper, were therefore fully prepared for ardent protest against the new taxes.[32] MacMaster says:

> Many a farmer gained his first information regarding it [the law] from the assessor, who, notebook and measure in hand, stood at his door to take the rates. After such a man beheld the official walk round his house, count every window, and carefully measure its size, no explanations, however lucid, no assurances, however solemn, could persuade him that he was not about to pay a tax on windows, which, with the single exception of the hearth-tax, was, to his mind, the most detestable that could be laid.[33]

Consequently, a protest was raised and ultimately an insurrection developed. Assessors were railed at, dogs were set upon them, and they were driven from the houses and premises of those whose properties they sought to assess. When judges and assessors sought to explain the tax, they were shouted down and sometimes jostled about.[34]

John Fries, the auctioneer, was in a good position while crying farm sales to spread propaganda against the assessors and the law. He not

---

[32] For the controversy over Jay's Treaty see Thorndike Pamphlets: Vol. 30, No. 8, *Features of Mr. Jay's treaty.* Philadelphia: printed by Lang and Ustick for M. Carey, 1795; Vol. 30, No. 14, *An address from Robert Goodloe Harper, of South Carolina, to his constituents, containing his reasons for approving of the Treaty of Amity, Commerce, and Navigation, with Great Britain.* New York: printed by T. and J. Swords, 1796. Also see pamphlets in the Duane Collection: Vol. 55, No. 2, *Remarks on the Treaty of Amity, Navigation, and Commerce, concluded between Lord Grenville and Mr. Jay, on the part of Great Britain and the United States, respectively.* Philadelphia: printed by Henry Tuckniss for M. Carey, 1796; Vol. 55, No. 3, *Remarks occasioned by the late conduct of Mr. Washington as President of the United States.* Philadelphia: printed for Benjamin Franklin Bache, 1797; Vol. 55, No. 5, *Examination of the Treaty of Amity, Commerce, and Navigation, between the United States and Great Britain,* by Cato, republished from the *Argus* by Thomas Greenleaf, 1795; Vol. 55, No. 6, *A defence of the Treaty of Amity, Commerce, and Navigation, entered into between the United States of America and Great Britain,* by Camillus (A. Hamilton). New York: printed by Francis Childs and Co., 1795.

[33] McMaster, Vol. II, p. 434. Reprinted by permission of Appleton-Century-Crofts, Inc.

[34] *Ibid.,* Vol. II, p. 435. *Aurora* (Philadelphia), April 13, 1799.

only did this, but assumed leadership of an angry group of farmers and other householders at Milford and openly commanded the assessors to stop their work. When this command was refused, two assessors were taken into custody and held as prisoners. The state courts attempted to deal with the offenders and in some counties arrested a number of them. This fact was made known to the insurrectionists by runners who were dispatched hither and yon; and on March 7, 1799, Fries led a mob which, accompanied by some of the militia, freed a number of prisoners. The government then took charge, marched the militia into the disaffected counties, explained to the people that the tax was constitutional and that they were engaged in acts of treason and rebellion. Fries was arrested, tried for treason and sentenced to be hanged, but was pardoned by President Adams.[35]

This action did not end the episode. The troops, on their way home, cut down a number of "sedition poles" which farmers and innkeepers had erected in protest against the sedition law. Rumors of brutalities practiced by the troopers spread throughout the area. After the troops had left, the editor of the *Reading Adler* denounced them bitterly, saying in part that "they had been seen whipping children and assaulting women with pistols and drawn swords." Some of the militiamen returned, dragged the editor to the market place, and flogged him. It was rumored that men, arrested because of their part in the insurrection, were "loaded with irons ... driven like cattle over long distances by day, and huddled at night into barns and damp cellars." [36]

William Duane, editor of the *Aurora* at Philadelphia, because of his part in reporting these occurrences and circulating these rumors, was also flogged by militiamen.[37] He, however, was not silenced by the beating which he received, but kept up his attack on the obnoxious tax laws and other acts of the Federalists. Two years later he was rewarded by his newspaper being made the best-known exponent of an agrarian administration which, when it came into power, eliminated the taxes against which he had protested, and on account of which taxes John Fries, a German-American farmer boy, had organized a farmer insurrection.

---

[35] See accounts given in *Aurora* in March, April, and May, 1799.
[36] McMaster, Vol. II, pp. 438-439. *Aurora,* April and May, 1799.
[37] *Aurora,* May 16, 20, 21, 25, 27, 1799.

JEFFERSONIAN AGRARIANISM

Parrington says that at the end of the Revolutionary War "agrarian and mercantile interests opposed each other openly and shaped their political programs in accordance with their special needs." [38] In the struggle, Thomas Jefferson was the recognized leader of the agrarian forces. He had not been altogether unsympathetic with Shays' Rebellion. In a letter written from Paris in 1786 he said, "These people are not entirely without excuse. . . . The Massachusetts Assembly . . . in their zeal for paying their public debt, had laid a tax too heavy to be paid in the circumstances of their state." [39] In another letter a year later, he stated that he hoped the so-called troublemakers would "provoke no severities from their governments." [40]

John Taylor of Caroline, Virginia, was an even more ardent exponent of agrarianism than Jefferson, and a far more voluminous writer. Beard cogently summarizes his arguments as follows:

1. The masses have always been exploited by ruling classes, royal, ecclesiastical, or feudal, which have been genuine economic castes sustaining their power by psychological devices such as "loyalty to throne and altar."

2. Within recent times, a new class, capitalistic in character, has sprung up, based on exploitation through inflated paper, bank stock, and a protective tariff, likewise with its psychological devices, "public faith, national integrity, and sacred credit."

3. In the United States, this class was built up by Hamilton's fiscal system, the bank, and protective tariff, all of which are schemes designed to filch wealth from productive labor, particularly labor upon the land.

4. Thus was created a fundamental conflict between the capitalists and agrarian interests which was the origin of parties in the United States.

5. Having no political principles, capitalism could fraternize with any party that promised protection, and in fact, after the

––––––

[38] V. L. Parrington, *Main currents in American thought*, Vol. I, p. 267. New York: Harcourt, Brace & Company, Inc., 1927.

[39] H. A. Washington, ed., *The writings of Thomas Jefferson*, Vol. II, p. 81. Washington, D. C.: Taylor and Maury, 1853.

[40] *Ibid.*, p. 104.

victory of the Republicans, capitalism successfully entrenched itself in power under new cover.

6. The only remedy is to follow the confiscatory examples of other classes and destroy special privilege without compensation.[41]

Jefferson won the Presidency in 1800. Thereby, the agrarians felt they had somewhat recouped from their setback at the hands of the Constitutional Convention. The campaign was bitter, the agrarians characterizing their opposition as "that stock jobbing crowd," "aristocrats," "fiscal corps," "stock gamblers," "plunderers of the people," "thieves on the farmers' backs," and the "corrupt squadron." [42] Jefferson appointed Gallatin, a sympathizer with the Whiskey Rebellion, as his Secretary of the Treasury, and William Duane, who had been flogged by militiamen in 1799 because of his sympathy with Fries' Rebellion, became one of his trusted counsellors.

Jefferson did not become, and no one could have become, a direct leader of a powerfully organized farmers' group. Such organizations were not possible under the transportation and communication conditions of that time. During his first administration, however, he did a number of things to alleviate the situation of distressed and protesting farmers. He abolished the newly established circuit courts, pared the ordinary expenditures of the federal government by $2,500,000 during the first year and by about $3,500,000 for each of the succeeding three years.[43] These economies made possible the abolition of the excise duties, which had been especially obnoxious to the farmers and the direct cause of the Whiskey Rebellion. During his two administrations, he reduced the public debt from $83,000,-000 to $57,000,000, thus further reducing taxes. In his second inaugural address, in 1805, he emphasized the fact that during his first administration "The suppression of unnecessary offices, of useless establishments and expenses, enabled us to discontinue our internal taxes." [44]

It is not to be assumed from the above-described facts that Jefferson

---

[41] Beard, *Economic origins of Jeffersonian democracy*, p. 351. Reprinted by permission of The Macmillan Company.

[42] *Ibid.*, p. 402.

[43] *Ibid.*, pp. 437-438.

[44] Washington, Vol. VIII, p. 40.

was acting solely vindictively. He had been opposed to the reign of the courts, the excise taxes, and the United States Bank from the beginning. He was author of the Kentucky resolutions of 1798, one of which was directed specifically against the right of the federal government "to lay and collect taxes, duties, imposts, and excises, to pay the debts, and provide for the common defence and general welfare of the United States." [45] His pronounced agrarianism had been well attested in numerous writings long before he became President. In 1785 in a private letter to John Jay he wrote, "Cultivators of the earth are the most valuable citizens. They are the most vigorous, the most independent, the most virtuous, and they are tied to their country, and wedded to its liberty and interests, by the most lasting bonds." [46]

In a letter to Colonel Arthur Campbell, in 1797, Jefferson wrote: "All can be done peaceably, by the people confining their choice of Representatives and Senators to persons attached to republican government and the principles of 1776, not office-hunters, but farmers, whose interests are entirely agricultural. Such men are the true representatives of the great American interest, and are alone to be relied on for expressing the proper American sentiments." [47]

Jefferson can hardly be said to have been the leader of a farmers' revolt, but he was just as much a party to the Farmers' Movement in his day as Ramsay MacDonald was to the labor movement in England for a quarter of a century before his elevation to the office of Prime Minister of his government at the end of World War I. He was only one among many intellectuals who believed devoutly in the necessity of keeping agriculture dominant among the economic enterprises of the nation and farmers well represented, if not dominant, in political affairs. His election was accomplished by a campaign among the farmers which, it is not too much to say, had been skillfully carried on for a full decade.[48] Both Federalists and Anti-Federalists accepted the issues of agrarianism as the

---

[45] *Ibid.*, Vol. IX, pp. 464-471.

[46] *Ibid.*, Vol. I, p. 403.

[47] *Ibid.*, Vol. IV, p. 198.

[48] Claude G. Bowers, *Jefferson and Hamilton: the struggle for democracy in America*, chap. vii, "Jefferson Mobilizes," pp. 140-160. Boston: Houghton Mifflin Company, 1925.

gauge of battle. The Anti-Federalists, or Republicans, won, and remained in power until the end of Monroe's administration in 1824.[49]

Charles Beard discusses the period from the beginning of Jefferson's administration to the end of Monroe's administration, and the struggle between the agrarian and mercantile interests, under the chapter heading, "Agricultural Imperialism and the Balance of Power." [50] It is not necessary to survey the details of agrarian dominance throughout the period. Suffice it to list a few of its evidences. The purchase of Louisiana in 1803 added millions of acres for agricultural settlement. The War of 1812 was fought primarily to keep foreign markets open for the agricultural products of the new West.[51] The struggle to keep the Mississippi River open for navigation was in behalf of the agricultural West. The protective tariff act of 1816 was passed under the argument that it would create eastern industrial markets for western agricultural products. The Florida Purchase served the same purpose as the Louisiana Purchase. The opening of western lands for settlement in small blocks at $1.25 per acre was for the purpose of inducing more families onto farms.

However, as Schlesinger reports:

> The America of Jefferson had begun to disappear before Jefferson had retired from the presidential chair. . . . The farm remained the statistical center of American life, but business enterprise was exerting stronger and stronger claims on the imagination of the

---

[49] In studying the electoral vote of 1800, it will be discovered that all of the dominantly agricultural states went for Jefferson and all of the dominantly commercial and industrial states went against him. Taking the gross electoral vote, all of the states south of Maryland, with the exception of a divided North Carolina vote, went for Jefferson. Pennsylvania and Maryland were divided, and New York was solid Republican. New England, Delaware, and New Jersey were solidly Federalist. See Beard, *Economic origins of Jeffersonian democracy*, pp. 353-414.

[50] Beards, Vol. I, chap. ix, pp. 391-436.

[51] According to McMaster, the vote in the House of Representatives on the declaration of war was 79 for and 49 against. New York was the only state with large agricultural interests, the majority of whose Congressmen failed to vote for war. The Pennsylvania delegation stood 16 to 2 for war, and the South Carolina, Georgia, Ohio, Kentucky, and Tennessee delegations were unanimously in the affirmative. "All over Massachusetts town-meeting after town-meeting was held to denounce the war." Petitions against war were sent to its legislature. See J. B. McMaster, *A history of the people of the United States*, Vol. III, pp. 457-458, 551-552. New York: Appleton-Century-Crofts, Inc., 1937. See also Beards, Vol. I, chap. ix, pp. 391-436. Julius W. Pratt, *Expansionists of 1812*. New York: The Macmillan Company, 1925.

people and the actions of the government. ... The new economic life acquired its appropriate institutions. The private business association was re-shaped into an effective agency of capitalist enterprise; and by its side the chartered corporation, created by special act of the state legislature, began its rise to dominance, first in banking, then in insurance and inland transportation, soon in manufacturing.[52]

Some followers of Jefferson, even Madison and Monroe, drifted with the change into what John Taylor, the abiding agrarian, described as the "slow and legal method by which the rich plundered the poor."

THE JACKSONIAN REVOLT

The thread of economic and political philosophy running between Jefferson and Jackson may be tenuous, but the thread of the Farmers' Movement between the times of Jefferson and Jackson is easily identified. Hofstader said of the Anti-Federalists, of whom Jefferson was certainly the chief one, that they insisted that Hamilton "through his methods of funding the national debt and through the national bank, subsidized those who invested in manufactures, commerce, and public securities, and threw as much of the tax burden as possible on the planters and farmers"; that "Jefferson, in common with eighteenth-century liberalism, thought of it chiefly as an unfair means of helping the rich through interest-bearing debts, taxation, tariffs, banks, privileges, and bounties."[53] Certainly the Jacksonian fight on the Second United States Bank was gauged directly on these issues.

Between 1800, when Jefferson was elected President, and 1828, when Jackson was elected, the people living west of the Allegheny and Appalachian mountains had increased in number from about one-twentieth to about one-third of the total population of the country. Furthermore, the economic interests of New England and the Middle Atlantic states had, during that period, shifted sharply from agriculture to manufacturing.

---

[52] Arthur M. J. Schlesinger, *The age of Jackson*, pp. 8-9. Boston: Little, Brown & Company, 1946.
[53] Richard Hofstader, *The American political tradition*, p. 32. New York: Alfred A. Knopf, Inc., 1948.

The Farmers' Movement became pretty much the index of a struggle between the Atlantic seaboard "business community" and the farmers of the West. As Beard says, the people of the West had built a classless society and rallied to Jackson because they believed he was one of their own. Others have described the struggle as one between creditors and debtors, but this is probably too simple a characterization. Western farmers were debtors only in the sense that they borrowed money to develop their farms, not in the sense of being bankrupt. They believed that Jackson's fight against the United States Bank was identical with their own revolt against eastern control of money and eastern interference with local control of credit.

The Farmers' Movement at that time was party to a contest between the people in terms of numbers and the so-called "natural aristocracy" in terms of wealth. Edward Everett, an anti-Jacksonian, told an English banker, "The present contest is nothing less than a war of numbers against prosperity." [54] Bancroft, an ardent Jacksonian, commenting on Jackson's veto of the bill to recharter the bank, wrote, "Political influence is steadily tending to the summit level of prosperity, and this political influence of wealth must be balanced by the political power of numbers. Even then this political influence often controls elections, and often with a giant tread stalks into the halls of legislation." [55]

Jackson, in his message vetoing the bill, said:

It is to be regretted that the rich and powerful too often bend the acts of government to their selfish purposes. Distinctions in society will always exist under every just government. Equality of talents, of education, or of wealth cannot be produced by human institutions ... but when laws undertake to add to these natural and just advantages artificial distinctions, to grant titles, gratuities, and exclusive privileges, to make the rich richer and the potent more powerful, the humble members of society—the farmers, mechanics, and laborers —who have neither the time nor the means of securing like favors for themselves, have a right to complain of the injustice of their government. [56]

---

[54] Arthur M. J. Schlesinger, *Problems in American civilization,* chap. ix., p. 96. Ed., George Rogers Taylor. Boston: D. C. Heath and Company, 1949.
[55] *Ibid.,* p. 35.
[56] *Ibid.,* p. 19. Reprinted by permission of D. C. Heath and Company.

Whether Jackson understood finance, whether "hard money" instead of paper money was a good thing at the time for western farmers, and whether Jackson was consistent throughout his public career on the issues of his political campaigns and administration, has been debated in numerous profound writings. Whether, or how, Jeffersonianism was transmitted through intervening political philosophies to Jackson, and whether he was one of the common people who elected him President are subjects which have also absorbed much time and attention on the part of scholars in history. That he represented, in his political expressions and official acts, the viewpoints of the farmers of his day on the issues of money, credit, taxes, and federal-government domination by industrial and commercial interests is probably not debatable. The Farmers' Movement was a part of the growing populist movement which increased as population moved westward, as something approaching geographic special interests developed, and as farmers got deeper into the price and market economy.

There were twenty-four states in the Union when Jackson was elected President, seven of them having been added since Jefferson went out of office. They were predominantly agricultural, and their representatives in Congress had steadily increased in number. As population drifted rapidly westward, the feeling became prevalent that political power should be shifted from the Atlantic seaboard inland. Hofstader says, "As poor farmers and workers gained the ballot, there developed a type of politician that had existed only in embryo in the Jeffersonian period—the technician of mass leadership, the caterer to mass sentiment; it was a coterie of such men in all parts of the country that converged upon the prominent figure of Jackson between 1815 and 1824." [57] Jackson was defeated by John Quincy Adams in 1824, but triumphed over the same opponent in 1828.

The campaign of 1828 was as fierce as the one of 1800 in which Jefferson had defeated the elder Adams, father of Jackson's current opponent. The large city newspapers, manufacturing and banking interests were all in favor of Adams's re-election. Arrayed against them were the farmers of the West and the workingmen of the towns and cities. Jackson himself was a Tennessee farmer, a military hero, and a violent opponent of the Second United States Bank. It is not too much to say that by joining

---

[57] Hofstader, p. 49. Reprinted by permission of Alfred A. Knopf, Inc.

hands with the "mechanics," as the laboring men of the cities were then called, the farmers of the nation, chiefly the western farmers, elected him President of the United States. Bowers says, concerning Jackson's campaign for re-election in 1832:

> A creature of another world, looking down from the skies upon the United States in the late summer and autumn of 1832, would have concluded that its people moved about in enormous processions on horseback, with waving flags, branches and banners. Great meetings were held in groves, addressed by fiery orators, furiously denouncing "The Monster" and the "Corporation" (chiefly referring to the United States Bank) and calling upon the people to "stand by the Hero." Men left their homes, bade farewell to their families as though enlisting for a war, and rode from one meeting to another for weeks at a time.[58]

The same author describes this campaign as "The first battle at the polls between the 'soulless corporation' and the 'sons of toil.'"

The chief issues of Jackson's campaigns and the eight years of his administration were: free public lands, expansion of the currency, cheap credit, and modification of the tariff. He argued that of the $28,000,000 of capital stock outstanding in private hands, the people of the West and Southwest held only $140,000; that of the annual profits of the United States Bank, $1,640,000 came from the nine western states where little or none of the stock was held, and therefore the people of the agricultural West were compelled continuously to pay tribute to eastern and foreign capitalists on money which they had borrowed to buy land.

Once in power, Jackson carried the demands of the western farmers into action by killing the United States Bank, opening up more western lands, and passing a new set of tariff schedules.[59] That some of these accomplishments failed to remedy the grievances of western farmers is not the point at issue, for however mistaken the demands may have been, they were the demands of farmers, not in terms of insurrection or rebellion,

---

[58] Claude G. Bowers, *The party battles of the Jackson period*, pp. 227, 245. Boston: Houghton Mifflin Company, 1922. For a consideration of the campaign of 1832, see chap. ix, "The Dramatic Battle of 1832," pp. 227-251. See also Nathan Sargent, *Public men and events*, Vol. I, pp. 247-249. Philadelphia: J. B. Lippincott Company, 1875.

[59] Beards, Vol. I, pp. 557-571.

but in terms of political action through the agency of a farmer President, and farmer Congressmen and senators who stood by their President's side in one of the fiercest political upheavals in the nation's history.

THE PANIC OF 1837 AND ITS POLITICAL AFTERMATH

With the elimination of the Second United States Bank, the charter of which expired in 1836 and was not renewed because of Jackson's successful opposition, private banks sprang up all over the nation. Between 1830 and 1837, 348 new banks were chartered, about 40 of them in the West, about 59 in the South, and the remaining 249 in the East. In Massachusetts alone, 72 banks were chartered in this period. Between 1803 and 1839, the population of the nation increased one and one-half times, while the banking capital increased twenty-five and one-half times, and the money in circulation per capita in the country four times.[60] Wildcat banking of the worst kind appeared all over the country. In Maine, bank commissioners discovered instances of loans having been made to stockholders before the capital had been paid in. In New York, stock was subscribed for on the promise of loans. Banks were issuing ten, fifteen, and even thirty paper dollars for every silver dollar they possessed. An era of false prosperity was on. The value of real estate in New York increased 150 per cent from 1830 to 1837. Millions of dollars were spent in the construction of roads and canals. States loaned fabulous sums to railroads, and midwestern states issued bonds to raise money to loan to railroad builders and to finance internal improvements.[61] Currency and credit expanded to meet the needs of expanding prosperity, and high rates of interest attracted capital and credit from England. In fact, it was a call for specie by the Bank of England that helped to force the questionable banking practices of American banks into the open and set the stage for the panic of 1837. "During the period from 1829 to 1837,

---

[60] Hunt's *Merchants' Magazine and Commercial Review*, Vol. III, No. 5 (November, 1840), p. 458; and Vol. II, No. 2 (February, 1840), pp. 159-160.

[61] Davis R. Dewey, *State banking before the Civil War*, pp. 14-16. National Monetary Commission. Washington, D. C.: Government Printing Office, 1910. Reginald C. McGrane, *The panic of 1837*, pp. 1-42. Chicago: University of Chicago Press, 1924. Hunt's *Merchants' Magazine and Commercial Review*, Vol. VII, No. 5 (November, 1842), p. 452.

state bank circulation increased from about $50,000,000 to over $149,000,-
000, and bank loans from $137,000,000 to $525,000,000. . . . From 1834 to
1837, bank circulation increased about 50 per cent in New England and
the Middle States, about 100 per cent in four Western States, and over
130 per cent in nine Southern States." [62]

The sale of public lands in 1834 was 4,658,219 acres; for 1835, 12,564,-
479 acres; and for 1836, 20,074,871 acres.[63] Contrary to the purpose of
Benton and Jackson, the sales of land during this period were in large
measure to men who bought in order to sell again at advanced prices.
Consequently, the market price of land frequently rose far above the
government selling price. Speculators borrowed from local banks to
finance newly purchased land, the government then redeposited the
money from whence it came, and it served as a loan to another speculator.
"These local banks and the government surplus thus became involved in
a common network of credits; banks were established to meet this temporary demand, so that the lender leaned upon the borrower." [64] President Jackson attempted to stem this tide of inflation and speculation by
the publication of his famous Specie Circular in July, 1836, which directed
that land sales must be effected in specie except for a period of three
months in the case of actual settlers.[65] The effect of the circular was to
discredit bank notes and cause private creditors to demand payment in
coin. This fact, coupled with the action of the Bank of England, brought
the era of prosperity suddenly to an end.

An act providing for distribution of surplus revenue, which had been
piling up from the sale of public lands since early in 1835, became a law
in June of 1836. This was followed by an order from the treasury transfer-
ring public money from points where it was collected to other places in
anticipation of its distribution among the states. The effect of this act
and the Specie Circular edict forced a large amount of specie from the

---

[62] Earl S. Sparks, *History and theory of agricultural credit in the United States*, p. 236.
New York: Thomas Y. Crowell Company, 1932. William G. Sumner, *A history of
American currency*, pp. 88-91, 117-120, 132-154. New York: Henry Holt and Com-
pany, Inc., 1874. McGrane, pp. 40-42.

[63] Benjamin H. Hibbard, *A history of the public land policies*, Table IX, p. 103. New
York: The Macmillan Company, 1924.

[64] Dewey, p. 350.

[65] Niles' *Weekly Register* (Baltimore), July 16 and 23, 1836.

Atlantic seaboard cities to the western states. The result was the quick weakening of credit. The government called on deposit banks and the banks in turn called on their customers. Money which had been abundant suddenly became scarce. On May 10, 1837, the New York banks suspended specie payments and were followed in a period of nine days in a similar action by the banks of thirteen other large cities from New Orleans in the South to Cincinnati and Louisville in the West.[66]

Coupled with these events was the fact that the cereal crops of 1835 and 1837 were short, and western farmers, therefore, had little or nothing to sell. The planters of the South had plenty of cotton, but the bottom had dropped out of prices. The panic, however, was more devastating in the cities than among the farmers. It is calculated that real estate in New York City alone depreciated $40,000,000 in six months' time. Two hundred and fifty bankruptcies occurred in that city in two months, 20,000 men were thrown out of employment, and the militia had to be called in to protect "terrified financiers." [67] Above everything else was the anomalous fact that farm prices of the West were high while money was scarce.[68] This, too, added to the misery of the city consumers.

The farmers, for the most part, escaped the devastating effects of the panic of 1837, but they suffered more than their share in the collapse of 1839, after a brief upturn in economic affairs in 1838. Specie payments were resumed for the most part in 1838, but apparently too quickly, for the situation collapsed again the following year, and the country did not return to hard money until 1842.[69]

It appeared that the great flow of people into the West had now created an agricultural production capacity beyond the purchasing capacity of those engaged in city enterprises. Money in the West was scarce, and

---

[66] McGrane, pp. 92-93. See also McGrane, chap. v, "Financial and Industrial Aspects of the Panic," pp. 91-144. Allan Nevins, ed., *The diary of Philip Hone*, Vol. I, pp. 257-259. New York: Dodd, Mead & Company, Inc. 1927.

[67] Katharine Coman, *The industrial history of the United States*, p. 230. New York: The Macmillan Company, 1912. *The diary of Philip Hone*, pp. 246-249. Sumner, pp. 138-139, 143. Niles' *Weekly Register*, July 23, 1836. Dewey, pp. 230-231. Thomas H. Benton, *Thirty years' view*, Vol. II, p. 18. New York: Appleton-Century-Crofts, Inc., 1856.

[68] *National Intelligencer* (Washington, D. C.), August 17, 1839, quoting from the Pittsburgh *Daily Advocate*.

[69] Dewey, pp. 232-233. Coman, 1912 edition, p. 231. *National Intelligencer*, August 17, 1839, quoting from the Pittsburgh *Daily Advocate*.

western indebtedness to eastern merchants had to be liquidated in produce sold at reduced prices. In Illinois, "Money was an almost unknown commodity, all business being transacted through the means of trade or barter. . . . Notes were given for value received, payable in a cow, or a horse, or other property." [70] The State of Virginia passed a stay and valuation law which deprived creditors of the power, under the state laws, to collect claims. [71] In North Carolina, a depreciation of 50 per cent on most tangible and active property was reported, and on land still more, with farms yielding about 2 per cent of their value. [72] In Mississippi, the value of Negro slaves fell from $1,200 and $1,500 to $200 and $250. [73] Losses to agriculture were variously calculated. One writer listed them as follows:

Losses on wool	$ 20,000,000
Losses on cotton	130,000,000
Losses on grain	150,000,000
Losses on capital vested in slave labor	400,000,000
Losses on capital vested in lands	2,500,000,000 [74]

The Whig party came to power out of this depression. William Henry Harrison, born in Virginia but then living in Ohio, who was an ex-Governor over the territory of Indiana and an ex-Congressman and senator from Ohio, was elected President in 1840. [75] He had represented the Northwest Territory as a delegate to Congress in 1799-1800 and succeeded

[70] S. J. Clarke, *History of McDonough County, Illinois*, p. 60. Springfield, Illinois: printed by D. W. Lusk, 1878.

[71] McGrane, pp. 113-114. Hunt's *Merchants' Magazine and Commercial Review*, Vol. VIII, No. 3 (March, 1843), pp. 272-273.

[72] *Journals of the senate and house of commons of the general assembly of the state of North Carolina, at its session in 1840-1841*, p. 335. Raleigh, North Carolina: printed by Thos. J. Lĕmay, 1841.

[73] *National Intelligencer*, May, 1837.

[74] Calvin Colton, *The life and times of Henry Clay*, Vol. II, p. 66. New York: A. S. Barnes and Company, 1846.

[75] The Indiana Territory at the time Harrison was territorial governor (1800-1812) included the present states of Indiana, Illinois, Michigan, Wisconsin, and part of Minnesota. See *The national cyclopaedia of American biography*, Vol. III, pp. 33-36. New York: James T. White and Co., 1893.

in securing the passage of a law relating to the sale of federal land in small parcels. He was therefore considered to be a westerner and a friend of the farmers and made his plea for nomination and election on this count. It was the western, southern, and agricultural vote from the East that elected him, although the hue and cry of the Whigs in general was to the effect that mercantile interests had all too long been made subservient to agrarian interests.[76] But as McGrane says, "A spirit of unrest seemed to pervade the West as a consequence of the hard times, and the people demanded a change."[77]

The Cincinnati *Daily Gazette* described the farmers' situation at the time in the following terms:

> In 1836 a farmer brought 100 bushels of wheat to market. He got for it $125 cash. He bought 100 pounds of coffee at 14 cents, $14.00; 10 pounds of tea at 75 cents, $7.50; 10 yards of cassimere at $1.50, $15.00; 8 yards of calico at $1.00, $8.00; one bridle, $2.00; and one pound of cavendish tobacco, 37½¢. He then had $85.12½ to carry home. He goes to market in June, 1840, with his 100 bushels of wheat; sells it, and buys the same articles. What does he now carry home? Twelve and a half cents! Is not the farmer the loser of $85 by the present state of things?[78]

This type of thinking prevailed widely among the farmers, with the result that a change in administration was demanded. The Whigs carried the agricultural states of Georgia, Indiana, Kentucky, Louisiana, Maine, Maryland, Mississippi, Michigan, North Carolina, Ohio, Pennsylvania, Tennessee, and Vermont.[79]

Garrison says that during the campaign "the Whigs, to make it appear

[76] See excerpts of a letter from Harrison to Giddings, December, 1838: George W. Julian, *The life of Joshua R. Giddings*, p. 55. Chicago: A. C. McClurg & Company, 1892. E. M. Carroll, *Origins of the Whig party*, pp. 149-170, 187-195, 216-220. Durham, North Carolina: Duke University Press, 1925. McGrane, chap. v., "Political Aftermath of the Panic," pp. 145-176. Beards, Vol. I, pp. 575-577. Calvin (Junius) Colton, *The crisis of the country*, second ed., p. 16. New York: E. Benson, 1840. Also see issues of *National Intelligencer* for 1840.

[77] McGrane, pp. 161, 174-175. See also Sargent, Vol. II, p. 110. Colton, *The crisis of the country*, p. 15.

[78] McGrane, p. 175, quoting from the Cincinnati *Daily Gazette*, March 5 and August 3, 1840.

[79] Thomas H. McKee, *The national conventions and platforms of all political parties, 1789 to 1905*, sixth ed., pp. 44-45. Baltimore: Friedenwald Company, 1906.

that their candidate was a man of the people and of the West, adopted the log cabin as their campaign symbol; and the effectiveness of the device was increased by adding a barrel of cider and adorning the cabin with a coon-skin or a live coon." [80]

The issues of the campaign were not at all clear, but the fact that it was the farmers of the West who primarily turned the tide of political battle is enough to mark the Whig victory, coming as it did just after the panics of 1837 and 1839, as a part of the Farmers' Movement.

The decade of 1830-1840 was a stormy political period. There were no organized farmer upheavals as such, but there are a number of similarities between this period and other periods of farmer discontent that are worthy of note. First, as a result of the industrial distress incident to the panic of 1837, there was an increased interest in agriculture, and apparently some movement from cities to farms. Second, planters of the South were led to doubt the wisdom of cash-crop farming and urged to follow a "live-at-home" program. Third, "stay laws," or temporary moratoria on debts, were enacted by state legislatures. Fourth, a new federal bankruptcy law was passed. Fifth, there was quite a general protest against the concentration of wealth and so-called "feudal privileges." Sixth, there was a shortage of money and a consequent demand for more currency. Seventh, there was a change in the national political administration, chiefly at the hands of farmers.

As with a number of other periods in the American Farmers' Movement, it is impossible to measure the progress or magnitude of this period in chronological or precise terms. It is, however, clearly evident that the farmer public was conscious of itself and was active a number of times before it took organized form in the Granger era following the Civil War. The focal issues of its interest were prices, markets, and credits. In their attempts to alleviate maladjustments in these fields, the farmers, wisely or not, rallied behind those politicians and statesmen who they believed best represented their views of the adjustments that should be accomplished.

----

[80] George Pierce Garrison, *Westward extension, 1841-1850* (A. B. Hart, ed., *The American nation: a history*, Vol. XVII), p. 48. New York: Harper & Brothers, 1906. For a description of the campaign, see also Sargent, Vol. II, pp. 105-111.

· 4 ·

EARLY FARMERS'

ORGANIZATIONS

AGRICULTURAL SOCIETIES

Until about 1860, farmers' organizations were for the most part concerned with technical problems of production rather than with problems of markets and prices. In fact, some members of early agricultural societies were not what we would today call farm leaders, nor were they even farmers. They were urban dwellers and often national leaders interested in agriculture only because it was one of the basic enterprises of a developing nation. In order to know how such organizations became the voice of the Farmers' Movement, it is necessary to know something of their history.

The earliest of them enlisted in their membership a number of signers of the Declaration of Independence and framers of the Federal Constitution. Despite their number and the status of some of their members, the influence of these early societies on the progress of agriculture was so slight as to be almost negligible. Bidwell says: "The older societies had confessed their inability to interest the common farmers in their theories and schemes for improvement. The reason was not far to seek. The working farmer of an inland community could not be interested in schemes to increase production until someone could show him a market for his surplus." [1] Such societies were in fact at first ridiculed by farmers. They were attempting to promote scientific production at the very time when such revolts as Shays' Rebellion, the Whiskey Rebellion, and Fries' Rebellion were representing the real concern of practical farmers.

The Philadelphia Society for Promoting Agriculture was organized in March, 1785, four years before Washington was elected President of the United States. Washington, Franklin, and Timothy Pickering were members of the organization. Little is known of its work during the first few years of its existence, but after its incorporation in 1809, it carried on work similar to that of the other agricultural societies to be briefly described here. [2] The Agricultural Society of South Carolina was also

---

[1] Percy W. Bidwell, "The Agricultural Revolution in New England," *American Historical Review,* Vol. XXVI, No. 4 (July, 1921), p. 686.

[2] For accounts of the Philadelphia Society, see *Memoirs of the Philadelphia Society for Promoting Agriculture,* Vol. I: Philadelphia: printed by Jane Aitken, 1808. Reprinted in 1815. Vol. II: Johnson and Warner, 1811. Vol. III: 1814. Vol. IV: Benjamin Warner, 1818. Vol. V: Robert H. Small, 1826. Vol. VI (*Sketch of the history of the Philadelphia Society for Promoting Agriculture*): 1939. *An address, from the Philadelphia Society for Promoting Agriculture, with a summary of its laws; and premiums offered.* Philadelphia: 1785. *Minutes of the Philadelphia Society for the Promotion of Agriculture, from its institution in February, 1785, to March, 1810.* Philadelphia: printed by John C. Clark and Son, 1854. Edward Wiest, *Agricultural organization in the United States* (*Studies in economics and sociology,* Vol. II), pp. 333-334. Lexington, Kentucky: University of Kentucky, April, 1923. Jonathan Periam, *The groundswell,* p. 64. Cincinnati: Hannaford and Thompson, 1874. William L. Wanlass, *The United States Department of Agriculture,* Johns Hopkins University Studies in Historical and Political Science, Series XXXVIII, No. 1, p. 18. Baltimore: Johns Hopkins Press, 1920. *Report of the Commissioner of Agriculture for the year 1866,* pp. 513-514. Washington, D. C.: Government Printing Office, 1867.

According to Carl R. Woodward, the oldest society in the United States actually termed an agricultural society was the New Jersey Society for Promoting Agriculture, Commerce and Arts established in 1781, rather than the Philadelphia Society, which is generally accepted as the oldest. Despite the fact that there is evidence of the existence of such a society (see *New Jersey Gazette* [Trenton, New Jersey], August 29 and September 5, 1781), no information is available concerning it. See Carl R. Woodward, *The development of agriculture in New Jersey, 1640-1880,* New Jersey Agr. Exp. Sta. Bull. 451, pp. 51-52. New Brunswick, New Jersey: Rutgers University, May, 1927.

For the New York Society, see *Transactions of the Society for the Promotion of Agriculture, Arts and Manufactures, instituted in the State of New York,* Vol. I. Second ed. rev. Albany, New York: Chas. R. and Geo. Webster, 1801. *Transactions of the Society for the Promotion of Useful Arts, in the State of New York,* Vol. II: Albany, New York: printed by John Barber, 1807. Vol. III: Albany, New York: printed by Websters and Skinners, 1814. Vol. IV, Part I: 1816. Vol. IV, Part II: 1819. U. P. Hedrick, *A history of agriculture in the State of New York,* pp. 113-119. New York Agricultural Society, 1933. Periam, p. 66.

For an account of the Massachusetts Society, see *Laws and regulations of the*

organized in 1785 (August), but was not incorporated until ten years later.[3] Its first president, Honorable Thomas Heyward, Jr., was a signer of the Declaration of Independence. It began to carry on activities which were typical of similar societies soon to be organized in other states—collecting and disseminating agricultural information and later conducting exhibits. According to the *Report of the Commissioner of Agriculture for the Year 1875,* "Its object was to institute a farm for agricultural experiments. . . . The Society early possessed itself of a tract of land near the city of Charleston. Agricultural experiments were continually made on this land up to the beginning of the late war." Irvine Walker, a historian of the Society, says, however, that experiments were not conducted on the Society's farm until the first decade of the twentieth century.[4]

———

Massachusetts Society for Promoting Agriculture. Boston: printed by Isaiah Thomas and Ebenezer T. Andrews, 1793. *Rules and regulations of the Massachusetts Society for Promoting Agriculture.* Boston: printed by Thomas Fleet, 1796. *Papers on agriculture: consisting of communications made to the Massachusetts Society for Promoting Agriculture, and extracts.* Boston: printed by Adams and Rhoades, 1807. *Georgick papers for 1809, consisting of letters and extracts communicated to the Massachusetts Society for Promoting Agriculture.* Boston: printed by Russell and Cutler, 1809. *Papers for 1810, communicated to the Massachusetts Society for Promoting Agriculture.* Boston: printed by Russell and Cutler, 1810. Periam, pp. 68-69.

For an account of the Society in Connecticut, see *Transactions of the Society for Promoting Agriculture in the State of Connecticut.* New Haven: printed by William W. Morse, 1802. Alfred C. True, *A history of agricultural education in the United States, 1785-1925,* United States Department of Agriculture, Misc. Publ. No. 36, p. 14. Washington, D. C.: Government Printing Office, 1929.

For an account of the Society in Virginia, see *Memoirs of the Society of Virginia for Promoting Agriculture.* Richmond: printed by Shepherd and Pollard, 1818. True, p. 15.

For general accounts of early agricultural societies, see Wiest, pp. 333-363. Kenyon L. Butterfield, "Farmers' Social Organizations," from L. H. Bailey, ed., *Cyclopedia of American agriculture,* Vol. IV, pp. 291-292. *Transactions of the Illinois State Agricultural Society, 1853-54,* Vol. I, p. 13. Springfield, Illinois: printed by Lanphier and Walker, 1855. *Report of the Commissioner of Agriculture, 1866,* pp. 513-522. *Report of the Commissioner of Agriculture, 1875,* pp. 437-438.

[3] The original name was The South Carolina Society for Promoting and Improving Agriculture and Other Rural Concerns.

[4] *Report of the Commissioner of Agriculture, 1875,* pp. 463-464. C. Irvine Walker, *History of the Agricultural Society of South Carolina,* pp. 3-8, 67-71. Charleston, South Carolina: published by the Society, 1919. Periam, p. 65. Wiest, p. 335. *Original communications made to the Agricultural Society of South Carolina; and extracts from select authors on agriculture.* Charleston, South Carolina: printed by Archibald E. Miller, 1824. *The Agricultural Society of South Carolina organized August 24, 1875,* mimeographed pamphlet prepared for the celebration of the 150th Anniversary of its Foundation, Charleston, South Carolina, January 14, 1936.

The Philadelphia and South Carolina organizations were followed by others, one in Maine in 1787, one in New York in 1791, one in Massachusetts incorporated in 1792, one in Connecticut in 1794, the Columbian Agricultural Society embracing Maryland, Virginia, and the District of Columbia in 1809, and societies in Georgia and Virginia by 1811. The one in South Carolina is still in existence, although a study of its records seems to indicate that there was a period from 1840 to 1869 when it was not active. President Heyward said in his first address to the Society, "Agriculture is the parent of commerce; and both together form the great sources from which the wants of individuals are supplied, and the principal riches and strength of every State flow. It becomes the duty, therefore, as well as the interest of every citizen to encourage and promote it." [5]

The New York Society for the Promotion of Agriculture, Arts, and Manufactures (organized in February, 1791) included in its membership John Jay, signer of the Declaration of Independence, author of the New York State Constitution, the second governor of the state, and first chief justice of the United States Supreme Court; Robert R. Livingston, Chancellor of the State and Minister to France; General George Clinton, army commander under Washington, first governor of the state, and Vice-President of the United States; John Sloss Hobart, jurist and United States Senator; Philip Van Cortland, general, Congressman, and wealthy landowner; Simeon De Witt, soldier, surveyor general of New York and Chancellor of the University of New York; General Horatio Gates, capturer of Burgoyne; Samuel L. Mitchell, professor of botany, chemistry, and agriculture at Columbia University; Elkanah Watson, proprietor of the Erie Canal; and many other persons prominent in political and business affairs. [6]

Rodney H. True says of the Albemarle (Virginia) Agricultural Society, organized in May, 1817:

> In this group of 30 men was one who had served his country eight years as its honored President, two others who were to be governors of Virginia, still another who was to represent that State in the United States Senate and his country at the Court of St. James, and another who closed his career on the Supreme Bench of the United

---

[5] Irvine Walker, p. 4.
[6] Hedrick, pp. 113-115.

States. There was a brigadier-general who was perhaps to deserve an even greater share of the gratitude of his fellow men by leading in the great movements of peace. There were also present a future head of the University of Virginia, and several who were destined to serve in the State legislature.[7]

The Berkshire Agricultural Society, organized in western Massachusetts in 1811, seems to have furnished a blueprint for a more direct attack upon what practical farmers considered their more urgent production problems. Its type of organization sprang up in a great number of counties in southern New England and served to keep before farmers the need for better markets, as well as for agricultural improvements along production lines. Elkanah Watson, the founder of the Society, tells in his history of the organization that his whole plan was to excite competition in an annual display of animals, domestic manufactures, and general farming—awarding, among others, a premium for the best-kept and most progressive farm in the community.[8] No doubt a large measure of the success of the Berkshire Societies lay in their ability to satisfy the farmer's need for a closer relationship with others in his community and for a greater number of social contacts.

These improvement types of societies were not confined to local or state scope. President Washington, in his last annual message to Congress, referred to the existence of such societies in other nations and said, "Institutions for promoting it [agriculture] grow up, supported by the public purse; and to what object can it be dedicated with greater propriety?"[9] His suggestion for an official governmental organization was taken up by the lower house of Congress and referred to a committee. The committee recommended the establishment at the seat of govern-

---

[7] Rodney H. True, "Early Days of the Albemarle Agricultural Society," *Annual report of the American Historical Association for the year 1918*, Vol. I, p. 243. Washington, D. C.: Government Printing Office, 1921.

[8] Elkanah Watson, *Rise, progress, and existing state of modern agricultural societies, on the Berkshire system, from 1807, to the establishment of the Board of Agriculture in the State of New York, January 10, 1820*. Albany: D. Steele, 1820. Bidwell, p. 686. Winslow C. Watson, ed., *Memoirs of Elkanah Watson*, chap. xxviii, pp. 364-381. New York: Dana and Co., 1856.

[9] James D. Richardson, ed., A compilation of the *Messages and papers of the Presidents*, Vol. I, "Eighth Annual Address," George Washington, December 7, 1796, p. 194. New York: Bureau of National Literature, 1912.

ment of "a society for the promotion of agriculture" to be known as The American Society of Agriculture. Such a society was to "be composed of the members of the Legislature of the United States, of the judges of the Supreme Court; of the Secretaries of State, Treasury, and War, and the Attorney General," and of such others as should be appointed. It was to hold annual meetings, elect officers, "and [elect] also a board of thirty members belonging to the society, to be called the Board of Agriculture," which was to carry on the bulk of the work throughout the year. The salary of the secretary and the expenses for stationery were to be paid from the public treasury, if the state of the treasury should render such advisable. The committee's report was never acted upon because it was submitted at a time when a bitter fight over tax legislation was absorbing all the time of Congress.[10] It is probable, however, that Washington's recommendation and the Congressional committee's report did something to stimulate the organization of a national society a few years later; at any rate, the Columbian Agricultural Society was organized in 1809 with members from Maryland, Virginia, and the District of Columbia, with headquarters at Washington, D. C. It enlisted the patronage of a great many influential men, but, like the state societies of its day, dealt with agricultural improvement rather than agrarian reform. It seems not to have survived the war period of 1812-1814.[11] Wiest remarks concerning this early type of organization, that they "virtually always lacked the spirit of the newer so-called farmers' organizations whose purpose is also largely educational but which exist primarily to promote the economic welfare of the farmers through cooperation and combination." [12]

These older societies were more definitely the forerunners of state and national departments of agriculture than they were of modern general

[10] *American state papers*, Class X. Miscellaneous, Vol. I, *Promotion of agriculture*, pp. 154-155.

[11] *Report of the Commissioner of Agriculture, 1866*, pp. 518-522. For the constitution of the Columbian Society, see *Agricultural Museum* (Georgetown, D. C.), Vol. I, No. 1 (July 4, 1810), pp. 8-11. For early proceedings and meetings of the standing committee, see *Agricultural Museum*, Vol. I, No. 1 (July 4, 1810), pp. 11-13; Vol. I, No. 2 (July 18, 1810), pp. 27-29; Vol. I, No. 11 (November 23, 1810), pp. 172-175; Vol. I, No. 22 (May 8, 1811), pp. 353-354; Vol. I, No. 23 (May 22, 1811), pp. 366-369; Vol. II, No. 1 (July, 1811), pp. 26-29; Vol. II, No. 5 (November, 1811), pp. 154-158; Vol. II, No. 6 (November, 1811), pp 189-191; Vol. II, No. 11 (May, 1812), pp. 325-329.

[12] Wiest, p. 333.

farmers' organizations. Their number in 1852 was approximately three hundred, and in 1860 reached almost one thousand. It was undoubtedly their leading members who responded to a call for agriculturists to meet at Washington, D. C., in 1852, at which time The United States Agricultural Society was organized. This society continued to carry on its scientific work until the United States Department of Agriculture was set up by law in 1862. These societies did much good, as similar societies are doing today, but they were only indirectly a part of the Farmers' Movement.[13]

FARMERS', MECHANICS', AND WORKINGMEN'S ORGANIZATIONS

The first farmers' organization to participate in what is thought of as a farmers' movement was a political organization—the New England Association of Farmers, Mechanics, and other Workingmen. How widespread and wholeheartedly the farmers of that time participated in the organization, however, is difficult to determine. They were considered natural allies of mechanics and other workingmen in that they were "producers," and the movement was one which attempted to settle issues between "producers," on the one hand, and "consumers" on the other. This organization was founded around 1830, following the rise of the first effective city central trade union of the world—the Mechanics' Union of Trade Associations—in Philadelphia, in 1827.[14] It is interesting to note that this organization sprang up during a period of falling prices. Unemployment was pronounced, hours of work in the factories were long, twelve to sixteen hours per day, and there was a large amount of woman and child labor in the mills. Many New England farmers' daughters were employed in industrial pursuits, and farmers were therefore concerned about unemployment, long hours, and low wages, as well as about low prices. Imprisonment for debt was practiced, compulsory militia drill was still the rule, and public education was by no means universal. The

---

[13] *Journal of the United States Agricultural Society*, Vol. I, No. 1 (August, 1852), p. iii. *Quarterly Journal of Agriculture*, Vol. VIII, No. 1 (April, 1860), p. 26. Wanlass, pp. 19-20. *Report of the Commissioner of Agriculture, 1866*, pp. 525-526.

[14] John R. Commons, *et al.*, *History of labour in the United States*, Vol. I, pp. 169-170, 290. New York: The Macmillan Company, 1921.

poor people, as in the time of Shays' Rebellion, felt that they were being asked to render far more service to the government than they were receiving from it. It was but natural, therefore, that they should be interested in reforms of all kinds. The farmers joined with the mechanics and other workingmen in demanding shorter hours, higher wages, public education, prison reform, and cheaper money.[15]

In 1829-1830, the Farmers, Mechanics and Workingmen of Allegheny County, Pennsylvania, and other similar organizations resolved that they would support only producers for office. They required candidates to pledge themselves, if elected, "to promote the interests and support the claims of the Working People"[16] and later demanded that candidates support definite measures. From 1828 to 1834, farmers' and mechanics' societies sprang up in New England, New York, New Jersey, Pennsylvania, Delaware, and Ohio. There was even the beginning of an organization as far west as Missouri.[17]

Commons lists the chief demands of these societies in the following statement, which is a description of the demands of the New England Association of Farmers, Mechanics, and other Workingmen:

This association, though at first rather an industrial than a political organization, eventually advocated a mechanics' lien law, reform in the militia system, simplification of the laws, extension of the suffrage, reform in the land tenure laws, in the system of taxation, and in banks and other incorporated monopolies, abolition of imprisonment for debt, protection of labour instead of capital, factory legislation, especially in the interest of women and children, a better

---

[15] *Ibid.*, pp. 170-184, for a survey account of the deplorable conditions of the producers of that period.

[16] *Ibid.*, pp. 209-210. Quotation is originally from *Mechanics Free Press* (Utica, New York), August 16 and 23, 1828. Also see issue of July 31, 1830. (Apparently the only adequate file of the *Mechanics Free Press* is to be found in Philadelphia, in the library of the Historical Society of Pennsylvania.)

The other material concerning Allegheny County is from the *Delaware Free Press* (Wilmington, Delaware), July 31, 1830. (This paper may be found at the Wilmington Historical Society of Delaware, in the Wilmington Institute Free Library, and at the New York Historical Society.)

For "other similar organizations," see *Mechanics Free Press,* November 14, 1829; July 31, 1830; September 18, 1830.

[17] *Ibid.*, pp. 185-332. Commons gives a detailed account of the various associations, cites statements from many workingmen's papers of the time, and records the demands of the societies in their various conventions.

system of education, in particular, provision for the education of children in factory districts, and shorter hours of labour.[18]

Although the New Haven delegates reported that the third convention of the New England Association was composed principally of farmers and mechanics and not of factory workers, there is also evidence that farmers were not very loyal or enthusiastic members of these societies.[19] The call for the second convention of the New England Association in 1832 made a special appeal to "the farming interests," [20] indicating that there was doubt about adequate farmer representation. The constitution of the association provided that, "Each and every person that shall sign this constitution, *except practical farmers*, shall, so long as he may remain a member of the Association stand pledged on his honor, to labor no more than ten hours for one day...." [21] These and other evidences would indicate that the name "farmers" might have been used to lend strength to the workingmen's movement, and that few farmers were, after all, really active members of the organization. Reading of newspaper notices and accounts of local meetings convinces one that farmers participated very little in these meetings. This brief account of the attempt to enlist them is presented because there have been more recent attempts on the part of organized laborers and organized farmers to join forces in reform movements.

FARMERS' SOCIETIES AND CLUBS, 1850-1860

If there is doubt about farmers' participation in the mechanics' and workingmen's organizations of 1828 to 1834, there can be no such doubt about their participation in the farmers' societies and clubs which devel-

---

[18] *Ibid.,* p. 318. Reprinted by permission of The Macmillan Company.

[19] Commons, p. 313. Commons quotes from *Carey's select excerpts*, Vol. IV, p. 435, which is a collection of clippings, both undated and unlabeled, made by Mathew Carey. They are available only in the Ridgeway Branch of the Library Co., Philadelphia.

[20] *Ibid.,* p. 308. For an account of this convention, see also the *Proceedings of the New England Association of Farmers, Mechanics and other Workingmen,* September, 1832, Boston.

[21] John R. Commons, *et al,* ed., *A documentary history of American industrial society,* Vol. V, *Labor movement, 1820-40,* p. 193. Cleveland, Ohio: Arthur H. Clark Co., 1910. Commons has reprinted this material from the *Co-operator* (Utica, New York), April 3, 1832. (The italics in the material quoted are mine.)

oped during the decade, 1850-1860. Such societies and clubs were organized in at least twenty states stretching from New York and Vermont to Oregon, Washington, and California. In 1859, there were known to be in existence 621 such organizations. More than half of them (350) were in the eight midwestern states of Ohio, Indiana, Illinois, Iowa, Missouri, Nebraska, Minnesota, and Wisconsin.[22] Delegates from the Illinois clubs and societies came together in Springfield in 1853 and organized the Illinois State Agricultural Society.[23] The state organization drafted a model constitution and promoted the formation of county societies. These county societies discussed technical and practical farming at their meetings, but in the early days apparently gave no consideration to price and market issues. Local country newspapers and the two agricultural journals of the area published regularly signed reports from local societies and clubs, and it is therefore possible to know something of the topics discussed at local meetings. The county societies conducted county fairs and the state society a state fair each year. Premiums were awarded and the local papers and agricultural journals gave much space to announcements before these events and to awards following them. News items and editorials dealt with such topics as "New Orchards," "The Sewing Machine," "Talks to Farmers," and "The Future of the Northwest," but only here and there did they indicate that state or federal legislation or prices and markets were discussed at meetings. In a few instances space was devoted to railroads, but freight rates, a topic that became a burning issue a decade later, were seldom mentioned.[24]

Emery's *Journal of Agriculture*, from its first issue—January, 1858—not only reported meetings of county agricultural societies and local clubs, but for a period actively promoted the organization of such clubs. The

---

[22] Belleville *Weekly Democrat* (Illinois), September 3, 1859, quoting from the Cleveland *Plain Dealer*.

[23] See *Transactions of the Illinois State Agricultural Society, 1853-54,* pp. 38-88, for an account of the Society in its first year of existence. See also Arthur Chas. Cole, *The era of the Civil War, 1848-1870,* Vol. III of *The centennial history of Illinois,* pp. 78-79. Springfield: Illinois Centennial Commission, 1919. *Prairie Farmer* (Chicago, Illinois), December, 1852, pp. 536-537. *Illinois State Register* (Springfield, Illinois), January 13, 1853.

[24] See Alton *Telegram* (Illinois), May 9, 1855. Amboy *Times* (Illinois), October 13, 1859. Grayville *Weekly Herald* (Illinois), September 12, 1857. Belleville *Weekly Democrat,* February 27, 1857, October 9, 1858, September 3, 1859. *Prairie Farmer,* 1855-1858. Emery's *Journal of Agriculture and the Prairie Farmer,* 1858-1859.

first issue of that journal carried an article signed by Worth on "Farmers' Clubs." In this article the author set forth their primary purposes: "First, They will give the farmer a professional character in his view, and heighten the dignity of his calling. . . . Second, They would furnish the best facilities for professional improvement. . . . Third, They will furnish the best possible facilities for acquiring a knowledge of the actual state of agriculture among us." Worth added, "At the present the merchant in town knows more about the prospect of any given district than many of its inhabitants know."[25] However, he in no way criticized merchants but only pleaded for the organization of farmers' clubs for the purposes he had described.

The city of Chicago was at that time developing at the very front door of midwestern farmers. One of its greatest enterprises was the grain trade. Not only the production but the prices of grain were important to midwestern farmers. Illinois, during the decade 1850-1860, came to be the greatest grain-producing state in the Union. It increased its corn production from 57,647,000 bushels in 1850 to 115,175,000 bushels in 1860, rose from fifth to first place in wheat production during that decade, and also became the leading oats, barley, and rye-producing state.[26] Heavy grain speculation developed in Chicago, out of which fortunes of from $20,000, to $30,000 were made in a few weeks. As Cole says, "The general effect upon the business of the city was extremely good, but the farmers were restive under this system and throughout the decade continued a spasmodic agitation for cooperative associations for the disposal of their produce."[27]

An article in Emery's *Journal of Agriculture* made the following statement: ". . . when our farmers have become associated to discuss and regulate their own interests, to enact as associations rules by which they will be governed, in the disposal as well as the production of crops, then shall there be less suffering from sharpers, less field for speculators among them, and a confidence in themselves created, which shall beget dire self-respect."[28] During that same month, an article quoted Professor J. B.

---

[25] Emery's *Journal of Agriculture* (Chicago), Vol. I, No. 1 (January, 1858).
[26] L. B. Schmidt, "The Westward Movement of the Corn-growing Industry in the United States," *Iowa Journal of History and Politics*, Vol. XXI (1923), pp. 112-141.
[27] Cole, pp. 75-76.
[28] Emery's *Journal of Agriculture*, January 7, 1858.

Turner as having at one time written to the farmers and mechanics of Illinois as follows:

> Let us besiege our Legislature and besiege Congress, and give no peace till they properly attend to all those interests of agriculture, which they now profess to attend to, and undertake all other enterprises which we so much need.
>
> That is the doctrine President Wilson [probably president of Illinois State Agricultural Society] preaches. Is it what we should practice? Do we want anything from government? If so let us ask for it. Have we any claim upon their attention? Who pays the taxes? Whose votes delegate power to Congress? Have we any representatives? What is done for us? [29]

But even before this, Professor Turner had struck a still more militant note. In the annual address made to the Illinois State Agricultural Society during the first year of its existence (1853-1854), he had said:

> But while our representatives and senators have thus with almost unparalleled unanimity manifested a disposition to do all in their power to aid us, we must bear in mind that they cannot help us unless we help ourselves. You must be first to move, first to resolve, petition and to act—talk—talk at home—talk abroad—and above all talk at the ballot-box—and then and not till then will your representatives in Congress stand ready to execute your will.[30]

There were thus appearing here and there statements which gave warning of the sentiments which were clearly stated a little later in the Farmers' Platform at Centralia, Illinois. The Belleville *Weekly Democrat*, in February, 1858, said, "We are opposed to the whole banking system, from beginning to end. They afford facilities to be sure, to men largely engaged in commercial business, but at the expense of the farmers and hard-working honest men." [31] And J. D. Porter, writing to Emery's *Journal of Agriculture and the Prairie Farmer*, told the editors, "Farmers want a paper devoted to *their interests* not only to show them how to produce greater crops, but to assist them in *getting better prices;* to be foremost

---

[29] *Ibid.*, January 21, 1858. Turner taught at the University of Illinois.
[30] *Transactions of the Illinois State Agricultural Society, 1853-1854,* p. 60.
[31] Belleville *Weekly Democrat,* February 27, 1858.

in pleading their cause in everything that pertains to their interest as farmers, as citizens, and as *men*. The time is fast approaching when farmers will *demand* and have the right which demagogues and the upper ten have so long denied them." [32]

At the Illinois State Fair, held at Centralia in September, 1858, a group of farmers formulated what might well be called the "Battle Cry of the Farmers' Movement," but there is little information concerning this so-called "convention." Emery's *Journal of Agriculture and the Prairie Farmer* claimed that it could find no evidence that such a meeting was held and implied that the platform was the work of one or a few men. This paper's published statement said in part, "It purports to have been a Congress representing the farmers of Illinois. We did not learn that there had been any meeting to discuss the creed, declaration, etc., until we saw it announced in the *Prairie Farmer* subsequently." The writer of the article said he went to the Cook County tent on the afternoon the meeting was supposed to have been held, but no one was there; returned an hour later and found a dozen men there, but heard no formal discussion. He then went on to say there was "not a single man of any note as an agriculturist among those we supposed to be delegates." [33]

Periam gives quite a different impression when he describes this meeting as "a general Convention or Congress" and says, "The discussions of this body were earnest in tone and comprehensive in scope." [34] He does not say that he was present, but he might well have been, for he was a leading member of an outstanding local farmers' club and later demonstrated great interest in affairs of this kind. Furthermore, his word cannot be taken lightly. He was a horticulturist of some note, and later was not only an outstanding agricultural editor, but also a member of the board of trustees of the Illinois Industrial University (now University of Illinois) and a professor at the Chicago Veterinary College. From 1873 to 1878, he served as vice-president of the Illinois State Board of Agriculture. [35]

Whatever the detailed facts about the technical call for this Centralia meeting are, and no matter who was there, it is evident that those who

---

[32] Emery's *Journal of Agriculture and the Prairie Farmer,* November 4, 1858.

[33] *Ibid.,* November 25, 1858.

[34] Periam, p. 204.

[35] *Dictionary of American biography,* Vol. XIV, pp. 463-464. New York: Charles Scribner's Sons, 1934.

formulated the statement, issued as the "Farmers' Platform," did little more than give voice to sentiments which were fairly prevalent among farmers of that area and had been partially expressed by them before the Centralia meeting. Periam, who later was editor of the *Western Rural* and the *Prairie Farmer,* says that farmers had seen great railroad magnates like Vanderbilt, Drew, and Gould grow rich through the control of not only railroads, but canal, lake, and river navigation; that they had seen merchants accumulating wealth from year to year with the result that intelligent farmers here and there had organized societies "to discuss their real or supposed grievances, and systems of cultivation..." [36] He named the beginning of their discontent with the railroads as about 1848, and with the merchants as about 1852. He says, "The feeling that relief must be had finally gained such strength that a general convention or congress was called, and held at Centralia, on the fifteenth of September, 1858." [37] The convention issued a "Farmers' Platform," a "Declaration of Principles," and a "Plan of Operations." Because of the significance of the sentiment expressed in these documents, we quote them here in their entirety.

FARMERS' PLATFORM OF 1858

We believe that the time has come when the producing classes should assert, not only their independence, but their supremacy; that nonproducers cannot be relied upon as guarantees of fairness; and that laws enacted and administered by lawyers are not a true standard of popular sentiment.

We believe that a general application to commerce of the principle that the majority should rule, would increase the income and diminish the outlay of producers, and, at the same time, elevate the standard of mercantile morality.

We believe that the producer of a commodity and the purchaser of it should, together, have more voice in fixing its price than he who simply carries it from one to the other.

We believe that the true method of guarding against commercial revulsions is to bring the producer and consumer as near together

[36] Periam, p. 201.
[37] *Ibid.,* p. 204. See pp. 196-204 for an account of the growth of farmers' grievances.

as possible, thus diminishing the alarming number and the more alarming power of nonproducers.

We believe that in union there is strength, and that in union alone can the necessarily isolated condition of farmers be so strengthened as to enable them to cope, on equal terms, with men whose callings are, in their very nature, a permanent and self-created combination of interests.

We believe that system of commerce to be the best which transacts the most business, with the least tax on production, and which, instead of being a master, is merely a servant.

We believe that good prices are as necessary to the prosperity of farmers as good crops,[38] and, in order to create such a power as to insure as much uniformity in prices as in products, farmers must keep out of debt; and that, in order to keep out of debt, they must pay for what they buy and exact the same from others.

DECLARATION OF PRINCIPLES

These truths we hold to be self-evident, that, as production both precedes barter and employs more labor and capital, it is more worthy the care and attention of governments and of individuals; that in the honorable transaction of a legitimate business there is no necessity for secret cost-marks; that, in all well-regulated communities, there should be the smallest possible number of nonproducers that is necessary to the welfare of the human race; that labor and capital employed in agriculture should receive as much reward as labor and capital employed in any other pursuit; that, as the exchanger is merely an agent between the producer and consumer, he should not have a chief voice in the establishment of prices; that the interests of agriculture and of commerce can only be considered as identical when each has an equal share in regulating barter; and that the principal road to honor and distinction, in this country, should lead through productive industry.

PLAN OF OPERATIONS

First. The formation of Farmers' Clubs wherever practical, the object of which shall be to produce concert of action on all matters connected with their interests.

---

[38] Underscored by author, to emphasize the battle cry of the Farmers' Movement.

Second. The establishment, as far as possible, of the ready pay system in all pecuniary transactions.

Third. The formation of wholesale purchasing and selling agencies in the great centers of commerce, so that producers may, in a great measure, have it in their power to save the profits of retailers.

Fourth. The organization of such a power as to insure the creation of a national agricultural bureau, the main object of which shall be an annual or semiannual census of all our national products, and the collection and dissemination of valuable seeds, plants, and facts.

Fifth. The election of producers to all places of public trust and honor the general rule, and the election of nonproducers the exception.[39]

The intervention of the Civil War to a considerable extent stopped a movement which might have grown to great proportions. Of that we cannot be sure, but we do know that the activities of similar clubs, with the assistance of the newly organized Grange, did launch a movement in Illinois shortly after the Civil War that constitutes one of the great tides of the Farmers' Movement in the United States. The "Granger Movement," so-called by Solon J. Buck,[40] of the late sixties and early seventies, did not have to start from the mark. It had a decade of prewar experience and organization back of it, and the leaders of this decade, among whom was Jonathan Periam, undoubtedly formed the connecting link between the Centralia convention and the Granger revolt.

Although the panic of 1857 was more a financial crisis than a general depression, it undoubtedly heightened farmers' thinking about prices and markets. The panic was the result of extreme speculation, stimulated more by railway expansion than by any other one thing. There was $1,350,000,000 poured into railway investments between 1830 and 1860. The greatest period of construction had been in 1856 and 1857.[41] While, therefore, the panic scarcely touched the farmers, the fact that great fortunes were being made out of an enterprise which was developing, as they believed, at the expense of farming caused them to protest and demand a greater voice in both government and economic affairs. Further-

[39] Periam, pp. 204-206.

[40] Solon J. Buck was the author of *The Granger Movement.*

[41] Katharine Coman, *The industrial history of the United States,* pp. 266-267, 302. New York: The Macmillan Company, 1910. Sumner, pp. 180-187.

more, it was the expansion of railroads into the Middle West that had converted a relatively self-sufficient agriculture into a commercial enterprise. It was therefore inevitable that the midwestern farmer should become concerned about prices and markets; and, as we have seen, it had been this concern which gave rise to the Farmers' Movement farther east more than one hundred years prior to this time. The panic of 1857 was not the cause or result of a farmer upheaval, but it was a result of wild money-making schemes—chiefly railroad expansion and grain speculation —and these were things against which the farmers at that time protested. Following the Civil War, the farmers organized in an attempt to wield definite influence against such practices.

· 5 ·

THE

AGRICULTURAL

REVOLUTION

FROM PIONEER TO SETTLED AGRICULTURAL
ECONOMY

Between the Civil War and the close of the century, an agricultural revolution took place in the United States which was as significant in its effects as the Industrial Revolution had been in England a century earlier. Agriculture moved deep into the commercial economy, and agricultural-economic issues became topics for discussion in an increasing number of agricultural periodicals. The era of canal building was completed, and railroad building was started well before 1860. The processing of one agricultural product after another moved from farm homes to city factories, and farm people therefore purchased an increasing amount of factory-made consumption goods. The McCormick reaper was patented in 1833, John Deere began manufacturing steel plows in 1837, and a practical grain drill in the same year. A mowing machine was patented in 1842. Other factory-made farm machinery followed rapidly, and farmers naturally purchased a greater amount and diversity of production goods.

Cotton had become the chief export product of the country, and the great corn and wheat commercial-farming belts were already partially settled before the war. In the face of this great expansion in agriculture, those engaged in nonfarm occupations had greatly increased, and agriculture was relatively less dominant than it had been at any time in the country's history. Commercial and industrial interests automatically grew stronger not only in the market but in political influence. During the forty-year period between 1820 and 1860, there arose some economic and political issues that have ever since been a part of the American Farmers' Movement.

Just prior to the war, as shown in the previous chapter, there had appeared the Farmers' Platform or Declaration of Independence, issued at Centralia, Illinois. Immediately following the war, farmers' clubs with both economic and political objectives were organized widely throughout the nation. These were followed by the Granger upheaval in the early seventies, accompanied by the Anti-Monopoly and Reform parties; the Greenback party in the late seventies and early eighties; the great Farmers' Alliance upheaval in the eighties and early nineties; and, finally, the titanic political struggle of the Populists in the middle nineties. Never before or since has there been such universal or sustained farmer protest as there was from 1867 to 1897. It was a sort of thirty-years' war, with the battles swinging from one front to another and the spirit of battle waxing and waning from decade to decade. But the gauge of battle was always the same, prices and markets, although often expressed in terms of monopolies and money. The dominance of agriculture in the nation was being challenged by other types of economic enterprise, and the farmer himself was being compelled to change from a relatively ignorant and isolated pioneer to a member of a capitalistic business system. This important change, while not consciously recognized by the farmers, demanded of them so many things to which they were not accustomed that they were kept in a ferment of confusion and protest. It meant that calculation was substituted for custom in producing those things for which it had always been supposed there was an unlimited demand, and that the owners of land, for the first time in American history, yielded social and political prestige to those engaged in other pursuits.

Before the Civil War, railroads had developed to such an extent that practically every city in the East was a market center. After the war came the great economic venture of pushing these new means of transportation and communication across the continent and furnishing to all sections of the nation these same market contacts. No one was more eager than the farmer that the task be accomplished. He therefore willingly lent himself and every unit of his government from township to federal government to the enterprise. States, counties, and cities bound themselves for unheard-of debts to help build railroads. Farmers and small townsmen invested their savings in railroad securities, and even European capital was induced to take heavy financial risks in helping to connect the granary of the world with the population and consumer centers of the world. Railroad mileage increased from 34,909 in 1866 to 163,562 in 1890, at the end of which period almost $10,000,000,000, about one-sixth of the estimated wealth of the nation, was invested in railroads.[1]

The great economic enterprise of railroad building gave the United States her first lesson in the real concentration of wealth, and farmers were faced with a fairly small group of financiers who challenged their supremacy in both economic and political affairs. As the Beards say, "The land of Washington, Franklin, Jefferson, and John Adams had become a land of millionaires and the supreme direction of its economy had passed from the owners of farms and isolated plants and banks to a few men and institutions near the center of its life." [2] It was, therefore, not surprising that the first and foremost protest of the Farmers' Movement for thirty years following the Civil War was against railroad domination, monopolies, and political corruption.

Coupled with the expansion of railroads, and partially resulting from it, was a great expansion of population into the West and Southwest and a consequent increase in agricultural production. Corn production increased from approximately 760,945,000 bushels in 1869 to 2,666,324,000 bushels in 1899, and wheat production from 287,746,000 to 658,534,000 bushels during the same period. Practically every other farm commodity produced by western farmers followed the same trend. The per capita production of every leading cereal, except rye, increased—in some cases doubled—during those thirty years. The production of cotton increased

---

[1] Beards, Vol. II, p. 192. Frederick Martin, *The statesman's year-book for the year 1870*, p. 590. London: Macmillan and Company, Ltd., 1870.

[2] Beards, Vol. II, p. 198.

from approximately 3,000,000 bales in 1869 to approximately 10,000,000 bales in 1899, and the acreage in harvested cotton tripled during this time.[3] Thus, year after year, as population from the ends of the earth poured into the West and Southwest, competition in American farm products increased. The inevitable result was an almost universal decline in farm commodity prices.

As is always the case during a war period, prices had skyrocketed during the sixties. Cotton had reached $1.01 per pound, wheat $2.06, and corn 78 cents per bushel during the period of inflated prices.[4] During the thirty-two years, 1864-1896, the wholesale farm price index (1914-1915 = 100) fell from 162 to 56. While the purchasing power of farm products in terms of nonagricultural products was a little better at the end of this period, it was very low in 1873 and 1880.[5] Cotton did not sell for as much as 11 cents per pound from 1880 until 1903; the price of corn rose above 50 cents per bushel only twice between 1870 and 1900; and the price of wheat, while fluctuating, exceeded $1.10 per bushel only twice between 1873 and 1900. There has never been a period in American history in which farm prices were depressed for so long a time as they were in the thirty years following the Civil War, and there has never been a period in which so large a percentage of American farmers rose in protest against the conditions under which they found themselves.

Farmers, of course, did not understand all of the complicated factors involved in this long period of depression. They did, however, know that a great era of agricultural expansion could not be paid for out of falling prices and currency deflation, and they did know that fixed charges, mortgage debts, and taxes became more burdensome as the value of money increased. They were, therefore, more than passively interested in the deflation program of the federal government following the Civil War. The per capita circulation of money had increased from $14 in 1861

---

[3] Louis B. Schmidt and Earle D. Ross, *Readings in the economic history of American agriculture*, p. 371. New York: The Macmillan Company, 1925. *Yearbook of agricultural statistics, 1939*, p. 44. Washington, D. C.: Government Printing Office, 1939.

[4] *Agricultural statistics, 1939*, pp. 9, 44. M. B. Hammond, *The cotton industry*, Part I, "The Cotton Culture and the Cotton Trade," Appendix I, Publications of the American Economic Association, New Series, No. 1 (December, 1897).

[5] "Wholesale Prices of Farm and Nonagricultural Products, 1798-1938," provided by the Division of Statistical and Historical Research, Bureau of Agricultural Economics, United States Department of Agriculture.

to $23.83 in 1865. Of the $770,000,000 of all kinds of money at the end of the war, $431,000,000 were United States notes—greenbacks.[6] This inflation had naturally contributed to high prices for all commodities. In these high prices farmers had shared with others, but their cash costs as well as their selling prices had been inflated. When deflation and falling prices came, their fixed costs—debts and taxes—did not decrease with decreasing prices and their debts, greatly increased during the period of agricultural expansion, continued to increase all during the thirty years of depression. The movement westward was undoubtedly overstimulated almost as much by mortgage companies, ready and anxious to loan money on farm real estate, as it was by the rapid development of railroads. Knox says:

> Mortgage companies also promptly appeared in the wake of settlement with active agents in all the towns. These largely handled English capital, which appeared to be pushing for investment in farm mortgages in this country at that time, the interest rate secured —ten per cent flat—being very enticing. The borrower paid from twelve to eighteen per cent, the difference going to the agent as his commission, and it became the practice in many cases to take a second mortgage in lieu of cash for such commission.
>
> The settler, after spending the money brought with him to the country in the establishment of his new home, found an agreeable response to his request for a short-time accommodation at the bank. When this fell due he was given bland attention by the agents of the mortgage companies, and urged to secure from them a mortgage loan for a term of years, being persuaded in many cases to ask for a larger sum than his needs required, the agent having in view his increased commission, and feeling secure in his knowledge of the avidity with which such securities were sought at the time by English and Eastern investors.[7]

Insurance companies and deposit banks entered the field of farm mortgages rapidly after 1880 and served, by offering credit in great volume, to help increase the farm mortgage debt.

---

[6] A. Barton Hepburn, *A history of currency in the United States,* p. 204. Rev. ed. New York: The Macmillan Company, 1924.

[7] John Jay Knox, *A history of banking in the United States,* p. 801. Cambridge, Massachusetts: Bankers Publishing Company, 1900.

The money issue vied with the railroad and monopoly issues during these three decades of depression. Farmers were convinced that the government's program of deflation was responsible for falling prices and that an increase in currency would not only bring back farm commodity price levels but make mortgages easier to pay. The per capita circulation of currency, however, did not again reach the high level of 1865 until 1892, and all during the seventies was little more than two-thirds of what it was at the end of the war, notwithstanding the fact that trade and commerce steadily increased all during the period.[8] The debates over the dozens of currency measures which were introduced in Congress during the period quite generally arrayed the legislative representatives of the West and Southwest against those of the East. The climax to this semisectional, semiclass struggle came in 1896, and the lines of battle were drawn by William Jennings Bryan when he sought to array the great democratic masses against what he was convinced was the domineering plutocracy of money. The speech which won him the presidential nomination of both the Democratic and People's parties swept into one grandiloquent statement the spirit of the farmers' revolt which had been brewing fully twenty-five years before the speech was delivered. Mr. Bryan said:

> The farmer who goes forth in the morning and toils all day—who begins in the spring and toils all summer—and who by the application of brain and muscle to the natural resources of the country creates wealth, is as much a business man as the man who goes upon the board of trade and bets upon the price of grain; the miners who go down a thousand feet into the earth, or climb two thousand feet upon the cliffs, and bring forth from their hiding places the precious metals to be poured into the channels of trade are as much business men as the few financial magnates who, in a back room, corner the money of the world. We come to speak for this broader class of business man.
>
> Ah, my friends, we say not one word against those who live upon the Atlantic coast, but the hardy pioneers who have braved all the dangers of the wilderness, who have made the desert to blossom as the rose—the pioneers away out there (pointing to the West), who rear their children near to Nature's heart, where they can mingle their voices with those of the birds—out there where they

---

[8] Hepburn, pp. 226, 251-252, 367, 384.

have erected schoolhouses for the education of their young, churches where they praise their Creator, and cemeteries where rest the ashes of their dead—these people, we say, are as deserving of the consideration of our party as any people in this country. It is for these that we speak. We do not come as aggressors. Our war is not a war of conquest; we are fighting in the defense of our homes, our families, and posterity. We have petitioned, and our petitions have been scorned; we have entreated, and our entreaties have been disregarded; we have begged, and they have mocked when our calamity came. We beg no longer; we entreat no more; we petition no more. We defy them.

You come to us and tell us that the great cities are in favor of the gold standard; we reply that the great cities rest upon our broad and fertile prairies. Burn down your cities and leave our farms, and your cities will spring up again as if by magic; but destroy our farms and the grass will grow in the streets of every city in the country. . . .

Having behind us the producing masses of this nation and the world, supported by the commercial interests, the laboring interests, and the toilers everywhere, we will answer their demand for a gold standard by saying to them: You shall not press down upon the brow of labor this crown of thorns, you shall not crucify mankind upon a cross of gold.[9]

THE ECONOMIC BACKGROUNDS OF REVOLT

Most students of the Farmers' Movement start their considerations with the organization of the Grange and its immediate antecedents—the agricultural clubs of the Middle West. This is but natural, due to the fact that from about 1870 to the present, the Farmers' Movement in the United States has been sponsored chiefly by general farmers' organizations, the earliest one of which was the Grange. Farmers' organizations are, however, as much results as causes of the Farmers' Movement. Most of them first came into existence at a period of high tide in the Farmers' Movement. It is, therefore, just as essential to understand the conditions out of which the high tides of the Farmers' Movement developed, after the Movement became attached to general farmers' organizations, as it is to

---

[9] William J. Bryan, *The first battle,* pp. 199-205. Chicago: W. B. Conkey Company, 1898.

understand those out of which Shays' Rebellion and other agrarian uprisings grew.

Conditions in both the North and South following the Civil War were
conducive to farmer discontent. In the South, agriculture was badly dis-
organized because of the compulsory abandonment of slave plantations,
the great loss of liquid capital, and the devastation of certain sections
over which northern armies had passed. In the North, a collapse of prices
followed the inflationary period of the Civil War. Returning soldiers
helped to increase production, and the inevitable backlash of overrapid
expansion of cultivated areas was setting in.

There was agricultural depression in both the West and South. The
volume of production in cotton more than doubled between 1866 and
1876, while the aggregate value for the total crop remained about the
same. The gross value of the corn crop for 1873 was almost identical with
that of 1866, although there had been an increase of almost 5,000,000
acres planted and something like a 65,000,000-bushel increase in volume
of production. Wheat acreage increased about 60 per cent from 1866 to
1875, while the gross value of the crop increased less than 15 per cent.
The price of cotton, which had reached $1.01 per pound in the New
York market in 1864, fell almost steadily to 8.16 cents per pound in
1878; the price of corn fell from 78.1 cents in 1867 to 31.3 cents per
bushel in 1878, and wheat fell from $2.06 per bushel in 1866 to 77.2 cents
in 1878. The development of new cotton lands in Texas, the necessity of
increased use of commercial fertilizers in the production of cotton in the
Old South, and the rapid development of the crop mortgage system in
the whole cotton belt all contributed to the plight of southern farmers.
These facts, coupled with the growth of mortgage debt and high freight
rates, created a state of mind on the part of farmers which, once focused
on their grievances and made vocal through the Grange and other farmers' associations, brought the Farmers' Movement to one of its highest
points in American history.

The expansion of farming in the Middle West had been accompanied
by an era of railroad building and was partly caused by the extension of
railroad mileage. Farmers had encouraged their states, counties, and
federal government to furnish financial assistance to the railroad companies upon the conviction that agricultural prosperity depended almost
solely upon transportation facilities. The first of the great land grants

was made in 1850 to the Illinois Central. In 1852, Congress passed an act making it possible to grant to railroads, then chartered or to be chartered within ten years, the right of way of 100 feet in width and free depots, watering places, and workshop sites, together with the privilege of taking stone, timber, and earth from adjoining government land for building and repair purposes.[10] Almost 20,000,000 acres of land were granted to railroad companies in the two years 1856 and 1857. The total grants finally reached more than 129,000,000 acres, almost 38,000,000 of which were granted by states. Illinois, Iowa, Missouri, Minnesota, and Michigan made total grants of about 20,000,000 acres.[11] In many instances, every other mile of frontage for six miles' distance back from the right of way was given to the railroads, and in some instances these lands were not sold until population had become sufficiently dense to greatly enhance their sale value.[12] States, counties, and municipalities issued bonds to raise money with which to subscribe for rail stocks and bonds.[13] These necessarily had to be liquidated out of tax receipts and, according to the report of the state auditor of Illinois in 1869, 48 per cent of all county, city, town and township indebtedness consisted of railroad obligations—debts and subscriptions.[14]

[10] Lewis H. Haney, *A congressional history of railways in the United States to 1850,* Bulletin of the University of Wisconsin, No. 211, Economic and Political Science Series, Vol. III, No. 2. Madison, Wisconsin: 1908. *Congressional Globe,* 32nd Congress, 1st Session, July 27, 1852.

[11] Benjamin H. Hibbard. *Report of the Commissioner of the General Land Office to the Secretary of the Interior for the fiscal year ended June 30, 1923.* Washington, D. C.: Government Printing Office, 1923.

[12] John B. Sanborn, *Congressional grants of land in aid of railways,* Bulletin of the University of Wisconsin, No. 30, Economics, Political Science and History Series, Vol. II, No. 3. Madison, Wisconsin: August, 1899. Frederick A. Cleveland and Fred W. Powell, *Railroad promotion and capitalization in the United States.* New York: Longmans, Green & Co., Inc., 1909.

[13] Emory R. Johnson, *American railway transportation,* chap. xxii, "Public Aid to Railway Construction." Second rev. ed. New York: Appleton-Century-Crofts, Inc., 1908. William W. Cook, *The corporation problem.* New York: G. P. Putnam's Sons, 1891. John W. Million, *State aid to railways in Missouri,* Economic Studies of the University of Chicago, No. 4. Chicago: University of Chicago Press, 1896. Charles W. Pierson, "The Rise of the Granger Movement," *Popular Science Monthly,* Vol. XXXII, No. 2 (December, 1887). Cleveland and Powell, chap. xii, "Individual and Local Subsidies to Private Companies"; chap. xiii, "State Aid to Private Corporations"; chap. xv, "National Aid to Private Companies."

[14] *Annual report of the Auditor of Public Accounts to the Governor of Illinois,* December 15, 1869, Statement No. 15. Springfield, Illinois: Illinois Journal Printing Office, 1869.

THE REVOLT BECOMES VOCAL

The reaction of the farmers of the Middle West against the railroads became quite violent when they discovered that freight rates ate up most of the low market prices of their products following the Civil War. Their dreams of cheap transportation turned into nightmares of high taxes. Their viewpoint at that time was probably well stated by D. C. Cloud in his book, *Monopolies and the People,* published in 1873 and read widely by leaders of discontented farmers:

> The aid granted to railroad companies has enabled them to get control of the commerce of the country. As a general rule, all of the railroads receiving subsidies in land, government, state, county, and city bonds, and large gifts in local taxes, have been owned or controlled by the same class of men, and not a few of the roads by the same ring or combination. Then speculators have visited all parts of the country, claiming to be men of "large hearts" who desire to benefit mankind. They talk of their large experience in railroad matters; of the great benefit the particular locality will derive from the construction of a certain line of road; of the great profit to be returned in the shape of dividends if local aid is voted, and after having by fraud, falsehood, and willful deception induced the people to move in the matter, they then turn their attention to state legislatures and to congress for more aid, and so perfect is their combination, that in almost all their attempts they are successful.... With their headquarters in New York and Boston; with Wall Street as the principal depot for all railroad stock and bonds, as well as the bonds of the United States, and of such states, counties, and cities as have been duped by them, these *raiders* upon the treasury and resources of a people have taken the absolute control of the railroad interest of the country, and "run it" for their own exclusive benefit, to the injury of the country and the absolute destruction of the agricultural interests of the great west.[15]

It was but natural, in the face of conditions and ideas such as prevailed, that wherever farmers met together they would discuss these matters, and not unnatural that the most prevalent shibboleth developed during the period was "antimonopoly."

---

[15] D. C. Cloud, *Monopolies and the people.* Davenport, Iowa: Day, Egbert and Fidlar, 1873.

It is to be remembered that the farmers of the Middle West had formulated a statement of their economic philosophy into a platform before the Civil War and that many farmers' clubs were in existence in Illinois and a number of other states. These organizations became exceptionally active as the effects of depression came to be felt. Documentary evidence of this new impulse to action is to be found in the 1870 issues of the *Prairie Farmer*.[16] Up to and including the issue of February 19, 1870, its reports of meetings of the St. Louis Farmers' Club and the Saint Clair Farmers' and Fruit Growers' Association indicate that discussion there related wholly to technical and scientific problems. But in the March 26, 1870, issue the title of the lead editorial was "The Time for Action." It began as follows:

> We publish in another column the call for a convention of those opposed to the present tendency to monopoly and extortionate charges by our transportation companies, to meet at Bloomington, Illinois, on the 20th day of April next, for the purposes that are therein set forth; namely, the consideration of the present charges for the transportation of freight by chartered companies and the devising of means that shall have the effect to reduce them.

The "call" referred to appeared on the editorial page and was signed by Henry C. Wheeler, Downer's Grove, DuPage County, Illinois. Further excerpts from the editorial and excerpts from the article by Wheeler reveal the dominant protest of the midwestern farmers at that time. Among other things, the editorial said:

> It is of little consequence to the farmer that the season is favorable and the soil productive, if half or two-thirds of the price of his crop is exhausted in getting it to market.
> That railroad companies are under moral, if not under legal obligations, to communities to transport persons and freights at a rate that shall be nearly uniform throughout their entire length, and at a price which shall not be considered exorbitant, seems evident from the fact that the companies received great privileges from the individuals through whose lands their lines pass. In the majority of cases the right of way was given, and in all instances legislatures

---

[16] The *Prairie Farmer* was published in Chicago. Henry D. Emery was editor in 1870.

granted the companies the power to take private property and to convert it to their own use.

And more than this, Subsidies have been granted to a very large number of roads in the West in the shape of lands, that would otherwise have been open to pre-emption and settlement by the citizens at a nominal cost. In many instances bonds to a very large amount have been issued by the different counties and towns through which the roads pass, from the sale of which the roads have been, in part, at least, made. To pay the interest on these bonds and to liquidate the principal, additional taxes are levied every year. In many instances, farmers, in order to raise money to pay taxes, are obliged to give a large portion of the value of their crops for the poor privilege of shipping them over a road which they helped to build. For a railroad to impel a man to pay extortionate freight on goods that are to be sold for the purpose of paying for making the road, particularly when the track runs over land once belonging to the farmer, seems, at least, like ingratitude.

Excerpts from the "Call" by Wheeler are as follows:

A crisis in our affairs is approaching and danger threatens.

Many of us are not aware of the gigantic proportions the carrying interest is assuming. Less than forty years since the first railroad fire was kindled on this continent, but which now, like a mighty conflagration, is crackling and roaring over every prairie and through every mountain gorge. The first year produced fifteen miles; the last, 5,000.

On the same mammoth scale goes on the work of organization and direction. By the use of almost unlimited means it enlists in its service the finest talents of the land as officers, attorneys, agents and lobbyists, gives free passes and splendid entertainments to the representatives of the people, and even transports whole legislatures into exceeding high mountains, showing them the kingdoms of the world with lavish promises of reward for fealty and support. . . .

What power can withstand the combined and concentrated force of the producing interest of this Republic? But what avails our strength if like Polyphemus in the fable, we are unable to use it for want of eyesight; or like a mighty army without discipline, every man fighting on his own hook, or were reposing in fancied security while the Delilahs of the enemy have well nigh shorn away the last lock of strength. In this respect we constitute a solitary exception, every other interest having long since protected itself by union and organization.

As a measure calculated to bring all interested, as it were, within speaking distance, and as a stepping stone to an efficient organization, I propose that the farmers of the great Northwest concentrate their efforts, power and means as the great transportation companies have done theirs, and accomplish something, instead of frittering away their efforts in doing nothing.

And to this end, I suggest a Convention of those opposed to the present tendency to monopoly and extortionate charges by our transportation companies, to meet at Bloomington, Illinois, on the 20th day of April next, for the purpose of discussion and the appointment of a committee to raise funds to be expended in the employment of the highest order of legal talent to put in form of report and argument an exposition of the rights, wrongs, interests and injuries (with their remedies) of the producing masses of the Northwest, and lay it before the authorities of each state and of the general government. Congress is now in session and the Constitutional Convention of this state will then again be convened. Farmers, now is the time for action.

On April 2, the *Prairie Farmer* published an article by Elmer Baldwin on "Rural Economy," which pointed out that farmers as a class have business interests which they must safeguard. A copy of the speech given by Senator Carpenter at the Wisconsin State Fair at Madison in 1869, entitled "Railroad Monopoly," was also in this issue; it dealt with the dangers of railroad consolidation and the power of Congress to regulate commerce. In addition, there was an article entitled "Railroads and Warehouses," which asserted that there was collusion between railroads and elevators in defiance of state law.

In the issue of April 16, an editorial entitled "Devote One Day to the Cause" said in part:

In the Bloomington convention, on the 20th of April, we shall see the first blow struck for a peaceful revolution that shall wrest from monopolies the power to oppress the people. . . .
The great need of the producers always has been in Organization.

Jonathan Periam says that "Wheeler's manifesto was published in the principal papers of the Northwest," but apparently only Illinois farmers attended. An organization was formed and a president and twelve vice-presidents were elected. Each vice-president was from a different county, and it is therefore probable that only thirteen counties were represented. Periam, however, says that "a large number of the leading farmers from various counties of Illinois met . . . in mass convention." They passed eight resolutions dealing chiefly with transportation costs, high taxes, need for agricultural information and organization.

Nothing came of this first attempt to organize, but about two and one-half years later a convention similar to the one at Bloomington was suggested to other clubs by the Farmers' Club of Avon, "in order to compare notes, discuss subjects of interest to the fraternity, inquire into the causes of the depressed condition of Agriculture in the West, and propose remedies therefor." The call was made by S. M. Smith of Kewanee, Illinois, for a meeting to be held at Kewanee on October 16 and 17, 1872, "for the purpose of comparing views, and consulting together on the best means of organizing a general union of farmers, for their mutual benefit and protection against the monopolizing tendencies of the age." Periam says that about fifty delegates attended; they "were eminent as farmers . . . and some of them were well known for their political prominence." The two items proposed for discussion by a committee appointed to draw an agenda were (1) "How can farmers, through their Clubs and other organizations, accomplish a saving to their members in purchasing, selling, and in transportation?" and (2) "Benefits and results obtainable through Farmers' Clubs and kindred organizations." The convention elected a president, a vice-president, and two secretaries, appointed an executive committee and a state central committee, and passed nine resolutions. We quote the two most pointed and elaborate resolutions:

Resolved, That the success of co-operative effort, as illustrated in the accumulation of capital for the carrying forward of immense business enterprises; in the combination of workingmen for the increase of wages, or the restriction of the hours of labor; in the formation of rings for controlling the price of agricultural or manufactured products, and for "bulling" or "bearing" the markets of every kind; and in the thorough and efficient organization of political parties for partisan ends, should teach the farmer the lesson, both of its efficiency and its adaptation to the particular needs, if applied with intelligence and wisdom.

Resolved, That it is the duty of Farmers' Clubs, and similar organizations, to put forth their best efforts for extending and multiplying
these organizations, until they shall compass the industrial interest
of the entire West.[17]

The executive committee elected at the Kewanee convention took its
obligation seriously and not only attempted to promote the organization
of more clubs, but called another farmers' convention to meet at Bloomington on January 15 and 16, 1873.

The call for the Bloomington convention was headed by the shibboleth,
"Equal and exact justice to all; special privilege to none," and its stated
purpose was

> to perfect the organization made at Kewanee, by the formation of
> a State Farmers' Association from said delegates, adoption of a
> constitution, and for securing the organization and representation
> of associations in every county, and, if possible, in every township,
> of the State; to discuss and insist upon reform in railway transporta-
> tion, the sale of agricultural implements, the sale of farm products
> by commission merchants, and such other abuses as have grown
> up in our midst, and are now taxing and impoverishing producers
> and consumers; and to transact such other business as may be
> brought before the Convention.

Two hundred and seventy-five regularly appointed delegates were
seated by the convention and a constitution and by-laws adopted. Permanent officers were elected and thirty resolutions passed. Most of the
resolutions dealt with the transportation problem, but a considerable
variety of other issues were also stated. The following were significant in
the light of what followed in Illinois and other midwestern states during
the next three years:

> *Resolved,* That the power of this, and all local organizations,
> should be wielded at the ballot-box by the election to all offices,
> from highest to lowest—legislative, executive, and judicial—of such,
> and only such, persons as sympathize with us in this movement,
> and believe, as we do, that there is a rightful remedy for this wrong,
> and that it can and must be enforced; and to this end we pledge our

[17] Periam, pp. 236-237.

votes at all elections where they will have a bearing against the wrong in question.

Resolved, That farmers buy no implements of those manufacturers or their agents who have entered into any conspiracy agreeing not to sell their implements to Farmers' Associations.[18]

Sentiments and ideas expressed by different speakers at this convention gave clear warning that a farmers' revolt was in the making, if indeed it had not already begun. Many of them are so pointed that we quote them in some detail:

If railway autocrats conspire to rob producers and consumers then the producers and consumers must organize for protection of their interests.

Poverty, if not bankruptcy, now stares us in the face. In the midst of such overwhelming abundance as to choke the marts of trade, and while the consumers on the seaboard and across the waters are hungry for our products, we cannot realize enough to pay our taxes and labor.

The railroads of Illinois stand in open defiance of the laws by charging rates greatly in excess of what the laws allow, and by unjust discriminations and extortions.

That the power of this, and all local organizations, should be wielded at the ballot box.... [19]

It was at this meeting that the Illinois State Farmers' Association was born. The next meeting of the Association was held at Springfield, in April, 1873. It met at the state capital during the session of the state legislature, had more than 300 delegates present from seventy-two counties, was addressed by Governor Beveridge and ex-Governor Palmer, passed a militant resolution against "all chartered monopolies" and a number of other resolutions demanding regulation and supervision of the railroads, demanded of Congress the repeal of all laws preventing competition between water and rail transportation, and expressed itself in favor of the immediate repeal of protective duties on iron, steel and

18 *Ibid.,* p. 258.
19 *Ibid.,* p. 280.

lumber, and all other products which enter into the making of agricultural implements. Periam says that within three months after adjournment of the second Bloomington convention in 1873, "over a thousand organizations had been perfected in the State, in response to the appeal made from Bloomington."

A few quotations from the proceedings of the second annual meeting, held in December, 1873, will serve to indicate that sentiment in favor of direct action had become pronounced. Witness the following:

> Resolved, That stealing is thieving, whether done by persons in the low walks of life or by high officials; and that we demand the utter repeal by Congress of the law known as the Salary-grab entire —Presidential, Congressional, and all.
>
> There are three ways of dealing with the monopolies that have risen in these latter days to oppress us.
>
> 1. One is to submit to them, and become the serfs of corporations. . . .
>
> 2. There is another way of dealing with monopolies . . . to put conspiracy against conspiracy—to fight the devil with fire. . . .
>
> 3. . . . there is a third way of dealing with monopolies, and that is to destroy them and have no monopolies to fight. . . .
>
> Whereas, the political parties of the country have criminally neglected the agricultural interest, and shamefully disregarded the rights of the people;
>
> Resolved, That the farmers cut themselves loose from all party association, and rally under a banner broad enough to embrace all in favor of just laws, and opposed to monopolies, to corruption, to extravagance, to the further donation of public lands to railroads, and to the creation of uncontrolled monopoly.[20]

In the platform adopted at this session, appeared, among others, these resolutions:

> Resolved, That the past record of the old political parties of this country is such as to forfeit the confidence and respect of the people, and that we are, therefore, absolved from all allegiance to them, and will act no longer with them.

---

[20] Proceedings of the second annual meeting of the Illinois State Farmers' Association held at Decatur, December 16, 17, and 18, 1873, pp. 32-33, 43. Chicago: printed by C. E. Southard. 1874.

Resolved, That we deprecate any further grants of public lands or loans of the public credit, and of National, State, or local subscriptions in aid of corporations.

Resolved, That we uncompromisingly condemn the practice of our public officials in receiving free passes from railroad managers.

Resolved, That, since a large number of plow manufacturers of the West have thrown down the gauntlet, we take it up, and recommend to the farmers of this State to patronize none of said manufacturers until they will sell to us direct at wholesale rates.[21]

Many farmers' organizations were in existence in the Middle West when these stirring events took place in Illinois. Most of these organizations were miniatures of such state and regional societies as those of Philadelphia, South Carolina, New York, and others discussed in the preceding chapter. They were more like literary or scientific societies than like local units of a militant movement. They were not related one to the other except in general purpose. They usually met once a month and attracted only the more intellectually-inclined farmers. As early as 1850, agricultural journals such as the *Prairie Farmer* had promoted their organization and had regularly reported accounts of their meetings and discussions. From such reports it is possible to trace the change in emphasis of their discussions and interests. The issues with which the Bloomington and Kewanee conventions were wrestling soon began to be reflected in the programs of these local societies. Freight rates, currency, and corporations as issues began to vie with those of technical farm production. These organizations did not move en masse into the farmers' revolt which was developing, but they furnished the forums in which the sentiments of the revolt developed.

In a great number of states, the organization of a state agricultural society antedated the organization of county or other local societies. The objectives, and to a considerable extent the activities, of the local societies, therefore, followed the lead of the state society. As the Farmers' Movement flowed into high tide in the 1870's, some of these local societies drifted or were swept along with it, some of them suffered decline because of it, and some continued their old types of interests and activities.

---

[21] *Ibid.,* pp. 100-101.

As one attempts to follow the development of the type of farmers' clubs which apparently largely composed the membership of the Bloomington convention, one often finds it impossible to distinguish between the old type of county or other local farmers' societies and a new type of farmers' club that was developing. The *Prairie Farmer* published reports from both types of organizations and in such reports, it is possible, in some societies, to trace the transfer from the old to the new issues being discussed almost as clearly as if one had been present at the meetings.[22]

The *Transactions of the Wisconsin State Agricultural Society* for 1871 reports on "State Societies," "District Societies," "County Societies," and "Township Societies and Clubs." It also gives reports on thirty-nine "County and District Agricultural Societies" which held fairs during the year. This was quite generally the one type of major project carried on by agricultural societies and was often the chief object of a society's existence. It is probably significant that not one of the twenty-four "Farmers' Clubs" discussed in the *Transactions* is reported as having conducted a fair during the year. They were quite universally discussion clubs, and as such were vehicles for carrying on the Farmers' Movement as it developed.[23]

There were organizations other than the Illinois Agricultural Association which went wholeheartedly with the tide, that attempted to combine consideration of technical agriculture and economic problems—sometimes even political considerations. They varied in their experience from going a long way in the direction of the Granger revolt to being very little influenced by it.

GENERAL FARMERS' ORGANIZATIONS AFTER THE CIVIL WAR

The State Agricultural Society of South Carolina was organized in 1839. Its founding followed previous attempts to organize such a society: one in Charleston in 1785 which stated that it was organized, "For the

---

[22] Issues of *Prairie Farmer* and *Western Rural* (Chicago), early 1869 to 1873. See especially *Prairie Farmer* issues of 1872-1873.

[23] *Transactions of the Wisconsin State Agricultural Society*, Vol. X (1871), pp. 11-12 and 478-479. Prepared by J. W. Hoyt, secretary, Madison, Wisconsin, 1872.

encouragement of agriculture in the State, and the promotion of the arts and sciences contributing thereto;" another, The United Agricultural Society of South Carolina, in 1826, which made its objectives more directly applicable to the science of agricultural production.[24] This organization was short-lived and was followed by another, The State Agricultural Society of South Carolina, in 1839, which in turn was active for about ten years and then went out of existence to be revived in 1855 under a new constitution. It held a state fair in 1856 and each succeeding year until the Civil War.

In 1869, The South Carolina Agricultural and Mechanical Society was organized and took up where its predecessor left off when the war intervened. Its object was "to develop and promote the entire material interests of the State." This is the organization that was in existence during the Granger period and continued, in spite of the Granger upheaval, to carry on its regular activities of holding an annual state fair and an annual convention at which problems of technical agriculture were discussed. It promoted the organization of county agricultural societies and solicited members of such societies to join the state society, but never established itself at the grass roots or attempted to mobilize masses of farmers for pressure purposes. It held meetings jointly with the state Grange, but apparently never became involved in any of the economic ventures of that organization.

The National Agricultural Congress, formed in St. Louis in 1872, was accomplished by joining two organizations which had come into existence during the two preceding years, one at Augusta, Georgia, and the other at Nashville, Tennessee. This Congress attempted to have affiliated with it all of the farmers' organizations and societies of the nation, but was never very successful in doing so. It clung too closely to the patterns of the state agricultural societies to attract the more direct-action farmers' organizations of the seventies.

In October, 1870, the Cotton States Agricultural and Mechanical As-

---

[24] See *History of the State Agricultural Society of South Carolina from 1839 to 1845, inclusive; of the State Agricultural Society of South Carolina from 1855 to 1861, inclusive; of the State Agricultural and Mechanical Society of South Carolina from 1869 to 1916 inclusive,* Introduction and chap. i, "The State Agricultural Society of South Carolina, 1839-1849," pp. 1-13. Published under the direction of the Society. Columbia, South Carolina: R. L. Bryan Co., 1916.

sociation, the Augusta Board of Trade, and the municipal authorities of the city of Augusta, Georgia, sponsored a three-day meeting at which delegates from eleven southern states assembled. They formed an organization, elected officers, and adjourned to meet at Selma, Alabama, in December, 1871. In the interim between these two meetings, the Tennessee Agricultural and Mechanical Association issued a call for a national meeting of agricultural organizations to assemble in Nashville, Tennessee, October 3, 1871. Delegates from eleven states "representing more than 40 different Agricultural Societies and Associations" came to this meeting. Among them was Mark A. Cooper, a delegate from the Congress which had been organized at Augusta. The National Agricultural Association was organized at this Nashville meeting and the decision reached to hold its next meeting at St. Louis in May, 1872. A committee of the newly formed Association was delegated to attend the forthcoming Selma meeting of the Agricultural Congress and invite them to consider meeting at St. Louis in May, 1872, to help perfect an amalgamation of the two organizations.[25] These two groups met at St. Louis and after holding separate preliminary meetings joined together and agreed to take the name, "National Agricultural Congress."

This new organization adopted a constitution but did not set forth a declaration of purpose or philosophy. In the preamble to the constitution, referring to the two groups which were joining to form it, these words were used: "for the purpose of taking into consideration the expediency of uniting the two into one grand organization, powerful and influential enough to command the respect of the whole country, by concentrating the usefulness of the various local associations and societies organized for promoting the interests of Agriculture in the United States." It provided that "Each State and Territory shall be entitled to two representatives for each and every State organization engaged in fostering agricultural pursuits." Other authorized representatives were to be the United States Department of Agriculture, agricultural schools or colleges,

---

[25] *Address to the agricultural organizations in the United States. Prepared by a committee in obedience to a resolution by the National Agricultural Association together with Constitution and Proceedings,* p. 27. Nashville, Tennessee: 1871. Also see W. C. Flagg, "Historical Sketch of National Agricultural Organizations," *Proceedings of the fifth annual session of the National Agricultural Congress, at Philadelphia, Pa., September 12th, 13th, and 14th, 1876,* pp. 4-5. Chicago: printed by Prairie Farmer Co., 1877. Periam, pp. 207-209. *Prairie Farmer,* November 26, 1870.

and "Each regularly organized Agricultural and Horticultural Society, of not less than fifty members," which contributed to the support of this organization.[26]

It is interesting to trace the history and spirit of this organization during the years in which the Grange, the Illinois Agricultural Association, and the farmer-supported independent political parties were in ascendancy. There is apparently no published record of the proceedings of either the Augusta or Selma meetings of the National Agricultural Congress, but there is one of the 1871 Nashville meeting of the National Agricultural Association. The only official action taken at this meeting, other than that essential to the establishment of the organization, was "to petition the United States Government . . . in favor of establishing, by international co-operation, of a general and systematic plan of meteorological observations and crop reports. . . ." The 1872 convention passed a resolution which read, "That this Congress do earnestly recommend to farmers, in the various districts and townships throughout the United States, to organize them-selves into clubs, and have monthly meetings, and with this organization disseminate, through the newspapers, the facts they may gather in the interests of practical agriculture."

But this convention did not entirely escape the impact of farmer senti-ment about railroads. It appointed a committee on transportation and passed some resolutions, one of which stated in part that "The consolida-tion now being made of the leading railroad lines, is calculated in their present workings to prevent the legitimate competition on which practi-cally the success of this planting and farming interests depend. . . ." Another resolution asked the Congress of the United States to remove the tariff on chemicals going into agricultural fertilizers. In opening the session the first day, Arthur B. Barrett said: "Societies among men are formed for the promotion of morals, good government, and self-protec-tion. . . . No Congress can stand before your will; you can dictate the policies of the country. . . ." President R. J. Spurr said that farmers were the toiling millions of the nation, that they were more poorly paid for their labor than any other class of people, but they had the power by association to control everything in the state and nation.

---

[26] *Proceedings of the National Agricultural Congress held at St. Louis, Missouri, May 27 to 30, 1872*, pp. 37-38. Indianapolis, Indiana: Sentinal Co., printers and binders, 1872. See also Periam, pp. 210-221. Periam was present at the St. Louis convention.

Notwithstanding these few indications of discontent, all other discussions were quite tame in comparison to what was happening in numerous farmers' organizations in the Middle West where conventions were being held. W. C. Flagg, president of the newly organized Illinois State Farmers' Association, was present and took part in the proceedings. He must have been impressed by the difference in the tenor of this meeting and the one held at Kewanee the following October.

Quite different from the St. Louis convention of the National Agricultural Congress was a meeting held at Topeka, Kansas, in March of the following year (1873). This meeting was called by the secretary of the State Board of Agriculture and was therefore tied up with the public organization of agriculture. But this fact did not keep it from following the pattern of behavior prevailing, or at least developing, at that time in the Farmers' Movement in the Middle West. The convention passed resolutions of protest, boldly asserted their demands, and threatened political action. The meeting was called at the request of the Manhattan Farmers' Club, a local organization. Sentiment on a much wider base must, however, have been evident else a state official would not have given it heed. The call of the meeting gives the complete story as follows:

> *Office Kansas State Board of Agriculture,*
> *Capitol Building, Topeka, February 27, 1873.*

To the Farmers of Kansas:

On the 10th inst., the following call for a "Farmers' State Convention" was issued:

The Farmers' Institution, held at Manhattan on the 23rd of January, 1873, adopted the following resolutions, to wit:

Resolved, That it is the opinion of this meeting that the farmers of Kansas should organize themselves into district clubs and at once place themselves in correspondence with the Secretary of the State Board of Agriculture, at Topeka. Furthermore, be it

Resolved, That whenever a sufficient number of clubs have reported to represent the public opinion of the State, the Secretary of the State Board be requested to call a delegate Farmers' State Convention, so that said farmers may meet to devise ways and means for their present relief and future protection.

In obedience to the request contained in the above resolutions, a delegate Farmers' Convention will be held in the hall of the

House of Representatives, Topeka, on Wednesday, the 26th day of March, 1873, at 2 o'clock P.M.

Each County Agricultural and Horticultural Society, and the farmers' clubs of each township in the State, will be entitled to one delegate. Application will be made to the different railroad corporations of the State for half fare rates to the Convention and return. If granted, notice will be duly given.

ALFRED GRAY, *Secretary.*

Subsequently the call was enlarged as follows:

Since issuing the above, applications have been received from the "Farmers' Union" of Douglas County, and from farmers of various parts of the State, requesting that Farmers' Unions, Granges of the Patrons of Husbandry, and all other farmers' organizations, as well as townships and counties having no such organizations, each have a representation in said Convention.

In view of the lively interest thus manifested, a cordial invitation is extended to the farmers of the whole State to send delegates to said Convention in pursuance of said request. But it is earnestly recommended that farmers do organize clubs and other agricultural societies, and send delegates therefrom wherever it is practicable to do so.

ALFRED GRAY, *Secretary State Board of Agriculture.*

Two hundred delegates representing all sections of the state came to Topeka in response to this call, stayed in session for two days, and organized themselves as The Farmers' Co-operative Association of the State of Kansas. Governor Robinson set the gauge of battle by strongly advising them to organize. Although he did not advise political action, he urged that they vote for the known friends of the farmer. The following excerpts from the resolutions indicate the tone of the meeting:

Whereas, Agriculture in its various departments is the basis of all material prosperity; and whereas, the burdens and impositions under which it lies have become intolerable, therefore, the farmers of Kansas, in convention assembled, do put forth this declaration of their desires and purposes, and state—

1. Farmers desire to unite in the form of clubs, unions, or stock association . . . for a common good, and for the moral effect it will have upon themselves and upon the rest of mankind.

2. They desire association for the purpose of controlling the prices of their products through their own boards of trade, or their own appointed agents...

3. They desire to unite for the purpose of getting their supplies at cost, with a reasonable per cent added to pay for collecting and distributing, and the use of capital.

4. They desire to cooperate for the purpose of securing a reduction in freight, and breaking the blockade between different parts of the country...

5. They desire tax reform, the abolition of sinecure offices, the reduction of salaries, rigid economy in public expenditures, and the repeal of our present iniquitous tax penalties.

6. They desire home manufactures...

7. They desire that the balance of our public domain should be kept [for]... actual settlement, and in no contingency be allowed to fall into the hands of railroad monopolies and land-sharks.

Resolved, That organization is the great want of the producing classes at the present time, and we recommend every farmer in the State to become a member of some farmers' club, grange of the Patrons of Husbandry, or other local organization.

Resolved, That the taxes assessed... are oppressive, unjust...

Resolved, That we... request our Senators and members of Congress to vote for and secure an amendment to the tariff laws of the United States, so that salt and lumber shall be placed on the free list, and that there shall be made a material reduction in the duty on iron, and, that such articles as do not pay the cost of collection be also placed on the free list.

Resolved, That we earnestly request the Legislature of our State ...to enact a law regulating freight and fares on our railroads... and that we... urge the favorable action of [Congress]... to the same end, and... to construct national highways at the expense of the Government.

Resolved, That the act passed by the last Legislature exempting bonds, notes, mortgages, and judgments from taxation is unjust, oppressive, and a palpable violation of our State constitution, and we call upon all assessors and the county boards to see that said securities are taxed at their fair value.

Resolved, That the practice of voting municipal bonds is pernicious in its effect and will inevitably bring bankruptcy and ruin upon the people . . .

Resolved, That giving banks a monopoly of the nation's currency . . . is but little less than legalized robbery of the agricultural classes.

Resolved, That, for the thorough and speedy accomplishment of all this, we pledge each other to ignore all political preferences and prejudices that have swayed us hitherto, to our hurt, and support only such men for office as are known to be true to our interests, and in whose integrity and honesty we have the most implicit confidence.[27]

Jonathan Periam says a meeting of an eastern organization was held sometime subsequent to the first Bloomington meeting of 1870. Its object, according to Periam, was to organize a great cooperative association to deal in grain. It was incorporated under the laws of New York as the Grain Growers' Transportation and Loan Association and provided for $10,000,000 capital stock in 200,000 shares. The writer does not know just who conceived the plan, but Periam reported that the board of trustees was composed of four men from Iowa, three from Wisconsin, four from Illinois, three from Minnesota, and one from Michigan. Practically all, if not all, members of the board were officers in midwestern state agricultural and horticultural societies; one of them was Henry C. Wheeler, who had issued the call for the first Bloomington convention; another was John Scott of Iowa, a delegate to the St. Louis meeting of the National Agricultural Congress in 1872; and still another was O. P. Whitcomb, president of the State Agricultural Society of Minnesota.

So far as is known, this organization was never perfected, the stock never subscribed, and the officers of the board of trustees never elected. It is possible, however, that it furnished the stimulus for the Farmers' and Producers' convention which was held in New York in May, 1873, at which convention was organized The National American Cheap Transportation Association. The stated object of this organization was "the cheapening and equalization of railroad transportation rates throughout

---

[27] W. G. Cutler, ed., *History of the State of Kansas,* pp. 263 ff. Chicago: A. T. Andreas, 1883. Or see p. 397 of the following edition: New York: Appleton-Century-Crofts, Inc., 1873.

the United States, and to make provision also for a subordinate association in each State, and regulate minor matters for the guidance and government of national and State associations." [28] The resolutions passed at the convention had to do altogether with the need for state and federal legislation regulating railroads. A subsequent convention was called to meet in Washington, D. C., in January, 1874, but since our only source of information concerning the organization is Periam's book, which was written before the time for the Washington meeting, we do not know what transpired after the official call for the meeting was issued in November, 1873, by Josiah Quincy of Boston.

A Northwestern Farmers' convention was held at Chicago in October, 1873, attended by about 300 delegates from Illinois, Wisconsin, Iowa, New York, Indiana, Nebraska, Minnesota, and Canada. Here again almost all the discussion for two days and all the resolutions had to do with transportation regulation and control. There were in attendance at this convention some of the prominent leaders of other organizations described in this chapter.

THE GRANGE IS BORN

It was during the period when farmer discontent, especially in the Middle West, was running high that the Grange came into prominence. The Patrons of Husbandry was not organized for the purpose of picking up and weaving together the threads of discontent, much less for the purpose of converting the discontent into organized action. As a matter of fact, the national Grange, to a considerable extent, fought against becoming the mouthpiece for the economic and political discontent which was raging among farmers during this period. It could not, however, withstand the demand that it grapple with the problems which were uppermost in the minds of farmers at that time.

---

[28] Periam, chap. xxvii.

· 6 ·

THE RISE

OF THE GRANGE[1]

ORIGIN AND ORGANIZATION

General farmers' organizations have not always meant to be, but have
never been able to escape being, the chief mouthpiece of the
Farmers' Movement in the United States. There is no better example of
this than the Grange in the 1870's. It started as a purely fraternal organization; but because it was a farmers' organization and because farmers at
the time of its rise demanded that it win its way by being militant, it led
one of the greatest American farmers' battles of all time. Space does not
permit telling the story of the rise of the Grange in all its details, but
enough of that story must be recorded to furnish the reader with a knowledge of the original purposes of its early leaders, its struggles during the
first few years of its existence, and its later change in emphasis. It started
as a farmers' fraternity, but made little progress as an organization until
it almost inadvertently became the mouthpiece of the discontent among

---

[1] The information for much of this chapter is necessarily from Oliver H. Kelley, *Origin
and progress of the order of Patrons of Husbandry in the United States: a history
from 1866 to 1873.* Philadelphia: J. A. Wagenseller, 1875. Specific citations will not
be made at the numerous places this book is quoted or otherwise referred to in the
following pages.

farmers which was running high in the early 1870's in the middle western states.

The organization of the Grange was conceived by Oliver H. Kelley, a Minnesota farmer, for a short time an associate in the United States Department of Agriculture, and an employee of the United States Post Office Department at the time the first Grange was formed. Kelley was a thirty-second degree Mason and had a deep appreciation of the values of such a fraternal organization to its members. It is easy to see how, with this background, he could conceive the idea of a farmers' fraternity of nationwide scope. Fortunately he recorded in a book, in 1875, not only an accurate history of the organization up to that time, but also gave a detailed account of his own thoughts and those of others about the purpose and problems of the Grange. Such a record is not available on any other of the early, large farmers' associations and societies.

Kelley was a farmer and an agricultural writer. Because of some articles on agriculture which he had written in 1864, he was invited to accept employment in the United States Department of Agriculture that winter. He remained in Washington only a short time, returning to his home in Minnesota in the spring of 1865, but was summoned back by Commissioner of Agriculture Newton in November of that year. Because of President Johnson's desire to encourage immigration into the South, a thing greatly desired by southern farmers, and because of Commissioner Newton's desire to have more detailed and reliable information about southern agricultural conditions than he was able to obtain in any other way, Kelley was sent into the South as an agent of the Department of Agriculture. His instructions were very brief, and he left Washington on January 13, 1866, with apparently little plan beyond that of making a general reconnaissance of conditions and serving as an ambassador of good will.

He traveled through Virginia and North Carolina for about two weeks and arrived at Charleston, South Carolina, on January 29, the morning of the day that news came from Washington that federal troops were to be recalled from the South. Kelley says that this news caused him to record in his diary "that politicians would never restore peace in the country; if it came at all, it must be through fraternity. The *people* North and South must know each other as members of the same great family, and all sectionalism be abolished." [2] It was an attempt to put this idea into action that gave rise to the Grange.

Kelley returned to Washington in April, 1866, and shortly afterward went to Minnesota, where he spent the summer on his farm, returning to Washington again in November of that year. In January, 1867, he received an appointment in the Post Office Department and found himself located in Washington with enough time to develop his idea of organizing "A Secret Society of Agriculturists." He had not been able to pursue the idea further than a conversation or two with friends while in Washington and Boston in April, 1866, but now, being again near those friends and in a location where he could form other friendships, he took up the task of formulating plans, purposes, and rituals for the proposed secret order. In a letter to William Saunders in August, 1867, he wrote, "while the order would aim to advance agriculture to a higher rank, by encouraging education, it would at the same time naturally embrace the benefits of its members guaranteed by Masonry."

This idea, that the Grange should be a fraternal organization, was shared by all of its founders. William Saunders, first national Master of the Grange, in its first official circular said:

> ... when we reflect upon the fact that certain associations have stood the test of ages and even centuries, as, for example, the Masonic Order ... why not embrace it in associations for the spread and increase of knowledge, and for the noble purpose of adding to national wealth and power?
>
> Reflections similar to the above have resulted in the formation of an order known as the Patrons of Husbandry.

In September, 1867, Kelley wrote to Anson Bartlett, of Ohio, who had become interested in the new organization:

> Among the objects in view may be mentioned a cordial and social fraternity of the farmers all over the country. Encourage them to read and think; to plant fruit and flowers,—beautify their homes; elevate them; make them progressive.

---

[2] See also John G. Wells, *The Grange illustrated; or Patron's handbook.* New York: Grange Publishing Co., 1874. Edward W. Martin, *History of the Grange movement; or, the farmer's war against monopolies.* Philadelphia: National Publishing Company, 1873.

Kelley enlisted the interest of a half dozen persons in Washington, and through the assistance of William Saunders, chief horticulturist of the United States Department of Agriculture, who traveled widely over the country, got in touch with some half dozen other persons with whom he carried on a lively correspondence during the fall of 1867 and the early part of 1868. He and the six other persons, all located in Washington, met on November 15, 1867, and definitely launched the organization under the name "Patrons of Husbandry." It was decided to call the local branches "Granges."

Various names for the new order and its locals had been suggested during the period of incubation: for the local units, "Fields," "Farms," "Bee-Hives," "Gardens," "Rustics," "Mushrooms," "Fungi," "Temple of Industry," etc.; and for the national organization, "Independent Order of Progressive Farmers," "Knights of the Plow," "Knights of the Sickle," "Knights of the Flail," "Independent Farmers," "Lords of the Soil," "Brethren of the Vine," "Companions of Labor," "Yeomen of Columbia," "Sons of the Soil," "Redemption in the Garden," "League of Husbandry," "Patrons of Industry," etc. In a letter to Bartlett, Kelley said that probably fifty different names had been suggested. He took the name "Grange" from a current novel and formulated the name "Patrons of Husbandry" by substituting the word "Husbandry" in the name of "Patrons of Industry" suggested by Bartlett.

It was decided that there should be four degrees, each representing a stage in the development of agriculture. Those for men were: Laborer, Cultivator, Harvester, and Husbandmen; and for the women: Maid, Shepherdess, Gleaner, and Matron. To these were added a fifth degree to be taken only in the state Grange, a sixth to be taken only in the national Grange, and a seventh bestowed only in the senate of the order. The senate was later abolished and an intermediate division, the Pomona Grange, generally a county organization, was added, so that now the fifth degree is bestowed by the Pomona, the sixth degree by the state Grange, and the seventh degree by the national Grange.

Kelley and his associates spent many hours and days in working out the ritual, the regalia, and the symbols of the order. To them all of these things were of profound importance in an organization which was to be built to a considerable extent upon the psychological satisfactions which come by way of participation in beautiful ritualistic work. The following excerpts from Kelley's correspondence reveal the value of these things in the minds of those who founded the Grange, and are presented in some detail to make clear that in the beginning there was not the slightest evidence that the Grange had any intention of becoming the militant voice of the Farmers' Movement.

Kelley wrote to Saunders in August, 1867:

> I should make it a secret order, with several degrees, and signs and passwords. The lectures in each degree should be practical, appertaining to agricultural work, at the same time convey a moral lesson.

He wrote to Bartlett, September 4, 1867:

> Now what I design is this: An Order that will create an interest, and keep it up. Country and town societies and clubs are interesting for a while, but soon lose their interest, and I see nothing that will be lasting, unless it combine with it the advantages which an Order similar to our Masonic fraternity will provide.

Bartlett replied, September 15:

> Would it not be better to drop the name "Lodges," and give the organized bodies of the Order some name derived from, or applied to, the cultivation of the soil? . . . The farm, the garden, or the vineyard, would be more appropriate, and not likely to excite opposition. "Work in the Vineyard," "Work in the Garden," instead of "Work in the Lodge." How does it strike you?

Kelley wrote to Bartlett on October 24:

> I feel very keenly the necessity of maintaining the most absolute secrecy in regard to what shall be the secret work of the Order. In regard to singing and music, I think you are right. Both words and music should be original, and of a lively character. Quotations from the Bible can be used in different parts of the work. Some of the finest passages are well adapted to the life of the farmer. The ideas are beautiful.

In another letter, he said:

> Now as to the sub-divisions in the Temple, it is to be presumed the Order that builds Temples must have lands (figuratively speaking). Within the wall that surrounds our Temple we have a field, a

vineyard, and a garden. Suppose we say we have field, vineyard, garden, and temple—four points made. These we otherwise designate as spring, summer, autumn, and winter. Again they indicate childhood, manhood, prime of life, and old age. Also preparation of the ground, planting the seed and trees, care of the crop while growing, and lastly the harvest. Again, the bud, the blossom, the fruit, and the fall of the leaf. The initiate is first a laborer in the field; second, advanced to more noble work in the vineyard—vine-dresser; third, placed in the garden where the culture of flowers adds refinement; fourth, being duly qualified, is assigned a seat at the intellectual feast in the Temple, and becomes a Husbandman.

In another letter to Bartlett on December 4, he reported:

I can send you the signs and passwords soon, and then we can commence organizing.

Second degree just received from you. I shall not make any further alterations in it. . . .

Make the third degree somewhat longer. I agree with you that we have lots of fun in that, including a picnic feast at the close of it. . . .

I will send dedication of Grange as soon as I can copy it.

Thus the Patrons of Husbandry was organized as a farmers' fraternity. Its purposes were social, fraternal, and educational. On the fourth of December, 1867, Kelley, Ireland, Thompson, and Saunders met in Saunders's office and elected officers. By each one of them assuming an office and electing Bartlett, Muir, and Moss, none of whom was present, each to an office, they were able to fill seven of the thirteen offices planned for in the organization. These seven constituted the total membership of the organization at that time. Two others were added before January 1, 1868, after which began the serious and strenuous efforts to promulgate the organization throughout the nation.

The seven authentic founders of the Grange were: Oliver H. Kelley, a Minnesota farmer, one-time employee of the Department of Agriculture and in 1867 a clerk in the Post Office Department; William Saunders, horticulturist or landscape architect, head of the Government Experiment Gardens and Grounds; William M. Ireland, chief clerk of the Finance Office, Post Office Department; Dr. John Trimble, an Episcopalian minister, a clerk in the Treasury Department; J. R. Thompson, a Civil War veteran, clerk in the Treasury Department; Aaron B. Grosh, a retired Universalist minister, clerk in the Department of Agriculture; and F. M. McDowell, a New York farmer. The fact is, however, that Kelley's correspondence and his own bank records show that Caroline Hall, his niece; Anson Bartlett, of Ohio; William Muir, of St. Louis, Missouri; and A. S. Moss, of New York, did more to help develop and refine the plan of organization and the philosophy of the Grange than did some of those who participated in its formal founding.[3]

Kelley had printed three hundred copies of a circular on November 1, setting forth an outline of the proposed organization, and mailed them to persons throughout the nation whose names he had obtained from his associates and from other sources. Writing seven years later he said, "These slips ... brought us some very encouraging replies, and established a lively correspondence with several persons, but at the present writing [1875] few of them hold any prominent position in the Order." It did, however, bring Bartlett of Ohio, Muir of Missouri, and Moss of New York into cooperation with the few men at Washington who were working on the project and got Kelley in touch with McDowell of New York, who later joined with the others in promoting the work of the order. A thousand copies of a second circular were printed on February 3, 1868. A trial subordinate Grange was set up in Washington as a school in which the ritual could be practiced, and the first actual initiation into the order took place in this Grange (Potomac Grange No. 1) on February 19, 1868.

Kelley resigned his position with the Post Office Department in February and gave all of his time to organization work. He stayed in Washington during February and March, perfected the organization of Harvest Grange (Potomac No. 1), completed the ritual and the constitution, had them printed, and then left on April 3 for his first organizing campaign. He wrote Bartlett on March 28, 1868, as follows:

I expect to leave here on Thursday next, enroute for Minnesota ... Most of the month of April I propose to give to organizing the Order

[3] See J. W. Darrow, *Origin and early history of the order of Patrons of Husbandry in the United States,* chap. i, "Origin of the Order of Patrons of Husbandry." Chatham, New York: 1904. Leonard L. Allen, *History of New York State Grange,* pp. 18, 23-33. Watertown, New York: Hungerford-Holbrook Co., 1934. D. Wyatt Aiken, *The Grange: its origin, progress and educational purposes,* pp. 4-5, Department of Agriculture, Special Report No. 55. Washington, D. C.: Government Printing Office, 1883.

on my way home. Spend a few weeks there and then start again. *I propose to make the Patrons my special business* until the order is firmly established.

The officers of the national Grange (it should be remembered that they alone constituted the national Grange) gave him "a letter of credit" which read in part:

> *This is to Certify,* That Brother O. H. Kelley is Secretary of the National Grange of the Patrons of Husbandry, and as such, is authorized to establish the Order in any State or Territory . . .
> He is hereby fully empowered to establish Subordinate Granges, to issue Dispensations, and to confer the degrees necessary for the organization and instructions of the same.
> Brother Kelley is also authorized to receive and receipt for all monies due or donated to the National Grange, and is heartily recommended to the sympathy and kindness of the farming community. . . .

Kelley remarks in his book, "This general letter, though very handsome, was of no particular value. I soon found 'pluck' and perseverance the most valuable requisites."

Kelley left Washington with $2.50 of Grange money in his pocket. This was all there was in the national Grange treasury; and although the members of the founding group had advanced $57.19 and the Harvest Grange had, up to that time, collected $35 in membership, these amounts had not been sufficient to liquidate printing and other costs. He borrowed $40 on the endorsement of four of his colleagues and departed with no doubt that he would be able to collect enough money for "dispensations" to pay his way from place to place, and liquidate the debts of the organization, as well as his own. He had written Bartlett in September the year before that he believed it possible to enroll a million members in twelve months. He was doomed to bitter disappointment. He says, "At 8:45 in the evening, I left the Depot at Washington for Harrisburg, little dreaming of the amount of hard labor that was to accompany the task I had undertaken, or that months would become years before success would follow."

He spent the remainder of the month of April on his way to his farm in Minnesota, but had collected for only four dispensations ($60) during that time. Only one Grange, at Fredonia, New York, became permanent. At Harrisburg, Pennsylvania, he collected $15 for a dispensation from three individuals, but no Grange was organized. From there he went to Penn Yan, New York, in a snowstorm and drove to Wayne, New York, the home of McDowell, where he was snowbound for three days. He failed to establish a Grange at Penn Yan, but McDowell gave him $50 and a great deal of encouragement. He arrived at Fredonia, the home of A. S. Moss, on April 15. There he organized his first Grange and collected the fees for his second dispensation. This subordinate Grange is still in existence and is therefore the oldest local of any general farmers' organization in the United States.

From Fredonia, Kelley went to Spencer, Ohio, for a meeting with Bartlett. He organized no Grange there and collected for no dispensation, but he did collect for a dispensation at Columbus. He arrived at Chicago on April 23, where H. D. Emery, publisher of the *Prairie Farmer*, informed him that he had a "club ready to be organized into a Grange." Thus he disposed of his fourth dispensation. From Chicago he went to Madison, Wisconsin, where he failed to organize a Grange, although he badly needed the fees for a dispensation to pay his way to St. Paul. He borrowed $15 from the Worthy Master of a Masonic Lodge in Madison, and after waiting a day at Prairie du Chien for the boat, he arrived at St. Paul on May 1, just four weeks after he had left Washington. Thus, after a month's hard work and expensive travel, Kelley had collected for four dispensations, set up one Grange, and was deeper in debt by $65 than when he left Washington.

He stayed in Minnesota for the remainder of the year, carrying on about as much correspondence with the creditors of the organization and his colleagues at Washington about these debts as he did about prospects for subordinate Granges. The year ended with nine dispensations having been placed, one each in New York, Pennsylvania, Ohio, Illinois, and Iowa, and four in Minnesota. But the fraternal organization, which Bartlett and Kelley had thought might sweep into its ranks a million dues-paying members during the first year, was not able to pay its current bills.

Kelley had borrowed $40 when leaving Washington, got $50 from McDowell while in New York, borrowed $15 from the Masonic Lodge at Madison, Wisconsin, and landed at his home with scarcely enough money to "purchase a postage stamp." The printers' bills were not paid and he was writing to Washington for "manuals" which the printers would not release until paid for. Some of his colleagues at Washington had lost faith and one or two of them were openly critical of what they considered a wild venture on Kelley's part. They held him personally responsible for debts which had been contracted, and he in turn believed that they were slackers in not pushing the work or even holding meetings among themselves. He says, "There were but *five* men to get together. If they felt inclined, they could *convene* any time at an hour's notice. I was beginning to look upon the National Grange as a farce." No one knows what would have become of this struggling farmers' fraternal order had the discontented farmers at that time not found it an appropriate instrument for mobilizing economic and political power.

A NEW IMPETUS

Thirty-eight new Granges were organized during 1869, thirty-three of them in Minnesota, and all of them in the Middle West, where they began to take root in the soil of discontent so prevalent among the farmers. Kelley still kept in touch with his eastern brothers, but it was the connections which he had made in the Middle West that furnished the dynamics for the real beginning of success. He had met Colonel D. A. Robertson of St. Paul in August, 1868, and with his assistance organized the North Star Grange No. 3 on September 2, the first local in Minnesota. Fifteen men paid $5.00 each to start the organization and, together with sixteen women, constituted the membership of a subordinate Grange whose influence was destined to change the motif of the Patrons of Husbandry for a full decade. It was under Robertson's guidance that the circular of the national organization was revised and printed. The first circular had emphasized only the fraternal and educational purposes. The second did not ignore these objects, for it said:

> The secrecy of the Ritual, and proceedings of the Order have been adopted, chiefly, for the purpose of accomplishing desired efficiency, extension and unity, and to secure among its members in the internal working of the Order—confidence, harmony and security.

But the important new note sounded in the circular read as follows:

> Among other advantages which may be desired from the Order, can be mentioned, systematic arrangements for procuring and disseminating, in the most expeditious manner, information relative to crops, demand and supply, prices, markets, and transportation throughout the country, and for the establishment of depots for the sale of special or general products in the cities; also for the purchase and exchange of stock, seeds, and desired varieties of plants and trees, and for the purpose of procuring help at home or from abroad, and situations for persons seeking employment; also for ascertaining and testing the merits of newly invented farming implements, and those not in general use, and for detecting and exposing those that are unworthy, and for protecting, by all available means, the farming interests from fraud and deception of every kind.

Although some of the Washington group did not like the changed emphasis, which from this time on became steadily more dominant, they passed resolutions commending Kelley and his new sponsors and authorized him to use their commendation in any way that would help him in his work. Kelley quotes Colonel Robertson as saying, when shown the communication, "By publishing it, there would be the appearance of an Association in existence, but we understand all about this National Grange. When we see you, we see all there is of it; but, of course, we know the advantages of having something behind to apparently give character to your decisions." Such a statement was an index to what later proved to be exceedingly important: that the leaders in the Middle West expected to use the Grange as a vehicle for mobilizing farmers in their class struggle.

Kelley fell in wholeheartedly with this change in emphasis. In December, 1868, he wrote McDowell:

> Among people the question is asked, "What benefits are we to derive?" I tell them that in every Grange there is to be kept a Blue Book and a Red Book. In the former all swindling concerns they come in contact with are to be recorded, *by vote of the Grange,* and information transmitted to other Granges, by which we become a secret detective and protective organization. In the Red Book we record reliable establishments, and anyone receiving a letter introduc-

tion *by vote of a Grange*, stating he is "duly recorded in the Red Book," is sure of cordial reception. I also advocate a Business Agent in each Grange, to be elected by ballot, who shall keep a record of real estate, produce, stock, etc. . . . We can secure discount to Granges on purchase of Books, Implements, etc., offered by publishers and manufacturers, and by systematic organization secure a reduction in rate of nearly everything purchased.

Kelley had much earlier than this informed the members of the national Grange that he believed such appeals as this would be necessary to make the order popular among practical farmers. He had reached this conviction as he traveled west through Ohio, Illinois, Wisconsin, and Minnesota.

Under the new impulse, things moved fairly rapidly in Minnesota. Kelley appointed deputies to assist in organization work, and six new Granges were added in that state between January 1 and February 20, 1869. On February 23, a state Grange was organized by the eleven subordinates then active in the state. The militancy of this state organization made itself immediately felt. At its organization meeting, the suggestion was made that "Subordinate Granges lease flouring mills in their respective localities, and flour their own wheat, keeping the bran and shorts for feed, and not send any raw materials into the Eastern market, but instead, appoint a business agent at St. Paul, who should receive the flour and ship it to the agent in New York City, who shall sell it on commission."

One or more new Granges were added in Minnesota in every month of the year 1869 except June—three in January, three in February, four in March, one in April, one in May, three in July, three in August, one in September, three in October, nine in November, and two in December— a total of thirty-three for the year. In addition to these, five were organized in other states—one in Iowa, two in Illinois, and two in Indiana. The collections for dispensations for new Granges, fees from those organized the year before, and donations totaled $902.61. In his annual report as secretary of the national Grange, Kelley reported forty-nine subordinate Granges and one state Grange, all except two of them in the Middle West. The report was made on January 25, 1870, to a national meeting composed of Saunders, Grosh, Trimble, Thompson, Ireland, McDowell, and Kelley, but it should be evident that the Grange had become a midwestern—for the most part, a Minnesota—farmers' organization for the time being.

In comparison to what followed, however, the movement was not yet on the march. During the year 1870, only thirty-eight subordinate Granges were organized, and Kelley therefore changed his tactics from spending most of his time in Minnesota to attempting to establish a few locals in a number of states out of which state Granges could be founded. His hope was that the state Granges would assume the responsibility of organizing locals, as had been the case in Minnesota. There were subordinate Granges in nine states by the end of the year, and a greatly widened interest in the order because of new contacts and new adherents scattered over a much wider territory. Kelley's report at the end of the year that the work was active in fifteen states was not technically correct so far as actual organizations were concerned, but did give a true picture of the areas in which vital interest had been demonstrated. A state Grange had been organized in Illinois in July, and a meeting was held in Iowa in October preliminary to organizing a state Grange which was due to be consummated in January, 1873. There were one or more organized Granges in Minnesota, Iowa, Missouri, Illinois, Indiana, Ohio, New York, California, and Tennessee. Inquiries had been received from Massachusetts, New Jersey, Kansas, Kentucky, Vermont, Georgia, and South Carolina.

The reader should remember that it was in April, 1870, that the first convention of what came to be the Illinois Farmers' Association was held at Bloomington, and also that Henry C. Wheeler was the prime sponsor of that meeting. Although invited, Kelley did not attend the meeting at Bloomington, and thus no direct connection was made at this time between the Grange and the organizations which were described in the preceding chapter. But through the good offices of Mr. W. W. Corbett, the then editor of the *Prairie Farmer*, Wheeler and Kelley were brought together in an attempt to make the Grange the vehicle through which the Illinois farmers might attack the problems which were troubling them. The convention named Corbett, Wheeler, and Reynolds as a committee on permanent organization, which looked promising for the Grange because Corbett was enthusiastic for the order. In July following the Bloomington convention, Wheeler was elected secretary of the temporary organization of the Illinois State Grange, an organization which

did not function until a few years later. For some reason, probably because the Grange was not prepared to carry out the immediate and direct action which the Illinois farmers desired, and because Wheeler had
his mind set on organizing a "Farmers' League," the two movements
failed to make a conjunction.

In Minnesota, the work of organization did not progress as rapidly
during 1870 as the year before, but the determination on the part of the
Grange leaders to grapple with practical business problems continued
to develop. They asked that the national Grange constitution be changed
so as to provide for county Granges, their object, according to Kelley,
being "to enable the County Granges 'to create a local corporation to buy
machinery or goods, and shipping produce.'"

Colonel Robertson was now publishing the *Minnesota Monthly* as an
organ of the state Grange, and the leaders there had won their right to
establish a state business agent by threatening to withdraw from the
national Grange, if need be, in order to accomplish their purpose. They
had opened an office in St. Paul during the previous year. Kelley had
read a letter from Corbett at the meeting of the Minnesota State Grange
in 1870 which said that the "Railroads, Insurance Companies, Warehouse
and Telegraph Companies, are crushing the life out of the producing
classes," and called upon the Grange to assist the people in war "against
the monstrous monopolies that are overshadowing us." The state Grange
ordered the complete letter to be presented for circulation.

The type of activities carried on in Minnesota is a cue to the fact that
the situation was ripe for further development in this direction in the
Middle West. Dudley W. Adams of Iowa expressed what might be characterized the call to arms, at the installation of a subordinate Grange at
Frankville, Iowa, in June, 1870:

> Through all the business relations of civilized life, unions of vari-
> ous kinds are the rule, and the more perfect they are the greater the
> strength. Merchants have their Board of Trade, Shoemakers have
> Knights of St. Crispin. Lawyers have their conventions, and Physi-
> cians their conclaves, where prices are fixed, and no one dare dis-
> obey the edicts of these unions. But how is it with the Agricultur-
> ist? Alas! we have nothing of the kind. Each one is working away
> against the world and against each other, unaided and alone. Im-
> mense in numbers and wealth; superior to any other calling in these

great sources of power—yet we are powerless. An immense helpless mob surging to and fro, without aim or method; the little squads of well-drilled lawyers and doctors charge through and through our poor disordered mass, and freely plunder our pockets. Railroads, telegraphs, commission men, mechanics, join in the pursuit with no fear of successful resistance. Like rabbits, we are the prey of hawks by day, and owls and foxes by night. Is there no remedy for this? Is there anything in the occupation of agriculture that makes a man legitimate prey for all the human vampires that infest the earth? Is the business of tilling the soil so benumbing to the mind and all the finer sensibilities, that we can contentedly accept and endure this state of affairs? Are we willing to admit that, strong as we are in numbers and wealth, we are incapable of self-defence?

Is there not enough of mind in our ranks to devise and execute a plan for our redemption from the position of slaves we now occupy? For one, when I look abroad upon these wide prairies, the granaries of the world, owned by those who till them, and holding in their hands such elements of power, I must admit shame mantles my face that no systematic effort is made for its use, at least in self-defence. A farmer has a field of wheat ready for the sickle, and it must be cut. Laborers fix the price at which they will assist in the harvest; the farmer submits. Threshers fix among themselves the price they will have for threshing, and again the farmer submits. The railroad companies fix the price at which they will carry the grain to Chicago; elevators fix the price of handling it; and buyers finally agree how much they will give for it; and each one of these middle men takes such a slice as he pleases, and the farmer timidly submits. This wheat now goes through steamers, sloops, more elevators, more speculators, canals, railroads, etc.; each one absolutely making his own terms, and only the producer and consumer are helpless. These two classes, the most deserving of all, are the victims of a few classes, small in numbers but strong by being determined and thoroughly united, yet having not another solitary element of strength at command. They do not produce a pound of meat, a bushel of wheat, a yard of cloth, or a pig of iron. They cannot subsist a month without us. We can without them. We have the power; we must use it. The farmers have got the lines, why don't they drive?

The year 1870 had been far from a success financially, only $1,696.45 having been received, $841.20 from dispensations, dues, sales of manuals and the like, and $855.25 from gifts, loans, and advances from leaders. Kelley himself had advanced $182.75, Saunders had contributed $55.50, and a new-found friend, Thomas B. Bryan of Chicago, had contributed and loaned a total of $400. But there were evidences from practically all sections of the nation that the order was on the eve of capturing thousands of discontented farmers as constituents.

During 1871, the organization moved forward with increasing acceleration; 130 new subordinates and two new state Granges were founded during that year.[4] The farmers of Iowa, who up to this time had not mobilized into any such fighting organizations as were described in Chapter 1, turned to the Grange as their mouthpiece and vehicle of action. General W. P. Wilson, editor of the *Iowa Homestead,* published at Des Moines, who through his paper for more than a year had been urging the organization of farmers' clubs, became a militant advocate of, and militant leader in, the organization.[5] The Iowa State Grange was organized on January 12, 1871, with eleven subordinate Granges represented. By April 22, deputies had increased the number to thirty-seven, and by the end of the year to 102. No other state made notable progress during the year except Wisconsin, where twenty subordinates were organized, most of them lapsing before the end of the year because of dissension between Deputy Burnham and the officers of the state Grange. Five subordinates were added in Illinois, six in Minnesota, three in Mississippi, and one each in South Carolina, Kentucky, Tennessee, Pennsylvania, Vermont, and New Jersey. State Granges were set up in Iowa and Wisconsin, although the one in Wisconsin had to be reorganized later. There were now about 180 Granges in sixteen states, and at least four other states had made requests for information and organizers. More than three-fourths of all local Granges were in Minnesota and Iowa.

The explanation of this rapid progress is to be found in the fact that such leaders as Wilson of the *Homestead* in Iowa, Corbett of the *Prairie Farmer* in Chicago, Jacques of the *Rural Carolinian* of South Carolina, took up the cause and pushed it steadily forward; and because, as Kelley

---

[4] Thomas C. Atkeson, *Semi-centennial history of the Patrons of Husbandry,* p. 42. New York: Orange Judd Publishing Co., Inc., 1916.

[5] See especially *Iowa Homestead* issues of August 6, November 19, December 17, 1869.

said, "'Co-operation' and 'down with monopolies,' were proving popular watch words." The change in emphasis which the Minnesota State Grange had initiated in 1869 was beginning to bear fruit.[6]

THE GRANGE CATCHES FIRE AS THE MOUTHPIECE OF THE FARMERS' MOVEMENT FROM 1872 TO 1875

In 1872, the Grange caught fire with the discontent among farmers which had been steadily increasing since the Civil War. The Iowa State Grange put into effect the establishment of a business agent, which Minnesota had suggested in 1869, and began making actual purchases for its members. Kelley had widely circulated reprints of four articles by Rufus Hatch which appeared in the New York *Independent* on stock watering and other railroad abuses, an issue that was already very hot in the Middle West. The Illinois farmers were not having any too great success in getting a permanent organization of their own established, but editors in both the North and South were beginning to give attention to the movement. Iowa and Minnesota were now dominant in Grange influence, and their points of view were coming to prevail in the national Grange. They were strong antimonopoly and anti-railroad-regulation states. As early as 1870, three bills had been introduced in the Iowa legislature proposing to set freight and passenger rates and create a railroad commission. In 1870-1871, Republican and Democratic state platforms contained planks asserting the state's right to regulate railroads and demanding legislation to that end. Minnesota had enacted a stringent railroad regulation law in 1871, following a transportation convention held at Owatonna in November, 1870.[7] Here, as in Illinois, the railroads had flaunted the laws and the farmers were incensed. When, therefore, the Grange finally came around to a willingness to lend itself to a considera-

---

[6] Those who are interested in following in detail the development of the Grange as a national farmers' organization during these years in which it was finding itself, or losing itself, according to the way one looks at it, can obtain a complete story of almost every detail in Kelley, chaps. ii-v; a less detailed account in Atkeson, chaps. i, ii; and a concise description in Solon J. Buck, *The Granger movement*, pp. 44-52. Cambridge, Massachusetts: Harvard University Press, 1913. The purpose here has not been to present a history of the Grange, but to show how it became the mouthpiece of the Farmers' Movement.

[7] Buck, *The Granger movement*, pp. 159-166.

tion of such issues as railroad abuses, monopolies, and middlemen, it had a program which appealed to the farmers of the Middle West, and they came into the organization by the thousands.

The year 1872 witnessed the conjunction of farmer discontent and Grange organization in terms of 1,150 new subordinate Granges, 652, or more than half of them, in Iowa. From less than 200 locals at the end of 1871, the number increased to 3,360 in May, to 5,062 in August, to 7,325 in October, 1873; to 14,365 in March, 1874, to 20,365 in September of that year, and to 21,697 by the end of the year. We probably cannot exaggerate the furor of sentiment which accompanied such activity. In Iowa alone, there were more than three new Granges organized per day during the months of May, June, and July, 1873. By September, 1874, there was a local Grange organization for every 806 people in the state, counting men, women and children, or about one Grange for every 400 rural adults. In Kansas, which was more sparsely settled, there was a Grange for every eighty-four persons engaged in agriculture, and in Indiana there was one Grange for every eighteen square miles, or two per township.[8] In the nation as a whole, almost forty Granges per day were added for the fifteen months from May, 1873, to September, 1874. Kelley lists the names of 1,968 deputies who had organized Granges before January 1, 1875. Eight of these men had organized 100 or more Granges each, and one, J. A. Barksdale of South Carolina, had organized 209. More than 1,000 Granges per month were added from March, 1873, to September, 1874, and more than 2,000 per month were organized during the first three months of 1874.

It would not be correct to assume that what Buck calls the "Granger Movement" of the seventies was wholly the work of the Grange, for some of the organizations described in Chapter 5 were actually more militant in the fight against "railroads and monopolies" than was the Grange. There can be no question, however, about the fact that a number of the state and subordinate Granges, especially of the Middle West, led the farmers' fight during this period.

The national Grange, while more conservative than the state and local Granges, had introduced into its annual meetings more and more of the spirit which had led to the rapid growth of the order. At the fifth annual

---

[8] *Ibid.,* chart between pp. 58 and 59; see also p. 67.

session, in January, 1872, Kelley said, "The educational and social features of our Order offer inducement to some to join, but the majority desire pecuniary benefits—advantages in purchase of machinery, and sales of produce. To bring all the Granges into direct communication, and to devise a system of co-operation, devolves upon the National Grange." Atkeson says concerning the trend of events in 1872, "The farmer and his family were beginning to realize their importance and power as never before in the history of the country. Indeed, before the end of the year even the politicians were beginning to realize the strength of the Patrons of Husbandry as a political force, and dealers in farm supplies its importance as a selling agency. Everywhere there was frantic wire-pulling to secure initiation into the now powerful Order."[9]

At the first regular delegate session of the national Grange, in January, 1873, national leadership passed definitely into the hands of state leaders, who were more militant than the national officers. Eleven of the sixteen officers elected were from fairly newly-established state Granges. Dudley W. Adams of Iowa was elected national Master; Thomas Taylor of South Carolina, Overseer; and T. A. Thompson of Minnesota, Lecturer.[10] The events of the year 1872 and the discussions at the annual session clearly revealed the readiness of the Grange to join in the fight for railroad control, and against "discrimination of railroads between individuals, and their corrupting of legislatures."

The 1874 annual session, held at St. Louis, was, according to Buck, "the most representative gathering of farmers which had ever taken place in the United States." Thirty-two state and territorial Granges were present, representing something like 500,000 members. At this meeting it was decided that membership should be restricted to farmers. This had not been the practice up to this time. The Declaration of Purposes adopted was dignified and fairly conservative, but among other things it said:

> We shall endeavor ... to discountenance the credit system, the mortgage system, the fashion system, and every other system tending to prodigality and bankruptcy.

We propose meeting together, talking together, working together,

---

[9] Atkeson, p. 48. Reprinted by permission of Orange Judd Publishing Co., Inc.
[10] *Proceedings of the sixth session of the national Grange of the Patrons of Husbandry* (Washington, D. C., 1873), p. 24. Washington, D. C.: Gibson Brothers, 1873.

buying together, selling together, and in general acting together for our mutual protection and advancement as occasion may require. . . .

For our business interests, we desire to bring producers and consumers, farmers and manufacturers into the most direct and friendly relations possible. Hence we must dispense with a surplus of middlemen, not that we are unfriendly to them, but we do not need them. Their surplus and their exactions diminish our profits. . . .

We are opposed to such spirit and management of any corporation or enterprise as tends to oppress the people and rob them of their just profits. We are not enemies to capital, but we oppose the tyranny of monopolies. . . . We are opposed to excessive salaries, high rates of interest, and exorbitant per cent profits in trade. They greatly increase our burdens and do not bear a proper proportion to the profits of producers.

. . . we appeal to all good citizens for their cordial cooperation to assist in our efforts toward reform, that we may eventually remove from our midst the last vestige of tyranny and corruption.[11]

Adams, of Iowa, was national Master for three years, 1873, 1874, and 1875. It was during this period that the Grange was at its height. In his three annual Master's addresses, he vigorously denounced overcapitalization and watered stock of railroads, suggested state and national control and regulation of rates, urged cooperative buying and selling, and insisted that the doors of the Grange be kept tightly closed against "hordes of speculators, demagogues, small politicians, grain-buyers, cotton-factors, and lawyers, who suddenly discover that they are 'interested in agricultural pursuits'; but only as a hawk is interested in the sparrow."[12] The national executive committee was giving much time and attention to the problems of transportation and cooperative buying and selling; the money question was much discussed, and the emphasis of the Grange had shifted from how to grow crops to how to sell them. Thus an organization which had started solely as a farmers' fraternal and educational organization, and had struggled along for five years with little success on the basis of that motive, by 1873 had caught fire with farmer discontent. Until that time it had few assets other than the enthusiasm of its founders and the loyalty of a few friends, and it was still in debt.

---

[11] *Proceedings of the seventh session* (1874).
[12] *Ibid.*, p. 18.

From 1873 to 1876, during panic and depression years, on the basis of reform motives, it mobilized into its membership more than 800,000 farm people and had the active cooperation and sympathy of twice that number; spread into every state in the Union except Rhode Island, and, coupled with other farmers' organizations, wielded an economic and political influence which was felt from one end of the nation to the other. James Truslow Adams says that the Grange membership reached 1,600,000 during this period.[13] Atkeson calculated a dues-paying membership of 858,050 for the year 1875, but says, "it is fair to assume that the living membership at any time is more than double the number that pay dues to the National Grange."[14]

THE GRANGE SKYROCKETS

No farmers' organization in American history, except the Alliance in the 1880's, better illustrates what happened in the Farmers' Movement when discontent and organization made conjunction than did the Grange from 1868 to 1876. We have noted to some extent how the prevailing discontent among farmers gradually changed the emphasis of the Grange from fraternity and education to an emphasis on economic reforms. Here is a panorama of what the economic reform movement did in turn to stimulate the growth of the Grange as a farmers' organization. When the order was founded in December, 1867, there were seven members. The total membership on January 1, 1875, was 858,050. The following brief summary description tells the story of this skyrocket evolution.

The national Grange was officially organized on December 4, 1867, the seven officers elected then constituting the entire membership of the Grange. The first session was held on January 7, 1868, with three persons—Saunders, Ireland, and Kelley—present. What Kelley calls the "First Annual Session of the National Grange," in fact the second annual session, was held on April 13, 1869, with only the six Washington faithfuls present. The third was held on January 25, 1870, with the same six and McDowell of New York present. The fourth annual session, held on Jan-

---

[13] James Truslow Adams, *The epic of America*, p. 209. London: George Routledge & Sons, Ltd., 1938.
[14] Atkeson, p. 350.

uary 4, 1871, had only five present, and the fifth, held on January 3, 1872, had six in attendance. It is notable, however, that Dudley W. Adams, Master of the Iowa State Grange, was one of the six at the 1872 meeting. He was elected National Lecturer at this session and the next year raised to the office of National Master. The sixth annual session was different— it was a delegate session with eleven states represented by twenty-three men and four women. The attendance was still so small that the meetings were held in Kelley's home during the four days of the session, January 8-11, 1873. The seventh annual session was the first to be held outside the city of Washington, D. C. It convened in St. Louis, Missouri, on February 4, 1874, with thirty-two state Granges duly represented by forty-three delegates. The following year, the meeting place was shifted into the South and was in session for fourteen days, February 3-16, at Charleston, South Carolina. Fifty-one delegates, representing thirty-three states, were in attendance. At the next meeting, in session from November 17 to December 2, 1875, in Louisville, Kentucky, thirty-one states were represented; and at the tenth annual session, held in Chicago, in November, 1876, only thirty states were represented. By this time the organization had passed its period of ascendancy and had started its decline.

The story of the national sessions just cited tells little in comparison to what the story of activities in various states reveals. Delegates to national conventions were restricted to state Masters and their wives. The numbers in attendance could therefore reveal little more than the number of active states in the organization. Some of the state conventions, whose delegates were the Masters of subordinate Granges and their wives, became almost too unwieldy to handle. There were nine states which, sometime between September, 1874 and July, 1876, had 1,000 or more Granges, and the number of locals (subordinate Granges) reached a national total of 21,697 by January 1, 1875. The total dues-paying membership in October of that year was 758,767.[15] If each local Grange had sent only its Master to the national convention at that time, such a convention would have numbered 43,394 delegates. The number of farms in the United States in 1875 was approximately 3,500,000, and the number of farm families approximately the same. There was thus a local Grange

[15] Buck, *The Granger movement,* table between pp. 58 and 59.

in existence for about every 160 farms and farm families of the nation. In 1874, Iowa, with 1,999 Granges, had a Grange for every 75 farm families; and, in 1875, Kansas, with 1,332 Granges, had a Grange for every 66 farm families.

The rapidity of periodic growth and decline is one characteristic of a movement. Some picture of this characteristic of the Farmers' Movement can be gained by a few illustrations. Iowa was the first state to surge forward in a big way. The first Grange was organized in that state in April, 1868. Only one more was organized in 1869, and nine in 1870. Iowa then caught on fire. It had 102 Granges in 1871, 652 in 1872, had more than doubled that number by May, 1873, and reached a peak of 1,999 by September, 1874. Illinois and Indiana followed quickly, with Ohio and Missouri not far behind. Illinois moved up from two Granges in 1869 to three in 1870, to eight in 1871, to 431 in May, 1873, to 676 in October of that year, to 1,533 by January 1, 1875. Indiana moved more slowly during the early years, but faster and farther in the later years. It had only two Granges in 1869, three in 1870, eight in 1871, and forty-six in 1872; but between October, 1873, and March, 1874, it increased from 467 to 1,502, and by January 1, 1875, had an even 2,000 Granges. Missouri and Ohio followed the same growth pattern. Missouri had 2,009 and Ohio 1,102 Granges on January 1, 1875.[16]

Two other bodies of data serve to show the speed and temper of the movement once it was on the march: the increases in membership, and funds collected and expended. It is impossible to know the dues-paying membership before 1874, when the national Grange became a well-systemized business organization. Atkeson presents national figures from 1874 to 1915 and states that he obtained the figures from the "actual amount of dues paid each year." They are as follows:

1874	268,368	1885	117,620
1875	858,050	1890	135,461
1876	728,313	1895	179,247
1877	411,244	1900	187,482
1878	324,782	1905	284,646
1879	246,383	1910	425,033
1880	124,420	1915	540,085

16 *Ibid.*, pp. 46-49. See also national Grange *Proceedings* for the years mentioned.

The lowest membership was in 1889, when it fell to 106,782; after this, it took the Grange more than forty years to again reach as large a number of dues-paying members as it had in 1875. In the interim, however, the Farmers' Alliance, Farmers' Union, Equity, Farm Bureau, and others had joined in carrying on the Farmers' Movement.

The records of collections and expenditures of the national Grange during the period of its ascendancy reveal much concerning the spirit and techniques as well as the magnitude of the movement. It collected $129,315 from applications for dispensations during the year 1873 and spent $29,314.40 for printing. Its total receipts for that year were $132,151.28 and its expenditures were $71,591.53. Its treasury was so overflowing that it invested $39,512.50 in United States currency certificates, held $7,742 in the contingency fund, and still had a balance over all these disbursements of $13,305.25. During the year, it had printed 140,000 manuals, 19,000 record books, 15,000 roll books, 165,000 copies of the constitution and by-laws, 46,240 miscellaneous circulars, and 68,405 songbooks. During the next year (1874), the total credited receipts were $229,533.72. During the first ten months of the year 1875, the total receipts were only $102,143.07.[17] The chief differences between income for the two years were in two major items, collections for applications, and the shorter period of collections in 1875. The collections for dispensations in 1874 yielded $148,900; in the first ten months of 1875, only $30,090. The high income in 1873 had been made possible by the sale of equipment and supplies, circulars, and songbooks to the amount of almost $47,000. Thus the annual income for the three years does not validly reflect the growth of the order. The growth is best reflected in the organization of new Granges, which was as follows: 1873, 8,667; 1874, 11,941; first ten months of 1875, 2,013. In his annual message, in November, 1875, the Worthy Master said, "In some localities Granges have from various causes languished and died."[18] There were 2,690 fewer Granges on October 1 than on January 1, 1875. Iowa, which had led the movement in organizing Granges, had 835 fewer than at its peak; Illinois, 744 fewer; Ohio, 135; Indiana, 515; Missouri, 108; and Kansas, 841 fewer. By July, 1876, the total number of Granges in the nation was

---

[17] *Proceedings* (1873, 1874, 1875).
[18] *Ibid.*

only 15,127, or 6,570 fewer than the maximum number in existence on January 1, 1875.[19]

The sentiment among farmers which led to the so-called "Granger movement" was not initially generated by the Grange. This sentiment had been in existence before the Civil War and had grown steadily, especially in the Middle West, after the war. Cloud's *Monopolies and the People*, Smith's *Grains for the Grangers*, Periam's *The Groundswell*, and Martin's *History of the Grange Movement; or the Farmer's War against Monopolies* were not Grange publications and did not deal primarily with the Grange. They constituted the literature of this time on the Farmers' Movement, of which the Grange inadvertently and temporarily became the chief mouthpiece. Farmers' clubs, associations, conventions, and their sponsors, like the *Prairie Farmer* and *Western Rural*, utilized the Grange as a piece of social, economic, and political organization to further a cause they had been agitating for more than two decades.

In January, 1873, the *Prairie Farmer* dedicated a column, which soon expanded into almost a page, to "Patrons of Husbandry." It had done about the same thing years before for farmers' clubs. All during the period of Grange ascendancy, it carried on the same page reports from farmers' clubs which were not members of the national or state Granges, and from the Illinois State Farmers' Association, which was in a way a rival, though not an enemy, of the Grange.[20]

The support, or at least the interest, of many newspapers, a thing essential to any movement, was not absent. The Granger movement had many papers regularly reporting its actions.[21] It was, however, primarily the extent and development of economic and political discontent of midwestern farmers which drove the Grange in the direction that will be described in the next chapter, and newspapers naturally reported this discontent. Some farm journals stimulated and guided it.

---

[19] Buck, *The Granger movement*, pp. 58-78.

[20] See issues of *Prairie Farmer*, 1873.

[21] See especially Chicago *Tribune*, issues from February, 1872, to 1876. *Western Rural* (Chicago), issues from 1873 to 1876. New York *Tribune*, from March, 1873, to 1876. Sioux City *Journal* (Iowa), March, 1873. Junction City *Tribune* (Kansas), March, 1874. Louisville *Commercial* (Kentucky), January, 1874. *The Kansas Daily Tribune* (Lawrence, Kansas), June, 1874. *News and Courier* (Charleston, South Carolina), April, 1874. *Iowa Homestead* (Des Moines), 1873 to 1876. *Rural Carolinian* (Charleston, South Carolina), 1869 to 1874. Oshkosh *Times* (Wisconsin), 1870 to 1876.

THE GRANGER REVOLT

1870-1880

THE COMPLAINTS OF THE FARMERS

The Granger revolt of the seventies has been variously interpreted as marking the end of the pioneer era in America, as a reaction to the coming of the Industrial Revolution in the nation's life, as the aftermath of the Civil War, and as one of the periodic ephemeral uprisings of American farmers. All of these interpretations are partially correct, but none of them furnishes an adequate explanation when taken by itself. From the point of view presented here, the period must be described as one of the high tides in the developing Farmers' Movement in the United States. In this instance, as in practically all other periods of high tides in the Farmers' Movement, the other side of the picture is a low tide in agricultural prosperity.

It is largely true that this period did mark the end of the pioneer period, in the sense that railroads had come to displace wagon trains and that the price, market, and credit system had swept away what had previously been a semi-self-sufficient midwestern agriculture. It is true that influences of the Industrial Revolution, as represented by the expansion of railroads, the development of factories, and especially the influence of corporate wealth, had greatly altered old economic arrangements. In the aftermath of the Civil War, as in most major wars, there was a price decline, especially in agricultural commodities, and a situation in which debtors were compelled to liquidate long-term obligations in money of a higher value than that which they borrowed. It is true that the farmers' revolt during this time was ephemeral in some of its aspects and undertakings. But it is also true that after the high tide of farmer discontent of the period had subsided, there was left in its wake a farmers' organization of national scope which has lived from that day to this, and a series of legislative enactments and established public policies which have helped to form not only the legal but the economic and social structure of American civilization. The Farmers' Movement did not die with the decline of Grange membership after 1875, and its influence would not have ceased had the Grange gone completely out of existence. The Farmers' Alliance did go out of existence after having followed somewhat the same path in the eighties and early nineties, that the Grange followed in the seventies, but the Farmers' Movement continued.

The story of the rise of farmers' organizations has already been sketched. There remains to be told the story of their spirit and accomplishments. The Grange was both the chief vehicle and spearhead, but by no means the only instrument used, in the Farmers' Movement during the decade 1870-1880. Other farmers' economic organizations were in the field, and a dozen different independent political parties were formed and used by discontented farmers in their attempt to remedy the situation in which they found themselves.

Two things were of supreme importance to the farmers at this time: one was cheap transportation; the other, cheap money. The railroads had invoked the right to run their lines across the farmers' fields, and had been granted about 130,000,000 acres of the "people's land" by the government and millions of dollars of the "people's money" in taxes necessary to liquidate railroad bonds. The farmers believed that the railroad companies should reciprocate by granting cheap freight and passenger rates to the people. Instead of this, some of the greatest fortunes of all times were being built up by eastern capitalists out of "exorbitant and unregulated rates." The pioneer farmers of the West had just completed the settlement of the Mississippi Valley and were still in debt for much of their land and working capital. The deflation program of the govern-

ment following the Civil War culminated in the "Crime of 1873," ° and
debtor farmers found themselves compelled to liquidate fixed obligations
with farm products which were steadily declining in value. The result
was an increasing burden of debt, an increasing volume of farmer discontent, and a consequent surge upward and forward in the Farmers'
Movement.

The farm-land mortgage debt in a typical county in the state of Iowa,
for instance, increased from about $4.90 to $7.72 per acre between 1865
and 1880. Not all of this was due to deflated currency and falling prices
for agricultural products, but part of it was. The creditors for these debts
in 1880 were different from those in 1860, 1865, or 1870. Seventy-six per
cent of the Iowa farm mortgage debt in 1860 was owed to private investors, 18 per cent to the state school fund, and 6 per cent to mortgage
brokers. In 1880, 31 per cent of it, or $48,360,000, was owed to mortgage
brokers, insurance companies, deposit banks—that is, to eastern capitalists.
The legal rate of interest was still 10 per cent in 1880.[1] The Middle West,
principally Illinois, Iowa, Minnesota, Wisconsin, Missouri, Indiana, and
Ohio, constituted the chief area of revolt against prevailing conditions and
practices. It was in these states that farmers' organizations, the Grange
and others, had been steadily gaining strength when the depression of the
early seventies tipped the scales in favor of open farmer revolt.

The first rumblings of discontent, represented in the Centralia Platform of 1858, had named prices and political representation as the basis
of contention. The Minnesota State Grange demands in 1868 had been
for grappling with "prices, markets, and transportation." Wheeler's call
for the first Bloomington Convention had dealt almost altogether with
the need of organization to combat "railroad domination and extortion";
and while some of the other organizations gave as much consideration to
other problems, it was the transportation problem which formed the

---

° *Crime of 1873.* This phrase refers to a law passed by Congress in 1873 abolishing
the silver dollar. The "silverites" called the law a "crime." Public orators thereafter
referred to it as the "crime of 1873."

[1] William G. Murray and Ronald C. Bentley, "Farm Mortgage Foreclosures," *The
agricultural emergency in Iowa.* Part IX, Circular No. 147, Agri. Exp. Sta., Iowa
State College of Agriculture and Mechanic Arts. Ames, Iowa: March, 1933. William
G. Murray, *An economic analysis of farm mortgages in Story County, Iowa, 1854-
1931,* Research Bulletin No. 156, Agri. Exp. Sta., Iowa State College of Agriculture
and Mechanic Arts. Ames, Iowa: January, 1933.

heart of the farmers' revolt in the decade 1870-1880. This was natural for two reasons: first, because of the immense importance of railroads to this inland area; and second, because of the public scandal resulting from the behavior of the railroad financiers and speculators.

Wheat was the main farm product shipped to market. The total wheat crop of the nation in 1870 was 287,745,626 bushels, of which the western states produced 202,000,000 bushels, or about 70 per cent. Edward Martin, writing a few years later, calculated that 130,000,000 bushels of the western crop that year moved into eastern and European markets.[2] All of it had to move to Chicago and most of it farther east over the railroads. The same thing was true of corn and livestock. Farmer supplies, implements, clothes, furniture, and food moved west over these same railroads. Railroads were, therefore, more important in the economic life of the West than any other one industrial thing. Freight rates were no higher than they had been ever since the railroads had been built, but the fact that they now absorbed so much more of the eastern market price of farm products caused the farmers to believe that high freight rates were the chief cause of their difficulty.

The case against the railroads was not so strong as the discontented farmers made it, but the history of railroad financing and speculation of this period, viewed in the most objective light, constituted nothing short of a national scandal. The railroads were built more rapidly than economic wisdom would have dictated, and many of them were, therefore, uneconomic ventures. Each road was an economic enterprise in itself, unregulated by either federal or state government, and subject to cutthroat competition of all other roads. Railroad companies were granted lands by federal and state governments which ultimately netted the companies hundreds of millions of dollars. They floated bond issues, and by other means increased their capital stock, and then charged rates high enough to pay dividends on their inflated stock values. They did not stop with these business practices, as unjust and unworthy as they were, but sought to control national and state legislative bodies and, failing in some cases to do this, flaunted railroad regulation laws passed by state legislatures. Their attitudes toward the public were arrogant and sometimes insolent. J. A. Coleman, in an article in the *Atlantic Monthly*

[2] Edward W. Martin, pp. 313-314.

in 1872, tells of being beaten and thrown off a train by railroad officials and employees because he did not have the exact form of ticket required, although the ticket was a type that was commonly accepted on all roads. He sued the road and was compelled to go through five trials, all of which he won. He quoted one of the leading railroad officials as saying, "the Road is determined to make it so terrible for the public to fight it, right or wrong, that they will stop it."[3] Samuel McNutt, for ten years, 1863-1873, a member of the Iowa state legislature, in a letter to D. C. Cloud in 1873 said that one railroad gave passes to those who had opposed railroad regulation in the Iowa legislature, but not to those who favored it, and that each pass was accompanied with a private note "stating that free passes were not now given generally, 'but only to their friends.' "[4]

One of the most elaborate systems of graft imaginable was used in some instances in financing railway construction. Contracts were let to dummy contractors for millions more than the cost of construction and the differences between cost and contract prices were pocketed by so-called financiers. An organization known as the "Credit Mobilier" was set up for the purpose of mobilizing capital to build the Union Pacific Railroad, but was used as the instrument by which its operators made millions of dollars, polluted some Congressmen, and systematically robbed minority stockholders. Because the "scandal of the Credit Mobilier" became one of the principal shibboleths of the Farmers' Movement for twenty years, we shall take space to describe briefly this corporation. We shall use Farmers' Movement literature of the time, for it is this literature that reflects what farmers were reading and hearing about the "railroad scandals."[5]

The Credit Mobilier Company was organized as a financial agent to build the Union Pacific Railroad from Omaha to the Pacific Coast. In 1866, Oakes Ames, a member of Congress from Massachusetts, and Oliver Ames, his brother, both men of considerable means, organized

---

[3] John A. Coleman, "The Fight of a Man with a Railroad," *Atlantic Monthly*, Vol. XXX, No. 182 (December, 1872), pp. 641-653.

[4] Cloud, p. 165.

[5] See Cloud and E. W. Martin. See also E. W. Martin, *Behind the scenes in Washington*. New York: Continental Publishing Co., 1873. These books furnish the chief Farmers' Movement literature of the period. The description of the Credit Mobilier given in these pages presents the case as they saw it.

a company with $2,500,000 capital stock. In 1867, they added $1,250,000 in stock and sold it to subscribers with the provision that each purchaser would receive as a bonus an equal amount of first mortgage bonds of the Union Pacific Company. The old stockholders were also granted this same bonus for the stock already owned. Oakes Ames then signed a contract with the Union Pacific Company to build 667 miles of road at prices ranging from $42,000 to $96,000 per mile, the total contract aggregating $47,000,000, an average of a little more than $74,000 per mile. The contract was transferred to seven trustees and later to the Credit Mobilier. Thus the Credit Mobilier literally contracted with itself to build a railroad at exorbitant prices. This would not have been so bad had there been no other factors involved, but there were, one of them being the federal government.

By an act of Congress the Union Pacific Company was endowed with one-half of the land for twenty miles on each side of its right of way. This meant that the Company received 12,800 acres of land for every mile of road which it built. In addition to this, the government loaned the railroad company an average of $32,000 per mile of construction contracted for. Over and above this, the Union Pacific Company issued stock of $10,000,000. When the Credit Mobilier was organized, all the assets of the road, including gifts from the government, were turned over to secure its shares (owned by the Ames brothers and others), and the federal government and all investors in the Union Pacific, other than those in the Credit Mobilier, were left with second liens. Thus everything of any value—the road itself, profits on construction, land granted by the government, and Union Pacific stocks—were literally in the hands of the Credit Mobilier. Placed in this position, the holding company, or financial agent, drained money as long as possible from the Union Pacific Company and the government and then allowed the road to be stripped of practically all of its earnings by diverting traffic to other competing roads, especially the Southern Pacific.

The contract to build the Union Pacific was made in October, 1867. On January 4, 1868, the stockholders of the Credit Mobilier received 80 per cent in Union Pacific first mortgage bonds and 100 per cent in its stock. On June 17, 1868, they received 60 per cent in cash and 40 per cent in the railroad's stocks; on July 5, 75 per cent in stock and 75 per cent in first mortgage bonds; on September 3, 1868, they received 100 per cent in stocks and 75 per cent in first mortgage bonds; and finally, on December 19, 1868, they received 200 per cent in stocks. In addition to all of this, the stockholders had received 200 per cent dividends in stock and 50 per cent of first mortgage bonds of the road before the contract to build the road was signed. From a study of all these facts and figures, this simple picture emerges: the Credit Mobilier collected from all sources combined more than twice what it cost to build the road, pocketed the excess cash—about $150,000,000—and retained the vast stretches of lands which the government had given them.

The above is an exaggerated account of what happened; but it was the story told over and over again at farmers' meetings and in Farmers' Movement literature in the seventies and for a considerable period afterward. Martin's statement epitomizes what the farmers believed, that "Reduced to plain English, the story of the Credit Mobilier is simply this: The men entrusted with the management of the Pacific Road made a bargain with themselves to build the road for a sum equal to about twice its actual cost, and pocketed the profits . . . this immense sum coming out of the pockets of the tax payers of the United States."

The fact that the chief promoter and a number of the leading stockholders of the Credit Mobilier were members of Congress, and that they and the company were all located in the eastern part of the United States, served to deepen the bitterness of the western farmers. It is easy to understand the transfer of their concern from local to national affairs on the hinge of the railroad issue. Railroads were vital to them where they lived and worked; they and their local governments had helped to promote and finance the roads; they were sure that freight rates were exorbitant, and that railroad companies were attempting to influence state legislatures. When they learned of the Credit Mobilier, they were confirmed in all their suspicions about railroad "racketeering." William Larrabee, ex-Governor of Iowa, in discussing the question, said:

So great was the estimate of convenience afforded by them (the railroads) and so strongly was public opinion prejudiced in their favor that it is no exaggeration to say that railroad companies as a rule were permitted to prepare their own charters, and that these charters almost invariably received legislative sanction. . . . Communities taxed themselves heavily for their benefit, and municipalities and individuals vied with each other in donating money, rights of way and sites for station buildings. ... So large were the public and private donations in several of the Western States that their value was equal to one-fifth of the total cost of all roads constructed.[6]

Now they claimed that eastern financiers, and even members of Congress, were using railroad building and financing to loot not only them but the federal government. This cast the railroad question as the dominant issue of the Farmers' Movement for almost two decades. The Credit Mobilier became a shibboleth which in that day was equal in opprobrium to "Wall Street" in later days.

Nor were the farmers and their leaders entirely incorrect in their interpretation of the Credit Mobilier. The whole affair was investigated by a congressional committee, which traced 160 shares of stock of the company for which contracts were made for delivery to different members of Congress. Oakes Ames had earlier written from Washington, "I shall put [the shares of stock for which he was trustee] where they will do most good to us. I am here on the spot, and can better judge where they should go."[7]

Concerning the findings of this congressional inquiry, the Beards write:

> Besides several other diverting truths, the investigation disclosed the fact that many men of the highest political standing had taken the profitable stock without realizing that they were "guilty of any impropriety or even indelicacy." Still Ames was censured; a Senator from New Hampshire was found guilty of corruption and perjury by the committee of his colleagues; all without making any change in the distribution of the Union Pacific returns.[8]

Rhodes describes the results of the investigation as follows:

> The Poland committee found Oakes Ames "guilty of selling to members of Congress" shares in the Credit Mobilier at prices much below their true value with the intent "to influence the votes and decisions of such members in matters to be brought before Congress for action"; and it recommended his expulsion from the House.

---

[6] Wm. Larrabee, *The railroad question*, p. 125. Chicago: The Schulte Publishing Co., 1893.

[7] Poland report, p. 4, H. R. 77, 42nd Congress, 3rd Session, December 12, 1872.

[8] Beards, Vol. II, p. 203. Reprinted by permission of The Macmillan Company.

It found James Brooks of New York guilty of corruption as a member of the House and as a government director of the Union Pacific Railroad and likewise recommended his expulsion. The House changed the resolution for expulsion in both cases to one of censure, which in the case of Ames was carried by 182:36 and in that of Brooks by 174:32. The fact is, the House had unwittingly executed on these unhappy men the extreme penalty of the law. The vote of censure was had February 27, 1873. Brooks died on April 30 following; Ames on the 8th of May. The deaths of both men were undoubtedly hastened by their mortification and disgrace.

The finding of the committee in the case of Brooks was just; that in the case of Ames strictly in accordance with the law.[9]

Other railroads were built with similar excess profits in construction going to so-called financiers. Railroad stocks were watered without conscience, rate discrimination practiced without apology, and exorbitant rates charged without recourse. James Truslow Adams says:

The rates charged were both exorbitant and discriminatory. In 1869, with wheat selling at 76 cents in the East, it cost the Western farmer over 52 cents for transportation, leaving him only 24 cents for his risk and labor. The railways could also make or break sections and businesses. The early rise of the Rockefeller fortune, for example, was notorious in this respect. Not only did the railroads carry his oil for less than they charged his competitors, but in one case, where they charged him 10 cents and his competitors 35, they even went further and paid to him the 25 cents extra they charged his competitors! [10]

---

[9] James F. Rhodes, *History of the United States from the Compromise of 1850 to the end of the Roosevelt administration,* Vol. VII (1872-1877), pp. 74-75. New York: The Macmillan Company, 1928. See also Wilson report and Poland report, H. R. 78 and 77, 42nd Congress, 3rd Session, 1873. See also Henry K. White, *History of the Union Pacific Railway.* Chicago: University of Chicago Press, 1895. John P. Davis, *The Union Pacific Railway,* especially chap. vi, "Credit Mobilier," pp. 163-202. Chicago: S. C. Griggs and Co., 1894. William Z. Ripley, *Railroads finance and organization,* Appendix III. New York: Longmans, Green and Co., 1920. *The Credit Mobilier investigation,* a speech by Hon. J. R. Hawley of Connecticut, delivered in the House of Representatives, January 25, 1873. Rowland Hazard, *The Credit Mobilier of America.* Rhode Island Historical Society. Providence, Rhode Island: Sidney S. Rider, 1881. In defense of Ames and others are such documents as *Oakes Ames and the Credit Mobilier,* prepared by Ames's sons. Boston: Frank Wood, 1880.

[10] James Truslow Adams, p. 299. Reprinted by permission of Little, Brown & Company and the Atlantic Monthly Press.

Other complaints of the farmers were those against patent laws, which they felt increased the cost of many things they had to buy; against high government salaries, which they thought raised taxes; against the domination of legislatures and Congress by lawyers and paid lobbies; and against the deflation of the currency. They not only passed resolutions in their Grange and club meetings against all of these things, but organized both economically and politically to remedy the conditions to which they objected.

THE GRANGE TAKES UP THE CUDGELS

It is interesting to trace the drift of the Grange into economic and political activity. It was not founded for the purpose of such activity, but it apparently had little or no possibility of growth and influence as a farmers' organization in the early 1870's if it failed to respond to the demands farmers were making for such action. Kelley was the first of the founders to recognize this fact, but there is no evidence that he was aware of it when he conceived the order or for some time afterward. In a letter of September 4, 1867, written to Anson Bartlett of North Madison, Ohio, he said:

Now what I design is this: An Order that will create an interest, and keep it. Country and town societies and clubs are interesting for a while, but soon lose their interest, and I see nothing that will be lasting, unless it combine with it the advantages which an Order similar to our Masonic fraternity will provide. Among the objects in view may be mentioned a cordial and social fraternity of farmers all over the country. Encourage them to read and think; to plant fruits and flowers,—beautify their homes; elevate them; make them progressive. In our lectures in the various degrees, just see what a fund of beautiful material we have to make them sublime. Every tool the farmer works with, and all his surroundings, the beauties of nature, can convey a moral illustrated lesson, and the labors of the farm also, the preparation of the soil (the mind) for the seed (ideas)—planting,—the harvest, etc. . . . Make it incumbent upon every member to plant at least one fruit tree and one vine annually. I long to see the great army of producers in our country turn their eyes up from their work; stir up those brains, now mere machines; get them in motion in the right direction; make them discard their old almanacs and signs of the moon; and just imagine what a volcanic eruption we can produce in this age. Everything is progressing. Why not the farmers? [11]

Bartlett, however, in his reply on September 15 said in part:

Something might be realized, it is true, by Fairs and Lectures, as well as fees and dues; but in this age "money makes the mare go." In my view of the matter, this Order ought to be a wealthy one, with money in the treasury, not only for assistance of distressed members, but also to loan to needy brothers and sisters, under proper limitations.

In his next letter, October 2, Bartlett went further:

The great majority of our countrymen are ruled by pecuniary considerations, although I would by no means make this a prime incentive for a person to unite with such an Order, but would rather so fashion the work and lectures as to lead the minds of the members into a higher and nobler sphere. Still taking society as we find it, I think we shall be compelled to so frame our work as to increase the chances for pecuniary success. This, however, I would have follow as a necessary corollary of the legitimate working of the Order, and not by the Order itself becoming a commercial or monied institution. To secure the attention and patronage of the masses, it must be made to appear that one of the legitimate consequences of being a member of the Order, will be to promote the pecuniary interests of those who belong to it.

There is no evidence in this exchange of correspondence that Bartlett or Kelley had marketing or manufacturing in mind. Rather, they were thinking of fraternal and educational benefits which could be accounted as "pecuniary." In a letter of October 15, 1867, to Bartlett, Kelley said:

Again, we want every member to take at least one newspaper. These we can get at reduced rates. Reports of the crops and prospects of prices will be kept constantly known and imparted to members. As you say, it will be a power in the land, and we can make it a powerful one.

----

[11] This and the other quotations appearing on the next few pages are from Kelley's *Origin and progress of the order of Patrons of Husbandry.*

In a letter of November 26, Bartlett said:

> In fact, this Order affords one of the most ample opportunities for collecting and diffusing trustworthy statistics, and if it is incorporated in the Constitution, there will then be no doubt about it, and a large number will be induced to join for the benefit such information will be to them.

When, however, the first circular was published, and through it information about the purposes of the order given to the public, none of these things was mentioned. This circular said:

> It [the order] is based upon the axioms that the products of the soil comprise the basis of all wealth; that individual happiness depends, in great degree, upon general prosperity, that the wealth of the country will depend altogether upon the general intelligence and mental culture of the producing classes. The best mode of securing a diffusion of knowledge, with a view to its application to the increase of the products of the soil, is therefore one of the most important questions that can be propounded, and we hope greatly to facilitate its solution by the results that will follow the work of the organization to which we allude, and concerning which we take the liberty of asking you to favor us with your considerate opinion, suggestions, and advice.

Bartlett, however, continued, through correspondence with Kelley, to point toward the type of activity which later became the battle cry of the Grange. In a letter of February 8, 1868, he wrote:

> My motion is just this: that unless we carefully read the signs of times, and plant ourselves, in fact, on advance ground, we will soon be left behind in the race of life. That here in the organization of this Order is the opportunity to initiate mighty reforms; that it will be expected of us to do so, and the world will be disappointed if we do not.

Kelley, in response to this letter, on February 12, said:

> Letters are continually coming in, asking "what pecuniary benefits are members to receive? If farmers see they can get good interest on their money that is paid for membership they will join in a body."

He wrote, however, that when he wanted to insert in a new circular a few words "relative to co-operation in protecting the members at large from imposition and frauds," Saunders did not favor it. Kelley adds, "I was satisfied we had got to have such a feature to make it popular."

He became more convinced of this necessity as soon as he began circulating among farmers attempting to establish Granges. He wrote to McDowell of New York, on April 19, 1868, after he had visited personally with Bartlett, at Spencer, Ohio, and George E. Blakelee, of the *Ohio Farmer*, at Columbus:

> Between ourselves, it will be an organization that will, in a few years' time, rule in this country. I know our associates in the National Grange do not see the Order in the same light as you and I do. They may by and by.

On April 21, while still on his trip west, he again wrote McDowell, saying this astounding thing:

> I have a good opportunity to get the sentiment of the farmers. In my humble opinion, this Order, with its influence, will inaugurate a party that will sweep the country of the present race of politicians. There is nothing else that can restore peace and quiet between North and South.
>
> Every kind of monopoly is now at work grinding the producer, and I find the people encourage our work, hoping to find relief.

Kelley was in the Middle West for a year before returning to Washington for the annual meeting of the national Grange in April, 1869. In the meantime, eleven local Granges and a state Grange had been organized in his home state of Minnesota. The Minnesota State Grange led the way into economic activities. At its first meeting, it was suggested:

> ...that the different Subordinate Granges lease flouring mills in their respective localities, and flour their own wheat, keeping the bran and shorts for feed, and not send any raw material into the Eastern market, but instead, appoint a business agent at St. Paul, who should receive the flour and ship it to the agent in New York City, who shall sell it on commission.

When, however, the suggestion was made in a letter from McDowell to the national Grange that it appoint "a general business agent of the

Order, also State agents to attend to buying and selling for the Subordinate Granges," the suggestion was laid on the table. This did not deter the Minnesota State Grange. It went ahead and appointed its business agent.

Minnesota was quickly surpassed in the number of Granges and in the number of Grange memberships by Iowa, Illinois, Missouri, Indiana, and Ohio. When the first delegate session of the national Grange was held in January, 1873, Dudley W. Adams of the booming Granger state of Iowa was elected National Master. In his Master's address on the opening day of the next annual session, he said:

> When the first subordinate granges had been organized, one of the first and most proper subjects for discussion was, how to make two blades of grass grow where one grew before. During these discussions, the fact soon became prominent that how to sell crops was fully as knotty a question as how to grow them. It came to the conviction of members, that we received 60 cents for a bushel of wheat, while the man who ate it paid $1.20 for it. We were selling corn at 20 cents per bushel, while the consumer was paying 80 cents for it. In what we bought, there was the same discrepancy between first cost and what we were obliged to pay. For mowers, sewing-machines, plows, musical instruments, etc., etc., we were paying from 30 to 200 per cent above the original cost. We asked ourselves whether the amazing difference was a necessity, or the result of circumstances over which we had control. The solution of this problem soon became the leading idea in the Order.[12]

In this address he referred to "cooperative stores," "freight rates," "Credit Mobilier," "tariffs," "speculators," "small politicians," "grain buyers," "cotton factors," and "lawyers."

National Worthy Lecturer, T. A. Thompson of Minnesota, in his address at the same meeting, said the order "has burst the chains of commercial servitude"; and the executive committee reported that it had "issued three business circulars during the year," "visited various cities and manufacturing stations in efforts to effect special arrangements for the benefit of the Order," and "placed themselves in correspondence with presidents and directors of railroad and other transportation companies." The com-

---

[12] *Proceedings of the seventh session* (1874), pp. 11-13.

mittee said: "The past experience of your committee induces it to suggest for your consideration the propriety of establishing a Business Agency in the office of the National Grange, to be under the direct and entire control of the Executive Committee." [13]

At the second day's session a committee "On Transportation and Co-operation" and another "On Commercial Relations" were appointed. The one on transportation and cooperation reported to this same session on the last day of the convention. In that report it made three especially significant statements:

> ... we feel the imperative necessity of some definite action, to the end that there may be an exchange of products between producers in the different sections of the country.

> It should be our purpose to arrange a business system by which an exchange of products may be made direct between the producer and consumer without the intervention of an unnecessary number of middle men.

> *Resolved,* That the Executive Committee of the National Grange be instructed to give especial attention to furnishing Patrons with tools and implements for the cultivation of our farms, and all family and farm supplies, at as low a price as a legitimate business profit will permit, and also to make arrangements by which a mutual exchange of products between different sections of the country may be made; and they are hereby authorized to employ, if in their judgment it may be necessary, competent agents to aid them in the work. [14]

This resolution was adopted.

In its report for the next annual session, the executive committee stated that it had acquired rights to the Werner harvester, a "walking cultivator," and a "seeder"; had secured exclusive control of "a sulky spring-toothed hay rake"; had arranged for "a combined self-raking reaper and mower"; and that additions to these were in progress. Its recommendation that it be allowed to establish national purchasing agencies in New York, Chicago, and New Orleans was, however, not approved. [15]

---

[13] *Ibid.,* pp. 29-30, 31.
[14] *Ibid.,* pp. 79, 80.
[15] *Proceedings of the eighth session* (1875), pp. 26, 30, 99.

THE ECONOMIC ATTACK ON PROBLEMS

At the ninth annual session—the fourth delegate session—held in November, 1875, the executive committee reported that it had visited manufacturers, gathered statistics, and communicated findings, by correspondence, to state Granges. It reported: "... in some of the states our agencies are doing a very large business for our Order, and saving for them in the aggregate millions of dollars, in others the results are unsatisfactory and disappointing to the expectations of the members of our Order, and in all they have fallen far short of the benefits which could be realized under a more perfect and uniform system." Its report criticized the commission system being used by some Granges, and asked for the opportunity to devise and submit to the Order a "permanent, uniform, cooperative business system." The committee was instructed to prepare such a plan and submit it to the order.

The executive committee of the national Grange—during much of that time composed of Aiken of South Carolina, Shankland of Iowa, and Saunders, one of the original seven—offered, it appears, as one looks back on what followed, wise counsel at every step of the Granger business ventures. They promoted sound principles of cooperation, sent a commission to England to study the English wholesale society and other British cooperatives, issued a circular setting forth and advocating Rochdale principles, and offered to lead in appointing three national purchasing agents who would operate under their direction.

The delegates either were far more conservative while operating as voting members of the national Grange, were afraid of domination of the executive committee, or could not control their own state and local Granges, for there seemed to be little hesitancy on the part of state and subordinate Granges to plunge into business ventures. Almost every program imaginable was made by these organizations in the period 1873-1876. They set up business organizations and negotiated business arrangements varying all the way from local buying clubs to banks and foreign marketing, accomplished a great deal, and created an economic upheaval of national magnitude and historical significance.

The first and most universal attack of the Grange on the economic problem was cooperative buying and selling. The simplest arrangement was one in which a subordinate Grange would promise to pool its buying orders and turn them over to a local merchant who would promise to grant concessions in price. The next most simple plan was for a county, district, or Pomona Grange to purchase fairly large quantities of staples at reduced prices because of "column purchases," that is, purchases made by checking a list of available goods. In a number of cases, state agents were appointed who made contracts with jobbers and even manufacturers and wholesalers, pooling the orders of a number of subordinate and Pomona Granges and distributing the supplies to local railroad stations. Twenty-six state Granges had adopted some sort of agency system by the end of the year 1874.[16]

A number of cooperative stores were established by county and district Granges, and although the national Grange did not participate financially in any of these economic projects, it did promulgate rules for organizing the Rochdale type of store, and a representative of the national executive committee made a trip to England during the summer of 1875 to perfect an arrangement for cooperation with the English Cooperative Union. Hundreds of local stores were organized throughout the nation, and the national Grange proceedings from 1875 to 1878 are filled with reports and discussions of these cooperative store projects. In a number of states, Grange supply houses or wholesale agencies were established to supply goods to the numerous local Grange stores.[17]

Cooperative selling was attempted in a number of places. In Missouri, a Grange livestock commission agent operated on the St. Louis market, and some of the southern states had agents in New York and Liverpool to handle consignments of cotton. In California, the state Grange shipped seventeen cargoes of wheat to foreign ports in 1874 through an employed agency. It later organized the Grangers' Business Association, with a capital stock of $1,000,000, to ship grain and other merchandise to foreign

---

[16] Buck, The Granger movement, p. 241.

[17] Prairie Farmer, December 26, 1874, p. 411. Kelley, pp. 35, 79, 112-114, 129, 168, 170, 171, 183, 298, 302-305, 385. A. E. Paine, The Granger movement in Illinois, The University Studies, Vol. I, No. 8 (September, 1904), p. 39, Urbana, Illinois: University of Illinois. Industrial Age (Chicago), January 31, 1874, pp. 5, 7. Ezra S. Carr, The Patrons of Husbandry on the Pacific Coast, pp. 134, 159-160, 177. San Francisco: A. L. Bancroft and Co., 1875. Proceedings of the seventh session (1874), pp. 31, 79-80. Eighth session (1875), pp. 23-31, 70, 98, 99. Ninth session (1876), pp. 89-93, 95-103, 141. Amos G. Warner, Three phases of cooperation in the West, Publications of the American Economic Association, Vol. II, No. 1 (March, 1887), p. 34.

ports. In Oregon, the Grangers also shipped grain abroad through the medium of commercial agencies.[18]

In one instance at least, an attempt was made, by the Illinois Grangers in 1878, to influence the price of hogs by withholding them from the market.[19] A resolution recommending the same thing was adopted by the Northwestern Farmers' Convention in 1873.

Even the executive committee of the national Grange compiled national price lists containing terms offered by manufacturers, and Secretary Kelley distributed a circular to subordinate Granges informing them of the offers of a New York patron to sell them seeds at wholesale prices. At another time, he circularized manufacturers offering to compile a confidential list of prices which they might be willing to offer to Granges if large orders could be compiled.

Somewhat discouraged by their attempts to deal directly with the "Harvester Ring," the "Plow Ring," and other "monopolies," as they called them, and considerably encouraged by their relative successes in cooperative purchasing, some of the state Granges determined to attack the problem of purchasing price at its core. Part of the immense funds that had piled up in the treasury of the national Grange during the years of its greatest growth were distributed as loans to state Granges on the basis of $2.50 for each subordinate Grange of good standing, and some outright donations to state Granges were made. The total amount thus distributed was $73,439.33, such states as Iowa and Missouri receiving large shares because of their great numbers of local Granges.[20] These loans gave the state Granges funds with which to attempt rather outstanding economic projects.

The Patrons, and other farmers, were especially incensed at the high price of harvesters, the "self-binder" being the most elaborate piece of farm machinery at that time and one of great importance in midwestern farming. For this reason, the Grangers began their own manufacture of farm machinery. In 1872, the Nebraska State Grange began manufacturing headers. In 1873, patents for the Werner harvester were purchased by the national Grange and 250 of these machines were manufactured in

[18] Buck, *The Granger movement*, pp. 249-253. Carr, pp. 203, 207-210.
[19] Paine, p. 44.
[20] *Proceedings of the eighth session* (1875).

Iowa, Minnesota, and Nebraska. During the year 1874, patents were purchased for a number of other farming implements. Harvester, sewing machine, threshing machine, and general implement factories were planned in Kansas, Iowa, Missouri, Wisconsin, Illinois, Indiana, and Kentucky; and some of them were actually established. A number of grist mills, a number of cheese and butter, linseed oil, starch, and hemp factories, a number of packing plants and cotton mills were planned and some of them projected. Where these projects were carried through they were partial successes, but in most cases they failed because of lack of capital, defective patent rights, or lack of managerial experience.

Even banking was attempted by some Grangers. The Grangers' Bank of California and two others in California were established in 1874 for the purpose of lending money on "landed security of the agriculturist." One of these had a paid-up capital stock of $500,000 and deposits of $2,000,000 in a few months' time. It loaned the farmers of the state upwards of $3,000,000 to assist them in holding wheat off the market, and saved them large amounts of money by this action.[21]

The insurance activities of the Granges did not strike at any major economic difficulty in which farmers found themselves, but they constituted one more attack on middlemen profits and were projects that were fairly easily accomplished. They became some of the most widespread and successful undertakings of the period. Mutual fire insurance companies were organized in every Grange state, usually as township and county organizations, but in four states—California, Kansas, New Hampshire, and Maine—as state organizations. Mutual Aid Societies—life insurance companies—were started in New York, Arkansas, Tennessee, Kansas, Wisconsin, North Carolina, South Carolina, Maine, and New Hampshire.

Thus the Grange, at its height in the seventies, made a direct economic attack on practically every problem which it recognized as troubling the farmer, except railroad building, and it attacked the railroad problem in another way more vigorously than any other thing. It is not an essential

---

[21] Carr, pp. 160-165, 175. *Proceedings of the fifteenth session* (1881), p. 36. Mortimer Whitehead, "Patrons of Husbandry," *Ninth annual report of the Bureau of Statistics of Labor and Industries of New Jersey, for the year ending October 31st, 1886,* Part VI, pp. 344-345. Trenton, New Jersey: John L. Murphy Publishing Co., 1886. *Prairie Farmer,* November 6, 1875. Warner, p. 36, also mentions a Granger bank being established at Olathe, Kansas, in 1883.

part of this story to tell of the tragic failure of most Grange undertakings, although most of these economic undertakings did fail. The chief causes for failures may, however, be briefly listed. First was the lack of previous cooperative experience. Second was a lack of capital and business knowledge in operating some of the larger projects. Third was the fact that they tried to build great business enterprises in too short a time. Fourth, they met opposition on the part of enterprises which were thrown in jeopardy by Grange activities. Fifth, the political activities of the Granges and other farmers' groups led to the disintegration of the organization before many of the economic experiments were fairly tested. Sixth, the fact that it would have been impossible under any circumstances to have fulfilled the exaggerated hopes of so many unsophisticated and harassed farmers fairly quickly caused discontent to grow up among members and they, as has been the repeated experience in farmers' organizations, destroyed their own cooperative enterprises by their disloyalty to them.

It should not, however, be assumed that there was no progress made toward the economic objectives which the Granges had set for themselves in the enthusiasm of their great strength during this period. That they saved their members considerable money in various ways, there is ample proof.[22] Some of the enterprises established during this period continued in existence for a number of years, and some are still in existence. They forced railroad regulation, which might have been delayed for a decade had it not been for their vigorous and powerful influence. But greater than all these, they stepped the Farmers' Movement forward a long stride by the things they learned from their successes and failures, and they left in existence a farmers' organization, The Patrons of Husbandry, whose membership has never been less than 106,000 since that time and now has more members than it had in 1875.[23]

---

[22] Warner, pp. 367-393. Daniel R. Randall, *Cooperation in Maryland and the South,* Johns Hopkins University Studies in Historical and Political Science, Sixth Series, Vols. XI-XII, pp. 502-507. Baltimore: 1888. Edward W. Bemis, *Cooperation in New England,* Johns Hopkins University Studies in Historical and Political Science, Sixth Series, Vols. I-II, chap. ii, pp. 33-36. Baltimore: 1888. Albert Shaw, *Cooperation in the Northwest,* Johns Hopkins University Studies in Historical and Political Science, Sixth Series, Vols. IV, V, VI, pp. 316-319, 333-344. Baltimore: 1888.

[23] While the information contained in this section has been obtained from many sources, the reader can secure an excellent and detailed account of the economic activities of the Grange during the decade 1870-1880 from Buck, *The Granger*

THE POLITICAL ATTACK

In the Declaration of Purposes, adopted at the first great delegate national annual session of 1874, it was asserted "that the Grange—National, State, or Subordinate—is not a political or party organization. No Grange, if true to its obligations, can discuss political or religious questions, nor call political conventions, nor nominate candidates, nor even discuss their merits in its meetings." Just as in the case of economic activities, however, this high purpose was to a considerable extent abandoned when the Grange became the mouthpiece of the Farmers' Movement. This was inevitable for two reasons: first, because when the organization grew powerful, politicians solicited its influence; and second, because it discovered quickly that to accomplish some of its economic objectives, state or federal legislation was necessary. Wells, writing in 1874, said, ". . . politicians with heavy boots worn over their pantaloons, rough coats and rougher hats, and 'hay-seed in their hair,' are telling gaping crowds that 'they were brought up as farmers,' that they always were 'interested in husbandry,' and that they are down on the railroads and middlemen; while men who never owned land enough to give them a decent burial plot, are trying frantically to recall some verses in praise of the farmer's wife." [24]

Oliver Kelley, as early as the spring of 1868, shortly after presenting the cause of the Grange to farmers and farm leaders of the Middle West, had written McDowell that nothing short of organized political action could effectively deal with monopolies.[25] Even that early, Kelley apparently was sensing the type of sentiment prevalent in farmers' clubs in the Middle West. It was just a year later that Wheeler issued his call through the *Prairie Farmer* for a convention of farmers which should plan to "concentrate their efforts, power and means as the great transportation companies have done theirs, and accomplish something, instead of fritter-

---

movement, chap. vii, "Business Cooperation," pp. 238-278. If it is desired to follow the proceedings of the national Grange year by year, this can be done fairly satisfactorily without perusing the annual proceedings, for Atkeson, in his *Semicentennial history of the Patrons of Husbandry*, reviews each annual session, presenting the trend of discussion and the main activities of the organization.

[24] Wells, p. 18.

[25] Kelley, p. 96.

ing away their efforts in doing nothing." [26] The *Prairie Farmer* and other
midwestern papers picked up the agitation and carried it forward between
1870 and 1874, when the national Grange held its first great delegate convention in St. Louis.

During the year before the St. Louis convention, Stephe Smith published *Grains for the Grangers*, which was dedicated by a poem entitled
"To the Toiling Hand." The last stanza of the poem read:

> God bless it with a special grace—
> Striking for Freedom's cause;
> Emancipation from the power
> Of Wealth and unjust laws;
> God give it strength, against the few
> Who rule but to be bribed,
> And speed the cause to which this page
> Is earnestly inscribed.[27]

In this book—half fiction, half facts—the author describes local Grangers
in their meetings as carrying on a type of political discussion which was
probably taking place at the time. Kelley, however, reports no evidence
of this sentiment being reflected in the 1873 session of the national
Grange; and Saunders, in his annual address before that body, said, "I
conceive that its [the national Grange's] main duties are: 1st. To collect
information; and 2nd. To disseminate it. Thus, it is simply an agency."

In the very beginning of the 1874 annual session, some reflection of the
demands for legislation which later was destined to make the Grangers a
powerful political pressure group was evident in Worthy Master Adams's
opening address before the convention, in which he said:

> While we readily assent to the proposition that railroads, even as
> now conducted, add immensely to the development of the country
> and the convenience of the people, still in our inmost soul we feel
> deeply wronged at the return made for the kind of liberal spirit
> we have shown them.
> I need not here repeat what the discussions of the last two years
> have developed concerning the rascalities of watered stock, con-
> struction companies buying legislators in State and nation, and

---

[26] *Prairie Farmer,* March 26, 1870.
[27] Stephe Smith, *Grains for the Grangers.*

Credit Mobilier. They have been fully ventilated till they are fully understood.

I see no solution of this problem but for Congress to avail itself of its constitutional right to regulate commerce between the States, and for the States themselves to regulate the tariffs within their own boundaries.[28]

That he became even more pointed than this furnishes evidence that Granges were discussing political issues at their meetings. He said in discussing the constitution of the national Grange:

Article 12 also demands most serious consideration to definitely decide what interpretation shall be put upon the word "political." I am gratified that our members are substantially a unit in the opinion that the Order should not in any sense become a political party. But at the same time, there are questions most fundamentally affecting our material interests, which can only be reached by legislation. It seems imperative, that such questions be discussed in the Grange. Shall it be ruled that such questions were political in the meaning of the constitution? The questions of transportation, taxation, finance, corruption in public places, were such as come home to the conscience and pockets of our members, and they wish to know whether they will be denied the privilege of canvassing them on the ground of politics. This body should clearly set forth an authoritative interpretation for the guidance of members.[29]

No such clarification was made. The committee on transportation and cooperation introduced a resolution concerning interstate transportation, but the resolution was not a memorial to Congress. It was at this session that the Declaration of Purposes was adopted, one section of which forbade even the discussion of candidates at Grange meetings.

But the Grange could not so easily side-step the farmer's demand for legislative action. In Illinois, the State Farmers' Association, which included in its membership both local farmers' clubs and subordinate Granges, had no aversion to direct political action. Its executive committee issued a call for a state farmers' convention to be held at Springfield, the state capital, April 2, 1873, in order to insure the enactment of effective

---

[28] *Proceedings of the seventh session* (1874), pp. 14-19.
[29] *Ibid.*

railway legislation.[30] In May of that same year, the farmers of the Illinois fifth district held a convention at which they nominated a candidate for chief justice of the state supreme court and passed resolutions demanding that the legislature pass certain railroad legislation.[31] This was followed by one in the second district and, later in the month, by a meeting of the farmers in Livingston County which adopted a political platform and started agitation for a complete state farmers' ticket.[32] This, in turn, was followed by a great number of farmers' meetings on what came to be known as the "Farmers' Fourth of July." The secretary of the State Farmers' Association prepared a "Farmers' Declaration of Independence" which was read at a great many of these meetings. This declaration was printed in the *Prairie Farmer* and the Chicago *Daily Tribune*,[33] and thus was undoubtedly read by many farmers who could not or did not attend the county "Fourth of July" meetings. Local Granges as well as farmers' clubs were passing strong resolutions in favor of railroad regulation and against monopolies, and it was inevitable that these same farmers should demand similar action when they sat as delegates in state Grange meetings.[34] The Granges had to go along with these demands or yield their leadership in the Farmers' Movement.

Illinois farmers led all others in political activities during the "Granger Era." In that state, it will be remembered, there were many farmers' clubs in addition to more than 1,500 local Granges, and these clubs had been agitating for railroad legislation before the Grange became an organization of much importance in the state. The new state constitution of 1870 had included mandatory provisions for legislation to control railway charges.[35] The legislature of 1871-1872 passed laws regulating fares, freight rates, and warehouses, and established a board of railway warehouse commissioners. The railroads only partially obeyed the laws until

---

[30] *Prairie Farmer*, March 29, 1873. Chicago *Daily Tribune*, March 21, 1873; see also March 29, 1873, for a discussion of "The Farmers' Movement."

[31] Periam, pp. 312-316. *Prairie Farmer*, May 17, 1873. Paine, pp. 34-35. Chicago *Daily Tribune*, May 15, 1873.

[32] Chicago *Daily Tribune*, June 3, 1873.

[33] *Prairie Farmer*, July 12, 1873. Chicago *Daily Tribune*, June 17, 1873.

[34] *Prairie Farmer*, especially issues of March 1, 15, 22, 29; April 5, 19; June 14; July 12; August 2; September 20; November 15; and December 20, 1873.

[35] Harvey B. Hurd, ed., *The revised statute of the State of Illinois*, A.D. *1874*, p. 79, Springfield, Illinois: Illinois Journal Co., 1874.

they could test them in the courts. The test came in January, 1873, when the Illinois State Supreme Court declared certain provisions of these laws to be against the spirit of the state constitution. Chief Justice Lawrence wrote the opinion, but the concurrence of the other members of the court was unanimous. This defeat at the hands of the court so incensed the farmers that they mobilized as never before. They met in a convention at the state capital in April while the legislature was in session and literally forced still more stringent railroad legislation, defeated Chief Justice Lawrence in the June election, and read the farmers' Declaration of Independence at dozens of farmers' meetings held on the Fourth of July. This "Declaration" started with a first sentence much like that of Jefferson's "Declaration of Independence":

> When in the course of human events it becomes necessary for a class of the people, suffering from long continued systems of oppression and abuse, to rouse themselves from an apathetic indifference to their own interests, which has become habitual ... a decent respect for the opinions of mankind requires that they should declare the causes that impel them to a course so necessary to their own protection.[36]

It then made a statement which constituted the firing of the first gun in a third-party movement in the Middle West. This statement was:

> We, therefore, the producers of the state in our several counties assembled ... do solemnly declare that we will use all lawful and peaceable means to free ourselves from the tyranny of monopoly, and that we will never cease our efforts for reform until every department of our government gives token that the reign of licentious extravagance is over, and something of the purity, honesty, and frugality with which our fathers inaugurated it, has taken its place.
>
> That to this end we hereby declare ourselves absolutely free and independent of all past political connections, and that we will give our suffrage only to such men for office ... as we have good reason to believe will use their best endeavors to the promotion of these ends; and for the support of this declaration, with a firm

---

[36] *Prairie Farmer*, July 12, 1873. Chicago *Daily Tribune*, July 17, 1873.

reliance in Divine Providence, we mutually pledge to each other our lives, our fortunes, and our sacred honor.[37]

We shall not tell the story of the development of independent political parties at this point further than to say that thousands of Illinois farmers made good on their declaration of independence in the fall elections of 1873 and were followed by farmers in Iowa, Minnesota, Wisconsin, and in other midwestern and some far-western states during the next fifteen years.

The Legislative Farmers' Club, made up of former representatives and senators in the Illinois legislature, was organized during the legislative session in 1871. It was a sort of farm bloc through which the farmers' organizations of the state brought pressure to bear on the legislature and the Governor. It not only sponsored the railroad legislation of 1871 and 1873, but mobilized enough farmers' petitions and resolutions to force the Governor to appoint two farmers on the Board of Railroad Commissioners in 1873.[38]

The Springfield convention of the State Farmers' Association (briefly described in Chapter 5, pages 103-105) was called by the executive committee of the association to meet in the state capital during the session of the legislature in the spring of 1873 "for the purpose of attending to our interests in the Legislature, and of giving that body and the Governor to understand that we mean business and are no longer to be trifled with; and that while we have no disposition to infringe upon the rights of others, we demand that protection at their hands from the intolerable wrongs now inflicted upon us by the railroads which they have a constitutional right to give us." [39] Mr. W. C. Flagg, who was president of the Association, had served as state senator in the session which passed the original railroad laws. He, therefore, formed a good liaison officer between the Legislative Farmers' Club and the 300 farmers who assembled at the convention. A new railroad law was passed which repealed the act of 1871 and was much more drastic. This new law was fought through the

---

[37] *Ibid.*

[38] *Journal of the senate of the twenty-eighth general assembly of the State of Illinois. Begun and held at Springfield, January 8, 1873,* pp. 154-155, 226-323, 325. Springfield, Illinois: State Journal Steam Print., 1873. Periam, pp. 302-311. *Prairie Farmer,* February 18 and 25, 1871.

[39] *Prairie Farmer,* January, 1873. Periam, pp. 256-262.

courts a number of times during the next few years, but was finally declared constitutional in 1880, and, according to Buck, "has remained the basis of railroad control in that state to the present day and has served as a model for legislation in other states." [40]

In Iowa, Minnesota, Wisconsin, and Missouri, legislative struggles between the farmers and the railroads were occurring at the same time as in Illinois; and in a great many other Granger states, agitation for regulation and control bore fruit during this decade. In surveying the state legislation of the decade, Buck says:

> Several of the principal features of American railway legislation can be looked upon as primarily Granger in their origin. Among these are (1) the establishment of schedules of maximum rates by direct legislative enactment, a method which has been generally superseded so far as freight charges are concerned; (2) the establishment of a commission with authority to draw up schedules of maximum rates; (3) the establishment of maximum rates, whether fixed by the legislature or by a commission, as *prima facie* evidence of reasonableness before the courts; (4) the attempt to prevent discrimination between places by *pro rata* "short haul" clauses; (5) the attempt to preserve competition by forbidding the consolidation of parallel lines; (6) the prohibition of the granting of free passes to public officials. [41]

Nothing better represents the mental attitudes and convictions of the farmers of the early seventies than the titles and subtitles of some of the Granger books which appeared during that time. The first edition of D. C. Cloud's book, *Monopolies and the People*, appeared in July, 1873. Its dedication reads:

> To the Patrons of Husbandry, who have become the pioneer corps in the efforts being made to reform the abuses now oppressing the country, and who are earnestly and efficiently laboring for the restoration of the rights of the people, with the hope that it may aid them in their patriotic work, this book is respectfully dedicated by the author.

———

[40] Buck, *The Granger movement*, p. 147.
[41] *Ibid.*, p. 205. Reprinted by permission of Harvard University Press.

The Granger Movement by E. W. Martin appeared in November, 1873. Its dedication is:

To the Farmers of the United States, the strong-armed, true-hearted hope of the Republic, now as in the past, the first to rise against oppression and wrong, the author dedicates this book as a token of his sympathy with them in their sufferings, and his admiration of the heroic battle they are waging for the oppressed of the whole country.

The title page of Stephe Smith's book, which appeared late in 1873, reads:

Grains for the Grangers, Discussing All Points Bearing upon the Farmers' Movement for the Emancipation of White Slaves from the Slave-Power of Monopoly.

Jonathan Periam's *The Groundswell* appeared in January, 1874. It is modestly dedicated "To the Producing Classes of America." Periam was much more temperate than the other three authors mentioned here, but sentences quoted from the early part of his book reveal a very deep conviction about the state of affairs at the time. The last sentence of his preface reads:

It is through this great quickening of the toiling masses, and their stimulation to higher endeavor, that either the renovation or overthrow of the effete and corrupt political parties of the day is to be effected.

On page 27, under the subtitle, "The Groundswell of Today," he says further:

If there be one danger of more threatening aspect than any other in the present juncture of the affairs in the United States, it is the disturbing and corrupting influences flowing out of the existence of great moneyed corporations that, year by year, take on more and more of the characteristics of conscienceless and irresponsible monopolies ... What wonder, then, that we behold today another popular uprising, in earnest protest against attempted wrongs; or, that the farmers, emphatically the great producing class of the whole community, should seek a closer union in council, business plans and influence, and thus to roll onward the waves of their mighty *groundswell?*

Smith's book is the only one appearing during the period of the greatest activity of the Farmers' Movement—the seventies—which describes scenes and events the spirit of which reveal the state of mind, both dour and enthusiastic, of the practical farmers at the time, although all the others express their own worries and enthusiasms. Martin, for instance, says:

> Four millions of voters united in a common cause, and seeking the triumph of a common principle, are capable of accomplishing anything.
>
> It will be a great and glorious revolution, and it will be peaceful.
>
> By presenting a solid front all over the Union upon questions vital to them, and by acting as one man in the hour of conflict with the enemy, the success of the farmers' movement will be as certain as the rising of the sun.
>
> The best opportunity ... is ... the "Order of the Patrons of Husbandry." [42]

Cloud, in the following word picture, probably presents the type of oratory which was used on many occasions at farmers' meetings during the seventies:

> No country in the world has been as bountifully supplied by the Creator with all the means to make a nation prosperous and happy as ours. It is vast in extent of territory. Its soil is rich, and most of it new. Lying in all latitudes, it produces fruits of every climate. The husbandman is assured of an abundant crop. All agricultural and horticultural pursuits are rewarded with large growths and bounteous harvests. Our shores are washed by oceans, which afford us highways, over which we can avail ourselves of the markets of the world; while flowing through the agricultural portions of our common country are our great rivers, upon whose waters the produce and manufactures of the land are transported to market. Our great lakes furnish us an outlet for the surplus product of the great west. Our sixty or seventy thousand miles of railroad traverse our country in all directions, reaching from the Atlantic to the Pacific, and spreading like a net-work from the lakes to the gulf. Our mines produce immense yields of the precious metals, while our hills and mountains

[42] Edward W. Martin, pp. 405-406.

are full of iron, coal, and lead. Petroleum flows in quantities which should add largely to the wealth of our common country. Our timber is not excelled by that of any growth in the world. Our lands are rich in fertility, and poor only in price. The Creator has done for us all that could be desired to make us prosperous and contented. Our government is, or was intended to be, based upon the will of the people. Our constitution recognizes no royal rulers, no lords, no titled gentry. Under it we are equal. They who administer the laws are selected by the people. In contemplation of law, all are equal—all are free and independent. With all these blessings and advantages we ought to be the happiest and most prosperous people on the earth. Peace, plenty, and contentment should reign supreme throughout the land. What are the facts?

Throughout the entire length and breadth of our land, mutterings and complainings are heard. From the farmers, the mechanics, and laborers alike, the complaint is heard, "We cannot pay our taxes and support our families"; "Our wages will not enable us to buy the necessaries of life, because of the large duties laid upon them." "Our farm products will not pay taxes, charges for transportation, and other burdens imposed upon us, and leave us any margin." "We had better let our lands lie idle than to attempt to cultivate them." These and like complaints are heard from the laboring and producing classes. Nor are their complaints without cause. Another interest has arisen in the land—it has become all-powerful. This interest penetrates the remotest portions of the country. It calls upon the laborer, the operative, the mechanic, the farmer, and all private citizens, for a division of the products of their labor. It enters the halls of legislatures and of congress, and demands, and not infrequently purchases, special privileges and powers. It visits the executive department of the government, and there secures special favors. It stalks boldly into the courts of the country and *there* procures unjust decisions in its interest. It indeed places its own men upon these *seats of justice,* that the judiciary of the country may not fail to support its aims. It has already obtained complete control of the finances of the country. It has corrupted legislatures and congressmen, until the law-making power has become a party to schemes of robbery and plunder. By corrupt legislation and *ex parte* judicial decisions, it has destroyed all the old republican landmarks, overridden the provisions of the constitution, and substituted for the government prepared for us by our forefathers an oligarchy that rules the land and holds the people at its mercy, and their property as its lawful booty. This great oppressor of the people is the railroad corporations and their associates, of which we have been treating. Railroad and other corporations, brokers, and stock-jobbers, have obtained such complete control over the government, the people, and the financial and commercial interests of the country, that they who depend upon agricultural pursuits, or upon their labor for a support, are deprived of these God-given rights which formed the base of our political superstructure.[43]

Smith presents what he thinks is the real voice of the farmer in the following excerpts from a speech by Delegate Burton, of Carroll County, Illinois:

"The Farmers' Movement—Already inaugurated in Twenty-four states. It will sweep Everything before it!"

"No more Republicans! No more Democrats! We want and *must have* Honest Men to fill Public Positions!"

"Who would be Free, himself must strike the Blow!"

"Corn must go up! Monopolies must come down!"

"Equal and Exact Justice to all! Special Privileges to no one!"

"Salary of our Congressman, One Hundred Bushels of Corn per day! Poor Fellows!"

"Farmers, to the front! Politicians, take back seats!"[44]

Smith presents these words from a Kansas Patron:

The reform movement goes bravely on, and the disinclination of the farmers, and those who sympathize with us in the war against monopolies, to be drawn into or to indorse any party, or to be ridden by any set of politicians, argues well for the future. It has not grown like a hot-house plant, but rather is it the result of deep convictions that the time has come when something must be done to break up old party ties. It is neither a Democratic nor Republican move, but welcomes all who will take part.[45]

---

[43] Cloud, pp. 248-249.
[44] Stephe Smith, pp. 84-85, 151-152.
[45] *Ibid.*

If the reader will turn back to pages 2 and 3 in Chapter 1 of this text, he can refresh his mind with a picture of a Grange scene in Indiana, which is probably typical of others that occurred often during the years 1873, 1874, and 1875.

One final excerpt is given from Smith, which expresses his own views and convictions, but also represents the type of thing many others were saying and thinking at the time:

> The war of 1812 was fought and won against the monopoly exercised by England on the high seas.
>
> The second declaration of independence was the war of the rebellion. Capital monopolized the labor of the slaves. The emancipation proclamation established the principle that labor and compensation must go together. An amendment to the constitution of the republic made that principle more binding and gave it the sanction of law. The first declaration was for white men; the second was for all men. Freedom under both was secured by the sword. You have announced the necessity of a third declaration—commercial freedom, emancipation from the slavery of monopolies, and personal independence.[46]

A movement cannot be completely understood from a cold analysis of its causes and effects. It is a human, palpitating experience in the lives of its leaders and followers. The excerpts quoted in this section are presented to acquaint the reader with the spirit—furious and uninformed though it may have been—of one of the high tides of the American Farmers' Movement.

[46] *Ibid.*, p. 35.

· 8 ·

THE FARMERS GO

INTO POLITICS

THE RISE OF THE THIRD PARTIES IN THE
SEVENTIES

The political activities of the farmers of the seventies created a great furor throughout the nation and caused President Grant in his fifth annual message to Congress on December 1, 1873, to say that "political partisanship has almost ceased to exist, especially in the agricultural regions." [1] A number of Independent, Anti-Monopoly, and Reform parties were organized in the Middle West and West, chiefly to fight the railroads. Granges and other farmers' organizations held their annual state conventions at state capitals while legislatures were in session, created public sentiment by continuous discussion and agitation in their thousands of local meetings, sanctioned or tabooed candidates for public offices, nominated and elected some of their own members to office, forced laws through state legislatures, and in one instance even dethroned a state supreme court judge and elected in his place one whom they thought would be more sympathetic with their activities and purposes. Their political activities caused many other persons and interests to be

---

[1] *A compilation of the messages and papers of the Presidents*, Vol. IX, p. 4189. See also pp. 4190-4209. New York: Bureau of National Literature, Inc., 1897.

arrayed against them, and probably had more than any other thing to do with the decline of the Grange which began after 1875.[2]

Threats of political independence in Grange and other farmer meetings during the first half of the decade 1870-1880 have already been noted. It will be remembered that Oliver Kelley, as early as 1868, had written to one of his colleagues, "In my humble opinion, this Order, with its influence, will inaugurate a party that will sweep the country of the present race of politicians." A letter from Editor Corbett, read by Kelley to the Minnesota State Grange in 1870 and later published as a circular of the national Grange, contained the following statement which served as a guide to Grangers' actions when they deemed political action necessary:

> We must not be political in the common acceptation of the term, only so far as to control politicians and office-holders—to make them talk, legislate and decide on the side of the people *all the time*—only so far as to protect our own just interests, doing injustice to no man who is in pursuit of a legitimate business that does harm to none. We must be a third party, to hold the balance of power (I think now we need not go beyond this), then, whichever party will declare itself to stand on our platform, and whichever candidate will unqualifiedly pledge himself to carry out the reforms we may demand, such party and such candidates should receive our vote.[3]

These suggestions were never followed by the Grange as an organization, but were used by Grange members as justification for individual action.

The national Grange did enter the political field deeply enough in 1876 to draw up resolutions touching subjects upon which legislation was desired, passing them on to state Granges, and from there to locals, from which letters were sent to Congressmen. They also set up a Grange lobby in Washington.[4] This mild type of action gave way rather quickly, however, to more direct and militant types of political activity. The beginnings of such activities were touched upon in Chapter 7. As noted there, the Illinois State Farmers' Association held a convention at Springfield in April, 1873, during the session of the legislature.[5] In Des Moines in

---

[2] *Nation*, Vol. XXII, January 27, 1876, pp. 57-58.

[3] Kelley, pp. 96. See also pp. 258-259.

[4] *Proceedings of the ninth session* (1876), pp. 85, 159-160.

[5] Chicago *Daily Tribune*, March 21, April 2, 3, 4, 1873. Periam, pp. 280-291. *The American annual cyclopaedia and register of important events of the year 1873*, Vol.

December of that year the Iowa State Grange held its annual session while the state legislature was in session and issued memorials to that body.[6] The first step toward more direct action was taken when the Illinois farmers held a convention of their own at Princeton in 1873, and nominated Alfred M. Craig as candidate for the supreme court judgeship to oppose Judge Lawrence, who had written the decision which declared the railroad regulation law of 1871 unconstitutional. As noted in Chapter 7, Judge Lawrence was defeated in the June election of that year.[7] These activities, however, were tame in comparison to what immediately followed.

Action was begun in Livingston County on May 31, 1873, when a group of farmers adopted a platform which they called the Livingston County Declaration of Principles. This Declaration was widely publicized and was quickly adopted by other farmers' groups.[8] Secretary S. M. Smith of the Illinois State Farmers' Association approved the platform and assisted in its promulgation. The Livingston County farmers appointed a committee to call a convention for the purpose of nominating candidates for county offices, and the executive committee of the State Farmers' Association urged that the Fourth of July be made the occasion for holding great farmers' meetings all over the state. As stated in the previous chapter, this suggestion was adopted widely, and a Farmers' Declaration of Independence was formulated to be read at such meetings. Secretary Smith delivered a fiery speech at Pontiac, and the Farmers' Declaration of Independence was read at many places.[9] These "Fourth of July" per-

---

XIII, pp. 367-368. New York: Appleton-Century-Crofts, Inc., 1874. (To be titled *Appleton's* in all further references.) *Prairie Farmer,* March 29, April 19, 1873.

[6] Periam, pp. 263-264, 557-560. Buck, *The Granger movement,* p. 170. Chicago *Daily Tribune,* December 10, 11, 12, 13, 14, 16, 1873.

[7] Chicago *Daily Tribune,* May 2, 15, June 4, 5, 6, 10, 1873. Periam, pp. 312-316. Paine, pp. 34-35. *Prairie Farmer,* May 17, 31, June 14, 1873.

[8] Chicago *Daily Tribune,* June 3, 1873. *Industrial Age,* August 20, 1873. See Chicago *Daily Tribune,* June, July, August, September, 1873, for various endorsements of the Livingston County Anti-Monopoly Platform and Declaration of Principles.

[9] For the Farmers' Declaration of Independence, see *Prairie Farmer,* June 21, July 12, 1873. Chicago *Daily Tribune,* June 16, 17, 1873. *American Agriculturist,* Vol. XXXII, No. 8 (August, 1873), p. 288.

For meetings held on July 4 and throughout the summer, see Chicago *Daily Tribune,* May, June, July, August, 1873.

The call for the July 4 meetings is to be found in Chicago *Daily Tribune,* June 16, 1873. *Prairie Farmer,* July 12, 1873, p. 19.

formances were followed by many picnics and other meetings during the summer; and that fall farmers' tickets appeared in sixty-six counties in the state.

The Livingston County Address, Declaration, and Platforms were as follows:

ADDRESS

The committee-men of the Farmers' Association of Livingston County, assembled here today, after careful deliberation and consultation upon the present status of the "Farmers' Movement," and believing that past experience has taught us that we can hope for no relief from either political party, and encouraged by past efforts, deem it both provident and advisable that, for the purpose of future action, a more thorough and perfect organization be formed in this county to carry out the various questions of reform which are so intimately connected with our material and political existence. We therefore invite the cordial cooperation of all classes in carrying out the following principles, which we submit for their careful consideration:

DECLARATION

This organization is opposed to railroad steals, tariff steals, salary-grab steals, bank steals, and every other form of thieving by which the farming and laboring classes are robbed of the legitimate fruits of their labor.

PLATFORMS

First—We are in favor of controlling by law the railroad corporations of our state. Second—We submit to direct taxation and duties to meet the necessities of the Government, but denounce as unjust and oppressive all taxation for the benefit of special classes. Third—We are in favor of the present banking system being so made that all men, by giving the proper security, should have equal privileges, so that supply and demand shall regulate our money-market. Fourth—We are opposed to all further grants of land to railroads or other corporations, and believe that the public domain should be held sacred to actual settlers.

We are in favor of a true system of Civil-Service Reform, making honesty and capacity the only valid claim for public employment;

and we believe that the office should seek the man, and not the man the office. [Unanimously and enthusiastically adopted.] [10]

The results of the November election were startling, especially to the leaders of the two old parties. The farmers were victorious in fifty-three of the sixty-six counties, registering 94,188 votes to a combined 82,075 for all opposing candidates.[11]

From 1873 to 1876, independent tickets were placed in the field in eleven midwestern and western states. They were known as Anti-Monopoly, Reform, Independent Reform, National Reform, Independent, and People's Independent parties in the different states. The states in which they were organized were Indiana, Illinois, Michigan, Wisconsin, Minnesota, Iowa, Missouri, Kansas, Nebraska, California, and Oregon. The most common plank in their platforms was one demanding regulation of railroads. In some cases the word "corporations," and in others "monopolies," instead of "railroads" was used. In some cases all three expressions appeared. These parties came to be widely known as Anti-Monopoly parties, but they were more than that, for they were as strong in their denunciation of corruption in and of government as they were in their denunciation of monopolies. They also demanded reduction in taxation, economy in public expenditures, the revision of tariffs, and the establishment of a system of civil service.[12]

The details of one third-party platform will serve as a typical illustration. The Minnesota convention was held at Owatonna, September 2, 1873. The following are some of the more pertinent planks of the platform adopted on that occasion. They are not quoted in their entirety, but nearly enough to reveal both their content and animus:

> *Whereas,* The leading issues ... hitherto [dividing] the people ... in political parties have ceased to exist, and it is unwise ... to continue the old party organization now that new and momentous questions have arisen; and

---

[10] Chicago *Daily Tribune,* June 3, 1873.

[11] For election returns, see *Appleton's, 1873,* p. 368. *The world almanac, 1874,* p. 23. *Prairie Farmer,* November 15, 1873. Chicago *Daily Tribune,* November 19, 1873.

[12] Buck, *The Granger movement,* pp. 100-101. William A. Dunning, *Reconstruction, po͡͡͡ economic, 1865-1877,* pp. 220-237 (Albert B. Hart, ed., *The American na͡   ͡   ͡ry,* Vol. XXII). New York: Harper & Brothers, 1907.

Whereas, The principal question . . . [involves] the privileges and powers of corporations as . . . operating in opposition to the well-being of the people; and

Whereas, . . . we recognize no party distinctions nor political issues . . . as worthy of more than minor consideration, be it therefore

Resolved, First: That the purpose of all proper government is the promotion of the entire people, and that . . . the conduct of any citizen, association, or copartnership . . . which may operate to the prejudice of this general welfare, is antagonistic to the true object of our Government . . .

Second: That we recognize no political party nor individual aspirant for office as worthy of our support, unless it or he will unite with us in declaring that the Government cannot alienate either in whole or in part to any person, association, or corporation for any purpose whatever . . .

Third: That we will not aid in elevating any man to any important public position . . . who will . . . deny or object to the exercise by the Legislature of the power to reverse or annul at any time any chartered privilege or so-called vested right or any privilege claimed to be involved in any charter to any corporation railroad or otherwise, which experience has shown is or may be exercised . . . to the detriment of the public welfare . . .

Fourth: . . . that the levying of imposts as inure to the benefit of a class or classes in the community, while being detrimental to other classes, is unjust and oppressive; and that tariffs levied on imported articles . . . are often so arranged as to become thus discriminative and injurious; . . . that it is . . . essential that the utmost care should be taken in framing such tariff laws, in order that . . . they may operate for the well being of the entire community.

Fifth: . . . that in the late act of Congress, increasing the official and Congressional salaries . . . we recognize only a corrupt and reprehensible avarice and reckless disregard of the public weal . . . and we demand the repeal of the law at the earliest practicable moment, and declare every man who supported and approved . . . unworthy the confidence of his fellow citizens and unfit for further occupancy of any position of public trust.

Sixth: That all participants in the Credit Mobilier and the corrupt transactions exposed by its investigation of the late Congress . . . deserve to have been punished as criminals. . . .

Seventh: . . . that public sentiment should . . . compel the resigna-

tion of all [public officers] who are guilty . . . of neglecting to execute faithfully the duties entrusted to them. . . .

Ninth: . . . we, as farmers and laborers despair of ever having our
wishes complied with or our interest subserved in the administration of public affairs until we shall take upon ourselves the discharge
of the duties we owe to ourselves and to each other of choosing and
electing our own candidates independently of the action of all other
political organizations, and we therefore . . . recommend to the farmers and laborers of the State that we shall do all in our power to
procure the nomination and election of full and complete county,
district, and State tickets, embracing candidates elected in the interests of the masses of the people for all positions in the Executive,
Legislative, and Judicial branches of the Government to be elected
this Fall, and that, to the end that the policy may generally obtain,
we solicit the cooperation of the industrial masses of the other States
in order that the influence of the movement may be extended to the
administration of our national affairs. . . .

Sixteenth: That we demand a State law that will pay out of the
public funds the costs . . . of all suits brought by individuals to
enforce the laws of the State against railroad corporations. . . .

Nineteenth: That the subserving of the present candidate for
Governor on Republican State ticket to the interest of railroads,
shows him to be an enemy to the rights of the farmers and laborers,
and a friend of monopoly.

The platform further asserted that all corporations should be "subject to
the sovereign authority and control of the Government"; "That our experience proves that persons elected by parties are subservient to the leaders
and wire-pullers of the parties electing them." [13]

Minnesota, Iowa, Illinois, and Wisconsin were the only states in which
the Anti-Monopolists were especially active during the 1873 elections.
The Iowa Anti-Monopoly convention was held on August 13 and the Wisconsin convention on September 23. Their platforms were very similar to
that of Minnesota. The Iowa platform demanded, among other things,
"the destruction of the banking monopoly," that there be no more land
grants made to the railroads, and asserted that Congressmen and other

---

[13] Edward W. Martin, pp. 510-513.

office holders "have enriched themselves from Credit Mobilier funds and salary swindles, and thus impoverished the people." [14]

In Iowa, the third party more or less fused with the Democrats, who normally constituted a minority party. The results of the election were that the Republican majority, which had been about 60,000 the year before, was cut to 22,000; state senators elected were divided thirty-four Republicans to sixteen Fusionists; and state representatives, fifty Republicans to fifty Fusionists. Seventy state legislators and Governor Carpenter were Grangers. Out of a total vote of 187,721, the Anti-Monopoly-Democrat fusion cast 82,578 votes.[15]

In Minnesota, the Republican majority for governor, which was normally from 15,000 to 20,000, was reduced to about 5,000; the Republican majority in the house was reduced to two; and the secretary of state and treasurer were elected by the Anti-Monopolists. As was the case in the state of Iowa, a number of the Republican legislators that were elected were Grangers.[16]

In Wisconsin, Governor Washburn, who had frequently recommended legislation for the regulation of the railroads, was renominated by the Republicans. Because of his known viewpoints, the railroad and liquor interests backed the Anti-Monopoly or Reform candidate who was elected.

---

[14] *Ibid.*, pp. 5, 10-13, 513-514. Chicago *Daily Tribune*, August 14, 15, September 2, 3, 25, 1873. *Appleton's, 1873*, pp. 381-382, 775-776.

[15] *Appleton's, 1873*, pp. 381-382. Fred E. Haynes, *Third party movements since the Civil War with special reference to Iowa*, pp. 67-73. Iowa City, Iowa: State Historical Society of Iowa, 1916. Chicago *Daily Tribune*, June to September, inclusive, 1873. *American Agriculturist*, Vol. XXXII, No. 11 (November, 1873), p. 439. *Industrial Age*, October 18, November 8, 15, 1873; February 7, 1874. *Appleton's, 1874*, pp. 413-419. Edward McPherson, *A handbook of politics for 1874*, p. 228. Washington, D. C.: Solomons and Chapman, 1874. Chicago *Daily Tribune*, October 25, November 7, 1873; January 8, 17, 1874. *The world almanac, 1874*, p. 26. *The world almanac, 1875*, p. 28. These sources are not in complete accord as to the political composition of the Iowa legislature; however, the differences are not enough to be significant.

[16] *Appleton's, 1873*, pp. 510-512. Chicago *Daily Tribune*, June to November, inclusive, 1873. *Industrial Age*, September 6, 1873. *Prairie Farmer*, September 13, 1873. Edward D. Neill, *The history of Minnesota*, pp. 760-763. Fourth ed. Minneapolis, Minnesota: Minnesota Historical Co., 1882. McPherson, *Handbook, 1874*, p. 228. Buck, *The Granger movement*, p. 91. In Minnesota, too, sources do not agree on the returns of the election; possibly the only significant disagreement pertained to which party elected the secretary of state.

The Anti-Monopoly-Democrat fusion ticket also elected a majority of the house and failed by only one to elect the majority of senators.[17]

In Kansas, there were no state-wide elections in 1873, but independent tickets were put in the field in a number of counties and succeeded in influencing the election enough to put a majority of about twenty in the lower house. As a result, ex-Governor Harvey, a farmer and reformer, was elected to the United States Senate by this legislature.[18]

In California, the People's Independent party elected forty-one members of the legislature to thirty-seven Republicans and forty-two Democrats. This legislature elected two United States Senators—Governor Newton Booth, a third-party man, for the long term, and John S. Hager, an "anti-railroad" Democrat, for the short term.[19]

There were some independent political activities in Nebraska, Ohio, and Indiana in 1873, but no parties were organized until 1874.[20]

———

[17] Charles R. Tuttle, *An illustrated history of the State of Wisconsin*, pp. 642-644. Madison, Wisconsin: B. B. Russell and Co., 1875. *Appleton's, 1873*, pp. 774-776. *Industrial Age*, September 6, November, 1873. *Prairie Farmer*, November 29, 1873. *The legislative manual for the State of Wisconsin for 1874*, pp. 325-359. Thirteenth annual edition, compiled by A. J. Turner under the direction of the Secretary of State. Madison, Wisconsin: printed by Atwood and Culver, 1874. George W. Peck, ed., *Wisconsin* (arranged in cyclopaedic form), pp. 309-310, 366. Madison, Wisconsin: Western Historical Association, 1906. Chicago *Daily Tribune*, June to December, inclusive, 1873; January, 1874. See especially issues of September 24, 25, November 8, December 2, 1873; and January 12, 1874.

[18] Chicago *Daily Tribune*, June, July, August, October, November, 1873; January, February, 1874. See especially issues of October 28, November 7, 1873; February 2, 3, 1874. *Industrial Age*, November 3, 15, 1873. Cutler, p. 264. Daniel W. Wilder, *The annals of Kansas*, pp. 635-639. Topeka, Kansas: George W. Martin Publishing House, 1875.

[19] Theodore H. Hittell, *History of California*, Vol. IV, pp. 518-520, 528. San Francisco: N. J. Stone and Co., 1897. Winfield J. Davis, *History of political conventions in California, 1849-1892*, pp. 321-324, 328-335. Publications of the California State Library, No. 1. Sacramento: 1893. Chicago *Daily Tribune*, August to December, inclusive, 1873; January, 1874. See especially issues of September 6, 11, December 22, 26, 1873; January 23, 1874. *Industrial Age*, October 18, December 27, 1873. *Appleton's, 1873*, pp. 83-84. Lauren E. Crane, ed., *Newton Booth, of California, his speeches and addresses*, pp. 124-138, 154-213. Haynes, pp. 56-57. Buck, *The Granger movement*, p. 93.

[20] Concerning activities in Nebraska in 1873, see *Appleton's, 1873*, p. 527. Chicago *Daily Tribune*, August 26, September 25, 1873. For Ohio, see Chicago *Daily Tribune*, June 9, 18, 24, 1873. For Indiana, see Chicago *Daily Tribune*, June 16, 18, August 23, 1873.

In Indiana, the local meetings in the fall of 1873 led to the state convention of Independents at Indianapolis in June, 1874, which adopted a Greenback platform.

The Chicago *Daily Tribune,* in response to an article in the *Nation,* presents a good, though probably a somewhat prejudiced, summary of the independent political movement in the Middle West at the end of 1873. It says:

> The *Nation* assumes, in a very dogmatical way, that the Farmers' movement has failed and come to an end, and it devotes several columns to a statement of the causes of its failure. It says:
>
> "Yet, notwithstanding all this, the Movement has failed—failed so completely that there is now little interest in the subject. No shipper expects to ship his goods any cheaper during the coming year for it; no traveler expects to carry his wife and family to the sea-side or the mountain at any less cost for it; no one who had a hand in the passage of the Illinois pro-rata law has the slightest expectation that it can ever be enforced; no railroad man believes that it will prevent his watering his stock; no newspaper editor any longer in private conversation—what he writes is, of course, another matter—professes to find it a serious subject."
>
> This is not the prevailing opinion in the West, where the Movement originated and has made most progress ... Every day's mail which we receive from the small towns in the West contains the records of the meetings of county associations, at which reports are read, giving the details of the year's progress, and of the increase of membership. In almost every part of the West these annual county conventions are now in session, and the newspapers are burdened with reports of their proceedings. In every instance they show accessions to membership. Instead of dying out, as a separate organization, they are absolving themselves more rapidly than ever from all allegiance to the old political parties, and declaring themselves independent of them. It is idle to talk of the failure of a movement which has gained the political control of the States of Wisconsin and California; which is dictating terms to the old parties in Iowa and Kansas; which has carried a majority of the counties of Illinois, and bids fair to carry the State at the next general election; which is making rapid headway in Minnesota and Michigan, and which has secured so fearless and able a leader as Gov. Booth in the United States Senate. ... The recent ripping-up of rotten Railway Boards in this State is one symptom of the strength of the movement, and, although the pro-rata law in Illinois has not worked well, the discontent which caused it to be enacted and the determination of those

who supported it have not been without a wholesome effect upon railway managers. To say that "No railroad man believes that it will prevent his watering his stock" betrays complete ignorance of the situation. We venture to say that no railway company in Illinois would attempt to issue watered stock to-day any more than it would attempt to issue fire and brimstone.

If there is any healthier political organization anywhere than that which the farmers have originated in the West, we do not know what name it is called by. . . .

It is not true, as the *Nation* insinuates, that corrupt and designing politicians and office-seekers have taken possession of the Movement, or have acquired any considerable standing or influence in it. They will come probably in due time, and in proportion to its strength and probabilities of success, but as yet they are few and powerless in its organization.[21]

From the standpoint of election successes, the results of the farmers' revolt in 1873 can be itemized as follows: election of one governor, of two United States Senators, of a control or balance of power in four state legislatures, election of two state officials in another state, and outstanding successes in local elections in an additional state.

During 1874, other states were added to the Anti-Monopoly crusade. Michigan came in with a National Reform party, none of whose candidates as such polled more than 7,100 votes.[22] In Missouri, the Independents fused with the minority Republicans, but lost to the Democrats by about 40,000 votes.[23] In Kansas, they fused with the minority Democrats, but lost to the Republicans by about 20,000 votes.[24] In Nebraska, where their candidates ran on a straight third-party ticket, they received very few votes.[25] In Oregon, however, where the Independent party made its first

21 Chicago *Daily Tribune,* January 26, 1874.

22 *Ibid.,* February 12, June 18, August 7, 1874. *Industrial Age,* February 28, July 11, August 15, September 12, 26, 1874. *Appleton's, 1874,* pp. 557, 559.

23 *Appleton's, 1874,* pp. 578-579. Chicago *Daily Tribune,* July 22, August 30, 1873; January 12, 1874. *Industrial Age,* May 16, 30, July 25, August 15, September 5 and 26, 1874. *Prairie Farmer,* March 7, 1874. McPherson, *Handbook, 1876,* p. 255.

24 *Industrial Age,* February 14, 28, June 13, July 25, August 8, 15, September 26, 1874. *Appleton's, 1874,* pp. 435-437. Wilder, pp. 641, 643-644, 646-648, 655-656, 659. Cutler, pp. 218, 264. McPherson, *Handbook, 1876,* p. 255.

25 *Appleton's, 1874,* pp. 586-587. *Industrial Age,* July 11, August 8, October 17, 1874. McPherson, *Handbook, 1876,* p. 255.

appearance that year, it polled about one-fourth of all votes, electing twenty-three representatives and six senators, thus giving it the balance of power in both houses.[26] In Illinois, an Independent Reform party was organized and nominated candidates for state treasurer and state superintendent of public instruction. The latter was elected by a majority of over 30,000. The Republicans elected the state treasurer.[27] In Indiana, the Independents elected eight representatives and five senators, gaining thereby the balance of power in the senate.[28] In Wisconsin, in 1874, a fusion of Republican opposition resulted in the election of three Reformers to the United States Congress; while in Iowa, one Anti-Monopoly Congressman was elected. In both Iowa and Minnesota, there were enough Reformers in the state legislature, with the aid of a few "anti-railroad" Republicans, to secure the enactment of anti-railroad legislation.[29]

After 1874, the so-called Anti-Monopoly parties wielded very little influence. The People's Independent party polled 30,000 or about one-fourth of the votes in California, and the Independent party candidates of Oregon polled about 800 votes in 1875. In Minnesota, a new Reform party polled about 2,000 votes in 1875. The Illinois and Indiana Independents apparently went over largely to the Greenback party that year.[30] In a number of states, however, fusions continued for a number of years.[31]

---

[26] *Appleton's, 1874*, pp. 673-674. Chicago *Daily Tribune*, April 16, 17, May 6, June 3, 4, 26, September 19, 1874. McPherson, *Handbook, 1876*, p. 255.

[27] Chicago *Daily Tribune*, May 6, 11, June 11, 22, 1874. *Prairie Farmer*, May 16, June 20, August 29, 1874. *Industrial Age*, January 10, 24, March 21, May 23, June 6, 13, 20, July 11, 25, August 29, September 5, 12, 19, 26, October 10, November 7, 14, 1874. *Appleton's, 1874*, pp. 402-404. John Moses, *Illinois: historical and statistical*, Vol. II, chap. ii, pp. 824-828. Chicago: Fergus Printing Co., 1892. *The world almanac, 1875*, pp. 24-25. *The Tribune almanac and political register for 1875*, pp. 47, 80-82. New York: Tribune Association, 1875.

[28] Chicago *Daily Tribune*, June 11, August 13, 1874. *Industrial Age*, April 18, June 13, 27, September 26, October 17, 24, 1874. *Appleton's, 1874*, pp. 412-413, 415. McPherson, *Handbook, 1874*, pp. 232-233.

[29] *Appleton's, 1874*, pp. 418-419, 564-565, 801-811. Tuttle, p. 649. *Industrial Age*, January 10, February 14, 28, March 7, May 23, June 27, July 4, 11, August 29, September 5, 12, 26, October 3, 17, November 7, 14, 1874. McPherson, *Handbook, 1874*, pp. 233-234. Also see issues of the Chicago *Daily Tribune* of the period.

[30] Winfield J. Davis, pp. 341-349, 355. Hittell, p. 566. *Appleton's, 1875*, pp. 99-101, 393, 509-511, 609-610. *Appleton's, 1876*, pp. 392, 410-411. McPherson, *Handbook, 1876*, p. 255. *Prairie Farmer*, May 22, June 19, 1875. *Western Rural* (Chicago), June 19, 1875.

[31] Buck, *The Granger movement*, chap. iii. Haynes, chap. vi.

The results of these few years of political upheaval do not appear very great when thrown into comparison with the political activities of the nation as a whole and all of the twenty-odd states where there were no independent parties. But when measured in terms of the fairly restricted area in which third parties did operate, and coupled with the influence of dozens of Grange members who were elected by the two other parties, this farmers' political movement was considerable in its influence. It not only took the nation by the ears and aroused a great deal of editorial comment in eastern metropolitan areas, but placed on the statutes of a number of states legislation which constituted the substantial beginning of railroad regulation, and began "that radical but tedious revolution of American ideas which is slowly bringing industry under the political power of democracy." [32]

THE GREENBACK PARTY

The Greenback party was more or less the successor of the Anti-Monopoly parties in the West. It developed out of demand for inflation of the currency, immediately after the "Crime of 1873." The short period of prosperity between 1870 and 1873 never reached the farmers, and in 1873 there was a nationwide depression that reached everybody. Prices fell to such an extent that it became impossible for debtors to meet their long-time, fixed obligations. Business houses by the hundreds went into bankruptcy; railway traffic dwindled away because of lack of general purchasing power; and many farmers lost their farms. Farmers and other people believed that the depression was due to a shortage of circulating medium and that the remedy was for the government to issue paper money. In the face of this sentiment, Congress, in 1873, passed an act demonetizing silver, thus further restricting the amount of "sound money." [33] The result was the rise of a new political party which demanded that the "Crime of 1873" be rescinded.

Attempts to deflate the Civil War currency had begun in Congress as early as 1865, but objections were so numerous and vigorous that a con-

---

[32] Commons, *A documentary history of American industrial society*, Vol. IX, *Labor movement, 1860-1880*, p. 49.

[33] Davis R. Dewey, *Financial history of the United States*, Twelfth ed., pp. 370-372, 403-405. New York: Longmans, Green & Co., Inc., 1934. Hepburn, pp. 271-274.

verse move was made in 1868. The issue was bandied back and forth for more than a decade, being settled finally by the resumption of specie payments in 1879. After the panic of 1873, Congress passed an act which would have increased the amount of greenbacks up to $400,000,000 and again established free banking, but President Grant vetoed the bill.[34] The sentiment which created the demand in Congress for inflation was generated largely in the Middle West and was a part of the Granger movement, although there were many leaders in the Grange itself who were opposed to cheap money.

Yet the Greenback movement did not receive its initial stimulus from farmers' organizations. It started at a convention of the National Labor Reform party at Columbus, Ohio, in February, 1872, when a Greenback platform was adopted and candidates were nominated for President and Vice-President. This proved to be a false start, however, due to the fact that their presidential candidate, Judge David Davis of Illinois, refused to run.[35] But in 1874, the movement was definitely started when the Independent party of Indiana issued the call for a conference to be held at Indianapolis in November. Representatives from seven states—New York, New Jersey, Connecticut, Illinois, Michigan, Kentucky, and Indiana —attended, many of them apparently from the industrial classes. The declaration of principles declared the most important issue before the people to be "the proper solution of the money question," and reported in favor "of a new political organization of the people, by the people, and for the people, to restrain the aggressions of combined capital upon the rights and interests of the masses, to reduce taxation, correct abuses, and to purify all departments of the Government."[36] The likeness of this declaration to the platform of the Anti-Monopoly and Reform parties of the farmers will be immediately recognized.

A national convention of the new party called to meet at Cleveland on March 11, 1875, was attended by about sixty representatives from

---

[34] Hepburn, pp. 205-236. Dewey, *Financial history of the United States,* pp. 331-378.
[35] McPherson, *Handbook, 1872,* pp. 210-212. Solon J. Buck, *The agrarian crusade,* p. 80. New Haven, Connecticut: Yale University Press, 1921.
[36] Buck, *The agrarian crusade,* pp. 79-82. Haynes, pp. 99, 105-107. Chicago *Daily Tribune,* November 26, 1874. Ellis B. Usher, *The Greenback movement of 1875-1884 and Wisconsin's part in it,* pp. 6-9, 10-15. Milwaukee, Wisconsin: published by the author, 1911.

twelve states and decided that an Independent party should be organized and should hold a nominating convention. The convention was held at Indianapolis in May, 1876, and approximately 240 delegates came from eighteen states and the District of Columbia. A platform was adopted, Peter Cooper nominated for President, and Samuel F. Cary for Vice-President. Peter Cooper was a liberal-minded New York philanthropist, founder of the famous Cooper Union, an adult education project for workingmen in New York. The Greenback platform of 1876 contained only a pointed preamble and five planks as follows:

> The Independent party is called into existence by the necessities of the people, whose industries are prostrated, whose labor is deprived of its just reward by a ruinous policy, which the Republican and Democratic parties refuse to change; and in view of the failure of these parties to furnish relief to the depressed industries of the country, thereby disappointing the just hopes and expectations of a suffering people, we declare our principles, and invite all independent and patriotic men to join our ranks in this movement for financial reform and industrial emancipation.

The five planks in the platform were:

> *First,* a demand for the immediate and unconditional repeal of the Specie-Resumption Act of 1875.
> *Second,* United States notes should be full legal tender for all purposes, except fixed contracts.
> *Third,* government should "keep in view the full development of all legitimate business—agricultural, mining, manufacturing, and commercial."
> *Fourth,* a "protest against any further issue of gold bonds for sale in foreign markets, by which we would be made for a long period 'hewers of wood and drawers of water' to foreigners."
> *Fifth,* against further purchase of silver which "will still further oppress, in taxation, an already overburdened people." [37]

Cooper accepted the nomination, but conducted no active campaign, with the result that little effort was made in the 1876 election contest. Considerable strength was developed in Indiana, and a number of pa-

[37] McKee, pp. 173-175. Haynes, pp. 109, 112-114. *Appleton's, 1876,* pp. 781-782. Chicago *Daily Tribune,* May 19, 1876. Indianapolis *Journal,* May 18, 19, 1876.

pers, the Indianapolis *Sun,* the *Industrial Age* of Chicago, and Ignatius Donnelly's *Anti-Monopolist* of St. Paul, vigorously backed the movement. Greenback clubs also played an important part in this campaign. It had been suggested by a resolution passed at a Greenback convention in Detroit, in 1875, that "Greenback clubs [be organized] in every state of the Union for the purposes of carrying out the principles and measures set forth" by the party. Marcus M. Brick Pomeroy was made chairman of the national committee for organizing these clubs, and supposedly organized over 8,000 during the Greenback period.[38]

The party polled only 81,737 votes out of a total of more than 8,000,000 cast that year in the Hayes-Tilden campaign. Most of the strength lay in the Middle West, where third-party sentiment had been developed by the Granger movement, although the Illinois vote of 17,233, the largest to be cast by any one state, was less than one-fourth as great as had been cast by the state Independent Reform party in 1874. Four other Granger states—Indiana, Michigan, Iowa, and Kansas—each cast more than 7,000 votes for the Greenback candidate; and ten midwestern states polled over 65,000, or more than three-fourths of all votes cast for the party. Pennsylvania was the only eastern state that made any showing.[39] It was thus apparent that while Independent-party sentiment had dwindled measurably since the Anti-Monopoly crusade of 1873 and 1874, the Greenback party, initiated in labor circles, had in 1876 become dominantly an agrarian party. Libby points out that for the most part the Greenback strength, by counties, lay in predominantly agricultural communities where the economic life was more undeveloped, the total valuation of land lower and the average value of mortgages on farms higher—i.e., in the inland poorer farming communities.[40]

Between the presidential campaigns of 1876 and 1880, the party gained strength and became even more dominantly agrarian. In 1876, it gained the balance of power in the Illinois legislature and the follow-

[38] Chicago *Daily Tribune,* August 26, 1875. Haynes, pp. 114-115. *Appleton's, 1896,* p. 579. Buck, *The agrarian crusade,* pp. 86, 93. *Extracts: from some of the communistic inflammatory and treasonable documents circulated by the National Greenback party.* Chicago: Honest Money League of the Northwest, 1878.

[39] *Appleton's, 1876,* p. 792. Buck, *The agrarian crusade,* pp. 85-86.

[40] Orin G. Libby, "A Study of the Greenback Movement, 1876-84," *Transactions of the Wisconsin Academy of Sciences, Arts, and Letters,* Vol. XII, Part II, 1890, pp. 530-548. Buck, *The agrarian crusade,* pp. 80-81, 90-91, 97-98.

ing year sent David Davis, its first choice for President in 1872, to the United States Senate and polled large votes in a number of eastern states. It polled more than 187,000 votes in 1877.[41]

In a meeting at Toledo, Ohio, in 1878, an alliance was formed with the Labor Reform party, which had been active in industrial states since 1870, and the name "National Party" was adopted.[42]

Agricultural states which cast large Greenback votes in the 1878 election were Iowa, Michigan, Missouri, Illinois, Indiana, California, Ohio, Wisconsin, Kansas, Minnesota, and Nebraska. The movement reached Texas for the first time that year, where it found strong backing because of the division among old party adherents resulting from Grange activities. In Texas, however, the Greenback candidates ran independently and polled 55,000 votes for governor and elected one Congressman and ten representatives to the lower house of the state legislature.[43]

In the elections of 1878, fifteen Greenbackers, or Nationals, were elected to Congress, six from the East, six from the Middle West, and three from the South, among them General James B. Weaver, destined to be the presidential candidate of the party in 1880.[44]

In a number of states, the party fused with the old-line party, which was normally the minority party in each given state. Throughout the nation, there were more than 1,000,000 votes cast for the National, or Greenback Labor, party and fusion candidates in 1878.[45]

The campaign and election of 1880 revealed some peculiarities of

----

[41] *Appleton's, 1877,* pp. 382-383. McPherson, *Handbook, 1878,* pp. 233, 807. Moses, Vol. II, pp. 848-850.

[42] *Appleton's, 1878,* p. 807. Chicago *Daily Tribune,* February 23, 1878. McPherson, *Handbook,* 1878, pp. 167-168.

[43] R. C. Martin, *The People's party in Texas,* p. 23, University of Texas Bulletin No. 3308. Austin, Texas: February 22, 1933. R. C. Martin, "The Greenback Party in Texas," *Southwestern Historical Quarterly,* Vol. XXX, No. 3 (January, 1927), pp. 165-169. Haynes, pp. 124-125.

[44] Buck, *The agrarian crusade,* pp. 88-91. Haynes, pp. 122-131. *Appleton's, 1878,* p. 807.

[45] *Appleton's, 1878,* p. 808. Thomas J. McCormack, *Memoirs of Gustave Koerner, 1809-1896,* Vol. II, pp. 629-631. Cedar Rapids, Iowa: The Torch Press, 1909. For a rebuttal of Greenbackism written at the time see, for example, George Wilson, Jr., *The Greenbackers and their doctrines.* Lexington, Missouri: Intelligencer News, 1878.

popular third-party movements. General Weaver, who had been elected to Congress from Iowa in 1878 on a fusion ticket and who was undoubtedly a most pleasing personality and effective political orator, was nominated as candidate for President. He made a vigorous campaign, but received only around 308,500 votes, less than one-third the number cast for the party in the side elections of 1878. The platform was much the same as in previous years, except that the plank calling for resumption of specie payment, and a number of others calling for woman's suffrage, a graduated income tax, and congressional regulation of interstate commerce were omitted. All of the issues stated in the platforms of the party in both 1878 and 1889 were strictly national, but the adherents of the party mobilized much greater strength in local and state elections than they did in the national election. Furthermore, the indication of returning farm prosperity apparently dampened the farmer's concern about cheap money and reform of the railroads.[46]

It was the campaign and not the votes of 1880 that marked it as a high tide in the Farmers' Movement. The platform contained fifteen planks, and its preamble was a preachment against "monopolies" and "international syndicates" which demand "dear money," "cheap labor," and a "strong government," and hence, a "weak people." The first plank stated "that the right to make and issue money is a sovereign power, to be maintained by the people for their common benefit."[47] General Weaver carried this populist doctrine about the country in the most vigorous popular campaign ever waged up to that time. In October of the campaign, he is quoted as saying that to date he had made more than 100 speeches, traveled 20,000 miles, shaken hands with 30,000 persons, and addressed 500,000 people in fifteen states. He gave some time to the campaign in Maine and spoke in both Boston and New York, but spent the greater part of his time in the southern states. He evidently believed that while the party probably would not win, it had a strong possibility of holding the balance of power in Congress. The Hayes-Tilden election of 1876 had been decided in the House of Representa-

---

[46] McKee, pp. 190-193. *The platform of the National Greenback party and the letter of acceptance of General J. B. Weaver.*

[47] *Appleton's, 1880,* pp. 696-697.

tives and the same might be the case in 1880, under which circumstances a goodly quota of Greenback Congressmen, holding the balance of power, could dictate the choice of President. If he had an idea that he might in that case be the choice for President, he never revealed that fact, and his campaign was carried on in every way as a battle of the people against vested interests. The high esteem in which he was held in his own state of Iowa was indicated by 32,701 votes cast for him for President, the largest ever cast in that state for any third-party candidate up to that time. But even then Iowa stood third in the number of Greenback ballots cast in 1880, the ten leading states being in order: Missouri, Michigan, Iowa, Texas, Illinois, Pennsylvania, Kansas, Indiana, New York, and Kentucky. Six of these states were old midwestern Grange states. They accounted for almost 162,000 of the approximate 308,000 total 1880 Greenback vote.[48]

The vote for the Greenback candidate in 1880 was practically four times as great as in 1876, but the demonstrated strength of the party was so slight in comparison to what the sentiment had seemed to indicate during the campaign, that the party never again rose to the heights gained in the Weaver campaign. Only two of the ten Greenback Congressmen elected in 1880 were re-elected in 1882, and the party's last appearance in national politics came in 1884. General Benjamin F. Butler was nominated for President by both the National (Greenback) party and "The Anti-Monopoly Organization of the United States" that year. Butler was from Massachusetts and much better known in labor than in agricultural circles and this, plus the fact that he did not make an active campaign, caused the party to be regarded by the farmers as an organization which could not redress their grievances. The National party polled around 175,370 votes that year. The ten leading contributing states were, in order: Michigan, Massachusetts, New York, Pennsylvania, Kansas, Illinois, Indiana, Ohio, Wisconsin, and Maine. Three eastern industrial states—Massachusetts, New York, and Pennsylvania—cast almost one-third of the total Greenback vote, and the six midwestern

---

[48] Fred E. Haynes, *James Baird Weaver.* Iowa City, Iowa: State Historical Society of Iowa, 1919. See chap. ix, "First Campaign for Presidency, 1880," pp. 155-178, for an excellent account of Weaver's campaign in 1880. *Appleton's, 1880*, p. 702. *Congressional record*, 46th Congress, 3rd Session, December 21, 1880, pp. 308-309. McPherson, *Handbook, 1882*, p. 186.

states which had cast 162,000 votes for Weaver in 1880 cast less than one-fourth that number for Butler in 1884.[49]

Once again a farmers' upheaval seemed to have failed. But General Weaver was nominated as candidate for President again by the Populists in 1892, and the political disruptions caused by the Greenback episode bore fruit for years to come. General Weaver's home state re-elected him to Congress in 1884 and 1886; and, as Haynes says, "... in a certain sense the first Democratic national victory since the Civil War [that of 1884] was the culmination of the 'Greenback Movement.'" He adds, "As has happened frequently in the history of third parties, real gains are recorded in the votes cast for, or taken away from, the two great parties."[50] Furthermore, the Farmers' Alliance was in the field to take up the political cudgels for the farmer before the demise of the Greenback party, and no farmers' revolt in the history of the nation has ever created as great a political upheaval as the Alliance did when it drifted into politics and created the Populist party.

The Greenback party is not generally thought of as one of the Granger parties, and in the main it was not. In most cases the Anti-Monopoly and Reform parties of the Middle West formed a link between it and the political agitation brewed by the Granger movement. It was, however, pretty much the successor of Granger third parties; and while its dominant plank in the beginning was one calling for an inflation of the currency, it never at any time failed to keep up the fight against the domination of railroad influence—an issue which had been raised and kept alive not only by the various third parties of the early seventies, but by the Grange itself.

In Texas, which the Grange did not enter until the last half of 1873 and where the railroad influence became dominant a few years later than in the Middle West, there had been no Anti-Monopoly or Reform party. The merest glance at the outstanding resolutions of the Texas State Grange for the years 1878 and 1880 and the planks of the Greenback party of that state for those years would be enough to convince

---

[49] McPherson, *Handbook, 1882*, pp. 1-3. *Handbook, 1884*, pp. 1-3. *Handbook, 1886*, pp. 1-3, 238. McKee, p. 229. All sources do not agree as to the number of Greenback and National Congressmen. For example, see Buck, *The agrarian crusade*, pp. 96-97. Usher, p. 14. *Appleton's, 1880*, p. 702.

[50] Haynes, *James Baird Weaver*, pp. 162-163.

one that the Grangers and the Greenbackers were pretty much the same persons in Texas. Both asked for repeal of the resumption act, remonetization of silver, repeal of the national bank law, that greenbacks be made legal tender, and for regulation of railroads, restriction of monopolies, and revision of the tariff. The Texas State Grange, in 1877, voted down a resolution which proposed to forbid officers of the Grange to hold political office; and the name of Worthy Master Lang, a member of the state legislature, was put in nomination for governor at the state Democratic convention in 1878.[51] Numerous other Grangers were prominent in third-party leadership in the Middle West and were undoubtedly Greenbackers from 1878 to 1884. This is to say that the Greenback movement in the Middle West and Southwest was not an interlude in the Farmers' Movement, but an integral part of it.

[51] R. C. Martin, *The People's party in Texas*, pp. 161-177. "The Grange as a Political Factor in Texas," *Southwestern Political and Social Science Quarterly*, Vol. VI, No. 4 (March, 1926), pp. 363-383. Ernest W. Winkler, ed., *Platforms of political parties in Texas*, University of Texas Bulletin No. 53. Austin, Texas: September 20, 1916. See pp. 179-180 for demands of Texas State Grange in 1878; pp. 193-194 for demands in 1880; pp. 180-181, 187-190 for copies of the Greenback platforms in 1878; pp. 198-201 for a copy of Greenback platform in 1880.

THE

FARMERS' ALLIANCE

1880-1890

THE FARMERS' ALLIANCE, A TREE WITH
MANY BRANCHES

One of the characteristics of a movement is that it generally arises out of the life of the masses and at numerous places. A number of abortive attempts at local organizations, however, do not constitute a movement. But when conditions are unsettled over a wide area and for a long period of time, a number of projects which start on a purely local basis are likely to furnish patterns for others to follow in their inclinations to do something about such conditions. Thus movements start. Furthermore, once the spirit of a movement gets going, it is likely to sweep into its wake organizations which were started with objectives quite different from the objects of the movement itself. The Grange was captured by the movement of the middle-western farmers in their fight for the control of railroads and for economic cooperation, although neither of these was part of the original objective of the order. The Farmers' Alliance started as an anti-horse-thief association at one place, as a debating club at another place, as a cemetery association at another, and as a group of farmers' clubs at still another. It became the farmers' vehicle for an organized attack on economic and political problems and developed into the largest farmers' organization of the world, its membership, at its height, probably being three times as great as that ever attained by the Grange.

The Alliance movement is generally said to have started in Texas, and so it did, as far as the earliest origins are concerned. Since, however, we shall include in that movement all the farmers' organizations of the decade 1880-1890, most of which became affiliated with the great Southern Alliance, we shall have to say that it started in at least six places —Texas, Louisiana, Arkansas, Chicago, southern Illinois, and North Carolina. It was, in its heyday, something like a great river with some half dozen tributaries, each with a separate and independent source. The story of the origin of the various farmers' organizations of the eighties, the amalgamation of most of them into one giant organization, and the meteoric career of the amalgamated organizations reads like a romance. Those vested interests which were disturbed by the Granger uprising and relieved by its decline in the late seventies were rudely shocked by what happened in the eighties and early nineties.

The story of the Farmers' Alliance will be told here in a little greater detail than a general survey of the Farmers' Movement warrants because, so far as the author knows, the history of the various branches of this organization has never been adequately analyzed elsewhere.

THE TEXAS FARMERS' ALLIANCE [1]

The Farmers' Alliance started in Texas as an anti-horse-thief and anti-land-grab farmers' organization. Dr. C. W. Macune, the outstanding leader of the Southern Farmers' Alliance in its early days, says that the Alliance was first organized "about the year 1873."[2] N. A. Dunning, probably its most trustworthy early historian, says its first local was organized

---

[1] Information on the Texas Alliance, unless otherwise documented, is from N. A. Dunning, *The farmers' alliance and agricultural digest.* Washington, D. C.: Alliance Publishing Company, 1891.

[2] *National Economist* (Washington, D. C.), March 14, 1889, p. 8. For a short sketch of Macune, see Annie L. Diggs, "The Farmers' Alliance and Some of its Leaders," *Arena,* Vol. V, No. 5 (April, 1892), pp. 598-600.

in either 1874 or 1875.[3] The exact date is not so significant as the fact that the organization arose just at the period when the Grange was beginning to decline. It is also significant that it was a weak and struggling organization until the Grange had declined pronouncedly, after which it became the leading mouthpiece of the Farmers' Movement, growing rapidly and to great magnitude.

The first organization in Texas was in Lampasas County, where a number of farmers' clubs were organized for the purpose of resisting land sharks, or claim jumpers, who were operating something like a racket in setting up fraudulent titles to lands on which others had settled. Because horse stealing was also still prevalent at that time in Texas and probably because of the romance attached to the capturing of cattle rustlers and horse thieves, the secret work of this early organization consisted of formulae for catching a horse thief. The signals and hailing signs were those which could be used in helping the sheriff and other club members to capture horse thieves. Bryan[4] makes the point that so-called cattle kings were in those days attempting to dominate the area and that something approaching an enclosure movement was being attempted by the large holders. These were the days of the fence wars in which local settlers protested against the fencing of large areas by the cattle kings. Bryan says that "crowds sometimes became angry mobs, and lawless acts were committed." The farmers believed that the fence laws were unjust and one-sided. These cattle wars and fence wars created stimuli which induced farmers to gather in meetings to protect their interests. The earliest local units of the Texas Farmers' Alliance grew out of this general situation in Lampasas County, and the movement gradually spread to nearby counties.

On February 22, 1878, the Lampasas County clubs, somewhere between twelve and twenty of them, joined together to organize a Grand County Alliance. The second county alliance was formed in Parker County, the third in Jack County, followed by similar organizations in several other counties. On May 4, 1878, twelve sub-Alliances from these counties met and organized the Texas Grand State Alliance. This organi-

---

[3] Robert Lee Hunt, *A history of farmer movements in the Southwest, 1873-1925*, p. 28. College Station, Texas: A. and M. Press, 1935.

[4] J. E. Bryan, *The Farmers' Alliance, its origin, progress and purpose*, pp. 1-5. Fayetteville, Arkansas: published by the author, 1891.

zation apparently never obtained a state charter and, after holding one meeting in addition to the organization meeting, seems to have gone out of existence. There is some evidence that it became involved in Greenback politics, which was rampant in Texas the year it was organized, and failed to develop because of this political fight. The second attempt at state organization, however, followed quickly. On July 29, 1879, the Parker County organization met to form a state Alliance, adopted the Lampasas declaration of purposes, slightly amended, and, on December 27, organized another Grand State Alliance. The Parker County Alliance, N. A. Dunning says, was about all there was to the Grand State Alliance during the following year. The organization was consummated by March, 1880, a total of four meetings having been held prior to that time.

The declaration of purposes of the state organization is exceedingly interesting for two reasons: first, because it set forth purposes of a general farmers' organization which were quite different from the purposes giving rise to the early Lampasas clubs; and second, because it did not presage anything of the great economic and political activities which came to dominate the organization when it grew to power. We quote this declaration of purposes *in toto:*

> Profoundly impressed that we as the Farmers' Alliance, united by the strong and faithful ties of financial and home interest, should set forth our declaration of intentions, we therefore *Resolve:*
>
> 1. To labor for the Alliance and its purposes, assured that a faithful observance of the following principles will insure our mental, moral, and financial improvement.
>
> 2. To endorse the motto, "In things essential, Unity, and in all things Charity."
>
> 3. To develop a better state, mentally, morally, socially, and financially.
>
> 4. To create a better understanding for sustaining our civil officers in maintaining law and order.
>
> 5. To constantly strive to secure entire harmony and good will among all mankind and brotherly love among ourselves.
>
> 6. To suppress personal, local, sectional, and national prejudices, all unhealthy rivalry and all selfish ambition.

The growth of this new farmers' organization, like that of the Grange a decade earlier, was slow. The Grand State Alliance was fearful that it might become involved in the question of entering politics or in other controversial issues. It held some of its early meetings in one-room school buildings with not more than five to ten delegates from the local district present. A state lecturer, however, was appointed in 1880 and a grand deputy lecturer in 1881. In the annual meeting of 1882, the secretary reported a total of 120 sub-Alliances in existence in twelve different counties. Not all of them, however, were represented at the state meeting. In 1883, only thirty sub-Alliances were present at the state meeting and all the officers except the lecturer and the secretary were absent. There were only about fifty sub-Alliances represented in 1884.

All during the first five years of its life, the State Alliance worked on rituals, regalia, burial services, and reorganization of degrees. Many members withdrew between 1882 and 1884 because of a resolution adopted at the 1882 meeting forbidding all political activities in the name of the Alliance. It was reported at the 1883 state meeting that in their "efforts to co-operate in buying and selling in the past, they had been treated with contempt by tradesmen" and little had been accomplished in this direction.

It was not until the state meeting of 1885 that the turning point in the organization came. A resolution had been passed at the 1884 state meeting urging that sub-Alliances and county Alliances organize joint-stock companies "for the the purpose of trade, and for the personal benefit of members financially." Delegates came to the meeting 600 strong, many of them determined to convert the organization into an instrument for militant activity. A resolution that year recommended "to the County Alliances (1) that the members of all Sub-Alliances act as a unit in the sale of their produce, and to this end the County Alliance set apart a day or days in which to put their produce on the market for sale," and (2) that none but Alliance members be allowed to participate in these cooperative activities. This was the spark that lighted the Alliance fire, which swept rapidly over the state. At the 1886 annual meeting, 2,700 sub-Alliances from eighty-four counties were represented. The organization had grown to such proportions that politicians were getting uneasy about it and state papers were warning it to keep out of politics. The convention passed a resolution declaring the strict nonpartisan spirit of the organization, but at the same time addressed a number of "demands" to the state and national governments.

The sharp turn in emphasis came near wrecking the organization from within. A militant segment of the membership insisted that there should be no restrictions whatever placed on the political activities of the organization. This caused those who were opposed to such action to withdraw, elect a rump set of officers, and apply to the secretary of state for a new charter. The split was avoided in a called meeting in January, 1887, at which Macune introduced a resolution stating that the organization would "labor for the education of the agricultural classes in the science of economical government, in a strictly non-partisan spirit." A sharp debate followed the introduction of this resolution, but it was finally adopted. The term "scientific and economical government" and similar ones were used often in the days when the Alliance was over its head in politics but still claiming to be nonpartisan.

A number of significant things happened at this consolidation meeting, probably the most important being the steps taken toward a definite program of economic cooperation. Acting-President Macune, in his address to the convention, emphasized the fact that other occupations were organized and said:

> The peculiar relations of large organizations to their own members, to the government, and to other organizations, is a subject worthy of the most profound study by all who exercise the right of citizenship.
>
> I hold that co-operation, properly understood and properly applied, will place a limit to the encroachments of organized monopoly, and will be the means by which the mortgage-burdened farmers can assert their freedom from the tyranny of organized capital, and obtain the reward for honesty, industry, and frugality, which they so richly deserve, and which they are now so unjustly denied.

He recommended that cotton mills be built in order to beat high freight rates and to keep from paying corporate monopolies; that steps be taken to assist county Alliances in perfecting a "system of purchasing supplies and sale of products"; that a board of fifteen trustees be elected to enact business and carry or assume the responsibility of the organization between general meetings. A committee of three appointed to report upon the expediency of securing an agency to sell cotton to manufacturers brought in recommendations that each county Alliance establish at least one cooperative store, cotton yard, and lumberyard, and that a state Alliance business agent of ability be appointed to sell cotton and other products and make wholesale purchases for the stores.

The organization had grown very rapidly since the 1885 meeting—from 700 to 3,500 sub-Alliances. Macune said, ". . . perhaps the most potent argument that organizing officers have used in securing this rapid accession to our ranks has been the individual benefits that would accrue from concentration of trade in purchasing supplies, and the bulking of products when offered for sale."

Following the pattern of the Grange, it had taken the Farmers' Alliance nine years to become the spokesman for the Farmers' Movement. Organized in terms of local farmers' clubs as early as 1878, it was in the annual meeting of 1887 of the Texas Grand State Alliance that the organization announced purposes which forewarned the general public that another high tide in the Farmers' Movement was imminent. A resolution was passed at this convention asking that organizers be sent into other states to set up Alliances and to cooperate with other agricultural societies. Another resolution asked that two delegates from each congressional district be appointed to represent the Texas Alliance in a meeting with J. A. Tetts of the Louisiana Farmers' Union. Mr. Tetts was in attendance at the Texas State Alliance meeting with full authority to negotiate for his organization. He had come to the meeting on the invitation of President Macune, who previous to this had sent Evan Jones, a prominent Texas Allianceman, to Louisiana to study the aims and purposes of the Louisiana Farmers' Union. This exchange of ambassadors, so to speak, of the two organizations predicated their later joining of forces.

THE LOUISIANA FARMERS' UNION

The Louisiana Farmers' Union was not so large or powerful an organization as the Texas Alliance, nor had it gone through any great conversion in purpose as the Texas organization had. From the date of its first organization, it had planned, among other things, to wrestle with the farmers' economic problems and insist on political behavior favorable to the farming interests. It was originated some time during 1880 by ten or twelve men who had met at the D'Arbonne Church in Lincoln Parish, Louisiana, for the purpose of cleaning up a graveyard, but who fell into a discussion of the farmers' problems and decided to form a farmers' club. This they did, making it a nonsecret organization so as not to exclude Primitive Baptists. The following excerpt states the objects of their club:

> The objects of this club are: First, to work for the elevation of agriculture to its true position among the industries of our country, by the mental, moral, social, and financial improvement of its members, which can be best effected by frequent meetings and free discussions, cultivating and developing their best talent for business; by experiments, adopting a more rational system of farming—one guided by the use of more brains—thereby commanding better returns for the labor expended; to encourage the practice of the cash system in buying and selling; to oppose special and class legislation and rebuke misguided and corrupt legislation; to endeavor to secure the nomination and election of good men to office, and spurn, as dangerous to liberty and economy, all professional politicians; to denounce and destroy, wherever possible, all political rings and defeat all machine candidates. In this club the largest liberty shall be allowed for the discussion of all questions, political, financial, and domestic, which can possibly interest the real farmers of our country.

The constitution further stated that the "club shall work for more favorable agricultural legislation, more equitable taxation, equal rights in transportation, lower rates of interest, cheaper administration of the laws, more respect for the true wants of the people, and especially more thorough representation in the halls of legislation."

It met twice a month for a while and grew to a membership of forty or more, but the attendance at meetings dwindled and the organization was abandoned after a little over one year's existence. J. A. Tetts, one of its founders, and a fellow farmer by the name of Skinner revived it four years later, this time to live until it and others like it in Louisiana amalgamated with the Texas Farmers' Alliance.

Tetts says that he and Skinner met on the streets of Ruston, Louisiana, one day in the fall of 1884 and in a discussion of the poor prices for cotton decided to organize again. The two met together in March, 1885, reworked the old Lincoln Parish Club's constitution and then called a meeting at Antioch Church in Lincoln Parish for the purpose of organizing. Nine men joined at that time. They decided to have no ritual, but did later construct some secret work.

This one club took in members from a wide area, but soon divided itself into other locals. "Unions" sprang up rapidly all over Lincoln Parish, and a mass meeting was called in July, 1885, to organize a parish (county) Union. This parish Union adopted a standard constitution for local Unions, modeled after that of the Texas Alliance, and adopted a ritual for one degree. It ordered a thousand copies of the constitution printed and apparently felt quite confident of rapid expansion. At a meeting the following August, the Lincoln Parish Union officers were voted to be the state Union officers, and all presidents of local Unions were deputized as organizers. At a meeting in the following October, in which four parish organizations were represented, Tetts reported that he had been in touch with the Agricultural Wheel of Arkansas (see below, page 203) and had received instructions to get in touch with any other such organization. An invitation was sent to the Texas Alliance to send delegates to a future meeting to explain the Alliance, and Evan Jones came. Tetts was sent to the Texas Alliance meeting, in Waco, in January, 1887, with full authority to help establish a national farmers' organization.[5]

The ground was thus laid for two substantial state farmers' organizations, one growing out of a local anti-horse-thief protective association, and the other out of a farmers' cemetery meeting, to join in developing an organization to take the place of the Grange in the farmers' battle for equity and justice. The Louisiana Union claimed 10,000 members at that time, and the Texas Alliance had probably ten times that number.[6]

———

[5] All the information given here on the Louisiana Farmers' Union is from N. A. Dunning, pp. 218-222, who quotes directly a letter from J. A. Tetts. Tetts, however, was apparently wrong in his date of the meeting of the Texas Alliance, giving it as January, 1886, rather than 1887. W. S. Morgan (*History of Wheel and Alliance*, p. 103. St. Louis: C. B. Woodward Publishing Company, 1891.) states the date of reorganizing the Union as 1886 instead of 1885. This is apparently correct, for it does not leave a full year unaccounted for as Dunning's quotation of Tetts does. When Dunning discusses the Waco meeting elsewhere, he gives the date as 1887.

[6] *Appleton's, 1891*, p. 299.

UNION OF TEXAS FARMERS' ALLIANCE AND
LOUISIANA FARMERS' UNION

Delegates appointed by the January 20, 1887, meeting of the Texas Farmers' Alliance met with J. A. Tetts, the representative of the Louisiana Farmers' Union, the following day and projected a national organization, electing Macune of the Alliance president and Tetts of the Union first vice-president. A constitution and declaration of purposes were adopted, the same as those of the Alliance, except that two articles were added. These two read as follows:

That we demand equal rights to all and special favors to none;
That we return to the old principle of letting the office seek the man, instead of the man seeking the office.

An interesting article in the constitution, which was to some extent a paraphrase of a similar one in the declaration of purposes of the Grange, and which N. A. Dunning says grew in favor with its repeated reading during Alliance history, read as follows:

The brightest jewels which it garners are the tears of widows and orphans, and its imperative commands are to visit the homes where lacerated hearts are bleeding; to assuage the sufferings of a brother or sister; bury the dead; care for the widows and educate the orphans; to exercise charity towards offenders; to construe words and deeds in their most favorable light, granting honesty of purpose and good intentions to others; and to protect the National Farmers' Alliance and Co-operative Union until death. Its laws are reason and equity; its cardinal doctrines inspire purity of thought and life; its intention is, "Peace on earth and good will to man."[7]

The name of the organization which combined the Louisiana Union and the Texas Alliance was to be the National Farmers' Alliance and Co-operative Union of America. Its constitution provided for the issuance of charters to state organizations and that no person should be admitted to membership unless he was "eligible to membership, under

---

[7] This last article is also interesting because Macune was a minister. For an account of this consolidation meeting, see N. A. Dunning, pp. 56-58. J. E. Bryan, pp. 9-11.

the constitution of the State Alliance of Texas, or the State Farmers Union of Louisiana." The Texas State Alliance voted a loan of $500 to assist in completing the national organization, which was to be chartered for ninety-nine years by the District of Columbia. The charter was prepared on January 27, 1887, and signed by the president and secretary of the new organization. The president was authorized to extend invitations to all labor organizations to send delegates to the next meeting, which was set for the fall of 1887 at Shreveport, Louisiana; and a representative was delegated to visit the Agricultural Wheel of Arkansas. This visit was made, and resulted in the Wheel having delegates at the Shreveport meeting.

During the spring of 1887, President Macune sent organizers into Missouri, North Carolina, Alabama, Mississippi, Georgia, Florida, Tennessee, and Kentucky, with the result that all of these states except Kentucky and Georgia had representatives at the Shreveport meeting.

THE ARKANSAS AGRICULTURAL WHEEL [8]

The Agricultural Wheel was another farmers' organization which started as a local club with no notion of growing into or being picked up by the Farmers' Movement. It started as a local debating or discussion club at McBee's schoolhouse near Des Arc, Arkansas, on February 15, 1882.

A general invitation had been issued, probably by W. W. Tedford, to the farmers of the neighborhood. Nine came to the meeting, seven of them participating in forming the organization. A committee of three—W. T. McBee, John W. McBee, and W. W. Tedford—was appointed to draft a constitution. The committee prepared the constitution and reported back a week later. The name adopted was the Wattensas Farmers' Club. The objects of the organization were stated to be "the improvement of its members in the theory and practice of agriculture, and the dissemination of knowledge relative to rural and farming affairs." Later its objectives were stated to be (1) "action in concert with all labor unions or organizations of laborers," and (2) "to secure beneficial legis-

---

[8] Information on the Agricultural Wheel, unless otherwise documented, is from W. Scott Morgan, *History of Wheel and Alliance*. St. Louis: C. B. Woodward Publishing Co., 1891.

lation to farmers."[9] Its officers were to be a president, two vice-presidents, a secretary, a treasurer, and a chaplain, who would constitute the executive committee, and two sentinels. At the third meeting the name of this local organization was changed to Agricultural Wheel, and the causes for this change express an interesting philosophy. Morgan quotes Tedford as giving the following reason for adopting the new name: "No machinery can be run without a great drive wheel, and as that wheel moves and governs the entire machinery, however complex, so agriculture is the great wheel or power that controls the entire machinery of the world's industries." The articles of incorporation for this new organization were signed on August 22, 1882, at which time, according to Morgan, "there were about 100 subscribers to the Articles of Association of Wheel No. 1." Four other locals were organized in Prairie County and three in Cleburne County, and the organization then quickly spread throughout the whole state of Arkansas. A state Wheel was organized on April 9, 1883, at McBee's schoolhouse, and at the state meeting in the following July, it was reported that there were thirty-nine subordinate Wheels in the state. By the following January, 1884, 114 locals were reported, with a total membership of 5,000.

Morgan states that the organization spread so rapidly that competent lecturers or organizers could not be supplied, that twenty counties were represented by sixty-two delegates at a meeting of the state Wheel on July 22, 1885; and that at a subsequent meeting, October 15 of that year, 462 subordinate Wheels had been chartered and the order was spreading into other states. "Ten Wheels had been chartered in Alabama, three in Mississippi, and four in Texas."

At the annual meeting in 1886, members from a number of other states were present and the proposition of organizing a national Wheel was discussed. This same matter had been discussed two years before, but now a committee composed of delegates from Arkansas, Tennessee, and Kentucky took definite steps to consummate the national organization. A national constitution and by-laws were adopted by the Arkansas State Wheel and plans were made to push organization in other states.

————

[9] Wattensas was the name of a creek in the McBee community. For a detailed account of this club, see *Biographical and historical memoirs of eastern Arkansas,* pp. 60, 678. Chicago: Goodspeed Publishing Co., 1890.

At the 1887 annual meeting of the Arkansas State Wheel, held in July, practically every county in Arkansas was represented. This convention appointed a committee "to confer with the Farmers' Alliance of Texas and the Co-operative Union of Louisiana, with a view to securing co-operative action in trade." The Wheel was at this time equally active in economic projects and more militant in its political attitudes than the Texas Alliance. Furthermore, it had spread into a number of states outside Arkansas and had organizations in Tennessee, Kentucky, Missouri, Texas, Alabama, Mississippi, Indian Territory, and even one substantial local in Wisconsin. At the meeting of the national Wheel held one month following the joint meeting with the Alliance and Union at Shreveport, the national membership was said to be 500,000. The year following, it was claimed that there were 1,947 subordinate Wheels and a total membership of 75,000 in the State of Arkansas.[10]

THE BROTHERS OF FREEDOM

In 1885, the Arkansas Agricultural Wheel had absorbed another quite substantial farmers' organization in that state. The Brothers of Freedom was organized in Arkansas in 1882, the same year as the founding of the Agricultural Wheel, and at the time of its amalgamation with the Wheel was said to have had 643 subordinate organizations. It was a secret organization of farmers, the purpose of which was "to incite a proper rivalry among merchants and dealers." The scheme was to organize local clubs, each of which would appoint a delegate to a Common Council. Delegates from the various Common Councils constituted county Councils, and the county Councils did the work of making contracts and driving deals with merchants. The organization apparently spread rapidly, for it soon organized a Grand Council and claimed a larger membership than the Wheel in 1885 when it amalgamated with that organization. Isaac McCracken, its president, was immediately made president of the amalgamated organization.

---

[10] It is more than likely that Morgan's estimate was overoptimistic. Others estimated the Arkansas membership at never more than 60,000, and still others at much less. There is no evidence at all that the national membership reached anything approaching 500,000. See *White County Citizen* (Searcy, Arkansas), August, 24, 1892. *Biographical and historical memoirs of eastern Arkansas*, p. 60. For the best all-around discussion of the Wheel, see W. S. Morgan, *History of Wheel and Alliance*, chap. iii.

The Declaration of Principles of the Brothers of Freedom had set forth not only its general objectives, but indicated that its spirit was typical of that which had come to prevail almost everywhere among the farmers of the West and South. It said:

> We believe there is a God, the great Creator of all things, and that he created all men free and equal, and endowed them with certain inalienable rights, such as life, liberty, and the pursuit of happiness, and that these rights are a common inheritance and should be respected by all mankind.
> We further believe that any power or influence that tends to restrict or circumscribe any class of our citizens in the free exercise of these God-given rights and privileges is detrimental to the best interests of a free people.
> While it is an established fact that the laboring classes of mankind are the real producers of wealth, we find that they are gradually becoming oppressed by combinations of capital, and the fruits of their toil absorbed by a class who propose not only to live on the labors of others, but to speedily amass fortunes at their expense. Therefore, in order to protect ourselves from the oppression of said combinations of capital, and to secure the co-operation of the laboring classes in obtaining a just reward for the fruits of honest labor, we ordain the following constitution, by-laws, and rules of order . . .

The Brothers of Freedom was more than a farmers' organization; it also included industrial laborers and other townspeople. Brick Pomeroy, the famous Greenback editor, said its "object is to combine together farmers and laboring men for the purpose of social intercourse and to lessen the burdens of the members by living economically, keeping out of debt, avoiding the crop mortgage system, and purchasing supplies as a body corporate and selling at a profit of ten per cent to the members.[11] It apparently leaned toward politics more strongly than did the Wheel in the early days, for some members of the Wheel feared combining the two organizations because of the political activities of the Brothers of Freedom. The union, however, had been voted for by the Grand Wheel

----

[11] Quoted from Brick Pomeroy's *Democrat* by the Nashville *News* (Nashville, Arkansas), December 5, 1885.

in December, 1884, and was ratified by one subordinate Wheel after another during 1885.[12]

THE AMALGAMATION OF THE WHEEL, ALLIANCE, AND UNION

In the fall of 1887, at a meeting at Shreveport, Louisiana, something approaching an amalgamation of all southern farmers' organizations was effected. The National Farmers' Alliance and Co-operative Union of America met in October of that year for its first delegate convention subsequent to its hasty formation in January, 1887, by J. A. Tetts of the Louisiana Farmers' Union and delegates from the Texas Grand State Alliance. The meeting was outstanding not so much because of what it accomplished, but because there appeared at the meeting outstanding agricultural leaders from at least ten southern states. Among them was Colonel L. L. Polk of North Carolina, editor of *The Progressive Farmer* and representing the North Carolina Farmers' Clubs, who was later to be president and most outstanding leader of the whole Alliance movement. Delegates from the states of Texas, Arkansas, Alabama, Florida, Kentucky, Louisiana, North Carolina, Mississippi, Missouri, and Tennessee were represented. Not least in importance among the new initiates were the president and secretary-treasurer of the state Agricultural Wheel of Kentucky, and the secretary and the treasurer of the national Agricultural Wheel.[13]

It is not perfectly clear that the representatives from the Agricultural Wheel came as official delegates with power to negotiate a union. Nevertheless, the following resolutions were recommended by a conference committee on which sat members of the Wheel:

> That we, as delegates of the Farmers' Alliance and Agricultural Wheel, agree to accept, as a basis of union, the secret work of the Alliance and the national constitution of the same; each State accepting this basis of union to retain such name as they now have, if they so desire.

---

[12] *State Wheel-Enterprise* (Searcy, Arkansas), July 24, 1885. This paper was the official organ of the Grand Agricultural Wheel of the State of Arkansas.

[13] C. S. Walker, "The Farmers' Alliance," *Andover Review*, Vol. XIV, No. 80 (August, 1890), p. 136. For the complete proceedings of this meeting, see N. A. Dunning, pp. 66-77. For a characterization of Polk, see Diggs, pp. 593-594.

That the eligibility clause in the National Alliance constitution be explained by statutory enactment, showing that the State Alliance of Texas, or the State Farmers' Union of Louisiana, has no power to change this eligibility.

These resolutions indicate on the one hand a spirit of willingness to form a single South-wide organization, and on the other a fear on the part of Wheel members that their organization might lose its identity if union were accomplished. Two additional steps were taken looking toward the complete mobilization of all the southern states into one organization, ten of which were represented at the Shreveport meeting. A committee of the national Farmers' Alliance and Co-operative Union was appointed to meet with representatives of state Wheels present at the meeting to formulate a policy upon which the national Alliance and national Wheel might consolidate. A committee was appointed to attend the January meeting of the state Farmers' Association of North Carolina to negotiate, if possible, the inclusion of that organization in the amalgamation of all existing southern farmers' organizations.

The next meeting of the Alliance and Union was set for Meridian, Mississippi, for the fall of 1888. The convention of the national Wheel at its McKenzie meeting also voted to meet at this same time and place, " 'for the purpose of meeting with the Farmers' Alliance and Co-operative Union of America,' with a view to consolidating the two bodies."

A few days before assembling at Meridian, in December, 1888, the Alliance and Union had appointed a conference committee of three to meet with a like committee from the Wheel for the purpose of bringing in recommendations for union. Immediately upon assembling at Meridian, the Wheel appointed its conference committee. W. S. Morgan, author of the *History of the Wheel and Alliance,* was a member of the Wheel committee, and Colonel L. L. Polk was a member of the Alliance committee, although the North Carolina farmers' society had not yet acted on the proposal for union with the Alliance. The following is a complete report of this joint conference:

We, your Joint Committee, appointed to consider a plan for the consolidation of the National Agricultural Wheel and National Farmers' Alliance and Co-operative Union of America, beg leave to submit the following report:

1. We most heartily recommend the proposed consolidation of the two orders.

2. We recommend that the name of the consolidated order be The National Alliance Wheel and Co-operative Union of America.

3. We recommend that the two bodies meet in the courthouse, in this city, at 3 o'clock this afternoon, in joint session or in committee of the whole, to be presided over by the president of the National Alliance.

4. We recommend that on all questions or matters relating to the organic laws of such consolidated body, each body shall be entitled to an equal number of votes, and on all committees appointed to perfect such consolidation, the two bodies are to have equal representation, to be determined by their respective presidents.

Each organization in separate sessions adopted the recommendations of their conference committee for union and the first joint session was held the afternoon of the first day. It was decided to call the amalgamated organization The Farmers' and Laborers' Union of America, a name adopted probably because of certain advances which had been made by the Knights of Labor. The constitution adopted was similar to that of the Alliance.[14] The new organization was to supersede the old ones when three-fourths of the state organizations of each had ratified the union, and a proclamation to that effect had been issued by the respective presidents. The new organization elected officers and agreed to hold its first annual meeting in St. Louis, in December, 1889.

A proclamation declaring that the condition prescribed by the Meridian meeting had been met was signed by President Macune of the Alliance, President McCracken of the Wheel, and President Evan Jones of the new organization on September 24, 1889, and the Farmers' and Laborers' Union was declared the consolidated organization on and after September 30 of that year. N. A. Dunning says concerning the completion of this act: "Within two years and eight months from the birth of the National Alliance, three national orders [referring, of course, to the Alliance, Wheel, and Union] had been united into one, all in excellent

---

[14] *National Economist*, April 13, 1889, pp. 50-51, gives the constitutions of the Alliance, the Wheel, and the new one of the Farmers' and Laborers' Union. For a brief but accurate account of the various proceedings involving the union of the Wheel and the Alliance, see *National Economist*, April 13, 1889, p. 57.

working condition, with a system well in hand, and a membership comprising eighteen States and Territories and numbering fully one million people."

Yet, what the memberships of the different organizations were at the time they amalgamated and therefore what the joint membership of the Farmers' and Laborers' Union was in 1888 are not known. But it was recorded in the proclamation of union that three-fourths or more of the state Wheels and the state Alliances had ratified the new constitution. The names of the states which did ratify are known, and since there is no evidence that any of the states refused to ratify the amalgamation, it can probably be taken for granted that the list of ratifying states is identical with those which had effective organizations at that time. Fourteen states and one territory were listed by the Alliance, namely: Texas, Tennessee, Alabama, Louisiana, Kentucky, Kansas, Missouri, Virginia, North Carolina, South Carolina, Georgia, Mississippi, Florida, New Mexico, and Indian Territory. Nine states and one territory were listed by the Wheel as follows: Arkansas, Tennessee, Kentucky, Texas, Missouri, Alabama, Mississippi, Louisiana, Wisconsin, and Indian Territory.[15] Thus all southern states except Maryland, West Virginia, and Oklahoma were present and participated in the founding of this great farmers' organization. Two of these, Oklahoma and Maryland, were present at the next convention, at St. Louis.

THE NORTH CAROLINA FARMERS' ASSOCIATION

When the Farmers' Alliance entered North Carolina in 1887, it found the farmers of that state already well organized. Their organization had grown up under the tutelage of Colonel L. L. Polk and was led by him almost en masse into the Southern Farmers' Alliance after 1888. Colonel Polk, a farmer, a Granger, an editor of a weekly newspaper, a one-time representative in the state legislature, and the first State Commissioner of Agriculture, became editor of *The Progressive Farmer* in 1886 and began with its first issue to promote the organization of farmers' clubs. He had called two state-wide mass meetings of North Carolina farmers in January, 1887, the second of which resulted in the organization of

---

[15] *Ibid.,* September 28, 1889, p. 24.

the North Carolina Farmers' Association. He had laid the groundwork for such an organization through the pages of his paper by urging farmers to organize local clubs, publishing a model constitution for such clubs, and suggesting that they be organized in every community and township of the state. He had proposed that the local or township clubs then be federated into a county organization, and the county organizations in turn organized into a state farmers' association. There were 400 local clubs in the state of North Carolina when Colonel Polk attached himself to the Farmers' Alliance.[16] He and North Carolina, therefore, should be counted as much the originators of the great Southern Farmers' Alliance as were Texas, Arkansas, and Louisiana with their local and state organizations, all of which joined in 1888 and 1889 to form the Farmers' and Laborers' Union of America.

In both his weekly paper and *The Progressive Farmer*, Polk had vigorously promoted agricultural reforms of all types. In an address before an Inter-State Convention of Farmers in Atlanta, in August, 1887, he recapitulated what he had been preaching for years: that "Defects in the Agricultural System of the Cotton States," were the one-crop system, the Negro tenant system, cultivating much land poorly rather than a little land well, "want of practical training and agricultural education of the masses," and "want of unity of action or co-operation among our farmers." At that convention, Polk introduced a resolution looking to closer union and cooperation of the farmers of the South, and, ". . . if practicable, the co-operation of the whole country." He had joined a local Farmers' Alliance in Wake County, North Carolina, the month before he went to the Inter-State Farmers' Convention, and at that convention he met Dr. Macune, organizer of the Texas Alliance, now leader of the National Farmers' Alliance and Co-operative Union. Polk was elected president of the Inter-State Farmers' Association by acclamation, and the next year's convention was held in Raleigh, North Carolina, his home town.

Polk had organized his first Farmers' Club in April, 1886, and the pages of his *Progressive Farmer* were literally filled with promotion of such

---

[16] *Ibid.*, April 6, 1889, p. 35. John D. Hicks, "The Farmers' Alliance in North Carolina," *North Carolina Historical Review*, Vol. II, No. 2 (April, 1925), p. 169. *The Progressive Farmer* (Raleigh, North Carolina), May 14, 26, June 2, 1887. *News and Observer* (Raleigh, North Carolina), January 19, 27, 28, February 6, 1887.

clubs during the following two and one-half years. Noblin, who, like the writer, has studied those pages, says: "Week after week during the following year [1886-1887] the *Progressive Farmer* happily announced the birth and noted the progress of clubs in various parts of the state." Concerning the origin and growth of no other segment of what came to be the Alliance is one able to so completely trace the development of a movement at its grass roots. The topics discussed at local meetings were reported and topics suggested for discussion by Polk were reported in *The Progressive Farmer*. No less interesting were the reports on Polk's constant travels to speak at and help organize clubs. The whole movement was a crusade for better farming, adult farmers' education, economic justice, and organization.[17]

A few of Polk's suggestions reflected his experience as a Granger, but none of them suggests the organization of a secret society. He at first proposed that clubs meet in the homes of members, but his final proposal was for larger and more substantial clubs, something that could, and probably would, become a general farmers' organization. The plan was for local school-district or township clubs, which would send delegates to county organizations, the counties to send delegates to a state farmers' convention; and eventually the various state organizations, he said, "might meet as a national body." The local clubs should meet as often as possible, the county organization should meet once a month, and the state organization should hold an annual convention. Such a state convention was held, and the state organization was accomplished in North Carolina in January, 1887.

The first local Alliance was organized in North Carolina in June, 1887, and a state Alliance was organized on October 4, 1887. When the state Alliance met jointly with the Inter-State Farmers' Association in August, 1888, it reported a total of 1,018 local Alliances and 53 county Alliances, with a total membership of 42,000. The North Carolina Farmers' Association had been officially absorbed by the state Farmers' Alliance in January, 1888, and Colonel Polk, together with S. B. Alexander, president of the state Alliance, attended the first annual meeting of the Texas Alliance and the Louisiana Union at Meridian, Mississippi, in December of that year.

———

[17] Stuart Noblin, *Leonidas LaFayette Polk, agrarian crusader*, especially chap. ix. Chapel Hill: University of North Carolina Press, 1949.

They returned to North Carolina and made it one of the strongest Farmers' Alliance states in the South in less than two years. In 1890, every county in the state except one had a county Alliance. There were 2,147 sub-Alliances with a total membership of 90,000.[18]

The North Carolina Farmers' Association did not contribute such great numbers to the amalgamated farmers' organization, by that time the Farmers' Alliance and Co-operative Union, as had the Texas Alliance or the Arkansas Wheel and Brothers of Freedom, but it did contribute a much more solidly organized constituency because of the preparation Colonel Polk had provided to the numerous farmers' clubs, which were organized from the ground up, and it contributed Colonel L. L. Polk, who, within two years, became president of the national organization and its greatest leader.[19]

This amalgamation of various farmers' organizations into a section-wide organization was something new in the Farmers' Movement. The Grange, fifteen years earlier, had fed upon the organization of farmers' local clubs, but never effected the absorption of any outstanding farmers' organization, unless the California Farmers' Union could be considered as such. The Farmers' and Laborers' Union, on the other hand, was the amalgamation of at least five farmers' organizations, each one of which had grown into some magnitude before it combined with the others. The Brothers of Freedom and the Agricultural Wheel had joined hands in 1885; the Louisiana Farmers' Union and the Texas Alliance had joined hands in 1887; the North Carolina Farmers' Association was absorbed by the Alliance in early 1888; and later that year, at the Meridian meeting, all of these were amalgamated into one organization. The first meeting of the amalgamated organization was set for St. Louis the following year, at which time and place similar organizations in the northern states also

---

[18] Adolph J. Honeycutt, *The Farmers' Alliance in North Carolina*, Master's Thesis, unpublished. Raleigh, North Carolina: North Carolina State College of Agriculture and Engineering, 1925. Hicks, "The Farmers' Alliance in North Carolina," p. 171.

[19] It is fortunate that Professor Noblin has contributed an authoritative biography of Colonel Polk—*Leonidas LaFayette Polk, Agrarian Crusader*. This book furnishes a record of events and the story of a personality, both of which are exceedingly valuable to an understanding of how a movement arises and develops. This book, plus Professor Honeycutt's thesis, and the writer's opportunity to read practically all of Colonel Polk's writings, has provided the understanding so greatly needed and not so far found on other early segments of the Farmers' Movement. The reader's attention is called especially to chaps. xii-xv in Noblin's book.

agreed to meet. Two of these northern organizations were comparatively large: the National Farmers' Alliance, popularly known as the Northern Farmers' Alliance, and the Farmers' Mutual Benefit Association.

Although the Agricultural Wheel was a southern organization, there was a Wheel in Wisconsin. It did not, however, have representation at either the Meridian or St. Louis meetings. Indiana, another northern state, did have delegates at the St. Louis convention of the Southern Alliance. They were representing the Mutual Benefit Association and were seated in the Alliance convention.

THE NATIONAL (NORTHERN OR NORTHWESTERN) FARMERS' ALLIANCE

While the powerful and militant Southern Alliance was being built from various sources throughout the South, things were again stirring among the farmers of the North and West. The *Western Rural*, an agricultural journal published in Chicago, began almost immediately upon the rapid decline of the Grange in the Middle West to agitate for a new farmers' organization. Discussion of taxes, money, and transportation injustice to farmers appeared in its pages regularly in 1877 and 1878. A series of articles on "Cheap Transportation" was published by it in the early part of 1879; and an editorial, in November, 1879, proposed the organization of "cheap transportation clubs" throughout the Middle West. This editorial suggested that such clubs have regular organic setups and meet once a month.[20] As far as is known, this suggestion was never followed, although the Granges that were left and other farmers' clubs undoubtedly discussed the matter at their regular meetings.

Finally Milton George, editor of the *Western Rural*, on March 6, 1880, through the pages of his paper, issued a call for an organization meeting. The call was followed by articles and editorials, and a meeting was held in the office of the *Western Rural* on April 15, 1880. How many persons appeared for this meeting is not known, but a farmers' organization of Cook County, Illinois, resulted. The organization called itself Cook County Farmers' Alliance No. 1. A constitution which had been previously published in the *Western Rural* was adopted, officers were elected, and the

---

[20] *Western Rural*, November 29, 1879; January 24, March 6, 1880; March 12, 1881.

decision made to constitute the Cook County local a temporary Central Alliance until twenty-five subordinates could be chartered to organize a national organization. The president and secretary were authorized to grant charters to any seven farmers who might make application and pay 25 cents. The Cook County Alliance was to meet every two weeks in the *Western Rural* office.[21]

Through the office of this farm journal a number of charters were distributed, and the organization began to grow in a loose sort of way. The National Alliance was organized on October 14, 1880, at a meeting held in Farwell Hall, Chicago. The *Western Rural* had offered to pay the expenses of delegates to a meeting for that purpose and about 500 farmers, Alliance delegates and others, came from thirteen different states—Illinois, Iowa, Nebraska, Wisconsin, Michigan, Missouri, Texas, Kentucky, Indiana, Ohio, Massachusetts, Rhode Island, and New York. The convention consumed most of the day in discussing transportation problems, but the resolutions passed covered the whole gamut of farmers' grievances prevalent for a decade. Seven rather wordy resolutions were passed, the contents of which demanded that Congress control the railroads, that political parties "nominate . . . men . . . who will work and vote to place the producers upon an equal footing with monopolies," and that those agricultural journals and farmers' organizations that would lead the fight should be supported. A constitution was adopted providing for local, state, and national Alliances. The objects of such organizations were stated to be as follows:

To unite the farmers of the United States for their protection against class legislation, the encroachments of concentrated capital, and the tyranny of monopoly; to provide against being imposed upon by swindlers, and swindling advertisements in the public prints; to oppose, in our respective political parties, the election of any candidate to office, state or national, who is not thoroughly in sympathy with the farmers' interests; to demand that the existing political parties shall nominate farmers, or those who are in sympathy with them, for all offices within the gift of the people; and to do anything, in a legitimate manner, that may serve to benefit the producer.

———

[21] *Ibid.*, March 6, 20, April 2, 10, 24, 1880. James W. Witham, *Fifty years on the firing line*, pp. 26-29, 50-51. Published by the author, 1924.

Mr. W. J. Fowler, secretary of the New York State Farmers' Alliance, was made president, and Milton George, editor of the *Western Rural*, was elected as one of the vice-presidents of the national organization.[22] George seems to have been left a free hand in issuing charters, and within a year's time it was claimed that not less than 1,000 locals had been organized.

Nebraska organized the first state Alliance on January 5 and 6, 1881, with delegates from twenty-five counties, and within eighteen months state Alliances had been organized in eight states—Nebraska, Kansas, Iowa, Wisconsin, Illinois, Minnesota, Michigan, and New York.[23] When the second annual convention was held in Chicago, October, 1881,[24] the secretary reported the organization had acquired a total membership of 24,500, with Nebraska, Kansas, and Iowa taking the lead in the order named. At the third annual meeting, in St. Louis, October, 1882, it was claimed that there were 2,000 locals with a combined membership of 100,000. The organization movement lagged somewhat with improved conditions in 1883 and 1884, but took on renewed life with the slump in wheat prices in 1885.[25] The Dakota Territorial Alliance was added in 1885 and the order was introduced into Colorado during that year.

———

[22] The only document which gives an authoritative account of the origin and early development of the national Farmers' Alliance, so far as the writer knows, is the *Western Rural year book*. The information thus far presented is largely from that document and the files of the *Western Rural*. See "History of Alliance Movement," *Western Rural year book, 1886*, pp. 130-143. Other sources carrying brief accounts are: Chicago *Daily Tribune*, October 15, 1880. Witham, p. 51. W. A. Peffer, "The Farmers' Defensive Movement," *Forum*, Vol. VIII, No. 4 (December, 1889), pp. 472-473. N. A. Dunning, p. 232. J. E. Bryan, pp. 57-58. Hicks, p. 99. Frank M. Drew, "The Present Farmers' Movement," *Political Science Quarterly*, Vol. VI, No. 2 (June, 1891), pp. 282-283.

[23] Witham, pp 51, 62. Hicks, pp. 99, 100-101. Omaha *Daily Bee*, January 7, 8, 1881. *Western Rural*, November 13, 1880; October 15, 1881. New York had a state Alliance in existence before the Chicago meeting. It had organized in March, 1877. The writer sees no object in discussing the controversy about either the New York Alliance or Kansas "Settlers' Protective Association," both of which claim the credit for being forerunners of both the Northern and Southern Alliances. It is doubtful that such was the case in any causal sense. Any reader interested in the controversy should see N. A. Dunning, pp. 10-13, 230-232. Hicks, pp. 97-98. *Western Rural*, October 23, November 20, December 4, 1880. E. G. Blood, *Handbook and history of the National Farmers' Alliance and Industrial Union*, Washington, D. C.: 1893.

[24] Chicago *Daily Tribune*, October 6, 7, 1881. J. E. Bryan, p. 59. Hicks, p. 101. Buck, *The Granger movement*, p. 119.

[25] See files of *Western Rural*, especially issues of October 15, 1881; May 27, November 4, 1882. Hicks, p. 101.

In his enthusiasm George began issuing honorary membership to anyone who demonstrated interest, and although the *Western Rural* gave
glowing accounts of progress from 1886 on, it is impossible to record any
accurate account of the growing strength of the Northern Alliance because it collected no dues, had practically no eligibility rules, and no
national records. The *Western Rural Year Book, 1886* says, "the object of
the Alliance to secure proper representation in the halls of legislation . . .
should not be lost sight of," [26] and thousands of farmers were meeting
in locally organized groups to discuss this objective.

There is no question about the steady growth of the Northern Alliance
between the time it was organized and 1889, when it held its national
convention at St. Louis and gave consideration to the possibility of joining with the Southern Alliance. Nationally, however, it was pretty much
a project of Milton George and the *Western Rural*. There were only seven
states and territories represented in the 1887 annual meeting, although
it is more than likely twice that number would have been entitled to
representation had they appeared at the meeting. In "The Farmers' Defensive Movement," Senator Peffer stated that "the membership of the National Farmers' Alliance is little, if at all, short of 400,000 and is spreading."
Its chief strength lay in the seven states of Kansas, New York, Nebraska,
Minnesota, Missouri, Illinois, Iowa, and Dakota Territory, with Kansas
probably the strongest, claiming 130,000 members.[27]

President Burrows had asked the executive committee of the Northern
Alliance as early as February, 1888, to give consideration to amalgamation
with the Southern Alliance, and President Macune of the Southern
Alliance spoke before the convention of the Northern Alliance in January, 1889.[28] The next meeting of the Northern Alliance was held in St.
Louis in December, 1889, at the same time as the meeting of the Southern Alliance.

———

[26] *Western Rural*, October 13, 1883; February 9, 1884.

[27] *Ibid.*, February 9, December 27, 1884; January 3, 17, March 7, 1885; May 22, 1886;
October 8, 15, 1887. N. A. Dunning, p. 225.
    For an account of the 1887 meeting, see Minneapolis *Tribune*, October 4, 5, 6,
1887. J. E. Bryan, pp. 60-63. Peffer, "The Farmers' Defensive Movement," p. 473.
Frank L. McVey, "The Populist Movement," *Economic Studies*, Vol. I, No. 3
(August, 1896), p. 196. Elizabeth N. Barr, "The Populist Uprising," from William
Connelly, ed., *A standard history of Kansas and Kansans*, Vol. II, p. 1141. New York:
Lewis Historical Publishing Company, 1918.

[28] *Western Rural*, February 16, 1889.

THE FARMERS' MUTUAL BENEFIT ASSOCIATION

At the same time that the Northern Alliance was picking up the Farmers' Movement in the western part of the corn belt, another organization had started in southern Illinois and was spreading over somewhat the same territory. The Farmers' Mutual Benefit Association arose in Johnson County, Illinois, in either 1882 or 1883. Its organization is said to have been inspired by the protest of five wheat farmers who formed a local shipping pool after they had tried and failed to get a number of different local buyers to compete for the purchase of their wheat. Their meeting to discuss the wheat-shipping project was the beginning of a regular club. Five clubs were formed in the county that winter; and sometime during the winter they met together, adopted a constitution and secret work, and formed the Farmers' Mutual Benefit Association. Each local club was constituted an agent to organize other clubs and promote the growth of the organization.[29]

The general scheme of organization was at that time a system of locals, the members of which met every three months in the General Assembly, the supreme body of the organization. Between the meetings of the General Assembly, new locals were organized as branches of existing locals and were chartered by the General Assembly when it met.

The details of the growth of the organization seem not to have been recorded, but a report to the *Western Rural* in 1887 stated that the organization increased its membership from 2,000 in 1886 to 15,000 in 1887. It apparently later followed somewhat the practice of the Northern Alliance in obtaining members, for in a report to the *Western Rural* in 1890, it was said that 127 applications had been received in one day at the headquarters of the organization and that there were 1,000 branches in the state. Another report said there were 2,000 members in Christian County, Illinois, alone.[30]

---

[29] This is a story gathered from N. A. Dunning, pp. 226-228, and from reports in the *Western Rural*. Winter debating clubs and literary societies were very general and widely attended in the rural districts of the Middle West during this period and for twenty years afterward. It may not, therefore, have been so much the wheat-shipping project as a combination of the ideas of secret organizations, stimulated by Grange experience, and the custom of holding literary meetings that gave rise to the F.M.B.A.

[30] *Western Rural*, November 26, 1887; February 22, March 22, 1890. Also see *National Economist*, November 8, 1890, p. 121.

The organization was incorporated in 1887 and the Articles of Incorporation states its objects to be as follows:

> ... to unite the farmers of the State of Illinois, and of the United States, in all matters pertaining to the interests of their calling; to devise ways and means whereby they may more effectually promote their general welfare; to improve the modes of agriculture, horticulture and stock raising; to adopt and encourage such rotation of crops as may improve rather than impoverish the soil; to devise and encourage such systems of concentration and co-operation as may diminish the cost of production, and of farm life and farm operations; to provide for the extension of the benefits of said association by organizing and chartering subordinate associations in such manner as may from time to time be prescribed by the rules and regulations of the association.

The motto of the organization was:

> Equal and exact justice to all; special privileges and immunities to none; charity to those in poverty, affliction or distress, and especially to those of our own Order.[31]

The scheme of organization after 1887 was a general assembly, state assemblies, county assemblies, and subordinate lodges. Ten male citizens, each over twenty-one years of age, could form a subordinate lodge and be furnished a charter by the General Assembly.[32]

The Farmers' Mutual Benefit Association had had representatives at the Meridian, Mississippi, meeting of the Southern Alliance in 1888 and also sent representatives to the meeting at St. Louis in December, 1889. At that time it had 2,180 subordinates and a national membership of about 150,000 in the ten states of Missouri, Iowa, Indiana, Ohio, West Virginia, Kentucky, Illinois, Kansas, Nebraska, and North Carolina.[33]

---

[31] E. A. Allen, *The life and public services of James Baird Weaver [and] ... James G. Field,* pp. 410, 413. People's Party Publishing Co., 1892. *General charter, declaration of purpose, and constitution and by-laws of the Farmers' Mutual Benefit Association,* pp. 4-5, 9. Mt. Vernon, Illinois: F.M.B.A. Printing Co., 1890.

[32] E. A. Allen, pp. 413, 415.

[33] *National Economist,* January 4, 1890, p. 242.

· 220 ·

NEGRO AGRICULTURAL WHEELS AND ALLIANCES

The Agricultural Wheel removed the word "white" from its eligibility rules in 1886, and made provisions for organizing Negroes into separate Wheels. Whether there were any Negro organizations of the Wheel formed prior to that time, the writer does not know. The Alliance of Colored Farmers of Texas, however, was formed in December, 1886, by a number of locals which had been organized just previous to this time. By 1890, there were state organizations of the Colored Farmers' National Alliance and Co-operative Union in ten southern states—Texas, Louisiana, Mississippi, Alabama, Georgia, Florida, South Carolina, North Carolina, Virginia, and Tennessee. In January, 1891, the national organization claimed to have 1,250,000 members in thirty different states, of which 700,000 were adult males and 150,000 were males under twenty-one years of age. At that time state associations were chartered in eleven states.[34] The Colored Alliance held its annual meeting in St. Louis in December, 1889, at the same time the other farmers' organizations held theirs.

OTHER AGRICULTURAL ORGANIZATIONS OF THE EIGHTIES

In order to make complete the story of farmers' organizations throughout the United States before the great gathering at St. Louis in December, 1889, it is necessary to mention a few others less well known than those thus far discussed. None of them created the furor which each of the major ones, just described, did, but each contributed to the growth and spirit of the Farmers' Movement during this decade.

First was the *Farmers' Congress,* the aims and purposes of which, as stated by its president, Colonel Robert Beverly of Virginia, in 1879 or 1880, were: "*First,* to arouse agriculturists themselves to a realization... that the tillers of the soil are a clear majority of *all the people*... and *secondly,* to enforce a recognition of it upon the representatives of the people who have been delegated to administer the State and national

---

[34] *Ibid.,* March 14, 1889, pp. 6-7; September 9, p. 409; December 14, pp. 200-201. N. A. Dunning, pp. 288-292. Drew, pp. 287-288. Hicks, pp. 114-115. The state organizations existent in 1890 as listed above are from N. A. Dunning. However, the *National Economist,* in December, 1889, listed Kentucky and Indian Territory as having state Negro associations and did not include Texas and Georgia.

governments." Seventeen states were represented at its fourth annual meeting in 1884, twelve at its 1885 meeting, and twenty-five at its 1886 convention. In 1887, it held its annual meeting in Washington, D. C. and claimed to have "made an impression on Congress, then in session." [35] Colonel Beverly said that the Farmers' Congress was the real forerunner of the Farmers' Alliance movement.

The *Farmers' League* was an organization which originated among the farmers of Massachusetts in 1889 and spread quickly throughout the New England states, New York, and Pennsylvania. It was based on township units and its sole condition of membership was that a person pay 50 cents and sign a pledge to work for the election of persons who would faithfully represent farmers in the enactment of legislation. N. A. Dunning says that it had about 50,000 members around 1890, and Herbert Myrick, its national secretary, said in 1891 that a sufficient number of local and county Leagues were being perfected to lead to the organization of state Leagues in twenty-two states in addition to the six already organized.[36] It was not the object of the League to compete with other farmers' organizations for membership, but to furnish a political instrument through which they could enforce their legislative demands.

The *Patrons of Industry*, while not strictly a farmers' organization, began trying just at the end of the decade to mobilize "agriculturists and laborers" into one organization, "to promote their rights and interests by protecting them by means of independent co-operative political action from the rapacious and avaricious greed of organized monopoly." It started in Michigan, where by 1890 it claimed a membership of 80,000, and soon spread to some thirteen northwestern states.

The *Grange*, of course, was still in existence in about thirty states all during the decade, and while the organization as a whole lost about six-

---

[35] *Farmers' congress of the United States, proceedings of the fifth annual session at Indianapolis (Indiana), 2nd and 3rd of December, 1885; farmers' congress of the United States, proceedings of the sixth annual session at St. Paul, Minnesota, August 25th to 30th, 1886.* Indianapolis: printed by A. R. Baker, 1886. For short considerations of this organization, see "The Farmers' Alliance," editorial in *The New York Times*, December 14, 1890. "A Non-Partisan Farmers' Organization," *Review of Reviews*, Vol. X, No. 56 (September, 1894), p. 303.

[36] E. A. Allen, pp. 450-468. N. A. Dunning, pp. 228-229. N. B. Ashby, *The riddle of the sphinx*, pp. 454-464. Chicago: Mercantile Publishing and Advertising Co., 1892. H. R. Chamberlain, "Farmers' Alliance and Other Political Parties," *Chautauqua*, Vol. XIII, No. 3 (June, 1891), p. 341.

sevenths of its 1875 membership, there were a few states in which it actually gained strength.

Not all of these organizations participated in the great farmers' convention that was held in St. Louis in December, 1889, but those which did represented about twenty-five states and probably spoke for well over one million members. Before we tell the story of that convention, the results of which were primarily felt in the next decade, a look should be taken at the causes for such a stupendous uprising as had occurred in the eighties, and a brief survey made of what the various farmers' organizations had attempted to accomplish.

· 10 ·

DEMANDS

AND ACCOMPLISHMENTS

OF THE ALLIANCE

THE ECONOMIC BACKGROUND AND CONDITIONS
IN THE EIGHTIES

The complaints of the farmers of the West and South were about the same in the eighties as they had been in the seventies, for the very good reason that their economic conditions were about the same. Wholesale prices of farm products recovered gradually from 1878 to 1882 and then began a decline which continued for almost fifteen years, with the exception of a slight -recovery in 1887 and 1888. The wholesale farm price index, which had stood at 99 in 1882, fell to 67 in 1889 and to 56 in 1896.[1] The prices of the three major farm products—cotton, wheat, and corn—upon which the West and South depended for cash, fell steadily all during the decade 1880-1890. Cotton sold as low as 6 cents per pound in Texas, corn as low as 10 cents per bushel in Kansas, and wheat as low as 42 cents per bushel in Nebraska during the eighties.[2] Economists

---

[1] "Wholesale Prices of Farm and Nonagricultural Products, 1798-1938."

[2] *First report of the Secretary of Agriculture, 1889,* pp. 261-263. Washington, D. C.: Government Printing Office, 1889.

claimed at the time that this decline in prices was due to a breakdown in world markets, but this meant nothing to the farmer, who was told of the rapid accumulation of fortunes running into the millions, earned largely out of railroad ventures and stock manipulations.[3] Nor were the things told him mere fairy stories. The truth is that the per capita wealth of the nation increased steadily after the close of the Civil War and there were approximately 4,000 millionaires and billionaires in the country in 1890, whose aggregate property was worth about $12,000,000,000.[4] The amount of capital invested in manufacturing establishments increased steadily from the end of the Civil War for thirty years, but the number of establishments steadily decreased. The capital value in cotton mills increased from $99,000,000 in 1860 to about $461,000,000 in 1890, but the number of establishments decreased 186. The establishments for the manu-facturing of agricultural machinery increased their capital value from $14,000,000 in 1860 to $145,000,000 in 1890, but the number of establish-ments decreased from 2,116 to 910.[5] Similar concentration was going on in a great many other industries. There was, therefore, a semblance of truth to the contention of farmers that monopolies were developing on all industrial fronts.

Furthermore, while the newer states of Nebraska, Kansas, and Texas were still making land grants and giving subsidies to the railroads, inves-tors in the earlier railroad projects were being squeezed out through liquidation processes. Many railroads went into the hands of receivers between 1880 and 1900. Between July, 1885, and November, 1886, Kansas municipalities, for instance, contributed $10,000,000 to railroads; and by 1890 the total assistance given by state and local sources was almost

---

[3] Herman C. Nixon, "The Economic Basis of the Populist Movement in Iowa," *Iowa Journal of History and Politics*, Vol. XXI, No. 3 (July, 1923), p. 387. Thorstein B. Veblen, "The Price of Wheat since 1867," *Journal of Political Economy*, Vol. I, No. 1 (December, 1892), pp. 68-103.

[4] George K. Holmes, "The Concentration of Wealth," *Political Science Quarterly*, Vol. VIII, No. 4 (December, 1893), p. 593.

[5] *Twelfth census of the United States, taken in the year 1900, Census reports,* Vol. IX: William R. Merriam, Director, *Manufactures*, Part III, p. 27. Washington, D. C.: United States Census Office, 1902. *Twelfth census of the United States, taken in the year 1900, Census reports,* Vol. X: Merriam, *Manufactures*, Part IV, p. 344. Wash-ington, D. C.: United States Census Office, 1903.

$75,000,000.[6] The railroad companies built 18,314 miles of road in 1882 and 1883, or 5,000 miles more than had been built in 1870 and 1871. Two years later, 1884 and 1885, eighty-one railway corporations having 19,000 miles of track were placed in receivership, while thirty-seven smaller railroads were sold under foreclosure.[7] These transactions, while not polluted with such private and public corruption as in the case of the Credit Mobilier, served to squeeze out most of the small investors, leave the chief ownership of the roads in the hands of a few such financiers as Morgan, Harriman, Gould, Vanderbilt, and Hill, and the debts for subsidies to be paid by the people through whose areas the roads had been built.[8] Not until 1887, when President Cleveland by executive order withdrew 21,000,000 acres of land from the contingent indemnity list and reopened them to settlement, did the federal government finally break what the farmers felt was a semimonopoly of the western lands by the railroad companies.[9]

Probably no great number of farmers, or other group of persons for that matter, saw clearly what was going on as a result of the great economic trends in the nation. But a movement does not rise or grow on the basis of cold analysis of any causal relationship of facts. It arises and grows out of the immediacy of conditions which impinge upon the everyday life of some great segment of a population. Detailed studies of the rise of the Farmers' Alliance in some half dozen states and a number of books written during the period in which that organization was in its ascendancy furnish a picture of the immediate conditions out of which the second

---

[6] Hallie Farmer, "The Economic Background of Frontier Populism," *Mississippi Valley Historical Review*, Vol. X, No. 4 (March, 1924), p. 413. Raymond C. Miller, "The Economic Background of Populism in Kansas," *Mississippi Valley Historical Review*, Vol. XI, No. 4 (March, 1925), pp. 470-471. John D. Hicks, *The Populist revolt, a history of the Farmers' Alliance and the People's party*, p. 69. Minneapolis: University of Minnesota Press, 1931.

[7] Katharine Coman, *The industrial history of the United States*, p. 348. New York: The Macmillan Company, 1912. *Statistical abstract of the United States, 1909*, p. 287. Prepared by the Bureau of Statistics, under the direction of the Secretary of Commerce and Labor. Washington, D. C.: Government Printing Office, 1910.

[8] Coman, pp. 349-352. Frank H. Spearman, *The strategy of great railroads*. New York: Charles Scribner's Sons, 1904.

[9] Benjamin H. Hibbard, *A history of the public land policies*, p. 249. New York: Peter Smith, 1939.

great tide of the Farmers' Movement following the Civil War swept the nation.[10]

In the old Granger states of Iowa and Illinois, farmers were being driven out of the production of wheat by the competition of wheat-producing areas farther west; the increased use of farm machinery was steadily increasing the cash costs of production; and farm-mortgage indebtedness, farm tenancy, and local taxes were all increasing. In the South, old plantations were crumbling under mortgage foreclosures; crop liens were becoming the established system of production credit; tenancy was increasing at an alarming rate; and the number of acres in farms, especially in the older sections, was actually decreasing. Colonel L. L. Polk, president of the Farmers' Alliance in 1890, probably expressed the feelings of thousands of farmers throughout the nation when he said:

> There is something radically wrong in our industrial system. There is a screw loose. The wheels have dropped out of balance. The railroads have never been so prosperous, and yet agriculture languishes. The banks have never done a better or more profitable business, and yet agriculture languishes. Manufacturing enterprises never made more money or were in a more flourishing condition, and yet agriculture languishes. Towns and cities flourish and "boom" and grow and "boom," and yet agriculture languishes. Salaries and fees were never so temptingly high and desirable, and yet agriculture languishes.[11]

THE GRIEVANCES AND DEMANDS OF THE ALLIANCE

The grievances of the farmers during the eighties were stated in the discussions and resolutions of the conventions of the great farm organizations of that decade and by the writers who spoke for them in books,

---

[10] The titles of some of the fugitive books and pamphlets which appeared during this period and the beginning of the following decade reflect the thinking of men who contributed greatly to the ideologies of the Farmers' Movement at that time. In addition to N. A. Dunning's and W. S. Morgan's books, which were attempts to record the history of farmers' organizations, were such as the following: Benjamin R. Davenport, *The crime of caste in our country.* Philadelphia: Keystone Publishing Co., 1893. N. B. Ashby, *The riddle of the sphinx,* previously cited. W. H. Harvey, *Coin's financial school.* Chicago: Coin Publishing Co., 1894. William A. Peffer, *The farmer's side,* previously cited.

[11] *The Progressive Farmer,* April 28, 1887.

pamphlets, and the current publications of the time. These grievances, for the most part, had to do with (1) railroads—freight and passenger rates, free passes, watered stocks, discrimination, thefts of land, connections of railroads with grain elevators, and subsidies of railroads as causes of high taxes; (2) monopolies—especially in manufacturing, transportation, and banking; (3) low prices for farm products; (4) debts—mortgages and crop liens; (5) tariffs; and (6) cheap money. The extent to which these grievances became matters of public concern is reflected by articles which appeared in periodicals that circulated widely among the whole reading public. The titles of some of these articles, and the names of the periodicals in which they appeared, will serve to indicate how a movement spreads to other segments of society than those immediately concerned. Note the following: "The Embattled Farmers," [12] "The Farmers' Defensive Movement," [13] "The Tariff and the Farmer," [14] The "Decadence of Farming," [15] "Western Feeling toward the East," [16] "Why the Farmer Is Not Prosperous," [17] "When the Farmer Will Be Prosperous," [18] "The Discontent of the Farmer," [19] "The Farmers' Alliance," [20] "A Bundle of Western Letters," [21] "The Discontent of the Farmer," [22] "The Farmers' Movement," [23] "The Farmers' Movement," [24] "Western Mortgages," [25] "Farmers' Alliance and Other Political Parties." [26] These are but a few of the dozens of similar magazine articles. Discussions were also appearing in metropolitan newspapers, and the pages of many country weeklies were dominated with farmer movement news for almost a decade.

———

[12] W. Gladden, *Forum*, November, 1890.

[13] W. A. Peffer, *Forum*, December, 1899.

[14] John G. Carlisle, *Forum*, January, 1890.

[15] J. Benton, *Popular Science Monthly*, November, 1889.

[16] W. V. Allen, *North American Review*, May, 1896.

[17] C. W. Davis, *Forum*, April, 1890.

[18] C. W. Davis, *Forum*, May, 1890.

[19] E. W. Bemis, *Journal of Political Economy*, March, 1893.

[20] C. S. Walker, *Andover Review*, August, 1890.

[21] *Review of Reviews*, July, 1894.

[22] J. R. Dodge, *Century Magazine*, January, 1892.

[23] *Public Opinion*, January 10, 1891.

[24] C. S. Walker, *Annals, American Academy of Political and Social Science*, March, 1894.

[25] J. W. Gleed, *Forum*, November, 1890.

[26] H. R. Chamberlain, *The Chautauquan*, June, 1891.

Most of the organizations started, just as the Grange did, with the avowal that they were nonpartisan and for the most part nonpolitical. All of them drifted rapidly into the habit of making legislative demands and finally ended their careers in a giant political upheaval.

The Texas Alliance complained in 1884 of middlemen costs and the manipulation of the cotton market. A little later (1886), they complained of the great amount of land held by railroads, the failure of corporations to pay their share of taxes, the lack of circulating currency, high freight rates, the lack of governmental regulation of railroads, and again stated their claim that the prices for cotton were "swallowed up" by the middlemen and manipulated by buyers and manufacturers.

No detailed records of the Louisiana Farmers' Union are available, but its constitution, adopted in 1885, specified that it would work for more equitable taxation, equal rights in transportation, lower rates of interest, and cheaper administration of laws.

The Agricultural Wheel and its joint organization, the Brothers of Freedom, were outspoken in their grievances and militant in their demands from the start. The Brothers of Freedom was organized for the specific purpose of forcing competition between local merchants. The Wheel, in the preamble to its constitution, stated in part:

> We hold to the principle that all monopolies are dangerous to the best interests of our country, tending to enslave a free people and subvert and finally overthrow the great principles purchased by Washington and his glorious compatriots.
>
> We hold to the principle that the laboring classes have an inherent right to sell and buy, when and wherever their best interests are served, and patronize none who dare, by word or action, oppose a just, fair and equitable exchange of the products of our labor.
>
> We denounce as unfair and unjust any set of men who sell at large profits, and gain the advantage over the laboring classes and obtain the product of their labor at greatly reduced prices, thus forcing patronage and constituting a hateful monopoly, making free and independent men slaves.[27]

In 1884, a resolution passed by the state meeting said, "The mortgage system in general is a blight upon the energy and industry of our com-

[27] W. S. Morgan, pp. 63-64.

mon country"; and the organization was especially bitter in its criticism of a state "law granting liens and mortgages upon stock or growing crops." [28]

After the Texas and Louisiana organizations amalgamated in 1887 into the National Farmers' Alliance and Co-operative Union of America, they complained about high protective tariffs, demonetization of silver, large land holdings of railroads, "syndicates or any other form or name of monopoly," high public debts and class legislation, and demanded free coinage of silver and a graduated income tax.

The St. Louis meeting in 1889 came near summarizing all the grievances and stating all the demands of the Southern Alliance. The organization, now officially known as the Farmers' and Laborers' Union of America, had swept into its ranks all of the southern organizations and was, by right of this fact and its almost ten years of discussion and experience, in a position to speak the mind of southern agriculture. President Jones, in his annual address, especially emphasized the "monopolization of finance," the "shrinking and insufficient volume" of money, the "enslavement by mortgages," the "wholesale absorption of land by aggregated capital," and the political power of "various rings, trusts, and combines, that now oppress our people and threaten the overthrow of our free institutions." [29] The demands of that convention constituted in a way the first step in the formation of a Populist party platform. These demands were:

1. That we demand the abolition of national banks, and the substitution of legal tender treasury notes in lieu of national bank notes, issued in sufficient volume to do the business of the country on a cash system; regulating the amount needed on a per capita basis, as the business interests of the country expand; and that all money issued by the government shall be legal tender in payment of all debts, both public and private.

2. That we demand that Congress shall pass such laws as shall effectually prevent the dealing in futures of all agricultural and mechanical productions; preserving a stringent system of procedure in trials as shall secure the prompt conviction, and imposing such penalties as shall secure the most perfect compliance with the law.

[28] *Ibid.*, pp. 70-71.
[29] For President Jones' address, see *National Economist*, December 21, 1889, pp. 210-211. Or N. A. Dunning, pp. 99-105.

3. That we demand the free and unlimited coinage of silver.

4. That we demand the passage of laws prohibiting the alien ownership of land, and that Congress take early steps to devise some plan to obtain all lands now owned by aliens and foreign syndicates; and that all lands now held by railroad and other corporations, in excess of such as is actually used and needed by them, be reclaimed by the government and held for actual settlers only.

5. Believing in the doctrine of "Equal rights to all and special privileges to none," we demand that taxation, national or State, shall not be used to build up one interest or class at the expense of another.

We believe that the money of the country should be kept as much as possible in the hands of the people, and hence we demand that all revenues, national, State, or county, shall be limited to the necessary expenses of the government, economically and honestly administered.

6. That Congress issue a sufficient amount of fractional paper currency to facilitate exchange through the medium of the United States mail.

7. We demand that the means of communication and transportation shall be owned by and operated in the interest of the people, as is the United States postal system.[30]

The detailed activities of the northern organizations were not as faithfully or elaborately recorded as those of the southern ones, but their contentions and complaints are well known. The Northern Alliance (National Farmers' Alliance) grew primarily out of a demand for railroad regulation, but in addition to its grievances against unfair discrimination and high freight rates, free passes, watered stock, and the political influence of the railroads, it denounced the plow, harvester, and other monopolies, cried out against low prices, and demanded more currency and lower tariffs.

The Farmers' Mutual Benefit Association arose out of a protest against middlemen and complained about low prices, farm mortgages, monopolies, concentration of wealth, patent laws, lack of adequate currency,

---

[30] *National Economist,* December 21, 1889, pp. 214-215. Or N. A. Dunning, pp. 122-123.

railroads, and national banks. It became more or less an appendage to the Southern Alliance, and it is therefore to be presumed that it agreed pretty thoroughly with the contentions of that organization.

The complaints of the farmers themselves, as represented in their organization resolutions, were mild in comparison to those of their leaders and sympathizers. The *Western Rural* was militant and almost bitter in its denunciation of the railroads and middlemen. As early as 1879 it said, "Farmers' work enriches the country even though the farmer himself abides in poverty." Later it called upon the Alliance to "protect farmers from schemes of boards of trade and speculators," and "to stem the current of unrepublican monopolies, that have gathered strength for these long years, until they threaten to engulf the basic industry of the Nation." [31] The *Pioneer Press* reported that the Minneapolis Board of Trade raised the question, "... how long, even with these cheap and wonderfully productive lands, can ... any agricultural community pay such enormous tribute to corporate organization in times like these, without final exhaustion and ruin?" [32] Jerry Simpson of Kansas argued that "We who use the [rail] roads are really paying interest on $600,000,000 instead of on $100,000,000 as we ought to"; [33] and the editor of *The Progressive Farmer* asked, "Do they [the railroads] not own the newspapers? Are not all the politicians their dependents? Has not every Judge in the State [North Carolina] a free pass in his pocket? Do they not control all the best legal talent of the State?" In another issue of his paper Colonel Polk said, "It [the depression] is the fault of the terrible financial system of the Government, a system that has placed on agriculture an undue, unjust proportion of the burden of taxation. Our currency has been contracted to a volume inadequate to the necessities of our people and trade, the result being high priced money and low priced articles." [34] Other editors and writers spoke of the eastern capitalists conspiring together to "levy tribute upon the productive energies of the West and South," [35] of railroads levying "freight and fares at their pleasure

---

[31] *Western Rural,* January 4, 1879; March 6, April 2, 1880.

[32] *Daily Pioneer Press* (St. Paul and Minneapolis), January 27, 1885.

[33] New York *Evening Post,* March 10, 1891.

[34] *The Progressive Farmer,* August 14, 1888; April 29, 1890.

[35] William E. Smythe, writing in "A Bundle of Western Letters," p. 44.

to the oppression of the citizens," [36] of politicians and trusts who "hold the people's hands and pick their pockets," [37] of a tariff that is a "hot-bed for the breeding of trusts and combines," [38] of the "concentration of agricultural land in the hands of merchants, loan agents, and a few of the financially strongest farmers," [39] of "tax-dodging" on the part of rail-roads,[40] and of national banks "conceived in infamy . . . for no other pur-pose but to rob the many for the benefit of the few." [41]

The authors of books which appeared during this period went into elaborate expositions of why farmers were in such dire circumstances, and presented the grievances of the agricultural masses in as militant terms as the most radical Farmers' Alliance could wish. N. A. Dunning, one of the most able of these, said:

> It is a question now between liberty and serfdom, and must be decided without delay. Some will ask: What shall we organize for? for the same reasons that our enemies do; for individual benefits through combined effort. Organize to watch them, to consider their motives, and, if possible, checkmate their designs, when aimed at you or your business.

W. S. Morgan, one of the leaders of the Agricultural Wheel and its most authoritative historian, says:

> The agricultural masses, the most numerous and important of any class of people forming the great body of the republic, and whose interests are identical, are kept divided upon the great issues which affect their welfare. They are robbed by an infamous system of finance; they are plundered by transportation companies; they are imposed upon by an unjust system of tariff laws; they are deprived of their lands and other property by an iniquitous system of usury; they are fleeced by the exorbitant exactions of numerous trusts; they

---

[36] *Journal of the senate of the general assembly of the State of North Carolina at its session of 1889:* "Message from the Governor," p. 37. Raleigh, North Carolina: Josephus Daniels, State Printer, 1889.

[37] *Farmers' Alliance* (Lincoln, Nebraska), September 20, 1890.

[38] John T. Morgan, "The Danger of the Farmers' Alliance," *Forum,* Vol. XII, No. 3 (November, 1891), p. 402.

[39] A. M. Arnett, *The Populist movement in Georgia,* p. 61. New York: Columbia University Press, 1922.

[40] Hicks, *The Populist revolt,* p. 86.

[41] Drew, p. 295.

are preyed upon by the merchants, imposed upon by the lawyers, misled by the politicians and seem to be regarded as the legitimate prey of all other classes. Monopoly names the price of what they have to sell, and charges them what it pleases for what they are compelled to buy.[42]

N. B. Ashby, Lecturer of the National (Northern) Farmers' Alliance, in *The Riddle of the Sphinx* sets the "riddle" in the following statements:

Could our forefathers have seen the material greatness of this age, they would have dreamed that the "Age of Saturn" had returned, and that Plenty was walking through the land; that every man had abundance and to spare, and that the lean wolf, Poverty, had famished for want of victims. But could they have seen the true condition of the farmers and laborers under the gild of all this outward pomp, pleased surprise would have given place to horrified amazement; for they, simple and guileless souls, believed in a supposed law of supply and demand powerful enough to secure to the farmer and the laborer the just rewards of their toil. They were not familiar with the patents, trusts, combines, and exactions which secure to those who do not work the lion's share of the harvest and the fruits of the laboring man's toil. Such a condition would have appeared to them a monster more terrible than the sphinx which depopulated Thebes, waiting an answer to its enigma.

In New England farms are standing deserted which are in sight and sound of the great factories, and this depopulation has gone on until the State authorities are busy with schemes of colonization by importation of poor people from Northern Europe. In the Middle States profits in farming are among the "lost arts," and lands and rents have depreciated greatly. In the Southern States land values are in the midst of the "Slough of Despond," and the condition of the farming classes hopeless, were it not for the fact and spirit of organization which now moves them as one man. In the Western States farm profits are an uncertain and often minus quantity, and the mortgaged indebtedness hangs a pall over every rainbow of promise. The farmers of the Eastern and Middle States are told that they are being ruined by the competition of the Western farmer living on cheap lands; the farmers of the South are told that their poverty is due to the devastation of the war and the lack of capital;

---

[42] W. S. Morgan, *History of Wheel and Alliance*, pp. 15-16.

the Western farmers are told that the trouble with them is over-production.[43]

It was out of attitudes of the kind and tenor expressed in these excerpts and quotations that the great Farmers' Alliance movement grew, and it was with the problems named by these various writers and resolutions that the farmers' organizations of the eighties struggled.

ECONOMIC PROJECTS OF THE ALLIANCE

The leading farmers' organizations of the eighties, like the Grange earlier, had other than economic objectives, but also like the Grange they quickly became dominated by their economic undertakings. The theory that only farmers and individual laborers are producers was almost universally accepted in farmer circles, and their first point of attack was therefore upon local middlemen. The attack soon moved beyond local purchasing to wholesale purchasing and finally to attempts at manufacturing. To these projects were added cooperative selling, insurance of all kinds, the furnishing of production credit, and the advocacy of a whole new scheme of marketing and finance—subtreasuries. These economic projects consisted in the main of seven types: (1) arrangements with local merchants, (2) cooperative stores, (3) state business agencies, (4) selling agencies of various types, (5) insurance companies, (6) manufacturing, and (7) the subtreasury plan.

In many southern states the Alliance and the Wheel were sufficiently powerful in membership to greatly disturb the local merchants. When, therefore, they approached a merchant with the proposition of guaranteeing him the patronage of a large number of Alliance customers in return for a reduction in prices, the merchant often accepted for two reasons: first, because he did not want to be boycotted; and second, because he believed that the greatly increased volume of business, guaranteed by so many farmers, would easily make it possible for him to reduce retail prices. In many instances the local Alliance specified the margin upon which merchants should operate, generally 10 per cent, but sometimes as low as 7 per cent.[44] In other instances a county committee was appointed

---

[43] Ashby, pp. 49-51.

[44] Information obtained from a local merchant at Austin, Texas, who was a party to one of these contracts. See also N. A. Dunning, p. 258. Honeycutt, p. 15.

to negotiate agreements with merchants, mobilize the patronage of Alliance members, and investigate complaints. Such committees generally demanded the right to study the merchants' invoices and quite generally insisted that at least one Alliance man be employed as a clerk in each store.[45] Northern Alliancemen followed this same practice to some extent.[46]

Because such agreements were often difficult to negotiate, because merchants found that they could not operate on such narrow margins, and because farmers believed that they could operate on even narrower margins, the system of agreements with local merchants was fairly quickly superseded either by cooperative stores or by county and state business agencies. Most often the cooperative stores, so-called, were joint-stock companies, the capital being furnished by relatively few enthusiastic Alliancemen, who then employed a manager and attempted to supervise his purchases and retail prices. Goods were sold both to Alliance members and nonmembers, the margins were low, the management often relatively incompetent, and the competition of other local stores unfair. As a result of these difficulties, it was inevitable that most of these independent stores would fail, leaving their enthusiastic owners to pay the losses.

The most widely used system of purchasing in both the northern and southern organizations was the business agency, either attached or unattached to a state exchange or other wholesale or jobbing firm. The simplest form of operation is illustrated by the Iowa, Minnesota, and Nebraska business agencies. Each state Alliance appointed a state purchasing agency whose duty it was to obtain options from manufacturers and wholesalers. Once these options were secured, lists were made up and sent to local and county Alliances. In some instances orders were taken at meetings. All orders were accompanied with cash, pooled, and sent to wholesale firms or manufacturers. The goods were shipped to the local agent or local organization for distribution to purchasers. The state agent for Iowa claimed to have done a very extensive business, especially in such staples as coal, flour, oil, binding twine, and farm machinery, and

—·—

[45] N. A. Dunning, pp. 356-357.
[46] Ashby, pp. 374-375.

to have saved the farmers of the state at least $100,000 per year in their purchases.[47]

State exchanges and other types of wholesale houses were developed by both northern and southern organizations. The Dakota Farmers' Alliance Company was probably the most outstanding in the North. It was a joint-stock company organized in July, 1887, with an authorized capital stock of $200,000. With $20,000 subscribed capital in $10 shares, it began business in January, 1888, and within the first year of operation did a business of more than $343,000. During 1888, it claimed that it had contracted for 20,000 cars of coal, and that it purchased 1,525,565 pounds of binding twine during the summer of 1888. It bought directly from mines and factories, made some of its contracts five years in advance, and claimed to take the whole output of some factories and mines. It had fifty local branches or agencies throughout the Dakota Territory, did business on a 2.5 per cent margin, paid 10 per cent dividends, and claimed to have saved its customers (in insurance and trade combined) a million dollars in one year.[48]

The Southern Alliance promoted state exchanges in a number of states —at least in Arkansas, Tennessee, Alabama, Louisiana, Florida, Mississippi, Georgia, South Carolina, Texas, and Kansas. Those in Arkansas, Tennessee, Georgia, Kansas, and Mississippi were apparently very successful, while the one in Texas failed because of its attempt to furnish production credit to its customers.[49]

---

[47] *Ibid.,* pp. 373-374. Hicks, *The Populist revolt,* p. 134. Blood, pp. 52-53. N. A. Dunning, pp. 357-358; Hicks, "The Farmers' Alliance in North Carolina," pp. 172-173. *Western Rural,* March 30, 1889. Honeycutt, pp. 26-29.

[48] Ashby, pp. 368-371, 374. *National Economist,* March 14, 1889, p. 14; March 30, 1889, p. 20. N. A. Dunning, pp. 367-369. *Western Rural,* January 26, 1889. W. S. Morgan, pp. 114, 238-244. *Appleton's,* 1890, p. 299. Wiest, pp. 465-467.

[49] For a detailed consideration of these exchanges and related business efforts, see W. S. Morgan, pp. 113, 115, 116-118, 122-123, 125, 126, 127, 129, 238-239. Files of the *National Economist;* for example, March 14, 1889, pp. 4, 5, 13, 14, 16; April 20, pp. 74-75; July 27, p. 297; August 10, p. 326; September 7, p. 386; December 14, p. 198; December 21, pp. 217-218; May 2, 1891, p. 102. N. A. Dunning, pp. 358-364, 367. Ashby, pp. 371-372, 376-377. Arnett, pp. 79-81. Blood, pp. 46, 49, 52, 53, 57. *Proceedings of the annual session of the Supreme Council of the National Farmers' Alliance and Industrial Union, at Ocala, Florida, Dec. 2-8, 1890,* pp. 43-53. Washington, D. C.: National Economist Publishing Co., 1891. Hicks, *The Populist revolt,* pp. 135-138. Modern I. Argus, *Minor chronicles of the goodly land of Texas.* Austin, Texas: N. J. McArthur, 1890. Clarence N. Ousley, "A Lesson in Co-operation," *Popular Science Monthly,* Vol. XXXVI, No. 6 (April, 1890), pp. 821-828.

The South Carolina state exchange plan became somewhat a model. It was formulated on the experience gained from successes and failures in other states and was an attempt to consolidate into one business organization all the Alliance business activities of the state. The following two paragraphs are excerpts from the South Carolina plan:

Art. 3. The purposes for which this corporation is organized are to conduct a general mercantile and brokerage business, and to act as agent for the purchase and sale of all kinds of farm supplies and products, and to do all that appertains to the receiving, handling, forwarding, and marketing of said products, and the purchase of supplies; to erect, manage, and operate warehouses, stock yards, grain elevators and packing establishments; to manufacture guano or other fertilizers, and all other such enterprises as may be found necessary or advisable to their profit and betterment.

Art. 7. It is hereby understood and agreed that each sub-Alliance adopting this exchange system and thereby ratifying this plan, is firmly bound to subscribe for and make settlement on stock, as above specified to the number of shares due from it, under the following schedule of ability, i. e., those having less than thirty-five (35) members shall be apportioned one share; thirty-five to sixty-five members, two shares; sixty-five to ninety-five members, three shares; all over ninety-five members, four shares; *Provided,* That this shall not prevent any Alliance from taking as many shares as it chooses.[50]

Between the sub-Alliance and the state organization were county organizations, but all were organically woven together by means of subscribed stock and elected trustees. Each sub-Alliance taking stock in the state corporation was entitled to one trustee stockholder. When there were three trustee stockholders in a county, they were permitted to elect a county trustee stockholder who represented the county in the state organization and had as many votes as there were shares of stock owned by all the sub-Alliances in his county.[51]

Wiest, pp. 464-467. W. L. Garvin and S. O. Daws, *History of the National Farmers' Alliance and Cooperative Union of America.* Jacksboro, Texas: J. N. Rogers and Co., 1887.

[50] *National Economist,* August 17, 1889, pp. 338-339.

[51] *Ibid.,* p. 339.

The name of the corporation was the Farmers' Alliance Exchange of South Carolina, Limited. Its charter was to run for ninety-nine years and its capital stock was $50,000—1,000 shares at $50 each. Its board of trustees, elected by state trustee stockholders, elected their own officers and operated the state exchange. The county trustee stockholders elected county business agents. Thus, a joint-stock company to handle all types of business for sub-Alliances was created. The state corporation was not permitted to make profits, "except what is sufficient to pay running expenses." [52]

The majority of the southern exchanges were not well established when the leaders of the Alliance became more interested in political than in economic activities. Macune had a rather bitter experience in the failure of the Texas State Exchange and did not, therefore, push the organization of such enterprises any too vigorously in the pages of the *National Economist,* of which he was editor. Indeed, he took a rather strong stand against allowing state business agencies to become too dominant in Southern Alliance affairs. He promoted what came to be known as the Macune Business System, but did not encourage the establishment of a national Exchange, a project that was often urged by the other Alliance leaders.

The Macune business system was quite lucidly explained in 1889 as follows:

> The idea of the Exchange plan is to provide a huge option house where everything the farmer uses may be bought at a fair profit but not such profits as a promiscuous credit business entails. This, then, will regulate the home market to margins of profit that will compel the dealer to sell for cash, or its equivalent, and when he does that he can successfully compete with the Exchange, and since the Exchange is not run for profit it will not desire a large volume of business, and it in no way interferes with its success and prosperity for the farmer to trade with his home merchant when he can buy at proper prices there; but whenever that merchant charges him too much, he will send to the option house and have his want supplied at the proper prices. [53]

[52] *Ibid.,* pp. 338-339.
[53] *Ibid.,* July 27, 1889, p. 297.

This idea was quite modern. It has been used by the Farmers' Equity Union for the last forty years, is the scheme of operation of many local "farmers' mutual exchanges" in southern states, and is in keeping with the Swedish "Middle Way," [54] a plan by which government factories operate as "stand-by" plants to enforce competition.

To what extent any of the farmers' organizations of this period were successful in cooperative selling, none of the writers or records of the time reveal. The Farmers' Mutual Benefit Association was originally organized for the pooling of wheat. The Texas State Alliance recommended the "bulking of cotton" for sale; the Texas Exchange did some selling of cotton and grain; and tobacco warehouses (auction markets) were operated in at least six towns in North Carolina. The Alliance Peanut Union was established at Suffolk, Virginia, and another one in Tennessee, the purposes of which were to standardize peanut bags and boycott all except those made of cotton, and to market cooperatively, if possible. An Alliance Elevator Company was established in Minneapolis, as a Dakota marketing business, and claimed to have paid "from 5 to 10 cents more for wheat consigned to it . . . than was paid by other wheat buyers . . ." [55] Numerous similar enterprises, mostly of small scope, were projected in various states, but for the most part the Southern Alliance, at least, made its marketing fight on the basis of the great subtreasury plan or in its advocacy of withholding farm produce from the market. In 1889, the national cotton committee passed a resolution for holding cotton which said, "The National cotton committee recommend that the farmers of the South shall sell no cotton during the month of September, except what may be absolutely necessary to meet the obligations which are past due." [56] There is no record showing to what extent this and similar resolutions were carried out.

The accomplishments of the business agents—chiefly the purchasing of supplies, fertilizers, tools and machinery—were undoubtedly substantial. The records of their accomplishment are more often verbal than statistical, and few precise data are available. N. B. Ashby, national lec-

---

[54] See Marquis W. Childs, *Sweden: the middle way.* New Haven, Connecticut: Yale University Press, 1936.

[55] *National Economist*, August 31, September 28, 1889.

[56] *Ibid.*, September 7, 1889.

turer for the Northern Alliance, said in June, 1889, "The fight of our Alliances of the North against the combine and binder-twine has been successful to a great degree, though the price of twine is not yet as low as we had confidently expected." [57] Other claims are stated more definitely. The proceedings of the Ocala (1890) convention of the Southern Alliance records that "The business done by the different members of the association aggregate about $10,000,000." There were eighteen state exchanges and business associations represented at this meeting. A National Association of Business Agents and State Exchanges had been organized in 1888 and this Ocala meeting was therefore their third annual convention. It is from their reported deliberations that the most consistent picture of business activities of the Alliance can be obtained.[58]

The following standing committees were appointed by the business agents on the first day of the Ocala convention: (1) transportation and freight charges; (2) agricultural implements and manufactures; (3) business agencies and exchanges. The president in his message said that "the prejudice of the wholesale dealers and manufacturers seems to be gradually melting away . . ." The secretary's speech was more belligerent and typically Farmers' Alliance in tone. He said, "Our enemy can not meet us successfully if we stand united, but if every agent attempts to work out this problem single-handed and alone, each will fall an easy prey to the powers of monopoly . . . it will take something more powerful than State agencies to give our people commercial reform." This sentiment prevailed to a sufficient extent to occasion the expansion of a gamut of committees to deal with the large problems of monopolies, viz.: "Committee on bagging for cotton"; "Committee on cotton arrangements and tare"; others on "binder twine and harvester machinery," "fruits and vegetables," and "tobacco." These, plus the three committees named on the first day, gave the business agents eight national committees which, had they been able to develop their work, would have ranked with the famous commodity committees of the Farm Bureau of the 1920's.

It is not, however, the purpose of this treatise to present in detail the business adventures, the successes and failures of the Farmers' Alliance, but rather to analyze the causes for the farmer's discontent and describe

---

[57] *Ibid.*, June 29, 1889.
[58] *Ocala proceedings*, pp. 34-35, 43-53.

the issues of his gauge of battle and its techniques. The proceedings of the Association of Business Agents and the columns of the *National Economist* furnish the most consistent sources of reference. The secretary of the Business Agents' Association at their Ocala meeting not only expressed the belief that their work in the Alliance was not clearly defined, but that it was actually looked upon as "an outside" activity.[59] This was indicative of the drift of the parent body away from primarily economic enterprises to political considerations. As a matter of fact, the "Reform Press" was considerably disturbed by the extent that the Business Agents' Association had become involved in their battle against commercially organized business. The Press wanted to deal with nation-wide, politico-economic issues rather than local stores, buying clubs, and the like, and furthermore they did not like to be boycotted by manufacturers and commercial firms in the field of advertising.[60] The Alliance had moved from the plane of local community conflicts between merchants and farmers to a national public of farmers, and in a public the press is a necessary and potent instrument. The Reform Press, therefore, was more influential than the Business Agents in Farmers' Alliance leadership after 1890-1891. There were certain types of issues which easily combined local grievances and public sentiment, and these became the rallying issues of greatest magnitude. They were in the South the Jute-Bagging Trust and the subtreasury plan; in the North, Railroads and Cheap Money.

Before these outstanding activities are discussed in some detail, a few other projects of significance should be mentioned. Insurance activities probably constituted the greatest success in Alliance business ventures, once again duplicating the experience of the Grange and in some instances carrying on Grange enterprises. In Iowa, a system of farmers' mutual fire and tornado local insurance companies was established in

---

[59] Particularly good discussions of the various aspects of the business activities of the Alliance appear in the pages of the *National Economist*. In addition to those already cited, see issues of August 10, 1889, p. 336; September 28, p. 31; October 5, p. 43; October 19, p. 67; February 15, 1890, p. 343; November 15, p. 140; January 10, 1891, p. 267.

[60] Just how much the Reform Press' fight with the Business Agents over the National Union Co. was because of its belief that the latter was corrupt, the author does not know. Be that as it may, the Reform Press succeeded in throwing the business emphasis of the Alliance pretty much out the window.

practically every county. The Iowa Mutual Tornado Insurance Company had risks in force in November, 1889, of more than $5,000,000; and in July, 1890, these had increased to almost $10,000,000. The hail and fire department of the Alliance Insurance Companies of the Dakotas, organized in 1886, claimed to have transacted business with more than 12,000 farmers by 1888. Life insurance companies were also organized in at least three states—Iowa, Minnesota, and the Dakota Territory [61]—and a National Alliance Aid Association was opened in Washington, D. C. in 1890.[62]

The Southern Alliance ventured into manufacturing projects. A cotton mill was built at Marble Falls, Texas, a dam was built across the Colorado River, machinery was purchased and shipped, but it was never installed.[63] The North Carolina Alliance purchased a building at Hillsboro, North Carolina, and started a shoe factory which, after a very short run, was abandoned. That building stood idle for more than thirty years. There were also at least six small tobacco factories started in North Carolina which operated for only a short time.[64] The Texas Exchange contemplated setting up woolen mills and implement and wagon factories. They launched some of these enterprises, but, as Ousley says, "From first to last several factories have been started, but without a single exception they have failed to reach the stage of successful operation." [65] The Dakota Farmers' Alliance Company at one time considered similar projects but never went further than to have a wagon called "The Alliance" made for it by a private firm.[66]

To "break the strangle hold of the jute-bagging monopoly" was a shibboleth that went back to Granger days in the South. Jute bagging was used as covering for bales of cotton, and the cost of this bagging was a middle cost in cotton just as were ginning, storing, and selling. Farmers believed that jute bagging was monopoly-controlled, and furthermore

---

[61] Ashby, pp. 359-365, 385. W. S. Morgan, p. 114. *National Economist,* March 30, 1889, p. 21; October 19, p. 65.

[62] *National Economist,* March 29, 1890, p. 28.

[63] The mill building stood idle and empty until the late 1920's when it was purchased by a private company and put into operation.

[64] Honeycutt, pp. 24-26.

[65] Ousley, p. 822.

[66] *National Economist,* March 14, 1889, p. 21. Ashby, p. 370.

that cotton instead of jute should be used for bagging. They talked about these matters in their meetings, passed resolutions about them, and finally organized something approaching a successful boycott of the "jute-bagging trust." In doing so, they demonstrated the effectiveness of organized group pressure and further developed their conviction concerning the efficacy of this type of action. The boycott carried beyond bagging for cotton bales to bagging for fertilizers and peanuts. A South Carolina resolution read, "*Resolved,* That the members of the State Alliance, in convention assembled, do earnestly appeal to every sub-Alliance in the State . . . that they use only cotton bagging, or if sufficient quantity of cotton bagging can not be obtained they will use any substitute—pine straw, or even common homespun—but jute." Another resolution recommended that each county Alliance resolve "to use no fertilizers put up in other than cotton sacks." [67] This type of action was apparently quite effective. The prices for jute bagging came down,[68] and most students of this and similar activities credit the boycott with being successful.[69]

THE GREAT SUBTREASURY PLAN

The most imposing project of any of the organizations of this period was the subtreasury plan of the Southern Alliance. Its plan to attack both the marketing and money problems warrants consideration in some detail. It was one of the issues upon which the northern and southern Alliances failed to agree in the 1889 St. Louis convention, and it was the issue upon which the southern organization was willing to stake its life in the late eighties and early nineties. The plan in brief was as follows:

1. That a branch of the United States Treasury be established in any county in the United States upon the petition of one hundred or more citizens of the county, provided the county clerk and sheriff furnished written evidence that the average gross amount of cotton, wheat, oats, corn, barley, rye, rice, wool, sugar, and/or tobacco had for two years sold for an average of $500,000 per year.

---

[67] *National Economist,* August 10, 1889, p. 327. See also *The Progressive Farmer,* August 7, 1888.

[68] *National Economist,* July 27, 1889, p. 297.

[69] Ashby, pp. 372-373. Hicks, *The Populist revolt,* p. 140. Arnett, p. 104. W. S. Morgan, p. 118.

2. That the county furnish a good and sufficient bond to the federal government for title to land upon which to locate a subtreasury building, and proof that the site for location had been selected by a popular vote of the citizens of the county.

3. That owners of the various farm products deposit their products in the nearest subtreasury (which would have adequate warehouse facilities) and receive a certificate of the deposit showing the amount and grade of the products, the value at time of deposit, and the amount charged for storage and insurance; these certificates to be negotiable by endorsement.

4. That United States paper money of full legal tender, receivable for customs, and for all private and public debts, and as part of the lawful reserve of any bank, equal to 80 per cent of the local current market value of products deposited in the warehouses of the subtreasuries, be advanced with interest at the rate of 1 per cent per annum.

5. That the products deposited may be withdrawn by the holder of warehouse certificates at any time by submitting the receipts and paying in money the amount of the marginal advance, all interest, insurance, and other charges against them; and when such withdrawals take place, the trustee of the subtreasury should send the money paid by the farmer to the United States Treasury where it would be destroyed.

6. That should the products not be redeemed within twelve months after deposit by the farmer who deposited them or by the holder of the warehouse certificates, then the trustee of the subtreasury should sell the products at public auction and use the money to satisfy the debt.[70]

It is clear that this elaborate and carefully worked-out plan was an attempt to accomplish two outstanding objects: to make it unnecessary for farmers to dump their products on sagged markets, and to expand the currency. It would also have provided an elaborate system of federal warehouses throughout the nation. A bill making provision for the estab-

---

[70] For a thorough presentation and analysis of the subtreasury plan, see N. A. Dunning, pp. 124-130, 336-354, 734-735. Ashby, pp. 302-316. Issues of the *National Economist* from December, 1889, through 1892. J. E. Bryan, pp. 86-109. Chamberlain, pp. 15-25, 49-51, 340. C. C. Post, "The Subtreasury Plan," *Arena*, Vol. V, No. 3 (February, 1892), pp. 342-353. *Southern Mercury* (Dallas, Texas), January 28, 1892; December 1, 1892, pp. 4-5. Thomas E. Watson, *The People's party campaign book, 1892*, pp. 199-205. Washington, D. C.: National Watchman Publishing Co., 1892.

lishment of the system was twice introduced in Congress and supported by a strong southern Alliance lobby; but the first time it was never reported out of the committee of either house, although it was given the courtesy of elaborate hearings in committees, and the second time it was forced out of committee on the last day of Congress and no record vote taken.[71]

Because of the likeness of this great scheme for farm relief to a number of others which have been proposed from time to time, it is worth while to summarize the arguments submitted by the Alliance in its behalf. It was argued that staple farm commodities constitute the most fundamental wealth in the world and are, therefore, a sound basis for currency, and that to use them for this purpose would be but to extend the operation of the principle upon which national bank notes were issued. Senator Peffer of Kansas called attention to the fact that "On the face of a national-bank note these words are printed: 'This note is secured by bonds of the United States deposited with the U. S. Treasurer at Washington,'" and asked, "What better is that endorsement than this— 'This note is secured by wheat deposited in the Government warehouse at Washington.'"[72] It was further argued that from the day of Adam Smith it had been admitted "that fluctuation in price is the only thing necessary to enable the exploiting class to appropriate all the results of productive industry except a bare subsistence to the laborer" and "that general prices always fall when the volume of money in the country is diminished, and vice versa"; that the volume of money needed for general trade and industry throughout most of the year was insufficient during the crop-moving season and that the only alternative to speculation in, and dumping of, farm products was to create a currency which would vary with the needs and demands of the season. The subtreasury plan, it was argued, not only provided this fluctuating currency but provided that it would fluctuate in exact ratio to the need.[73] Dr. Macune urged that the plan resolve itself into a scheme whereby farmers might raise

---

[71] See *Congressional record*, 51st Congress, 1st Session, February 18, 1890, p. 1468; February 24, p. 1645. 2nd Session, December 9, 1890, p. 237. 52nd Congress, 1st Session, May 19, 1892, p. 4432; May 20, p. 4480; May 21, p. 4515; May 23, p. 4563. *House Reports*, No. 2143. See also issues of *National Economist* for the period.

[72] Peffer, *The farmer's side*, p. 245.

[73] Ashby, pp. 306-309.

money while holding their grain for a rise in the market, and thus squeeze out the speculator and middleman.

It was assumed that another vicious evil would be attacked by the operation of the subtreasury plan, in that a source of cheap credit would be established through which the farmer could escape the slavery imposed by the crop-lien system. It was estimated that at least $550,000,000 of new currency would be placed in the hands of farmers at each harvest time and that this money not only would make possible the payment of fall obligations but, because of the low rate of interest, would soon permit the farmer to escape merchant credit altogether.[74]

OTHER ECONOMIC ADJUSTMENTS URGED

There were certain other economic adjustments which farmers desired but which, like the subtreasury scheme, could not be put into operation except through either national or state legislation. Such was the proposal made by the Northern Alliance for increasing the volume of money by issuing currency based on land securities. The national Grange in 1889 endorsed this proposal, and Senator Leland Stanford of California introduced a bill in the United States Senate providing for such a scheme.[75] Such also were the demands for reduction in taxation, economy in all phases of government, railroad regulation, corporation control, the abolition of national banks, the establishment of income taxes, the elimination of patent royalties, the elimination of dealing in futures, and the free coinage of silver. In fact, it was the growing conviction on the part of farm organization leaders that the most important economic adjustments could be made only by legislative action that turned the last and greatest farmers' meeting in the decade into something approaching a political convention. At the St. Louis meeting in December, 1889, practically all of the farm organizations of the nation gathered, and while the attempted union of the northern and southern Alliances failed, both organizations from that time on drifted so rapidly into politics that it was difficult to distinguish them from the Populist party.

---

[74] A complete analysis of the subtreasury plan is given by John D. Hicks, "The Subtreasury: A Forgotten Plan for the Relief of Agriculture," *Mississippi Valley Historical Review*, Vol. XV, No. 3 (December, 1928), pp. 355-373.

[75] *Congressional record*, 51st Congress, 1st Session, May 23, 1890, pp. 5169-5170. Ashby, pp. 316-328.

THE ALLIANCES
AFTER ATTEMPTS
AT UNION

ATTEMPTS AT UNION OF ALL ORGANIZATIONS

When the two great farmer Alliance organizations met concurrently in annual convention in St. Louis in December, 1889, they represented the greatest percentage of American farmers ever to cooperate in one convention. Actually they met separately in their respective annual conventions, but they had a number of meetings in joint session and cooperated throughout the session in an effort to effect consolidation. The Southern Alliance was represented by ninety-five delegates from eighteen states and one territory, while the Northern Alliance delegates numbered sixty-five and represented eight states. Committees of delegates were sent to this great meeting from the Knights of Labor and the Farmers' Mutual Benefit Association, both committees having been authorized by their organizations to work for closer cooperation with the Southern Alliance. In addition, the Colored Alliance was meeting in separate annual convention in the city at the same time.

There were various claims as to the number of farmers present. The

St. Louis *Globe-Democrat*, December 4, 1889, speaking only of the Southern Alliance, vividly related: "Yesterday morning, at 10 o'clock, Entertainment Hall of the Exposition building resounding with the stentorian voices of 150 delegates who compose the National Farmers' and Laborers' Union Convention, and who represent about 2,000,000 horny-handed sons of toil west of the Alleghenies." *Appleton's Annual Cyclopaedia and Register of Important Events for the Year 1890* says that, on the basis of an official census of the Southern Alliance taken in July, by the end of 1890, a year after the St. Louis convention, "the claim that the Southern Alliance alone contains 3,000,000 members is perhaps correct."

There is little doubt that it was hoped by both Alliances that they might leave St. Louis with only one great national farmers' organization in the field. The Farmers' Mutual Benefit Association had had representatives at the Southern Alliance convention the year before at Meridian, Mississippi; and Evan Jones, president of the amalgamated southern organizations at the time of the St. Louis convention, had met with the executive committee of the Northern Alliance in February, 1888, to explain the nature of the southern order with a view toward consolidation.[1] Dr. Macune, up to that time chief spokesman of the southern organization, had spoken at the convention of the Northern Alliance in January, 1889, and had explained the action taken the year before at Meridian by the southern group.[2] On September 28, a little over two months before the St. Louis meeting, President Jay Burrows of the Northern Alliance had published an official notice which was addressed to all officers of state and territorial Alliances in North and South Dakota, Wisconsin, Minnesota, Ohio, Illinois, Kansas, Nebraska, Colorado, and Washington Territory, and to all subordinate Alliances in New York, Pennsylvania, Indiana, California, and Oregon. He had suggested that each state or territorial Alliance discuss the matter of union and send its delegates to St. Louis prepared to vote on the matter. He had, however, been very careful to leave the matter of what to do to each state and had said, "You need not, however, confine your action to the adoption or rejection of that document, but rather instruct your delegates upon the broad prin-

---

[1] *National Economist*, October 19, 1889, pp. 72-73; January 4, 1890, p. 242.
[2] *Western Rural*, January 26, February 16, March 30, April 6, 13, October 5, 1889.

ciple of union, upon whatever terms may be agreed upon at St. Louis." [3]
The document to which he referred was the constitution adopted by the
Southern Alliance at Meridian, Mississippi, the year before. This official
statement of Burrows to his own state Alliances had been published in
the *National Economist*, the official organ of the Southern Alliance, and
may have been interpreted by the southern group to the effect that each
northern state Alliance would come to St. Louis prepared to act autono-
mously concerning union. It is not probable that Burrows had any such
idea in mind, but rather that the delegates from each state would come
prepared to discuss the issue in the National (Northern) Alliance meeting and that any action that was taken would be by majority vote and
as a national body.

The Southern Alliance had already penetrated the northern states of
Indiana, Missouri, Colorado, and Kansas; and the Agricultural Wheel had
organized local units in Wisconsin as early as 1887. The Southern Alliance
probably believed that it would be able to capture the whole northern
movement because of the latter's loose type of national organization. It
is also apparent that some of the leaders in the northern organization
were anxious for such union.[4] Others apparently desired only cooperation or collaboration between them as two independent organizations.
Immediately after the convention was over and as long as the two organizations were in existence, there were differences of opinion as to why
union or cooperation was not accomplished and disputes about what
transpired at the 1889 St. Louis convention.

The chronology of events at St. Louis, according to the most authoritative sources, is as follows: The Southern Alliance met in Entertainment
Hall of the Exposition building and the Northern Alliance at the Planter's House. At 10:00 A.M. of the first day, however, they met in joint session and were welcomed by Mayor Noonan and Governor Francis of
Missouri. Responses were made by J. H. McDowell of Tennessee for the
Southern Alliance and by A. J. Streeter of Illinois for the Northern Al-

---

[3] *National Economist,* October 19, 1889, pp. 72-73.
[4] A. J. Streeter, one of these leaders of the northern group, was very much in favor
of consolidation and worked for it throughout the convention. See his speech in the
St. Louis *Republic,* December 4, 1889.

liance.[5] The two bodies then separated for independent meetings. During the afternoon session, the Northern Alliance sent a committee of nine, "duly elected" as "a committee of conference," to the meeting place of the Southern Alliance for the purpose of meeting with a "like committee" from the southern organization. The northern committee was formally received and escorted to the platform. After an exchange of views, they withdrew and the Southern Alliance took immediate action by appointing a committee of nine "to confer with the National Alliance of the Northwest [the northern body]," and a committee of five to confer with the Mutual Benefit Association.[6]

President Jones, in his opening address to the Southern Alliance, said:

... whereas there have been negotiations between the National Farmers' Alliance and the Farmers' Mutual Benefit Association of the Northwestern States, looking to a consolidation of these two great agricultural organizations with the Farmers' and Laborers' Union of America, and as delegates from the National Farmers' Alliance and National Mutual Benefit Association are now in the city, I would recommend that you give this matter your immediate attention, and if possible agree upon a basis of union, or at least cooperation.[7]

President Burrows, in his address to the Northern Alliance, did not refer to this issue, but called upon the farmers of the nation to unite in a fight for reform in the fields of transportation, monopoly, and money.[8]

The minutes of the Southern Alliance, recording the next step in negotiations for union, stated:

The committee on conference then made a report as follows:

The joint committee agree to recommend to our respective organizations the adoption of the following resolutions, to wit:

First, That a joint committee of five on the part of the National Farmers' Alliance and a like number on the part of the National Farmers' and Laborers' Union be appointed with authority to for-

---

[5] W. S. Morgan, p. 148. N. A. Dunning, p. 96. *National Economist*, December 21, 1889, p. 210. St. Louis *Republic*, December 4, 1889.

[6] *National Economist*, December 21, 1889, p. 210.

[7] *Ibid.*, December 21, 1889, p. 210.

[8] *Farmers' Alliance* (Lincoln, Nebraska), December 21, 1889.

mulate a plan for a confederation of said organizations and of other known agricultural and industrial organizations in the United States, to the end that immediate and practical cooperation may be secured for the accomplishment of the objects common to all.

Second, that the autonomy of said organization be preserved intact until such time as the way may be found clear to effect organic union if the same should hereafter be found necessary.[9]

The minutes do not record a formal motion concerning this recommendation, but do record the names of the committee of five appointed by the Southern Alliance and state that, "On motion the Farmers' Mutual Benefit Association was allowed representation on conference committee, to confer with Northwestern Alliance."[10]

Early in the afternoon of the third day's session of the southern group, the report of the joint committee on conference with Northwestern Alliance was read and adopted as follows:

The joint committee of the National Alliance and National Farmers' and Laborers' Union, appointed to formulate a plan to secure practical co-operation of said organizations and of other kindred organizations for the accomplishment of the objects common to all, recommend the adoption of the following resolutions, to wit:

Resolved, 1. That the presidents and other authorized representatives chosen by the executive board of each national and State agricultural and industrial organization in the United States be requested to assemble in the city of Washington, on 22d day of February, A.D., 1890, to consider and agree upon a basis for a federation of such organizations for the purpose of securing needed reform and remedial national and state legislation, and for the promotion of such other objects as may be found to be of common interest to such organizations; it being understood that such plans as agreed upon shall be submitted to the various national and State organizations participating therein for ratification and adoption.

2. That an executive committee of two each on the part of the National Farmers' Alliance and the National Farmers' and Laborers' Union be appointed, with authority to take all necessary steps to carry out the foregoing resolution and to arrange for an immediate federation of said organizations, if same be now possible.

---

9 *National Economist*, December 21, 1889, pp. 211-212. N. A. Dunning, pp. 98-99.
10 *National Economist*, December 21, 1889, p. 212.

3. That the President of the National Farmers' Alliance and National Farmers' and Laborers' Union and the General Master Workman of the Knights of Labor now in this city be authorized and requested to take all necessary steps to carry out the foregoing resolutions, and to arrange for an immediate federation, if the same be now possible.

The following resolution was read by Brother Patty, of Mississippi:

Resolved, That the National Farmers' and Laborers' Union declare in favor of organic union with the National Farmers' Alliance.

That a committee of five be appointed to meet a like committee on part of the National Farmers' Alliance to prepare a constitution and plan of consolidation for said organizations. Adopted.[11]

Later on this same day the Southern Alliance passed the following resolution:

That the communication from the National Farmers' Alliance proposing articles of federation be received and placed in the hands of the members of the proposed joint committee to prepare constitution and plan of consolidation of the Union and said National Alliance, and that said committee inform the National Alliance of the action this body had on the subject of federation and organic union, and that this body will not consider the subject of federation and respectfully decline it.[12]

The "articles of federation" referred to in this action were exceedingly important to the Northern Alliance. They described the plan by means of which the northern organization believed union could be effected. The failure of the southern organization even to consider them (they are not even recorded in the southern minutes) was later named by N. B. Ashby, lecturer of the Northern Alliance, as the chief cause of failure to consolidate. The articles read:

ARTICLES OF FEDERATION
ARTICLE I

1. This Federation shall be known as the Federated Farmers' Alliance and Industrial Union of America.

---

[11] N. A. Dunning, pp. 120-121.
[12] *National Economist*, December 21, 1889, p. 213.

2. It shall be composed of ten delegates from each National body composing this Federation, chosen at the annual meeting of each National organization for the term of one year. The President of each National organization shall be members ex-officio.

3. Its officers shall consist of a President, Vice-president, Secretary and Treasurer from its members, to be elected for the term of one year.

4. The duties of said officers shall be the same as those usually pertaining to said officers respectively.

5. The first meeting shall be on the 6th inst., at the Planter's House, in St. Louis, Missouri. The time and place of its next annual meeting shall be fixed by the Federation at this meeting.

6. The President and Secretary of this Federation and the President of each National body composing this Federation shall constitute its Executive Board.

7. The Executive Board shall call special meetings whenever they deem it necessary.

8. The Federation shall have power to adopt rules and regulations for its government.

9. This Federation shall continue until such time as the National organizations composing it may unite in an organic union.

ARTICLE II

1. The objects of this Federation shall be to unify and carry into practical effect the principles which may be adopted by the National bodies composing this Federation, and to secure legislation in the interest of these principles.

2. Its special duty shall be to secure practical reform in the interests of the producers of the country in money, land and transportation.

ARTICLE III

1. Each National body composing this Federation shall defray the expenses of its delegates to the meetings of Federation, and shall, by annual appropriation, by the Executive Board, contribute its equal share of the general expenses of the Federation.

2. The Executive Board shall report to the annual meeting of the Federation a full statement of all expenditures during the past year and for what purpose expended, and shall submit their estimate of the expenses for the coming year for approval by the Federation.

During the following day, the Southern Alliance spent the whole fore-
noon session in presenting and adopting a new constitution which gave
no consideration to the idea of union.[13] The minutes record that during
the afternoon, "On motion a committee from the Northwestern [North-
ern] Alliance was received, and considerable time given to a conference
with this body."[14] Nothing is told as to the contents of this conference,
but the minutes for the evening session record these negotiations:

The following propositions were received from the National Alliance:

1. The name of the organization shall be changed from the National Farmers' and Laborers' Union of America to that of National
Farmers' Alliance and Industrial Union.

On motion this proposition was agreed to.

2. To strike out the word "white" in the constitution.

This proposition had already been practically complied with in
the new constitution.

3. To leave the secret work optional with each State.

Not granted, but a substitute was adopted that the States not
ready to receive the secret work at once shall be allowed one year
for preparation.

The delegation from the Northern Alliance was escorted in, and
the following communication was read and referred to the committee on the constitution:

1. That we perfect our present organization as two separate
bodies.

2. That we meet together in joint session for the purpose of adopting a constitution for a united body, and for the election of officers.

3. That the question of the adoption or ratification of said action
be left to the several State Alliances of the National Farmers' Alliance represented here, and when two-thirds of said Alliances have
ratified, that the president be authorized to issue a proclamation
perfecting the new organization; provided that where State Alliances have already passed upon the question of union, action of
their executive committee will be sufficient.

---

[13] *Ibid.*, pp. 213-214.
[14] *Ibid.*, December 21, 1889, p. 214.

The committee on the constitution reported as follows:

We suggest that the committee from the National Farmers' Alliance now in waiting, be informed that this body has perfected its organization, by adopting a constitution and electing officers, and announces as ready to contend for the farmers' interest in every way, and would be glad to receive any accessions or assistance from the National Farmers' Alliance, but respectfully decline to enter into the proposed new federation for lack of time.

The report was adopted, and the National Alliance informed of the action.[15]

At the next day's session (the last day of the convention), Kansas, South Dakota, and North Dakota were voted into the Southern Alliance and their delegates seated in the convention.[16] It is impossible to tell from the proceedings whether or not North Dakota actually did go over to the Southern Alliance. The president of the North Dakota organization was seated in the southern convention, but nothing was said about issuing North Dakota a charter, a procedure definitely indicated in the cases of Kansas and South Dakota. Perhaps the fact that the two Dakota Alliances had been separated less than two weeks before the St. Louis convention tended to complicate the issue. The following resolution was unanimously adopted: "That a committee consisting of Bros. Tracy, Blood, and Erwin be instructed to inform the National Farmers' Alliance that this body will stand firmly to the propositions made yesterday, and invite them to appear before this body for obligation and secret work, as well as participation in the further business of the session."[17] The Southern Alliance had, in the meantime, worked out an agreement for economic and political cooperation with the Knights of Labor.[18]

The minutes of the Northern Alliance apparently were not preserved,[19] and it is, therefore, impossible to know what its detailed actions concerning consolidation were, except as they were recorded in the minutes

----

[15] *Ibid.*, December 21, 1889, p. 215.

[16] *Ibid,* December 14, 1889, p. 193; December 21, pp. 215, 217.

[17] *Ibid.*, December 21, 1889, p. 215.

[18] *Ibid,* pp. 213-215. N. A. Dunning, pp. 122-123. St. Louis *Republic,* December 2-7, 1889. St. Louis *Globe-Democrat,* December 5-6, 1889.

[19] For brief summaries of the meetings of the Northern Alliance, see St. Louis *Republic,* December 3, 4, 5, 6, 7, 1889.

of the Southern Alliance. We do know that it was the northern group which took the initiative in attempts at consolidation during the St. Louis convention. It was their committee which went to the southern meetings and not vice versa. It was they who made propositions to which the southern group responded. Furthermore, two, and possibly three, of the northern state Alliances actually joined the Southern Alliance while still at St. Louis. These facts and what transpired later would seem to indicate that there was division in the ranks of the Northern Alliance at St. Louis. Also, this division continued after the delegates returned to their homes. President Burrows, editor of the *Farmers' Alliance*, official organ of the Northern Alliance and the paper which came nearest to reporting the story of the Northern Alliance's transactions during this period, for a while continued the attempt at consolidation. The first issue of his paper following the convention carried the following headlines:

THE NATIONAL ALLIANCE MEETING AT ST. LOUIS

A UNION

On a Platform by the National Alliance,
the Farmers' and Laborers' Co-operative
Union and the Knights of Labor

A Grand Declaration

United on this Platform, a Final Victory
Is Certain!

His article said:

The following is the joint declaration of the Farmers and the committee of the Knights of Labor assembled in St. Louis last week. The demands of this declaration are the demands of all the societies represented, unanimous, and without reserve or qualification. The time has at last arrived when these three great societies can go before the country united upon one platform, and united upon the further demand that all candidates for office should unqualifiedly endorse these demands, as an indispensable condition of support...

While a complete organic union was not made between the Northern and Southern Alliances, the ground was cleared, and all or nearly all points of difference removed, so that union may be considered practically accomplished. Two Northern States, Iowa and

Minnesota, being entirely without instructions, refused to complete an organic union without an opportunity to refer the matter back to their State Alliance. The southern men were strenuous that a final union should be accomplished without delay. This placed our people in a very embarrassing position, as they were very loath to take action which would force a secession of two states. The time to which the session could be prolonged had about arrived, on account of limitation of railroad tickets. At this juncture President Loucks, of Dakota, proposed as a final compromise, that the two bodies should join together and, the constitution which had been proposed having been accepted by both bodies, they should proceed to the election of officers for the new organization and that upon such election the action should be referred back to the states for ratification, and when two-thirds of the states had ratified, the union should be announced by proclamation. This proposition was rejected by the Southern Alliance, whereupon the Northern Alliance adjourned sine die. It is probable that there might have been some misunderstanding as to the nature of this proposition. Previous to its submission both bodies had elected their officers for the ensuing year. In the southern body we are informed the election was prolonged and exciting. The delegates were tired out with the long uninterrupted work of the session, and perhaps felt indisposed to enter into another election.

However all this may be, all important points of difference between the two bodies being removed, a final union will undoubtedly take place at the next meeting. And it may be better, and may conduce to our final strength, that this temporary delay has taken place. We will know each other better at the next meeting than we did at this. It is well to say, however, that no differences of a sectional nature could be seen at St. Louis. The color line was nearly obliterated, and our people from all sections met as one indivisible people, with identical interests and a common cause. The only real embarrassment arose from the refusal of two states to ratify without referring to their states. And in the case of these states their delegates were in favor of union.[20]

The proceedings of the Southern convention seemingly contradict this, in that the proviso (actually an additional resolution) of which Ashby

---

[20] *Farmers' Alliance*, December 14, 1889.

speaks below, providing for the appointment of a "committee of five," was adopted by the southern body. Subsequent action provided that the Southern Alliance's committee on constitution should act in the capacity of this negotiating committee.[21]

A few issues later, Ashby wrote concerning the report of the St. Louis joint committee on conference:

> It failed to pass the Farmers' and Laborers' Union [the Southern Alliance].... Coupled with the resolution was the proviso "that a committee of five be appointed to meet a like committee on part of the National Farmers' Alliance to prepare a constitution and plan of consolidation for said organization." No such committee was appointed by the brethren from the South. No plan of consolidation was formulated or presented. The Farmers' and Laborers' Union offered us their constitution to adopt or nothing.[22]

Two years later, N. A. Dunning wrote:

> It was both hoped and expected that the Alliance of the Northwest would consolidate with the National Farmers' Alliance and Industrial Union as had the Union and Wheel, and form one grand agricultural organization. All efforts in that direction proved futile, through the persistent opposition of a few men who have since been relegated to obscurity ... A careful analysis of the causes which conspired to bring about this result disclosed the fact that sectionalism, that old enemy of national organized labor, was the controlling factor.[23]

Who the "few men" referred to by Dunning were was not revealed. It is clear, however, that Macune of the Southern Alliance in his address to the joint meeting of the two bodies was very pointed in his remarks. He said, among other things, that the matter was discussed when the Louisiana Union and the Texas Alliance were amalgamating and that the Texas organization "was not willing to join itself to that order [the Northern Alliance]" for three reasons: first, because the Northern Alliance "was a nonsecret and very loose organization, with neither fees nor dues, and charters seemed to be sent out by the National Secretary, Mr.

---

[21] See *National Economist*, December 21, 1889, p. 212.

[22] *Farmers' Alliance*, January 11, 1890.

[23] N. A. Dunning, p. 133.

George, to anybody who would request them on very little evidence as to the qualifications of those applying. Second, the published rulings as to the qualifications of membership made Negroes eligible; and third, the National Secretary published a ruling that any person raised on a farm was considered a practical farmer, and was therefore eligible regardless of his present occupation." He added that "The membership of the Texas State Alliance and the Louisiana Union were at that time [1887] unanimously opposed to each of these three methods," and thought that it would be "a needless waste of time to lose a year in order to ask the National Farmers' Alliance to modify its methods that they might join it . . ." [24] This speech of Macune's presented the uncompromising position of the Southern Alliance. President Jay Burrows of the Northern Alliance did not speak as bluntly as Macune, but he did say that the expansion of the northern organization had been "purely voluntary, and that the National Alliance has not employed any national officers in proselyting work." [25] He doubtless meant to accuse the Southern Alliance of such proselyting.

It is not the primary purpose of this book to thread out the minute details of situations such as the one just described. This exception is made because no one else has apparently taken the time to gather together and carefully analyze the relatively few documentary evidences which are available. Furthermore, the author uses the St. Louis convention of 1889 to illustrate the difficulty which has appeared at other periods in attempts to unite all farm organizations even when they seemed to be fighting the same battles.

Nixon lists an elaborate set of causes for the failure of the northern and southern Alliances to unite, viz: a greater tendency of the Southern than the Northern Alliance toward third-party politics; an unwillingness on the part of the Southern Alliance that each organization exercise considerable autonomy; a fear that the spoils of office might not be evenly distributed; disagreement on eligibility of Negroes to membership; differences in fundamental economic problems of the two sections represented by the organizations; and disagreement on the subtreasury plan. [26]

---

[24] See N. A. Dunning, pp. 105-120, for Macune's speech.

[25] *Farmers' Alliance*, December 21, 1889.

[26] Herman C. Nixon, "The Cleavage within the Farmers' Alliance Movement," *Mississippi Valley Historical Review*, Vol. XV, No. 1 (June, 1928), pp. 22-33. See

As Hicks points out, however, the negotiations between the two organizations revealed a willingness of northern and southern farmers to work for common ends and a conviction on the part of all that "the time was ripe for a series of political demands that, if carried into effect, might accomplish a sort of 'bloodless revolution.'" [27] Both conventions at St. Louis demanded abolition of national banks, the issue of legal tender paper money, some more comprehensive system of regulating railroads, retrenchment in government expenses, reform in taxation, and the restriction of land ownership to settlers.

THE SOUTHERN ALLIANCE IN THE EARLY NINETIES

The Southern Alliance changed its form of organization at the St. Louis convention and, as a result of the negotiation efforts toward consolidation, had agreed with the proposal of the Northern Alliance that the organization be known as the National Farmers' Alliance and Industrial Union. The new scheme provided that the organization be divided into three departments—legislative, executive, and judiciary. The legislative department, or Supreme Council, was composed of the officers of the organization and delegates elected by the states. The executive department was composed of the national officers, with the president as head and having power to direct all other officers and all executive work, subject to regulations made by the Supreme Council. The judiciary department was composed of three judges, whose duties were to pass upon rulings of the president, to pass upon grievances of the Supreme Council, and to listen to appeals from states.[28]

The treasury was in good condition at that time and salaries of $3,000 to the president, $900 for a stenographer, $2,000 to the secretary, $3,000 to the lecturer, $2,000 to the chairman of the executive board, $500 to the treasurer and to each member of the executive board were voted before election of officers took place. Colonel L. L. Polk of North Caro-

---

especially pp. 23-25. For additional accounts as to why consolidation failed, see Drew, pp. 290-303. Blood, pp. 39-40. Hicks, *The Populist revolt*, pp. 121-124. *Appleton's, 1890*, pp. 300-301. *Western Rural*, June 6, 1891. St. Louis Globe-Democrat, December 8, 1889. Herman C. Nixon, "The Populist Movement in Iowa," *Iowa Journal of History and Politics*, Vol. XXIV, No. 1 (January, 1926), pp. 44-45.

[27] Hicks, *The Populist revolt*, p. 123.

[28] *National Economist*, December 21, 1889, p. 213.

lina was elected president; B. H. Clover of Kansas, vice-president; J. H. Turner of Georgia, secretary; H. W. Hickman of Missouri, treasurer; and Ben Terrell of Texas, lecturer. Colonel Polk established national headquarters at Washington, D. C., where Dr. Macune had already been issuing the *National Economist* for almost a year.[29]

Polk immediately began a vigorous campaign for the extension of the organization, especially into northern and western states. As a result, he reported to the next annual convention—held in Ocala, Florida, in December, 1890—that since the "last annual meeting in the city of St. Louis, the states of Illinois, Indiana, Michigan, North Dakota, California, Colorado, West Virginia, Pennsylvania, and Oklahoma have been added to the roll call of our Supreme Council. Organizers are at work in the states of Washington, Oregon, Ohio, New York, New Jersey, and Arizona." He added that he had "visited officially twenty-four states, and everywhere . . . found a zealous interest and harmonious spirit among the brotherhood."[30]

On the basis of the reports of the credentials committee at the time of the 1889 and 1890 meetings, Illinois, Colorado, North Dakota, South Dakota, Pennsylvania, Michigan, West Virginia, New York, Minnesota, and California were represented for the first time in 1890. Indiana had a representative at the 1889 meeting, but evidently was not adequately organized until the following year.[31]

In the meantime, Macune, as head of the legislative committee, had put up a vigorous fight in Washington for the subtreasury bill, had mailed out thousands of circulars, kept up a diligent campaign through the *National Economist,* and had seen that Congress was flooded with thousands of petitions in behalf of the Alliance legislative program.[32]

The annual convention of 1890 was held in December, at Ocala, Florida. According to the official proceedings, delegates were present from twenty-five states and one territory.[33] Undoubtedly a number of other

---

[29] *Ibid.*, December 21, 1889.

[30] *Ibid.*, December 13, 1890, pp. 197-200.

[31] *Ibid.*, December 21, 1889, p. 210; December 13, 1890, p. 201.

[32] N. A. Dunning, pp. 133-134, 137. Also see issues of the *National Economist* for this period.

[33] N. A. Dunning, pp. 138-177. J. E. Bryan, pp. 114-138. Blood, pp. 40-41. *The New York Times,* December 1, 3, 4, 5, 6, 14, 1890.

states and a great many visiting delegates were present that were not recorded by the credentials committee. This possibly accounts for the often-repeated assertion that there were around 500 delegates present from thirty-five or so states. The official proceedings also indicate a larger attendance. A resolution was passed that "delegates from States not having State organizations be accorded privilege on the floor without the mileage and per diem, and without a vote." [34]

The whole convention was rather disturbed by confusion of various types. The total expenditures for the year had been $19,551.65, which was $6,021.10 more than receipts. The organization had apparently overshot the mark in its attempt to expand, and retrenchment was in order. The president's salary was reduced to $1,000 and the salaries of the chairman and members of the executive board and the treasurer were abolished. It was decided that neither the president nor chairman of the executive board need remain at Washington full time, and there was considerable criticism of both Polk's and Macune's militancy. [35]

The Southern Alliance was never stronger in national dues-paying members than during 1890, and yet less than 250,000 persons had financially supported the organization during that year. The constitution provided that the national dues be 5 cents. The total amount of 1890 dues equaled $12,150.22. Thus, the organization that was claiming a membership of from one to three million members could in its best year show dues collected from only 243,000 persons. [36] Its followers undoubtedly numbered hundreds of thousands, but its financial supporters were relatively few.

The *Proceedings* of the Ocala convention show how rapidly the organization was drifting into politics. In his presidential address, Polk gave due emphasis to educational and business activities, but also said:

It is the fixed purpose of this organization to secure, if possible, certain needed legislative reforms. However urgent and emphatic may be our demands, experience teaches us that they are of no avail unless

---

[34] *Ocala proceedings*, pp. 13-14.

[35] N. A. Dunning, pp. 158-162, 170. *The New York Times*, December 3, 4, 1890. *Ocala proceedings*, pp. 17, 27.

[36] See N. A. Dunning, pp. 158, 170. *Ocala proceedings*, pp. 23, 30.

supported and enforced by such practical methods as will convince the law-making power of our determination and ability to prosecute them to a successful issue. Let this Supreme Council, representing all parts of the country, and that great interest that pays over eighty per cent of all taxes of the country, assert and maintain its dignity and its solemn purpose to protect and advance the interests of its constituency, by declaring their legislative needs, and by showing to the American Congress that when its demands on paper are ignored, it can and will vindicate and maintain its claims at the ballot box.[37]

The chairman of the executive board, in his report, referred to the question of direct political action and proposed that a meeting of "delegates from all organizations of producers" be held about February, 1892, just preceding the next national campaign, to determine action. He said, "If the people by delegates coming direct from them agree that a third party move is necessary, it need not be feared . . ."[38] This suggestion was adopted by the convention at the time it was read; and later a separate resolution was adopted calling for the election of "a committee composed of one from each State here represented, to be known as the National Executive Committee, for the special purpose of conferring with like committees from other organizations" to decide what action should be taken. A legislative council was also set up, consisting of the national president and all state presidents, to look after and urge the legislative demands of the organization before Congress.[39]

Before we turn to later events, for which the ideas and plans just described furnished the basis, a few further facts concerning the Ocala convention should be given. Representatives, whether official or not, from the Farmers' Mutual Benefit Association were again present, and another committee from the Southern Alliance was appointed to confer with them about confederation. The Colored Alliance held its convention at the same time and place, and by conference between it and the white organization, it was agreed that they would work in cooperation for all their objectives and demands. The convention again asserted its

---

[37] *National Economist,* December 13, 1890, p. 198.
[38] *Ocala proceedings,* p. 25.
[39] *Ibid.,* pp. 25, 29-30, 37.

intention to stand and fight for the St. Louis platform, and the Knights of Labor assured the Alliance that it also was standing steadfastly by the St. Louis agreement.[40] The influence of the western states, in which third-party revolts had already won notable success during the year, was sufficiently great in the convention to give it a sharp and ultimate turn in the direction of political action.[41]

Indeed it is not too much to say that the Ocala meeting was the last real convention of the Southern Alliance as a general farmers' organization; for between the Ocala meeting and the proposed meeting of "delegates from all organizations of producers" to be held in February, 1892, a drive for a third party came in, so to speak, from the side, and so colored the complexion of public sentiment that the next Farmers' Alliance meeting was little more than a political convention.

The state of Kansas, which had elected W. A. Peffer to the United States Senate and "Sockless" Jerry Simpson, B. H. Clover, John Davis, J. G. Otis, and William Baker to the House of Representatives in the 1890 election, furnished the leadership for this new drive. A call was issued for a convention to be held in Cincinnati, in May, 1891, to which were invited representatives of any and all organizations which might be interested in a third-party movement. Actually the call originally planned the convention for February, 1891; but because that date conflicted with the meeting of the Kansas legislature, it was later changed to May 19 of that year.[42] Congressman Davis, in an interview to *The New York Times*,[43] said that the call was drawn up by Professor C. Vincent and his two brothers, H. and L. Vincent, all of Winfield, Kansas, the latter two being editors and publishers of the *Non-Conformist*. He further stated that they were aided in the work by C. A. Power of Indiana and General J. H. Rice of Kansas, and that they submitted a rough draft of the call to him for suggestions and changes. The calling of this

---

[40] *Ibid.*, pp. 13, 14, 16, 21-22, 31-32.

[41] *The New York Times*, December 3, 1890. *National Economist*, May 16, 1891, pp. 129-130.

[42] See Haynes, *Third party movements since the Civil War, with special reference to Iowa*, p. 246.

[43] *The New York Times*, December 5, 1890. For additional consideration of the circumstances surrounding the calling of this convention, see the *National Economist*, April 4, 1891, p. 34; May 2, p. 106. Cincinnati *Enquirer*, May 20, 1891. *The New York Times*, December 25, 1890; May 18, 1891.

convention was not an Alliance move and probably would not have received the open approval of either the northern or southern Alliance. As a matter of fact, Congressman Davis said that consideration was given to the proposition of presenting it to the Ocala convention, but the decision was made not to do so because its initiators would not want it to be known solely as an Alliance movement. It is doubtful if it would have received the approval had it been presented, for the Ocala convention apparently went just as far in the direction of a third-party movement as its constituents could be carried at that time.

It was planned that delegates from the Alliance and all other national organizations in sympathy with the St. Louis platform would be invited to take part in the Cincinnati convention, that the call would be circulated for signature in Alliance states, but that the Alliance would not be asked to endorse it per se. When the convention finally assembled, the Southern Alliance was very well represented. Yet it was more a midwestern than a southern meeting and was certainly a political convention and not a farm-organization meeting. Of the 1,412 delegates seated by the credentials committee, 411 were from Kansas, 317 from Ohio, 154 from Indiana, and 1,258 were from the nine states of Kansas, Ohio, Indiana, Nebraska, Illinois, Missouri, Kentucky, Iowa, and Minnesota.[44]

The Cincinnati conference, while not entirely a farmers' convention, is one of the highlights in the Farmers' Movement. It picked up the threads of discontent in farmer and labor circles, mobilized the advocates of reform, and crystalized the drive for political action into a party platform. The convention itself, while carried on by strict parliamentary procedure, at times almost degenerated into mob action. The organizations represented were not in any exact sense responsible for their delegates, with the consequence that the mass power of those in attendance served to dominate the organization and vote of the convention. It is an interesting commentary on the occasion that James B. Weaver, who had been the Greenback candidate for the Presidency in 1880 and was to be the Populist candidate for President in 1892, led the conservative bloc in the convention against such extremists as Ignatius Donnelly of

---

[44] Cincinnati *Enquirer*, May 21, 1891. Cincinnati *Commercial Gazette*, May 21, 1891. Cincinnati *Times-Star*, May 20, 1891. *The New York Times*, May 21, 1891. New York *Daily Tribune*, May 21, 1891. Sources do not agree on the exact number of total delegates, or the number from each state, but the difference is very slight.

Minnesota, J. A. Streeter of Illinois, and the great majority of the Kansas delegation.[45]

The Cincinnati *Enquirer*, whose reporters were in a position to observe the convention closely, and which reported the proceedings in greater detail than any other newspaper of the nation, ran headlines during the four days of the meeting as follows:

May 18, page 1:

THEY'RE HERE—THE GREAT INDUSTRIAL ARMY—THOUSANDS OF OTHERS ARE ON THE WAY—DELEGATES TO THE NATIONAL UNION CONFERENCE —SIMPSON, WEAVER AND OTHER SHINING LIGHTS ARE ON THE GROUND AND READY FOR BUSINESS—VIEWS OF THE PROBABLE WORK OF THE CONVENTION—NAMES OF THE DELEGATES ALREADY IN THE CITY

May 19, page 9:

BY THOUSANDS—COMES THE INDUSTRIAL ARMY—TO THE NATIONAL CONFERENCE IN THIS CITY—REMARKABLE GATHERING OF REFORMERS TO DISCUSS THEIR WOES—THE FARMERS OF KANSAS AND THE GREAT WEST HERE IN LARGE NUMBERS—ALL THE CENTRAL STATES WELL REPRESENTED AT THE CONVENTION—BUT THE EAST AND SOUTH SEND VERY FEW AND WILL CUT NO FIGURE—THE LEADING ISSUE IS THAT OF A THIRD PARTY AT THIS TIME—BOTH SIDES OF THE CONTROVERSY PREPARED FOR A VIGOROUS FIGHT—THE ST. LOUIS DEMANDS OF 1890 LIKELY TO BE THE PLATFORM ADOPTED—PROBABILITY OF AN AMICABLE AGREEMENT

May 20, page 9:

STARTED—THE NATIONAL UNION CONFERENCE—COMMENCES ITS SESSIONS AT MUSIC HALL—DELEGATES FROM THE WEST AND NORTHWEST PRESENT IN FORCE, WHILE THE REPRESENTATION FROM THE SOUTH AND EAST IS LIMITED—OHIO MAKES A GOOD SHOWING WITH HER DELEGATION—C. CUNNINGHAM, OF ARKANSAS, SELECTED TEMPORARY CHAIRMAN—SENTIMENT OVERWHELMINGLY IN FAVOR OF THE NEW PARTY MOVEMENT

May 21, page 9:

PEOPLE'S PARTY—BIRTH OF THE NEW POLITICAL POWER, WHICH WILL ENTER THE NEXT PRESIDENTIAL FIGHT—THE NATIONAL CONFERENCE

---

[45] Cincinnati *Enquirer*, May 20, 1891.

COMPLETES ITS WORK AND ORGANIZES FOR THE GREAT POLITICAL BATTLE OF '92–TUMULTUOUS SCENE FOLLOWS WHEN THE BLUE AND GRAY SHAKE HANDS ACROSS THE BLOODY CHASM AND BURY THE HATCHET

A few headlines from the Cincinnati *Commercial Gazette* give similar pictures of the convention:

May 18, page 1:

AT HAND–THE BIRTH THROES OF THE NEW PARTY–A SUCCESSFUL ACCOUCHEMENT WILL BE DIFFICULT–FOR THE DOCTORS DIFFER WIDELY AND RADICALLY–THEIR FLAG, THOUGH NOT RED, HAS A CRIMSON TONE–WITH LITTLE WHITE OR BLUE TO RELIEVE IT

May 19, page 1:

ALLIANCE ALIVE–BUT ONLY A FACTOR IN TODAY'S GREAT CONFERENCE–MANY MEN OF MANY MINDS TAKE PART–FARMERS, NATIONALISTS, SINGLE TAXERS AND LABORERS–LAND, MONEY AND TRANSPORTATION LEADING–A NEW PARTY IMMINENT UNLESS DEFECTIVE MACHINERY AND INHARMONIOUS POLICIES PREVENT

May 20, page 1:

9,000,000 MORTGAGED HOMES–ONE OF THE TEXTS OF U. S. SENATOR PEFFER–WHO PREDICTS THE FORMATION OF A THIRD PARTY–WHOSE MISSION IS TO CREATE, NOT TO DESTROY–THE CLASSES DRIFTING AWAY FROM THE MASSES–ONE GOING UPWARD, THE OTHER DOWNWARD–FULL REPORT OF A REMARKABLE SPEECH–VOICING THE PRINCIPLES UNDERLYING THE "NATIONAL UNION CONFERENCE"–WHICH ORGANIZED WITHOUT MUCH CONFUSION YESTERDAY NOON.

May 21, page 1:

THE PEOPLE'S PARTY–BORN AND BAPTIZED–SHORT, SHARP WORK AT MUSIC HALL–AMID SURROUNDINGS OF INTENSE EXCITEMENT–SCENES THAT WERE DRAMATIC AND IMPRESSIVE–THE NET RESULT A STRIKING PLATFORM

The reports of the Cincinnati convention contained in the *National Economist* were much less picturesque and sensational. Excerpts from its report of the meeting read as follows:

This meeting and the platform . . . are now matters of history . . . . There are many views which can be presented of the causes for the meeting, the work of the body assembled, its methods and the immediate effect and ultimate results of the action, all worthy to challenge the most careful thought and consideration on the part of every loyal and true citizen of this country.

It was not an Alliance meeting. Those who called it did not desire or intend that it should be an Alliance meeting. The Alliance at its last national session, at Ocala, Florida, had provided for a general conference of all organizations of producers willing to cooperate to secure political reform, to be held in February, 1892, and agreed that delegates from all such organizations should meet at that time upon an equitable basis of representation and agree upon a set of demands and upon a method for enforcing such demands.[46]

The conference was called to order by Judge W. F. Rightmire of Kansas; and United States Senator William A. Peffer, newly elected by a third-party group in Kansas, was made permanent chairman. Not a single southerner served on an important committee nor took a prominent part in the discussions. President Polk of the Southern Alliance, in a letter to the convention, advised against the formation of a third party until a year later; but Polk's suggestion was listened to with "painful silence."[47] The convention built its platform largely out of the St. Louis and Ocala demands, and the party founded by the convention served as the chief instrument by which the Alliance got its demands before the public. At the same time, it served inadvertently as the move by which the Alliance ultimately lost its national identity in the oncoming Populist revolt.[48] Technically, the Southern Alliance remained in the hands of southerners, but as a national movement it was never again able to dominate the stage now set for a political drama which soon swept it and all other farm organizations of the time except the Grange into oblivion.

[46] *National Economist*, May 30, 1891, p. 161.

[47] Cincinnati *Enquirer*, May 21, 1891. Cincinnati *Commercial Gazette*, May 21, 1891. *National Economist*, April 4, 1891, p. 24. New York *Daily Tribune*, May 21, 1891.

[48] For detailed and excellent accounts of the Cincinnati convention, see *Appleton's, 1891*. *National Economist*, February 21, 1891, p. 357; May 16, pp. 129-130; May 30, pp. 161-162; June 13, pp. 196-197, 199; November 21, p. 145. New York *Daily Tribune*, May 20-22, June 2, 1891. *The New York Times*, May 19-22, 1891. Cincinnati *Commercial Gazette*, May 18-22, 1891. Cincinnati *Enquirer*, May 17-21, 1891. Cincinnati *Times-Star*, May 19-21, 1891. *Western Rural*, June 6, 1891. Hicks, *The Populist revolt*, pp. 209, 211-217. Haynes, *Third party movements*, pp. 246-249.

SOUTHERN ALLIANCE DRIFTS INTO POLITICS

As a result of Dr. Macune's suggestion—in his report to the Ocala convention as chairman of the executive board—recommending the authorization of a call for a convention in February, 1892, of all organizations of producers willing to cooperate for political reform, and because of the growing agitation for third-party action, the Southern Alliance passed a resolution providing the skeleton machinery for such action, and the details for putting the plan into effect were referred to a committee on confederation.[49] The committee met in Washington, D. C., in January, 1891, with like committees from the Knights of Labor, the Farmers' Mutual Benefit Association, the National Colored Farmers' Alliance, and the National Citizens' Alliance, and organized themselves into the Confederation of Industrial Organizations with Ben Terrell of the Southern Alliance as its president and with a slightly modified Ocala platform as its basis. They scheduled their next meeting for February 22, 1892, and "delegates from every industrial organization in the country were invited to meet with them" at that time.[50] Thus was the stage set for the St. Louis meeting in February, 1892, the overture of the Southern Alliance to the demands for third-party action.

Early in June, 1891, representatives of the Farmers' Alliance and Industrial Union from Missouri, Kansas, Colorado, Nebraska, and the Indian Territory met in Kansas City to establish an interstate union, the object being "to effect a business organization and to establish an Alliance newspaper."[51] This was a perfectly legitimate thing for these state organizations to do, but it served to show the militancy and to an extent the independence of the western Alliancemen at this time. A similar meeting of the business departments of the Alliance of twenty-two states was also held in New York in November, 1891, for the purpose of organizing the National Union Company, the program of which was "to buy out a merchant in every trade center of importance, stock him up with everything he wants in the line of general everyday goods demanded

---

[49] *Ocala proceedings*, pp. 25, 37.
[50] *National Economist*, January 31, 1891, pp. 309-310; April 4, p. 34; May 30, p. 161. Blood, pp. 66-67. Hicks, *The Populist revolt*, pp. 210-211.
[51] Haynes, *Third party movements*, pp. 252-253. *Appleton's, 1890*, p. 299.

by the farmers, and make him the local manager of the concern." [52]
Again this was a project not sponsored by Southern Alliance leaders and
was a further indication that Alliance affairs were drifting rapidly out of
the hands of the officers of the southern organization.

In the interim between the Cincinnati convention held in May, 1891,
at which the People's party was founded, and the annual meeting of the
Farmers' Alliance held at Indianapolis in 1891, the *National Economist*
took great pains to emphasize the fact that the People's party and the
Farmers' Alliance were absolutely separate organizations. The elections
of 1891 had transpired in the meantime and the People's party had not
fared too well in these elections. The Alliance was therefore very anxious not to be the recipient of any adverse public opinion which had
developed on account of the third-party movement. The leading article
in the *National Economist,* November 21, 1891, said in part:

> Because the People's party did not win at the recent election the
> Alliance is going to pieces. This is the logic of the old party organs
> all over the country. This is done to discourage and dishearten mem-
> bers of the Alliance and win them back to their old party allegiance.
> To some extent this sort of misconstruction is having its effect, but
> as a rule it does no harm. The Alliance and the People's party are
> two separate and distinct organizations and will always remain so,
> despite the efforts of the partisan press to force them together...
> The Alliance as an order has received no injury, but will receive a
> positive benefit. The meeting at Cincinnati... was not an Alliance
> meeting in any sense of the term, and was not so considered at
> that time nor since. In fact the Alliance and its conservatism has
> been roundly abused by the more radical reform press because it
> did not take a part in that meeting. Since this meeting all political
> action outside of Kansas has been in the hands of those who did
> not belong to the Order. [53]

The program for the Indianapolis convention, published in advance
in the *National Economist,* proved that the meeting was planned quite
definitely as a farmers' meeting and not as a political convention. Nevertheless, it had sprinkled among the assigned speakers such third-party

---

[52] Haynes, *Third party movements,* pp. 253-255. St. Louis *Globe-Democrat,* February
23, 1892.

[53] *National Economist,* November 21, 1891, pp. 145, 152.

sympathizers as Loucks of South Dakota and of the Southern Alliance, Stelle of the Farmers' Mutual Benefit Association, and such political leaders as James B. Weaver, Jerry Simpson, Senator Peffer, and Ignatius Donnelly.[54] The stage was, therefore, almost perfectly set for just what happened, namely, a convention which played halfway between the old Farmers' Alliance purposes and third-party politics.

The Supreme Council—the delegate body of the Southern Alliance—held its authorized 1891 annual meeting at Indianapolis in November. The convention moved forward from the first day as a regular annual meeting. Colonel Polk, in his presidential address, once more emphasized the educational features of the organization, but at the same time laid great emphasis upon the demands of the organization, most of which called for definite political action. Although he declared that the Alliance must be kept free from entanglement with any party, he also said that the farmer had "resolved to present his case before the supreme tribunal of public opinion and ask for its decision through the ballot-box." One whole section—in fact, the concluding section of his address—was under the subtitle "Our Duty Politically." The following few sentences taken from this section of Polk's speech will illustrate its tenor.

When it [the Alliance] shall fail to elevate its membership above the arrogant domination of party mandate—when it shall fail to impress the individual member with the fearful responsibility which attaches to his action as a citizen—when it shall fail to teach him that it is a great political and moral crime to subordinate his honest and enlightened convictions to the ascendancy of mere party policy, the hour for its decay, dissolution, and death will have come.[55]

Polk, Macune, Livingstone, and Terrell, all outstanding leaders of the old Southern Alliance group, joined by Tillman of South Carolina, did their best to stem the tide which they felt was drifting permanently toward third-party action. These southerners believed that the farmers of the South would have a greater chance of gaining power by capturing the Democratic party than by organizing a new party. Taylor had done so in Tennessee, Tillman in South Carolina, and Watson in Georgia. But General James B. Weaver of Iowa and Congressman Jerry Simpson of

[54] *Ibid.*, October 31, 1891, p. 103.
[55] *Ibid.*, November 28, 1891, pp. 162-166.

Kansas, both strong third-party advocates, addressed the convention and, together with other northern leaders, swung the organization toward political action. Polk was re-elected president, but H. L. Loucks of South Dakota, a member of the national committee of the newly organized People's party, was made vice-president.

The general movement for reform had broken up and become organized into so many different agencies, each trying to furnish leadership and guidance to one trend of events, that the whole meeting was one of confusion as far as the old Southern Alliance program was concerned. The Reform Press Association, the Committee on Confederation of Industrial Organization, the State Business Agents, and the national committee of the People's party all held meetings during the convention, each striving to give direction to the great dynamic power represented there. There was only one thing upon which there was a semblance of agreement, and that was the need for some sort of political action based upon the St. Louis and Ocala platforms. While, therefore, the southern leaders sought in vain to guide things into nonpartisan channels, it seemed inevitable that the third-party advocates would ultimately triumph. The minutes of the convention, together with the newspaper reports of the time, show the shift which had taken place in the activities and purposes of the Southern Farmers' Alliance. No longer did the business enterprises of the national organization or of the state organizations receive major consideration. As a matter of fact, the organization of business agencies was severed from the national organization. The proceedings of the convention do not show such activities in detail; however, they do record that the state business agencies were made an organization separate from the Alliance as a result of action taken by the Supreme Council of the Southern Alliance.[56]

The *National Economist* reported in its columns that at the convention "all was peace and harmony, no discord, no jar, no contention... The harmony of sentiment was truly remarkable; nearly all the action had was practically unanimous." In another place it said, "The most prominent and remarkable feature of the recent national meeting was the perfect unity which prevailed."[57] Press reports from the Indianapo-

---

[56] *Ibid.*, December 5, 1891, p. 181.
[57] *Ibid.*, November 28, 1891, p. 162; December 5, p. 177.

lis papers, whose reporters were undoubtedly in attendance whenever possible and who interviewed many outstanding personages participating in the convention, indicated, however, that harmony was not so pronounced; in fact, they clearly recorded that the transfer in emphasis which was taking place in this giant farmers' organization from economic to political action was not without great disturbance and confusion. The Indianapolis *Sentinel* carried these headlines on three days of the convention:

November 20, page 1:

SPLIT AND CAUGHT DESCRIBES THE SITUATION OF THE ALLIANCE —THE ANTI-SUB-TREASURY MEN WILL BREAK AWAY AND THE OTHERS JOIN THE PEOPLE'S PARTY—ALL MASKS ARE REMOVED— THE THIRD-PARTY COMMITTEE GATHERS THEM IN—GETTING ALL THE NATIONAL OFFICERS OF THE ALLIANCE—THE FMBA QUIETLY DROPS INTO LINE—THE CONFEDERATE CONVENTION NEXT FEB. WILL PROBABLY CALL FOR A PRESIDENTIAL NOMINATING COM- MITTEE—THE ANTI-SUB-TREASURY MEN WILL IMMEDIATELY PRO- CEED TO ORGANIZE A NEW ALLIANCE—THE REFORM PRESS ASSO- CIATION AND THE NATIONAL UNION—DOINGS OF THE VARIOUS ORGANIZATIONS

November 21, page 1:

HAPPY AS CLAMS ARE THE PEOPLE'S PARTY'S REPRESENTATIVES, HAVING SECURED ALL THEY CAME HERE FOR—THEY ISSUE AN ADDRESS TO THE PEOPLE—A TICKET BEFORE JUNE—THE ANTI- SUB-TREASURY ALLIANCE TO MEET IN MEMPHIS—A CALL ISSUED BY THE EXECUTIVE COMMITTEE—JERRY SIMPSON THINKS THE THIRD PARTY WILL WIN

November 23, page 2:

THE FARMERS GO HOME FEELING WELL PLEASED WITH THEIR WEEK'S WORK—BUT NOT HALF SO JUBILANT AS THE PEOPLE'S PARTY MANAGERS, WHO SEEM TO HAVE SECURED EVERYTHING THEY CAME AFTER—DR. MACUNE'S GREAT VICTORY [58]

[58] For excellent accounts of the Indianapolis convention, see *National Economist*, November 28, 1891, pp. 161-169; December 5, pp. 177-178, 180-183. Hicks, *The Populist revolt*, pp. 221-222. Haynes, *Third party movements*, pp. 254-255. Blood, pp. 41-42. Indianapolis *Sentinel*, November 14-23, 1891. Indianapolis *Journal*, November 16-23, 1891.

The subtreasury split was another difficulty reported by the Indianapolis press. It was probably somewhat overemphasized because the anti-subtreasury group issued a call during the Indianapolis meeting for a separate convention to be held the following month. As far as the author knows, this meeting was never held. If it was, it did not affect enough Alliance members to be significant. The following excerpt from the *National Economist* probably gives a fair picture of the situation:

> ... the action of that body [the Southern Alliance] upon the sub-treasury plan was unanimous. It is perhaps true that there are many members of the Order who do not accept the sub-treasury plan in full, but it is not true that they are fighting the demands of the Order on that account. True, there had been a few who have adopted that course (less than a hundred in the United States), and they have as a rule been expelled from the Order, and are now seeking notoriety by reporting organizations that never existed and never will. These men who are fighting the demands held a meeting in St. Louis last September, and appointed a committee to visit the Supreme Council in their behalf. The committee came to Indianapolis and made their presence known to the Supreme Council. A Committee was appointed to confer with them and report. They presented to the committee their objections to the demands, which were carefully considered by the committee, and the proposition made by the committee in response, was that they should reduce their objections to the demands to writing, file a copy with the committee, and the next night they would discuss the question publicly, they to first read their paper and defend it, and a member to respond. This they refused to accept. These facts are submitted to the public, believing that it is unfair, unkind and unjust for the press of the country to persistently circulate reports of a split and division in an order of over a million members on account of the opposition to it by less than a hundred members who have been expelled as unworthy.[59]

A meeting of the confederated organizations (the Confederation of Industrial Organizations) was held during the progress of the Indianapolis convention and the basis of representation for various national or-

---

[59] *National Economist,* December 5, 1891, p. 177. See also Indianapolis *Sentinel,* November 21-22, 1891.

ganizations was decided upon for the delegate convention to be held in St. Louis the following February. The resolutions adopted read as follows:

> That representation in the convention shall be governed by the following rules:
>
> 1. Each of the following organizations shall be entitled to twenty-five votes as an organization:
>
> The National Farmers' Alliance and Industrial Union
> The National Farmers' Alliance
> The Colored Farmers' National Alliance and Co-Operative Union
> The Farmers' Mutual Benefit Association
> The Knights of Labor
> The National Citizens' Alliance
> The National Citizens' Industrial Alliance
> The Patrons of Husbandry
> The National Patrons of Industry, and such other organizations as may be accepted and indorsed by the executive committee prior to the first day of February
>
> 2. Each of the above organizations acting with the confederation shall be entitled to an additional vote for each 10,000 voting members and major fraction part thereof. Adopted.[60]

The meeting first mentioned in the Ocala convention and planned by the Confederation of Industrial Organizations was held according to schedule in St. Louis in February, 1892. It was a Southern Alliance project to the extent that Macune had suggested such a meeting originally, that the Southern Alliance had participated in the organization of the Confederation of Industrial Organizations, and that the Indianapolis convention had agreed to it. All the organizations represented at Indianapolis and others were present. Ben Terrell, past national lecturer of the Southern Alliance and president of the Confederation, called the meeting to order and urged the convention to "confine [its] demands to land, transportation, taxation, and money," leaving "moral reform" till they had more time. President Polk was the first to address the convention, and while he confined his remarks chiefly to the money question, in closing, he said, "... we must have relief if we have to wipe the two old par-

---

[60] *National Economist,* December 19, 1891, p. 213.

ties from the face of the earth."[61] Others moved forward with the full intention of perfecting a complete third-party program. The speechmaking was concluded by Ignatius Donnelly of Minnesota, who predicted the union of the Democrats and Republicans to defeat the reformers and said their wedding "ceremony would be performed at the altar of plutocracy, Grover Cleveland and Ben Harrison would act as bridesmen, the devil himself would give away the bride, and Jay Gould pronounce the benediction."[62]

Twenty-two different organizations, some of them never heard of by the chief leaders or the credentials committee, were given delegate representation in the 1892 St. Louis convention. The call had been issued in the name of nine organizations which were finally allotted approximately 675 out of a total of nearly 765 seats in the convention. Of these, the National Farmers' Alliance and Industrial Union (Southern Alliance) was allotted 246, and the Colored Alliance, 97. Thus, a total of 343, or almost one-half of the delegates, were from the southern group. Ranking in order of strength below them were: Knights of Labor, 82; Patrons of Industry, 75; Farmers' Mutual Benefit Association, 53; National Farmers' Alliance (Northern Alliance), 49; National Citizens' Industrial Alliance, 25; Patrons of Husbandry, 25; and National Citizens' Alliance, 25.[63] Colonel Polk, national president of the Southern Alliance, and Ben Terrell, past national lecturer of that organization, were nominated for permanent chairmen. Polk was in favor of the third-party movement and Terrell opposed to it. Polk was elected. His election can well be marked as the official act by which the Southern Alliance was carried into the Populist party. But for the moment, and in the convention itself, there was enough third-party opposition to forestall a direct third-party move, and the convention adjourned after having adopted a platform which

---

[61] *Ibid.*, March 5, 1892, p. 394; February 27, p. 380. *The New York Times*, February 23, 1892. St. Louis *Republic*, February 23, 1892.

[62] *The New York Times*, February 23, 1892. *National Economist*, February 27, 1892, p. 380.

[63] The Citizens' Alliance was an organization largely confined to Kansas, which was set up for the small townspeople who were barred from membership in the Alliance, but who were followers of the Alliance and Populist movements. According to the *National Economist*, October 11, 1890, the organization at the time had more than 16,000 members and was "rapidly increasing." See *National Economist*, October 11, 1890, p. 60; January 17, 1891, p. 283.

followed closely the demands of the Southern Alliance made in its St. Louis meeting in 1889 and repeated at the Ocala convention in 1890.

Sources differ as to the total number of delegates and the relative delegate strength of various organizations seated, the only significant difference being that some sources give the Northern Alliance 97 delegates rather than 49. Some sources also mention that 25 delegates-at-large were credited to the Southern Alliance, but this is not substantiated. Neither is it exactly clear whether there were eight or nine organizations which took part in issuing the call, the participation of the Patrons of Husbandry in this regard being questionable. The National Citizens' Industrial Alliance is referred to by some sources as the National Citizens' Independent Alliance.[64]

A meeting of "individual and independent citizens who love their country" immediately followed adjournment. Macune called the meeting to order and James B. Weaver was made presiding officer. A committee of fifteen was appointed to confer with the executive committee of the People's party with regard to the calling of a nominating convention. That night the two committees met and decided to hold such a convention on July 4, 1892.[65] At the nominating convention held in Omaha, the Populist party became a blazing reality, and the Southern Alliance was literally buried.[66] Colonel Polk died on June 11, between the time of the St. Louis and Omaha meetings, and H. L. Loucks of South Dakota, vice-president of the Southern Alliance and member of the national com-

---

[64] The *National Economist*, March 5, 1892, p. 395. St. Louis *Globe-Democrat*, February 24, 1892. St. Louis *Republic*, February 24, 1892. *The New York Times*, February 24, 1892. *Southern Mercury*, February 25, 1892. For detailed accounts of the St. Louis convention, see *National Economist*, February 27, 1892, p. 380; March 5, pp. 385, 392, 394-397; March 12, pp. 401-402. *The New York Times*, February 23-25, 1892. St. Louis *Globe-Democrat*, February 22-26, 1892. St. Louis *Republic*, February 22-25, 1892. *People's Party Paper* (Atlanta, Georgia), February 25, March 3, 1892. Hicks, *The Populist revolt*, pp. 223-228. Haynes, *Third party movements*, pp. 257-259. Arnett, pp. 132-134.

[65] *National Economist*, March 5, 1892, pp. 385, 396-397. Blood, p. 67. *The New York Times*, February 25-26, 1892. Hicks, *The Populist revolt*, pp. 228-229. Haynes, *Third party movements*, pp. 259-260.

[66] For accounts of the Omaha convention, see *National Economist*, July 9, 1892, pp. 257-258; July 16, pp. 279, 288. New York *Daily Tribune*, July 3-6, 1892. Chicago *Daily Tribune*, July 4-5, 1892. *Morning World-Herald* (Omaha, Nebraska), July 2-6, 1892. Hicks, *The Populist revolt*, pp. 230-237. Haynes, *Third party movements*, pp. 261-264.

mittee of the People's party, became president. He had been president of the National (Northern) Farmers' Alliance during the year 1890, and through him it was easy to swing large segments of both organizations quickly into the Populist party movement.

THE NORTHERN ALLIANCE IN THE EARLY NINETIES

The Northern Alliance left the 1889 St. Louis convention with its ranks divided. The Kansas, South Dakota, and North Dakota delegations had gone over to the Southern Alliance and had been seated in the Southern convention. President Burrows of the Northern Alliance had said in his presidential address at St. Louis that

> New state organizations have been formed in Ohio, Washington, and Colorado. The Alliance has been reorganized in Illinois on a basis that promises to give that great state a distinctively farmers' organization commensurate with the magnitude of its agricultural industries. New Alliances have been chartered in California, Oregon, Pennsylvania, Indiana, New York and Missouri, and only a little effort is required to secure state organizations in those states.[67]

All of these states except California and Oregon were represented in its next national annual convention.

Northern and western states listed by the credentials committee at St. Louis in 1889 included Indiana, Missouri, Kansas, Nebraska, and Oklahoma. In 1890, additional northern and western states sending representatives were Illinois, Colorado, North Dakota, South Dakota, Pennsylvania, Michigan, New York, Minnesota, and California; however, Nebraska and Oklahoma were not present. In 1891, Wisconsin, New Jersey, Ohio, Washington, Oregon, and Iowa were the new western and northern states present, with Oklahoma also having representatives at this meeting.

The failure at union led the militant president of the Southern Alliance—Colonel L. L. Polk—to efforts to enlist northern states in his organization. In this he was fairly successful for, as we have seen, nine northern and western states had delegates at the 1890 Southern Alliance conven-

[67] *Farmers' Alliance*, December 21, 1889.

tion at Ocala for the first time and seven more were at its 1891 convention.[68] The Northern Alliance, however, continued its existence and, in the states of Nebraska, Ohio, and Iowa, continued to gain strength. It held its next annual convention in Omaha in January, 1891, to which eleven states sent representatives. The credentials committee seated 105 delegates as follows: Nebraska, 42; Ohio, 18; Iowa, 17; Illinois, 6; Indiana, 5; Wisconsin and Washington, each 4; Pennsylvania, 3; New York, Missouri, and Minnesota, each 2. The constitution provided for two delegates-at-large from each state and one delegate from each twenty-five local Alliances or major fraction thereof. It would thus appear that the Northern Alliance could claim something over 2,000 locals at that time, about one-half of them in Nebraska. The secretary, however, stated in his report that two states not represented at the convention had state Alliances and that three additional states were preparing to organize.[69]

President Powers, in his address, stated that "there are interests which are common to all [industrial classes], and for which some general organization is necessary," and that it was in the relation of these organizations to the government that cooperation was most needed. He called attention to recent successes of political moves which had arisen "on the spur of the moment" and said, ". . . it does seem reasonable that by following out a definite, plain system for such action every year, that success would be the rule and not the exception." He believed that the issues upon which the concerted action was urgently needed at that time were: "Money reform, land reform, transportation reform, ballot reform, and the suppression of any vice that is tolerated by law to the peril of our national prosperity." In his address he laid greatest emphasis on money reform. One of the convention's resolutions called for "the free and unlimited coinage of silver on an equality with gold."[70]

The convention listened to Ben Terrell of the Southern Alliance explain the Ocala platform of that organization, but after some discussion tabled all consideration of the matter. It also voted that it could not see its way clear at that time to enter into an elaborate system of co-

---

[68] N. A. Dunning, pp. 96-97, 152-153. *National Economist*, November 28, 1891, p. 166. *Ocala proceedings*, pp. 12-13.

[69] E. A. Allen, pp. 519, 522. Ashby, pp. 412-413.

[70] E. A. Allen, pp. 519-522, 532-533. Omaha *Daily Bee*, January 28, 1891.

operative enterprises proposed by delegates from the Farmers' Mutual Benefit Association, although it did agree to work in cooperation with that organization for common objectives.

Probably the most important action taken by the convention was contained in a resolution calling for a convention on February 22, 1892, "to fix a date and place for the holding of a convention to nominate candidates for the office of President and Vice-President of the United States." It demanded, however, that representatives to that convention consist of "one delegate from each State in the Union." [71] The first part of the declaration at least was in harmony with the Southern Alliance, and with the Southern Alliance it moved, through the steps already described, into a second Omaha convention, July 4, 1892, and into the Populist party movement.

THE FARMERS' MUTUAL BENEFIT ASSOCIATION IN THE NINETIES

The Farmers' Mutual Benefit Association continued to flirt with both the northern and southern Alliances after the St. Louis, 1889, convention. It had representatives at every meeting of each organization, and each time joint committees were appointed to work on federation. Organic union was never accomplished with either, however; and it came into the second St. Louis convention, in February, 1892, with enough separate strength to be allotted fifty-three delegates to help make the plans for a third-party convention.[72]

---

[71] *National Economist*, February 7, 1891, p. 333. For a detailed account of the Omaha convention, see proceedings in E. A. Allen, pp. 519-536. Hicks, *The Populist revolt*, p. 210. New York *Daily Tribune*, January 28, 30, 1891. Omaha *Daily Bee*, January 28, 1891.

[72] *National Economist*, March 5, 1892, p. 395. Haynes, *Third party movements*, p. 258.

· 12 ·

THE POPULIST REVOLT

ECONOMIC CONDITIONS OF AGRICULTURE IN
THE EARLY NINETIES

T he economic conditions which prevailed in the eighties had stimulated the growth of farmers' organizations beyond anything that had
ever been accomplished in that field before that time. Once the organizations had felt their power and formulated their programs, it would
have required a startling turn for the better in farm economic outlook
to have diverted them from the path they had charted. Never were all
the issues around which the American Farmers' Movement revolved more
clearly seen and never were so many slogans of the Movement coined.

No such turn for the better in the economic outlook came to pass, except for a slight improvement in general prices during 1890 and 1891.
The wholesale farm price index, which had declined to 67 in 1889, rose
to 76 in 1891 and then started a decline which, with some fluctuations,
continued for five years, dropping to 56 in 1896. The purchasing power
of farm commodities never dipped so low as the wholesale farm price
index during this period, for the wholesale price index of nonagricultural
products was also falling; but the purchasing power of farm products
was down for the third time since the Civil War and was exceedingly low
in 1890.[1] Even had the purchasing capacity of farmers remained the

---

[1] "Wholesale Prices of Farm and Nonagricultural Products, 1798-1938."

same, discontent would not have been averted, for while farmers would have in that case remained relatively as well off, the slump in prices would have had its effect. So crude a reaction as a movement operates upon obvious comparisons and contrasts and is most subtly tuned to general trends, but it is never capable of detailed analysis of intricate facts. The fact that prices for corn, wheat, hogs, cotton, and other major farm products fell lower year after year was sufficient to carry farm revolt to one of its highest peaks in American history. In an attempt, therefore, to understand the Populist movement in terms of its economic background, a comparison of the nominal prices of specific farm products is more important than indexes of longtime trends.

Cotton on the New Orleans market averaged 9.08 cents per pound in 1890, 7.28 cents in 1891, 8.15 cents in 1892, 7.3 cents in 1893, and 5.86 cents in 1894. The price of corn, while fluctuating considerably during the first half of the decade, fell quite steadily on the Chicago market from 58 cents a bushel in 1890 to 25 cents in 1896. Wheat prices followed the same trend, falling from 97 cents a bushel in 1890 to 57 cents in 1894.[2] The farm price for cotton averaged 8.4 cents per pound for the four years 1888-1891, but fell to an average of 6.9 cents for the four years 1892-1895. The farm price of corn dropped to 21 cents per bushel in 1896, the farm price of wheat to 49 cents in 1894, and the farm price of tobacco to 6 cents per pound in 1896.[3] In some special localities, farm prices dipped considerably below their national averages. Wheat, for instance, sold for an average of 42 cents per bushel in Kansas and 40 cents in Nebraska in 1893, and cotton sold for 4.1 cents per pound in Mississippi in 1894.[4] These decreasing prices were not offset by corresponding decreases in the costs of production and distribution. Freight rates declined only slightly during the period, taxes stayed the same or increased, farm wages declined only slightly, and interest payments on farm mortgages remained fixed.[5] Only the slightest calculation is neces-

---

[2] *Agricultural statistics, 1939*, pp. 9, 44, 102. United States Department of Agriculture. Washington, D. C.: Government Printing Office, 1939.

[3] Ward C. Jensen, *Price economics of what farmers sell*, p. 6. Bulletin 226. South Carolina Agricultural Experiment Station of Clemson College, May, 1926.

[4] *Yearbook of the United States Department of Agriculture, 1894*, p. 545.

[5] C. E. Emerick, "An Analysis of Agricultural Discontent in the United States," II, *Political Science Quarterly*, Vol. XI, No. 4 (December, 1896), pp. 606-607. Buck, *The Granger movement*, pp. 104-109.

sary to prove that farmers had just cause for discontent with the situation. A farm mortgage of $1,000, for instance, contracted by a wheat farmer in 1890 pledged him to pay the then farm selling price of 1,031 bushels of wheat. In 1894 he found himself compelled to sell 1,775 bushels to liquidate the debt. A debt contracted in 1890 in terms of 1,000 bushels of corn required 2,320 bushels in 1896 to liquidate it. This sort of picture was painted over and over again to farmers during the Populist campaigns of the nineties. Nor was it an exaggerated picture, for 75 per cent of mortgage debt in force in 1890 had been incurred during the five years just passed, and only 8.02 per cent was incurred before 1880.[6]

Mrs. Mary Elizabeth Lease of Kansas, one of the Alliance orators of the times, describes the situation as follows:

> Wall Street owns the country. It is no longer a government of the people, by the people and for the people, but a government of Wall Street, by Wall Street, and for Wall Street. The great common people of this country are slaves, and monopoly is the master. The West and South are bound and prostrate before the manufacturing East. Money rules, and our Vice President is a London banker. Our laws are the output of a system which clothes rascals in robes and honesty in rags. The parties lie to us and the political speakers mislead us . . . the politicians say we suffered from overproduction. Overproduction when 10,000 little children, so statistics tell us, starve to death every year in the United States, and over 100,000 shop-girls in New York are forced to sell their virtue for the bread their niggardly wages deny them . . . Kansas suffers from two great robbers, the Santa Fe Railroad and the loan companies. The common people are robbed to enrich their masters . . . There are thirty men in the United States whose aggregate wealth is over one and one-half billion dollars. There are half a million looking for work . . . We want money, land and transportation. We want the abolition of the National Banks, and we want the power to make loans direct from the government. We want the accursed foreclosure system wiped out. Land equal to a tract thirty miles wide and ninety miles long has been foreclosed and bought in by loan companies of Kansas in a year. We will stand by our homes and stay by our firesides by force

---

[6] *Report on real estate mortgages in the United States at the eleventh census: 1890,* p. 313. Department of the Interior, Census Office, George K. Holmes and John S. Lord, Special Agents. Washington, D. C.: Government Printing Office, 1895.

if necessary, and we will not pay our debts to the loan-shark companies until the government pays its debt to us. The people are at bay, let the blood-hounds of money who have dogged us thus far beware.[7]

At another time Mrs. Lease said, "It is a conflict between the debtor class and the creditor class, is a conflict between the wheat, pork, and beef, and cotton, and corn, against the bond holders, the bonds and gold of the nation."[8]

Most of the farm mortgage debt which burdened farmers in the nineties had been incurred in a perfectly normal way. Men borrowed money to buy land and improve it with the expectation that farm income acquired by hard labor, normal seasons, and normal prices would enable them gradually but surely to pay it back. Creditors made loans in this same faith. Nor, over a long period of time, were these calculations and this faith incorrect. Iowa farm-land values, for instance, increased 678 per cent between 1880 and 1910, while the farm-mortgage debt increased only 376 per cent.[9] But for the period 1891-1896, practically all such calculations went awry because of the general disturbance resulting from the panic of 1893 and, in some of the western states, because of repeated crop failures.

The panic of 1893 was a financial panic. It started by the failure of the Philadelphia and Reading Railway Company in February, followed by the failure of the National Cordage Company in May. These failures, as is always the case in a panic, punctured the thin skin of credit structure in New York, and the whole stock market collapsed. The scare was on; the people by the thousands rushed to get their money out of banks. In self-protection the eastern banks tightened on credit and restricted loans to interior banks. Western and southern banks in small towns and farming communities went to the wall first—and quickly. Out of a total of 158 national bank failures of that year, 153 were in the West and South. In addition to national banks, 425 state, private, and savings banks and loan,

---

[7] Barr, Vol. II, pp. 1150-1151. Reprinted by permission of the Lewis Historical Publishing Company, Inc. Annie L. Diggs, "The Women in the Alliance Movement," *Arena*, Vol. VI, No. 2 (July, 1892), pp. 165-167.

[8] *Joint debate between Mrs. M. E. Lease and J. M. Brumbaugh*, p. 6. Concordia, Kansas: F. A. Filson, Times Print.

[9] William G. Murray, p. 371.

trust, and mortgage companies suspended operations.[10] These conditions, added to those which had resulted from low farm prices for the two years before and a crop failure over wide areas of the Middle West, converted the panic of 1893 into a general economic depression for agriculture.

Kansas was probably harder hit than any other state. The great avalanche of population that flowed into the West from 1850 to 1890 had run well past the areas of safe farming into arid lands. Railroad advertisements and land boomers had caused farms to be opened up and towns built which had no chance of survival in a country subject to severe drought. The droughts of 1887, 1888, and 1893-1897 served practically to depopulate many western Kansas counties. Families traded whole farms for teams and wagons with which to move farther west or return to the East. What happened in western Kansas also happened in western Nebraska, the Dakotas, and eastern Colorado. In 1891 no less than 18,000 prairie schooners crossed from Nebraska to the Iowa side of the Missouri River. Twenty-six counties in South Dakota lost 30,000 population during the nineties. Kansas's population as a whole decreased more than 92,000 between 1890 and 1895, most of the loss being in western counties. Twenty well-built towns in that part of the state were reputed to be left without a single inhabitant, and 11,000 farm mortgages were foreclosed between 1889 and 1893. A great number of one-time farm owners were reduced to the status of tenants and hired men.[11] With conditions such as these prevailing, it is little wonder that farm revolt resulted and that Kansas led the way.

In addition to the immediate circumstances which caused farmers to rebel, there was another set of factors working slowly but surely to alter the whole economic and social status of farmers. The westward move-

---

[10] Alexander D. Noyes, *Forty years of American finance*, pp. 188-194. New York: G. P. Putnam's Sons, 1909. *Annual report of the Comptroller of the Currency to the second session of the fifty-third Congress of the United States*, Vol. I, p. 80. Washington, D. C.: Government Printing Office, 1893.

[11] Farmer, pp. 406-427. Miller, pp. 469-489. James C. Malin, "The Turnover of Farm Population in Kansas," *Kansas Historical Quarterly*, Vol. IV, No. 4 (November, 1935), pp. 339-372. A. D. Edwards, *Influence of drought and depression on a rural community, a case study in Haskell County, Kansas*, pp. 29-30, 36. Social Research Report No. VII. Washington, D. C.: United States Department of Agriculture, January, 1939. Hicks, *The Populist revolt*, pp. 11-35. Buck, *The Granger movement*, pp. 19-24.

ment of population had overshot its mark and resulted not only in the settlement of submarginal lands, but also in an overproduction of farm products. Low prices for farm products and high prices for farm lands— an economic anomaly—were both inevitable. Farmers were not, however, schooled to the idea that their enterprise was less worthy of economic reward than others and so rebelled against the forces of urbanization which were coming to dominate the economic and social life of the nation. In the decade 1880-1890, there was probably more talk among farmers about the "concentration of wealth" than at any time before or since. In this decade the national population increased 24.86 per cent; the rural population, 15 per cent; and the urban population, 61 per cent. The per capita wealth of the nation increased from $870 to $1,036, and the rural share of it decreased from 28 per cent to 25 per cent.[12] These detailed facts were not, of course, generally known by farmers; but they did know that others were making fortunes while farmers were accumulating debts, that eastern capital was financing farm mortgages, that the day had passed when young men could make an easy ascent from farm hired man or tenant to owner, and that the obvious level of living was higher in towns and cities than on farms. Farmers, therefore, counted themselves as an oppressed class—oppressed by railroads, banks, Wall Street, monopolies, and even by the government. W. S. Morgan concludes his book, which was adopted by the St. Louis convention (1889) as an authoritative history of the Farmers' Movement, as follows:

> Laboring men of America! The voice of Patrick Henry and the fathers of American Independence rings down through the corridors of time and tells you to strike. Not with glittering musket, flaming sword and deadly cannon; but with the silent, potent and all-powerful ballot, the only vestige of liberty left. Strike from yourselves the shackles of party slavery, and exercise independent manhood.
>
> Strike at the foundation of the evils which are threatening the existence of the Republic.
>
> Strike for yourselves, your families, your fellow man, your country and your God.
>
> Strike from the face of the land the monopolies and combinations that are eating out the heart of the Nation.

---

[12] Emerick, p. 435.

Let the manhood of the Nation rise up in defense of liberty, justice and equality. Let the battle go on until all the people, from North to South and East to West, shall join in one loud acclaim, "Victory is ours, and the people are free!" [13]

ALLIANCEMEN TURN TO POLITICS

The political upheaval created by the farmers' organizations in the nineties was more startling than the Granger revolt of the seventies. Like the Grange and farmers' clubs two decades earlier, Alliancemen at first attempted to pledge candidates to support measures which they advocated, but were usually disappointed with the results. Farm organization memberships were so large that some of their own members were bound to be candidates for office, and although in such instances Alliance leaders argued that these candidates were not farm organization candidates, they nevertheless urged that they should be accorded support because they were farmers.[14] It was only natural that when some outstanding Alliance leader became a candidate, he should receive the loyal and enthusiastic support of the individual members of his organization, and almost inevitable that the organization itself would sooner or later become involved in politics by that support. It was also natural that politicians or would-be politicians should seek influence and even leadership in the organizations in order to further their own political objectives. Both of these things happened, with the result that by 1890 the Alliance in various states was deep in politics. A discussion of the political bickering which took place during this period is presented by Josephus Daniels of North Carolina. He tells not only how Polk struggled with himself over the issue, but how Senator Vance was caught in the middle, so to speak, and how Senator Butler used the Alliance to further his own political interests.[15]

There were not so many third parties organized in the nineties as in the seventies and eighties, but fusions with minority parties or domination of

---

[13] W. S. Morgan, *History of Wheel and Alliance*, p. 774.

[14] The increasing emphasis of the Alliance upon political action was clearly reflected in the pages of the *National Economist*. See issues of September 7, 1889, p. 386; November 2, p. 103; December 7, p. 191; December 14, p. 193; January 11, 1890, p. 263; February 1, p. 305; December 27, p. 235. See also *Farmers' Alliance*, July 5, 1890.

[15] Josephus Daniels, *Tar heel editor*, chaps. xxxix, xliii. Chapel Hill: University of North Carolina Press, 1939.

one of the old parties turned more state elections and placed far more farmer candidates in both state and national offices than had been elected by the Grangers twenty years earlier. A short résumé of what had already transpired in outstanding Alliance states before the establishment of the national People's party will serve to convince anyone that the farmers' organizations of the nation had more to do with the rise of Populism than any other organization, and probably more than all other organizations combined. In fact, it was the revolt of the farmers in 1890 that caused editors during that year and the following years to predict that a national third party was almost a certainty in 1892. An excerpt from an article in a national periodical shortly after the 1890 political campaign gives a vivid picture of the spirit of revolt which was ablaze in the Middle West. It reads as follows:

> That campaign of 1890 was the most thrilling ever known in the West. The country school-houses were packed with excited throngs. County, district and State conventions were attended by great crowds of eager, earnest and indignant farmers. The excitement and enthusiasm were contagious, and the Alliance men deserted their former parties by thousands. Putting a gill of fact and grievance into a gallon of falsehood and lurid declamation, these oratorical Alliance quacks doled out an intoxicating mixture. In vain the reports of the meetings were suppressed by the partisan press. In vain the Republican and Democratic leaders sneered at and ridiculed this new gospel, while they talked tariff and War issues to small audiences ... All the ridicule, abuse and evasion aided wonderfully the Alliance cause. Its members shouted that they were being persecuted in their "battle for human rights," and converts came more rapidly. Thus was produced that clamoring brood of Peffers, Simpsons, Kems and McKeighans and the hundred other political rain-makers who proclaimed their virtue on the Western prairies in 1890.[16]

The political upheaval in Kansas in 1890 was greater than that in any other state. There, a People's party ticket was put in the field by the Farmers' Alliance and came near capturing the entire election. The Republican governor's plurality was reduced to one-tenth of what it had been in 1888, with Willitts, the farmers' candidate, losing to his Republi-

---

[16] Frank B. Tracy, "Rise and Doom of the Populist Party," *Forum*, Vol. XVI, No. 2 (October, 1893), pp. 243-244.

can opponent by a vote of 106, 972 to 115,025. The People's party elected ninety members to the lower house of the state legislature. The Republicans and Democrats combined elected only thirty-five state representatives, and while there was a sufficient number of holdovers to keep the state senate in the hands of the Republicans, the state legislature as a whole was safely in the hands of the third party after the 1890 state election. Five Congressmen out of seven were elected at the polls by the farmers, and William A. Peffer, editor of the *Kansas Farmer*, was elected to the United States Senate a little later by the farmer-dominated state legislature.[17]

The campaign in Kansas illustrated better than any other the intense earnestness of the Populists, who asserted that the struggle for control of the Kansas legislature was

> ... not between the Populists and Republicans as political organizations, but between the common people of the State and the Eastern mortgagers and alien railroad owners; between the common people and those scheming, purse-proud foreigners, who seek to make of this beautiful, fertile state another Ireland, between the common people and the miscreants, who, by low-shielded, pitiless oppression, would drive struggling Adams and Eves from the prairie Edens they have labored in poverty, in privation, in tears, but in hope, to make beautiful and fruitful.[18]

The state committee prepared "suggestions and plans for local organization, drill, and work" in the various counties of the state and instructed local organizers not "to let the enemy" get hold of the instructions. A few lines from these suggestions are indicative of the whole body of instructions:

---

[17] The figures cited are from *Appleton's*. Other sources differ slightly. For accounts of the Populist movement in Kansas in 1890, see *Appleton's, 1891*, pp. 411-412. Hicks, *The Populist revolt*, pp. 155-156, 159-162, 165-170, 179-180, 182-183. Haynes, *Third party movements*, pp. 239-240, 244-245, 251. Drew, p. 308. *Tribune almanac and political register for 1891*, pp. 284-287. *Nation*, Vol. LII, No. 1336 (February 5, 1891), p. 104. *National Economist*, December 6, 1890, p. 192. W. A. Peffer, "The Farmers' Alliance," *Cosmopolitan*, Vol. X, No. 6 (April, 1891), p. 698. J. W. Gleed, "Is New York More Civilized Than Kansas?" *Forum*, Vol. XVII, No. 2 (April, 1894), pp. 232-233. *The New York Times*, December 14, 1890. New York *Herald Tribune*, January 28, 31, 1891.

[18] *Points for Populists as to organizing the House of Representatives*. Issued by the Kansas Populist Headquarters in 1890. In Kansas State Historical Library, Topeka.

The conditions are ripe for proselyting. Victory is within our grasp, but it will require detailed organization and earnest personal work in every community to secure it . . .

Each of you has a few personal Republican friends who will support you. This plan will not estrange these friends. It will multiply your power for yourself and the ticket, on the principle that he accomplishes most who puts others to work . . .

The proposition is to find a true fusionist in each road district in the State who has the fitness and the will to take charge of the work in that district . . . there are 9,000 road districts in the State, and the loss of one man to the district means a loss of 9,000 votes, which is more than we can stand . . .

Do not think of the whole mass. They cannot be won. We do not want them. Single but one, two, or three in his district who are known to be disaffected and concentrate all effort upon these few . . . If we can convert one Republican to the district, it means 9,000 taken from them and added to us, or a difference of 18,000 in the final result . . .

In the event of the fusion rally in your county, he is to urge the fusionist of his district to attend . . . Insist upon their attendance with their families to swell the crowd.

Our Committees have no money except as the people send it in. This is a fight between the people and the trusts . . . There are many nickels, dimes, and quarters laying around in his road district that the State Committee would be welcome to if they had a chance to get them . . .

Now, Mr. County Candidate, by the time you have drilled two or three road district men in the presence of the township committeeman, you have him drilled and you can let him go home. When you are done with the townships assigned to you, there is a force at work for you and the entire ticket while you go elsewhere. . . .

Show these men that the work the State Committees want them to do can be largely done at home and in the field.[19]

In Nebraska, a People's Independent party was organized by representatives of the state Grange, the Farmers' Alliance, and the Knights of Labor. In the election such inroads were made on the Republican party

---

[19] *Ibid.*, "A Message and Plan for County Candidates."

that a Democrat was elected governor and the Independents gained control of the senate and elected fifty of the one hundred representatives. The gubernatorial election was so close that the Independent candidate contested it, claiming that the 1,144 majority of the Republicans was obtained by fraud. The farmers could also claim two clear victories out of the three congressional contests and an upset in the other, there being elected that year one Democrat, one Democrat-Independent, and one Independent. The state legislature would undoubtedly have sent a farmer representative to the United States Senate had it been its privilege to elect a Senator that year.[20]

In South Dakota, a convention of the Farmers' Alliance and Knights of Labor formed an Independent party and nominated H. L. Loucks, president of the State Farmers' Alliance, for governor. The Republicans won the governorship with a majority reduced considerably below normal, but the Independents elected fourteen members to the state senate and forty-five members to the house of representatives. A United States Senator was elected by the new legislature, and while the person elected— Rev. James H. Kyle—was not solely a third-party candidate, he had been elected to the state senate as an Independent and should therefore be counted among the victories of the third party.[21]

In Minnesota, the third-party campaign was directly under the sponsorship of the Farmers' Alliance. The Independent candidates for state offices made a respectable showing and forty-five Alliancemen were elected to the state legislature—twelve to the senate and thirty-three to the house. Three Democrats, one Republican, and one Allianceman were elected to Congress.[22]

---

[20] Haynes, *Third party movements*, pp. 240-241. *Appleton's, 1890*, pp. 584-585. *Tribune almanac, 1891*, pp. 297-298. John D. Barnhart, "Rainfall and the Populist party in Nebraska," *American Political Science Review*, Vol. XIX, No. 3 (August, 1925), pp. 527-540. John D. Barnhart, *The history of the Farmers' Alliance and of the People's party in Nebraska*, pp. 240-241. Doctoral Dissertation. Harvard University, 1929.

[21] For accounts of the Populist movement in South Dakota in 1890, see *Appleton's, 1890*, pp. 782-783. Haynes, *Third party movements*, pp. 241-242, 251-252. *Tribune almanac, 1891*, p. 311. Hicks, *The Populist revolt*, pp. 157, 181.

[22] *Appleton's, 1890*, pp. 556-557. Haynes, *Third party movements*, p. 242. *Tribune almanac*, pp. 294-295. Hicks, *The Populist revolt*, pp. 157-158, 162-164, 185. John D. Hicks, "The People's Party in Minnesota," *Minnesota History Bulletin*, Vol. V, No. 8 (November, 1924), pp. 537-539.

In Michigan, the Industrial party was formed by the Patrons of Industry, the Alliance, and various labor organizations, and a state ticket nominated. The party's candidate for governor polled only 13,198 votes; but the state went Democratic for the first time since 1854, and eight Democratic Congressmen were elected as opposed to three Republicans.[23]

In Indiana, a People's party was formed at a convention made up of delegates from the Greenback-Labor party, the Farmers' Mutual Benefit Association, the Farmers' Alliance, and the Grange. The governor was not up for election in 1890 and the party's candidate for secretary of state received only 17,354 votes, but the upheaval created by the party served to elect eleven Democrats to two Republicans to Congress.[24]

In North Dakota, Colorado, Illinois, and Iowa, third parties were not organized. Fusion tickets, however, were agreed upon in Colorado and North Dakota, and revolting farmers in Iowa and Illinois cut down the normal vote of Republican candidates. In Illinois, seven Republican Congressmen lost their seats to Democrats.[25]

In the South, the great strength of the Alliance caused it literally to capture the Democratic party in a number of states. It elected its candidate for governor in three states—Tennessee, South Carolina, and Georgia—and the candidate whom it approved in Texas won. It elected enough of its adherents to state legislatures to dominate eight of them—in Alabama, Georgia, Florida, Missouri, Mississippi, North Carolina, South Carolina, and Tennessee. In Georgia, six Congressmen out of ten were defeated because they did not receive either the approval or support of the Farmers' Alliance. In North Carolina, the Democratic state platform read almost like the Ocala, Florida, Southern Farmers' Alliance platform. In

---

[23] *Appleton's, 1890,* pp. 552-553. Haynes, *Third party movements,* pp. 242-243. *Tribune almanac, 1891,* p. 294. Hicks, *The Populist revolt,* p. 181.

[24] *Appleton's, 1890,* pp. 239-240. Haynes, *Third party movements,* p. 243. *Tribune almanac, 1891,* pp. 280-281.

[25] For an account of the Populist movement in North Dakota in 1890, see *Appleton's, 1890,* p. 629. Paul R. Fossum, *The agrarian movement in North Dakota,* p. 37. Johns Hopkins Studies in Historical and Political Science, Series XLIII, No. 1. Baltimore: Johns Hopkins Press, 1925.

For Colorado, see *Appleton's, 1890,* p. 153. Hicks, *The Populist revolt,* p. 181.

For Illinois, see Hicks, *The Populist revolt,* p. 181. *Appleton's, 1890,* p. 429.

For Iowa, see Haynes, *Third party movements,* pp. 304-312. Hicks, *The Populist revolt,* p. 181. *Appleton's, 1890,* pp. 445-446, 448. Drew, p. 308.

South Carolina, the support of the Alliance was thrown to Tillman. In Texas, the Democratic candidate for governor, William Hogg, was literally the farmers' candidate.[26] Throughout the United States, about forty-four Congressmen and six United States Senators elected in 1890 were claimed as Alliance supporters.[27] Notwithstanding this fact, Colonel L. L. Polk, president of the Southern Alliance, said as late as November, 1891,

Our organization is plainly and forcibly political, but non-partisan. The man or the party that gives us the best proof that they will

———

[26] For a discussion of the Populist movement in Tennessee in 1890, see *Appleton's, 1890*, p. 796. Arnett, pp. 122-123. Daniel M. Robison, *Bob Taylor and the agrarian revolt in Tennessee*, p. 148. Chapel Hill: University of North Carolina Press, 1935. Hicks, *The Populist revolt*, pp. 177-178.

For South Carolina, see *Appleton's, 1890*, pp. 778-779. Haynes, *Third party movements*, pp. 238-239. Arnett, p. 122. Francis B. Simkins, *The Tillman movement in South Carolina*, chap. v, pp. 103-134. Durham, North Carolina: Duke University Press, 1926. Hicks, *The Populist revolt*, pp. 171-174, 178, 181-182.

For Georgia, see *Appleton's, 1890*, pp. 365-366. Arnett, pp. 102-116. Haynes, *Third party movements*, p. 238. Hicks, *The Populist revolt*, pp. 175-177, 178, 182.

For Alabama, see *Appleton's, 1890*, pp. 5-6. Arnett, p. 123. John B. Clark, *Populism in Alabama*, p. 127. Auburn, Alabama: Auburn Printing Company, 1927. Hicks, *The Populist revolt*, pp. 177-178.

For Florida, see *Appleton's, 1890*, pp. 319-320. Haynes, *Third party movements*, p. 238. Arnett, p. 123. Hicks, *The Populist revolt*, p. 178.

For Missouri, see *Appleton's, 1890*, p. 564. Hicks, *The Populist revolt*, p. 178.

For Mississippi, see *Appleton's, 1890*, p. 561. Arnett, p. 123. Drew, p. 307. Hicks, *The Populist revolt*, p. 178.

For North Carolina, see *Appleton's, 1890*, p. 625. Arnett, p. 123. Haynes, *Third party movements*, p. 238. Joseph G. de Roulhac Hamilton, *North Carolina since 1860* (*History of North Carolina*, Vol. III), pp. 229-233. Chicago: Lewis Publishing Co., 1919. *Tribune almanac, 1891*, pp. 71-72. Hicks, *The Populist revolt*, pp. 170, 174-175, 178, 182.

For Texas, see *Appleton's, 1890*, p. 800. R. C. Martin, *The People's party in Texas*, pp. 25-26. Hicks, *The Populist revolt*, p. 177.

See also *The New York Times*, September 15, 1890, for a discussion of the "Alliance in the South."

[27] *National Economist*, November 15, 1890, p. 1. Drew, p. 308.

Appleton's, 1890, p. 301, says, "A total of 38 members of the Farmers' Alliance is claimed in the Fifty-second Congress. The Alliance has elected several United States Senators."

Hamlin Garland, "The Alliance Wedge in Congress," *Arena*, Vol. V, No. 4 (March, 1892), pp. 447-457, characterizes Alliance Congressmen and Senators.

For general discussion of election, see *National Economist*, January 24, 1891, pp. 293-294. Edward Stanwood, *A history of the Presidency from 1788 to 1897*, p. 491. Boston: Houghton Mifflin Company, 1897.

stand by our demands will receive our votes... The Kansas and California alliances are strong for the third party, but such action is against the principles of the Alliance in general. We desire to educate our members in the great principles of economy involved and then let them choose the party that best represents and indorses their principles.[28]

It is generally assumed that the two Farmers' Alliances were forced into third-party activities by minority groups within their ranks and by outsiders who insinuated themselves into their ranks. This was undoubtedly true to a degree. When, however, the platforms of the St. Louis (1889) and Ocala (1890) conventions of the Southern Alliance, and the Omaha (January, 1891) platform of the Northern Alliance are studied, and when the story of the participation of Alliancemen in the independent political activities of the 1890 state elections is known, it becomes apparent that the farmers, if not the farmers' organizations as well, were rather willingly led into the movement which set up a National People's party in 1892.

THE FARMERS WRITE THEIR POLITICAL PLATFORM

It will be remembered that a move to call a national third-party convention was first made at the Southern Alliance convention at Ocala, Florida, in December, 1890. This action was especially urged by the Kansas delegation, which had allied itself with the southern organization a year before because of the outstanding political demands made in the St. Louis platform. The Supreme Council of the Southern Alliance, however, went no further than to set up a Committee of Confederation at that time, looking toward a rather mature consideration of the third-party suggestion. The Northern Alliance meeting, held in Omaha, a month later, also made a third-party demand, but like its southern ally counseled mature consideration of the plans for such a move.[29] In Kansas, however, the State Alliance was not so cautious. In August, 1890, it had organized a People's party and been through a remarkably successful political

---

[28] See Indianapolis *Sentinel,* November 15, 1891.
[29] Blood, p. 41. *National Economist,* February 17, 1891, p. 333. *The New York Times,* December 5, 1890.

campaign just before its delegates went to the Ocala convention.[30] It was natural, therefore, that there should come from Kansas a demand for speedier action than seemed to be promised by either of the two national Alliances. This demand was met in the Cincinnati conference held in May, 1891. William A. Peffer, newly elected United States Senator from Kansas, was permanent chairman of that conference.[31]

A national executive committee was set up by the Cincinnati conference; and five members of that committee met in St. Louis in June, 1891, and began making preparations for the 1892 presidential campaign. The plans outlined provided for furnishing materials to the six or seven hundred reform newspapers and the organization of People's party clubs in wards, townships, and counties, with a central club in every county.[32] When, therefore, the Populist hosts gathered at Omaha in July, 1892, the groundwork for launching a new political party was well laid. The farmers' organizations had been swung into line through a series of meetings, including the Cincinnati conference of May, 1891; the annual convention of the Southern Alliance held in Indianapolis in November, 1891; and a meeting of the Confederation of Industrial Organizations held in St. Louis in February, 1892.[33] After the St. Louis meeting adjourned, the delegates met as "individual and independent" citizens and appointed a committee of fifteen to confer with the executive committee of the People's party.[34]

The *National Economist,* official organ of the Southern Alliance, was quite conservative in its use of headlines, much more so than other Alliance papers. In its issue of July 2, 1892, however, it broke loose with something approaching yellow journalism headlines. The following is taken from the front page of that issue:

---

[30] Hicks, *The Populist revolt,* p. 211. *Appleton's, 1890,* p. 471. Cincinnati *Enquirer,* May 19, 1891. *National Economist,* July 2, 1892, p. 247. Miller, p. 469. Peffer, *The farmers' side,* pp. 697-698.

[31] Cincinnati *Enquirer,* May 20-21, 1891. E. A. Allen, pp. 512-518.

[32] Haynes, *Third party movements,* pp. 249-250. *The Weekly Iowa State Register,* June 19, 1891.

[33] *National Economist,* November 28, 1891, pp. 161-169.

[34] *Ibid.,* March 5, pp. 383, 394-397. March 12, 1892, pp. 401-402. Omaha *Daily Bee,* February 25, 1892. St. Louis *Republic,* February 25, 1892. St. Louis *Globe-Democrat,* February 25, 1892.

THE REVOLT

THE FARMERS AND LABORERS OF THE DEMOCRATIC PARTY REFUSE TO SWALLOW WALL STREET'S CANDIDATE NOMINATED BY BRIBERY AND CORRUPTION

WITH ONE ACCORD FROM MAINE TO TEXAS THEY SPEW HIM OUT

NEARLY EVERY DEMOCRATIC STATE HEARD FROM AND ALL DENOUNCE BOTH PLATFORM AND NOMINEE

THE REPUBLICAN PARTY WILL NOT CARRY A SINGLE STATE WEST OF THE MISSISSIPPI

THE DEMOCRATIC PARTY WILL NOT CARRY A STATE SOUTH OF THE OHIO

RING RULE HAS ENRAGED THE PEOPLE AND OPENED THEIR EYES

CLEVELAND AND HARRISON HAVE BOTH BEEN WEIGHED IN THE BALANCE AND FOUND WANTING

DOWN WITH THE TYRANTS WHO WINK AT THE ROB-BERIES COMMITTED BY TRUSTS AND COMBINES BECAUSE THEY DONATE CORRUPTION FUNDS TO CONTROL ELECTIONS

THE PEOPLE ARE LEAVING THE DEMOCRATIC PARTY LIKE RATS DESERT A SINKING SHIP. IT IS DOOMED.

THE REVOLT AGAINST THE DEMOCRATIC PARTY THREATENS TO LEAD THE REVOLT OF A YEAR AGO AGAINST THE REPUBLICAN PARTY.

THE TWO GREAT REVOLTS ARE A MATTER OF HISTORY THAT ASTOUND THE WORLD AND TOGETHER THE REVOLTERS OF THE SOUTH AND WEST WILL MARCH HAND IN HAND TO VICTORY IN NOVEMBER

AT LAST

The die is cast. The spell is broken. The mists have cleared away. The record is complete to the last word and letter, the book is closed. The *Economist* recognizes the fact that no longer can any man claim devotion to the demands of the Alliance and consistently affiliate with the Democratic or the Republican parties, because both those parties have announced against the demands and have nominated men who are thoroughly identified with those whose interests are inimical to those of the agriculturists of America.[35]

The Omaha convention was originally called for July 4, but because of the desire to make nominations on Independence Day, the 1,366 delegates assembled on Saturday, July 2, heard the report of the credentials committee, elected a temporary chairman, appointed committees on platform and resolutions, rules and order of business, and permanent organization, and adjourned. When the convention reassembled on Monday, H. L. Loucks of South Dakota, then president of the Southern Farmers' Alliance and past president of the Northern Alliance, was elected permanent chairman. A platform following fairly closely those of St. Louis and Ocala was quickly adopted and nominations were in order. General James B. Weaver, past Greenback Congressman from Iowa and Greenback party candidate for President in 1880, and Independent United States Senator James H. Kyle of South Dakota, were the two leading persons nominated as candidates for President of the United States. Weaver won on the first ballot with 995 votes to 275 for Kyle. James G. Field of Virginia was nominated as candidate for Vice-President over Ben Terrell of Texas by a vote of 733 to 554.[36] General Weaver, in an extemporaneuos speech to the convention after his nomination, said in part:

This is the grandest movement of our civilization. It is rallying the best hearts and best heads of the nation around the three con-

[35] *National Economist*, July 2, 1892, p. 241.
[36] The figures cited are from *National Economist*, July 18, 1892, p. 279. Other sources disagree slightly. See *Southern Mercury*, July 14, 1892. Omaha *Daily Bee*, July 5, 1892. *The New York Times*, July 6, 1892. Haynes, *Third party movements*, pp. 262-263. E. A. Allen, p. 118. McPherson, *A handbook of politics for 1892*, p. 271. *Appleton's, 1892*, p. 753. Joseph C. Manning, *Fadeout of Populism*, pp. 29-33. New York: T. A. Hebbons, 1928.

tentions of modern times—the great land problem, the great currency or financial problem, and the great and overshadowing problem of transportation. (Applause). These are the centers around which this great movement is rallying. You are right, and you will be triumphant as certain as we are assembled in this hall. (Prolonged applause.) Your faith and your work will conquer. This is no longer a country governed by the people, and it is the great duty today devolving upon the party which you represent to rescue the government from the grasping federated monopolies, and restore it to the great common people to which it belongs. (Applause).[37]

The major planks of the Omaha platform dealt with *Finance*—the free coinage of silver, circulating medium to the amount of $50 per capita, a graduated income tax, economical government, and the establishment of postal savings banks; *Transportation*—government ownership of railroads, telephone and telegraph lines; and *Land*—including all natural resources, "the heritage of the people," prohibition of alien ownership, and the return of land held by railroads for settlement. Other planks called for tariff revision, restrictions of pensions, popular election of senators, adoption of secret ballot, abolition of contract labor, and the eight-hour working day. The preamble to the platform gives a better picture of the spirit of the new party movement than any other item ever to be written concerning it. It reads, in part, as follows:

> The conditions which surround us best justify our cooperation. We meet in the midst of a nation brought to the verge of moral, political and material ruin. Corruption dominates the ballot box, the legislatures, the congress, and touches even the ermine of the bench. The people are demoralized, most of the states have been compelled to isolate the voters at the polling places to prevent universal intimidation or bribery. The newspapers are largely subsidized or muzzled, public opinion silenced, business prostrated, our homes covered with mortgages, labor impoverished, and the land concentrating in the hands of the capitalists. The urban workmen are denied the rights of organization for self-protection; imported pauperized labor beats down their wages; a hireling standing army, unrecognized by our laws, is established to shoot them down, and they are rapidly degenerating into European conditions. The fruits of the toil of

---

[37] E. A. Allen, pp. 119-120. Omaha *Daily Bee*, July 6, 1892, p. 2.

millions are boldly stolen to build up colossal fortunes for a few, unprecedented in the history of mankind, and the possessors of these, in turn, despise the republic and endanger liberty. From the same prolific womb of governmental injustice we breed the two great classes—tramps and millionaires.

The national power to create money is appropriated to enrich bondholders. A vast public debt, payable in legal tender currency, has been funded into gold-bearing bonds, thereby adding millions to the burdens of the people.

We have witnessed for more than a quarter of a century the struggles of the two great political parties for power and plunder, while grievous wrongs have been inflicted upon the suffering people. We charge that the controlling influences dominating both these parties have permitted the existing dreadful conditions to develop without serious effort to prevent or restrain them. Neither do they now promise us any substantial reform. They have agreed together to ignore in the coming campaign every issue but one. They propose to drown the outcries of a plundered people with the uproar of a sham battle over the tariff, so that capitalists, corporations, national banks, rings, trusts, watered stock, the demonetization of silver, and the oppressions of the usurers may all be lost sight of. They propose to sacrifice our homes, lives and children on the altar of Mammon; to destroy the multitude in order to secure corruption funds from the millionaires.

Our country finds itself confronted by conditions for which there is no precedent in the history of the world—our annual agricultural productions amount to billions of dollars in value, which must within a few weeks or months be exchanged for billions of dollars of commodities consumed in their production; the existing currency supply is wholly inadequate to make this exchange; the results are falling prices, the formation of combines and rings and the impoverishment of the producing class. We pledge ourselves that if given power we will labor to correct these evils by wise and reasonable legislation in accordance with the terms of our platform.

... believing that the forces of reform this day organized will never cease to move forward until every wrong is remedied and the equal rights and equal privileges securely established for all the men and women of the country. We declare therefore,

First, That the union of the labor forces of the United States, this day consummated, shall be permanent and perpetual. May its spirit enter into all hearts for the salvation of the republic and the uplifting of mankind.

Second, Wealth belongs to him who creates it, and every dollar taken from industry without an equivalent is robbery. "If any will not work, neither shall he eat." The interests of rural and civic labor are the same; their enemies are identical.

Third, We believe that the time has come when the railroad corporations will either own the people or the people must own the railroads, and should the government enter upon the work of owning and managing any or all railroads we should favor an amendment to the constitution by which all persons engaged in the government service shall be placed under civil service regulation of the most rigid character, so as to prevent the increase of the power of the national administration by the use of such additional government employees.[38]

THE CAMPAIGNS OF 1892 AND 1894

The support of the 1892 Populist candidates was by no means confined to farmers, but the election returns showed very definitely that it was farm organization states which cast the majority of the People's party vote. The ticket polled 1,041,577 votes, of which twenty-five Farmers' Alliance states cast almost 900,000. Kansas led with 163,111, followed in order by Texas, 99,638; Alabama, 85,181; Nebraska, 83,134; Colorado, 53,584; North Carolina, 44,732; Georgia, 42,939; and Missouri, 41,183. The states of California, Illinois, Indiana, Iowa, Kentucky, Minnesota, Oregon, South Dakota, and Tennessee each cast more than 20,000 ballots for the ticket. Kansas, Colorado, Idaho, Nevada, North Dakota, and Oregon cast electoral votes for the ticket; and five United States Senators, ten Congressmen, about fifty state officials, and over 1,500 county officers and legislators were elected.[39] How overwhelmingly agrarian the Populist

---

[38] Omaha *Daily Bee*, July 5, 1892. E. A. Allen, pp. 96-99. *National Economist*, July 23, 1892, p. 303. *People's Party Paper*, July 8, 1892. McVey, pp. 143-150. T. C. Jory, *What is Populism? An exposition of the principles of the Omaha platform adopted by the People's party.* Salem, Oregon: Ross E. Moores and Co., 1895. "The Farmers' Alliance," *Public Opinion*, Vol. X, No. 10 (December 13, 1890), pp. 217-220. Nixon, "The Populist Movement in Iowa."

[39] McPherson, *A handbook of politics for 1894*, pp. 272-273. *Appleton's*, 1892, pp. 755-756. McKee, pp. 287-288. *Southern Mercury*, November 17, 1892, p. 9. C. S. Walker, "The Farmers' Movement."

vote was, is also indicated by a comparison of the presidential vote of the People's party in 1892 and the Union Labor party in 1888. The Union Labor vote was only one-seventh of the People's party vote, and twenty states which cast no votes at all for the Union Labor party in 1888 did cast votes for the Populist party in 1892. Eighteen of these twenty were predominantly rural states.

During the 1892 campaign the People's party fused with the Republicans in the South and with the Democrats in the West in a number of states. In Georgia, for instance, the People's party placed the Republican nominee for governor on their ticket and made no nominations for Congress. In Kansas and North Dakota, the Democrats accepted the Populist nominee. In Louisiana, the Republicans and Populists divided electoral nominations between them, and in Alabama a thorough-going fusion was worked out.[40]

In a number of southern states, notably Florida, Louisiana, Mississippi, South Carolina, and Texas, the Democrats, either through their candidates or through their platforms, conceded enough to the Populists to hold down serious division in their ranks; and in some states of the Middle West the third-party group was unable or refused to fuse with the Republicans.[41]

A few outstanding results may well be noted in certain of the strong farmers' organization states. In Kansas, the entire Populist ticket and five out of seven Congressmen were elected. In Nebraska, the Populists helped elect Bryan—a Democrat—and the Democrats helped elect Kem—a Populist—to Congress. One other Congressman was elected on a fusion ticket. In North Dakota, the whole fusion state ticket except secretary of state was elected. In Minnesota, one Populist was elected to Congress, and the Populists held the balance of power in the state legislature. The popular vote cast for the People's party by eight western states was as follows: in Nevada, 66.76 per cent; in Colorado, 57.07 per cent; in Idaho, 54.66 per cent; in North Dakota, 48.96 per cent; in Kansas, 48.44 per cent; in Wyoming, 46.14 per cent; in South Dakota, 37.58 per cent; and in Ala-

[40] Arnett, p. 153. Fossum, p. 37. *Appleton's, 1892*, pp. 3-5, 370-371, 425, 529-530. Haynes, *Third party movements*, pp. 265-268. Hicks, *The Populist revolt*, pp. 245-247, 255-257. Stanwood, pp. 515-516.

[41] *Appleton's, 1892*, pp. 279, 425, 472, 705, 740-741. Hicks, *The Populist revolt*, pp. 245-261.

bama, 36.60 per cent. Texas and Washington each cast more than 20 per cent of their vote for the ticket.[42]

The Populists as such did not gain absolute control of a single state government and received only twenty-two of the electoral votes, but they had created the greatest furor of twenty years in American politics and were greatly encouraged by their showing. In a number of states where fusion tickets gained control of the state government, it is difficult to separate Populist votes from those of the other party tickets with which they fused. After the election, General Weaver, in a letter to H. E. Taubeneck, chairman of the national committee of the People's party, said:

> ... unaided by money our grand young party has made an enviable record and achieved surprising success at the polls. We are but little behind the Republican party in the number of states carried ... we will doubtless hold the balance of power in the Senate of the United States, have doubled the number of our adherents in the house of representatives, secured control of a number of state governments, hold the balance of power in a majority of the states in the Union, and have succeeded in arousing a spirit of political independence among the people of the Northwest which cannot be disregarded in the future.[43]

The *Southern Mercury*, official organ of the Texas State Alliance, summed up the results of the election as follows:

> The conflict is over, and while the democrats elect the president, vice-president, a majority of congress and will have control of the senate also, still the people's party have gained a great victory. They have carried six states (the first time in thirty years that a third party has had a voice in the electoral college), have defeated the republican party and are on the highway to ultimate success.[44]

---

[42] *Appleton's, 1892*, pp. 269-270, 371, 485-486, 529-530. Hicks, "The People's Party in Minnesota," pp. 545-546. Hicks, *The Populist revolt*, pp. 261-269. "Record of Political Events," *Political Science Quarterly*, Vol. VIII, No. 2 (June, 1893), pp. 378-379. Haynes, *Third party movements*, pp. 264-270. "The Pending Presidential Campaign," *Arena*, Vol. VI, No. 3 (August, 1892), pp. 300-310. *Southern Mercury*, December 1, 1892, p. 7.

[43] Cited by Haynes, *Third party movements*, p. 270, from *The Weekly Iowa State Register*, November 18, 1892, and Clinton *Weekly Age* (Clinton, Iowa), November 18, 1892.

[44] *Southern Mercury*, November 17, 1892, p. 9. This campaign received quite a bit of attention in the magazines of this period, of which the following is a sample: Wm.

In 1893, the Independents and Democrats of the Nebraska legislature elected William V. Allen, a Populist judge, to the United States Senate. The Kansas Populist legislators joined the Democrats that year in electing Judge John Martin, a Free Silver Democrat, to the United States Senate. Considerable reform legislation was passed in Kansas, Nebraska, and South Dakota; and Populist agitation was kept at as high pitch as could be expected in an off-election year. In Kansas, the fight for control of the lower house of the state legislature was so severe that both Populist and Republican contestants were backed by armed forces and final control of the house was gained only after days of contest by a court decision.[45] In the South, the sprinkling of Populists in the state legislature caused but little disturbance with the solid Democratic regimes, but the Farmers' Alliance was still strong enough and still unsettled enough in its political policies to keep fusion negotiations active during 1893. In Alabama, for instance, conventions of the Jefferson Democrats and Populists were held simultaneously and at the same place in May of that year; in North Carolina, politically minded Alliancemen were growing more and more determined to enter the Populist party; and in Texas, a strong reform press and an outstanding set of third-party leaders kept up a continuous bombardment of propaganda between the 1892 and 1894 political campaigns.[46]

State political campaigns of 1894 furnished opportunity for further consolidation of Populist forces, and although they were not so successful

---

M. Springer, "Why the Democratic Party Should Elect the Next President"; T. E. Watson, "Why the People's Party Should Elect the Next President"; J. C. Burrows, "Why the Republicans Should Elect the Next President." These three were printed in the *Arena*, Vol. VI, No. 2 (July, 1892), pp. 198-207. See also, "The Pending Presidential Campaign," cited above.

[45] *Appleton's, 1894*, pp. 42-43, 503-504. Hicks, *The Populist revolt*, pp. 274-281, 281-286, 693-694. Albert Shaw, "William V. Allen: Populist. A Character Sketch and Interview," *Review of Reviews*, Vol. X, No. 54 (July, 1894), pp. 30-42. For a general discussion, see also Tracy, pp. 247-248. Haynes, *Third party movements*, pp. 275-276. Gleed, "Is New York More Civilized than Kansas?" p. 234. "The Elections," *Political Science Quarterly*, Vol. VIII, No. 2 (June, 1893), pp. 378-379, 384-385.

[46] Clark, pp. 148-150. Simeon A. Delap, "The Populist party in North Carolina," *Historical papers*, Series XIV, pp. 53-54. Durham, North Carolina: Trinity College Historical Society, 1922. R. C. Martin, *The People's party in Texas*, pp. 113-141, 183, 191, 192, 200. *Review of Reviews*, Vol. X, No. 54 (July, 1894), pp. 6-11; Vol. X, No. 55 (August, 1894), pp. 188-190. *Political Science Quarterly*, Vol. VIII, No. 4 (December, 1893), pp. 771-773.

in electing their candidates in western states as they had been in 1892, due to a combination of local influences, they gained in numerical strength, and in the South considerable gains were shown in the election results. The vote in Kansas decreased from 163,000 in 1892 to 118,000 in 1894. However, gains of more than 10,000 were made in Arkansas, Colorado, Georgia, Illinois, Iowa, Michigan, Minnesota, Nebraska, North Carolina, Ohio, Pennsylvania, Texas, Virginia, Washington, and Wisconsin. Something approaching complete fusion with the Republicans was accomplished in Alabama, Texas, and North Carolina; and while this served to lose about 2,000 votes for the party in Alabama, it served to gain about 104,000 in North Carolina and 52,000 in Texas. There were also outstanding gains in Georgia, Minnesota, Virginia, and Washington. The party that year polled 1,471,590 votes, 430,562 more than in 1892. Six United States Senators, seven Congressmen, 153 state senators, and 315 state representatives were in the control of the Populists as a result of that year's election.[47]

THE ELECTION OF 1896

During the years from 1890 to 1894, the Farmers' Movement was drifting more and more out of the hands of general farmers' organizations and into the hands of the new political party. In the campaign of 1896, this transfer was completed. The Populists and Democrats both nominated William Jennings Bryan as their candidate for President, the free coinage of silver dominated all other party issues, and so many forces and counterforces operated in the campaign and election that it is quite impossible to judge the strength of the Farmers' Movement by that year's election returns. The state election returns of 1895 indicated that the Populist party had not held the farmers in line to the same extent as in either 1892 or 1894. This off-year election was marked in the North by Republicans regaining some of the ground they had lost in various elections since 1890.[48] Now that there was to be a national fusion with the

---

[47] McVey, p. 197. *Review of Reviews*, Vol. X, No. 58 (November, 1894), pp. 473-475; Vol. X, No. 59 (December, 1894), pp. 595-597, 600, 621-625; Vol. XI, No. 61 (February, 1895), pp. 142-143. *Tribune almanac, 1895*, Vol. VII, No. 1; Vol. VIII, No. 1. *Appleton's, 1894*, by states. Hicks, *The Populist revolt*, pp. 326-339.

[48] Haynes, *Third party movements*, pp. 284-289. *Review of Reviews*, Vol. XII, No. 71 (December, 1895), pp. 646-647, 666-667. Hicks, *The Populist revolt*, pp. 346-349. *Appleton's, 1895*, pp. 368-370.

Democrats, it is easy to see that southern strength would be lost because of bitterness which had developed between the Populists and Democrats in that section.[49]

In an analysis of the Farmers' Movement, there is no point in going into the 1896 campaign in any great detail.[50] The Populist platform was very similar to that of 1892, and thus very similar to the demands of the farmers' organizations from the late eighties on. The Democratic platform was not dissimilar, but with one issue dominating the campaign platforms, this meant little. There are a few facts and incidents, however, which should be related to show the strength of sentiments and doctrines which had been developing for years in farmers' organizations and which could not be completely ignored by the politicians now in power. In the first place, the Populists refused to accept Sewell, the vice-presidential candidate of the Democrats, because he was "president of a bank, director in railroads and other corporations, and a wealthy employer of labor." Instead, they nominated Populist ex-Congressman Thomas E. Watson of Georgia, a country editor and one of the most fiery reformers of the whole period.[51] The Populists retained in their platform the old planks for government ownership of railroads and irredeemable currency as opposed to regulation of railroads and redeemable currency in the Democratic platform.[52]

There is a good bit of evidence that the Populists were not so overwhelmingly sold on the silver issue. It was William Jennings Bryan's leadership in the Democratic party and the fusion of the Democratic and Populist parties in 1896 that has led to the popular belief that free silver

---

[49] Arnett, pp. 203-205. *Review of Reviews,* Vol. XIV, No. 83 (December, 1896), p. 646. Henry D. Lloyd, "The Populists at St. Louis," *Review of Reviews,* Vol. XIV, No. 80 (September, 1896), pp. 299-300. Hicks, *The Populist revolt,* pp. 369-370.

[50] For methods and tactics of the campaign, see Newell D. Hills, "An Outlook upon the Agrarian Propaganda in the West," *Review of Reviews,* Vol. XIV, No. 80 (September, 1896), pp. 304-305. W. B. Shaw, "Methods and Tactics of the Campaign," *Review of Reviews,* Vol. XIV, No. 82 (November, 1896), pp. 550-559.

[51] *Review of Reviews,* Vol. XIV, No. 79 (August, 1896), p. 140; (September, 1896), pp. 289-297. Lloyd, pp. 298-303. *Political Science Quarterly,* Vol. XI, No. 4 (December, 1896), pp. 768-772. *Southern Mercury,* July 30, 1896; September 10, 1896. William DuBose Sheldon, *Populism in the old dominion,* pp. 130-131. Princeton, New Jersey: Princeton University Press, 1935.

[52] McKee, pp. 292-297, 306-310. Arnett, pp. 201-202. *Southern Mercury,* July 16, 1896, p. 4.

and Populism were almost identical terms during that period. An article printed in September, 1896, concerning the Populist convention at St. Louis, stated:

> The tumultuous refusal of the convention to allow Senator Stewart of the silver convention an extension of time when he was addressing them, was one of the many signs that the convention cared less for silver than did the Democratic convention. Most of the Democrats really believe free silver is a great reform. That is as far as they have got. But it was hard to find among the Populists any who would not privately admit that they know silver was only the most trifling installment of reform, and many—a great many—did not conceal their belief that it was no reform at all ... The People's Party believes really in a currency redeemable in all the products of human labor, and not in gold alone, nor in gold and silver. A party which hates Democracy accepted the Democratic nominee, and a party which has no faith in silver as a panacea accepted silver practically as the sole issue of the campaign.[53]

The campaign was not conducted especially on agricultural issues, and the popular vote did not altogether reflect differences between agrarian and other interests. This was necessarily true due to the fact that free silver was the sole dominating issue, and because hundreds of northerners and westerners were traditionally Republican and such agricultural states as Michigan, Wisconsin, Nebraska, Iowa, Illinois, and Ohio had for years cast their electoral votes for the Republican ticket. The best indices, therefore, to the part agrarian sentiment played in the campaign and election are the nominating ballots in the Democratic convention and the turnover of popular votes in agrarian states. There is some significance in the fact that the only six states which did not as a whole or in part cast their vote for Bryan on the fifth ballot of the Democratic nomination were all eastern states—Connecticut, New Hampshire, New Jersey, New York, Pennsylvania, and Rhode Island; and only one of these—New Hampshire—was an agrarian state.[54] The popular votes in the election returns showed that none of the rock-ribbed Republican

---

[53] Lloyd, p. 302. See also *Review of Reviews*, Vol. XIV, No. 79 (August, 1896), pp. 131-143. Stanwood, pp. 550-555.

[54] William Jennings Bryan, p. 218. Stanwood, pp. 548-549.

states, except Bryan's home state of Nebraska, turned in a majority to the Democratic-Populist candidates, although the vote was closer than usual in Indiana, Illinois, and Ohio, and much closer in Michigan and Iowa. Oregon, one of the old farm-organization and third-party states, went Republican; and while all the other western states, except California, went Democratic-Populist, the silver-mining influence was probably more responsible than the agricultural interest for this fact. The purely Populist sentiment as measured in the vote for Watson—vice-presidential candidate on that ticket—is not a true index, for undoubtedly thousands of Populists voted the Bryan-Sewall rather than the Bryan-Watson ticket. Watson received only 222,207 popular votes out of a total of 13,930,783, Texas and Kansas combined contributing 125,766, or well over one-half, of all the Watson vote.[55] Bryan's vote, however, exceeded the Cleveland vote of 1892 in all agrarian states except Alabama, Georgia, Louisiana, and Virginia in the South, and Wisconsin in the North.

Mr. Bryan traveled 18,000 miles in his campaign, spoke about 600 times, and addressed something like 5,000,000 people. He never went as far west as Colorado nor farther south than North Carolina and Tennessee. He made only one trip into the East and confined his personal campaign chiefly to the Middle West.[56] Farmers by the hundreds of thousands poured out to see and hear him and at some places carried banners typical of Alliance rallies, such as "Our barns are full, but our pockets are empty" and "We mean business." Ready orator that he was, Bryan picked up these slogans as texts for such statements as the following: "Nature smiles upon your husbandry; your soil gives forth its rich abundance, but, according to the experience of the farmer, with all his industry, economy and patient toil, he finds that the lot of the

---

[55] *Appleton's, 1896*, pp. 770-774. W. J. Bryan, pp. 606-611. *Review of Reviews*, Vol. XIV, No. 83 (December, 1896), pp. 643-647. McKee, pp. 326-329. *The world almanac and encyclopedia, 1897*, pp. 423-471. New York: Press Publishing Co., 1897. "Post-Election Reflections," *Review of Reviews*, Vol. XV, No. 84 (January, 1897), pp. 88-92.

[56] Bryan, pp. 384-385, 600-601, 618. In *The first battle*, Bryan gives a detailed account of his itinerary, the things he did, and the audiences to which he spoke. *Review of Reviews*, Vol. XIV, No. 82 (November, 1896), p. 519. Willis J. Abbot, "William Jennings Bryan—A Character Sketch," *Review of Reviews*, Vol. XIV, No. 79 (August, 1896), pp. 161-173.

American farmer grows harder every year." In one instance he quoted a Flint, Michigan, banker as saying to a farmer: "If Bryan is elected President, I shall foreclose the mortgage on your farm"; and the farmer replying: "If McKinley is elected you can have the farm, because I will not be able to pay for it, but if Bryan is elected you cannot foreclose the mortgage because under bimetallism I will be able to pay it off." [57] On other occasions, he referred to Jefferson's conviction "that without prosperity among those who till the soil . . . there can be no permanent prosperity anywhere"; said he would not favor free coinage of silver if he did not believe that it would be beneficial to farmers; and declared that "the farmer had reached the point where the income from his farm is not more than sufficient to pay his debts, his taxes, and his fixed charges." [58]

For the most part, however, he made no great plea for the farmers' cause except as it was a part of the cause of the "masses" against the "classes," nor did he spend much time in consideration of any other issue except free silver. Practically every issue which farmers' organizations had raised and wrestled with was resolved into a money issue. In his Washington, D. C., speech, he said: "Talk about monopolies! Talk about trusts! My friends, they propose to establish the most gigantic of all trusts—a money trust, and let the few men who hold the gold dole it out at such price as they will to all the other seventy millions of American people." [59] In his Goldsboro, North Carolina, speech, he said: "Democrats who believe in tariff reform and Republicans who believe in protection are able to come together when both recognize that the money question is the paramount issue." [60] He did not discuss the transportation issue at all, although this had been one of the burning issues in farm organizations for thirty years. In *The First Battle*, where he reviewed the campaign in 630 pages, he gives no space to the part Watson played in the campaign, due, he says, to a request from Watson himself that these things be left out. In the final chapters, titled "Reminiscences," "Explanations," and "The Future," he makes no allusion to farmers, farm organizations, or farm problems, but does give words of appreciation to the

---

[57] W. J. Bryan, pp. 448, 562.
[58] *Ibid.*, pp. 521, 536, 544.
[59] *Ibid.*, p. 461.
[60] *Ibid.*, pp. 455-456.

Populists and Silver Republicans; pays special tribute to Senators and Congressmen who had been elected by farmers, but does not refer to the fact that they were farmer representatives; praises the Bimetallism and Bryan Clubs, but never mentions the Farmers' Alliance.[61] So far, therefore, as Mr. Bryan was concerned, the 1896 campaign was not in any peculiar way a part of the Farmers' Movement.

Minor campaign speakers and political leaders made special appeals to farmers as their localities and constituencies dictated. The writer remembers as a young boy attending a "Popocrat" rally at which a song entitled "The Farmer Is the Man That Feeds Them All" was sung, and he remembers local politicians in Iowa holding schoolhouse and courthouse meetings at which special appeals were made to farmers. In the main, however, the Farmers' Movement was lost in the political movement which included many others besides farmers, and lost many farmers who clung to their old party affiliations. As a matter of fact, there was scarcely an outstanding farm-organization man who played a prominent part in the councils of the campaign. Senator Butler of North Carolina was chairman of the People's Party National Committee,[62] but he had come into the Alliance late in its development and was accused by many farm leaders of his state of having little interest in the movement beyond his own political aggrandizement through it. Harry Tracy, editor of the *Southern Mercury,* an organ of the Southern Alliance, was on the National Committee, but the names of Loucks, Wardall, Jones, Buchanan, Alexander, Terrell, Fields, Morgan, Post, Ashby, Dunning, Stelle—all of them outstanding farm-organization leaders—do not appear anywhere in the accounts of the campaign.

The transition from Farmers' Movement to Populist movement was made through two steps: first, the gradual transfer from fraternal, social, and economic activities to political activities in terms of backing candidates for office; and second, the taking over and re-focusing of the whole movement by the political leaders whom the farmers had elected. Both of these steps were contested most bitterly by some farm-organization leaders; and the split caused by the contest, particularly in a number of

---

[61] *Ibid.,* pp. 612-629.
[62] Carl Snyder, "Marion Butler," *Review of Reviews,* Vol. XIV, No. 81 (October, 1896), pp. 429-433. *World almanac, 1897,* p. 103.

southern states, was one of the chief reasons that the Farmers' Alliance did not survive long after the Populist revolt.[63]

The results of the 1896 campaign were these: a loss in offices held by men who had been elected by farmers during the few preceding years, the quick death of all farmers' organizations of that period except the Grange, and the slow demise of the People's party. In some of the western states, where the People's party fused with the Silver Republicans and Democrats, as in Washington, Populism reached its greatest strength in the 1896 election. The fusion carried the state of Washington that year, electing a majority of both houses of the state legislature, the governor, and his subordinates.[64]

The Populists, however, were never again a serious factor in American politics, although they continued to put a ticket in the field until 1908. They never again captured an electoral vote or polled as much as 1 per cent of the popular vote. Gradually, one after the other of their representatives dropped out of state office and out of the United States Congress. The group of farmers' organizations which had carried the Farmers' Movement to its highest tide in the history of the nation all went down with the Populist movement, and there was a period of six years following 1896 in which the Farmers' Movement was at a lower ebb than it had been for forty years, or has been since.

The People's party did not, however, go out of existence with the 1896 election. It continued on the national ballot until the election of 1908, its banner being carried during most of this time by Thomas E. Watson, vice-presidential candidate on the People's party ticket in 1896 and probably the most thoroughgoing Populist of the whole movement.

Thus far we have said little about Watson. Bryan was apparently disappointed when the Populists did not accept Sewell as their vice-presidential candidate, and Watson was thoroughly convinced that Populism was injured by a tie-up with the National Democratic party. He thoroughly disapproved of Sewell, criticized him terrifically all during the campaign, and was even critical of Bryan himself, although he cam-

---

[63] Arnett, chap. iv, "Blasting at the Solid South," pp. 117-155; chap. vi, "The Party Revolution of 1896," pp. 185-210. Daniels, chap. xxxix.

[64] Carroll H. Wooddy, "Populism in Washington: A Study of the Legislature of 1897," *Washington Historical Quarterly*, Vol. XXI, No. 2 (April, 1930), pp. 103-119.

paigned for him in 1896.[65] He issued a statement during the campaign which was given wide circulation; in it he said:

> The menace that endangers Mr. Bryan's success to-day is the profound dissatisfaction which exists among the humble, honest, earnest Populists who have built up the People's party ... The Populist voters are dissatisfied and suspicious ... They feel that the principles they love are being used as political merchandise and that the Populist vote is being auctioned off to the highest bidder.[66]

TOM WATSON, "PITCHFORK" BEN TILLMAN, AND BOB TAYLOR

The Populist party was far more than an agrarian movement, but the agrarian movement of the time was also considerably more than the Populist movement. Tom Watson's influence in Georgia, Bob Taylor's influence in Tennessee, and Ben Tillman's influence in South Carolina went far beyond anything that is indicated in the Populist vote in those three states. Tillman, by definite design and shrewd political maneuvering, kept the agrarian rebels of South Carolina in line by his capture of the Democratic party of that state. Robert L. Taylor of Tennessee had been the farmers' successful candidate for governor before the Alliance became strong in that state. He was governor of Tennessee three times and, although he was never an avowed Populist, he served as the recognized leader of the agrarian revolt in Tennessee during most of the period of the Alliance and Populist upheaval. Watson started his rebellion within the Democratic party in Georgia as early as 1880, was elected to the state legislature on the Democratic ticket in 1882, but resigned before his term expired. He took no part in the national campaign of 1884, but supported Cleveland on the Democratic ticket in 1888.[67]

In the meantime, the Farmers' Alliance had gathered strength in Georgia and thereby furnished the springboard for Watson's departure from the Democratic party. Watson did not join the Alliance and ad-

---

[65] C. Vann Woodward, *Tom Watson, agrarian rebel*, chap. xvii, "The Debacle of 1896," pp. 302-331. New York: The Macmillan Company, 1938. William W. Brewton, *The life of Thomas E. Watson*, chap. xxxi, "The Presidential Campaign of 1896," pp. 266-273. Atlanta, Georgia: published by the author, 1926.

[66] New York *World*, September 28, 1896.

[67] C. Vann Woodward, pp. 73-77, 96-102, 112, 122. Brewton, pp. 165, 184-185, 196.

vised against its entering into politics, but nevertheless welcomed its growing strength and regained some of his lost influence upon the basis of sentiment and popular opinion which the Alliance developed.[68] As Woodward says:

> Of this bracing intellectual ferment Tom Watson drank thirstily and responded to it as to an intoxicant. "A new era has dawned in Georgia politics. The old order of things is passing away. The masses are beginning to arouse themselves, reading for themselves, thinking for themselves. The great currents of thought quicken new impulses. At the bar of public opinion the people are pressing their demands and insisting that they be heard." [69]

As the Populist party grew to power, Watson was opposed to its fusion with the Democrats in the North and with the Republicans in the South. In the first issue of his paper to appear after the 1896 election he said:

> Our party, as a party, does not exist any more . . . Fusionists sold the national candidate of the People's Party for the highest price they could get in each state, and the result is that while the fusionists have succeeded in getting some local pie, the national organization is almost dead . . . The sentiment is still there, the votes are still there, but confidence is gone, and the party organization is almost gone . . .[70]

Watson, however, did not retire or give up the Populist fight. He did withdraw from political life for approximately eight years after what to him was the Populist debacle of 1896, but he continued the publication of his paper and through its columns promoted the cause of Populism. He refused to accept the candidacy for governor of Georgia on the Populist ticket in 1898, but during that same year he wrote:

> If . . . you mean to ask me how goes it with the *Principles* of Populism, I say to you that they never commanded more respect, never

---

[68] *People's Party Paper*, January 7, 8, 21, 1892. From January 7 to February 4, 1892, the *People's Party Paper* ran a feature on the front page entitled, "Speaking Out— The Alliance Endorsing Thos. E. Watson and Falling in Line with the People's Party."

[69] C. Vann Woodward, p. 139. Reprinted by permission of the author. *Atlanta Journal*, August 31, 1889.

[70] *People's Party Paper*, November 13, 1896.

met with the approval of a larger proportion of you fellow citizens, than they do today.[71]

He took no part in the national campaign in 1900, but received the unsolicited nomination for President on the People's party ticket in 1904, was presidential candidate again in 1908, and in 1910 returned to the Democratic party, which he had deserted twenty years before, and was elected to the United States Senate as a Democrat in 1920. Two years later he died. His last public utterance was in behalf of ejected striking coal miners in Pennsylvania.[72]

He had begun preaching reform in the Democratic party in Georgia as early as 1878, was elected to the lower house of the Georgia legislature in 1882, and immediately took up the cudgels in behalf of the farmers against the railroads. He was not a member of the Alliance, but he fought on parallel lines with it all during its heyday in Georgia and in the nation. His own comment was: "I did not lead the Alliance; I followed the Alliance, and I am proud that I did follow it." [73] When, however, the Farmers' Alliance literally lost itself in the Populist party, Watson did lead that party in Georgia, later led it in the nation, and was its last presidential candidate.[74]

During the period of Watson's agrarian leadership in Georgia two other southern states, never strong Populist states, experienced agrarian revivals which should be accounted as aberrant to the Populist upheaval. That these revivals did not attach themselves entirely to the Populist bandwagon can be accounted for by the danger inherent in breaking the ranks of the Democratic party so shortly after it had gained ascendancy over carpetbag rule. The crusade was led by Ben Tillman in South Carolina and by Bob Taylor in Tennessee.

No fusion ticket appeared in South Carolina during the Populist era, but Ben Tillman so completely broke the rule of what he called "rings" and "cliques" by mobilizing farmer sentiment and using the Farmers' Alliance that his rise to power must be counted as part of the general

---

[71] C. Vann Woodward, p. 333.

[72] *Congressional record*, 67th Congress, 2nd Session, September 22, 1922, pp. 13, 141.

[73] C. Vann Woodward, p. 140.

[74] *Ibid.*, pp. 398-401. Edward Stanwood, *A history of the Presidency from 1897 to 1909*, pp. 158-161, 201. Boston: Houghton Mifflin Company, 1912.

Farmers' Movement of the time. His entrance into public life was on an agrarian platform; his first organizational project was the founding of a county agricultural club, and when he entered politics his challenge was couched in the following statement: "The farmers have acted like cowards and idiots in the past; whether or not they are going to run the State in the future is for them to say." [75] He was called "Farmer Tillman" and "the agricultural Moses" [76] by those whom he assembled in the Farmers' Convention each November about election time. In an address at the first meeting of this convention he said: "Say, you men who own the soil of South Carolina . . . how do you like this wet nursing, this patronizing, this assumption of superiority, this insufferable insolence? . . . Let us agree on what we consider just for us and the State and see to it that in the next Democratic primaries men are chosen who will loyally carry out our wishes." [77]

He never broke with the Democratic party but instead captured it for his cause, first by lobbying as a member of the legislative committee of his Farmers' Convention, then publicly campaigning for men and legislative measures, and finally by running for governor of his state and the United States Senate. In all of these activities he was successful. His opponents referred to him and his followers as Independents, a title which undoubtedly carried Populist connotations at that time. Tillman continually insisted that the old-line politicians "did not represent the people," which was certainly a Populist doctrine. Furthermore, the issues for which he fought were the Populist issues of the day: regulation of the railroads; practical, rather than theoretical agricultural education; elimination of the dominance of lawyers in politics; and shifting of taxes from farm land to corporations. He was president of his county Alliance, wrote the Alliance call for the meeting and the organization of the state Farmers' Association, was claimed as an Alliance candidate by H. R. Chamberlain, one of the official historians of that organization,[78]

---

[75] *News and Courier*, January 8, 1886.

[76] Simkins, p. 64.

[77] *Ibid.*, p. 68. Reprinted by permission of Duke University Press.

[78] H. R. Chamberlain, *The Farmers' Alliance, what it aims to accomplish*, p. 28. New York: The Minerva Publishing Co., January, 1891.

and said himself: "I was put into office by the Farmers' Movement and my successor should be a farmer."[79]

Tillman's official paper, the *Daily Register* (Columbia, South Carolina), was edited by T. Larry Gantt, who had made an outstanding reputation in Georgia, a strong Populist state, as a partisan of the Farmers' Alliance. Gantt, Tillman himself, and the Tillmanites were thoroughly committed to the Ocala platform of the National Farmers' Alliance, and this platform was practically identical with the platform of the Populist party. Even so, Tillman, while he opposed the nomination of Cleveland in the national Democratic convention, supported him against James B. Weaver, the People's party candidate, in the 1892 election. Weaver received only one-thirtieth of the vote in South Carolina that year. Ben Tillman was, therefore, never a bona fide Populist nor was South Carolina a Populist state. Nevertheless, Tillmanism was a part of Populism, and the reform movement led by him in South Carolina was a part of the Populist movement.[80]

One other southern state, which was for the most part dominated by agrarian politics during the Alliance-Populist period, and its leading crusader need to be given consideration. Robert L. Taylor—three times governor of Tennessee—was never a Populist candidate or even a Populist, but the part he played in the agrarian revolt in that state was part and parcel of the agrarian revolt of the times. He was first elected governor of Tennessee in 1886, one year before the Alliance came into that state. The Agricultural Wheel had, however, entered the state two years earlier and developed considerable strength in the western part. Taylor was governor from 1886 to 1890, was followed by an Allianceman from 1890 to 1892, a reactionary Democrat from 1892 to 1896, and was then drafted by the farmers and small townsmen again in 1896.[81] His failure to go "whole hog" for Populism or fusionism probably kept his state from the political confusion which reigned in the sister state of North Carolina for a decade, but at the same time guaranteed the overthrow of

[79] Simkins, p. 182.

[80] For a detailed and well-documented account of the facts presented here, see Simkins. Chamberlain, *The Farmers' Alliance, what it aims to accomplish*, p. 28. Manning, pp. 17-18.

[81] Robison, pp. 70-72, 148, 174-175, 184-187, 192-204.

the old-guard Democrats as completely as fusionism did in some other southern states or as Tillmanism did in South Carolina.

Tennessee, like most other southern states, was a dominantly rural state, and like them also had always been governed by wealthy planters, "whose aristocratic tendencies," says Robison, "brought them socially, if not economically, much nearer the rich merchants and bankers of the cities than to the small farmer . . ." [82] Now, however, labor unions as well as such farmers' organizations as the Agricultural Wheel and Farmers' Alliance were sounding notes of discontent with this type of political domination. Bob Taylor may not have thought of himself as a crusader in their behalf, much less as the prophet of the small farmers, but he believed in them, spoke their language, was immensely liked by them and hailed by them as "Our Bob." He "fiddled" his way into their hearts during his campaign and, when they elected him governor, he took their point of view in relation to money and railroad issues. In his first message to the state legislature he complained about taxes that discriminated against small real-estate holders and urged a revision of the state's revenue laws.[83] In 1896, he took his stand unequivocally in favor of free silver.[84]

By 1890 the Farmers' Alliance had reached such strength in Tennessee that it nominated its president, J. P. Buchanan, for governor on the Democratic ticket and elected him with a pronounced majority. Robison asserts that the people that elected him "were the same people who had supported Robert L. Taylor" and that "On many state problems Buchanan's recommendations did not differ greatly from those previously made by Governor Taylor." [85] Buchanan was not re-elected because the Democratic party in Tennessee was threatened by third-party politics. Although Buchanan had made a good governor and had never publicly endorsed the St. Louis platform but as a state official, he was forced to commit himself on the yet more radical Ocala pronouncements that were being circulated at that time. His declaration in favor of these principles

---

[82] *Ibid.*, p. 5.

[83] *Journal of the house of representatives of the forty-fifth general assembly of the State of Tennessee*, pp. 367-368. Nashville: Marshall and Bruce, Printers to the State, 1887.

[84] Robison, p. 198.

[85] *Ibid.*, pp. 138-140, 148-149.

led to the belief that to nominate him would be "running . . . a Democrat on a third-party platform."[86]

Four years of reactionary administration brought a popular demand by the farmers and liberals for Bob Taylor as governor, and while he accepted the nomination with some reluctance, he made the race in the Populist-Democratic year of 1896 and was again elected by the rural voters of the state.[87] That he was by and large acceptable to the Populists was indicated by the fact that their state ticket polled just about one-half as many votes as it had in 1892. There were, however, 7,000 more votes cast for the Populist state ticket than for the Populist national ticket in Tennessee in 1896, and Taylor polled between seven and eight thousand votes less than Bryan in that election.[88] While, therefore, he won his state back for the farmers, he never received the unanimous support of the Populists. He was probably less a Populist than Ben Tillman of South Carolina, but like Tillman he must be counted among the leaders of agrarianism in the 1880's and 1890's when Populism was rising to influence.

―

[86] Memphis *Appeal-Avalanche,* April 20, 1892.
[87] Robison, p. 204.
[88] *Ibid.,* p. 203.

· 13 ·

A LOW TIDE

IN THE

FARMERS' MOVEMENT

AFTER THE CRASH

The highest tide of the Farmers' Movement in all American history was reached in the late 1880's and early 1890's. A real groundswell, starting in practically all sections of the country, in the early eighties, developed a farmer public which by the early nineties came near being the most powerful pressure group of the nation. Farmers were operating economic enterprises of many kinds at many places. Middlemen, newspapermen, and politicians were highly conscious of the potential strength of these hundreds of thousands of aroused agrarians. To what extent the farmers themselves would have moved into the political arena had they not been stimulated to do so by the politicians and the Reform Press, it is impossible to say. That they did enter the political arena, and in doing so largely neglected their grass-roots structure, is very clear. By 1896 the Farmers' Alliance group of organizations was so definitely political that outstanding success in the state and national elections of that year was essential to its survival.

It could hardly be said that Bryan was the farmers' presidential candidate; but he was the candidate of the Populist party, and the Populist party came nearer being the weathervane of farmer sentiment in 1896 than any single farmers' organization or combination of farmers' organizations. The debacle in the Farmers' Movement which came in the middle nineties was the end-product of a steady, though rapid, evolution of the movement from local neighborhood and community enterprises in buying and selling through the stage of larger and larger economic enterprises, and finally into the stage of complete public action. In other words, by 1896 the Farmers' Movement was pretty well separated from its own grass roots of local organization, had cast its destiny in the success or failure of a great farmer public, and, failing, went down as a public.

THE PEOPLE'S PARTY AFTER 1896

The People's party had come into existence in 1892 as the end-product of from fifteen to twenty years of developing third-party sentiment. It therefore picked up the dynamics which had been developed by the Independent, Anti-Monopoly, and Greenback parties. It was by no means a one-hundred per cent agrarian party. It became rather dominantly agrarian because it swept into its ranks so many Farmers' Alliancemen. Tom Watson, probably the longest-lived, dyed-in-the-wool Populist of the nation, advised the Farmers' Alliance against going into politics. He also advised against and fought fusion with minority parties. He was the vice-presidential candidate on the People's party ticket in 1896 and was quite convinced that real and fundamental Populism was sold out during that campaign to pragmatic and variegated fusionism on all hands. After the debacle of that campaign, Watson withdrew from politics completely for eight years. The Populists nominated him as their gubernatorial candidate in Georgia in 1898, but he refused to accept the nomination.[1]

In the campaign of 1898 many Populist candidates were still in the field, but the most significant results were those obtained by fusion of

---

[1] Thomas E. Watson, "The Honest Ignorance of the Average Southern Democratic Editor," *Watson's Jeffersonian Magazine,* Vol. V, No. 4 (October, 1910), p. 817. C. Vann Woodward, p. 334.

the Populist party with the Republicans in the South and with the Democrats and Silver Republicans in the North and West. Twenty-five states held Populist or fusion conventions that year.[2] The Populists and fusionists continued to hold sway in the West and North to a much greater extent and for a longer period of time than they did in the South. The West had been independent for a generation, while the South had always been solidly Democratic. Yet, in 1898 there continued to be Populist activity in Alabama, Arkansas, Georgia, Mississippi, North Carolina, Texas, and Virginia. The Populists in Alabama nominated a complete state ticket, and the candidate for governor received 31.08 per cent of the total vote. In Arkansas, the Populist nominee for governor received only 7.44 per cent of the total vote; in Georgia, 30.21 per cent. In Mississippi there were Populist candidates for Congress, but no Populist was elected. In North Carolina, candidates for Congress claimed to be either "Populist-Republican-Independent" or "Populist-Democratic-Independent." One Congressman was elected on each of these tickets. There was a big carry-over of Populists in the North Carolina state legislature of 1899, twenty-four in the senate and thirty-two in the house. In Texas, the only two tickets placed before the voters were the Democratic and Populist, resulting in a complete Democratic victory. Nine Populists continued to represent that party in the house of the state legislature. In Virginia there was one Populist in the state senate in 1899.

In the North and West the fusionists and Populists were more active and more successful. They elected one Congressman in California, and their gubernatorial candidate received 45 per cent of the total vote. In Colorado the fusion candidate, a Democrat, was elected governor; and two fusion candidates, one Silver Republican and one Populist, were elected to Congress. There were also nine Populists in the state senate and twenty in the house. In Idaho, the Populist candidate for governor did not fare so well, receiving slightly less than 14 per cent of the total vote; the state legislature of 1899 had two Populists in the senate and six in the house. In Oregon the fusionist and the "Middle-of-the-Road Populist" candidates for governor together received 44 per cent of the total vote. In Washington the Silver Republicans, Democrats, and Populists combined, but lost to the Republicans by a large majority. As in

---

[2] *Appleton's, 1899.* See under names of states.

other states, there were Populist holdovers in the state legislature, in this case enough to prevent a Republican majority in the upper house. In Montana, the fusionists elected a supreme court judge and won four out of six congressional seats. Nebraska elected a complete fusionist state ticket and four out of six United States Congressmen. In Kansas, the fusionist gubernatorial candidate lost the election by about 3 per cent of the vote and there were no Populist victories. There was, however, a heavy carry-over in the state legislature. The fusionist candidate for governor in Michigan received approximately 40 per cent of the vote. In Minnesota, he was elected by 52 per cent of the vote. In Missouri, the fusionist faction of the Populist party accepted the Democratic nominees. In North Dakota, the fusionist candidate for governor received more than 41 per cent of the total vote, and in South Dakota he was elected by a small majority. In Wisconsin, the vote for the Populist candidate was negligible. The eastern states of Maine and New Jersey had Populist candidates for governor, but neither received any appreciable vote.

In the 1900 presidential election, a great many of Bryan's Populist adherents followed him back into the Democratic party, although the Middle-of-the-Road Populists also had a national ticket. Their candidates, Wharton Barker of Pennsylvania, and Ignatius Donnelly of Minnesota, polled only 50,599 votes, Texas contributing more than two-fifths of the total. The only states to cast more than 1,500 votes for the Populist candidates were agrarian—Texas, Georgia, Missouri, Alabama, Kentucky, and Mississippi. Fusionist governors won in Colorado, Idaho, and Washington in the 1900 state election. Some fusionist Congressmen won in Colorado, Idaho, Kansas, and Nebraska, and a number of states elected Populists or fusionists to their state legislatures. Such industrial states as Connecticut, Delaware, Massachusetts, and Rhode Island dropped completely out of the Populist columns.[3]

In the 1902 state elections, there were no outstanding Populist victories; and gradually Populist and fusionist candidates, elected in earlier years, were dropping out of the state legislatures, governorships, and Congress.

Tom Watson entered the field again in 1904 as Populist presidential

---

[3] Woody, pp. 103-104. Stanwood, *A history of the presidency from 1897 to 1909*, pp. 38-43, 75. *World almanac, 1901*, p. 437. *Tribune almanac, 1905*, p. 377.

candidate and received 114,546 votes, more than twice the number cast for the Populist ticket in 1900. The strongest Populist states in that year were again agrarian, led in the order named by Georgia, Nebraska, and Texas.[4] In 1908 Watson was again presidential candidate, but received only 29,146 votes, 16,969 from his own home state of Georgia. Only seven other states—Alabama, Arkansas, Florida, Indiana, Mississippi, Missouri, and Tennessee—cast as many as a thousand votes for the Populist party.

J. C. Manning, himself a prominent Populist and Allianceman in 1890, argued as late as 1928 that it was a combination of political accidents which caused the death of the Populist party. He argued that "had Bryan not come upon the scene, had he failed to capture the Democratic National Convention in 1896, if free silver had not been written into the Democratic platform, then there would have been much to follow in the South and West to strengthen Governor Waite as a political prognosticator."[5] Davis H. Waite, to whom he referred, was elected governor of Colorado in 1893 as a People's party candidate. He was the country's leading free silver advocate, and Manning believed that the West and South would have continued to be Populists on this one issue had Bryan and the Democratic party not stolen the issue.

Manning described many local scenes in the South in which he saw Populists gradually but ruthlessly pushed out of political leadership by aspiring Democratic politicians. He as much as says that hill farmers stuck to Populism to the last, and that Negroes would have done the same had they not been led to believe that by backing such candidates as Tillman in South Carolina they were voting for a third party. He described in detail the process of transition back to the Democratic party in Alabama, where he was at one time a Populist state senator. He said, "The answer of the Democratic Party in Alabama was 'yes, we counted you out—what are you going to do about it.'"

In 1910, Watson returned to the Democratic party. It had taken fifteen years for the Populist skyrocket to fade from the skies. In the meantime, two other farmers' organizations had come into existence—the Farmers' Union in the South and the American Society of Equity in the North.

---

[4] Stanwood, *A history of the presidency from 1897 to 1909,* pp. 114-117, 137. *World almanac, 1905,* p. 445. *Tribune almanac, 1905,* p. 377. C. Vann Woodward, pp. 357-363.

[5] Manning, pp. 5-10.

Neither of them went heavily into politics, but each became the mouth-piece of the Farmers' Movement in its own region.

THE FARMERS' ALLIANCE AFTER 1896

The decline of those farmers' organizations which had been swept into the Populist movement was far more precipitate than the decline of the People's party itself. The decline of Alliance organizations in the local communities had begun with the drift of the Alliance into politics. The payment of dues to support the development of small business enterprises was no longer the passion or purpose of Alliancemen.

Fusion party arrangements tended to estrange strong Populist party adherents. In the South, the Populists were accused of being clever politicians seeking to overthrow the Democratic party; in the North, they were accused of trying to overthrow the Republican party. Naturally, strong Democratic party adherents in the South did not like to be accused of collusion with the Republicans, and strong Republican adherents in the North did not like to be accused of having joined hands with the Democrats. If to be loyal Alliancemen meant such fusion or coalition, they preferred to, and did, drop out of the Alliance. Both the southern and the northern Alliances, therefore, were practically extinct by the time Populism had gained ascendancy in their ranks and caused them to cast their destinies on that particular political wheel of fortune. It is doubtful that they would have survived as farmers' organizations even had the Populists won in 1896.

Many Alliance economic enterprises had been started and were operating successfully in the late 1880's and early 1890's. They did not stop abruptly or go out of existence with the demise of their national organizations. Most of them were joint-stock companies, supported by investments of loyal Alliance members, and therefore suffered from loss in patronage and support as this intense loyalty cooled off or diminished. Furthermore, the strong public sanction of the Farmers' Movement, which had made it unpopular for either big or little commercial businesses to fight Alliance economic projects, no longer existed to any extent after the Alliance had gone so thoroughly into politics. One after the other, Alliance business enterprises fell by the wayside, often catching local Alliance leaders with legal economic obligations from which they could not escape. Many a leader paid hundreds and sometimes thousands of dollars out of his pocket in the liquidation of Alliance enterprises because he could be held legally responsible for such obligations and because his neighbors were no longer enthusiastic about the movement.[6]

There were, until as late as 1940, still some direct organizational carry-overs of the Farmers' Alliance in existence. Probably the most interesting of all was the North Carolina State Farmers' Alliance. During the last forty years of its existence, it was not an organization of any great size or influence, but met regularly each year, elected officers, appointed committees, and passed resolutions in somewhat the same manner that it did in the days of its greatest strength. It continued through all of these years primarily because it retained in its treasury something like $25,000 worth of securities which had accumulated during the days of the operation of its state business agency. The existence of this fund and the fact that some of the men who were members of the Alliance in the 1890's were still alive kept this vestigial organization in existence. A brief sample of some of the minutes of its annual meetings in its later years will suffice to show the types of activity in which it engaged.

In 1926, the original declaration of purposes of the Alliance was reaffirmed, and still other purposes of community service and cooperation were added; the organization "expressed its approval of co-operative marketing," and urged its members "to give their best efforts in perfecting it"; appropriated $300 as awards to tenant farmers and their wives and to club boys and girls. In 1928, it passed resolutions in support of the State College of Agriculture, Smith-Hughes Schools, and the State Department of Agriculture; on taxation of intangible wealth; in favor of co-operative marketing; in encouragement of farm-home ownership; on the development of forestry; and said, "We plead for support of a state-wide farm organization with local, county, and state units in order that all phases of agricultural production, business and rural welfare may be more effectively promoted and that the farmer's voice may be heard in the councils of state and nation." This last resolution was passed as a compromise between an attempt on the part of some of the younger members to carry the organization as a whole into the Grange, which

---

[6] The writer's father was obliged personally to discharge a debt of some $900 in order to liquidate a local Alliance enterprise.

was just then re-entering the state, and the older members who objected
to abandoning the state Alliance organization.[7]

The writer joined the North Carolina State Farmers' Alliance in 1926
and attended the meetings of the State Alliance quite regularly for five
years. After the 1928 state meeting, he recorded his observations as follows:

> I walked into the room just a few minutes before the meeting was
> called to order. I felt that I knew most of the agricultural leaders
> in the state, but I recognized only four people in the assemblage
> of about thirty.
>
> The president took the chair and opened the meeting according
> to the ritual formulated almost fifty years ago. The steward was
> asked to ascertain whether the persons assembled there knew the
> "word." I had joined the organization two years before, but no
> "word" had ever been given to me. The chairman of the executive
> committee sat next to me and when I asked him what the "word"
> was he said he did not know anything about any "word." Since the
> "word," if there was one, was given in a whisper, I do not know
> how many others were in the same fix as the chairman of the executive committee and myself.
>
> As the oath was repeated, I, not knowing the signs, spent my time
> observing the audience and discovered that less than half the persons there went through with the signs. The chairman overlooked
> the fact that the meeting was supposed to be opened with prayer,
> but the chaplain, one of the oldest members present, reminded
> him of this slip. All during the meeting there were many promptings from the older members, who apparently remembered the ritualistic way in which Alliance meetings had been conducted thirty
> or forty years ago.
>
> The oldest man in the group was over eighty and, with the exception of three who had joined within the last two years, I am
> sure there was no man or woman in the audience under fifty years
> of age.
>
> When the executive committee and the treasurer made reports,
> it became known that there was in the state treasury over $24,000.
> This was a carry-over from the heyday of the great Farmers' Alliance organization of the late eighties and early nineties. In view

---

[7] See minutes of North Carolina State Farmers' Alliance meetings for years mentioned.

of the fact that every other Alliance has died, it is apparent that the existence of this fund is the only thing which has held the North Carolina State Alliance together.

The executive committee presented a report for alterations in the constitution which provided for the changing of the name, the abolition of the ritual and all secret work, and the construction of the organization on modern farming organization lines. This proposition was debated pro and con in three sessions, covering a period of probably eight hours all told. It was only a few of the progressive older men and three of us younger men who approved of the change and attempted to get it made. We were overwhelmingly outvoted on the basis of arguments presented on both the sacred name "Alliance" and the ancient traditions which would be sacrificed if any change in the purposes and name of the organization was made.

Two or three of us attempted to say as judiciously and adroitly as possible that this organization had but two alternatives: one, to lose its whole identity by using its influence and its name to establish a state organization of farmers which could do for the future what the Alliance did in the past; or, to stick by its old traditions, attempt to conserve its funds and see its old members one by one step off into the grave. It has lost 30 per cent of its members in the last year. The defenders of the old regime made no pretense of having any outstanding purposes or projects, and a son of one of the older members said that he was sure they had no purpose whatsoever except to keep their funds intact as long as they were alive.

The collapse of the Alliance and Populist movements was more precipitate than their rise and represented even better than the collapse of the Granger movement in the seventies the episodic character of the Farmers' Movement up to that time. The collapse was much more apparent than real, for farmers' organizations did not completely fade from the public scene; and when they returned in force, they came to stay. Furthermore, many parts of the Populist legislative program were placed into government structure during the 1880's and 1890's and many more have been adopted since. When the 1889 St. Louis resolutions are checked with decade-by-decade accomplishments in legislation from 1890 to 1940, the extent of their adoption into law during that fifty-year period becomes almost startling.

The Populist movement, and therefore the Alliance movement to a great extent, was a people's movement against concentration of power, whether in industry or politics. The Alliancemen and Populists inveighed against monopolies, money and banking concentration, plutocratic government officials, and extreme partisan politics. They demanded the Australian ballot, the popular election of United States Senators, primary elections, the initiative, referendum, and recall—all of which have become state or federal practices. A number of additional demands have found their answer in less direct but nevertheless recognizable form.[8] The famous subtreasury plan was not altogether a wild idea when thought of in terms of the "Ever-Normal Granary" and millions of bushels of "sealed grain" and stored cotton.

Not all of these things came to pass because the Farmers' Alliance and the People's party advocated them. A movement does not work in such a direct fashion except in a very fragmentary way. Its very genius is to deal with longstanding maladjustments and to accomplish adjustments by long-time, persistent attack. The muckraking episode of the late nineties of the last century and the first decade of the present century was a part of the people's movement. Woodrow Wilson's first administration, in terms of laws passed, was almost a Populist regime.[9] The farm relief agitation of the 1920's and the whole gamut of farm programs since then are part of the Farmers' Movement. The fact that much of the latter-day legislation is different from the specifications prescribed by the Alliance does not alter the truth of the statement that the Alliance was pleading for reform in the very field to which reform agricultural legislation has later applied. The Farmers' Alliances and their allied organizations and the Populist movement arose like a skyrocket and came down like a meteor, but the heat and light they engendered endured in later decades of the Farmers' Movement.

———

[8] For a detailed discussion of the Populist contributions, see Hicks, *The Populist revolt*, chap. xv, "The Populist Contribution," pp. 404-423. Manning, pp. 33-35.

[9] Charles W. Eliot, "The Achievements of the Democratic Party and its Leader since March 4, 1913," *Atlantic Monthly*, Vol. CXVIII, No. 4 (October, 1916), pp. 433-440. Carl R. Woodward, "Woodrow Wilson's Agricultural Philosophy," *Agricultural History*, Vol. XIV, No. 4 (October, 1940), pp. 129-142.

THE GRANGE IN THE NINETIES

The membership of the national Grange declined almost steadily after 1876 and very rapidly after the Farmers' Alliance took the field. It had risen to 858,050 dues-paying members in 1875, but had fallen to 106,782 in 1889.[10] One after the other of the reports from the various states, presented to the national Grange in November, 1889, tells of the difficulty that the Grange was having in the face of Alliance competition. The Alabama report said:

It affords me pleasure to be able to report for Alabama, that notwithstanding a tidal wave has swept over the State in the interest of another farmers' organization . . . several Granges have been reorganized and accessions are being added to our Granges . . . Nothing but Herculean efforts and untiring energy and constant vigilance can hold the field against such forces as are now and have been applied to secure co-operative efforts by other farmers' organizations in Alabama.[11]

The Kansas report said:

Other farmers' organizations, wisely recognizing the needs of the people, and adapting their fees to the farmers' changed condition, have rapidly increased in the State.

The Nebraska report said:

Other farmers' organizations are springing up in many parts of the State that to-day command the admiration of many of the farmers, and many are joining these organizations, not because they are better than the Grange, but because they are cheaper. We are cultivating a friendly relation between ourselves and all other associations, for we believe there is room for us all and material enough to work upon to build up and maintain the Grange and the other organizations within our State . . .

The South Carolina report read in part as follows:

A new farmers' organization known as the Alliance, has swept over our State like a wave. This organization is the outgrowth of the

---

[10] Atkeson, p. 350.

[11] *Proceedings of the twenty-third session of the national Grange,* 1889, p. 41. In National Grange Headquarters, Washington, D. C.

Grange, but it is an instance in which the child has outgrown its parent. In consequence of this we have thought it best to merely make efforts to keep up our old Granges, lest an active exertion to organize new Granges might be construed as antagonistic to other farmers' organizations.[12]

Virginia reported:

The Farmers' Alliance has come into our State, and [these Alliances] are rapidly organizing in most every county, and are crippling our Grange work, as they organize much cheaper than we can; hence the farmers say they can join an organization so much cheaper than the Grange, and by organizing the Alliance they can do us much good and get the same benefits. They will not lend a listening ear to us when we try to tell them as best we can of the advantages they have over the Alliance by joining our Order. Our State Grange treasury is depleted, the National Grange treasury has money—why not come to the help of the needy.

Missouri said:

We have reorganized forty-six Granges in our State during the last year, and have added thirteen hundred and fifty-seven members. The "Agricultural Wheel," "Farmers' Alliance," "Patrons of Industry," "Farmers' Mutual Benefit Association," and other kindred farmers' organizations are all in the field and some of them doing a good work. We most emphatically favor the appointment of a Committee from the National Grange to meet with the "Farmers' and Labor Union" at St. Louis, during the second week in December, and cordially invite the farmers there assembled to return to the paternal roof.

The North Carolina report was exceedingly gloomy:

It is painful to acknowledge that the Grange is at a low ebb in North Carolina. Last year it was booming. We were leading. A great movement, called the Farmers' Alliance, has about ruined the Grange. They say they have the same ends in view, with better trade arrangements (taken from the Grange), cheaper and less autocratic. They claim to be only the child of the Grange, and whilst

---

[12] *Ibid.*, pp. 45, 49, 54.

professing not to do anything to antagonize the Grange, they are absorbing it.[13]

These quotations from the national proceedings of the Grange reflect sentiments and activities for a period just preceding the great St. Louis Farmers' Alliance convention. A few quotations from the next year's proceedings (1890) serve to show that the devastation among Granges still continued. The Kansas report said:

We have but little of interest to report as to the work of the Order in Kansas during the year just closed. The number of Granges continues the same as shown in my last report, with an increase in membership of 214 over the number shown one year ago, which, in view of the extraordinary growth in the State of the "Farmers' Alliance and Industrial Union," should in my judgment, be accepted as satisfactory, if not encouraging.[14]

A report from Topeka, Kansas, in the Topeka *Capital* was noted in the *National Economist,* as follows:

The Kansas State Grange devoted a large part of yesterday's session to discussing the question as to the practicability of cooperating with the Farmers' Alliance in securing legislation for the relief of farmer interests and for the furtherance of all measures which will benefit the farmer.

The North Carolina report stated:

North Carolina remains about *status quo,* compared with last year's report. The few remaining Granges are steadfast and hopeful. They mostly went into the Alliance. We have had within the last few months a few Granges reorganized that are now buoyant and determined. We need Lecturers in the field; the want of means is the great deficiency, especially as our Alliance brethren ever appear "flush" and fill the field requirements.[15]

New York reported in a different tenor:

Several new farmers' organizations have sought to gain a foothold in the State, but Grange principles are too firmly established in the

---

[13] *Ibid.,* pp. 56, 65-66.
[14] *Proceedings of the Grange, 1890,* p. 29.
[15] *Ibid.,* p. 48.

old Empire State to be overthrown by misrepresentation, diminutive fees, or extravagant promises. Our faith in the future of our noble Order is strengthened by each passing year's experience. We are endeavoring to impress upon our membership the fact that there is no excellence without labor, no success without persistent energetic effort, and our hope and trust is that the lustre of our past experience may in no wise be dimmed by our work in the future.[16]

Somewhat the same tone as of other years continued in the reports of the 1891 sessions, but discouragement was less prevalent and less pronounced. Kansas said:

We have just passed through a great political campaign in our State, which seemed to preclude the possibility of effective work. And we find that the decline in our Order above reported, comes from counties where there are strong organizations of the Farmers' and Citizens' Alliance. As you are doubtless aware, the period of the last eighteen months in Kansas has been a peculiar one in relation to politics, and many of our members united with other organizations for political purposes, and while this has been the case in Kansas, yet we realize the fact that to the conservative membership of the Patrons of Husbandry one great truth has been clearly demonstrated, to wit: That education and co-operation is the grand bulwark upon which the future prosperity and perpetuity of our noble Order depend, and while the past move in our State may redound to the good of the Order in the future, we shall endeavor to watch the opportune time and with unwavering faith, hope, charity and renewed fidelity will do what we can toward reviving and building up our organization during the coming year.

Iowa reported:

I think I may safely say that we have held our own during the year. Many of our Granges do something in the way of cooperative purchases, and many avail themselves of the offer of the National Alliance, who generously extend to our membership all the benefits of their trade arrangements. The longest and most bitterly contested political contest in the history of the State has just closed. This so absorbed the attention of the people that it was not deemed advisable to attempt any extended Grange work.

---

16 *Ibid.,* p. 53.

North Carolina reported:

> Two causes are operating against us—bad crops, and the Alliance organization. The latter do not antagonize, but they inculcate that they are enough, and that the Grange is played out. I believe if we could get assistance that reaction would set in in 1892, and the Grange would revive again.[17]

The Grange did begin growing in membership after 1889. It grew slowly but steadily during the next ten years and by 1900 had an annual dues-paying national membership of 187,482. Its dues fell off sharply during the great campaign year of 1896, and the ground lost during that year was not gained back for almost three years. It has grown steadily from that time to the present.[18]

As the Grange regained membership, the geography of its strength and weakness reflected the inroads of the Alliance movement. The ten leading Grange states in 1889 were, in order, Maine, Pennsylvania, Michigan, New York, Ohio, Massachusetts, Texas, New Hampshire, Connecticut, and Illinois. Texas dropped out of this list of ten leaders and Oregon was added during the next year (1890). In other words, the Grange and the Alliance tended somewhat to divide the field between them during the decade of the eighties. The Grange tended to hold its own where the Alliance was not strong, but lost heavily where the Alliance was growing. The following strong Alliance states dropped completely out of the Grange columns on or before 1896: Alabama, Georgia, Kansas, North Carolina, South Carolina, and Tennessee. Some of these states did not return to the Grange fold until thirty-five or forty years later.

As Grange strength was gradually recouped, those states which had gone headlong into the Alliance failed for a long while to participate in its recovery. Between 1890 and 1900 there were 1,765 new Granges organized, or an average of about 160 new local Granges a year. Pennsylvania and New York each contributed 299 of them; Ohio, 193; Michigan, 179; and New Hampshire, 148. Thus five states, no one of which was

---

[17] *Journal of proceedings, twenty-fifth session of the national Grange* of the Patrons of Husbandry, Springfield, Ohio, 1891, pp. 42, 73. Philadelphia: J. A. Wagenseller, 1891.

[18] Atkeson, p. 350.

ever a strong Alliance state, contributed more than 63 per cent of all the new Granges organized in the first decade of the Grange's recovery.[19]

Loss in membership on the part of the Grange was not the only impact of the Farmers' Alliance and Populist movement upon it. It had declared for free silver in 1889 and was allotted twenty-five delegates at the 1892 St. Louis convention, which was a Populist meeting.[20] It cooperated with the Farmers' Alliance in both economic and political undertakings, but as a national organization it did not go headlong into the Populist movement as the Alliance did, and for this reason survived the 1892 and 1896 political campaigns with more strength than it had in 1889. And because all during this time it continued to operate consistently through the framework of its subordinate Granges, it retained the framework of an organization which made it possible for it to live after the debacle of the early nineties and grow stronger decade by decade thereafter.

THE ANCIENT ORDER OF GLEANERS

The decade 1890-1900 is the only one from 1860 to 1920 in which there did not arise one or more general farmers' organizations which grew to national magnitude. Presumably this was due to the fact that for the first half of the decade all the old farm organizations, except the Grange, were so deep in politics that it was impossible to get farmers to be concerned with other issues until those for which they were fighting by means of the ballot were settled. This decade was, however, not destined to be wholly without its contribution in this field. The Ancient Order of Gleaners was organized by Messrs. Slocum, England, Ealy, and Chase at Caro, Michigan, in October, 1894, and had a comparatively steady growth during the decade. During the nineties it did not reach beyond the boundaries of Michigan, but in that state it attained a membership of about 10,000.

Just how it happened to be organized at a time when the Northern Alliance and the Grange were operating in that state is not clear, but

---

[19] The above information is taken from records of dues paid at the national annual conventions of the Grange from 1889 to 1900.

[20] Atkeson, p. 154. *National Economist*, March 4, 1892, p. 395.

the type of activities in which it engaged would suggest that the Alliance did not furnish the fraternal features which its founders desired and the Grange was unwilling to engage as directly in economic cooperation as was felt to be necessary. At any rate, the order was organized with secret and ritualistic features similar to those of the Grange and with cooperative features similar to those of the Alliance in the Dakotas, Iowa, and Minnesota. Its first project was the establishment of an "Emergency Fund" into which members paid twenty-five cents—one-half their annual dues—"to create funds to care for members during disability or death." This emergency fund has since been converted into an incorporated insurance company with about 50,000 policies and almost $50,000,000 worth of insurance in force.

This organization began its economic campaign by fighting the "binder-twine trust" and the middlemen, and during the early years of its existence claimed to wield a large political influence in Michigan. It purchased farm supplies cooperatively, set up a mutual benefit fund, and organized local lodges, known as "Arbors," through which members could enjoy social activities. Its activities since 1900 have not been greatly enlarged, but its rise and considerable growth in the nineties must be given to make the record of farmer organizations during that decade complete.[21] It is now little more than a small insurance company.

——

[21] Information on the early history of the Gleaners is difficult to obtain because the enlarged insurance program in later years overshadowed everything else, even the concern of its members in its origin. Such information as is presented here has been obtained from pamphlets published by the organization, especially, *A national marketing system, Stepping stones, Ancient order of Gleaners* (Ritual). Caro, Michigan: 1895. *Constitutional provisions and by-laws of the ancient order of Gleaners.* Caro, Michigan: State Arbor and Secretary's Office, 1895. *The Gleaners, Gleaner protection for children, The Gleaner juvenile department.* Information has also been obtained from correspondence and personal interviews with officials, and from the files of the *National Gleaner*, mouthpiece of the organization.

· 14 ·

THE FARMERS' UNION

There was no period of pronounced depression from the middle 1890's until after World War I; and yet two new general farmers' organizations, which are often said to have been depression-born, came into existence just after 1900 and grew rapidly. Both the Farmers' Educational and Cooperative Union and the American Society of Equity were organized in 1902, the former in the South, the latter in the North. Furthermore, the Grange recovered and grew steadily, through depression and prosperity, after 1890. The Farmers' Movement, which up to that time had appeared to consist of a series of episodic upheavals, often separated one from the other by decades, settled into the pattern of successful activities.

Since the rise of the Union and Equity, general farmers' organizations have consistently carried the torch of the Farmers' Movement. There have been two violent farmer upheavals since that time—the Kentucky Night Riders in 1907-1908 and the Farmers' Holiday Association in 1932-1933. These were, of course, a part of the Farmers' Movement, but neither they nor the Nonpartisan League have represented the genius of the movement in the same way as have general farmers' organizations. The movement, thirty years earlier, had been picked up by the Grange and carried forward by the Alliance. In each instance, a great balloon-type of farmer public was developed on behalf of the farmers' cause. In each case the balloon burst because it became inflated with political sentiment. Since 1900, no such thing has occurred. Instead, an American farm public has been constantly in existence and functionally operative.

The Farmers' Union, like all other farmers' organizations before it, built its strength in cash-crop areas. It started in the cotton states, shifted to the wheat states, and for a number of years had great strength in some of the big tobacco-producing states.

THE RISE OF THE FARMERS' UNION

The Farmers' Educational and Cooperative Union was conceived by Isaac Newton Gresham, a newspaperman and an old Allianceman, at Point, a little town in Rains County, Texas. A person who came as near as any to being his biographer says:

> Newt. Gresham was sitting on a log one day at a cross-roads country store, and observed the few woebegone and debt-depressed farmers who came and went. Doubtless Newt. Gresham recalled the time when the Grange, the Wheel and the Farmers' Alliance had made heroic but unsuccessful effort to break away from such conditions as he was then witnessing, and in his heart of hearts he desired to aid them. There came to him, as if by inspiration, a hope that he might be able to assist them and thus redress their many wrongs.[1]

Gresham revealed his thoughts and his plans for a farmers' organization first to O. P. Pyle, the editor of the Mineola *Courier*, whom he had met two years earlier at a state press convention, and was encouraged by Pyle to go forward with his plans. He therefore invited a few of his neighbors and friends to meet with him and listen to his plan. Nine of those who came joined him in starting a new organization. He was soon invited to a nearby community to explain his plan, and then to another, and another. This process continued so rapidly that it was only a comparatively short time before it was decided to send organizers into nearby states. They went into Arkansas, Oklahoma, Indian Territory, Mississippi, Louisiana, Alabama, and Georgia. In a remarkably few years the organization had spread over the whole South and for a decade and

---

[1] C. S. Barrett, *The mission, history and times of the Farmers' Union*, p. 103. Nashville, Tennessee: Marshall and Bruce Co., 1909.

a half was a powerful and in many ways more effective organization than the Alliance had been in its heyday twenty to thirty years earlier.

Space will not be taken to describe in detail just how the Union got going. Enough of that story should be told, however, to illustrate certain typical techniques of a movement. Hunt, in the following quotation, describes the characteristics and role of the man who initiated this particular segment of the Farmers' Movement:

> After locating in Point, Gresham apparently did not do so well financially. He worked continuously on plans for organizing farmers, drawing upon his experience in the Grange and Farmers' Alliance for ideas. No one had any faith in his plans, and he worked alone. A local merchant, who had the only typewriter in Point, says that Gresham used his typewriter to copy his outline for an organization. This merchant says that Gresham worked day after day in trying to get into satisfactory language what he had in mind, but had difficulty in doing so. He had experienced the emotional appeal and sentimental language of the Grange and Alliance, but on account of his limited education, he had difficulty in getting his emotions and sentiments into written form. He soon exhausted his finances and credit and found difficulty in securing food for his family. The local merchants had no faith in his plans, and they looked upon his activities as a waste of time. Finally, none of the credit merchants would longer extend credit to him, and he appealed to a cash merchant, a Mr. W. A. Harris, for aid. Mr. Harris states that Gresham came to him almost crying, saying that all the other merchants had refused him further credit. He appealed to Mr. Harris to violate his strict rule of selling for cash only, saying that he was sure that his plans for organizing the farmers would succeed, and when they did, Harris would profit by the success of the new organization, meaning that he would turn as much trade to Harris as possible. Suffice it to say here, he lived up to his promise. Gresham asked Harris for only the staple foods for his family. "Flour, sugar, sow belly with buttons on it, etc.," was what he asked for his family. He asked for nothing for himself, as he promised to seek elsewhere for his food, if only he could get barest necessities for his family. Mr. W. S. Sisk, who later became one of the charter members, says he boarded Gresham for some time. Sisk had little confidence at first in the plans of his guest, but he says Gresham had complete faith in the outcome. Mr. Sisk relates how Gresham would

look up at the stars at night and say: "Sisk, the world will revolve around this place some time." He meant, of course, that he and the founders of the new order he was planning would be great bene-factors to farmers, and that the country would look to them for leadership.[2]

There were ten charter members of the organization including Gre-sham. Divided by occupation, they consisted of one newspaperman, one county clerk, one physician, one country schoolteacher, and six farm-ers; by political party, they numbered three Populists, one Socialist, one Independent, and five Democrats. Hunt tells of interviews with four of these men, and gives their somewhat contradictory versions on the found-ing of the Union. The author interviewed James S. Turner, one of the three appearing before the notary public for the charter, who was living on a farm about fifteen miles from Atoka, Oklahoma, in 1926, and got a slightly different picture from that which Hunt's interviews yielded. Barrett, writing much earlier and from personal acquaintance, but prob-ably imbued with some organizational pride, gives a brief history and description of all early Union leaders.[3] Probably the most important fact about these leaders was that some of them, including Gresham, had been active in the Farmers' Alliance, and probably the most important eco-nomic fact of that time is that the price of cotton fluctuated between 7 cents and 11 cents a pound between 1900 and 1909.[4]

Gresham and his friends received a state charter on August 28, 1902. Officers and directors (the ten charter members) were named in the charter, which was to run for fifty years. It was considered to be a private charter with altruistic purposes, and read as follows:

CHARTER

The State of Texas
County of Rains

Be it known that we, the undersigned citizens of Rains County, Texas hereby make application for a charter for the following pur-poses, to wit:

———

[2] Hunt, p. 46. Reprinted by permission of the author, Robert Lee Hunt, Texas Agri-cultural and Mechanical College.

[3] Barrett, pp. 103, 259-414. Hunt, pp. 45-52.

[4] Jenson, p. 6.

1. The name of the Corporation shall be "The Farmers' Educational and Cooperative Union of America."

2. The purpose for which it is formed is to organize and charter subordinate Unions at various places in Texas and the United States, to assist them in marketing and obtaining better prices for their products, for fraternal purposes, and to cooperate with them in the protection of their interest; to initiate members, and collect a fee therefor.

3. Its place of business is to be the State of Texas, and its business is to be transacted in Texas.

4. It shall exist for a term of fifty years.

The number of its officers and directors shall be ten, as follows: Dr. Lee Seamster, Emory, Texas, President; J. B. Morris, Emory, Texas, vice-President; O. H. Rhodes, Emory, Texas, Secretary; W. T. Cochran, Emory, Texas, Treasurer; Newt Gresham, Point, Texas, General Organizer; T. J. Pound, J. S. Turner, T. W. Donaldson, Jessie Adams, W. S. Sisk, all of Emory, Texas, Directors.

It shall have no capital stock paid in, and shall not be divided into shares.

Witness our hands this 28th day of August, A.D. 1902.

DR. LEE SEAMSTER,
O. H. RHODES,
J. S. TURNER

The State of Texas
County of Rains

... before, me, the undersigned authority, on this day personally appeared before me Dr. Lee Seamster, O. H. Rhodes, and J. S. Turner, known to me to be the persons whose names are subscribed to the foregoing instrument and acknowledged to me that they executed the same for the purpose and consideration therein expressed.

Given under my hand and seal of this office, the 28th day of August, A.D. 1902.

(Seal)   T. S. MAGEE
J. P. and Ex-Officio Notary Public, Rains County, Texas

Filed in the office of the Secretary of State this 17th day of September, 1902.

JOHN G. TODD
Secretary of State[5]

---

[5] Hunt, pp. 49-50. Reprinted by permission of the author.

The ten charter members decided that the first attempt at organization should be made at Smyrna community, a few miles west of Emory. To W. S. Sisk, W. T. Cochran, and James S. Turner, residents of the community and officers in the corporation, goes the credit for the organization of the first local Union. Almost immediately, the next local was organized at Emory.[6]

Farmers joined readily for a fee of $1.00 and monthly dues of 5 cents. Old Alliancemen and Populists offered their services in great numbers as organizers and things moved so fast and loosely that they were soon out of hand. Twelve and a half dollars of the first $15.00 collected by a local Union for initiation fees went to the organizer, the remaining $2.50 to the home office for the charter and traveling expenses. An organizer could sublet his rights to other individuals for a commission of $2.50 for each local organized, and some organizers thereby found their jobs quite profitable.

Gresham, named as organizer in the charter, was more interested in promotion than he was adept at keeping accounts, with the result that by the time the membership of the organization had grown to notable size, no one knew how much money had been collected or where it had gone. This resulted in accusations of various kinds and sooner or later the elimination from leadership in the Texas State Union of practically all the charter members.[7]

The incorporators of the organization, either because they were so busy with booming affairs that they did not think of a systematic scheme of organization or because they did not desire to share their responsibilities, failed to promote an operative state Union. The first state meeting was called for February, 1904, eighteen months after the charter was granted. The following is an excerpt from Hunt's account of this meeting:

> The first call for a state meeting came in February 1904. It should be kept in mind that the Union at this time was legally a private corporation. The promoters charged an initiation fee of $1.00 for

[6] *Ibid.*, p. 52.

[7] The authorities for all the information in the following pages are: Barrett, Hunt, and C. B. Fisher, *The Farmers' Union*. Studies in Economics and Sociology, No. 2. Publications of the University of Kentucky, Vol. I, No. 2. Lexington, Kentucky: 1920. Practically all of the detailed information on actions of conventions is from Hunt.

each member of the newly organized Unions and annual dues of
60¢ each; all of which went into the pockets of the promoters, and
out of which expenses were paid. It was thought by the outsiders
that it was a good paying venture. The farmers made no serious
complaint about it being a private affair until rumors began circulating freely. So firm was the belief that the charter members were
making good profits out of it, that a local physician in Emory got
together a group of farmers and tried to imitate the Union, but with
no success. At all events, after eighteen months of operating the
Union as a private business, the owners called, in response to growing demands, a meeting for February 16 to 19, 1904.

A newspaper reporter in Mineola reporting the meeting says men
began to arrive on the 14th. "They are from pretty much every
part of Texas, and one or two from Arkansas. The total number of
delegates and visitors now here considerably exceed 100.

"The preliminary business of the meeting began yesterday with
a session of Farmers' Union organizers. About 40 organizers were
present, and had a kind of experience meeting, comparing notes and
reviewing the work they had done."

This was the first time the organizers had had an opportunity
to check with one another to see what each was doing.

President J. B. Morris of Rains county called the meeting to order, and after the usual welcome address and response, a temporary organization was effected, with the election of O. P. Pyle, editor
of the Mineola *Courier,* as chairman, and A. M. Colwick, another
newspaperman, as secretary. The meetings were all secret, and
none but members was permitted to enter. A committee on credentials was appointed . . . One hundred and five delegates were
duly seated.

The object of this meeting was to organize a Texas State Union,
but it should be kept in mind that the officers here elected later
became officers of both state and national unions. This should be
kept in mind because this peculiar arrangement later caused a good
deal of confusion and bickering among the leaders.

The Mineola *Courier* claimed at this time the membership had
reached 50,000. Pyle was the editor of this paper, and knew equally
as much as anyone as to the probable membership, but it is doubtful if anyone actually knew how many members there were. A fire
had recently destroyed all books and papers, and all figures were
a guess.

On February 9, 1904, the *Password*, official mouth organ for the Union, edited by Gresham, stated:

"The ten Rains County men who started the Farmers' Union do not claim perfection. They have made mistakes, but said mistakes were not fatal. They have been cursed from within and without. They have been charged with everything but a pure motive. They have pursued the even tenor of their way, and have today an organization the like of which has never before been seen for strength and beauty—age considered. Curse us if you will, but we are with you on February 16 to bid you good morning, and to turn over to you the truth which was never given us, but which we assumed at the beginning."

The original charter was left in the hands of the ten charter members, and was not acquired by the Texas State Union until some time later.

Some other states were represented at the Mineola meeting, but they had no voice in the deliberations. It was strictly a Texas affair.[8]

The second state convention was held at Fort Worth, on August 9 of the same year, and was attended by delegates from seventy-nine Texas counties. The secretary reported: "Work is in progress in the following states: Alabama, Georgia, Tennessee, Arkansas, Texas and two territories." He claimed 700 locals had been formed in Texas, and the president claimed that the Texas membership had reached 100,000.

The third state convention, held in Fort Worth, in February, 1905, was a landmark in Farmers' Union history. It was attended by about 300 delegates, representing ninety Texas counties, and fraternal delegates from the states of Arkansas, Alabama, Oklahoma, Indian Territory, Louisiana, and South Carolina. The original charterholders sold their rights to the state and national organization, which up to this time were identical, and states other than Texas were granted the right to organize state Unions when they had as many as 5,000 members. It was claimed that the national membership at the time was 200,000, with 4,264 locals distributed among the states as follows: Texas, 2,926; Indian Territory, 524; Oklahoma Territory, 315; Louisiana, 238; Georgia, 114; Alabama, 58; Mississippi, 24; Missouri, 23; Tennessee, 23; South Caro-

---

[8] Hunt, pp. 64-66. Reprinted by permission of the author.

lina, 16; North Carolina, 2; Kentucky, 1. All officers elected at the convention were Texans.

During and after this meeting, a lot of strife developed between the dirt farmers and some of the officers who were newspapermen or other nonfarmers. Texas organizers had gone into other states and collected charter fees and dues with the result that the money went back to Texas, a situation highly objectionable to the other states. Hunt, however, quotes Calvin, vice-president of the Texas Union, as saying that "the row at Ft. Worth was a baby in comparison to the one in Waco," when the fourth convention was held in that city in August, 1905. The determination of the bona fide farmers to eliminate all others from leadership, and even membership, was so pronounced and vocal that someone with a sense of humor introduced the following resolution:

> Resolved, that the portion of the constitution that refers to actual farmers be amended so as to read as follows:
> "He is a man who holds the plow handles from early morning till dewy eve; he must make his living only by the sweat of his brow, while he holds the plow. If he sharpens his plow himself, then he is a blacksmith; if he builds a corn-crib, he is a carpenter; and in either case he is not eligible to membership in the Union. He must swear he has no ambition to ever get able to quit plowing; and he must teach his children to follow in his footsteps, and have no greater ambition than his own, provided he always shall be allowed to attend the various organizations to which he belongs, discuss politics, and perform other like services, while his wife and children represent him at the plow handles." [9]

The Union in Texas lost membership because of the strife which had developed. Furthermore, it was not yet a real national organization. Once again all the officers elected at Waco were Texans, but they considered themselves the authorized officers of both the Texas and national Unions. This state of affairs could not possibly continue with other states now

---

[9] Hunt, pp. 72-73. Quoted by Hunt from Waco *Daily Times Herald*, August 11, 1905, p. 6. Reprinted by permission of Waco *News-Tribune*. Hunt quotes accounts of this convention from Texas newspapers in detail and thereby gives a vivid picture of the fight which eliminated Gresham and other old leaders from control of the organization.

forming their own state Unions. The old deposed Texas leaders aided and abetted the leaders in other states in their fight against their subservient status.

The first necessary step in accomplishing change was a real national convention with voting delegates from all organized states. Such a meeting was called for Texarkana, Texas, for early in December, 1905. The committee on credentials, composed of one member from each state present, recommended the seating of the following number of delegates: Texas, 61; Arkansas, 33; "Indiahoma," 31; Georgia, 17; Louisiana, 8; Tennessee, 3; Kansas, 1; Alabama, 1. The Texas delegation thus had slightly less than two-fifths of the voting strength of the convention, not quite as many as the next two strongest delegations combined.

Texas local Unions had instructed their delegates to vote for no man for office unless he was an actual farmer, but this was to no avail. Other states, and probably some Texas friends of the original leaders, combined against them and elected O. P. Pyle, a newspaper editor of Mineola, Texas, as president, and Newt Gresham, another newspaperman, as national organizer. The newly elected vice-president was from Alabama, the secretary-treasurer from Arkansas, the doorkeeper from Missouri, the sergeant-at-arms from Georgia, and the six members of the executive committee from Alabama, Arkansas, Louisiana, Georgia, Indian Territory, and Texas. One member of the executive committee was C. S. Barrett of Georgia, soon to become president and the guiding light of the organization for the next twenty-odd years.

The old Texas constitution was adopted with only minor changes; and soon after the Texarkana meeting, a national charter was obtained from the Texas secretary of state, using the original name of the organization, the National Farmers' Educational and Cooperative Union of America. But the life of the new organization was short-lived. The Texas State Union, which had quite summarily shunted aside the local men who had founded the order, refused to be equally easily shunted aside by members from other states. Calvin, president of the Texas Union, called a meeting in March, 1906, after securing an injunction preventing the officers of the national Union from using the official and legal name of the original organization and from taking any action thereunder. He and his faction so completely dominated the convention that they had no difficulty in having the officers of the Texas Union declared the officers of the national Union. Some of the officers elected at the Texarkana meeting were present and were allowed to speak but not to vote.

After the action of the Texarkana convention was officially repudiated, a resolution was adopted which provided that Calvin and his staff resign as national officers, that the officials elected at Texarkana agree to abandon the charter which they had secured, and that an entirely new set of officers be elected to serve until the next annual national convention was held.

The next national convention was held in Texarkana in September, 1906, and a full quota of officers elected in regular order. C. S. Barrett of Georgia was elected president and served continuously in that capacity until 1928. What else, if anything, was done except to "fix the price of cotton" is not clear. In his book Barrett gives one paragraph to this meeting, and regular publication of the annual proceedings are not available until a year later. The published proceedings of the Texas annual state meeting, held in August preceding the national meeting, refers only four times to the national: one reference stated that the article "relating to the unorganized States, should be entirely eliminated from the Constitution, for the reason that Texas has no control over unorganized States"; another mentioned a conflict with the Indiahoma Union over national dues; the third recorded the election and instructions of the Texas delegates to the "National Convention, to be held at Texarkana, September 5"; and the fourth was a resolution which read, "That we favor the perfection of the Farmers' Educational and Co-operative Union of America as now organized, on as inexpensive a plan as possible, commensurate with the magnitude of the organization." The board of directors of the national Union at the next annual convention (Little Rock, September, 1907) said in the last paragraph of its report:

We meet you at the close of our term of office with clean hands and clear consciences. We feel justified in saying to you that the Farmers' Union is in better condition today than at any time since its organization. Its membership is stronger and better educated. They understand each other better, are more determined and more loyal, and ready if need be to make greater sacrifices than ever before. To be able to truthfully make this statement is reward enough for us for the part we have been permitted to take in bringing about such a condition.[10]

The breach was apparently healed and the Farmers' Union was on its way as a thriving national farmers' organization five years after Newt Gresham conceived and founded it.

Gresham died in April, 1906, a poor man, thus proving to his friends and thousands of followers that he had never profited financially from all he had done in behalf of the organization. The Texas convention passed a resolution of sympathy to the family and referred to him as "our beloved brother and founder." The national convention, a year later, adopted his daughter, Miss Lutie, "as the daughter of the National Union"; and voted to copyright an official button with Newt Gresham's picture on it and turn the copyright over to Mrs. Newt Gresham. Gresham's daughter was also placed on the payroll of the national organization.[11]

The growth of the Farmers' Union between September, 1906, and September, 1907, was as phenomenal as that of the Grange and the Alliance in the days of their ascendancies. President Barrett, in his annual address, said, "There is not today in the republic in which we live any one body of men engaged in a single profession whose motives are so clear, whose plans are so coherent, whose unity is so perfect and inspiring, and whose members are so magnificent as the Farmers' Union of America."[12] Seventy-two delegates, representing twenty states, were officially seated in this convention. The financial statement showed $15,-779.23 collected in dues and $2,245.47 "received from charters issued" during the year. The secretary said in his report, "We now have thirteen chartered State Unions, with 17,938 chartered locals and ten other States with 736 chartered locals, a total membership of 935,837 active Union workers, an increase during the year of four State Unions, 673 local Unions and 339,250 members."

The organization had been in debt $3,000 at the beginning of that

---

[10] Barrett, p. 158. Reprinted by permission of the National Farmers' Union.

[11] *Minutes of the National Farmers' Educational and Co-operative Union of America, held in Little Rock, Arkansas, September 3-5, 1907*, p. 10, Conway, Arkansas: Arkansas *Union Tribune*, 1908.

[12] *Ibid.*, p. 5. Reprinted by permission of the National Farmers' Union.

fiscal year, but with an assessment which netted more than $9,000, plus regular dues and charter fees, the Union had collected $27,340.08 and showed "cash in bank to balance," $10,490.55. President Barrett claimed that more than 2,000 warehouses had been built, but did not say that they had all been built during the current year.

GROWTH AND EXPANSION [13]

Like the Farmers' Alliance, the Farmers' Union was prone in its heyday to exaggerate its estimates of membership, but it would be difficult to overestimate its influence in the South during the first decade of its existence. The Arkansas Union surged to the front during the first year of its national life, followed closely by the Mississippi and Alabama Unions. Oklahoma came up quickly in 1908, California in 1909, after which North Carolina led all other states for five years. This was followed by a rapid development in Kansas and Nebraska, one or the other holding first place after 1915. From 1910 to 1918 North Carolina contributed 19 per cent of all national receipts. For the fiscal year 1913, it contributed more than 30 per cent. Kansas contributed almost 19 per cent of all national receipts from 1913 to 1919, and Nebraska's share was nearly 20 per cent from 1914 to 1919. These three states paid 52 per cent of all national Union income for the six years, 1914-1919.[14]

It is fairly easy to visualize the stir that the organization of from 200 to 300 locals in one state in a single year created, and that sort of thing happened again and again over a period of fifteen years. Florida organized 203 in 1907; Kentucky, 226 in 1908; California, 114 in 1909; Nebraska, 70 in 1912 and 119 in 1913.[15] While this was going on, business agents were being appointed, warehouses built, cooperative stores established, and even various types of manufacturing plants set up and operated. One need not use his imagination to know that politicians were

---

[13] The data that follow for the next few pages are primarily from Barrett.

[14] *Published minutes, 1907.* Conway, Arkansas: Arkansas *Union Tribune*, 1908. Little Rock, Arkansas: Central Printing Co., 1908. Texarkana: Arkansas-Texas, 1912. Texarkana: Four States Press, 1913.

[15] *Minutes of the National Farmers Educational and Co-operative Union of America, ninth annual session, held in Salina, Kansas, September 2, 3, 4, 1913,* p. 17. Texarkana: Four States Press, 1913.

interested in activities of the Union and Union men interested in the activities of their legislators and Congressmen. The Alliance was never as consistently influential as the Farmers' Union in Texas, Arkansas, and North Carolina in the South, or in Kansas and Nebraska in the North, notwithstanding the fact these were all strong Farmers' Alliance states in the eighties and nineties.

The Union had penetrated all of the cotton states by 1908 and had state organizations in each of them except Virginia at that time. It had also made progress in other states, entering Kentucky, Kansas, and California in 1906; Colorado, Indiana, Iowa, New Mexico, Illinois, and Washington in 1907; Idaho, Oregon, and Arizona in 1908. By 1912, when it came to its maximum strength in the cotton belt, it had locals in twenty-nine states, but the twelve cotton states were contributing 77 per cent of the national Union's receipts. The ranks of states in these contributions were as follows: North Carolina, Texas, Arkansas, Alabama, Tennessee, Mississippi, Georgia, Virginia, South Carolina, Oklahoma, Louisiana, and Florida. All of them except North Carolina had some years before been stronger than they were at this time.

After 1912, the Union's center of strength and influence began moving into the wheat states. North Carolina continued as the leading Union state through 1914 and did not drop below second place among the states until 1916. Kansas was first in 1915 and Nebraska in 1916. By 1920 the twelve cotton states listed above were contributing only 20 per cent of the national Union's receipts; and seven wheat states—Minnesota, South Dakota, Nebraska, Kansas, Colorado, Washington, and Oregon—which in 1912 were contributing 12 per cent of the nation's Union receipts were in 1920 contributing 55 per cent. These wheat states for the following five years, 1921-1925, contributed 58 per cent and the cotton states only 27 per cent.

If looked at from the view of cash or commercial crop-producing states, it will be seen that the cotton, wheat, and tobacco-producing states have always been the strongest Farmers' Union states. With the exception of 1909, when California flared up for a single year, some cotton or wheat states have always led in Union membership. As a matter of fact, the ten leading Union states, listed year by year during the whole history of the organization, find few exceptions to this generalization. Illinois appears in the list three times, but always as the ninth or tenth in strength. Indiana appeared once in seventh place, and Ohio appeared once in seventh place. The chief exception is Iowa, where the militant leadership of Milo Reno brought that state into high rank and held it there from 1920 to 1936. Virginia and Kentucky, both of which were strong Union states for a number of years, mobilized their strength from tobacco-producing areas where another farmers' organization, the Equity, was also strong.

The growth of the Union on a national scale took place quickly. The amount of dues received from state Unions by the national Union was greater in 1908 than any year thereafter until 1917. The amount has remained remarkably constant throughout the whole life of the organization. The lowest point during the first twenty-year period was $15,503.39 in 1913, and the highest was $35,051.65 in 1921.

Membership in the Farmers' Union, however, is difficult to estimate. Until recently, the constitution provided that each state Union should transmit to the national Union 16 cents per member per year. Two practices, however, have tended to vitiate an analysis made by dividing the total dues paid to the national Union by 16 cents. One is the practice of state Unions to pay more than 16 cents per dues-paying member in order to collect mileage and per diem of delegates to the national convention.[16] The other is the well-known, and almost universal, practice of locals and even state Unions to be actually representative of many more persons than the number that pay their dues consistently. Furthermore, women, although loyal Union members, pay no dues as they do in the Grange, and the same is true of children. There can be no question that the second of these two practices is far more prevalent than the first and that the national membership has therefore always been considerably larger than state payments to the national Union would indicate.

The membership in 1907, the first year of a real national Union, calculated at 16 cents per member paid into the national treasury, was 98,620. The next year it was 130,282. Then followed four years with an average of about 118,500; two years with an average of only 110,059;

---

[16] Information from prominent officials of the national Union. A few dollars in addition to the 16 cents per member, paid by delegates, when added to the legitimate dues, guarantee payment of all expenses in attendance at the national convention. The cost to delegates paying this difference was often far less than it would be if he had to pay his own expenses. Furthermore, unless the money was remitted by the state Union, the credentials of the delegate were not valid.

then back to an average of about 136,000 from 1915 to 1919.[17] The actual adherents of the Farmers' Union were probably four times as many as these figures indicate for any one or all of these periods of growth. Whatever the facts about the actual number of farmers who claimed membership in the Union at different stages of its growth, it is known that when it was started, in 1902, at a crossroads town in Texas, it had only ten members and in 1920 it had locals in thirty-three states and organized state Unions in twenty-six of them.[18]

While the Farmers' Union did not grow into national proportions by means of any such outstanding amalgamation as helped to build the Southern Alliance, it did accomplish one consolidation of significance at the time the action was taken. An organization known as the Farmers' Social and Economic Union had been organized in Illinois in April, 1900. The Farmers' Relief Association had sprung up in this same state, and these two organizations joined with the remnants of the old Farmers' Mutual Benefit Association in 1906 to form a Farmers' Union which, with considerable membership in Illinois and some strength in adjacent states, came into the Farmers' Educational and Cooperative Union of America a year later. This merger did two things: it gave the southern organization entrance into a midwestern state, and tied in the remnants of one of the lesser farm organizations of the eighties with an organization which is still in existence.

ECONOMIC ACTIVITIES OF THE FARMERS' UNION, 1902 TO 1920

The Texas charter obtained by Newt Gresham and his colleagues stated that it was the purpose of the Farmers' Union "to assist them [subordinate Unions] in marketing and obtaining better prices for their products . . . and to co-operate with them in the protection of their interests . . ." The first local at Smyrna, together with other locals in Rains

---

[17] Calculations based upon dues paid any one year are less trustworthy than an average for a number of years because it is the habit of members in all national farm organizations to pay past dues in following years. These calculations are made from figures given in national proceedings. Fisher, by using three-year averages, estimates average membership from 1908-1910 as 121,826 and from 1917-1919 as 140,066. See Fisher, p. 15.

[18] Fisher, Table I following p. 12.

County, Texas, made a contract with cotton ginners of the county in 1903 as their first step in carrying out this purpose. They claimed to have saved the farmers of the county $6,000 by this contract and nearly $500 by shipping their own cottonseed. In 1904, the Texas State Union (at that time also called the National Union) decided to sponsor a movement to withhold cotton from the market. The plan was to hold one bale out of every five off the market altogether and market the other four bales slowly. A special meeting of the executive committee was called and $50 was spent on night telegrams "to prominent farmers, to governors, to senators and others in the cotton States, asking that a meeting be held on November 17th, in all the counties of the South for the purpose of asking the farmers to withhold their cotton from the market." A price of 10 cents per pound was demanded. Cotton went above 10 cents by July, 1905, and the Union officials claimed credit for having saved or made the farmers of the South $160,000,000 by their holding campaign. Hunt quotes a statement of a Union man published in the Fort Worth *Record* of August, 1907, as follows:

PERCENTAGE OF THE COTTON CROP MARKETED FROM
SEPTEMBER TO NOVEMBER, 1901-1908 °

Year	Per Cent Marketed
1901-1902	45.34
1902-1903	47.17
1903-1904	50.19
1904-1905	45.20
1905-1906	48.49
1906-1907	42.32
1907-1908	39.92
1908-1909	45.91

° Reprinted by permission of Fort Worth *Star-Telegram*.

The national Union consistently followed the plan of attempting to fix the price for cotton, conducted reduction in acreage campaigns, and one year (1908) claimed to have induced a good many farmers to plow up a large amount of cotton after it was planted and growing.

It did not take the Union long, however, to recognize that something more than pronouncements by officials, resolutions by conventions, and expected individual action on the part of hundreds of thousands of farmers was necessary for the effective holding and marketing of cotton. A plan for cotton warehouses was presented to the 1904 convention and a committee appointed to give consideration to such a plan. The committee, reporting in August, 1905, recommended "that the Farmers' Union of each county do build standard warehouses and that each state president and executive committee be empowered to formulate such plans and send copies to the various local unions in the state." The Texas Union followed these suggestions with the result that 323 warehouses were built in a little over two years. Other states followed suit; and buying or building cotton warehouses became, at least in the early years, the greatest business enterprise of Union members. The president of the Oklahoma Union in 1907 said:

We have adopted definite plans in the hope of destroying the mighty and tyrannical power of the Cotton Exchange. Beginning with the plan of locally bulking, which was soon followed by holding one-fourth or one-fifth of the cotton crop, and the establishment of a minimum price; but by this means you remember we succeeded in securing only partial cooperation. But through the warehouse system we can revolutionize the present system and enthrone the farmer as absolute master in fixing the price upon his own products. The warehouse is now recognized as an indispensable addenda in stable and profitable marketing. We have already in cooperation in the two territories quite a number, and reports from all over the State indicate that the first season's operation has been quite a success. I do not know how many have been built, or how many are now under construction, but the Farmers' Union in greater Oklahoma should have warehouse storage for at least one-fourth of her cotton production. I want to impress upon this convention the great, and, as I see it, paramount, importance of constructing warehouses, at least in every central cotton market in every county in the State. Do not let us falter, but let us push the work until we have accomplished all we started out to do.[19]

The national Union had a standing "committee on warehouses"; and at its regular meeting in 1908, this committee recommended "the continua-

---

[19] Barrett, p. 205.

tion of the building of warehouses throughout the entire South." It said, "We believe that every town that markets as much as 500 bales of cotton should have a warehouse of sufficient capacity to accommodate the people." In 1909 it said, ". . . we find that the building of Warehouses has been carried to almost every nook and corner of the country. . . ." The reports of 1908 recommended the building of grain elevators, and those of 1909 and 1910 indicated that this program had been put into effect. The report for 1911 listed thirty-six warehouses built during the year, the known costs of twenty-eight of them being $60,166.50. The 1912 proceedings showed nine built in Oregon, at the cost of $30,500, and eight in Washington, at the cost of $19,165. The next year's proceedings show Oregon, Washington, and Idaho to have built an additional eighteen warehouses at the cost of $83,069 and a flouring mill at the cost of $17,981.[20] Powell, writing in 1913, says, "The Farmers' Union has 1,600 warehouses in the cotton states," and quotes the Commissioner of Corporations as reporting 1,500 in 1909.[21]

In addition to the warehouse system as a means of controlling the supply of cotton delivered to the market were the activities of different state Unions in selling cotton directly to American and foreign factories. The Farmers' Union Cotton Company of Memphis maintained offices in both Liverpool and Manchester, England, and sold cotton directly from county warehouses to mills. The South Carolina Union made some attempts at foreign selling, and the Texas Union negotiated with New England mills. Barrett claims that the cotton activities of the Union saved the farmers of the South millions of dollars by consistent propaganda for acreage controls, warehousing, grading, selling, holding, reducing freight rates, and contract giving.[22]

Like the Alliance and the Grange, the state Unions early attempted to operate local and state business agencies. Hunt says that members of the first locals "followed the example of the Alliance and made arrangements with certain merchants to sell to members at a 10 per cent discount under

[20] *Minutes* of various years.
[21] Harold G. Powell, *Cooperation in agriculture,* pp. 191, 193. New York: The Macmillan Co., 1913.
[22] Barrett, pp. 134-136, 199, 226, 233-234. See also T. J. Brooks, *Origin, history and principles of the Farmers' Educational and Co-operative Union of America,* p. 10. National Union Farmers Print, n. d.

regular retail price. Members had to show their membership cards in order to get the discount. . . ." [23]

A business department of the state Union was established in Texas in 1904, in Alabama in 1905, in Georgia in 1906, and in North Carolina in 1909. The Georgia project was probably the only outstanding one. It organized a $50,000 capital stock implement company and built a fertilizer plant. Its manager, J. G. Eubanks, speaking before the Missouri State Union in 1908, said that he estimated a savings for Georgia farmers of $1,008,000 during the previous year. The Alabama department was successful for a few years. During the year preceding the 1907 annual convention, it did a business of $350,257.16, dealing mostly in flour and fertilizers. And the North Carolina Business Agency handled $231,626.18 worth of business in 1910. Other states had similar but less outstanding enterprises. In April, 1914, *The National Field,* official organ of the national Union, published a "Partial List of Farmers' Union Enterprises" which included 323 different business firms. More than one hundred of them were in Washington and Idaho, forty-four in North Carolina, and thirty-nine in Alabama.[24] There could very well have been twice that number in existence, for many were not reported and others started by Union members were not designated as Union enterprises.

In addition to the chief projects of selling cotton, building warehouses, and operating business agencies, the state Unions, almost as soon as they were organized, took up a number of other economic enterprises. In Colorado, a coal mine was purchased and operated; in Mississippi, the first steps were taken toward the establishing of a Farmers' Union Bank and Trust Company in 1908; and Florida attempted to organize a Union stock company during this same year.[25] Hundreds of business ventures were attempted by county and local Unions in the way of purchasing clubs, and buying fertilizers and other supplies in carload lots. For the most part, however, these projects were sporadic and ephemeral, creating about the same disturbance as the projects of the Alliance but not developing into permanent organizations. They met with consistent resistance from middlemen and wholesalers and were not organized or operated on

---

[23] Hunt, p. 61.

[24] *The National Field* (Atlanta, Georgia), Vol. I, No. 25 (1914), pp. 7, 12.

[25] Barrett, chap. xiii.

stable business principles or with enough volume to guarantee their success. This same thing cannot be said of many Farmers' Union economic enterprises since 1910, for, as will be recounted later, this organization has probably contributed more by way of successful enterprises than any other farmers' organization, unless it be the Farmers' Equity Union.

If the early business ventures of the Union in the South were not as permanent as the organization might have wished, that did not discourage its leaders. The board of directors, in the fifteenth annual national convention in 1919, asserted that the future success of the Farmers' Union depended very largely upon the development of business institutions.[26] This idea became even more prevalent after the strength of the organization shifted to the West than it was while it was predominantly a cotton states' organization. State and regional exchanges or wholesale business houses were established in California, Colorado, Iowa, Kansas, Kentucky, Nebraska, Oklahoma, South Dakota, and Washington, the one in Washington serving the three states of Washington, Oregon, and Idaho. The one in Kansas was a jobbing enterprise. Many of these exchanges or business houses are still in existence and doing a large volume of business. The Nebraska State Exchange, for instance, for a number of years quite consistently handled more than a million dollars of business annually. It at times served more than one hundred local cooperatives throughout the state of Nebraska, and in addition operated a retail store at its home plant in Omaha.[27] The Farmers' Union Jobbing Association, located at Kansas City, Kansas, was described by the *Literary Digest* in 1920 as "the largest cooperative institution in the world, doing a business of more than $150,000,000 in 1919."[28] It served 435 cooperative enterprises, 100 of which were stores, operated a livestock exchange, made contracts with farm machinery manufacturers, operated an insurance company, and all told did probably a larger business than all other Union enterprises combined, with the exception of the Live Stock Commission.[29]

Gradually the Union came to sponsor the Rochdale system of local stores, although many of the Farmers' Union stores have not been

---

[26] *Minutes, 1919.*

[27] Data from personal examination of the Nebraska Exchange books.

[28] "Kansas Has World's Greatest Cooperative Enterprise," *Literary Digest,* May 8, 1920, p. 136.

[29] Fisher, p. 45. *Minutes, 1920,* p. 8.

operated on Rochdale principles. Mr. W. C. Lansdon, national lecturer, attempted to carry on a systematic education in these principles of cooperation in 1915, and published a pamphlet in which he told the story not only of the Rochdale weavers, but also the story of other outstanding European cooperatives.[30] Members of local and county Farmers' Unions probably organized more local farmers' stores than all other agencies combined in the period between 1900 and 1920; and while many of them failed, there were still many of them in existence in 1920.

Probably the most outstanding, and in many ways most successful, types of business ventures started by the Union in the period under discussion were its livestock and grain commission enterprises. The Farmers' Union Live Stock Commission was set up in Omaha in 1917, and claimed to have made savings for its patrons of almost $12,000 during the first year of operation. By 1920, it had increased these savings to more than $62,000, and since that time has more than doubled them. Operation was started on the Omaha market on April 1, 1917, and on the St. Joseph market in August of that year. The next year, the Sioux City market was entered, and since that time agencies have been set up in Kansas City, Denver, Wichita, Chicago, St. Paul, and St. Louis. These enterprises were organized as joint-stock companies, and because they handled a great volume of business for non-Union members, but rebate only to Union patrons, it was possible to declare a dividend of 38 per cent the first year and a 60 per cent dividend in 1920. Since that time dividends have a number of times been as high as 70 per cent.[31] The National Commission Company was organized in 1919 and was planned to be a federation of cooperative elevators. This plan had to be altered because the organization was denied a seat upon the Omaha Grain Exchange, and did not therefore start functioning within the period under consideration. The Nebraska Farmers' Union later organized the federation as a stock company; it obtained a seat upon the Grain Exchange, and moved steadily forward after 1923.

It is not necessary to go further with proof that the Farmers' Union was aggressive, and to a great extent successful, in carrying on the Farm-

_____

[30] W. C. Lansdon, *Cooperation—history, necessity, methods.* Salina, Kansas: 1915.

[31] *Farmers' Union Live Stock Commission.* Pontiac, Illinois: Bulletin published by Farmers' Union of Illinois, n. d.

ers' Movement which the Alliance had so tragically dropped almost a decade before this new organization came on the scene. As brief a summary as possible of the economic undertakings must include mention of the following, not already given space in this chapter: cooperative gins in Arkansas, Georgia, Louisiana, North Carolina, Oklahoma, and Tennessee; cooperative stores in Arkansas, California, Colorado, Georgia, Kansas, Kentucky, Indiana, Iowa, Missouri, Nebraska, North Carolina, South Dakota, Tennessee, Virginia, Washington, Oregon, and Idaho; mutual insurance in Colorado, Indiana, Kansas, Montana, and Nebraska; grain elevators in Colorado, Kansas, Montana, Nebraska, Oklahoma, South Dakota, Washington, Oregon, and Idaho; livestock and poultry shipping associations, local creameries, and purchasing clubs in a number of states; and in addition to all these, the big enterprises of state exchanges, livestock and grain commissions.

Reporting in 1921, Secretary Davis listed Farmers' Union enterprises in nine states, with combined capital assets of $14,610,000, which had done a business of $286,300,000 in the preceding twelve months. He stated that the report was fragmentary and that a conservative estimate for the Union enterprise in the nation as a whole would be $30,000,000 capital invested and an annual turnover of $605,000,000.[32] Indeed, the Farmers' Union by the latter part of this period had become so thoroughly engrossed in economic cooperation that the fraternal feature, except as represented in annual picnics, had been literally dropped from the order.[33]

THE FARMERS' UNION AND POLITICS

The Farmers' Union, knowing what had happened to the Grange and Alliance when they entered the political field, started, and for a number of years operated, with a dogmatic determination to avoid the political mistakes of their forerunners. Newt Gresham, who had been an Alliance-

---

[32] *Proceedings of the mass meeting of the Farmers' Union, held in Washington, D. C., April 20, 21, 22, 1921*, p. 11. Texarkana: Four States Press, 1921.

[33] So much of the information included in this section has been obtained by personal visits by the writer to the headquarters of these various enterprises, by correspondence with various Farmers' Union papers, that specific citations have often been impossible. Much information, some of it duplicated by personal investigations, has been obtained from Fisher, chap. ii, especially pp. 44-47. A. G. Davis, *Supplement A to the Farmers' Union, what it is and what it is doing*, pp. 5-19, 21-28. Texarkana: Four States Press, n. d.

man and a Populist, wrote into the introduction of the first Farmers' Union constitution, "This is in no degree a political party, and shall forever abstain from even so much as a discussion of partyism." In the 1905 convention, the constitution was amended so as to absolutely forbid any member of the Union from even discussing politics at a Union meeting.[34] The Texas state charter was later revoked for a time by the national Union because of its political activities; and Barrett says, "A local union in Mississippi endorsed a candidate and the charter was immediately revoked" by the state president.[35] Nevertheless, the Union did to some extent follow the path of its predecessors. It never created or endorsed a given political party, but almost from the beginning passed resolutions concerning legislation, endorsed and promoted legislative measures, appointed legislative committees, and maintained legislative representatives at state capitals and in Washington.

In his first presidential address, in 1907, Barrett said:

I trust in the Almighty God that we shall never see a time when the Farmers' Union shall be fretted by political demagogues within its ranks . . . I plead with you never to suffer the Union to be contaminated by an affiliation with any political party. But while we hold fast to the splendid neutrality of our position, we must never hesitate in political life to defend and to advance the original purposes of this organization. To this end as individuals and as an organized body without party names, we must not hesitate *to ballot as a unit* against those things which would seek to oppress or degrade us, and we must give the world to understand that by joining this non-political union, we have not surrendered a single political right that belongs to each and every citizen in the American republic.[36]

This was a pretty broad charter for political action. It literally said that the Union as an organized pressure group expected to wield political influence. This it began at once to do.

At a Texas Union convention two years before Barrett became president, "A resolution was adopted making it a fixed policy of the Union to keep a man at Austin during the sessions of the legislature to look after

---

[34] Hunt, pp. 69, 132.
[35] Barrett, pp. 103, 119.
[36] *Minutes, 1907*, pp. 6-7. Reprinted by permission of the National Farmers' Union.

the farmers' interests and cooperate with the railroad brotherhoods and the Texas State Federation of Labor in matters affecting the interest of labor in any form within the state." [37] State Unions early began appointing committees on legislation, and the national Union from the beginning had such a committee. State conventions, county Unions, and sometimes local Unions formulated legislative programs and demands, and Union officials had no hesitancy in claiming credit for the enactment of much legislation. Legislators, other state officials, and Congressmen from strong Farmers' Union territory naturally tried to win Union support by offering to do the farmers' bidding in legislation and government administration. All of these things combined to make the Union a strong political force in many southern states from 1905 to 1915, in midwestern and western states after 1915, and at the national capital all during this time.

Barrett said in 1909, "The Farmers' Union is out of politics only in the partisan sense . . . There is certain legislation of a national character which the organization is demanding, and for which it is quietly but determinedly working"; and he said frankly, "The farmer must go into politics, and when I say the farmer, it necessarily follows that I mean, to an extent, the Farmers' Union . . . The time has come . . . when we must utterly disregard kind and benevolent advice from our would-be friends, free and unlimited counsel from our would-be saviors, and use the horse sense with which the Almighty has endowed us. The dictates of that horse sense point our entrance into the field of political activity if we would take practical and not oratorical steps toward the materialization of our mission." Like the leaders of the Alliance who, two decades before, had argued that there was a difference between "politics" and the "science of government," the national president of the Farmers' Union made a sharp distinction between "politics" and "partisanry." He pointed to the lobbies of other economic interests, the example of labor unions, and said, "The ballot is the deadliest weapon known to modern history"; and concluded by declaring, ". . . it is settled beyond peradventure that going into politics is our sole salvation. Until we do, we will be trying to turn over the earth with a tooth pick." [38]

The Union never placed a ticket or even a candidate in the field, but it

---

[37] Hunt, p. 76. Reprinted by permission of the author.
[38] Barrett, pp. 46, 47-48, 257.

influenced political conventions, platforms, and candidates. In 1916, *The Progressive Farmer* of Raleigh, North Carolina, declared, ". . . the Farmers' Union has been the most potent factor that has ever been brought to bear in legislative matters that affect the life and business of agriculture" in the state; [39] and the Colorado Union claims credit not only for the passage of many favorable laws, and for defeating numerous reactionary legislators, but also accepts responsibility for the defeat of Governor Carlson and the election of Governor Sweet.[40]

The North Carolina Union, for the first three years of existence, had a state advisory council consisting of the executive committee, president, vice-president, secretary-treasurer, and state organizer-lecturer, to which was delegated the responsibility of looking after state legislation. After 1910, a legislative committee was appointed to work with the advisory council of the state Union and the Washington representative of the national Union.[41] The political activities of the organization grew steadily more militant until 1919, when it withdrew from the national organization because it favored more direct political action than the national would sanction. In North Carolina the activities began in resolutions and demands passed in Farmers' Union conventions. These were followed by lobbies, first at the state capital and later at Washington, and by hundreds of petitions from Union members to state and national legislators. In some cases the advisory council prepared a standard resolution or petition and asked the general membership to sponsor it. In other cases it asked locals to prepare their own petitions. Copies of the resolutions passed by the state Union conventions were sent to all legislators, and those passed by locals were sent to local senators and representatives. The advisory council held meetings at the offices of the *Progressive Farmer*, and conferences were held there with legislators who were asked to draft or sponsor bills desired by farmers. On special occasions, large delegations were called to Raleigh to attend legislative committee meetings, at which time the two houses of the state legislature sometimes sat as a committee of the whole and listened to speeches of Union leaders, flanked by hundreds of farm-

---

[39] *The Progressive Farmer*, January 22, 1916.
[40] Fisher, p. 59.
[41] C. P. Loomis, "Activities of the North Carolina Farmers' Union," *The North Carolina Historical Review*, Vol. VII, No. 4, pp. 443-462.

ers who filled the legislative halls. Candidates were requested to make public their stand on certain measures which the Union supported. Questionnaires were mailed to those seeking office, and their replies were published in the *Progressive Farmer*.[42] A list of issues upon which candidates were asked to express themselves was circulated in 1916 and in 1917; the names of representatives who voted for or against measures supported by the Union were printed in the *Progressive Farmer*.[43] In 1920, a candidate for governor in the primaries was defeated because he refused to make a public reply to a Farmers' Union questionnaire.

A Farmers' Union Legislative Committee in Colorado followed the plan of sending questionnaires to candidates for public office, publishing their replies, and publishing also a completely tabulated statement of how all legislators voted on Union measures. The following is an abridged copy of a Colorado Farmers' Union questionnaire:

> Representing about 20,000 voters, and a rapidly growing constituency, recognizing the fact that to secure just and equitable legislation, effective administration of the laws and justice in the courts, the officials and lawmakers must have adequate knowledge of the needs and demands of the people they serve.
>
> Therefore we present to you some of the more important problems that will concern the citizens of our State during the next few months.
>
> We have a strong, active legislative committee and secure our information from every part of the state and fully believe that these are some of the most important and vital questions that concern the people of our commonwealth.
>
> We present nothing that we cannot comprehensively outline and stand ready to interpret at any and all times.
>
> (*Signed*) STATE LEGISLATIVE COMMITTEE
>
> 1. Will you support and vote for a law that will permit the establishment of co-operative banks in Colorado?
>
> (————————) [44]
> *Yes or No.*

---

[42] *The Progressive Farmer*, January 9, February 27, 1915; May 20, 1916; January 27, April 14, 1917.

[43] *Ibid.*, March 24, 1917.

[44] Fisher, p. 60.

Questions were asked on seven other problems: primaries, rural education, a herd law, state mining of coal, child and animal protection, a pure-seed law, and opportunities for hearings before committees of the legislature. The candidate was asked to answer the questionnaire or to give his reasons for not doing so, sign it, and state his occupation. This action and a constant watch on activities in the legislature were followed up by a report to the state Union. The committee said in part: "Your committee was on the job during the entire session of the Legislature. We made the following demands for the farmers of the State." [45] Then follows a list of the demands, after which the report stated the results obtained, and among other things, said:

> The Governor has been a disappointment.
> There seems to be but one course for the farmers to pursue in the future; do as did North Dakota. Why should we spend our votes for partisan politicians switching from one party to another and smarting under the party lash? The farmers can unite with the laboring man and elect every State officer and legislator in the State from the ranks of the common people . . .
> We got just what is coming to us for this negligence. The men in overalls and jumpers are the fellows who keep the world alive and moving, why not give these men of brawn and brain a chance to run the State's affairs as they do the State's industries? [46]

While the Colorado Union claimed some very definite legislative accomplishments, those of which it was most proud were the Mutual Insurance Law of 1913, and the Cooperative Marketing Act of 1922. Its chief accomplishment has been the systematic and persistent way it has kept its program before the state legislature ever since it came into existence in 1907.[47]

Barrett, in his 1910 presidential address, told of a "certain Southern United States Senator of some prominence" who failed to respond to an inquiry about "the stand of Congress on six measures of vital importance to the Farmers' Union" who later "got in a tight place . . . and set about

---

[45] *Ibid.*, p. 61.

[46] *Ibid.*, p. 62.

[47] A. T. Steinel, and D. W. Working, *History of agriculture in Colorado*, pp. 343-344. Fort Collins, Colorado: State Agricultural College, August 1, 1926.

explaining and defending and excusing himself," but was nevertheless defeated in the next election. In his address to the 1913 convention he said, "The National Congress is waking up and is giving heed more and more to the voice of the agriculturist." The national Union, at its first real national convention, in 1907, appointed a committee on legislation which in its report recommended that the Union "elect at this time three competent men to be known as a National Legislative Committee, whose duty it shall be to go to the city of Washington when Congress convenes and present our claims, and, if possible, have our demands enacted into law." This recommendation was repeated at the 1908 convention and again in 1910 and 1914.[48]

Such a lobbying committee was never appointed, but members of the legislative committee did go to Washington from time to time. For the most part, however, President Barrett carried this responsibility and was without question the most powerful agricultural lobbyist in Washington for at least fifteen years.

As was stated early in this chapter, the Farmers' Union formed no new political parties. Neither has it, so far as the writer knows, favored one old party against the other. But as Barrett said in 1923, ". . . we seated and unseated members of Congress, members of State legislatures and others . . . We sought the great in their seats in Washington . . . Farmers with their own hands, more used to guiding the plow than the pen, wrote letters. Some of them were not constructed according to rules of modern grammar . . . But they all breathed a demand that an honest man had a right to make to those who were proposing to serve him in Congress." [49]

The three old issues of transportation, monopolies, and cheap money, legislation concerning which the Grange and the Alliance had so ardently fought, were at no time the heart of the Union program. In certain states it contended for lower freight rates, and even lower passenger rates, but it never made the railroads the brunt of any of its major attacks. It advocated better rural credits and wanted government loans made directly to the farmers without banks and associations acting as intermediaries, but in its early history it never insisted on the same degree of inflation as the

---

[48] *Minutes, 1907-1913.*

[49] C. S. Barrett, *Uncle Reuben in Washington,* p. 167. Washington, D. C.: Farmers' National Publishing Co., Inc., 1923.

Greenbackers or the Populists demanded. It did not often deliver scath-
ing tirades against "trusts, combines and monopolies," as the Grangers,
Wheelers, and Alliancemen had, but it constantly took its stand in behalf
of a more equitable distribution of wealth; and in the later years of the
period which we have been discussing it declared in favor of "Government ownership or control of all natural resources; as minerals, oil, coal,
phosphates, lime, building stone, timbers and water powers." It also asked
for a limitation on large holdings of land and government ownership of
railroads.[50] For the most part, however, this great farm organization,
during the first twenty years of its existence, spent its major effort in a
more or less systematic attack on the price and market problems of the
farmer, and in so doing it clarified the issues which had lain at the roots
of the Farmers' Movement during all the preceding decades.

More clearly than any that preceded them, the two general farmers'
organizations founded at the turn of the century, and after a low tide in
the Farmers' Movement, directly stated their purpose in terms of the
issues about which the American Farmers' Movement has revolved. The
first issue of *The National Field* said, "*The National Field* stands for
certain definite things, but above all else it will stand for trying to solve
the vital problem—adequate marketing of the crops you produce, with
full and just returns upon the fruits of your toil." [51] All through the pages
of the official organ of the Union, year after year, this and other issues
of the Farmers' Movement were stated and discussed: prices, money and
credit, monopolies and trusts, storage and holding of farm products, farm
legislation, and, above all, farmers' cooperatives. The pages of this national
paper and a number of state Union papers published photographs of
delegates to state and national conventions, of cooperative warehouses and
stores and gins, published Union poems and songs, and in every other
way reflected and used the types of promotion which further a movement.

[50] *Minutes, 1919*, pp. 46-49.
[51] *The National Field*, Vol. I, No. 1, p. 1.

THE AMERICAN SOCIETY

OF EQUITY

THE BASIC IDEA OF "EQUITY"

There is real significance in the fact that the American Society of Equity, organized at Indianapolis, Indiana, in 1902, and its sister organization, the Equity Union, organized in 1910, developed in an area and during a period of great agricultural prosperity. Secretary of Agriculture James Wilson said in his annual report for 1909, "The value of farm products is so incomprehensively large that it has become merely a row of figures"; and the Country Life Commission report stated, "There has never been a time when the American farmer was as well off as he is today..." [1] But by this time, the Farmers' Movement in the United States had developed to the stage where its continuance did not depend on the occurrence of depressions. The Equity did not arise because of depression and it did not decline because of either prosperity or depression. It was the first large farmers' organization about which this can be said.

It is true that J. A. Everitt, the founder of the American Society of Equity, said in the preface to *The Third Power*, "If there is a place or

---

[1] Quoted by John D. Hicks, "Western Middle West, 1900-1914," *Agricultural History,* Vol. 30, No. 2 (April, 1946), p. 72.

corner anywhere in the world where the producers of our food and clothing suppliers (commonly called farmers) are not ready to revolt against
the absolute domination of non-producing classes in pricing their products, I am not aware of it." That he was not referring to a general discontent but only to the price and market systems is evidenced by an earlier
sentence in which he said, "'That the old and thoroughly bad system can
speedily be changed—the producers regulate the marketing of their products and make their own prices—I am thoroughly convinced."[2] Everitt
believed that the solution to the age-old problem of the farmer was to put
business methods and business organization into the whole system of
farming, from production to marketing of farm products; that this could
be done and that no other class should oppose the farmers' organizing
themselves into a "Third Power" to compete with the two other great
powers—Business and Labor.[3] To him this was equity. It is interesting that
he should have sounded this note twenty years before the McNary-
Haugen "Battle for Equality" and thirty years before the "Farm Parity
Prices Program" came into existence.

The central idea and slogan of the Equity was "controlled marketing
to compel profitable prices for all farm products." Everitt's faith was
clearly expressed by the following statements:

> The awakening of the agricultural classes, the organization of them
> into national and international co-operative bodies, which is now
> being accomplished, will remove agriculture from the list of un-
> certain industries and place it on a basis of certainty—for prices
> equal to that enjoyed by the best regulated manufacturing or com-
> mercial enterprises.

> You now have, for the first time, the right plan and are directed for
> the right objects. Give this society the same membership that you
> gave the Grange or Alliance and the work will be done now and
> forever. Give the members one-tenth of the benefits this society is
> capable of giving and they will never abandon it. Before many
> years, yes, I believe before many months, equity, which is next to
> righteousness, will be established.[4]

---

[2] J. A. Everitt, *The third power.* Fourth Edition, pp. v, vii. Indianapolis: published by
the author, 1907.

[3] *Ibid.,* chap. i.

[4] *Ibid.,* pp. vii, 243.

The growth of the Society of Equity is difficult to appraise during its first five years of existence because it was loosely organized. Its development was impeded by internal dissension and the necessary reorganization which followed. In terms of the techniques of a movement, its failure to grow rapidly can be accounted for chiefly by the facts that it did not have grass-roots locals and did not capture the support of newspapers and farm journals which could carry its ideas to the masses of farmers and their friends.

THE RISE OF THE AMERICAN SOCIETY OF EQUITY

J. A. Everitt said he had been thinking over the plan of Equity for a year before presenting it to two or three farmers who helped him to form the organization.[5] Mr. M. W. Tubbs, later editor of the *Wisconsin Equity News*, who was closely associated with the organization from 1903 on, says, "H. L. Hearron, of Carlville, Illinois, a farmer of little wealth, influence, and education seems to have first conceived the idea of forming an organization of farmers to 'control marketing' . . ." In his immediate locality, some thirty or forty local Unions sprang into existence between 1898 and 1901. Tubbs says that Hearron wrote Everitt telling him of his idea, what he and his friends had done by way of organization, and soliciting Everitt's assistance. Tubbs adds that "this was undoubtedly the germ that set to work in Mr. Everitt's fertile brain, and caused him to investigate conditions and publish in his paper during 1902 a series of articles on Marketing Conditions, Supply and Demand, Visible Supply, Controlled Marketing, Organization of Farmers, Boards of Trade, Manipulation, etc. etc." [6]

Everitt—owner and publisher of *Up-to-Date Farming*—even more than Oliver H. Kelley in the case of the Grange, agitated, planned, promoted, and finally organized the American Society of Equity. He wrote in August, 1901, "If it was possible to control and limit the production of our chief farm crops, within the action of the farmers themselves, it would be possible to control prices." [7] In September of the same year he pub-

---

[5] From an interview with Mr. Everitt.

[6] *Wisconsin Equity News,* June 10, 1912.

[7] *Up-to-Date Farming,* August 15, 1901.

lished an article calling attention to the fact that the larger the national yield of any farm crop the smaller the total monetary return to the producers of that crop. In the same issue of his paper, he announced that he would soon publish a plan for "controlling production and prices of farm products." [8] This he did in a series of articles published in December, 1901, and in January and February, 1902. [9] Because his plan was clearly stated and because it was, in some ways, a forerunner of similar proposals made two decades later, it merits rather complete exposition.

Everitt's theory started with the conviction that farmers, like workers and businessmen, should organize in defense of their economic interests; that they fed the world and if need be they could starve it by control of production. His proposal was not that the farmers starve the world, but that they organize to make profits in their own business. He believed that this could be much more successfully accomplished by attempting to regulate their own business than by trying to regulate the other man's business as had been attempted by the Grange and Alliance. He therefore advocated a coalition of businessmen and farmers, and in his first drive for membership invited "friends of farmers" to join the organization. [10] He believed that it was the dumping of products on the market where others than farmers could take advantage of surpluses that kept farmers from reaping the benefits of ever-expanding markets for their products. But he did not believe there was much danger of price-breaking surpluses if farmers could be made intelligent about the market by means of monthly crop reports, and if fluctuating surpluses could be stored on the farms to take care of fluctuating deficits. [11]

Everitt said, "If my argument is sound it is clear that the farmers need not look to lawmakers, Divine Providence, or anywhere but to themselves." [12] He planned for them to join the American Society of Equity in great enough numbers to keep down the "visible supply" of market crops

---

[8] *Ibid.*, September 15, 1901.

[9] *Ibid.*, December 15, 1901, January 15, February 15, 1902.

[10] *Ibid.*, August 15, December 15, 1901.

[11] *Ibid.*, January 15, February 15, October 15, 1902; April 1, 1904. Mr. Everitt loaned the writer an elaborate article which he prepared, but never published, during the McNary-Haugen days, advocating what might very well be described as an "Ever-Normal-Granary" plan.

[12] Everitt, *The third power*, p. 44.

by storing part of them in their own granaries. They were to make crop reports through their county unions, these reports to be compiled for the nation and published monthly in *Up-to-Date Farming*, the official organ of the Society. Here all members and subscribers would read the reports and govern both their planting and marketing according to the knowledge of what was best for their own interests.[13] The membership, however, was not forthcoming; and the dues, which had been set at $1 per year, including a subscription to *Up-to-Date Farming*, were lowered first to 50 cents and then to 25 cents per year, the subscription to the official organ—*Up-to-Date Farming*—still being included. Tubbs says the organization had hard sledding because the "Agricultural Press, Colleges of Agriculture, and Farm Institute workers commenced 'knocking' the idea as a 'one-man organization,' a visionary scheme to fool the farmers and to build up a tremendous circulation for *Up-to-Date Farming*," and that while Everitt "had expected to enroll several hundred thousand members during the first six or eight months, only about twenty or thirty thousand had been enrolled." [14]

The purpose of the society was "to secure equity and fair dealing in all the business relations of human life." Its objects are fully set forth in the Articles of Incorporation, the chief of which was "to secure equitable and profitable prices for all products of the farm, garden, and orchard, including livestock and dairy products and poultry." [15] More elaborately set forth in a pamphlet published immediately after its organization, the objects were:

No. 1. To obtain profitable prices for all farm products, including grain, fruit, vegetables, stock, and their equivalents. No. 2. To buy advantageously. No. 3. To secure equitable rates of transportation, storage in warehouses, etc. No. 4. Insurance features. No. 5. To secure legislation in the interests of agriculture, open up new markets and enlarge old ones. No. 6. To establish institutions for educating farmers, their sons and daughters, and the general advancement of agriculture. No. 7. Crop reports and securing new seeds, grains, fruits, vegetables, etc. No. 8. To improve our highways. No.

---

[13] *Up-to-Date Farming*, December 15, 1901; January 15, 1902; April 15, 1903; April 1, 1904; October 15, 1905. Everitt, *The third power*, chaps. x, xi.
[14] *Wisconsin Equity News*, June 10, 1912.
[15] "Constitution and By-Laws," *Up-to-Date Farming*, May 1, 1905, p. 4.

9. To irrigate our land. No. 10. To establish similar societies in foreign countries, as the Russian Society of Equity, etc., but societies only in surplus-producing countries. No. 11. To prevent adulteration of food and marketing of same. No. 12. To promote social intercourse. No. 13. To settle disputes without recourse to the courts.[16]

The objects and purposes of the society were sufficiently elaborate and diverse to encompass almost anything, and apparently the founder intended that they should be, for in his very elaborate exposition of them he said:

I realized fully, the conditions four years ago when I devised the plan of the American Society of Equity and intended it, when established, to strengthen congress, legislatures, presidents, and all who sincerely want to help the common people in their demand for equity. It was my purpose to build a mighty machine of the farmers and their friends. This machine will take the energy of the hundreds of writers, and instead of allowing it to waste, like the waters of Niagara, we will confine it in carefully prepared channels and direct it against all inequity and all inequality. The power will be irresistible . . .[17]

For two years following its organization, Equity was pretty completely an Indiana—in fact, an *Up-to-Date Farming*—organization. The officers who incorporated the society were Everitt, owner and publisher of *Up-to-Date Farming*, president; A. D. McKinney, one-time editor of *Up-to-Date Farming*, secretary; H. W. Miller, farmer-banker of Marion County, Indiana, treasurer; S. R. Williams, editor of the *Texas Farm Journal, Texas Stock Journal*, and *Kansas City Farm Journal*, vice-president; Mark P. Turner, lawyer of Indianapolis, counsel; Sid Conger, poultry farmer and member of the Indiana State Board of Agriculture, organizer; and Eli A. Hirshfield of Indianapolis, press agent.[18]

The 1903 national convention, held in Indianapolis in December, was only a one-day meeting and was attended by very few delegates. The only recorded minutes in existence appeared in *Up-to-Date Farming.*

---

[16] *The plan of the American Society of Equity.* American Society of Equity. Indianapolis: *Up-to-Date Farming*, 1903.

[17] Everitt, *The third power*, pp. 38-40.

[18] R. H. Bahmer, "The American Society of Equity," *Agricultural History*, Vol. 14, No. 1 (January, 1940).

Election of officers was by mail, and Everitt was unanimously elected president. Thirty-two vice-presidents were elected, one from each of the following states: Alabama, California, Florida, Iowa, Michigan, Missouri, Nebraska, North Carolina, Ohio, Tennessee, Texas, and Virginia; two from each of the states of Arkansas, Oklahoma, and Pennsylvania; three from Kansas, three from Kentucky, four from Indiana, and four from Illinois. They were all "unanimously elected," which would indicate that the few men present simply elected all who had been nominated by mail. The minutes show the participation of only eight persons. The organization claimed a membership of 59,000 at that time. Everitt announced in his paper that there would "be no annual dues until the Society is built, whether it requires another year or five years," but said he would expect everyone to renew his subscription to the paper. It is thus clear that there was no way of separating members from mere subscribers.

The announcement of the date of the 1904 annual meeting and the ballot for nominations were published in October. The meeting date was to be December 8; the place, Indianapolis.[19] The list of nominees was published on November 1 and again on November 15 and December 1.[20] For some reason the December 15 issue of *Up-to-Date Farming* carried no account of the annual meeting, a one-column running story in the January 1, 1905 issue indicating that there had been no actual assembly. Presumably the Board of Directors, or those who were at headquarters, counted the ballots, and that was all there was to the annual meeting. The story said, "As is well known, there is no provision for direct representation at the annual meeting, as the officers are elected by direct vote of the members in their local unions, and transmitted by mail to the National Union." The article claimed "very nearly one hundred thousand enrolled, and half as many more co-operating for our purposes, but not yet actually enrolled as members." It mentioned lack of strength in the cotton belt and extreme northwestern wheat region and said, "There is quite a prevalent opinion that we have reached a point where our general system of organization may be profitably revised . . ." and suggested that "where three or more local unions exist

---

[19] *Up-to-Date Farming*, October 15, 1904.
[20] *Ibid.*, November 1, 15, December 1, 1904.

in a county they are advised to organize county unions . . ." The result of the election was announced, showing thirty-eight states and one territory each represented by one vice-president. The ten states not represented were Arizona, Connecticut, Delaware, Maine, Massachusetts, New Mexico, Nevada, Rhode Island, Vermont, and Utah.

The 1905 national convention was much nearer a bona fide delegate meeting. The secretary's report showed a membership of 143,661. Kentucky led with 13,497; followed by Illinois, 10,395; Indiana, 10,138; Michigan, 9,175; Ohio, 8,141; Louisiana, 7,799; and Arkansas, Missouri, Oklahoma, Pennsylvania, and Virginia each with more than 5,000. The remaining membership was scattered throughout other states, Indian Territory, and Canada.[21] It was thus evident that the special drive made to organize wheat farmers had not been an outstanding success. Kansas membership was reported as only 3,267; Nebraska, 2,954; and North Dakota, 2,526.[22] That Kentucky, predominantly a tobacco-producing state, was leading in membership was significant as an index to the part which some past Equity members were to play a few years later in the so-called "Night Riding" episode in that state. Significant also was an unwillingness on the part of delegates to approve the new constitution which Everitt had promulgated the preceding May in response to discontent he had sensed with regard to the scheme of organization. His new constitution, issued by proclamation, had made provisions for county unions, in addition to local unions, and for a definite scheme of representation at national conventions.[23] Previous to this time he had advocated voting by mail and had not cared to see county unions organized. The delegates to the convention took things in their own hands and adopted a new constitution, thus starting an organizational conflict which two years later split the society and eliminated Everitt as its guiding genius.

The new constitution provided for state and county unions, each with a full set of officers; for division of dues between them and the national union; for local unions to meet twice each month, county unions quar-

---

[21] *Ibid.*, December 1, 1905, p. 11. This report was for "Members and Subscribers to Official Paper" and was thus only a loose calculation of actual membership. It showed 47,968 for 1903 and 81,515 for 1904. See also Bahmer, p. 44.

[22] *Up-to-Date Farming*, December 1, 1905, p. 11. Bahmer, pp. 44-45.

[23] *Up-to-Date Farming*, May 1, 1905, pp. 4-7.

terly, and state unions semiannually. The Equity program was to be carried out by the county unions taking care of the crop reporting, state unions having general supervision over all Equity activities within their boundaries, and the national union having committees representing special agricultural interests, each to give special consideration to marketing problems in its field. Everitt was re-elected president and Tubbs re-elected secretary. Outwardly, therefore, it was not apparent that there had been a disturbance in the ranks of the Equity. The Board set prices for wheat, corn, barley, and cotton, and adjourned. But state unions were organized immediately, the first in Wisconsin in February, 1906, followed by others in Illinois, Oklahoma, Kentucky, Michigan, Arkansas, Nebraska, Virginia, New York, Indiana, Minnesota, North Dakota, and South Dakota.[24] A number of business organizations were also started during that year.

From the beginning the American Society of Equity more or less specialized in an attempt to influence the price of wheat. It began a "Hold Your Wheat" campaign in 1903.[25] The price was set at $1 per bushel on the Chicago market at that time. In 1904, this campaign was extended to include beans, barley, timothy hay, cotton, corn, potatoes, and tobacco.[26] During this year the price set for wheat was advanced to $1.20 per bushel, and special efforts were made to organize the hard-wheat belt. Because the price of wheat did advance to $1.20 a bushel in late 1903 and early 1904, the Equity claimed that its holding campaign had been a success. The price fell in 1905, however, and the Equity lowered its "set price" to $1 per bushel.[27] All during the years 1903, 1904, and 1905 headlines in *Up-to-Date Farming* reflected this drive for price-fixing. Some of them were:

May 1, 1903:

AN APPALLING CONSPIRACY

THE FARMERS OF THE UNITED STATES TO BE ROBBED OF $116,000,000 IN TWO CROPS, WHEAT AND OATS

---

[24] *Ibid.*, November 15, 1905; February 15, 1906.
[25] *Ibid.*, June 1, July 1, 1903.
[26] *Ibid.*, May 1, August 1, September 1, September 15, October 15, November 1, December 1, 1904.
[27] *Ibid.*, August 1, 1905.

July 1, 1903:

DOLLAR WHEAT IS COMING

August 15, 1903:

WAR ON BETWEEN FARMERS AND SPECULATORS

December 1, 1904:

AT LYNCHBURG: THE FIRST CONVENTION BY AMERICAN FARMERS TO ESTABLISH PRICES

January 1, 1905:

HOW TO SECURE PROFITABLE PRICES

January 15, 1905:

HOLD COTTON FOR 12¢

April 1, 1905:

$1.00 FOR 1905 WHEAT

June 1, 1905:

THE DEVIL'S OWN—DEALING IN FUTURES—THE PIT— THE MOST DEMORALIZING INFLUENCE IN THE BUSINESS WORLD

July 1, 1905:

A NEW DECLARATION OF INDEPENDENCE

Everitt was president of the new society from its founding to 1907, when there was a split in the organization and new headquarters of the American Society of Equity were set up in Chicago.[28] He had pushed the organization vigorously through the columns of his paper, under such slogans as "Dollar Wheat," "Pool Your Tobacco," and "Equity for All." In four years' time, the Society had state organizations in twelve states—Indiana, Illinois, Kentucky, Wisconsin, Michigan, Minnesota,

---

[28] The first issue of the new official organ of the American Society of Equity, the *Equity Farm Journal,* was released by the Equity Publishing Co. in Chicago in November, 1907. Beginning in December, 1907, Everitt called his *Up-to-Date Farming* the official organ of the "Farmers' Society of Equity."

North Dakota, Nebraska, Kansas, Oklahoma, Arkansas, and New York. The ground for organization was fertile because of the demise of the Farmers' Alliance and because the Grange had been receding into conservatism.

The founder of Equity was not primarily interested in local or county units to begin with. He was fundamentally concerned about commodity price control and believed that such control could be accomplished by sign-up campaigns which would mobilize hundreds of thousands for common action. As the society evolved, it represented a compromise between the ideas of the founder and of those who more closely followed the patterns of the Farmers' Alliance.[29] The compromise provided for a hierarchy of organizations from locals to a national with two additional features—sections and departments. Local unions were federated into county unions, counties into district unions, districts into state unions, states into section unions, and sections into the national union. The two new features in a farmers' organization were the "sections," which provided for regional organizations, and "departments," which provided for commodity organizations. The purposes and plans of the Society did not change materially as the years went by, but none of the actual projects was ever put into effect on a national scale. The control of the organization shifted out of Everitt's hands after the split in 1907; and from then until its final decline, its chief center of strength resided in Wisconsin, where it set up numerous local enterprises and made considerable efforts at commodity marketing.

CONFLICT AND CHANGE IN ORGANIZATION

When the annual convention met in East St. Louis in October, 1906, it was immediately apparent that those opposed to Everitt's original plan of a large national price-fixing organization were in control. The constitution was amended to provide for department unions, one for each commodity group, each department to organize and handle its

---

[29] A series of articles by Everitt in *Up-to-Date Farming* entitled "Conspiracy and Rebellion" set forth the difference in viewpoints which went into the final compromise. See *Up-to-Date Farming*, November 15, 1907, p. 2; November 22, p. 2; December 1, p. 2; December 8, p. 2; January 1, 1908, pp. 13-15; January 15, pp. 16-17.

own affairs, subject only to the constitution and by-laws of the national union. The country was to be divided into seven areas or sections, each with headquarters at a principal market rather than all at one place. Everitt tried to stem the tide away from his original plan, but was refused the opportunity to make his full argument. He was re-elected president, but the shift in the purposes and structure of the organization had been so great and the leadership of others had developed so far that ultimate rupture was inevitable.

The break came at the 1907 national convention at Indianapolis. Everitt had been outvoted four to three all year in the Board of Directors' meetings. He was not elected president for the ensuing year, and the contract with his paper, *Up-to-Date Farming*, was annulled. He and his loyal followers held a rump convention and elected another set of officers: W. H. Mitchell of Kansas, president, and Everitt, vice-president. The split in the society was complete and lasting. C. M. Barnett of Kentucky had been duly elected president of the old society; L. N. Staats of Illinois, vice-president, and O. D. Pauley of North Dakota, secretary-treasurer. The leaders of the anti-Everitt group did not place themselves in office, but did dictate whom the officers should be, and led in the further revision of the constitution. They decided to establish their national headquarters in Chicago. Their actions served fairly quickly to destine the American Society of Equity to being a midwest organization, whose chief influence from that time forward was in Wisconsin, Minnesota, North and South Dakota, Montana, and northern Iowa.

The national union undoubtedly reached its maximum membership strength before the split came, and, although it gained strength in the middle northern states until 1913 or 1914, it was never again a nationwide organization. Its ranks were again divided, though not by open conflict, when, in 1910, a few of its loyal members and leaders founded the Farmers' Equity Union.[30]

There were local unions in Wisconsin and Minnesota in 1912 whose combined official numbers were above 6,000, indicating that there had been that many locals organized in about ten years' time. The dues-

---

[30] Bahmer gives a fairly detailed and completely objective account of the conflict between the two factions of the Equity during 1906 and 1907. Everitt gives a much more detailed, though less objective, account, in the columns of *Up-to-Date Farming* during the period.

paying membership in Wisconsin in 1910-1911 was 7,798 and that of Minnesota probably 5,000. All during the years 1911, 1912, and 1913 the *Wisconsin Equity News* carried reports of new locals being organized, dues for membership coming in, rousing meetings, and successes in various undertakings. In Wisconsin, 1,888 new members were added from October, 1910, to October, 1911, and 1,500 were added the next year.[31] The eight states of Wisconsin, Minnesota, South Dakota, North Dakota, Illinois, Indiana, Kentucky, and New York contributed to the "National Union Defense Fund" that year; and seven states had delegates at the national convention, New York and South Dakota not being represented, but Ohio having a representative. All newly elected national officers were from Wisconsin, Minnesota, and North Dakota, with the exception of one from Kentucky,[32] and the society from that time forward was pretty much a wheat-belt organization. In March, 1912, there were 12,000 members in good standing claimed in Wisconsin, and the *Wisconsin Equity News* had a circulation of 40,000.[33] Minnesota, with Magnus Johnson as state president, carried on a drive for 10,000 members, and North Dakota was reporting good progress. As a general farm organization, however, the American Society of Equity seemed never to have increased its membership beyond what it was in 1912—probably 30,000 to 40,000. It was as a sponsor of economic enterprises, and not as a farmers' general society, that it made its influence most widely felt.

The National Woman's Auxiliary to the American Society of Equity was organized in 1908 and became a live organization in 1911, but seemed to be confined chiefly, if not solely, to Wisconsin. All of its officers were from that state and all its conventions were held there. Mrs. M. Mollery, its national president, stated its "motives" to be "to promote the intellectual, moral, and social side of farm life," and "to help the American Society of Equity in every way possible." The resolutions of the women's conventions had to do with the problems of economic cooperation, legislation, social welfare, taxes, education, woman's suffrage,

---

[31] For accounts of the continuation of conflict between factions of the American Society of Equity, and for the growth of the organization in the middle northern states, see the files of *Up-to-Date Farming* for 1906-1908; those of the *Equity Farm Journal,* the *Wisconsin Equity News,* and the *Co-operators' Herald.*

[32] *Wisconsin Equity News,* November 10, 1911; November 25, 1912.

[33] *Ibid.,* December 10, 25, 1911, p. 3; March 10, 25, 1912.

and similar problems.[34] Men apparently were allowed to attend the auxiliary conventions, which generally lasted two or three days, and these conventions were considered quite important by the main society. The woman's branch claimed to have added zest and entertainment to local union meetings, and of course assisted in forming sentiment and maintaining loyalty, both of which are necessary parts of any movement.

A report of the Wisconsin state convention in 1911 shows that the Wisconsin organization still maintained that "The Wisconsin State Union, American Society of Equity, is not a business organization as it is at present organized, but it is an Educational Organization fitted to carry on propaganda of cooperation."[35] At the same time, the *News* carried block typefillers in every issue asking, "Are You Doing Business?" In 1916, the dominant center of the Society became Minneapolis and St. Paul, and its one great project became the marketing of grain, organized about the Equity Cooperative Exchange which had been started in 1911. The original purposes and plans were preached to the last, but the emphasis in practice became less grandiose and the million members necessary to establish complete control of markets was never attained or even approached. In 1924, the remnants of the Society began discussions with the Farmers' Union concerning the combining of the two groups, a move that had been discussed by some members of both organizations twenty years before.

In Wisconsin, the Equity made conjunction with the La Follette movement, gathered strength from the twenty years' growth of that movement, and, in turn, lent considerable organized strength to the views which Senator Robert La Follette, Sr. was agitating.[36] La Follette was first elected governor of Wisconsin in 1900, farmers constituting the bulk of his support. The Equity entered that state in 1903, and Wisconsin ultimately became the leading Equity state of the nation. On October 1, 1903, it claimed a membership of only 459; by 1907, it had a paid-up membership of 10,000, and began the next year to publish its own official paper, the *Wisconsin Equity News*. Its membership was located chiefly

---

[34] *Ibid.*, February 25, May 25, December 10, 25, 1912; March 25, April 25, 1913.

[35] *Ibid.*, September 11, 1911.

[36] A. P. Wilder, "Governor La Follette and What He Stands For," *Outlook*, March 8, 1902. T. Saloutos, "The Wisconsin Society of Equity," *Agricultural History*, Vol. 14, No. 2 (April, 1940).

in the western and northern sections of the state, areas of great La Follette strength. Wisconsin, Minnesota, and the Dakotas remained the stronghold of Equity for a decade after it had practically disappeared in other states.

ECONOMIC PROJECTS AND ATTAINMENTS OF THE AMERICAN SOCIETY OF EQUITY

Foremost among the cooperative projects of the Society were its grain-marketing, livestock-shipping, and tobacco-marketing projects, but in addition to these, it operated elevators and other warehouses, meat-packing plants, flour mills, creameries and cheese factories, wool pools, beef rings, buying clubs, cooperative stores, a cooperative laundry, a great central wholesale exchange, and other wholesale and jobbing enterprises. It organized property and fire insurance companies, and in one instance at least, a project was urged but never set up for manufacturing woolen goods. In 1912 Minnesota claimed to have 1,072 cooperatives and to be organizing a new one every day.[37] These types of projects, as conducted by other farmers' organizations, have been described in preceding chapters, and it is therefore not necessary to describe any of the Equity projects except those that were unique or that made advances over those of other farmers' organizations.

Everitt originally planned to organize a capital-stock company to carry out the marketing objectives of the Society. The capital was to be $100,000, and no one was to own more than one of the $1 shares. This plan was never carried out because the Indiana law governing such companies did not permit as wide or free activities as were thought desirable.[38] When the constitution was amended, providing for departments, it was expected that each department would in fact be a commodity organization. Thus the major economic activities and accomplishments were to be in the field of marketing grain, tobacco, potatoes, etc. on a nationwide or section-wide scale.

The first move was taken on May 25, 1903, when the famous "Hold Your Wheat" bulletin was issued.[39] The price demanded was $1 per

---

[37] Wisconsin Equity News, December 25, 1912.
[38] Up-to-Date Farming, December 15, 1902; January 15, 1903.
[39] Ibid., June 1, 1903.

bushel on the Chicago market, and farmers were urged to withhold delivery until paid that price. This was followed by prices being set for oats, barley, beans, potatoes, corn, hay, cotton, and tobacco.[40] By 1906, however, the Equity was convinced that something more drastic than holding and verbal price-setting were necessary. A great many Equity members suggested reduction in acreage, some advocating complete abandonment of planting for a year. The Society argued that the five states of Minnesota, Nebraska, Kansas, Iowa, and Illinois could control the price of wheat, corn, oats, barley, hogs, and cattle.

Intensive campaigns were conducted in these states with marked success. A large amount of wheat was held off the market that fall and the price rose during the winter of 1906-1907. The Equity promoted, and to a limited extent conducted, a "farmers' strike" during this period. Its action probably had some effect on wheat prices.

About 200 farmers, representing about a dozen states, met at the National Grain Growers' Convention in Omaha in June, 1907, and formed an organization "to regulate production; to direct the marketing and to do everything that may be necessary to secure profitable prices." [41] As Bahmer says, no final figures were ever released on the sign-up campaign which followed for the pooling of grain. It was, however, reported that in North Dakota over 10,000 members pledged a million acres of wheat; a half dozen other states, Kansas the most outstanding after North Dakota, had more or less successful campaigns; and the Equity leaders claimed that their pool kept prices up during the panic of 1907.[42] They came to realize, however, that they would have to provide a marketing agency to help the farmer sell the wheat he had pledged to withhold. They therefore negotiated agreements through private commission firms, and Exchanges were established in St. Louis, Kansas City, Chicago, and Minneapolis.

Similar, though even more drastic, action was taken by Kentucky and Tennessee tobacco growers. The Equity can neither claim the credit nor should it receive the blame for the Night Riders' activities, but the National Tobacco Growers' Association was organized as a branch of

---

[40] Bahmer, p. 44. See also issues of *Up-to-Date Farming* for all of 1904. Saloutos, p. 83.
[41] Bahmer, p. 51.
[42] *Ibid.*, pp. 51-52.

the Equity in 1904, and the early activities of the Planters' Protective Association were strictly in line with Equity policies.

Except for the Equity Cooperative Exchange, the most ambitious business organization set up by the Society was the Equity Producers' and Consumers' Exchange. This was a joint-stock association with an authorized capital of $150,000. It was promoted by Tubbs and other Wisconsin Equity leaders who, as early as 1906, assumed that they had been authorized to promote farmer-labor cooperatives. After they obtained control of the Society, they assiduously promoted Equity Exchanges, the first at Chicago, the second at Detroit, and the third at Scranton, Pennsylvania. They even went so far as to charter an International Equity Exchange under New Jersey law, with an authorized capital of a million dollars. The stock of this organization was to be held by local Equity Exchanges. Locals were to be of two types: shipping exchanges, organized by farmers and located at county points, and city exchanges, organized for the purpose of storage and distribution. Numerous smaller business ventures, many of them successful, were organized and operated by Equity members. Only a few samples are briefly described here.

A number of counties in Wisconsin first began operating local wool pools in 1909, and in 1911 a "State Wool Department" was set up. Warehouses were established in at least ten counties and the manager of the State Wool Department marketed for all of them.

The Consumers' Co-operative Trading Company—a store—was organized at Madison, Wisconsin, in 1911 as a model for others to follow. Members of the University of Wisconsin faculty assisted in this project.

The Bay View Co-operative Company, organized in Milwaukee in November, 1912, reported that it was doing a business of $2,500 per month in less than two months after starting. By 1913, there were fifty Equity stores in Wisconsin, practically all of them stock companies. The shares were often issued for only $10, and interest rates or dividends could not exceed 6 per cent. The remainder of earnings were distributed as patronage dividends, the nonstockholders receiving only one-half the rate of stockholders. Thus the Rochdale principle was followed in such cases.

The Equity, like practically every other farmers' organization of the grain belt, fought what it called the "Binder Twine Trust." The organization took credit for the 1911 Wisconsin law which established a twine plant at the State's Prison. One of the state organization's chief projects was the purchasing of binder twine in wholesale quantities, which it then shipped out to local unions, stores, and warehouses. Before the Wisconsin prison plant was established, a number of Wisconsin locals purchased in job lots from the Minnesota state prison plant, and claimed to have saved almost one-half the purchase price by doing so.

The Wisconsin State Union operated an exchange, doing chiefly a jobbing business and acting as a go-between for those who had apples, potatoes, dried fruit, fence posts, and even farms for sale. One of this organization's interesting projects was the handling of woolen blankets which it secured from a cooperative mill in New Mexico. It dealt chiefly, however, in such staples as coal, flour, fencing materials, rope, and other nonperishable products.

Probably the most unique cooperative project was the Farmers' Cooperative Laundry of Chatfield, Minnesota. It was operated in conjunction with the Farmers' Cooperative Creamery, but had an authorized capital stock of its own of $5,000 and shares were sold at $5 each. It began operation in December, 1912, and during the third week of operation "put out about ninety washings, exclusive of the hotel work, more than 50 per cent of which came from rural homes.[43] It was operated, like many of the stores, on the Rochdale plan, but later followed the practice of rebating to all patrons. Farmers never paid cash, but instead had their laundry bill—generally $2—deducted from their cream checks.

The Equity cannot claim to be the originator of livestock-shipping associations. The Grange had made a start in this field as early as 1873, and other organized farmers' groups had attained some success in it before the Equity began its projects.[44] Indeed pioneer attempts to grapple with the problem of marketing livestock cooperatively had been made fifty years before the Grange came on the scene.[45] But it was the American Society of Equity which first placed the modern livestock-shipping associations on the scene to stay. The earliest local was organized at

---

[43] *Wisconsin Equity News,* January 10, 1913.

[44] Herman Steen, *Cooperative marketing: the golden rule in agriculture,* p. 106. New York: Doubleday & Company, Inc., 1923.

[45] Edwin G. Nourse and Joseph G. Knapp, *The Cooperative marketing of livestock.* Institute of Economics Publication No. 40, pp. 10-11. Washington, D. C.: Brookings Institution, 1931.

Postville, Iowa, in 1904, followed by one at Durand, Wisconsin, in 1906, and another at Litchfield, Minnesota, in 1908.[46] The Wisconsin Co-operative Law of 1912, strongly urged by the Equity, cleared the way of obstacles. This was followed by similar laws in other states, and local associations began to develop rapidly. The *Wisconsin Equity News,* in February 1913, published a model constitution and by-laws for an Equity Co-operative Shipping Association, which had been put out by the Minnesota State Union, and thereafter gave reports from various locals. In April, 1913, it published a list of "Authorized Representatives" located in St. Paul, Minneapolis, Milwaukee, Duluth, Superior, and Chicago to which local associations should ship, and a department manager was appointed in the Wisconsin State Union to assist in the various central market sales. One of these authorized agencies in South St. Paul handled almost $13,000 worth of business for the farmers during the month of January, 1913.[47]

Many shipping associations were organized under other than Equity auspices, Minnesota leading the way for the first few years. There were 115 in that state in 1913 and 143 in 1916.[48] Wisconsin had 120 and Iowa 57 in October, 1916, when the Equity Cooperative Exchange opened a livestock branch in St. Paul. This new organization received 1,585 cars of livestock at St. Paul during 1917, and reached 3,383 during the year of 1920. In August, a branch was opened in Chicago which, though not doing so well as the one at St. Paul, handled 1,924 cars in 1920. In addition to furnishing a central sales agency for local shipping associations, the Exchange furnished a medium through which stockers and feeders could be purchased outside the speculative market. Steen records that "the Equity was severely handicapped by a factional warfare within the Minnesota Equity Society; by a severe boycott engineered by exchange firms; and by employment of some inexperienced salesmen,"

[46] E. G. Nourse and C. W. Hammans, "Cooperative Livestock Shipping in Iowa in 1920," Agricultural Experiment Station Bulletin 200. Ames, Iowa: 1921. Theodore Macklin and M. A. Schaars, "Marketing Livestock Cooperatively," Agricultural Experiment Station Bulletin 381. Madison, Wisconsin: 1926. Louis D. H. Weld, "Statistics of Cooperation among Farmers in Minnesota, 1913." Agricultural Experiment Station Bulletin 146. St. Paul, Minnesota: 1914.

[47] *Wisconsin Equity News,* April 10, 1913.

[48] Edward D. Durand, "Cooperative Livestock Shipping Associations in Minnesota." Agricultural Experiment Station Bulletin 156. St. Paul, Minnesota: 1916.

but that "it rose to second place among St. Paul firms in 1921," the year before it sold this department to the Iowa Farmers' Union.[49]

Just as in the case of shipping associations, the Equity cannot claim credit for the origin of the cooperative elevator movement, or even for the first attempt to pool grain on a large scale. The movement had started in Nebraska in the eighties, and there were about 1,800 farmer grain elevator companies in the United States in 1911 when the Equity Exchange was established; almost two-thirds of them were in Iowa, Minnesota, the Dakotas, and Wisconsin.[50] But as Steen says, "For nearly a decade the Equity alone upheld the standard of cooperation in the grain trade of the Northwest . . . and paved the way for later organizations to obtain a foothold . . ."[51]

The Equity's part in the marketing of tobacco, which in 1907 and 1908 developed into one of the bitterest fights in the long history of the American Farmers' Movement, will be recounted in a later chapter dealing with the Kentucky Night Riders. Equity tobacco pools were as outstanding in Kentucky as their grain pools were in the North, but the Night Riders, who were not Equity men, overshadowed what they were doing.

POLITICAL ACTIVITIES AND INFLUENCE OF THE AMERICAN SOCIETY OF EQUITY

The founder of the American Society of Equity did not plan that the organization should ever engage in politics. He believed there were altogether too few farmer representatives in Congress and that farmers had too little influence on legislation. He believed, however, that once farmers were strongly organized they would be able to demand legislation in the interest of agriculture without going into politics. He believed further that the Society had "the strongest safe-guards to keep it out of politics."[52] Had this been true, it would have been one of the few exceptions among general farmers' organizations.

The inclination to influence politics, and especially legislative action,

[49] Steen, p. 107.
[50] Powell, p. 122.
[51] Steen, p. 213.
[52] Everitt, *The third power*, chap. xv.

began to develop as soon as state unions grew strong. State conventions at first passed resolutions setting forth programs and issues with which farmers were concerned. Gradually these resolutions took the form of requests and demands. In due time, legislative committees were established, followed by lobbying, by questionnaires to candidates, by approval and disapproval of candidates and platforms, and finally by election of Equity leaders to public offices and insistence that farmers be appointed to state boards and commissions.

As usual, this evolution did not take place without the opposition of some members. In 1908, the editor of the *Wisconsin Equity News* said, "We already have persons who have considered the three dollar membership fee simply as an investment against the time when they can declare themselves for some office and ask for our support on the grounds of fraternal fellowship. Such men should be spotted and turned down." [53] Two months later, however, the *News* carried an article under the headline, "THE WISCONSIN IDEA—A WORD WITH ALL DELEGATES," to the forthcoming national convention, in which it set forth "legislation" as one of the "objects" of the Society. Six months later, it put out the "Special Legislative Issue," which listed the personnel of committees in the state legislature and the "Texts of Proposed Bills, Showing to which Committee Referred, and Editorial Comment." One headline read, "POSTAL REFORM COMING. WHOM THE GODS WOULD DESTROY THEY FIRST MAKE MAD." The following issue carried a picture of the state capitol with this caption: "New State Capitol. Where Bills that will Start the State Binder Twine Plant will be Passed in Spite of the Opposition of the Manufacturers and Dealers."

The annual convention of 1909 passed resolutions suggesting that local unions study and discuss such questions as tariff, money, marketing of farm products, guarantee of bank deposits, direct vote on such subjects as election of United States Senators, woman's suffrage, etc., benefits from national and state departments of agriculture, and farmers' institutes. The convention restated its demands for a binder-twine plant and condemned the Aldrich banking bill and "the last tariff bill." [54] At

---

[53] *Wisconsin Equity News,* August 1, 1908.

[54] *Ibid.,* October 1, 1908; April 1, 15, 1910; November 25, December 10, 25, 1909; January 10, 1910.

other times, the national Society and state Societies declared in favor of good roads, taxation reform, adequate rural schools, parcel post, postal savings, antitrust laws, rural credit legislation, cooperative marketing laws, etc.[55]

The *Wisconsin Equity News* carried articles by different writers who advocated political action, published the stand of certain candidates on public issues, urged farmers to write their Congressmen in behalf of certain legislative measures, and once published an elaborate questionnaire of the Farmers' Union type, which the editor thought all candidates for office should be asked to answer. From time to time, some Equity member would write an article advocating currency reform, revision of the tariff, tax reform, or some other economic and social reform. The American Society of Equity itself, however, could not be said to have taken a stand on any of the great issues which had formed the battle cry of preceding farmers' organizations. It pretty much stuck to its knitting as a cooperative business advocate, and tried to influence legislation only when some specific measure was up which it felt was of vital importance to marketing. The *Co-operators' Herald*—house organ of the Equity Cooperative Exchange—was being published during the life of the Nonpartisan League and the rise of the Farmer-Labor party, both of which had strong followings in Equity territory; but all it did by way of advocacy of either of these movements was to publish news about them, their platforms and demands.

Equity, like the Grange and Alliance before it, wrestled with the issue of what is political economy and what is partisan politics. In October of 1908, the first page of the *Equity Farm Journal* carried two articles or editorials, one entitled "Politics and Business," the first two sentences of which were as follows: "It is impossible to separate the two. Politics has to do with the business of the nation." The same editorial said, "There are honest men in all parties and there are dishonest ones. If you know an honest man on the other ticket and a dishonest one on your own for the same place, vote for the other ticket . . ." The other editorial was entitled "The Political Situation." Its first sentence was, "This is the last issue before election, and while the American Society

---

[55] *Ibid.*, March 15, 1909; January 10, 1913. *Equity Farm Journal*, April, October, 1908; December, 1909; February, 1911. Saloutos, p. 61.

of Equity is not in politics, it behooves our people to pay attention to the situation and the candidates."[56] When the Farmers' Union sponsored a great farmers' convention in May, 1910, the editor of the *Equity Farm Journal* foresaw the possibility of the organization of a farmers' and laborers' third party. Had this happened, there is every reason to believe that thousands of Equity members would have gone into this political undertaking.[57]

Within the states, Equity men actually dabbled in direct political action. In April, 1920, a writer in the *Wisconsin Equity News* said, "We have been letting political sharks skin us ... We want our man on the ticket, and if we cannot get our man on, for God's sake let us put up a man ... of our own and paddle our own little boat."[58] As early as 1914, Ira M. J. Chryst of Wisconsin was quoted as saying, "We just made a little platform of our own and said, 'Gentlemen, here is our platform. How many of you are big enough to stand on our platform?' We did not ask him whether he wanted his name to appear on the Democratic ticket or the Republican ticket. It is the man we want and not the name of any political party." Magnus Johnson, past president of the Minnesota State Union said, when testifying before the Rules Committee of the House of Representatives in 1914, "But there is one thing I want to mention, and that is, we have put into our State legislature and we have helped to put into this Congress men with progressive ideas, that we know will stand by the farmer and will work for the farmer, and we are going in the future to put every man who runs for office on record in this great Northwest country, and if that man does not obey the wishes of his constituents over there in Minnesota, Wisconsin, North Dakota and South Dakota, we will elect that man to stay at home."[59] Johnson himself was elected to the State legislature, as was A. F. Teigan, both strong Equity men.

Probably the most outstanding political influence of the Equity was the part it played in the organization of the Nonpartisan League and the Farmer-Labor party. It did not, as a society, enter either of these

---

[56] *Equity Farm Journal*, October, 1908, p. 1.

[57] *Ibid.*, April 1-June 1, 1910.

[58] *Wisconsin Equity News*, April 21, 1920.

[59] Bahmer, p. 62. (Quoted from *National Grain Grower* and *Equity Farm News*, January, 1914.)

organizations, but its followers by the thousands furnished the constituents of these movements. It was at a called meeting of the North Dakota State Equity Society that the germ of the Nonpartisan League was planted; and it was George Loftus, dynamic Equity leader, who first furnished the technique of calling the roll of the North Dakota state legislature to see where the members stood on Equity (soon to be Nonpartisan League) demands.

The American Society of Equity was organized primarily with economic objectives. It was not a secret society, had no fraternal features, engaged very little in party politics, and was the first example in the United States of a general farmers' organization which did not start with some other purpose—either educational or fraternal—and later shift to economic and political behavior. Its founder's dominant objective was to attack the price and market problem with a frontal attack.[60] In his book, which argues the whole case for the Equity, he said:

> My purpose in all this is, frankly, to make the farmer discontented, not so much with conditions as with himself for allowing them to exist . . . If we admit that it is right for those who sell to the farmer to fix the prices at which they sell, and we don't dispute it, we must also admit that it is right for the farmer to fix the prices at which others shall buy from him. But really it is not a question of right at all—it is a question of power. If the farmer is to free himself from the compulsion to which he is now subjected, he must do so by his own act. And it is better so. A prosperity won by one's own effort is better and more securely based than that created and guaranteed by government. The solution of the problem is not to be found in Washington, but on the farms.[61]

The American Society of Equity did not grow as large or live as long as some other farmers' organizations, but no organization more closely adhered to its first principle of attack in all of its economic behavior.

It must be admitted that as long as Everitt was its national president and dominant leader, and his paper its leading spokesman, most of the Society's efforts were expended in trying to mobilize a gigantic membership. He did not believe that its one grand objective could be gained

---

[60] *Up-to-Date Farming,* January 15, 1903.
[61] Everitt, *The third power,* pp. 41, 43.

with less than a million farmers acting in enlightened union. Within a few years after the leadership shifted into the hands of others and became more diversified, various and sundry economic projects sprang up and worked themselves into a degree of economic success.

THE DECLINE OF THE EQUITY

The decline and demise of the American Society of Equity did not come at the hands of a heroic national battle, as was the case of the Alliance in 1896. C. O. Drayton, who was its revered and enthusiastic president for one and one-half years after its complete reorganization in 1908, resigned early in his second term and organized the Farmers' Equity Union. The Kentucky Equity, next strongest to Wisconsin, was never able to completely disentangle its relations with the Night Riders in the minds of a great many people. The Wisconsin Society therefore so nearly became the whole of the American Society that the fate of the Society pretty much depended on what happened in that state. There, internal squabbles for control of the Society, accusations of disloyalty during World War I, and the rise of the Nonpartisan League served to fairly quickly dissipate the 40,000 members which the Wisconsin State Society claimed at its height. It would be difficult to say just when the American Society of Equity went out of existence. Milo Reno told the writer in 1924 that the Iowa Farmers' Union had taken over Equity. More of this accretion apparently continued. When, therefore, formal amalgamation with the Farmers' Union occurred in 1934, it was a vote to ratify what had already happened.

Few, if any, farmers' organizations ever struck more directly at the issues about which the Farmers' Movement revolves, and probably none has had less national influence on those issues. J. A. Everitt's idea of the farmers as the "Third Power" was discarded in 1907 when he was ousted as president. When the Society began to go to pieces, those who had discarded him re-issued his book in an attempt to recapture the impulse he had given to the revival of the Farmers' Movement in 1902, but to no avail. The Equity Cooperative Exchange, an organization which originated out of Everitt's "Dollar Wheat" campaign, had become a separate entity. The Nonpartisan League, which was organized on the hinge of Equity doctrine, took over the farmers' political fight in the

Northwest, and all that remained of Equity enterprises were the local "Exchanges," shipping associations, elevators, and stores, many of which still exist. But the American Society of Equity was not a national or powerful organization after 1917.[62]

[62] See Saloutos, "The Decline of the Wisconsin Society of Equity," *Agricultural History*, Vol. 15, No. 3 (July, 1941), pp. 137-150, for an excellent analysis and detailed account of the last few years of turmoil, and ultimate failure, of Equity.

· 16 ·

OTHER EQUITY
ORGANIZATIONS

THE FARMERS' SOCIETY OF EQUITY

When the split came in the American Society of Equity in 1907, Everitt, its founder, objected to both the removal of its headquarters to Chicago and to what he thought was a changed emphasis in the purposes of the organization. He therefore withdrew and formed the Farmers' Society of Equity. Those who differed with him said that while the objectives of his organization were excellent in theory, the aim of obtaining a million members for the purpose of controlling markets and fixing prices was neither necessary nor attainable. Those who followed Everitt contended that it was a desire on the part of others to form something like farmer-labor unions which led him to revolt. Everitt himself says that labor representatives were present at the 1907 convention and were permitted to vote on the policies of the organization.[1]

There is little need of discussing the Farmers' Society of Equity in detail. It adopted a constitution, by-laws, purposes and objectives very similar to those of the original organization, except that it made "farmers and co-workers" rather than just "farmers" eligible for membership. It

---

[1] *A glance backward and an earnest look forward.* Indianapolis, Indiana: *Up-to-Date Farming*, n. d.

assumed an even more liberal attitude toward other economic classes and attempted to work out a scheme of cooperation between farmers, merchants, and consumers. The plan was that residents of cities and towns appoint committees to call upon various receivers of farm produce and make terms with the fairest of them for handling such produce. The committees were then to notify the Farmers' Society of Equity headquarters at Indianapolis concerning the merchants selected, and the organization would see that local unions delivered the produce to these merchants. By this practice it was hoped to remove all "speculative elements" from both the farmers' and consumers' markets.[2]

The national organization was to be known as "The Clearing House"; state and county organizations, as "Unions"; and the county and local units, as "Clearing Houses." The annual dues of $1.50 per person were to be divided as follows: 50 cents to the national clearing house, 25 cents to the state union, 10 cents to the county clearing house, 40 cents to the local clearing house, and 25 cents to the official paper (*Up-to-Date Farming*). Each farm crop was to have a "department" to provide or care for the "production, price and manner of marketing it. Each department was to hold a meeting at each annual convention, at which time the producers of the different crops would make their decisions on production, price, and marketing, these decisions to be binding on the whole convention and on the national clearing house."[3] None of these provisions ever diverted Everitt from his original purpose of obtaining a million members, who by their concerted action could control the surpluses of farm products and thus control their price. Everything else was subsidiary to this supreme project. How large the membership was in 1916 when the Society ceased to function, it is not possible to determine. Mr. Everitt says the circulation of *Up-to-Date Farming* was 250,000, but it had many subscribers who were only casually, if at all, interested in the Farmers' Society of Equity.[4]

As we follow the various directions which Equity enterprises took following the original split, it will be seen that Everitt's original plan was

---

[2] J. A. Everitt, *Cooperation by farmers, merchants, and the consumer of farm products.* Farmers Problems, No. 10. In Indiana State Library, Indianapolis, Indiana, n. d.

[3] *Constitution and by-laws* (Farmers' Society of Equity). Indianapolis, Indiana: 1907.

[4] Personal interview with Mr. J. A. Everitt.

in keeping with the general ideas which were very widespread, especially among cash-crop farmers. An article which he prepared in the 1920's, but never published, was not too unlike "McNary-Haugenism" of the period and yet not unlike his original Equity ideas.[5]

THE FARMERS' EQUITY UNION

The resignation of C. O. Drayton during his presidency of the American Society of Equity and his almost immediate organization of the Farmers' Equity Union in 1910 did not constitute an open split, or even any great upheaval in the organization of which he had been a member from earliest Equity days. It is not difficult to see, however, that there were two current ideas about how to promote the objectives for which Equity was organized. Those who favored organizing large pools for marketing grain, tobacco, and potatoes constituted the militant wing of the Society's membership. The Kentucky Equity program was chiefly that of pooling tobacco. The North Dakota Equity led the grain-pooling activities, followed by Minnesota and South Dakota. Drayton was from Illinois, not primarily a cash-crop area, and never a strong Equity state. He did not object to pooling, but objected to organizing giant marketing organizations outside of the parent society. In his presidential address in 1909, he said, "Equity Terminals in large centers for handling all our members' grain, hay and produce, will come naturally as the Equity Exchanges (locals) grow up in the country." [6] Not being able to lead the American Society of Equity in this direction, he quietly withdrew during his second term as president, and seven months later organized the Farmers' Equity Union.

The story of Drayton's disagreement with the militant wing of the American Society of Equity furnishes part of the explanation of the type of new society which he organized. He joined the American Society in 1903 under Everitt's leadership, but did not follow Everitt when the split came in 1906 and 1907. He was president of the Illinois State Union when he went to the reorganization meeting of the American Society of Equity in Milwaukee in October, 1908. He had been an organizer for the Society in Kentucky, Tennessee, Kansas, Indiana, Michigan, Minne-

---

[5] Copy furnished the author by Mr. Everitt.

[6] *Equity Farm Journal*, December, 1909, p. 10.

sota, North Dakota, and Missouri.[7] In the Milwaukee meeting, 110 delegates were seated, 88 per cent of them from Kentucky, North Dakota, and Wisconsin. They and others apparently knew Drayton well and respected him. The minutes of that convention record only one remark by him in addition to his presentation of the report of the Committee on Constitution and By-Laws, of which he had been named chairman. When the delegates assembled again in December for their annual constitutional meeting (the October meeting was a special one), he was the only candidate nominated for president, although Illinois had a very small delegation. The rules were suspended and he was elected by acclamation. In his published greetings to the members, he said he would hold twenty meetings in each of the Equity states during the coming year, which he did, apparently promoting the idea which he announced at the next annual convention.

His idea was the organization of hundreds of local exchanges, owned and operated by a local board of directors. In his presidential address in 1909, he said two things which are cues to the reason for his later quitting the Society and organizing a new one:

The salvation of Equity is indirect revenue sufficient for a continual campaign of organization and education.

Ship out all farm produce. Ship in flour, feed, twine, apples, fencing, cement, salt, etc. Buy and sell on a safe margin. Have a Board of Directors who direct. Hire honest manager at living salary. Out of gross earnings pay running expenses, each membership's dues, and 5 per cent for use of money as dividends on the stock. The balance is net earnings. Pay ¼ of 1 per cent of net earnings to national union. Prorate the balance among stockholders according to business given.

This was clearly his platform. He did not, however, stop with it, but struck sharply at the idea of organizing great independent central exchanges. He said, "Brothers, let us get away, once and forever, from the idea that we need an organization outside of, and independent or separate from, the American Society of Equity to do business for us."[8]

---

[7] *Ibid.*, November, 1909, p. 6.
[8] *Ibid.*, December, 1909, p. 10.

There was no adverse discussion of his ideas recorded in the minutes of the convention, although a delegate from Wisconsin, in seconding Drayton's nomination for re-election as president said, "We believe the Honorable C. O. Drayton is beyond contamination, whatever insinuations have gained their way into the public press. Wisconsin wants to bear testimony that although he may have made mistakes, we have made mistakes. God deliver us from the men who don't make them." He went on to urge Drayton's unanimous election, which soon followed. There is evidence, however, that already the adherents of organizations separate from Equity were carrying out ideas in conflict with those of Drayton. This fact was emphasized by the seating of three delegates of the Grain Growers' Department, and one delegate from each of two District Grain Growers' Unions. Those who believed in this type of activity ultimately gained the day and helped to organize the Equity Cooperative Exchange, which will be discussed later in this chapter.

A little space is given at this point to these divergent views within the American Society of Equity in order to document the fact that at this time, as earlier in the Grange and Alliance and later in other general farmers' organizations, one is able to clearly identify the departure of more militant members from a faith in the slow methods of education and the organization of local cooperative groups as bases for a later direct attack on the all-pervading price and market problem. President Drayton was holding general organization meetings, chiefly dedicated to organizing various types of cooperatives in all Equity states, each an independent business unit but each known as a local Equity Union. Reporting on such meetings in North Dakota, he wrote, "In many of my meetings I will reach ten or more local unions. I am endeavoring to get the local unions at each shipping point to thoroughly canvass the territory for dues, for new members, and for stock in an Equity Exchange." [9] At this very time, the Grain Growers' Department was carrying on a militant campaign for pledging farmers to pool their grain and purchase a terminal elevator, paying little attention to local Unions.

A few months later, Drayton wrote, "If we continue the idea of Department Unions, in a few years we will have seven or eight weak, separate organizations, in conflict more or less with each other, and neither

_____

[9] *Ibid.,* July 1, 1909, p. 2.

of them answering the full needs of that farmer who sells, each year, a car load of hogs, a car of wheat, a car of hay, a car of apples and ships milk to the city." [10] The national convention of the Society began the day after this article appeared. The only delegates present from North Dakota and Minnesota were representatives of the Grain Growers' Department. President Drayton was re-elected by acclamation. He stated his position even more strongly in his presidential address, saying: "Let our organized forms be local, county, state, district and national. Five wheels are enough for any wagon. The great danger is that after stock, wool, produce, grain and tobacco departments are established at great labor and expense by the parent organization, they will become independent and drift to themselves, deny their allegiance and refuse financial support to the parent organization . . ." [11] This is exactly what they did, but before we tell their stories, there should be recorded a brief history of the organization which Drayton founded after he resigned as president of the parent society.

The Farmers' Equity Union was chartered by the State of Illinois, Drayton's home state, on December 16, 1910, seven months after he resigned as president of the American Society of Equity. Two weeks later "action was taken" by the Board of the American Society of Equity "to instruct the members that neither Mr. Drayton nor Theron Fisk are authorized representatives of the American Society of Equity." [12]

This new organization had no fraternal or social features, but was to be a purely business organization. It provided for no types of pooling or holding of products to influence prices. It is still in existence, and two pamphlets, published forty years after it was founded, reveal how faithfully it has followed the ideas Drayton was advancing in the face of the drift into more direct attacks upon price and market problems. One of these pamphlets says, "Through the years the Farmers' Equity Union has not deviated from Mr. Drayton's plan, which is to organize strong local companies on a firm business around market centers and to organize centralized companies to serve locals in a trade territory." [13] The

---

[10] *Ibid.,* November 15, 1909, p. 11.

[11] *Ibid.,* December 1, 1909, p. 1.

[12] *Ibid.,* January, 1911, p. 7.

[13] *History and facts—1910-1950,* p. 3. Greenville, Illinois: Farmers' Equity Union, 1950.

other said, "The Equity organization is a purely democratic organization, controlled by the farmers out at the crossroads. This is shown in that the local depends upon the voluntary support of its members, the centralized company on the locals, and the national depends upon the voluntary support of the entire organization."[14]

The Farmers' Equity Union is thus based primarily on the local Equity Exchange, which is purely a business organization, neither a fraternal lodge nor a unit in a market pressure group. Each local exchange is totally independent of all other locals and independent of the centralized companies. If it wants to send voting delegates to the Society's national convention, it must pay small dues to that society. It may employ the services of the Equity Audit Company, one of the early-organized centralized companies, but it need not do so. It may use any other Equity centralized company, but need not do so. It carries on no propaganda campaigns except through its national house organ, *Equity Union Exchange*, and the few pamphlets it publishes. But by the early 1920's, it had issued approximately 600 charters to local exchanges and to centralized companies, many of which are still in operation.

The Equity Union has never been a noisy part of the Farmers' Movement, but it has attacked the farmers' price and market problem at the grass roots by recognized, sound methods of cooperation. It has gone one step beyond that in organizing centralized companies which act as wholesale buying and selling companies for the local exchange. Interestingly enough, one of the first centralized companies organized was the Equity Union Grain Company. It was placed at Kansas City, Kansas, where it could handle grain from Oklahoma, Kansas, Nebraska, and Colorado and was therefore operating alongside the Equity Cooperative Exchange—to be described in the next section of this chapter—which was serving the grain growers of the Northwest. Interestingly enough also, the Equity Union Grain Company is still operating, while the Cooperative Exchange, which created a much greater stir in the Farmers' Movement, passed out of existence twenty-five years ago.[15]

The Equity Union Grain Company was established by stock sub-

14 H. C. Pollhast, *Some principles of Equity cooperation*, p. 1. Greenville, Illinois: Farmers' Equity Union, 1950.
15 L. Melton, *Plan and purpose of the Farmers' Equity Union*. Greenville, Illinois: Farmers' Equity Union, 1924.

scribed by local Equities of the four states named in the above paragraph, and thus follows Drayton's ideas of the proper type of organization by which to enter the central grain market. Melton reported in 1924 that it had handled five million bushels of grain the previous year and owned two seats on the Kansas City Board of Trade.[16] There were four centralized companies in existence in 1924. Besides the Grain Company at Kansas City, Kansas, there was the Equity Union Coal and Mercantile Company at Denver, which handled not only coal but lumber, fencing, fruits and vegetables, automobile tires, and other farmers' supplies. It was established by, and served about, one hundred local exchanges. The Chicago Equity Union Exchange was the third centralized company to be organized. It handled farm supplies, but chiefly was the selling agency for Equity Union centralized creameries. It owned a seat on the Chicago Mercantile Exchange. The Ohio Central Equity Exchange Company was the other centralized company which came into existence during this early period. It was established at Lima, Ohio, to act as purchasing agent for Ohio and eastern Illinois local exchanges and to act as a grain broker for them. There were three large Equity Union creameries—one at Aberdeen, South Dakota; one at Orleans, Nebraska; and one at Lima, Ohio—which were using the Chicago Equity Union Exchange as sales agent in the early 1920's.

The Farmers' Equity Union has grown steadily in volume of business done since the date at which this account ends. It has never abandoned the principle of building from the local up to central-market companies, and it has never abandoned the purpose of nationwide marketing. It has, moreover, worked patiently at this task and toward this end. The reader will be interested in the stories of the grain- and tobacco-marketing organizations which followed a different path. These stories constitute the remainder of this chapter.

THE EQUITY COOPERATIVE EXCHANGE

In contrast to the Farmers' Equity Union, which carried out Drayton's ideas of how to attack the farmers' price and market problems, was the Equity Cooperative Exchange. The latter followed the other school of

---

[16] *Ibid.,* p. 4.

thought, that which had gained so much ground in the American Society of Equity by 1910 that Drayton felt impelled to resign as president of that society. The story of such organizations as the Equity Cooperative Exchange is sometimes thought symbolic of the whole history of the Farmers' Movement. This, of course, is not true, but the fight of the Northwest Grain Growers does offer an opportunity to see more clearly the actual fabric of the Farmers' Movement than does any other episode up to 1920.

Outstanding as a contribution to an analysis of the Equity Cooperative Exchange are the facts about grain marketing which were developed in the detailed investigation of the Federal Trade Commission, made and published during the period when the Cooperative Exchange was at its peak and during the period of its decline. It is impossible to present here even a synopsis of the facts published in a report of more than 1,700 pages by that Commission. Those who will study this report will be convinced that the farmers' complaints about control of local elevators by terminal companies and railroads, about the organic relationship of terminal elevators and grain exchanges, about Boards of Trade and Chambers of Commerce, about excessive dockage and demurrage charges, about ineffective grades' inspection, and about manipulation of grades through practices of mixing grains at terminal elevators were validated by the Commission's investigation.[17] As is typical of those involved in movements, the farmers did not possess or use all the types of objective understanding which the Federal Trade Commission developed. But their knowledge of, and experience in, marketing had by the beginning of the twentieth century developed to the point where they made more valid diagnoses of their problems than had earlier generations of farmers.

The first step in the northwestern farmer's diagnosis of his problems grew directly out of a very real and widespread condition incident to the production of a cash crop in a semiarid area. Boyle, in attempting to explain the origin of the Equity Cooperative Exchange and the Nonpartisan League, said:

—

[17] U. S. Federal Trade Commission, *Report on grain trade.* Seven volumes, published serially from 1920 to 1926. Washington, D. C.: Government Printing Office. Facts especially pertinent to the complaints of the Equity Cooperative Exchange will be found in Vol. I, chaps. iv, v, vi, xi; Vol. II, chaps. ii, iv, vi; Vol. III, chaps. iii, iv, vii; Vol. III, "Letters of Submittal."

The economic life of the region is very simple. It is based on wheat
...It is a one-crop section...Local flour mills have not been developed to form a market for this grain...The North Dakota wheat
crop not only goes far to market, but goes into another state. It finds
its way to the great mills of Minneapolis or to the exporters at
Duluth...a market so far away from the farmer gives rise in him
to two powerful psychological conditions concerning this market
—ignorance and superstition.[18]

This problem and these conditions had existed long before the Exchange
was organized in 1908, or even before the American Society was organized in 1902. The Dakotas had been strong Farmers' Alliance states
in the late 1880's and early 1890's. The North Dakota Alliance, together
with other states of that region, had insisted that the Alliance include
terminal elevators among its economic projects. A Farmers' Protective
Association was organized in 1891 which, for a number of years, maintained an agent in Duluth to take care of the grain of its members.
Through their own organizations and with the assistance of local businessmen whose economic life also depended on wheat, they struggled
against what they were convinced was terminal elevator and railroad
control and manipulation of grain prices and transportation costs. Finally, in 1907, the First District of the American Society of Equity, comprising the Dakotas and Minnesota, organized a wheat pool and claimed
to have signed up approximately thirty million bushels in a "dollar
wheat" campaign. The next year, a conference of Equity leaders established the Equity Cooperative Exchange.[19]

It will be remembered that the American Society of Equity had sponsored a National Grain Growers' Convention at Omaha, Nebraska, in
1907, had decided to establish Exchanges at St. Louis, Kansas City,
Chicago, and Minneapolis, and had promoted the sign-up and withholding campaign of which the Dakotas' and Minnesota campaign, mentioned
in the preceding paragraph, was a part. From 1908 on, one has no difficulty in seeing the dominance of those sponsoring these ideas in the

---

[18] J. E. Boyle, "The Agrarian Movement in the Northwest," *The American Economic
Review*, Vol. VIII, No. 3 (September, 1918), pp. 504-505. Reprinted by permission
of the American Economic Association.

[19] Fossum tells the story in detail of the struggle of more than two decades which
culminated in this act. See Fossum, chaps. ii, iii.

American Society of Equity. The Equity program from the beginning was in keeping with the idea that farmers could control the prices of their products by controlling their flow to the market and, if necessary, by controlling the amount of their production.[20] It was when Equity moved into the Northwest, especially into North Dakota, and made conjunction with the farmer-thinking which had developed out of the problems of cash-crop farming, that it began to increase in membership and sharpen its methods of attack.

The wheat growers had learned that to own and operate county elevators did not solve their price and market problems, because none of the final price or market decisions was made at points where the farmer delivered his grain to the local elevator or railroad. Some of them had discovered that even when they by-passed local elevator middlemen and shipped their grain, in carload lots, to central grain-market centers, membership on grain exchanges was essential for wholesale marketing to millers and exporters. The Minnesota Farmers' Exchange, organized in 1902, with a capital stock of $500,000, had attempted to purchase a seat on the Minneapolis Chamber of Commerce—in fact, a central grain exchange—and being unable to do so, had failed.

Farmer-owned local elevators had been established in great numbers but the farmer-owners claimed that they not only had difficulty in breaking into the grain exchanges, and thus had difficulty in selling their grain, but that they were charged excessive demurrage on cars of wheat that couldn't be unloaded. They furthermore claimed that their competitors, the "line elevators," [21] were given lower freight rates than they were from local shipping points to central city grain markets. These contentions, and the fact that farmers' grain was mixed at terminal elevators in such a way as to raise grades after purchased from the farmer, were all validated by an elaborate investigation of the Federal Trade Commission.[22]

The Equity Exchange was developed within the American Society of Equity by members of that society who believed in more effective direct action than the society seemed willing to take. It developed in an area

---

[20] See Everitt, *The third power*, p. 43.

[21] *Line elevators*. Elevators owned by railroads or terminal elevator companies.

[22] *Cooperative marketing*. Senate Document No. 95, 70th Congress. See especially chap. ii. Washington, D. C.: Government Printing Office, 1928.

where not only farming but all local business depended on cash grain crops which passed out of the farmers' and local businessmen's hands at local shipping points. No better statement of farmer ideas about what this meant can be presented than the following, written two years after the Exchange enterprise was launched:

> Prior to this [the beginning of the farmers' cooperative elevator movement], companies having large elevators in the great terminal markets of Minneapolis and Duluth and smaller elevators along the different railroads had absolute control of the grain business. They were monarchs of the grain buyers' world and the farmers were the serfs. In these days there was little if any legislation curtailing the operations of the large grain combines. They had the power to punish their enemies and reward their friends as they saw fit. They had their own system of grading. They did their own weighing and and, what is worse, they set their own prices. In those days there was one price for all and this ranged from 15 to 25 cents below the terminal quotations.[23]

Saloutos describes "the Equity grain marketing program in the spring-wheat country" in four stages:

> ... first, the pre-Equity Cooperative Exchange period, 1903-1907, when the grain marketing operations were under the control of the American Society of Equity in Indianapolis; second, 1908-1912, the period beginning with the founding of the Exchange, a passive phase, and ending with the appointment as sales manager of the pugnacious George S. Loftus, a crusader for terminal market reform and bitter foe of the Minneapolis Chamber of Commerce; third, 1912-1915, [a period] beginning with launching of a bitter campaign against the Chamber of Commerce and ending with the defeat by the North Dakota legislature of a bill for a state-owned terminal elevator; fourth, the period from 1915-1923, during which phase the Exchange had successfully competed with the Nonpartisan League for farmer support, and ending with the Exchange being adjudged insolvent.[24]

---

[23] *Co-operation in marketing of grain*, p. 3. Issued by the Equity Co-operative Exchange. Minneapolis: printed by Improvement Gazettes, 1910.

[24] Saloutos, T., "The Rise of the Equity Cooperative Exchange," *Mississippi Valley Historical Review*, Vol. XXXII, No. 1 (June, 1945), pp. 42-43.

The first stage has already been briefly described and will be referred to again in the chapter on the Nonpartisan League. In terms of the Farmers' Movement, data on the second stage are the most important because they show the ideological characteristics of the movement.

Theodore G. Nelson, president of the Grain Growers' Department of the American Society of Equity, writing in 1911, said:

On May 30, 1908, the secretaries of Minnesota and South Dakota State Unions, American Society of Equity, and the president of the Grain Growers' Department of the society, to wit, R. H. Aldridge, C. W. Pierson, W. I. Lowthian, and Theodore G. Nelson, assembled in a little room at the St. James Hotel in Minneapolis, and there, with information and assistance given by some of the most active war-horses in the ill-fated Minnesota Farmers' Exchange, among whom were O. G. Major, M. S. Blair and others, well known among the farmers of the Northwest, wrestled with the perplexing problem for two days.

The men comprising this committee concluded that the real problem was not only a matter of raising sufficient money with which to handle grain and operate terminal elevators, but conditions had to be produced which would make it possible for farmers to patronize the institution when once launched. Indeed it was not only a matter of making it possible. *There had to be an awakening in the rank and file of the farmers* to the fact that merely condemning of existing conditions would not alter these conditions. *It was necessary for the farmers themselves to get in earnest* [25] about wanting to ship their grain to their own agency . . ." [26]

A number of important things are revealed in this statement. Most important is that the conference was between Society of Equity members and some of those who had been leaders in the old Minnesota Farmers' Exchange. Equally important to an understanding of what followed is that the president of the Grain Growers' Department of the Society of Equity took a leading part. Also important is the fact that none of the Equity members was officially representing the Society. Two of them

---

[25] Italics are the author's.

[26] *Co-operators' Guide* (*Equity Farm Journal*), February, 1911, p. 4. *Co-operators' Guide* was for a short time the title of *Equity Farm Journal*.

were presidents of state Unions of the Society and three of them were leaders in the Grain Growers' Department of the Society. They were joined by some of those who had been tried by fire in the old Minnesota Farmers' Exchange.

During the stage of development which Saloutos calls "the passive phase," 1908-1912, those sponsoring the Exchange proposition were by no means passive. In terms of developing sentiment and soliciting support, the Grain Growers' Department, which was leading the fight for terminal elevator ownership, was by no means idle. The evidence is that the leaders of this Department intended to move forward either within or outside of the American Society of Equity. In the announcement of the second annual convention of the Grain Growers' Department of the American Society of Equity to be held at Fargo, North Dakota, October 28, 1908, there was listed, by states, the number of 319 delegates to be seated— North Dakota, 105; Wisconsin, 79; Minnesota, 30; a total of 214, or 67 per cent of the total number of delegates.[27] At this convention, action was taken which gave the Board of the Grain Growers' Department the greatest degree of independence possible within the Equity Society.[28] At a meeting of District Union Number One—composed of North Dakota, South Dakota, and Minnesota—held at Fargo, North Dakota, October 27-29, 1908, only those delegates who had "pledged" their grain for the "selling and pricing program" to be established were permitted to vote on that program.[29]

Theodore G. Nelson, President of the Grain Growers' Department, in announcing a series of mobilization meetings in an article entitled, "The Speculators and Grain Gamblers Must Go," said:

> Grain Growers are writing that message on the walls of time at present. Here is how it looks. Monster mass meetings at Fargo, North Dakota, June 9 and 10; at Madison, Minnesota, June 4 and 5; at some point in Nebraska to be determined later, probably June 18 and 19. Then a final meeting at Fargo, July 27, to which all grain growers who pledge their grain in the Dakotas and Minnesota will go for the purpose of devising ways and means to market this year's

---

[27] *Equity Farm Journal,* October, 1908, p. 14.
[28] *Ibid.,* November, 1908, p. 9.
[29] *Ibid.,* December, 1908, p. 8.

crop without giving the speculators and gamblers a single kernel to handle.[30]

Another article in the same issue of the *Equity Farm Journal* was headed,

BIG MASS MEETING OF EQUITY MEMBERS AND GRAIN GROWERS, TO BE HELD IN FARGO, JUNE 9 AND 10. 3,000 DELEGATES WILL ATTEND FROM THE SPRING WHEAT STATES. THE MEETING TO BE A DECLARATION OF INDEPENDENCE. THE SOCIETY TO SHOW THE WORLD THAT THE WHEAT GROWER CAN MARKET HIS OWN PRODUCTS WITHOUT THE INTERVENTION OF PARASITES. BOARD OF TRADE DOOMED.[31]

So far as the author can determine, this giant convention was never held. Whether it was or not, public sentiment and opinion were in pronounced ferment.

It was three years later that the Equity Cooperative Exchange was incorporated, in North Dakota. Under its constitution, no one who was not a member of the American Society of Equity could be a member, but neither could an Equity member join it who had not "pledged" to place all his grain in the grain pool and sell it through the Exchange. Thus the Exchange was organized out of Equity members but did not include all of them, did not require approval of the Board of Directors of the Equity Society for what it did, and was in no way subject to the control or supervision of the so-called parent society.

The July issue of the *Equity Farm Journal* carried an article with immense headlines which read: "GREAT ORGANIZING AND PLEDGING CONTEST IN MINNESOTA, NORTH AND SOUTH DAKOTA." The article started with the following sentence: "The American Society of Equity wants 50,000 new members and 50,000,000 bushels of grain pledged in North and South Dakota by next Fall." [32] Later issues carried reports on the "pledging campaign."

Three months later, the president of the Grain Growers' Department reported that arrangements had been made to use "special bins, port

———

[30] *Ibid.*, May 15, 1909, p. 8.
[31] *Ibid.*, p. 9.
[32] *Ibid.*, p. 11.

elevators, loading platforms, etc., to ship and sell in carload lots our pledged grain through our present selling agency, the Equity Cooperative Exchange, of Duluth and Minneapolis, Minnesota, and Superior, Wisconsin." [33] Two months later, President Nelson argued in an article, "It does not concern the grain growers directly how tobacco or potatoes are graded nor the tobacco or potato grower how grain is graded . . ." [34] He was, of course, arguing for special commodity marketing organizations. J. M. Anderson, Secretary-Treasurer of the North Dakota State Union, reported in January, 1910: "The Equity Cooperative Exchange is operating under the direct arrangement of District Union No. 1 of the American Society of Equity. This is the first step taken toward the establishment of a grain marketing machine." [35]

Two weeks later it was reported:

> The afternoon of January 20th was Equity Day at a great four days' meeting at Fargo, North Dakota. Hundreds of people could not even get inside the doors of the largest building in Fargo, the Opera House, on that afternoon. . . . At four o'clock the meeting was resolved into a business session for the purpose of promoting the American Society of Equity Terminal Elevator proposition. . . . The enthusiasm ran high and Theo. G. Nelson, President of the Grain Growers' Department of the Society had his hands full in keeping order. J. M. Anderson and E. Biesbarth, Secretary and Treasurer respectively of District Union No. 1, had to keep going at a lively gait to enroll members and receipt for subscriptions to the terminal elevator proposition as fast as they were offered. We do not have definite information as to what the final tabulation showed the subscriptions to amount to at that meeting, but we know it ran close to $10,000 and it may have exceeded that mark.[36]

The next issue of the *Journal* carried a statement headed "TERMINAL ELEVATOR PROPOSITION A SURE GO." The first sentence read: "That the terminal elevator proposition is sweeping the Northwest like a tidal wave there is no longer any doubt of, and now is the golden hour for grain growers of the country to get together about this promising

------

[33] *Ibid.*, September 15, 1909, p. 16.
[34] *Ibid.*, November 1, 1909, p. 12.
[35] *Ibid.*, January 15, 1910, p. 11.
[36] *Ibid.*, February 15, 1910, p. 16.

institution and be sure that the $50,000 are subscribed before spring work sets in." Another article in the same issue said over $30,000 had been subscribed.[37]

Although the campaign was pushed hard, a report of the meeting of District Union No. 1 held late in July said: "The big question was whether or not the terminal elevator and commission house project should be launched in full blast, or only half blast, or not at all this year." A committee of three was elected to decide this question and another committee of five was appointed "to draw up a set of articles of incorporation and by-laws to be reported to a meeting of share subscribers which is to be held when the $50,000 have been subscribed for." [38]

Probably better than to describe the period just before 1912 as a "passive phase" is to designate it a period of trial and error. During this period the Equity organization did get millions of bushels of grain pledged and did operate through a special agent in Minneapolis. In other words, it tried to break into central grain-exchange marketing and had the grain to do so. It was thwarted because it was not permitted to purchase a seat on the Minneapolis Chamber of Commerce. It had therefore handled only 805 cars of grain by the end of 1912.[39] No one would deny that this accomplishment was slight in comparison to what it later did, or that its attitudes and behavior were relatively passive in comparison to what followed when George Loftus became its business manager. The story of the terrific fight that occurred between the Exchange and the Minneapolis Chamber of Commerce has been told many times and from many angles. Undoubtedly the most authoritative account is that of the Federal Trade Commission, but its report is mundane in comparison with those which reveal the economic and human drama in which Loftus played a major part.

Loftus.played the same role in the Equity Cooperative Exchange that many less capable persons have played in various episodes of the Farmers' Movement. He was a rabble-rousing orator; but far more important, he knew intimately the ins and outs of those practices in the existent system of marketing grain against which the farmers complained. He was born

---

[37] *Ibid.*, March 1, 1910, pp. 8, 9.
[38] *Ibid.*, August 15, 1910, p. 8.
[39] Fossum, p. 83.

on a Wisconsin farm of Irish immigrant parents, and while he lived there only until he was nine years of age, he could claim to be and was always accepted as "a farm boy." As a young man he began working for a railroad as chief clerk in the office of the general freight agent of the St. Paul and Duluth railroad at St. Paul. At twenty-seven years of age, he joined ex-Governor Hubbard in establishing and operating a hay and grain receiving business in St. Paul. This partnership had an elevator on the Northern Pacific tracks at Stillwater, Minnesota, which was in competition with a "line elevator" at that same location. Through what Loftus proved in the courts was discrimination in freight rates between these competitors, his company was forced to the wall. It was this suit, followed by one after another over a number of years, that led him into the farmers' fight about freight rates, demurrage, inspection, grading and mixing of grains, terminal elevator control of line elevators, and domination of central grain marketing by the Minneapolis Chamber of Commerce. When, on September 1, 1912, he was appointed sales manager of the Equity Cooperative Exchange, it is easy to understand, with his backlog of experience, why he became the leading genius of that organization until his death in July, 1916. He could understand the validity of the farmers' complaints better than they could, and he had both the personal drive and the oratorical ability to mobilize them by the thousands for a show-down fight.

Fossum's thesis is that Loftus, because of the animus he had developed against central grain markets and especially against the Minneapolis Chamber of Commerce, and because of his personal misfortunes in the grain business, did the Equity Exchange and the whole cooperative movement considerable damage.[40] Whether this was true or not cannot be determined by the evidence Fossum presents. That Loftus made a tactical mistake in the way he handled some members of the North Dakota legislature in one rough-and-tumble fight was evidenced by some loss of followers in that state. But the fact that the Equity Exchange made progress under his leadership and for a number of years afterward is evidence that his personal talents played a dominant role in the Farmers' Movement. Ex-Senator Usher L. Burdick, in his praise of Loftus, probably fairly validly describes this role as it was accepted by the farmers of the North-

40 *Ibid.*, especially pp. 83-93.

west. He said, "George Loftus served the people and fought corporate greed and selfishness; he abandoned business positions and independent income to serve the farmers for what they could afford to give; he forgot himself and never once in his eventful career abandoned the cause in which he was enlisted." [41] Senator Robert La Follette, Sr., added to the description of the techniques of Loftus's leadership in a tribute to him on the floor of the United States Senate when he said, "Loftus was much more than a detective. His other great side was as a creator of public sentiment. He was a master of men. He stirred men up. He made them think. No man could be bored in any meeting of which Loftus had charge. There was something doing every minute. The audience did not simply sit and listen. Loftus wouldn't let them. Every man had to take sides, either for Loftus or against him." [42]

Enough has been said to show how thoroughly the Equity Cooperative Exchange was a part of the Farmers' Movement. Its pattern of behavior as a part of that movement has been described. Unfortunately its decline as a major episode also somewhat followed the pattern of previous episodes. Its decline did not begin with the death of George Loftus; movements are stronger than their most dynamic leaders. It declined because, as it grew in size and expanded into wider geographic areas, it could not keep all of its complex machinery in balance. Its credit became impaired, conflict developed, and it was finally absorbed by the Farmers' Union in 1934. The profile of its existence and activities had been as follows. It started in 1907 with a grain-holding pledge, buttressed with no marketing machinery except some farmer-owned country elevators; became a terminal elevator, by resolution of a small group, in 1908; was incorporated as a business organization in 1911; had handled only about 800 carloads of grain by 1912; was handling something like ten times that amount per year by 1915; moved from Minneapolis, where it had been unable to purchase a seat on the grain exchange, to St. Paul in 1914; on January 1, 1917, began operating a terminal elevator of its own; it had already purchased two seats on the St. Paul Grain Exchange. It claimed 40,000 stockholders at its peak and had 500 employees, claimed to be operating 70

---

[41] Usher L. Burdick, *The life of George Sperry Loftus, militant leader of the northwest,* Introduction. Second edition. Baltimore, Maryland: Wirth Brothers, 1940.
[42] Quoted by Burdick, p. 73. Reprinted by permission of the author.

country elevators in addition to its terminal elevator. It entered the live-stock-marketing field in 1916 in South St. Paul, and in 1920 made more than six million dollars on livestock sales. It came into conflict with the drive in North Dakota for a state-owned terminal elevator, sponsored by the Nonpartisan League, expanded into undeveloped areas in Montana, and probably overextended credit to local elevators. The end result was squabbling in public, weakening of its financial structure, and absorption by another farmers' organization.

Saloutos concludes his analysis of the decline of the Equity Cooperative Exchange by saying:

> It [the Exchange], no doubt, influenced the local if not the terminal market price; yet sight must not be lost of the fact that the Exchange operated in a period of generally rising price levels. The Exchange influenced the inspecting, weighing, and grading of grain on both the local and terminal markets. The Exchange carried to greater lengths the struggle for better warehousing and credit facilities, something which the Grange, the Alliance, and the Farmers' Union previously had advocated ...
>
> The Exchange came to an untimely ending; yet the fact remains that it bridged the gap between the Grangers, Alliancemen, and Populists, on the one hand, and the Nonpartisan League, the Minnesota Farmer-Labor Party, and the Farmers' Union on the other.[43]

TOBACCO MARKETING AND THE
KENTUCKY NIGHT RIDERS

The same thing happened in the Dark Fire and Burley tobacco areas as in the spring-wheat area and for the same reasons. Both were pronounced commercialized farming areas. There was the same conviction about the need for an all-out commodity marketing attack in Kentucky as existed in North Dakota. There was the same difference in thinking among members of the American Society of Equity on this issue in the two areas. There was the same experience in the two areas of attempts to solve central marketing problems before the Equity Society came on the scene. By 1905, Kentucky was the strongest Equity state in the country,

---

[43] Saloutos, "The Rise of the Equity Cooperative Exchange," p. 62. Reprinted by permission of T. Saloutos and the *Mississippi Valley Historical Review.*

probably because Everitt's marketing plan appealed to its tobacco farmers. It remained strong after Everitt split with the Equity Society and was second only to Wisconsin when the reorganization was accomplished in 1908.

Kentucky organized its tobacco pool in 1904, but believed in the Equity plan of pooling many farm products and believed that poolers should be members of the Society rather than of the Planters' Protective Association, whose plan included all producers of tobacco irrespective of their other affiliations. M. F. Sharp, state organizer for Equity in Kentucky, said, "It seems to me the height of folly to narrow our efforts down to one crop when Kentucky farmers are interested in so many crops." [44] C. O. Drayton said on the same page of the *Equity Farm Journal,* "Let American Society of Equity tobacco growers stick to the American Society of Equity and help us build up the national Union." From these and other published statements, it was evident that Equity was having difficulty keeping its members from affiliating themselves with other more militant tobacco-pooling organizations, first the Protective Association and later the Burley Tobacco Society. The public did not always know the difference between these various tobacco-pooling organizations, and Equity was compelled to defend its good name against the accusations that it was involved in the activities of the more militant organizations.

The Dark Tobacco District Planters' Protective Association of Kentucky and Tennessee was organized in 1904. It was a cooperative that included large and small growers, owners and tenants, Negroes and whites. Its announced purpose was "to protect itself from illegal combination in restraint of trade." Equity organizers were present at its organization meeting to see whether a compromise could be worked out between the two groups, but reported that "the promoters wanted an independent association and were opposed to a national movement." [45] It wanted to include all dark-tobacco growers in order to control, as nearly as possible, the whole supply, and did not therefore want any other eligibility rules for participation except a pledge to deliver tobacco to the Association's pool or to restrict production if need be.

A vigorous campaign for members was carried on by the Planters'

---

[44] *Equity Farm Journal,* July, 1908, p. 9.
[45] *Up-to-Date Farming,* October 1, 1904, p. 6.

Protective Association, with speakers, organizers, and other assistants traveling from headquarters into the local areas asking farmers to sign pledges for the reduction of acreage and the holding of tobacco. The overhead organization consisted of a board of directors, composed of a representative from each district of each county represented in the association, together with an executive committee composed of one person from each county. Membership was not confined to farmers, but included also local and county officials, doctors, lawyers, and other interested citizens.

The movement served quickly to divide the sheep from the goats, and those who did not sign were dubbed "Hill Billies," because, for the most part, they consisted of small growers in the hillier sections of the tobacco area, whose financial destinies were not so completely tied up with the market price of tobacco as were those of the large commercial growers. The tobacco companies naturally made the greatest possible use of the division in the ranks of the farmers by raising the price of tobacco of nonmembers and boycotting the Association's salesmen. This move made it difficult for the Association to hold its members who wanted to participate in the increased prices which the companies were paying for tobacco. The Association, however, weathered its first difficult year by selling several thousand hogsheads of tobacco to an eastern buyer at a slightly lower price than the big companies were paying to the Hill Billies. It entered its second year with a membership of 7,000 in twenty-two counties and with the determination to drive for expanded organization. A mass meeting held in Guthrie, Kentucky, September 23, 1905, was said to include 18,000 people. Tension was high and the farmers determined.

In February, 1906, Virginia joined the protective movement. Tennessee was already in. The sign-up that year was for three-year pledges, or contracts, based on the crop years of 1906, 1907, and 1908. Virginia did not come through with its campaign, but the Kentucky and Tennessee membership was raised to about 12,000. The Association continued to sell some tobacco, but the Hill Billies were receiving greater benefits than the Association members on account of the movement because buyers paid a premium for their tobacco, probably at least partially to encourage others to break their contracts. Another mass meeting was staged at Guthrie, September 22, 1906, attended by 25,000 people. A huge parade led the way to the fairgrounds, where a barbecue dinner was served and many speeches heard. The members and other adherents of the movement left this meeting enthusiastic, but convinced that sign-up pledges were not enough to meet the situation.

In October, thirty-two farmers met one night in a schoolhouse and passed a set of resolutions called "the Resolutions of the Committee of 32 of the Possum Hunters' Organization." [46] The object of the resolutions was to give notice to all nonmembers of the Association that they would be given the opportunity to join and pledge their tobacco; but if they refused, they were to be instructed as to their future course of action. A copy of the resolutions was sent to each county Association for consideration and action. The first thing approaching night riding came when the farmers carried handbills containing these resolutions to the various local meetings of the Association. They went at night chiefly because they were busy in the daytime, but they did not wear masks or carry guns. They said they intended no violence, and when the resolutions were adopted, the Association officials cautioned "no excitement, no indiscretion, no violence." This mandate, however, was not followed to the letter. In December, several tobacco factories were destroyed and at least one tobacco buyer was forced to leave the state.

In response to the Kentucky governor's protest to the chairman of the executive committee of the Planters' Association concerning night visits, the officer replied that "visitations made to certain very aggressive and offensive buyers of the large corporations were only remonstrances." Another officer of the Association, however, stated that lawlessness and night riding must cease, in order not to bring discredit to the Association. This indicated that violence had been practiced. The chief result of these actions was that the small secret group changed its name from "Possum Hunters" to "Night Riders."

During May and June, a few plant beds of Hill Billies were destroyed, and in September and October, a few tobacco barns were burned. In November, a tobacco factory was dynamited. These were not acts of the Protective Association as such. The Night Riders called themselves "The Silent Brigade" or "The Inner Circle."

---

[46] James O. Nall, *The tobacco Night Riders of Kentucky and Tennessee, 1905-1909,* p. 43. Louisville, Kentucky: The Standard Printing Company, 1939.

Their purpose was to force all growers to join the Protective Association, to force independent dealers to cooperate with the Association and to force the trust companies to buy tobacco only from the Association at its set prices. Their intentions were to whip and manhandle persons who opposed them, to destroy the plant beds, tobacco barns, and other property of Hill Billies, to burn the factories and associated holdings of the trust companies and their agents, and to raid towns and cities if these acts were necessary to gain their ends.[47]

Their organization was a fraternal order with a solemn "blood oath" taken by its members. The oath read, "By standing up in this meeting I solemnly pledge myself to take arms and shed blood for the association."[48] Meetings were held at night, and all plans were strictly secret. The organization had a code of signals, a password, and a badge of white cloth for identification. Most of the men wore masks when out on night-riding activities. They carried shotguns, revolvers, or rifles; rode horses, or mules, or drove buggies. Their organization was set up in a military fashion with a general and lieutenant in charge who sent out orders to colonels, captains, and lieutenants under them. A colonel was in charge of each county; a captain was in charge of each lodge of twelve men; and lieutenants were appointed to assist the captains. The rank and file were organized into groups of eight men—seven privates and a lieutenant—and were known by numbers instead of by their names.

Robert Penn Warren, in his novel *Night Rider*, probably rather validly described the sentiment and experiences of the men who joined in this tragic episode. The following is an excerpt from his description:

Mr. Munn went to the table, which stood some ten feet away from the lantern and directly in front of it. He touched his fingers to the table-top, and waited. On the table a book lay, a Bible, an ordinary kind of Bible with worn, imitation leather covers. He had seen many a Bible like that, many a one, lying on the table in the family room of a farmhouse, or on the mantelpiece beside a carved wood clock, probably, and a glass vase full of paper spills, and a spectacle case.

----

[47] *Ibid.*, p. 52. Reprinted by permission of The Standard Printing Company.
[48] Quoted by *Equity Farm Journal,* March, 1908, from the *Henderson* (Kentucky) *Journal.*

"Percy Munn," the voice said, "you are about to take a most serious step. It is not necessary to impress upon you the gravity of that step. And about to take a most sacred oath. If you are to turn back, now is the time to turn back."

Someone coughed twice in the darkness. Mr. Munn turned his head slightly toward that direction.

"You can turn your back now and go out of this room and mount your horse and ride away and never speak one word of your coming here tonight, and no single soul will think the less of your manhood. But now is the time. Look in your heart and mind, and consider."

Mr. Munn waited with his eyes raised above the direct rays of the light. There was silence for some thirty or forty seconds.

"Percy Munn," the voice said, "Are you clear in your mind, and determined?"

"I am," Mr. Munn said.

"You are about to take the oath of membership in the Free Farmers' Brotherhood for Protection and Control. The sole purpose of this organization is to see that a fair price is paid for dark fired tobacco, and it will adopt such means as seem advisable to further that purpose. Are you, Percy Munn, prepared to take the oath?"

"I am," Mr. Munn said.

"Place your left hand upon that book."

Mr. Munn did so.

"That book, Percy Munn, is the Holy Bible. An oath taken upon it and in God's name is sacred for all time and eternity. Will you swear upon it?"

"I will," Mr. Munn said.

"Raise your right hand and repeat these words," and the voice proceeded: "I, Percy Munn, knowing the injustice under which our people groan—" and it paused for Mr. Munn to repeat the words.

"I, Percy Munn, knowing the injustice under which our people groan—" Mr. Munn said slowly and distinctly.

"—and being willing to abide it no longer—"

Mr. Munn repeated: "—and being willing to abide it no longer—"

The voice resumed: "—do swear on this holy book and on the name of God our Creator . . . that I will steadfastly support the purpose of the Free Farmers' Brotherhood for Protection and Control . . . and whatever measures may be deemed advisable for the accomplishment of that purpose—and that I will loyally obey the commands of the truly elected officers superior to me in this organization—and that never, under any circumstances, will I speak one word of this organization or its affairs—to any man or woman not of this organization—not excepting the wife of my bosom.—This I solemnly swear."

"—This I solemnly swear," Mr. Munn concluded. He removed his hand from the book.

"Come forward," the voice said, and he walked across the intervening ten feet or so of floor toward the lantern and the voice. He passed beyond the range of the lantern's rays, was completely blind for an instant before his eyes could accustom themselves to the dark, and then saw the man standing behind the table that supported the lantern, and the other men sitting on benches and boxes beyond. The man behind the lantern shook Mr. Munn's hand, and said, "Well, sir, we're happy to welcome you in."

"Thank you," Mr. Munn said. He peered at the man's face, thinking he had seen it somewhere before, but in that light he couldn't be sure.

"If you'll just have a seat, we'll be proceeding," the man said.

One of the men on the bench just behind the table moved over, and Mr. Munn sat down beside him.

He watched the other men, one after another, come through the door over there across the wide floor, and stand motionless just inside it until the voice gave the command, and then move slowly forward, blinking at the light. Some of them peered hard at a spot just by the light, straining, apparently, to penetrate the depth of darkness where people were; and others, as Mr. Munn himself had done, lifted their eyes toward the obscurity of the ceiling. The first kind were nervous, and they would wet the lips with the tongue before they began to repeat the words of the oath. Mr. Munn tried to recall whether or not he himself had wet his lips that way. He had not been nervous, he decided. He had really felt nothing, nothing at all, when he stood out there in the middle of the floor in the full beam of the light. That was what surprised him. A man was due to feel something out there, taking the oath. Then he began to think how the taking of the oath changed the relation of all those men to each other there beside him in the dark. The oath had said, God our Creator. He wondered how many of those men believed in God. And then if he himself did. It had been a long time since he had thought of that, he remembered. The man who was, at that moment, taking the oath finished, and at the command, advanced to join the group in the shadow.[49]

When the Night Riders were fully organized and ready for action, they gave public notice of this fact through a proclamation, sent through the mails to the county newspapers. The Protective Association disavowed any connection with the Night Riders and passed a formal resolution expressing disapproval of any lawlessness or acts of violence, but this did not impede the Night Riders nor did it prove that Association members had nothing to do with the episode. The Night Riders themselves claimed they were an inner circle of the Association. Their chief activities were: (1) to destroy the plant beds of nonmembers; (2) to destroy the property of the tobacco companies. This latter activity was accomplished in a highly organized and effective manner. When an attack was made upon a town where tobacco company properties were located, the Night Riders destroyed all telephone and telegraphic communications by cutting wires; announced their approach to the general citizenry by a volley of gun fire, and then went about their business of dynamiting warehouses and factories. Properties in the three Kentucky towns of Princeton, Hopkinsville, and Russellville, estimated at the value of $160,000 to $185,000, were destroyed in these activities.[50]

Such activities, of course, led to sharp reaction, but not until after a number of farmers had their plant beds destroyed, a number of them had been whipped, and a few had been forced to leave the area of operation. Some deaths resulted, although they were few in number, and killing was never a deliberate intention on the part of the Night Riders. Court actions followed by convictions were ineffective because it was almost impossible to assemble juries who were not, to some extent, in sympathy with the distressed growers. The Hill Billies did some night riding of their own, scraped tobacco beds of Association members, and burned some barns.

The Night Riders claimed they succeeded in bringing the membership

---

[49] Robert Penn Warren, *Night Rider*, pp. 154-157. Reprinted by permission of Random House, Inc. Copyright, 1930 by Robert Penn Warren.

[50] See Martha McCulloch-Williams, "The Tobacco War in Kentucky," *American Review of Reviews*, February, 1908. H. L. Beach, "The Great Tobacco War," *The Saturday Evening Post*, August 3, 1907; January 18, 1908. "Night Riders," *Outlook*, February 29, 1908.

of the Protective Association up to 30,000 in Kentucky and Tennessee, and precipitated a crisis which was beyond the capacity of the local officials to control. The old-line tobacco companies, however, purchased as little Association tobacco as possible and consistently paid lower prices than they did to non-Association growers. Townspeople formed a Law and Order League, organized volunteer groups to guard their towns against raids, and called out the militia. By 1909, the people were tired of violence and desperately wanted peace. Court action, use of militia, counter organization, and the desire for peace in the area caused the Night Riders to disband. The Protective Association lost members rapidly, declined in influence, and was disbanded after a few years.

In the period of greatest activity of the Night Riders, the American Society of Equity, although not sponsoring or even agreeing with either the Night Riders or the Protective Association, gained members and continued to operate tobacco warehouses in Kentucky. They claimed an 80 per cent sign-up of "pooling pledges" in the "Green River District," and at one stage of successful operation issued an "ultimatum" to non-members that they would have to sign up or be denied the use of Equity warehouses.[51] Such a move might indicate that Equity itself had degenerated into a purely tobacco-pooling organization. That this was not the case is clearly evident from the part Equity members in Kentucky were at that time and afterward playing in the broader program of the American Society. It did resist and condemn the Night Riders and it at first stringently opposed such strong action, even in marketing, as the Protective Association practiced. It, however, later joined hands with the Burley Tobacco Society in a direct-action attack on the price and market problems of the tobacco growers.

In 1909, the Burley Tobacco Society conducted a big sign-up campaign which not only pledged growers to deliver to a pool all the tobacco they grew or controlled, but to pay "liquidated damages" if they failed to do so.[52]

Two articles in the *Equity Farm Journal* in July, 1909, showed how opposed the Society was to this method and how anxious it was not to

---

[51] *Up-to-Date Farming*, October 1, 1906.
[52] *Equity Farm Journal*, August 1, 1909, p. 11.

be identified in the public mind with the Burley Society. One article said:

> We have received several letters from Kentucky, some of them very forceful in expression, about the Burley Tobacco Society and some of them saying that if this is the way the American Society of Equity proposes to do they will drop it at once and never have a thing to do with it again.

The other article said:

> The National Union of the American Society of Equity and the State Union of Kentucky should rush every available man who loves his fellow man and would save him from signing such a cunningly devised cut-throat scheme, as that pledge would run him into the Burley section and warn them to beware before they wreck with one stroke of the pen the fruits of their previous efforts to better their conditions.[53]

The next issue of the *Journal* gave its explanation of what had happened. It said that a large number of Equity men had pooled their tobacco with the Burley Society under the impression that it was a part of the American Society of Equity; that the Burley Society had asserted that it was a part of Equity, but that "no sooner did the managers of the Burley Tobacco Society get their fingers on more than $300,000 as their margin of expenses than they decided they were strong enough to cut loose from all pretense of connection with the American Society of Equity."[54]

This conflict was more in the open than the one between the Co-operative Exchange and the Society of Equity in the spring-wheat area because the Society itself was attempting to operate a tobacco pool. The object here is to emphasize that in the two great cash-crop areas of wheat and tobacco, the indirect and slower methods of the American Society of Equity in attacking the price and market problem were not considered adequate by those farmers who were deeply involved in commercial production, and that in both areas those favoring more direct action prevailed. As a matter of fact, the Burley Society and the Ken-

---

[53] *Ibid.*, July 15, 1909, p. 5.
[54] *Ibid.*, August 1, 1909, p. 4.

tucky Union of the Society of Equity joined hands in October, 1909, in order that they might more nearly control the whole Burley crop and not be played off one against the other by the "tobacco trust." [55] This coalition by no means solved the marketing problems of tobacco growers. The joint-tobacco pool suffered the same fate as the Equity Cooperative Exchange, and did so much more quickly.

The Night Riders were not Equity men, and their activities were not even sanctioned by the Tobacco Protective Association, but they staged one of the few demonstrations of violence in the long history of the American Farmers' Movement. Their display of violence, like the revolt of the Virginia and Maryland tobacco growers one hundred and fifty years earlier, came at the hands of farmers whose almost complete financial destiny rested on the price and market problems of a cash crop.

[55] *Ibid.*, October 1, 1909, p. 10.

· 1 7 ·

THE

NONPARTISAN LEAGUE

THE LEAGUE AS PART OF THE
FARMERS' MOVEMENT

The Nonpartisan League had a number of important roots, but its taproot was sunk deep in the centuries-old Farmers' Movement. The general economic conditions of North Dakota nurtured it and socialistic sentiment fertilized it. It made conjunction with the Progressive political movement of the Northwest, and itself became a thoroughgoing political organization. But the almost countless accounts that have been written on one or another of its activities, together tell the story of one of the most exciting episodes in the Farmers' Movement. Its political activities were by no means unrelated to the old grain-growers' economic battle against the railroads, terminal elevators, and grain exchanges. It developed out of the same economic situation and wrestled with the same price and market problems as the Equity Cooperative Exchange.

During the course of the League's history, its leaders and protagonists just about ran the gamut of complaints about which the Farmers' Movement had revolved for the previous fifty years. They said the federal government had given extensive and valuable land grants to the railroads to induce them to bring the northern plains into market production; that the same financial interests that developed the railroads also developed and controlled the central grain markets of Duluth, Minneapolis, St. Paul, and Chicago; that the boards of trade of these cities were tools of these interests; and therefore that railroads, elevators, mills, and all credit facilities essential not only to marketing but to farming were in the hands of a virtual monopoly. They said this system involved control of freight rates, interest rates, grading, inspection, dockage, storage, and milling of grain—in short, all the marketing, financing, and processing steps which served to spread costs between producer and consumer. It was frequently said in North Dakota, "The farmer raised a bushel [of wheat] and got paid for a peck; the consumer received a peck and paid for a bushel." [1]

The farmers of the wheat-growing states had registered many protests against the methods by which the grain business was conducted. As early as 1892, there was an uprising in North Dakota as the result of a veto by the Governor of a bill favored by the Farmers' Alliance, to force railroads to lease sites on their rights of way for grain elevators and warehouses. A fusion of the Farmers' Alliance, the Populists, and the Democrats resulted in the election of their own man as Governor, and under his administration a small amount of money was appropriated for a farmer-controlled terminal elevator at Duluth. This effort was short-lived, due to the panic of 1893 or other reasons, and nothing further was done about the elevator for some time.

In 1906 there was a more determined effort, inspired by the same economic grievances on the part of the farmers, but outwardly by a political battle between the conservative Republican machine and the "insurgents," headed nationally by Senator Robert M. La Follette of Wisconsin, and organized within North Dakota by George Winship, then editor and owner of the Grand Forks *Herald,* and Burleigh F. Spalding and John Sorley, organizers. These three men, dissatisfied with the methods of the administration in office, sensing the wide discontent of the farmers, and favoring replacing the caucus and convention system of nominating candidates with primary elections, set about to organize a "revolution." Sorley formed the "Scandinavian Voters' League," com-

---

[1] Chas. E. Russell, *The story of the Nonpartisan League,* p. 11. New York: Harper & Brothers, 1920.

posed largely of Norwegians who then represented about 40 per cent of the voters of North Dakota. Spalding, whose renomination for Congress had been withheld by the Republican convention of 1903, and given to Ansel Gronna instead, organized his followers. The Norwegians, traditionally Republican, became convinced that the old Republican machine represented "Big Business," which was charging too much interest on their money, manipulating the price of wheat, and controlling their vote; and they lined up solidly with the insurgents. Their "war cry was 'North Dakota for North Dakotans' and the object of their anathema was 'Big Business.'" [2] A coalition of insurgent Republicans with the Democrats elected a farmers' Governor. They also gained control of both houses of the legislature.

The episode of the Equity Cooperative Exchange was told in an earlier chapter, but it should be recalled that the Exchange movement was spearheaded by North Dakotans. It had traveled a rocky road up to 1914 and, as will be seen later, was party to the founding of the Nonpartisan League.

The militant action on the part of the cash grain growers was accompanied by milder attacks on them and their other farming problems by nonfarmers. The "Better Farming Movement" was sponsored by the banks, lumber companies, grain houses, implement dealers, and mail-order houses. Its objective was to convince farmers that they could solve many of their problems by better farming methods. This movement was well supported by lectures and circulars and was capped in 1915 by an "Appreciation Week" set aside by the Governor of the state as a general week of "thanksgiving for the great resources of the state." The slogan for this occasion was, "Boost, don't knock." These were probably laudable undertakings, but like the advice given to Alliancemen "to raise more corn and less hell," it was received by the distraught grain growers as an insult. Both "Better Farming" literature and "Appreciation Week" were supported by advertising of the businessmen, and the farmers saw this fact and the whole effort as proof of a countermove on the part of the "interests" they were fighting.

After repeated unsuccessful efforts to improve their situation, the

---

[2] A. A. Bruce, *The Non-Partisan League*, pp. 21, 28; chap. x. Third Edition. New York: Henry Holt and Company, 1927.

farmers of North Dakota finally became convinced that a state-owned terminal elevator at the important terminal market of Minneapolis, St. Paul, or Duluth was their only way into central markets, and that they must get into central markets directly to keep from being slaves of a system over which they had no control. As early as 1912, the people of the state had ratified by a vote of three to one a constitutional amendment to provide for the erection of a state-owned terminal elevator outside of North Dakota. Two years later, a popular vote ratified another constitutional amendment, by the same margin, for such an elevator within or outside of the state. The 1914 legislature, after passing a special assessment for the state elevator ($75,000), instructed the State Board of Control to go ahead with plans. The Board of Control, however, used the fund, with the aid of a special committee, to investigate the feasibility of the elevator. The result was a 600-page report showing a terminal elevator unnecessary. The legislature, acting on this report, then repealed the tax that was to have provided funds to build the elevator. When the 1915 legislature convened, the farmers petitioned it to carry out the mandate of the people, twice expressed very decisively on this question. The house of representatives turned the demand down by a vote of 64 to 40.[3] This action planted the seeds that grew into the revolt that followed.

Each major episode in the development of a movement brings the movement to high tide by a sharply focused public, and the development of a public is accomplished by the exposition of issues in which an increasing number and diversity of persons participate. Newspaper editors, journalists, politicians, ministers, educators, and nearly-always-self-seeking propagandists sooner or later become involved. Their contributions are varied and the viewpoints of some of them are highly colored. But they all help to develop the public which is forming or in operation. Because the Nonpartisan League episode was near enough to our time to make a record of its almost every move, we shall attempt to exploit that record for the purpose of laboratory observation.

As early as 1900, Robert M. La Follette, of Wisconsin, in a good many ways the spiritual father of the Nonpartisan League, began publicly to

---

[3] *Legislative manual.* Bismarck, North Dakota: North Dakota Department of State, 1915.

expose facts concerning railroad freight rates and discriminatory practices, tariffs, line elevators, trusts, local and state government scandals,
and to carry these findings to the people of Wisconsin and other states
by means of lecture tours. His vigorous, militant, spellbinding messages
were heard by many thousands throughout the Middlewest and Northwest. Perhaps his most vehement attack was on the railroads and their
"monopolistic practices." In a speech delivered in Des Moines, Iowa, in
October of 1905, entitled "Shall It Be the Railways or the People?" he
is quoted as saying:

> The will of combinations, and chiefly the railroads, is now the
> law of the land. The people have fallen under an industrial servi-
> tude because the prices of their products and the particles they
> consume are fixed for them. Industrial servitude and political liberty
> cannot exist simultaneously . . . there is no line of important business
> which is not controlled by a trust . . . The railroad is the most pow-
> erful of all of these interests. . . The railroads are as much highways
> as the roads which the state maintains through the state of Iowa,
> but the people have given the private corporations which operate
> them the right to establish uncontrolled toll gates upon them; these
> highways are public institutions, for the people built them, giving
> them land equal to the area of Ohio, Indiana, Iowa, Missouri, Illi-
> nois and Wisconsin. It is established that transportation is a function
> of the government. It is for the government to try to control rates
> and if unsuccessful to take over the railroads.[4]

Regarding the line elevator and grain-marketing situation, chief issues
of the grain growers, he had this to say on the floor of Congress in 1906:

> Within the last few years the system of marketing our grain
> crops has completely changed . . . In the days of an open market
> . . . the bidding was genuine, and the grain was sold to the highest
> bidder in a real competitive market. Today the farmer must hunt
> the different buyers in their offices and ask the price. Each quotes
> him the same price. They have little concern as to which one buys
> the grain, as the profits are pooled. If any buyer purchases more
> than his share, he is subject to a penalty.
> The farmer has no alternative. He must sell his grain to one of

---

[4] *Register and Leader* (Des Moines, Iowa), October 10, 1905. Reprinted by permission
of *The Des Moines Register.*

the elevators at his local station. He cannot ship it himself. The railroad will not give him cars, and if he could get cars he could hardly find a dealer who would handle his grain in the market. The need of the farmer for money is in almost all cases urgent. The merchant is impatient for a settlement of his account; the banker demands payment of his notes; the harvest hands must be paid in cash.[5]

The whole enterprise of North Dakota agriculture, especially wheat farming, was tied up with this system. The farmers' complaint was that when he needed money for seed, fertilizer, machinery, or labor to put in a wheat crop, he paid interest rates of from 10 to 14 per cent, in some cases in the early days 15 to 24 per cent, and for small loans even as high as 28 to 48 per cent.[6] After the crop was harvested, he had to obtain transportation facilities at freight rates which he claimed were dictated by absentee stockholders in the railroad companies. Sometimes he was forced to let his shipment stand idle on a railroad siding while the prices on the Minneapolis market "mysteriously went downhill." At the line elevator, owned for the most part by the railroad companies, the farmer's wheat was weighed and the freight rate and handling charges involved in transporting the wheat to Minneapolis were "fixed" by the company. After the wheat got to market, it was again weighed, inspected, and graded. At this point, the farmer, who had paid for transporting the uncleaned wheat, received credit only for the cleaned wheat; the dockage (screenings) was kept and sold by and for the company for livestock feed at about $8.00 per ton. In addition to this, the farmer felt sure that much of the wheat he sold as No. 2 or 3 came out on the market as No. 1, but that he was paid for No. 2 or 3 and was at the mercy of the company inspector as to which grade turned up.[7]

What the farmer called the "game of selling" the wheat was carried on in markets in Chicago, New York, and Liverpool, where trading in futures was practiced, a kind of trading never understood by the farm-

---

[5] *Congressional record*, 59th Congress, 1st Session, p. 9091. June 25, 1906, Robert M. La Follette, speaking to his resolution that the Interstate Commerce Commission investigate the elevator and grain forwarding business of the country.

[6] Russell, p. 35.

[7] *Ibid.*, chap. iii. See also Herbert E. Gaston, *The Nonpartisan League*, chap. iii. New York: Harcourt, Brace & Company, Inc., 1920.

ers. This trading was handled by private brokers on a commission basis, with the possibility—in fact, probability—of the same shipment changing hands three or four times. To the farmer this was pure gambling with a commodity into which he had put money and hard work. He felt that numerous middlemen dipped into the potential or prospective profits of the shipment of wheat, and finally the farmer received only a "miserable little pittance" with which to pay back his banker, live until the next season's crop had been sold, and start the new crop for "someone else to make money on." The whole elaborate system seemed to the farmer to protect everyone except the producer of wheat. He said he was producing "the staff of life"—wheat—"and was going broke doing it." [8]

Probably the best evidence of how all-encompassing a specialized public can be, once it is in process of formation, was the part played by the North Dakota Agricultural Experiment Station in dealing with some of the issues which the farmers of that state believed were involved in the marketing and prices of wheat. As early as 1905 the state legislature had passed a law which made it the duty of the state agricultural experiment station "to conduct experiments and determine the comparative milling values of the different grades of wheat and baking tests of flours made therefrom." This law was on the trail of what the farmers of the state were convinced was a double-barreled racket—the mixing of grades after the wheat was shipped out of the state, and a discrimination against the flour made from lower grades. [9]

Experiments were begun in 1907, and, in January of 1915, Professor E. F. Ladd of the North Dakota State College of Agriculture published the first report on the 1907-1914 findings. [10] This was followed by another report in January, 1916; another in November, 1916; and still another in January, 1917. The first paragraph of Professor Ladd's first bulletin read as follows:

———

[8] "North Dakota's 'Revolution,'" *Literary Digest,* Vol. IX, No. 13 (March 29, 1919), pp. 12-13. Quoting from Arthur Capper's *Farmers' Mail and Breeze* (Topeka, Kansas).

[9] *Legislative manual.* North Dakota Department of State.

[10] E. F. Ladd, *Is the present system of grading wheat equitable?* North Dakota Agricultural Experiment Station Special Bulletin, Food Department, Vol. III, No. 14. North Dakota: Agricultural College, January, 1915.

Does the producer receive a fair price for all grades of wheat? This question has been repeatedly asked, and in comparing the different types and grades of wheat coming under observation one has been forced to take note of this question in previous years but never before has the question been so forcibly presented as with the 1914 crop.[11]

In his second bulletin, published after the state legislature had refused to follow the mandate of the referendum to establish a state-owned terminal elevator, he said:

> It would seem, therefore, that we would be justified in concluding that the present system of grading wheat is not equitable, and that the difference between No. 1 and No. 4 and Rejected is too large a margin, and the farmer whose wheat grades low does not receive a fair compensation in proportion to its true value for milling purposes.[12]

These were strong statements from an authoritative source and were used liberally by the leaders of farmer discontent.

In his third bulletin, published after the Nonpartisan League had won in the 1916 election, Professor Ladd made a statement which furnished the League with its slogan, "the racket in Grade D Feed Wheat." The statement was:

> For example, in Grade D Feed, the carload cost $653.01, as compared with $1,526.75 for Grade No. 1 Northern; while the increase in selling price over that of the cost price for Feed A wheat would be $1,454.02 and only $1,031.72 on No. 1 Northern. This would seem to lead back to the original question as given in our first bulletin,—"Is the Present System of Grading Wheat Equitable?" [13]

Because Professor Ladd used direct rather than restrained language, because his findings validated the farmers' complaints, and because he was later elected to the United States Senate by the League, some of his

---

[11] *Ibid.,* p. 233.
[12] E. F. Ladd, *Chemical and physical constants for wheat and mill products,* p. 294. North Dakota Agricultural Experiment Station Bulletin No. 114. North Dakota: Agricultural College, January, 1916.
[13] E. F. Ladd, *North Dakota wheat for 1916.* Bulletin No. 119, 1916. Ladd, *Practical milling tests.* Circular No. 15, 1917.

intellectual colleagues have been inclined to discount his findings. The point made here is that he, as a scientist and an employee of the State Agricultural Experiment Station, made a contribution, whether wittingly or not, to the opinion and sentiment involved in the Nonpartisan League public. It should, however, be recorded that Federal Trade Commission investigations corroborated his findings. The Commission found that the Minneapolis market in 1912-1913 reported "in" 46.1 per cent No. 1 Northern wheat, but reported "out" 56.5 per cent; that it reported "in" 30.2 per cent No. 2 Northern, but reported "out" only 26.1 per cent. They graded up some No. 3 also. The records for the succeeding four years showed the same practices. During the five years covered by the Commission's investigation, the elevators of Minneapolis disposed of almost nine million more bushels of No. 1 Northern than they purchased, disposed of more than three million more bushels of No. 2 Northern than they purchased, and disposed of almost four million more bushels of No. 3 than they purchased; but they disposed of almost eleven million bushels less of "Lower" grades than they purchased. They could and did do this by mixing lower with higher grades as far as possible without diluting the higher grades below established and inspected standards.[14]

The farmers, of course, sold their wheat at the lower grades at which the elevators purchased. Professor Ladd not only revealed these facts to North Dakota farmers in terms of their own losses, but, by systematic experiments and tests, proved that the baking qualities of the lower grades did not justify the wide difference in prices which prevailed in local markets between them and the higher grades. He calculated that North Dakota farmers lost, through terminal elevator mixing operations, $1,978,060 on every 100,000,000 bushels of wheat they sent to market.[15] Furthermore, they failed to collect for any of the by-products (screenings, bran, and shorts) which were sold back to farmers for stock feed by the millers. His bulletins were given wide circulation by the Nonpartisan League, and their official paper, *The Nonpartisan Leader*, saw to it that these "crimes against the farmers" were given wide and constant publicity.

[14] *Report of the Federal Trade Commission on the grain trade*, Vol. III: "Terminal Grain Marketing," pp. 313-315. Washington, D. C.: Government Printing Office, 1922.

[15] Ladd, Bulletin 114, p. 287.

THE NORTH DAKOTA FARMERS MOBILIZE
FOR ACTION

It was not by accident that George Loftus of the Equity Exchange called a state-wide meeting of the American Society of Equity in Bismarck while the legislature was in session in 1915. The Equity farmers were enraged at the indifference of the legislature and were eager to demonstrate their wrath by meeting at the state capital in impressive numbers. At a joint session of the legislature one afternoon, Loftus even called the roll of the state legislators, compelling them to go on record, one after the other, on the farmers' demands, chiefly for a state-owned elevator.[16]

It happened that at this same time A. E. Bowen, a prominent Socialist organizer, was conducting meetings in Bismarck in which he was presenting facts and figures on the economic conditions of the North Dakota wheat farmers, including Professor E. F. Ladd's investigations on D Feed wheat and other matters. Some Equity farmers were undoubtedly members of Bowen's audience.

The Bismarck meetings of the legislature and the Equity served as a magnet to another very interested spectator—Arthur C. Townley, a bankrupt bonanza wheat and flax farmer of Beach, North Dakota, a former Socialist organizer, and soon to be the founder of the Nonpartisan League. The story of how he made conjunction with, and helped to develop, a powerful farmers' public in North Dakota needs to be related as a part of the tactics of a movement.

The role Townley played as leader in the Nonpartisan League warrants a brief description of his personality and earlier experiences. Like George Loftus, leader of the Equity Cooperative Exchange, he had a compelling personality, and like Loftus he had had a bitter experience in the grain business. It cannot be claimed that these two men provide a pattern of Farmers' Movement leadership, but attention should be called to the fact that no movement succeeds unless, in its stage of ascendancy, it does have some such type of leadership.

Charles Edward Russell, editor of *The Nonpartisan Leader*, described

---

[16] Interview with Congressman William Lemke of North Dakota, November 28, 1940.

Townley as a man with eager determination, resourcefulness, and with a cool, calculating intellect; a person who could devote his boundless energies to a single purpose with near-fanaticism, using every means possible to advance that cause. He said Townley also proved to be a master at organization and difficult to excel in platform speaking.[17]

In 1910, Townley had borrowed money, rented land in the Golden Valley of North Dakota near the Montana border, and obtained farm machinery on credit. His first crop of flax was a success, so the next year he reinvested his profits and as much more as he could borrow and raised flax on a larger scale. This year was even more profitable than the first, netting him about $50,000. Again he invested all of his profits, borrowed all he could, rented more land, bought more tractors, and started the season of 1912 with a real bonanza flax farm. But this time his luck failed to hold, the weather ruined part of the crop, the bottom dropped out of prices, and his venture left him not only bankrupt but something like $100,000 in debt.[18] He is said to have resolved after this experience to "break the grain trust," which he believed manipulated the market that ruined him.[19]

About a year after the complete collapse of the costly flax venture, Townley turned his energies toward obtaining memberships for the Socialist party. He had decided that the only hope for the farmer lay in breaking the "system" which was keeping him broke—the farm machinery companies, the controllers of "usury" rates, and the grain speculators. He was convinced that this could be accomplished only through political control of the state; he was equally convinced that the two major parties in the state could not be counted on to solve the farmer's problem. Hence, he turned to the Socialist party and became one of its paid organizers. Saloutos says, "the Socialist Party of North Dakota was a fairly well-organized unit from 1908 to 1914, despite the predominance of agricultural population in the state, and the party's influence was greater than its membership figures would indicate"; that it

---

[17] Interview with Russell, October 18, 1940.

[18] Chester H. Rowell, "The Political Cyclone in North Dakota and the Economic Cycle Which Is at the Heart of the Trouble," *World's Work,* Vol. XLVI, No. 3 (July, 1923). Gaston, p. 49.

[19] O. M. Thomason, *The beginning and the end of the Nonpartisan League.* St. Paul, Minnesota: 1920.

had espoused the causes of state-owned elevators and mills, credit, banks, and other farmer reforms. It had established an "organization department" which could solicit farmer membership without requiring them to join the party. It was for this organization department that Townley was working.[20]

Townley persuaded a farmer friend to sign a note for the necessary cash with which to buy a Ford car and was soon traveling over the state enlisting Republicans and Democrats in the organization department of the Socialist party, which he told them would do something about the farmers' problems. When he discovered how many more memberships he was able to secure than he had been able to get when he had traveled on foot, he decided that there should be many more organizers and many more Fords. He presented this idea to the Socialist state committee, but they said his plan was too irregular. They were also suspicious of the brand of socialism he was preaching, and, in fact, abolished the organization department of the party because it was getting out of hand. Townley was disgusted. He said, "Too many of them didn't want to get anywhere, it seemed to me. In methods they were as conservative as the old parties. Offer them a plan by which they could really accomplish something instead of mere talking, and they were afraid of it."[21]

It was not long after his break with the Socialist party that Townley went to the Equity Society meeting at Bismarck, called by George Loftus. While there, he talked to many Equity and Equity Exchange men. One of his most important talks was with F. B. Wood, a prominent Equity member from Deering, North Dakota, whom he had known previously. In the following February (1915), he went to Wood's farm to talk with him further. Wood was interested but at first wary of Townley's grandiose scheme. He was, however, interested in Townley as a person who compelled his attention with shrewd arguments, and he admired his determination, faith, and energy.[22] Townley remained at the Woods'

[20] Saloutos describes these relationships and gives much detail on the Socialist party and Townley which are not included here. See T. Saloutos, "The Rise of the Nonpartisan League in North Dakota, 1915-1917, *Agricultural History*, Vol. XX, January, 1946, pp. 43-61.

[21] Theodore Saloutos, "The Expansion and Decline of the Nonpartisan League in the Western Middle West, 1917-1921," *Agricultural History*, Vol. XX, No. 4 (October, 1946), pp. 235-252.

[22] Gaston, p. 54.

farmhouse for several days, long enough to win completely the support of Mr. Wood and his two sons, Howard and Edwin.

Townley and Howard Wood started out at once in Wood's old Ford, going from farmhouse to farmhouse to spread their faith in organization and to explain how they believed it could be successfully done. They were armed with only a pledge of support, signed first by the three Woods, which carried with it annual dues of $2.50.[23] On the first day, they obtained the signatures of nine farmers; in six days they had seventy-nine, with no refusals. They proceeded to organize three townships in that county, but since the farmers had all paid their dues in postdated checks, they soon ran out of cash for gasoline. Howard Wood then got a note for $1,200 discounted at the bank, and they used the money to buy gasoline for three cars to put into the membership campaign. A meeting was called at Glenburn and $925 subscribed, which was immediately used to send out two more cars.

Organizers were then sent out on a commission basis to enroll still more farmers; this brought many volunteers into the campaign and the number of cars grew steadily from ten to twenty, then forty, and later sixty, operating in all parts of the state. By July, 10,000 farmers had banded themselves together in a common purpose. That they were organizing the Nonpartisan League was not at first announced; for months, the League membership campaign was kept a carefully guarded secret. Towns of any size were assiduously avoided and work was always begun in the most rural sections of a county.

Townley's plan of organizing the farmers, based partly on his former experience as a Socialist organizer, was carefully worked out in all details. He and his lieutenants would meet at night in the lobby of the post office at Beach, where John Baer, later cartoonist and Congressman for the League, was then postmaster. Townley would instruct the organizers in the general line of argument, how to answer opposition, and what some of the facts were that would give weight to their cause. Scandinavians would go into Scandinavian territory, Catholics to the Catholic farmers. To each farmhouse would go an organizer, a lecturer

---

[23] The dues were for a short time $2.50 per year, but were soon raised to $6.00, then $9.00 per year, and later were changed to $16.00 for a two-year membership. The dues at first included a year's subscription to *Pearson's Magazine* and *The Nonpartisan Leader*, but after the first year or so included only the *Leader*.

or speaker, and a neighbor or at least another farmer. One of these men would approach the farmer himself, talk to him about the ideals of the movement, give him figures on economic conditions in the wheat trade, and use all possible salesmanship to sign him up. The two men who came with the organizer were present to lend moral support, and if necessary to head off the farmer's wife by engaging her in conversation lest she intervene and prevent her husband from signing up. Usually the organizer was kept free of interruptions and came out triumphantly with the farmer's signature and a postdated check.[24]

At the end of a week of membership campaigning, Townley would call a meeting of his organizers, speakers, and workers to take inventory and improve the selling technique. The man who brought in the most memberships for that week was asked to present his sales talk to the meeting. The others would take notes on it, incorporate the best points in their own speeches, and use them in the campaign the following week. In the very earliest days of the League, when the organizers were all carefully hand-picked and conditions were ripe for the movement, this was about all the sales training the workers needed or received. It was not very difficult to get good organizers because they received $2.00 to $5.00 for each cash membership as their commission, and some of them were able to make sizeable earnings.[25]

The crowning event in the membership campaign was the big picnic or schoolhouse gathering to which Townley and the best League speakers came to address the farmers, arouse their enthusiasm, and prepare the way for organizers to sign up all who had not yet done so. Townley was at his best at a meeting of this kind, speaking to the crowd as their trusted confidante and advisor, and he usually succeeded in turning the meeting into something reminiscent of a Billy Sunday revival or one of the early Populist gatherings.[26] This type of meeting was a very effective device in reaching large numbers of farmers with their best talent. This public kind of assembly was not held, however, until the League membership drive was well under way and known to the opposition.

---

[24] Interview with John Baer, Washington, D. C., September, 1940.
[25] A. A. Bruce, p. 72. Organizers were later paid even higher commissions—see John E. Pickett, "A Prairie Fire," *Country Gentleman*, Vol. LXXXIII, No. 20 (May 18, 1918), p. 4.
[26] Pickett, p. 4. "North Dakota's 'Revolution,'" *Literary Digest*, p. 12.

The method of opening up new territory after the League was well established in North Dakota and had its own paper was quite similar to the early campaigning and was equally well mapped out. Organizers would go into a county and start working quietly among the farmers, overcoming opposition by locating the farmer's chief grievance and dwelling on it until he was won. After a few farmers were signed up, the organizers would move into other territory, leaving these farmers to spread the word themselves among their friends and neighbors, usually with the help of a few issues of *The Nonpartisan Leader.* When this leaven had had a chance to work, the organizers would come back to sign up the county. When the job was nearly finished, the League workers would hold meetings in schoolhouses or county halls, where memberships would pile up in great numbers. The small-town businessman, who had believed that the organizers had given up the county because they had gone away, woke up with a start and the opposition began. As nearly always happens, outside opposition acts as a cohesive force to the group opposed, and the League fights were no exception. Many a small-town businessman lived to regret bitterly his opposition to the League when an organized farmer boycott eventually forced him out of business.[27]

It was in September (1915)—when the first issue of *The Nonpartisan Leader,* the League's own paper, announced a membership of 22,000, which had been organized in only seven months—that the "Interests" became aware of the substantial movement that had been gaining momentum and crystallizing without their taking cognizance of it. The opposing forces became alarmed and tried to use the weapon of ridicule by calling League members the "Six-Dollar Suckers."[28] Some newspapers tried to frighten those already signed up and used every means to keep others from joining the cause, even going so far as to arrest canvassers on the charge of conspiring to get money under false pretenses. Ridicule, however, failed completely and, in fact, served to unite the farmers even more in their struggle against a "common enemy."

----

[27] Interview with Senator Lynn J. Frazier, October 7, 1940.
[28] Gaston, chap. viii. Russell, p. 204.

THE NONPARTISAN LEAGUE TAKES OVER THE GOVERNMENT OF NORTH DAKOTA

The first objective of the Nonpartisan League was to control the North Dakota state primaries in June of 1916. Their plan was to choose candidates to run on the regular Republican ticket for all state offices, men who would sign an agreement to carry out the League program if elected. The candidates were nominated at a state convention, held in Fargo on April 1, to which one delegate was sent from each legislative district, these delegates having been chosen at precinct and county meetings of League members. Precinct and county meetings were open only to farmers, and voting power given only to League members, one of whom was chosen chairman of the meeting. The meetings were conducted by the League members themselves, and the delegates thus elected at precinct, and then county meetings were sent to the state convention to choose the complete slate of candidates.

When the delegates thus elected came to the state convention, the first issue before the caucus was to choose the best man they could find to head the ticket as candidate for Governor. Several names were suggested, but none seemed to quite "fill the bill." During the discussion of candidates Beecher Moore, one of the League organizers, happened to mention Pembina County, and the thought flashed through William Lemke's mind that Lynn Frazier, his college friend and fellow football player, lived in that county and would be just the man they wanted. He therefore told the group about Frazier and his assets for that job—first, and most important, that he was a dirt farmer; second, that he was a graduate of the University of North Dakota. He was a prominent football player and therefore rather widely known over the state; he had been captain of the team for two years, showing real leadership in that capacity, and real ability to do teamwork during the third year when he played under Lemke's captaincy. He was honest and dependable. The members of the caucus were so taken with Lemke's word picture of the man that they insisted upon getting Frazier down to Fargo immediately. Lemke telephoned him and asked him to come to Fargo on the pretext of asking his advice on whether or not he, Lemke, should accept the League nomination for Lieutenant Governor.

Frazier came to Fargo and attended the caucus meeting the next day. He looked over the caucus and the caucus looked him over, without Frazier's knowing their reason for so doing. He went back to his farm "concerned about the Socialist influence in the group," although Lemke had assured him that the League was not a Socialist organization even though there were Socialists prominent in it. When the convention itself assembled, Frazier was nominated for Governor on the first ballot and knew nothing of what the convention had done until he read it in the paper on the way down to Fargo after a second telephone call from Lemke. After some hesitation, he decided to accept the nomination.[29]

The convention wanted to nominate Lemke for the supreme court, but Townley insisted that the League needed him in his position of legal and political advisor. However, they nominated Lemke's law partner, Robinson, for supreme-court candidate. William Langer, who had some reputation as a Prohibitionist and local state's attorney in cleaning up "blind pigs," was nominated for attorney general. Thomas Hall was nominated as secretary of state and Carl Kositzky as state auditor. The League, which then claimed 40,000 members, threw its full support behind all the candidates nominated by the convention and also behind the following five-point program: State-owned Terminal Elevators, Flour Mills, Stockyards, Packing Houses, and Cold Storage Plants; State Hail Insurance on the Acreage Tax Basis; Exemption of Farm Improvements from Taxation; State Inspection of Grain Dockage and Grading; Rural Credit Banks Operated at Cost.[30]

The League's opponents had many epithets for this program—they said it was "anarchistic," "of the torch and ax," "extravagant," "destructive," "vilely radical." They warned of it as a "lower class uprising." They sought to propagandize the League convention and mobilized every resource to fight its progress. But by this time, the League was thoroughly organized, strong in numbers, and was attempting to fight money with money by raising the annual dues from $6.00 to $9.00, or 75 cents a month, including a subscription to *The Nonpartisan Leader* and *Pearson's Magazine.*[31]

———

[29] Interview with Representative William Lemke, November 28, 1940.
[30] Gaston, p. 60. Russell, p. 213.
[31] Russell, pp. 214-215.

The League members campaigned vigorously, making a complete circuit of the state in a special train with speakers, candidates, and League leaders, and carried the primaries with pluralities of 17,000 votes. All of the candidates for state offices selected by the League were elected, with the single exception of the state treasurer. They elected three members of the state supreme court, eighty-seven members of the house of representatives, and eighteen members of the senate.[32]

Although the Farmers' Legislature of 1917 failed to get a satisfactory terminal elevator bill, they passed, among others, the following reform laws: (1) three laws dealing with the railroads—one to force the railroads to furnish cars to all shippers alike, one to force them to furnish sites for elevators and warehouses along their rights of way, and one to furnish side-tracks at mines; (2) a law requiring all elevators and grain warehouses to be licensed by the state, to better the practices of grain weighing and grading; (3) a law to encourage and protect cooperative societies; (4) creation of a highway commission; (5) a law creating a dairy commission to protect and foster the dairying industry; (6) taxation reform, directed chiefly at the railroads and other corporations, and providing for a graduated income tax upon large fortunes; (7) a law giving women suffrage for national elections; (8) laws to establish county agricultural and training schools, evening schools for young men and women above ordinary school age, and to standardize rural schools; (9) a law guaranteeing bank deposits, assessing all banks to provide the guaranty fund; (10) administrative reform—laws combining certain offices, to reduce duplication in duties, reducing allowances to certain programs, etc.; and (11) reduction of the rate of assessment on farm improvements to 5 per cent of their actual value.

The most drastic piece of legislation sponsored by the first League caucus was a bill in which the very constitution of the state itself was to be redrafted and on which depended the League's whole state-ownership program. The opposition fought this bill with all the resources they could muster because they realized what the full implications of the bill were, and more especially because they feared it was within the legal rights of the legislature.[33] It was called the "Farmer's Bill of Rights" and proposed

---

[32] *Legislative manual.* North Dakota Department of State.
[33] Bruce, p. 88. Russell, pp. 226-228. Gaston, p. 150. Pickett, "A Prairie Fire."

a new state constitution to be submitted to the people for approval through a special election. It was to provide a natural market-way to the producer by giving power to the state to enter any manufacturing or industrial field and to increase its debts by $500,000, giving the state sufficient financial leeway to build a terminal elevator and flour mill through bond issues. The principal purpose of encompassing so much vital legislation in one bill was to focus the issues sharply and quickly, to get a short constitution that the voters would read and understand, and to make their whole state-ownership program possible.[34]

Although the new constitution was proposed primarily to get the state-ownership program, there were other provisions in the bill also: a short ballot, recall of public officials, extension of term of elective office from two to four years, and removal of the court's right to declare unconstitutional any law adopted by the vote of the people. The whole idea was branded as revolutionary and socialistic by the opposition, but what they disliked most was the idea of the state going into business and using bond issues to finance its ventures.

The "Farmer's Bill of Rights" (House Bill 44) failed to reach the statute books because the holdover, anti-League membership of the senate that year was large enough to defeat it. Its provisions, however, were eventually put into the constitution one by one when the League gained complete control of the legislature. The League was of course enraged over the blocking of this vital piece of legislation at this time, and Townley is quoted as saying that the "suffering of the poor, the weeping and wailing and gnashing of teeth in the city of New York can be traced directly to the State of North Dakota, and to those twenty-eight hold-over Senators and their kind, who are responsible for their misery."[35] The League leaders took its failure to pass as merely a temporary setback, indignant though they were, and planned at once to attempt to get the same result by petition. This was a two-year process and the League organizers were quick to seize on the plan as a good argument for getting two-year, paid-in-advance membership fees of $16.00.

The real triumph of the League in North Dakota came in the election

----

[34] Interview with Representative William Lemke.
[35] Charles Merz, "Political Revolt in the Northwest," *New Republic*, November 10, 1917.

of November, 1918, and the so-called "League's Legislature" of 1919.
Governor Frazier was re-elected, carrying the state by more than 17,000
votes. The League, in fact, elected a complete state ticket that year,
including control of the legislature, with a majority in both the house and
senate. The opponents were badly whipped and feared what might be
the outcome of this top-heavy control. Some newspapers were bolder
than ever in their denunciation, saying that "bolshevistic, red-radical
Townleyism" was now supreme. Rumors were rampant as to the violent
"innovations" which were sure to take place. Some of the eastern newspapers were so confident of an impending cataclysm that they sent
reporters to the capital of North Dakota in January, 1919, to be eye-
witnesses to the special disasters that would occur when the "League's
Legislature" convened.[36]

But no "special disasters" occurred and the legislature of 1919 established something of an all-time record. Its session was the shortest one in
history, having adjourned in less than the sixty days allotted, having
introduced only one-fourth of the usual number of bills, having enacted
the lowest number in history (360), and was one of the least expensive
legislatures that ever sat in North Dakota, having cost $50,000 less than
the one preceding it. But this had not been accomplished without careful
planning and a rather unique "educational" program for its members.

Almost complete lack of political knowledge and experience had proved
to be an asset to the Nonpartisan League candidates in their first campaign in North Dakota. What the people wanted was a farmer regime.
It is claimed that many farmers who were elected to the state legislature
could scarcely speak and write English, and very few knew anything
about legislative procedures. Hence, the League faced one of its first
big jobs—to transform these farmers into legislators by an educational
program.

In characteristic fashion, the League set about doing this task
thoroughly. They rented the entire Northwest Hotel in Bismarck and all
League members lived there. Every night the ballroom of this hotel would
be the scene of a secret caucus meeting of all Leaguers, for the purpose
of instructing the representatives on the next day's legislation. These

---

[36] Russell, pp. 250-251. See also *The New York Times*, January 26, March 10, 1919.
William MacDonald, "An Ideal State in the Northwest," *World's Work*, Vol.
XXXVII, No. 5 (March, 1919), pp. 495-496.

meetings were very carefully guarded against intruders from the outside, and all proceedings were kept secret. Each night, the bills to be presented in the legislature the next day would be read before the caucus meeting by the "Steering Committee," and the bills would be discussed and amended from the floor in regular parliamentary form. The whole process of making a bill into a law would take place except for the formal public proceedings of the following day which would place the bill on the statute books of North Dakota. The majority vote of the caucus at night on bills or resolutions was automatically the majority vote in the house and senate the next day.[37]

The Steering Committee, composed of the League leaders, was of course all-powerful in this legislative process. All bills which were reported to the caucus were reported first to the Steering Committee and approved there. Anyone outside of the legislature wishing to appear before the caucus had to get permission to do so either from the Steering Committee or from the caucus itself. All changes that were made in bills in committee had to be brought before the Steering Committee and all important changes had to be approved by the caucus.[38]

The caucus "training school" for the legislators is said to have proved its effectiveness by the time the special session of the legislature was called in January, 1918. The farmer legislators had learned the business of putting through a bill and they were well posted on their legislative program. They carried out this program at the rate of two important bills a day and adjourned in about a week, said to have been one of the briefest and busiest sessions in the United States. No longer was it necessary to employ the device which opposition leaders claimed was used during the preceding session—having a red-haired clerk read a bill on which Leaguers were to vote "yes" and a black-haired clerk when they were to vote "no," or vice versa.

The major laws passed during the historic session of 1919 set up the legislative machinery for the League's comprehensive program of state-owned industries. They created: (1) an Industrial Commission, to be composed of the Governor (Chairman), the Commissioner of Agriculture

---

[37] Bruce, p. 65. Russell, p. 253. Gaston, pp. 132-134.
[38] J. D. Bacon, *North Dakota's reward for electing Nonpartisan League officers.* Grand Forks, North Dakota: 1921.

and Labor, and the Attorney General, to be in charge of the League's program of state-owned industries and enterprises; [39] (2) the Bank of North Dakota, to be run by the Industrial Commission, to be capitalized at $2,000,000 from a state bond issue, and to be the sole depository of all public funds; [40] (3) The North Dakota Mill and Elevator Association, to engage in the business of manufacturing and marketing of farm products and to establish a state-owned warehouse, elevator, and flour-mill system to be operated by the Industrial Commission, and to be financed by a state bond issue not to exceed $5,000,000; [41] (4) the Home Building Association of North Dakota, also under the direction of the Industrial Commission, designed to promote home building and ownership among residents of the state; [42] (5) a system of state hail insurance whereby a flat tax of 3 cents an acre was levied on all tillable land in the state, to provide for administrative expenses, and an indemnity tax on all cultivated and crop land, except hay and meadow land, of not more than 50 cents an acre.

In addition, legislation passed by the 1919 session provided among other things for the following: (1) a graduated tax on incomes, attempting to distinguish between earned and unearned incomes; (2) exemption of all farm and some town improvements from taxation; (3) a workmen's compensation act, to be operated on a fund obtained through a levy on employers, in proportion to the amount of danger involved in the work; (4) an official newspaper in each county, to be first selected by the Industrial Commission, and after 1920 by a vote of the people of the county at each regular election; (5) revision of railroad freight rates designed to remove discrimination against North Dakota; (6) an amendment to the grain-inspection law of 1917, creating the office of State Inspector of Grades, Weights, and Measures, to see that all weighing and inspecting were fair and accurate, and to make sure that the farmer

---

[39] "Law Creating Industrial Commission," *Laws of North Dakota, 1919*, chap. cli, House Bill No. 17. Issued by Committee on State Affairs.

[40] "Law Creating Bank of North Dakota," *Laws of North Dakota, 1919*, chap. cxlvii, House Bill No. 18. Issued by Committee on State Affairs.

[41] "Law Creating Mill and Elevator Association," *Laws of North Dakota, 1919*, chap. clii; Senate Bill No. 75. Issued by Committee on State Affairs. "Bonds of North Dakota Mill and Elevator Association, *Laws of North Dakota, 1919*, chap. cliii, Senate Bill No. 75. Issued by Committee on State Affairs.

[42] "Law Creating Home Building Association," *Laws of North Dakota, 1919*, chap. cl. Senate Bill No. 19. Issued by Committee on State Affairs.

received payment for dockage that was valuable; (7) an absent voter's law permitting all persons expecting to be absent on election day, and all women living more than half a mile from their polling places, to vote by mail; (8) establishment of an inheritance tax; and (9) further assistance to cooperatives.

This legislative program was both extensive and experimental. It provided all the necessary machinery for the state of North Dakota to go into business—banking; grading, storing, milling and marketing of wheat; building houses; and insurance. It set up new forms of taxation to finance the program and dictated new methods of running the state's business. To the farmers, it was their answer to previous legislatures' failure to give them a state-owned elevator or to improve the conditions under which they conducted their business. In other quarters, the program was branded as socialistic, revolutionary, and radical, but it was interpreted by the League as the "go-ahead signal" for the overwhelming victory at the polls in the last election.

· 18 ·

THE
GROWTH AND DECLINE
OF THE
NONPARTISAN LEAGUE

THE ECONOMIC PROGRAM OF THE LEAGUE
IN NORTH DAKOTA

One of the most important acts of the League was the establishment of a powerful state industrial commission to "manage, operate, control and govern all utilities, industries, enterprises and business projects now or hereafter established, owned, undertaken, administered or operated by the State of North Dakota except those carried on in penal, charitable or educational institutions." It was empowered to purchase, lease, or acquire sites by eminent domain, as provided by law; hold or dispose of any such property; fix prices of things bought and sold by the industries under its control, and provide for the necessary funds for carrying on these industries by negotiating the bonds of the state in such amounts as provided by law. The manager and subordinate officers and employees of each enterprise were to be appointed by the Commission and were subject to its supervision and control. The Commission was given authority to conduct investigations on all matters directly or indirectly connected with the operation of the state enterprises and was required to prepare an annual report to be filed in the office of the secretary of state not later than the first of February of each year. A sum of $200,000 out of the general funds of the state was made immediately available to carry out the provisions of this act. The *Nonpartisan Leader*, showing pictures of Governor Frazier, Attorney General William Langer, and Commissioner of Agriculture and Labor John N. Hagan announced: "STATE INDUSTRIAL COMMISSION FORMED—LEAGUE CAUCUS IN NORTH DAKOTA DECIDES ON BODY OF THREE MEN TO HANDLE PUBLICLY OWNED ENTERPRISES—ADEQUATE POWERS GRANTED." [1] Anything so nearly approaching a corporate state certainly went way beyond what had ever before been considered as essential to gaining the objectives of the Farmers' Movement.

The Bank of North Dakota was the key enterprise in the whole state ownership program because it provided the chief credit facilities for all other activities. The opening section of the law stated that, "For the purpose of encouraging and promoting agriculture, commerce and industry, the State of North Dakota shall engage in the business of banking, and for that purpose shall, and does hereby, establish a system of banking owned, controlled and operated by it, under the name of the Bank of North Dakota." [2] The bank was to be capitalized at two million dollars to be obtained by a state bond issue and was to be located, maintained, operated, managed, and controlled by the Industrial Commission. Special legislation was passed to provide for the Bonds of North Dakota, Bank Series. [3] The bank was to be made the depository of all state funds and all the funds of state penal, educational, and industrial institutions. It was permitted to make loans to individuals only on a first mortgage on North Dakota real estate, not to exceed one-half the value of the security;

---

[1] *Nonpartisan Leader*, February 3, 1919, p. 4.

[2] "Law Creating Bank of North Dakota," p. 36. See also *Constitution—laws and amendments thereto authorizing the North Dakota industrial program*. Issued by Industrial Commission. Bismarck, North Dakota: June 1, 1921.

[3] "Bonds of North Dakota Bank Series," *Laws of North Dakota, 1919*, chap. cxlviii, House Bill No. 49. Issued by Committee on State Affairs. *Laws of North Dakota, 1919*, chap. cliv, Senate Bill No. 130. Issued by Committee on State Affairs.

and the law was later amended by initiative to read that "real estate loans could be made only to actual farmers who were residents of the state." The bank, however, could "transfer funds to other departments, institutions, utilities, industries or business projects of the state." It could also "make loans to counties, cities, or political subdivisions of the state or to state or national banks, on such terms, and under such rules and regulations as the Industrial Commission may determine." It could act as reserve or rediscount bank for state banks depositing funds there and all its deposits were guaranteed by the state. The bank was the answer to the League's original platform demand for "rural credits at cost" with its special Farm Loan Department, and became the central unit in the League's banking system.

The people of North Dakota were kept apprised of the League's progress in establishing the State Bank through the pages of the League-controlled press. A few headlines from the *Nonpartisan Leader* between January and August of 1919 briefly tell the story:

"NORTH DAKOTA STATE BANK PLAN WELL UNDER WAY —NONPARTISAN LEAGUE CAUCUS APPROVES COMPREHENSIVE MEASURE TO FREE THE STATE FROM FINANCIAL PIRATES—FARMER MAJORITY MAKES PASSAGE CERTAIN"; "NORTH DAKOTA STATE BANK HAS MANY PRECEDENTS—FUNDAMENTAL PART OF LEGISLATION FOR THE PEOPLE MODELED ON FEDERAL RESERVE AND FARM LOAN ACTS—MANY COUNTRIES OFFER EXPERIENCE"; "NORTH DAKOTA STATE BANK READY TO OPEN SOON"; "NORTH DAKOTA BANKERS BACK STATE PLAN—COOPERATION TO MAKE INSTITUTION A BUSINESS IS PLEDGED TO INDUSTRIAL COMMISSION AND MANAGER WATERS AT CONFERENCE IN BISMARCK"; "FEDERAL FARM LOANS AND STATE BANKS—RURAL CREDIT SYSTEM ESTABLISHED IN NORTH DAKOTA IS ENDORSED BY PRESIDENT OF ST. PAUL FEDERAL LAND BANK"; "NORTH DAKOTA INITIATES RURAL CREDITS—NEW PEOPLE'S BANK OFFERS FARM LOANS AT SIX PER CENT, WITH THIRTY YEARS TO REPAY AT SEVENTY DOLLARS PER THOUSAND." [4]

---

[4] *Nonpartisan Leader*, January 27, February 10, April 21 and 28, May 19, and August 11, 1919.

The answer to the farmers' demands of many years for their own terminal elevator came with the passage of the bill creating the North Dakota Mill and Elevator Association under the direction of the Industrial Commission. This bill enabled the state to "engage in the business of manufacturing and marketing farm products and for that purpose shall establish a system of warehouses, elevators, flour mills, factories, plants, machinery and equipments owned, controlled and operated by and under the name of North Dakota Mill and Elevator Association." The Industrial Commission was to locate and maintain the places of business, acquire the necessary property and equipment by whatever means necessary, and could "buy, manufacture, store, mortgage, pledge, sell, exchange or otherwise acquire or dispose of all kinds of manufactured and raw farm and food products and by-products, and may for such purposes establish and operate exchanges, bureaus, markets and agencies, within or without the State, including foreign countries, on such terms and conditions, and under such rules and regulation as the Commission may determine." The Commission also fixed buying and selling prices, service charges, and other costs. Another bill was passed to provide the means of financing the mill and elevator project, authorizing a bond issue not exceeding $5,000,000, to be called the "Mill and Elevator Series," to bear not more than 6 per cent interest payable semiannually, and to be secured by first mortgages on the property used by the North Dakota Mill and Elevator Association.

Before building a new mill, the Industrial Commission bought a small one at Drake, in the northcentral part of the state, to run on an experimental basis. The *Nonpartisan Leader* of September 1, 1919, announced this plan: "NORTH DAKOTA BUYS ITS FIRST FLOUR MILL— PLANT AT DRAKE IS PURCHASED TO BEGIN NEW STATE ENTERPRISE—ORDERS FOR FLOUR POUR IN FROM MANY STATES—EXTENSION ON SITE IS ALREADY PLANNED." And a week later: "NORTH DAKOTA MILL GRINDS FIRST WHEAT— PEOPLE OF DRAKE CELEBRATE OPENING OF STATE ENTER- PRISE—FARMERS ARE PAID FULL MILLING VALUE FOR GRAIN." The *Leader* of November 3 reported: "STATE MILL EARNS 150 PER CENT PROFIT—AUDIT AFTER FIRST TWENTY-SIX DAYS SHOWS $2,349 GAIN ABOVE OPERATING COSTS—FARMER GETS MORE FOR WHEAT, CONSUMER PAYS LESS FOR FLOUR." For several years, the mill paid an average of 12 cents a bushel above the market price for wheat and sold flour and mill feeds considerably under market prices.

With the Drake mill operating successfully, it was announced through the League newspapers that inducements from various cities in the state would be helpful in deciding where to locate mills the League was planning to build. The *Leader* of June 9, under the headline of "GETTING FARMERS' PROGRAM UNDER WAY," stated that "J. A. McGovern, Chief Deputy Grain Inspector, to Manage Mill and Elevator Association in North Dakota," and "Cities Clamoring for State Enterprises." Competition for the new mills greatly stimulated the sale of the mill and elevator bonds and aided materially in developing favorable conditions under which to launch the project. Bismarck and Grand Forks became the leading contenders for the new mill, while Fargo businessmen seemed to remain apathetic. It was decided to locate the mill in Grand Forks, despite its relatively undesirable geographic location, chiefly because this city offered to donate a free site and to purchase a million dollars' worth of the mill and elevator bonds.[5] On May 5, 1920, the state started construction on the new and modern mill and elevator which was to have a total storage capacity of about 1,500,000 bushels and a milling capacity of 3,000 barrels a day. It was to be the most up-to-date mill of its kind anywhere, and its construction was said to be in the hands of one of the foremost construction engineering companies of the country.[6]

A third League enterprise, the Home Building Association, was created in "An Act declaring the purpose of the state of North Dakota to engage in the enterprise of providing homes for residents of this state and to that end establish a business system operated by the state under the name of the Home Building Association of North Dakota..." It was announced by the *Leader* in February in the following headline: "NORTH DAKOTA TO BOOM HOME OWNING—SERVICE OF LARGE STATE BUILDING AND LOAN AGENCY WILL BE AT COST—LOAN LIMITS PUT AT $5,000 IN TOWN AND $10,000 ON FARM." The next month, the *Leader* stated that the home building project was also to be used in connection with aid to soldiers returning from the World War: "LEAGUE

---

[5] Gaston, p. 302.

[6] Henry G. Teigan, "The National Nonpartisan League," *American Labor year book, 1921-1922*, Vol. 4, pp. 421-426. New York: Rand School of Social Science, 1922.

STATE HAS REAL SOLDIER PLAN—MEN RETURNING FROM SERVICE IN FIGHTING FORCES TO GET $25 FOR EACH MONTH OF SERVICE—HOME BUILDERS ACT WILL PROVIDE FARMS." The further scope of the plan for the farmers of the state was revealed in a July issue: "THE NORTH DAKOTA HOME BUILDING ACT— MANAGER OF NEW STATE ENTERPRISE HOPES TO BRING LABOR-SAVING DEVICES TO EVERY FARMHOUSE IN THE STATE." [7]

The Home Building Association was under the direction of the Industrial Commission, could accept deposits on which it could pay not more than 6 per cent interest, and could be assisted by bond issues authorized by the state or by legislative appropriations. The plan was that a group of ten or more depositors in the Association would organize themselves into a Home Buyers' League within the Association. As soon as a member of this League had deposited in the Association at least 20 per cent of the cost of the home or farm dwelling he wanted to buy or have built, the Association furnished the balance of the money required, taking a mortgage for that amount, and bought or built the house. Repayment of the amount forwarded by the Association was to be in monthly installments large enough to liquidate the debt in not less than ten or more than twenty years. The sum of $100,000 was appropriated to carry out the provisions of this act. By September the Association was functioning. The fourth anniversary issue of the *Nonpartisan Leader* announced: "NORTH DAKOTA BUILDING WORKER'S HOME—FIRST HOUSE OF MEMBER OF STATE HOME BUILDING ASSOCIATION NOW UNDER CONSTRUCTION IN BISMARCK—DETAILS OF THE NEW PLAN." [8]

One of the most elaborate activities undertaken by the League leaders was the so-called Consumers' United Stores Company.[9] The purposes outlined in the Articles of Incorporation were pretty broad, some of which were stated as follows:

---

[7] *Nonpartisan Leader,* February 3, March 10, July 28, 1919.

[8] *Ibid.,* September 22, 1919; October 4, 1920.

[9] Jerry D. Bacon, *The farmer and Townleyism, the inside story of the National Nonpartisan League under Townley dictatorship.* Grand Forks, North Dakota: Jerry D. Bacon, 1918.

...to buy, lease, establish or otherwise acquire, and dispose of all kinds of personal and real property which the corporation may deem necessary or convenient for the purpose of its business; to buy, sell, own, lease, transfer, assign, improve, exchange or otherwise acquire and dispose of all kinds of personal property, including bills, drafts, notes, bonds, mortgages, stocks and all other commercial paper and securities, whether negotiable or non-negotiable, of corporations and individuals; to endorse and guarantee payment of bills, drafts, notes, bonds, mortgages, stocks, and all other kinds of commercial paper and securities, whether negotiable or non-negotiable, of corporations and individuals; to make loans with or without security upon personal or real property, and to invest all the funds of the corporation in any way deemed advisable by the Board of Directors.

There were other provisions for transactions of a financial nature, together with two articles of a still broader character:

...to carry on educational work or propaganda along all lines deemed by the Board of Directors to be in the interest of or beneficial to the economic· educational or political welfare of the producers and consumers of this nation; ...

to aid and assist the producers and consumers of this nation in educating themselves to efficient cooperative buying and selling, and to assist in making democracy a real factor in our political, educational and economic life.

This economic program was only partly tuned to the issues over which the Farmers' Movement had struggled. A farmer who wished to participate in this plan paid $100 for a buyer's certificate guaranteeing him the right to trade in the farmers' store in his community when established. He was to receive merchandise at wholesale prices plus freight and a 10 per cent operating charge. When enough farmers in a given community (usually about thirty) had subscribed $100 each, the store was set up with 90 per cent of the total amount of money subscribed; the rest went into a general fund of the Company. If a local store failed, the farmer was entitled to the return of his $100, less $10 for each year he had traded with the store, if the assets of the local establishment were sufficient to cover this amount; if not, the claims of the various subscribers were prorated up to the limit of the assets. The general fund was not subject to claims made by members of a store that failed. If a store in one locality was a success, all the profit above the initial cost of establishing the store went into the general fund, but the converse was not true; that is, the general fund took surpluses of successful stores, but did not pay the deficits of stores that failed. The local farmers' stores sold chiefly staple groceries, some clothing, shoes, hardware, furniture, and farm implements; and the Company had its own warehouse for these products in Fargo. Management of the Company was in the hands of a board of directors of three, who were to be elected at the first meeting of the incorporators and stockholders, and who were empowered to elect a president, secretary, and treasurer, and any other officers and assistants needed.

Probably the most successful of the League activities was the state hail insurance department, which was part of a larger program including insurance of public buildings against fire and tornado and the bonding of public officials. This, like the State Bank and flour mill, was called for in the League's original platform. A hail insurance department was set up in the state insurance commissioner's office by law, and its plan of operation was announced in the *Leader* in February in this headline: "STATE HAIL INSURANCE PLAN DECIDED—RATES OF FIFTEEN CENTS ON CROP LAND AND TEN CENTS ON UNUSED TILLABLE LAND TO COVER COSTS—SLACKER ACRES THUS MUST BEAR PART." The larger plans were introduced in March through the *Leader:* "NEW INSURANCE LAWS FOR NORTH DAKOTA—HAIL RISKS, WORK-MEN'S COMPENSATION AND FIRE RISKS ON PUBLIC BUILD-INGS TO BE CARRIED BY STATE—WILL SAVE BIG OPERATION EXPENSES." In May, the League announced that the state had hired a noted risk expert to come into the state to fix the insurance rates for their program.[10] Meanwhile, the private insurance companies were vigorously fighting the invasion of the state in the insurance field. The League, however, continued with its plans; and in June, the *Leader* carried this headline: "THE HAIL INSURANCE FIGHT—NORTH DAKOTA STATE PLAN WILL REDUCE PREMIUMS AND CUT AWAY $600,-000 ANNUAL PROFIT OF RISK FIRMS." [11] A bulletin of the Non-partisan League claimed that hail insurance through private companies

[10] *Nonpartisan Leader,* February 3, March 10, May 26, 1919.
[11] *Ibid.,* June 2, 1919, p. 12.

was costing $60 per $1,000, and that under the new law it would cost from $8 to $10 per $1,000, meaning "a saving of at least $100 every year to the average farmer carrying $2,000 in insurance." [12]

The hail insurance plan as worked out by the League provided for a flat tax of 3 cents an acre on all the tillable land in the state. The maximum payment for damage was set at $7 per acre, in case of total loss. A farmer's land was considered insured unless he notified the County Auditor and the State Hail Insurance Commissioner before June 15 each year that he wanted his land withdrawn from state hail insurance protection.

THE NATIONAL ORGANIZATION OF THE NONPARTISAN LEAGUE

The Nonpartisan League reached its highest peak in North Dakota, but its influence was not limited to that state. League organizers were sent to the western part of Minnesota as early as July, 1916, and soon after that to the neighboring states of Montana and South Dakota. By January, 1917, the League claimed 10,000 members outside of North Dakota, and that summer opened membership campaigns in Idaho, Washington, Colorado, Nebraska, Kansas, Oklahoma, Texas, Iowa, and Wisconsin.

The League made its first real move for expansion into other states in 1917 and moved into the political campaign in Minnesota in a big way in 1918. This was its most promising new territory for a number of reasons: Minnesota had been North Dakota's closest and most faithful colleague in the Equity Cooperative Exchange; the farmers of western Minnesota and North Dakota faced the same farming and marketing problems; they were pretty much alike in ethnic composition; and they were of course physically adjacent. The League's campaign machinery was moved into Minnesota and immediately thrown into full gear. It started with a series of local meetings on February 22, 1918, in which delegates were named to district conventions which were in turn to name delegates to a state convention. Two hundred and sixty Ford cars were purchased, and organizers were brought in from almost a dozen other states. The purpose was to capture the dominant (Republican) party, but since the League itself was nonpartisan, it enrolled many

---

[12] *Where the people rule, North Dakota, a state where democracy is safe. The Nonpartisan League state*, p. 11. St. Paul, Minnesota: Nonpartisan League, 1919.

Democrats, and by so doing reduced the vote of the Democratic party from 93,112 in 1916 to 32,649 in 1918. The vote for the Republican party was increased from around 200,000 to approximately 350,000. The League carried 30 counties and, with the aid of labor, nominated 80 out of 130 members of the lower house and 42 out of 67 members of the senate. This accomplishment was, however, not as great a League triumph as it appeared because most of its nominees ran as Farmer-Labor party candidates and were defeated. The results showed only 15 Farmer-Labor members elected to the senate and 36 to the lower house.[13]

The League entered Nebraska attempting to elect only county and legislative officers, but met with no success. It entered Kansas, but contented itself with expressing preference for Senator Capper. In South Dakota, it assisted in nominating an Independent for Governor, who lost in the election. It backed the Wisconsin Society of Equity in Wisconsin in 1920. In Montana, it nominated 40 out of 95 members of the lower house and 14 members of the senate. Saloutos says it also claimed success in organizing Washington and helped to elect a Democratic Governor in Idaho. It had followers—in fact, members—in still other states, but staged no organized political campaigns in them.

With a substantial membership outside of North Dakota, the name of the organization was changed to National Nonpartisan League, and its headquarters were moved from Fargo to St. Paul in January, 1918. By its appearance, the office of the national headquarters might have been the home office of any large industrial concern. It was said to be teeming with activity, was equipped with the most up-to-date office machinery, and was staffed by experts in many fields. As one writer said, "They have printing presses of the very latest type—the best money can buy. In addition they have equipped their offices with multigraphing, mailing, sealing, stamping and addressing machinery, so they can print, fold, put in envelopes, stamp and address forty-five hundred circular letters per hour."[14] There were library experts, a staff of accountants, a book department for the sale of League-endorsed literature, a cor-

---

[13] Analyses of the campaigns in other states are made by Saloutos in his article, "The Expansion and Decline of the Nonpartisan League in the Western Middle West, 1917-1921." He fully documents his findings, but his citations of sources will not be repeated here.

[14] Teigan, p. 34.

respondence school for the organizers, and a staff of regular lecturers. There was a constant stream of literature flowing out to farmers and other interested persons in many states. All lines of League activity—economic, political, educational, and social—converged in this office. In addition to the national office, there were six to one hundred organizers in each of about twelve states, a state office and staff in states which had a substantial membership, and outside speakers from time to time.

As national membership in the League faded out and the circulation figures of the *Leader* decreased, the activities of national headquarters were drastically curtailed. State organs of the League which had once flourished in at least eight states, in addition to several dailies and more than one hundred farmer-labor-owned weekly papers in League states, eventually went out of existence or into other hands. It was said that, "All that was left of the League in 1923 was its office furniture, a large volume of uncollected postdated checks, a fleet of old Ford cars, and the *Nonpartisan Leader,* which was printed monthly, mailed to about 100,000 old League members, with the cost of printing paid from a dwindling advertising patronage." [15]

The spread of the Nonpartisan League has been likened to a prairie fire by one writer, and this is an apt figure of speech. It will be recalled that the League piled up a membership of 10,000 within the first five months of its history in North Dakota. Neighboring states were quick to follow suit, organizers were sent out on a commission basis in great numbers, and the campaign was constantly stimulated by correspondence, pamphlets, books, speakers, and copies of the *Nonpartisan Leader.* League correspondence indicates that their organization was unable to fill all the requests for organizers that were received from interested groups in states all over the country.

By the end of 1918, the League is said to have been nearly 200,000 strong, with North Dakota, Minnesota, South Dakota, and Montana accounting for about half of that number, and the nine states of Nebraska, Idaho, Colorado, Wisconsin, Texas, Iowa, Kansas, Oklahoma, and Washington making up the balance.[16] During the latter part of

---

[15] A. W. Ricker, "The Birth and Growth of the Northwest Farmers' Union," *Farmers' Union Herald,* July, 1937, pp. 1, 4.

[16] Nathan Fine, *Labor and farmer parties in the U. S., 1828-1928,* pp. 363-438. New York: Rand School of Social Science, 1928. See also Gaston, p. 238.

1919 and the early part of 1920, the League grew to between 225,000 and 250,000 members in thirteen or fourteen states.[17] The *Nonpartisan Leader* claimed by this time to have a million readers.[18] In 1920, the League claimed over 200 representatives in the state legislatures of nine states.[19] By the spring of 1922, however, the membership of the League and the circulation of the *Leader* had dropped to about 150,000.[20] From this point on, membership figures dwindled with fading political power, and the League fire which had once burned so brightly gradually died out. It did not die, however, without having left embers which were rekindled in the farmer-labor movement soon to take its place in the northwest country.

OPPOSITION TO AND DECLINE OF THE LEAGUE

During the North Dakota legislative session of 1917, much of the reform legislation sponsored by the Nonpartisan League members was killed by the anti-League, holdover membership of the senate. By 1919, however, the League was in control of both houses of the North Dakota legislature and all other branches of government, and was able, therefore, to enact its entire program. This was not done without vigorous opposition from anti-League forces both within and outside of North Dakota. The *Nonpartisan Leader* carried headlines and stories on this opposition; pamphlets were issued in a number of states; newspapers throughout the Northwest were full of the controversy; and national magazines and newspapers discussed the League program pro and con.

A few headlines from the *Nonpartisan Leader* will show some of the sources of this opposition:

"THE COPPER-COLORED PRESS OF *MONTANA*—CORPORA-TION CONTROL SUPPLIES TAINTED NEWS TO THE PEO-

---

[17] Bruce, p. 8.

[18] *Nonpartisan Leader*, September 22, 1919. (As early as August 26, 1918, the front page of the *Leader* carried the statement, "More Than a Million Readers Each Week.")

[19] F. A. Teigan, *The Nonpartisan League, its origin, development and secret purpose,* p. 4. St. Paul: Economic Research and Publishing Company, 1918.

[20] See *National Nonpartisan League Papers,* filed in Minnesota State Library, St. Paul, Boxes 1-6, 1916-1922.

PLE OF A GREAT STATE—FEAR THE FARMER VOTE AND STRIVE TO KEEP IT SPLIT"; "KEEP YOUR EYES ON *WASH-INGTON* STATE—ALL ATTEMPTS OF POLITICAL GANGS TO BULLY FARMERS AND WIVES FAIL, AND THE LEAGUE IS BOOMING AS NEVER BEFORE"; "HATING THE FARM-ERS AND THEIR UNIONS—AN ACCOUNT OF FUTILE ATTEMPTS TO STOP THE NONPARTISAN LEAGUE IN *WISCONSIN* AND *NEBRASKA*"; "ATTACK ON LEAGUE NOW NATION-WIDE—SPECIAL INTERESTS MENACED BY PRO-GRAM OF ORGANIZED FARMERS WIN SUPPORT OF SAT-URDAY EVENING POST PUBLISHERS, WHO ORIGINALLY FAVORED FARMERS." [21]

The industrial program of the League had a rather turbulent his-tory. The conditions making possible state-owned business enterprises were, as shown before, born of long-standing demands by farmers chiefly for control of their own markets and for better credit arrangements. These were the very issues on which the League met its severest oppo-sition from the beginning at the hands of the business interests. An overwhelming League victory at the polls finally made the industrial pro-gram possible and with it the answer to the farmers' demands.

The state bank was one of the chief targets of anti-Leaguers from the time of its establishment. When they initiated a measure permitting public funds to be deposited in other banks, they were directing a hit at the core of the League program. This measure was passed and had a somewhat disorganizing influence on the bank and therefore on the whole program.[22] Another handicap suffered by the Bank was the diffi-culty encountered in the sale of its bonds. It was claimed that they were boycotted at the dictates of Wall Street, the North Dakota Bankers' Association, and the Federal Reserve Bank at Minneapolis. The League finally established offices in Chicago, New York, and Washington to sell the bonds, and labor unions were asked to cooperate. Within three months after these offices were opened, the League claimed to have $1,500,000 pledged for the purchase of its bonds.[23]

---

[21] *Nonpartisan Leader*, July 8, August 5, October 7 and 28, 1918.
[22] Fossum, p. 116.
[23] H. G. Teigan, pp. 421-426.

The Bank of North Dakota opened for business on July 28, 1919, and claimed to have more than $17,000,000 in resources by November 15, and to have completed in three and one-half months nearly $2,000,000 worth of farm loans at lower rates of interest than ever known in North Dakota, saving the farmers about $45,000 in interest and cutting the rate about 2.5 per cent. By February 15, 1920, resources of the bank were said to be nearly $20,000,000.[24] The League claimed that by July 1, 1921, the Bank had made approximately $3,000,000 worth of loans to farmers at rates saving them $90,000 a year or $180,000 up to that date, and had financed state industries to the extent of $1,000,000.[25] The League also had this to say about the operation of the bank:

> No bank anywhere at any time has ever undergone the savage sabotage and pitiless publicity to which the Bank of North Dakota has been subjected from the hour it opened for business down to this date and come through the ordeal unbroken. No other bank has ever been attacked as viciously by the enemy within and without, as has been the Bank of N. D., and survived the assault. No private bank on earth could have stood for twenty days, much less twenty months, the lying propaganda spread by its enemies and the runs, garnishments, "investigations" and suits engineered against it, that have been successfully withstood by the Bank of N. D.[26]

A legislative report published in 1921 stated that the bank had little but state deposits, and that more than 50 per cent of the total loans and discounts consisted of League enterprise paper. The report was chiefly an indictment of the Industrial Commission and served as a forerunner to the recall election on October 28, 1921.[27] The new anti-League Industrial Commission took office on November 23, 1921, and made another damaging report on the state industries just five weeks

---

[24] Russell, pp. 299-300.

[25] *Townleyism, a true story of the operation of the Nonpartisan League program in North Dakota, as told in official reports of the various departments of the state government.* Fargo, North Dakota: Elliott Printing Co., 1921. This pamphlet contained the League's answer to its critics.

[26] *Ibid.*, pp. 93-94.

[27] *Report of House Audit Committee investigating the Bank of North Dakota and other state industries.* Filed March 4, 1921. St. Paul: Temple, Webb & Co., 1921.

later, stating in part, "The losses of the Bank, it would seem, have come largely from an effort to be of service to political friends." [28]

In the summer of 1922, when Nestos was campaigning for the governorship and the continuation of his administration of the state's affairs, he stated that the Bank of North Dakota lost approximately $220,000 in 1921, and charged League speakers and writers with claiming that the bank was making money when they knew it was operating at a loss. The Independent Voters' Association charged that the Townley administration had ruined North Dakota's credit outside of the state, had caused the flight of capital for investment elsewhere, and was guilty of extravagance and mismanagement in running the bank.[29] From 1922 on, with a program of gradual curtailment of the bank's activities and with a drastically reduced program of state-owned business, the Bank of North Dakota became chiefly a rural credit agency.

The North Dakota Mill and Elevator Association represented the culmination of the farmers' most insistent demands and was bitterly attacked by the anti-League forces from the very beginning. The League started its business operations in this field, it will be recalled, by buying a small mill at Drake, and claimed to have made 83 per cent profit on the total purchase price in the first 111 days of operation. They also claimed to have paid an average of 12 cents a bushel more for grain, asked 50 cents to $1.00 less per barrel for flour, and to have sold the by-products of shorts, bran, etc. for $7.50 per ton less than it was sold by private concerns. On the amount of grain milled here, another writer said the Drake mill had saved growers and consumers approximately $40,000 a year besides rendering the service of stabilizing prices in the area.

———

[28] *Report of the Industrial Commission for year ending December 31, 1921.* Bismarck, North Dakota. For other reports on the State Bank and Mill and Elevator, see later *Reports of the Industrial Commission. North Dakota Bonds.* Issued by the Bank of North Dakota, Bismarck. Mandan, North Dakota: printed by Mandan News, 1921. *Condensed audit report of state mill and elevator and the Bank of North Dakota.* Presented by State Board of Auditors, Bismarck, North Dakota, 1929. The audit report covers the period July 1, 1926-June 30, 1928. *Report of the State Board of Auditors, State of North Dakota,* July 1, 1928-Oct. 31, 1930. Bismarck, North Dakota.

[29] R. A. Nestos, "The Campaign Issues," June 5, 1922. "Effect of Townleyism on State and Individual Credit." Fargo, North Dakota: Independent Voters' Association. Two speeches by Governor Nestos, included in a publication by his campaign committee, which is now in the Minnesota State Library Collection.

With the Drake mill in operation for nearly a year, the League started construction of the new mill and elevator at Grand Forks in May, 1920. When the project was about one-half done, work was discontinued on it due to lack of funds. When the Nestos administration came into office the following year, with an endorsement by the voters of the League industrial program, the new Industrial Commission sold bonds and started building operations again in April, 1922. This mill opened for business in October of that year and is still in operation.

The Home Building Association never reached the proportions envisioned in the original League plans and was not a financial success. There was said to be a total deficit of $400,000, including the cost of maintaining the Association and construction costs.[30] The 1922 report of the Industrial Commission was very sharp in its criticism of this program, saying:

> In so far as building activity is concerned, the Home Building Association has been in a condition of suspended animation since in the fall of 1920. A few homes already begun at that date were finished and for two years nothing has been done except to close out the stocks of material on hand and try to get matters in shape so that contracts might be entered into. The Association's assets are gradually shrinking, its liabilities daily growing larger; there is no way to prevent the one or retard the other.[31]

When the courts had finished the cases regarding the oral contracts under which the houses had been built, and after the houses had been resold, the affairs of the Association were wound up and the home building program of the League came to an end.

The state hail insurance program was started in 1919. Eight million acres were said to have been insured the first year, saving the farmers $3,150,000 by the difference- in rates between the League and private companies. The *Nonpartisan Leader* pointed this out as the test of the value of the hail insurance law: "COST OF POLICIES CUT ONE-HALF IN MOST DISASTROUS YEAR IN NORTH DAKOTA HISTORY—

---

[30] Gilbert W. Cooke, "The North Dakota Industrial Program." Doctoral dissertation. Madison, Wisconsin: University of Wisconsin, n.d.

[31] *Report of the Industrial Commission on Home Building Association,* December 31, 1922, Bismarck, North Dakota, p. 33. See also *Report of the Home Building Association to Industrial Commission,* September 26, 1922.

TWELVE THOUSAND CLAIMS RECEIVED BY STATE DEPART-
MENT." [32] The first year, the League claimed to have reduced the rate
from 77 cents per acre to 28 cents for $7 indemnity.[33] According to the
Commissioner of Insurance, the same sort of record was made the next
year, saving the farmers about $9,000,000 during a two-year period.
The Nestos administration continued the hail insurance program with
some changes, and while a program of state hail insurance continues in
North Dakota, it is said to be still in an experimental stage.

While the League administration of the state's business was on public
trial, pamphlets were issued and the League-controlled press carried
articles in defense of its policies and program.[34] The opposition maintained a steady barrage of criticism by means of pamphlets and newspaper articles, and succeeded in hampering the progress of the industrial
program by initiative measures, hearings, investigations, audits, and
critical legislative reports. The League charged that "the opposition to
the progress of state industries in North Dakota have no intention of
any fair presentation of the facts," and that "their purpose only is to
gain political advantage even at the cost of misrepresentations and deceit
to the people of the State of North Dakota." [35] A legislative committee
of the opposition administration said that the "impractical theorists have
launched the state into an orgy of financial excesses and delirium of
socialistic experimentation, born in hate and nurtured in prejudice, the
results of which are such that it will require years of conservative, practical administration of public affairs to eliminate the nefarious consequences resultant therefrom . . . The Committee recommends that the
state confine its business activities to those matters which are, in their
nature at least, quasi-government in character . . ." [36]

According to one writer, the industrial program cost North Dakota,
fiscally, something over $10,000,000 up to 1934, which amount was raised
by a general property tax levy, but that socially the program has at least
the following benefits to its credit: it has lowered insurance rates by

---

[32] *Nonpartisan Leader*, September 15, 1919.

[33] Ladd, *Congressional record*, p. 920. *Nonpartisan Leader*, December 22, 1919.

[34] For example, *Where the people rule, North Dakota*, . . .

[35] Nestos, "The Campaign Issues."

[36] *Report of House Audit Committee investigating the Bank of North Dakota and
other state industries*, p. 65.

one-third; it has protected the funds of governmental units as private banks have failed; it has fostered the protein content measurement of wheat; and has reduced interest rates to western farmers.

Discussion and evaluation of the North Dakota industrial program have by no means been limited to the League and anti-League forces. The experiment was watched with interest by writers throughout the nation, and articles appeared on the subject in many national magazines and newspapers. Chester H. Rowell, writing in *World's Work,* said that the various institutions were, except for the state bank, League-promoted rather than governmental institutions and that only part of them failed. He stated that many of the smaller newspapers were still running, and some of the chain stores still operating. He called the Home Building Association a clear business failure and described the Bank of North Dakota as a state farm loan bank.[37]

In reply to an article in the *Nation's Business,* in which the author condemned the whole industrial program because it raised the taxes too high,[38] Bruce Bliven said that while the League made many errors and tried to do too much too quickly, the program suffered from the crisis of 1920-1921 and from the continuous and powerful opposition of great financial interests; that the Bank of North Dakota saved many thousands of dollars to the farmers through the lowering of the interest rate alone, and that the mill and elevator got good prices for the farmer and on the whole was a successful enterprise.[39]

Opposition to the League reached its height, particularly in Minnesota, after America's entrance into World War I, when charges of disloyalty, pro-Germanism, and Pacifism were hurled from every direction; public halls were closed to League gatherings; meetings were broken up; League leaders were tarred and feathered; and some of the officials were even covered constantly by Secret Service men and spies. Opposition to the League during the first six months of the United States' participation in the World War I was so severe, and its disorganizing effects so great, that a League official claimed that if the war had not

[37] Rowell, "The Political Cyclone in North Dakota . . ."

[38] William S. Neal, "North Dakota Returns to Sanity," *Nation's Business,* Vol. XIV, No. 3 (March, 1926), pp. 13-17.

[39] Bruce Bliven, "North Dakota Five Years After," *New Republic,* April 28, 1926, pp. 292-293.

intervened, the League would have spread over the nation and "would have elected Lynn Frazier President of the United States."[40] The League, however, never fully recovered from the setback to its organization due to the disloyalty charges of the early period of the World War I.

The most militant critic of the League during its entire history was Jerry D. Bacon, owner of the Grand Forks *Herald* and the town's leading hotel, one of the founders of the anti-League Independent Voters' Association, and author and publisher of many anti-League pamphlets and articles. The principal aim of Bacon's attacks, as of many others who fought the League, was to prove that the whole League program was a socialistic experiment, that the League leaders were all Socialists and I.W.W.'s, and that the aim of the League was to establish state socialism in North Dakota. Bacon's "Carry-the-Truth-to-the-People" series of three pamphlets was designed to "tell the Story of the Remarkable Socialist Autocracy in North Dakota."[41] He accused the League of having become "a distinctively partisan affair in which class has been arrayed against class, the farmer against the town resident and businessman, the farmer against the banker," and said that his exposé was "an effort to show convincingly that Nationwide Socialism is the true purpose of the Townley propaganda and that the farmers of the state of North Dakota, and of other states possibly, have gone into it without having the least suspicion of the real purpose of Townley and his allied Socialists, Pacifists and I.W.W. leaders—not to say disloyalists."[42] He went on in this pamphlet to list most of the leaders and workers in the League organization, showing in each case his Socialist connections, even inserting a copy of Townley's registration blank as a member of the Socialist party in Golden Valley County, North Dakota, in 1914.

Another ardent critic of the League was Ferdinand A. Teigan, a former member of the League, who wrote an eighty-two-page diatribe

---

[40] Interview with William Lemke, November 28, 1940.

[41] This series of three pamphlets consisted of: *The Farmer and Townleyism, The inside story of the National Nonpartisan League under Townley dictatorship,* cited above. *A. (After) C. (Cash) Townley smoked out, whistles a new tune, but only to aid his huge profiteering schemes.* Grand Forks: 1918. *Townleyism unmasked now stands before the world in its true light as radical socialism!* Grand Forks: n.d.

[42] *The farmer and Townleyism,* pp. 7-8.

in which he said, "The Nonpartisan League is a Socialist organization. It was conceived by Socialists, planned by Socialists, builded by Socialist organizers, and its editors, writers and public speakers are, and from the beginning have been Socialists. It was organized for the express purpose of spreading broadcast Socialist ideals." [43]

A publication coming out a little later was still dwelling on the same theme; it listed thirty-one people prominent in the League, from Townley down to state managers and organizers, who had been prominent in the Socialist party, in most cases giving photostatic copies of their signatures in their Socialistic connections. The booklet showed how practically every radical organization in the United States, and especially in the West, tied into or backed the Nonpartisan League. [44]

The volume of literature that poured off anti-League presses, written by disgruntled or disillusioned ex-Leaguers, by officials in rival organizations, by bankers, millers, businessmen, conservative politicians, and all the natural enemies of the League is too great to be reviewed or even listed here. Jerry Bacon's pamphlets and the two booklets described above are probably the outstanding exposés and the most elaborate anti-League documents that were offered to the public. Of course Bacon wrote other pamphlets [45] and through his own newspaper and the Independent Voters' Association kept hammering away at the League through the opposition press. Attacks also came from organizers who had been replaced for one reason or another, [46] from the head of a rival organization in a nearby state who did not want the League

[43] Ferdinand A. Teigan, *The Nonpartisan League, its origin, development and secret purposes*, p. 8.

[44] Asher Howard, compiler, *The leaders of the Nonpartisan League, their aims, purposes and records*. Minneapolis, Minnesota, 1920.

[45] Jerry D. Bacon, *Sovietians—wreckers of Americanism*, 1921. *Who is Arthur C. Townley? North Dakota's reward for electing Nonpartisan League officers*, 1921(?). *National Nonpartisan League* (Resumé of the League, their officers, methods, laws and the effect on economic conditions in North Dakota furnished by Farmer Jerry D. Bacon of Grand Forks, N. D. for publication in states where requested). Typed mss. in Mss. Div. of Minn. State Historical Society, St. Paul, Minnesota. *A. C. Townley, pretending to be the farmers' friend plays into the hands of Socialists and I.W.W.'s by assisting in keeping the price of wheat down*, 1919(?).

[46] Rev. William Henry Talmage, *The Mad Captain*, and *We'll Stick*, Two Nonpartisan League Lectures, October 15, 1918. Redfield, South Dakota: Redfield *Press*, October 15, 1918. S. R. Maxwell, *The Nonpartisan League from the inside*. St. Paul, Minnesota: Dispatch Printing Co., 1918.

to come into that state,[47] from League officials who turned against the organization and ran for office on the conservative ticket.[48] These are but a few of the many sources of anti-League literature in the area, and it must be remembered that the League "experiment" was being discussed by newspapers and magazines all over the United States. In addition, two magazines were started by Minneapolis businessmen for the express purpose of presenting anti-League propaganda; one of these, *The Red Flame*,[49] appeared first in November, 1919, and lasted only through September, 1920; and the other, *On the Square*, A Magazine for the Farm and Home,[50] survived only two issues, May and June, 1918. A "fake League" was also started in Minnesota by Twin Cities' businessmen to try to get members away from the farmers' League. The organization, which called itself the Minnesota Nonpartisan League, Inc., survived only eighteen months, and its paper, *The Nonpartisan*, was published for only five months.[51]

The Independent Voters' Association was the chief opposition organization which came into being to fight the League. It was composed of "Anti-Radical Republicans," Democrats, and disgruntled Leaguers; and its function was stated to be "that of an educational and propaganda organization, but its plan of organization is such that its membership can readily get into formation for election campaigns within any unit of political government."[52] The Independent Voters' Association had

[47] J. N. Tittemore and A. A. Vissers, authors and compilers, *The Non-Partisan League vs. the home*. Milwaukee, Wisconsin: Burdick-Allen Co., printers, 1922.

[48] William Langer, *The Nonpartisan League; its birth, activities and leaders*. Published under penalty of the Anti-Liar's Law of North Dakota providing for one year in the penitentiary. Mandan, North Dakota: Morton County Farmers Press, 1920. See also J. Edmund Buttree, *The despoilers, stories of the North Dakota grain fields*. Boston: The Christopher Publishing House, 1920.

[49] *The Red Flame*, monthly magazine published by the Red Flame Publishing Co., Bismarck, North Dakota, November 1919—September 1920. This magazine was published by the Citizens' Economy League from March to September, 1920. The complete file is available at the Minnesota State Historical Library, St. Paul, Minnesota.

[50] *On the Square*, A Magazine for the Farm and Home. St. Paul, Minnesota: On the Square Publishing Co., May and June, 1918.

[51] *Nonpartisan Leader*, June 9, 1919, and following issues. *The Nonpartisan*. Official Organ of the Minnesota Non-Partisan League, Incorporated under the Laws of Minnesota. St. Paul, Minnesota: August 1 to December 1, 1917.

[52] *The I.V.A., its plan of organization and operation*, p. 2. Fargo, North Dakota: State Headquarters, 1921. For background of the I.V.A., see also Theodore G.

articles of incorporation and by-laws, officers, a state executive committee of twenty-one members, dues-paying membership, its own weekly paper, the *Independent Politician,* and local units which were granted charters by the state headquarters at Fargo. The chief activities of the Independent Voters' Association were "initiating and referending legislation" and conducting "a finish fight with Townleyism." Before the 1922 election, they issued this militant statement: "Until the government of North Dakota is taken entirely away from the gang of imported and home grown radical Socialists and I.W.W.'s that still have their hands on a great part of our government, every intelligent, active citizen in the state should be lined up either with the gang in control of the Nonpartisan League or with the I.V.A." [53] This organization remained active until the League went out of power.

The first important political result of the opposition's efforts was the holding of a referendum election in June, 1919, on seven League laws. This election was promoted by the Independent Voters' Association and three state officials who turned against the League—Thomas Hall, secretary of state; Carl Kositzky, state auditor; and William Langer, attorney general. The League came through with a victory on all seven measures, and the *Leader* made much of this in the headlines of its July 14 issue: "THE BIG NORTH DAKOTA VICTORY—LEAGUE MEASURES CARRYING OUT PROGRAM POLL BIGGEST VOTE IN STATE'S HISTORY"; "NORTH DAKOTA REFERENDUM CAMPAIGN—TACTICS OF LEAGUE OPPOSITION AND BETRAYAL OF PEOPLE BY THREE STATE OFFICIALS FAIL TO SWAY FARMERS FROM PURPOSE."

Attempts by the opposition to tie up League laws through court action were likewise unsuccessful, and the *Leader* of June 30 announced the League victory thus: "LEAGUE WINS TWO BIG COURT VICTORIES—SUPREME COURT OF NORTH DAKOTA ORDERS SECRETARY OF STATE TO SIGN BANK BONDS—INDUSTRIAL PROGRAM UPHELD BY UNITED STATES JUDGE."

The most effective technique employed by the opposition was in

---

Nelson, *A Volume of truth in words and pictures,* pp. 3-16. Fargo, North Dakota, June 17, 1917.

[53] *The I.V.A., its plan of organization and operation,* p. 13.

actually supporting candidates for office, at first on a modified League program and later in opposition to practically everything the League stood for. Coalitions were formed between the Republicans and Democrats, and a joint campaign committee was formed to promote the candidacy of those who ran against League candidates. Pamphlets were issued by the dozen purporting to show why and how the League administration had been a failure and urgently asking that it be replaced. League leaders were charged with mismanagement of public money, with Socialistic and I.W.W. connections, with autocracy, radicalism, and similar charges.[54]

In 1920, the opposition succeeded in getting approval by the electorate of two I.V.A.-initiated measures curtailing the activities of the Bank of North Dakota,[55] but the League administration continued to hold nearly all of the state offices. In October, 1921, however, the powerful Industrial Commission was deposed in a recall election, and Frazier was replaced as governor by R. A. Nestos, a young lawyer from Minot with I.V.A. endorsement. The industrial program was again saved by the defeat of four initiated measures designed to dissolve or curtail the Bank of North Dakota and to limit the powers of the Industrial Commission. Through a coalition of Republicans and Democrats, Nestos defeated William Lemke for the governorship in 1922, but Lynn J. Frazier was elected to the United States Senate, and all other Republican candidates, League and conservative, were elected; all Independents were snowed under in a Republican landslide. This election dealt another

---

[54] Some of the pamphlets issued by the Joint Campaign Committee were: *Voters' guide*, Fargo, North Dakota, 31 pages. Printed at Grand Forks. *Trade unionism and Townleyism*, Grand Forks, North Dakota, 13 pages. *Legislative purposes of the League leadership and procedure to attain it*, Grand Forks, North Dakota, 15 pages. *An enemy of church and home*, Fargo, North Dakota. *Reasons for the recall*, Fargo, 4 pages. Other pamphlets "paid for and distributed by the I.V.A." were: *Our taxes and the cost of our state government; Labor legislation in the last session of North Dakota's legislature; Our Socialist autocracy; Frank and Tom discuss the primary election; Reasons why good citizens cannot vote for Lynn J. Frazier for United States Senator if they want to be honest with themselves and loyal to their state and nation.* Statement by Joint Anti-Townley Republican-Democratic and Independent Voters Association Campaign Committee. Fargo, North Dakota, 1922.

[55] For discussion of these initiated measures, see *N. D. Publicity Pamphlet*. Constitutional Amendments Initiated and Referred Measures. Issued under authority of law by Thomas Hall, Secretary of State. Bismarck, North Dakota: Bismarck Tribune, State Printers, 1920.

stunning blow to the League in North Dakota, virtually writing the finale to its regime in that state. Control of all important state offices and of both houses of the legislature was gone and only two representatives in the halls of the United States Congress were left to carry the League banner. The opposition had done a very thorough job in removing the Townley administration from its once all-powerful position in North Dakota.

THE LEAGUE AND THE FARMERS' MOVEMENT

The story of the decline of the Nonpartisan League, though told as briefly as possible, reveals that it was political involvements and conflicts, not primarily its economic program, that caused its demise. Townley, who conceived the political attack on the farmers' problems, apparently came to believe that this was a mistake. In his letter of resignation from the presidency of the League in 1922, he said:

> I have finally reached the conclusion that a strong, active and numerous membership in each state is the only basis upon which political and economic success can be built, and that in striving for the election of candidates we have lost sight of the important things. In other words, we have devoted all our force and energy to seeking the election of our candidates and have neglected the re-enrollment of old and securing new members.
>
> And finally and most important of all, I have concluded that this neglect of enrollments and failure to give it first attention was due to the fact that in each state we have been endeavoring to carry on both political and economic functions through one set of executives. It is my opinion that this work of enrolling members is a business function, requiring specialized training, and is inevitably bound to be neglected and fail, if required of men who are at the same time engaged in the business of looking after the political activities of the League.[56]

Townley was speaking of the internal organization and the day-by-day work of that organization. Probably a more important commentary is one concerning the role and character of a public as an instrument of

---

[56] Saloutos, *Decline of the Nonpartisan League,* p. 251. Reprinted by permission of the Agricultural History Society.

a movement. As Bogardus says: "a person is a member of several publics at the same time." [57] A necessary corollary of this fact is that not all members of any given public do, or can, give their major attention and energy to that public. Furthermore, some who have attached themselves to a going public do so in order to have standing in it which they can use for other purposes in which they are interested. Equity members became a part of the Nonpartisan League public because its prime objectives were those for which they were already mobilized. The Socialist party formed a temporary liaison with the League because of its public ownership ideas. The Farmer-Labor party, like the League, was interested in a realignment of party affiliations. The La Follette forces, and La Follette himself, believed in the basic reforms which the League was attempting to accomplish. Many outsiders who went to North Dakota to help the League were believers in socialism, cooperatives, third parties, or broad liberalism. Such a diversity of sentiments may focus temporarily on a clearly defined set of pertinent issues, but they can seldom be kept in balance long enough to carry out a specific program. This was illustrated in the Nonpartisan League episode. The Socialist party of North Dakota abolished its organization department when it became convinced that other than its own prime interests were being served. The League probably sowed seeds in Minnesota which grew into segments of the Farmer-Labor party. The League public later proved that it was loyal to La Follette, but when it tried to enter Wisconsin, it appears that La Follette could not afford to have it dilute his powerfully established public in that state.

As we shall see later, a political party is seldom a movement, and all American movements have dissolved when they have become political parties. As Saloutos says, "Mass movements are of temporary duration unless founded upon economic organization that functions every day of the year..." [58] They may not be "economic organizations" at all, but they are not movements unless they consistently and constantly and effectively attack the same set of issues. Even the old Equity Exchange leaders abandoned the League and fought it when its day-by-day activi-

---

[57] E. S. Bogardus, *Fundamentals of social psychology*, p. 275. New York: Appleton-Century-Crofts, Inc., 1924.

[58] Saloutos, *Decline of the Nonpartisan League*, p. 251.

ties came to have more to do with politics than with the farmers' price and market problems. Some of its strongest early political backers abandoned it when it showed signs of returning to these prime issues of the Farmers' Movement. Thus the League was a fairly ephemeral political episode. To the extent that it, more clearly than any other episode in the Farmers' Movement, defined the issues at stake, it was, and is, a part of the American Farmers' Movement.

THE COOPERATIVE

MARKETING MOVEMENT

F^{armers' cooperatives have always wrestled with the specific prob-}
lems that constitute the core issues of the Farmers' Movement.
In striving for a larger portion of the consumer's dollar they have shot
directly at the bull's-eye issues of prices and markets. Their purposes
have always been the same and their activities have been so persistent
and so consistent that the history of farmers' cooperative marketing undertakings constitutes a movement in and of itself.

The Grange, Alliance, Union, and Equity launched many cooperative
undertakings. Some associations set up by them are still in existence and
prospering. Many of them failed and the vast majority went down during periods of decline in the strength and influence of general farmers'
organizations. Farmers' cooperatives, however, began their development
in the United States long before the first general farmers' organization,
the Grange, was organized in 1869; and by no means are all cooperative
associations currently operating under the sponsorship of general farmers' organizations. In a number of instances independently organized
cooperatives were picked up by, or covered by the programs of, general
farmers' organizations. The Grange in the 1870's and 1880's attached
itself to a fairly well-developed farmers' elevator movement, and some

State Farm Bureaus were organized in the 1920's as sponsoring agencies for large cooperatives which were already launched. Cooperatives have contributed to the Farmers' Movement both as parts of general farmers' organizations and independently of them.

A comprehensive story of the evolving Farmers' Movement therefore requires an analysis of the different tactics employed by many farmers' cooperatives as well as those employed by farmers in many of the episodes described in earlier chapters. Most of the problems which cooperatives ran into as they moved deeper and deeper into marketing activities were the same as those with which the Grange, Alliance, Union, and Equity dealt from 1870 to 1920: inadequate inspection, railroad company control of marketing channels and facilities, large corporate commission firms, lack of credits, terminal elevators and stockyards, problems of weights and measures, and even political domination by others than farmers. It is the purpose of this chapter to describe the types of experiences farmers' cooperatives have had and the tactics they employed or evolved as they wrestled with these problems.

While some American farmers were attacking price and market problems by restricting production, withholding products from the market, and even destroying portions of products ready for the market, others were forming themselves into local neighborhood and community groups to improve the marketability of their products. While general farmers' organizations were building or buying terminal storage facilities and even establishing banks and other big businesses, hundreds of local groups were building, buying, or renting local elevators and organizing local livestock-shipping associations in order to take just one or two short steps down the channels of trade which ran between them and the large central urban markets. While more militant farmers were organizing legislative pressure groups and even organizing political parties, many local farmers' cooperative associations were federating in order to be able to take a few more steps toward controlling or at least influencing other than local processes involved in the marketing of their products. This step-by-step entrance into the price and market economy is the story of cooperative marketing.

In the days when American farmers delivered their products to town consumers by peddling eggs, vegetables, meat, butter, cheese, etc., they had no great price and market problems. They were processors, transporters, and salesmen, as well as producers. When modern and elaborate systems of transportation widened their markets and created great distances between them and consumers, they could no longer market their products directly. Even some of the processing which had previously been done on farms and in farm homes passed into the hands of factories controlled by others. A number of other businesses were established along the market road which ran between the farmers and the consumers. The history of cooperative marketing is the story of the attempts of farmers to retain or recapture control of some of the functions they lost in this economic development. This story cannot be told in detail here. All that will be presented are illustrations which show how, through attempts at direct marketing, farmers have discovered that they are involved in all the price, market, credit, and other issues with which the Farmers' Movement has dealt. The illustrations selected are the cooperative marketing of dairy products, grain, cotton, and citrus fruit.

DAIRY PRODUCTS COOPERATIVES [1]

Farmers had been making butter and cheese in their own homes and selling them to local consumers long before commercial markets developed. When more distant markets opened up, some of their home-processed products were already prepared to be shipped. All they needed to do was to produce them in greater volume and standardize them. It is thus easy to understand why dairy products cooperatives were the first to be founded by American farmers. Early cheese rings were simply composed of small groups of neighboring farmers, each a home processor, who pooled their milk in large enough volume to make cheese of various types and sizes. No adequate account of the earliest undertakings in this field has been recorded in detail, but it appears that as early as 1810 some dairy producers in Connecticut attempted to make and sell butter cooperatively. The first successful attempt at such cooperation however, was made in 1841 by the dairy farmers of Jefferson County, Wisconsin. Then in 1851 some farmers in Oneida County, New York, banded together to make and sell cheese. A cooperative creamery

---

[1] For a discussion of dairy cooperatives, the most easily obtainable single source of information is the *Annual proceedings of the American Institute of Cooperation, 1920.* See especially pp. 43-68, 535-538.

was founded in Orange County, New York, five years later; and another one in Montgomery County, New York, in 1863. These cooperatives were followed by others in the next two decades in Vermont, Massachusetts, Pennsylvania, Ohio, Illinois, Michigan, and Wisconsin. By 1920, there were 4,000 of them in the United States.

Cooperative creameries were also processing plants in which farmers followed one farm product one step down the road to market by converting fluid milk into butter. At the same time the farmers set up wholesale selling institutions to dispose of the product. Specialized dairy farmers could market their whole farm product through these cooperatives, and dozens of general farmers could market smaller amounts of milk through these same institutions. They were thus operated in many other than in specialized dairy areas, milk and cream routes being established to gather the excess milk and cream from general farms. They freed the farmer from customary barter practices with local stores, freed the housewife from the irksomeness of making "small dabs" of butter, and, above all, placed the farmer in a position to produce standardized quality, and even branded butter. Once this was done, actual merchandising of dairy products could be accomplished. To bring this about in any effective way, however, required a volume of business, inspection, advertising, and all the machinery essential to large-scale, standardized overhead operation. These steps automatically followed.

An illustration of how these steps were taken is the story of the Sheboygan County Cheese Producers' Federation, later the Wisconsin Cheese Producers' Federation. It was formed in 1913 by forty-three local cooperative cheese factories, each holding one membership. The Federation then formed the Farmers' Federated Warehouse Company and built storage facilities in order not to be rushed into the necessity of dumping its products on the market. During its first year of operation, it handled 6,108,500 pounds of cheese, enough to make it a substantial sales agent for all the local factories which owned it. In 1921, it handled almost 14,000,000 pounds of cheese, 5.5 per cent of the total Wisconsin state production. A Federal Trade Commission report, written in 1926, tells of the continued growth of this organization up to that time. It was then the selling organization for 205 cheese factories, which had a combined farmer membership of 8,000. It handled 33,614,000 pounds of cheese that year, 11 per cent of all Wisconsin production. It also sold cheese for 27 factories located in Minnesota. It was marketing to jobbers, wholesalers, packers, and processed-cheese manufacturers and returning sales receipts, less handling charges, to its members. It had thus traveled all the way down the market road from the farmer to the consumer except for the final step of retail selling.

A local cooperative creamery or cheese factory was, of course, a comparatively small business unit in the total field of dairy production. It could not support a central-market sales agent, and therefore had to sell to traveling country buyers or depend on its manager to sell through some other middleman. There was at least one middleman still between them and the central markets. Furthermore, each cooperative was a competitor of all other cooperatives in wholesale markets.

It is not necessary to repeat similar stories of the development of cooperative creameries. It has already been noted that some of them were organized before 1860. They spread slowly but steadily into practically all areas of the country, not only where dairy farming prevailed, but wherever any goodly number of farmers had small amounts of excess fluid milk. As there came to be many of them in fairly concentrated areas, such as Minnesota, Iowa, and Wisconsin, they developed centralized cooperatives by federating local creameries into selling and marketing agencies. Probably the earliest of these were the cooperative at Tulare, California, in 1911, and the Minnesota Cooperative Creameries Association established that same year. The latter was a stock company owned by 130 cooperative creameries which later established and operated a commission house in New York City. This company thus took all steps in marketing from local assembling and processing to shipping, storing, financing, and selling in world markets. By 1921 this Association included 345 creameries. The Federal Trade Commission reported in 1926 that it then included 503 creameries, which together had 75,000 farmer members. It is known today as Land O'Lakes Creameries and its products are as well known as almost any brand product purchased by American housewives.

The cooperative attack that affects the greatest number of producers of dairy products consists of fluid-milk bargaining and operating organizations. These organizations are made up of farmers who seek to have some influence on the amount and price of milk that flows into given large urban centers. They are of two types, those which operate marketing facilities and those which only bargain concerning prices, quantities, standards, etc. In a great many instances, organizations which started as groups of farmers bargaining with distributors later became convinced that they must own processing plants and shipping and distributing facilities of their own. This was true of one of the outstanding organizations of the nation, the Dairyman's League of New York State. After a period of operation, this organization became convinced that local cooperatives were neither efficient nor sufficiently powerful. It now owns about 200 plants, all controlled by the central organization. Fluid-milk cooperatives have thus passed rapidly from groups of farmers who joined hands to eliminate competing city milk routes, through the stages of bargaining with distributors, to well-organized and disciplined groups of milk producers which are more numerous than any other type of cooperative in the nation.

LIVESTOCK COOPERATIVES

In the history of the cooperative marketing of farm products, that of livestock is probably the least spectacular, but it is a better illustration, in some ways, than any other of how farmers have attempted to keep control of those steps nearest to them in the marketing process. When livestock began to move to distant markets, the first function beyond the farm in marketing was performed by the shipper who assembled hogs, sheep, or cattle in great enough numbers to ship to central markets in carload lots. He was, in most cases, an entrepreneur who actually purchased the stock from the farmer, and shipped and sold it in his own name. He was therefore the first middleman between the farmer and consumer. Although he was generally a person well-known to the farmers, it was his function that farmers sought to take over by organizing local cooperative shipping associations. Having done this, the cooperative shipping associations naturally began to deal with terminal stockyards, commission men, and packers in selling their stock.

General farmers' organizations—the Grange, Alliance, Union, and Equity—had attacked livestock-marketing problems in their programs, but for the most part by attempting to establish terminal-market sales agencies. The Missouri State Grange had its own sales agency in St.

Louis in the 1870's. The Kansas State Grange and the Farmers' Alliances of Kansas, Nebraska, and Missouri established the American Livestock Commission Company and opened offices in Chicago, Kansas City, East St. Louis, and Omaha in 1889. This company did a substantial business for two years, but under the opposition of commission firms it ceased operation in 1891. The Equity Cooperative Exchange established a livestock division in 1916 to serve the many local livestock shipping associations which the American Society of Equity had organized in the Middle West and continued in operation until the Exchange sold its livestock division to the Iowa Farmers' Union in 1922. The Nebraska Farmers' Union established the Farmers' Union Livestock Commission in Omaha in 1917, and during the next year established commissions in St. Joseph and Sioux City. The Kansas Union established one in Kansas City in 1919, and the Colorado Union established one in Denver that same year. These five cooperative commission companies added St. Paul and Chicago to their markets when they purchased the livestock division of the Equity Cooperative Exchange in 1922.

Although few of these early general farmer organization associations continued to operate for any great length of time, the association at Superior, Nebraska, was an exception. Briefly, the story of that association concerns twenty farmers who met at a country schoolhouse to organize in protest against what they believed were rake-offs of local buyers. They did not necessarily believe these buyers were crooked, but were convinced that they bought on too wide margins, found that they refused to pay premiums for superior animals, and suspected the relationship between the buyer and the railroads and commission men. They took over this first step in marketing by organizing a cooperative shipping association.

It will be remembered that the American Society of Equity (not the Equity Cooperative Exchange) specialized in organizing local exchanges and that in the Middle West most of these exchanges were grain elevators or local livestock-shipping associations. Three of the earliest shipping associations were at Postville, Iowa (1904); Durand, Wisconsin (1906); and Litchfield, Minnesota (1908). After that, they multiplied rapidly. By 1916 there were 143 in Minnesota, 120 in Wisconsin, and 57 in Iowa. When the Farmers' Union became strong in Nebraska and Kansas, shipping associations developed rapidly in that area. The development was slower in other corn-belt states, but it was estimated that there were not less than 500 livestock-shipping associations in 1916. By 1920, there were approximately twice that number.

The purposes of local shipping associations were "to obtain for every farmer what his stock were worth" and to handle shipments from the farm to terminal markets at cost, both of which it was believed would increase prices. Many, if not most, of the early local shipping associations were unincorporated. Membership dues were nominal, most often only $1.00, and generally collected out of sales. Nonmembers were often permitted to ship through the association and members were not compelled to do so. Sometimes the shipping association was an adjunct of a local Equity Exchange or Farmers' Union elevator, or other local cooperative. The functions they performed were: assembling livestock in carload lots, consigning them to the market, and distributing the proceeds of sale. Someone, of course, had to be responsible for securing listings from farmers to deliver their stock to the local shipping point, securing the car, loading it and billing it out, keeping the accounts, and dispersing the sales receipts. This required a local, part-time or full-time manager; once such a manager was employed, the shipping association had completely taken over the local middleman function for their members.

Immediately after this was accomplished, farmers began to discover some of the business intricacies or complexities that existed on the market road which they had decided to travel. The first thing they learned was that it was very uneconomical, almost literally impossible, for stockyards to handle and commission men to sell a carload of stock in the five to twenty separate lots which represented the individual ownerships of the shippers. It not only took time and yard space, but scale charges were higher and the animals themselves lost weight because of so much sorting and resorting. The terminal commission men therefore passed the problem back to the local cooperative shipping associations, and the local manager had to assume the responsibility of grading and docking. When this was done, shipping associations discovered that some of their members preferred to trust their own talents in dickering with a local buyer to taking the dockage assigned by their own manager, or to trust him to assign premiums which they believed their stock deserved. The only way around this was to establish more formal associations, adopt binding contracts for delivery of stock and acceptance of the responsibilities and obligations necessary to cooperative operation.

When local shipping associations began taking responsibility for delivering their livestock to terminal markets, they of course discovered that there were transit problems: stock in transit had to be watered and fed; delays in transit had to be ironed out; and railroad damage to stock had to be taken into account. These problems, plus the fact that a great number of local shipping associations had come into existence, suggested the desirability of federation of locals into larger, more efficient, and more powerful organizations. The first of these was the Minnesota Central Cooperative Livestock Shipping Association, organized in 1915. It began immediately to tackle not only the problem of securing more adequate settlement of claims against railroads for damage or loss in transit, but to obtain better stockyard facilities at local shipping points, adjustment of train schedules, and even legislation which required inspection and efficiency of terminal market operation. This organization was, of course, interested primarily in the St. Paul livestock market, and in about five years prepared to enter that central market with its own sales agency.

Livestock-shipping associations did not experience the bitter fights with which some other commodity groups have had to contend. Of course, they were not generally well received by local buyers whom they sought to replace; and they were, at some places, conscious of the opposition of other local businessmen and organizations. Some of them thought they were discriminated against by railroads in local stockyards and in obtaining cars for shipping stock. Many commission firms and central markets were unfriendly. But the cooperative marketing of livestock by local shipping associations had a comparatively tranquil development. Livestock producers' central marketing organizations had a different experience when, a few years later, they began to be real competitors in central markets.[2]

---

[2] For the best general source on livestock cooperatives, see Nourse and Knapp, *The cooperative marketing of livestock*. Washington, D. C.: The Brookings Institution, 1931.

GRAIN COOPERATIVES

The farmers' elevator movement had an early history very similar to that of livestock shipping associations and dairy cooperatives. Discontent on the part of grain growers began almost with the settlement of the Middle West, due, first, to inadequate grain assembling facilities at local shipping points, and, second, to a conviction that local grain traders and railroads were making more money out of grain than were the farmers. Nourse records the organization of at least two farmers' elevator companies in Iowa before Granger days and postulates, probably correctly, that the Grange grew as much on the basis of discontent which caused these early elevators to be organized, as elevators during and immediately after 1872 grew at the hands of Grange promotion. He, however, gives the Grange credit for what he calls the first farmers' elevator movement in Iowa. It reached its high tide in 1874, when there were thirty-three farmers' elevators in that state. The *Proceedings* of the 1873 Iowa State Grange reported that one-third of the grain elevators and warehouses in the state were owned or controlled by Granges and that five million bushels of grain had been shipped directly to Chicago through Grange agents. Some elevators established during the Alliance days in the 1880's—at Cedar Bluffs, Nebraska; Rockwell, Iowa; and Goodwine, Illinois—were still operating fifty years later.

The protest of five farmers against local grain dealers gave rise to the Farmers' Mutual Benefit Association in 1882; and the American Society of Equity, organized in 1902, within ten years fathered the outstanding attack of the Equity Cooperative Exchange on the whole grain-marketing system. The Farmers' Union, once it was well established in the Pacific Northwest, led the fight of the grain growers in that region. These general farmers' organizations cannot, however, claim the sole credit for the widespread growth of farmers' local cooperative elevators. The elevators sprang up in all the wheat belts of the nation and illustrate better than any other type of farmers' local cooperatives the movement which gained force for two decades, and finally became an almost nationwide issue in the wheat and other grain pools in the early twenties of this century.

Local elevator companies, whether under the auspices of general farmers' organizations or not, and whether cooperatives or stock companies, attempted to take over some of the steps in marketing during the evolution of our commercial and industrial economy. Not all of the bitter struggles against those who had previously performed these functions were carried on by general farmers' organizations, but the farmers' elevator movement thrived on the sentiments stirred up by such struggles. There were 100 cooperative elevators in 1904, 1,000 in 1907, 1,866 in 1911, and, as calculated by Steen, more than 5,000 in 1921. In this movement, the farmers eliminated excessive dockage at country elevators, got safe storage places for their grain, were to some extent in charge of their own grading, and undoubtedly narrowed the margin between farm and central-market grain prices. But they still had to sell to, or use, terminal elevators which belonged to others, and they had no direct contacts with the millers or other wholesale buyers, into whose hands their grain had to flow after it was shipped from country elevators. They had thus taken only the first relatively successful step on the road which the Grangers and Alliancemen had trod when they tried to influence the grain markets of the nation by handling their products all the way from the farm to the flour mill or tried to influence world grain prices by holding.[3]

COTTON COOPERATIVES [4]

Cotton was pretty much a market crop from its earliest production in the United States, but the fact that it was produced mostly on plantations which were large enough business organizations to maintain business connections in Central American and European markets was not conducive to cooperative endeavors. When, however, these conditions no longer prevailed, smaller farmers began to join hands in the marketing of their cotton. The Grange furnished the first organized vehicle for

---

[3] Probably the best single, broad yet brief review and analysis of grain cooperatives is *Letter from the Chairman of the Federal Trade Commission transmitting that Commission's analysis of Cooperative Marketing,* chap. iii, pp. 47-78. Washington, D. C.: Government Printing Office, 1928.

[4] The one document that presents the greatest amount of information on the cooperative marketing of cotton, in brief terms, is O. W. Herrmann and C. Gardner, *Early developments in cooperative cotton marketing.* Circular No. C-101, 1936, Farm Credit Administration, Washington, D. C. See also R. H. Montgomery, *The cooperative pattern in cotton.* New York: The Macmillan Company, 1929.

their endeavors. State Grangers in practically all cotton-growing states began attempting to market cotton in bulk. They appointed state sales agents to handle their members' cotton, placed them under bond, sometimes established sales agents in New York, New Orleans, and even in Liverpool. When it became apparent that these types of activity did little to influence prices, they attempted acreage limitation. Nine cotton-producing states presented "A Memorial to the Cotton States" at the National Grange Convention, in 1874, urging the Grange members in these states to reduce their cotton acreage.

The Farmers' Alliance and the Farmers' Union continued these same types of endeavors, but no outstanding cotton cooperatives were established until after 1920. Even before the turn of the century, and thus before the organization of the Farmers' Union, associations of cotton growers put on campaigns for acreage reduction and withholding. The Southern Cotton Growers' Protective Association for years conducted a campaign to induce farmers to plant fewer acres and hold cotton until it would sell for the price set by the association. In 1905, with the assistance of the Farmers' Union, it became the Southern Cotton Association, including in its membership bankers, merchants, and other business people in the cotton belt. Meetings were held all over the South advocating not only reduction of cotton acreage, but reduction in the amount of fertilizer used.

Another organization, the National Cotton Association, was organized in 1908, the main object of which was "to establish and maintain at all times a minimum 'bread-and-meat' line of 10 cents per pound." It, and similar associations less well known, attempted some cooperative marketing, but they were all chiefly reduction-of-acreage and holding movements. Even the activities of the Farmers' Union followed this pattern to a greater or less extent. As an outgrowth of these holding movements, one basic step was taken on the market road from farmer to consumer. Hundreds of local warehouses were built to protect cotton from "country damage" while it was being withheld from the market. Cotton thus stored could be and was used as collateral for loans, and thus a second step was brought partly under control. Few of these warehouse companies were, however, cooperatives.

Likewise a goodly number of so-called "cooperative gins" were built during this period, probably the earliest one by a group of Texas Farmers' Alliancemen in 1887. The Farmers' Union, especially in Texas and Oklahoma, organized a great many such companies between 1905 and 1920. Most of them were joint-stock companies, but they paid patronage dividends. Herrmann tells the story of one such association organized in 1913 by the Texas Farmers' Union District No. 28, including Knox and Haskell counties. It was a success from the start and has been in existence ever since. He also tells the story of the Scott Cotton Growers' Association, organized in 1912 by twenty-four large cotton growers in Arkansas, which was a real cotton-marketing cooperative. It did not attempt to limit acreage or influence price by other than efficient functioning. The purposes provided in its charter were:

(1) to produce cotton from pure seed; (2) to obtain uniformity in ginning; (3) to sell cotton in even running lots; (4) to deal as nearly direct with the mills as possible; (5) to act in cooperation with the United States Department of Agriculture towards accomplishing these objectives; and (6) to take such further action as might be practicable to produce better cotton and improve the prevailing methods of handling and marketing the same.

This association operated successfully until 1922, when it was absorbed by the Arkansas Cotton Growers' Cooperative Association, which in turn was a part of the cooperative marketing movement which swept the South in the early 1920's.

The agitation for better prices for, and more efficient marketing of, cotton built both the Farmers' Alliance and the Farmers' Union into giant organizations in the South. It built one cotton association after another. Still, the cooperative marketing of cotton, one of the great cash crops of the country, made no outstanding contribution to cooperative marketing before 1920. Just before, during, and after 1920, cotton growers, together with hundreds of thousands of other farmers, were swept into the most furious cooperative marketing campaign ever staged in the history of the nation.

Cotton growers, and grain and tobacco growers, have played leading roles in the Farmers' Movement throughout its history. Their products were for a long while the leading cash crops of the country and were therefore the first to enter completely the market economy. Their ultimate consumers and some of the middlemen who handled them were more distant from farmers than was the case with some other farm products. It therefore appeared to these farmers that they must strike a more distant target than was possible through local cooperatives. The outstanding success of combining both types of attack was illustrated by the rise of so-called "commodity marketing associations." (See below.)

MARKETING OTHER COMMODITIES

Other cooperatives have repeated this same type of experience. Potato pools, along with grain and tobacco pools, constituted one of the major marketing pools of the American Society of Equity. The Eastern Shore of Virginia Produce Exchange, organized in 1910, is a good illustration of another cash-crop cooperative marketing association. Its chief business has been the marketing of potatoes. Local associations of truckers have, for more than three-quarters of a century, practiced different degrees of cooperation in marketing vegetables. In fact, farmers have attempted cooperative marketing of every type of farm product which flows to market in any considerable volume. In all cases, they have attempted to recapture a degree of control over the movement of products which they lost when they entered the price and market economy.

When they became involved in the price and market economy, they of course increased their purchases as well as their sales. The history of their purchasing cooperatives in the United States is therefore as old as the history of their marketing cooperatives. That history will not be related in this volume because, by and large, it did not take on the characteristics of a movement until after 1920.

COMMODITY MARKETING ON THE PACIFIC COAST

While the farmers' cooperative marketing movement was gaining ground through the medium of local organizations in other sections of the country, the farmers of the Pacific Coast, mainly those of California, were developing a different approach to the problem, which later came to be known as the "commodity" cooperative marketing approach. The fundamental theory of this form of marketing was that producers never could be really influential in central and national markets unless they controlled the major portion of a given market product, or at least until they had organized a majority of the producers of that product or commodity into one marketing association. This type of organization was first represented in this country by the citrus-fruit growers in California.

The first carload of oranges was shipped out of California in 1877, but in less than ten years the shipments exceeded 2,000 cars per year, and the growers found themselves in a precarious financial condition because of heavy investments in orange groves and declining prices. The custom was for the farmer to sell his crop outright to a buyer, who offered either a lump sum or a given price per pound or bushel. Thus the buyer assumed all risks of shipping, of glutted eastern markets, and of unpredictable and fluctuating market prices. This was a proper middleman responsibility, but in the case of oranges, which were perishable and an agricultural specialty at that time, middlemen had to buy on exceedingly wide margins to cover their risks. The producers were convinced that, in addition to these inevitable conditions of speculative buying, there was an agreement between buyers to apportion the producing areas among themselves. There was no documentary proof that this was true, but growers did know that they received bids from one buyer and no others, and that prices offered by all buyers to all farmers were uniform in comparison to fluctuating central market prices.[5]

The first organized step taken by the growers was that of the Orange Growers' Protective Union, which met in Los Angeles on October 24, 1885. After all-day and evening sessions for several days, the assembled growers recorded the following in their minutes:

> The disastrous results in the prices obtained [and] the apparent dishonesty of many commission houses in handling the orange crop of Southern California set the producers to thinking and inquiring what shall we do to make our crops remunerative. The few who were fortunate to receive returns that were satisfactory were only lucky, whereas their neighbors everywhere marketed their oranges at a loss.[6]

---

[5] William W. Cumberland, *Cooperative marketing*, pp. 43-44. Princeton, New Jersey: Princeton University Press, 1917.

[6] R. M. MacCurdy, *The history of the California Fruit Growers Exchange*, p. 10. Los Angeles, California: G. Rice and Sons, printer, 1925. Reprinted by permission of the California Fruit Growers Exchange.

A board of directors was elected and an executive committee of five was appointed to carry out the will of the convention. Two salaried representatives were sent east that winter to arrange with commission firms for the sale of fruit. The following February (1886), a contract for members was adopted which provided for payment to the Corporation (Protective Union) of two and one-half cents on every box of oranges or lemons sold by members, whether sold by the organization or personally. The money collected from these payments was to be used

> to defray the expenses of the Corporation, incurred by it in carrying out the purposes for which it was formed; viz:
> To regulate the shipments of citrus fruits and distribute the same in such manner as to prevent the overstocking of markets, and thereby prevent such competition among the stockholders or their fruits as is prejudicial to their interests;
> To seek out the best markets and by careful inquiry ascertain the most reliable and responsible commission merchants in the eastern cities and in San Francisco, and to keep its stockholders informed of such markets and merchants;
> To make the best terms with such merchants for the stockholders of this Company;
> And, generally, to promote the interests of the stockholders in this company in all matters arising in the course of the trade.[7]

Indicative of the animus of the growers was a resolution adopted by the Union, in December, 1885, which read as follows:

> That it is the sense of this board of directors that the Orange Growers Protective Union should not enter into entangling alliances with fruit dealers, but should avail themselves, when proper, of the facilities that they may have to offer, bearing in mind that this Union is one of growers and for the interests of growers.[8]

The secretary of the Union claimed that it shipped more than 1,000 cars of fruit and returned $23 per car as dividends to its members. The

---

[7] *Ibid.*, p. 11. Reprinted by permission.
[8] *Ibid.*, p. 13. Reprinted by permission.

Union, however, ". . . succumbed, due to the persistent opposition of the commission men and buyers, who were able to make larger profits by dealing with the growers individually." [9]

Because there was concerted and successful opposition to the activities of the Union by speculative buyers and because it was not organized to offer effective and efficient substitute methods of marketing for the old speculative system, the Union went out of existence and things grew steadily worse. The number of cars of citrus fruit—oranges and lemons— shipped out of California increased steadily year after year, but the complaint was widespread that growers were not only producing and giving away their crops for nothing, but were receiving bills instead of profits at the end of the year. Often prices would not cover the costs of packing and transporting, let alone yielding anything toward the expenses of production. It frequently happened that the larger the crop a grower produced, the more he was indebted to a packer or shipper at the end of the season.[10]

While the abortive effort of the Protective Union was going on, there was a local group of growers near Riverside, California, and another at Claremont who were starting at the grass roots of cooperation and making effective headway. The one near Riverside was the Pachappa Orange Growers' Association, now generally recognized as the originator of the form of cooperative marketing which the California Fruit Growers' Exchange made famous. Eleven neighboring growers banded themselves together in 1888 and agreed to pool their fruit and sell as a group to a packer. Later they contracted with a packer to sell their own product. They formally incorporated in 1892, and during the season of 1893 operated with a packer under a contract which provided: (a) that their entire crops would be delivered to the packer to be "weighed, culled, graded, packed, sold, shipped, or otherwise disposed of under the management and supervision of the Pachappa Orange Growers Association," (b) that they share expenses (presumably per units of product each had in the pool), (c) that they should "fully participate in the shipment of their fruit," and (d) that they would "receive their pro-rata share of the

———

[9] *Ibid.*
[10] Cumberland, p. 47.

net proceeds of the fruit so shipped according to varieties delivered and in the manner prescribed for the distribution of the same." [11]

With discontent among growers widespread and with the successful experience of the Pachappa Association in mind, a large meeting of growers was called in Los Angeles in 1893, and under the guidance of the leader of the Pachappa Growers, a plan was worked out and placed in operation during the period 1893-1895. The plan was later somewhat revised and the Southern California Fruit Exchange was organized in the fall of 1895. It operated successfully for eight seasons, and then some of its members unfortunately attempted to combine with the "dealers" into the California Fruit Agency and suffered a setback. The recovery from this mistake was rapid, however; and with an expanded membership, because of a geographically expanded area of production, it reincorporated into the California Fruit Growers' Exchange in September, 1905, and has operated under that name since that time. [12] The number of boxes of fruit shipped by the Exchange increased from 4,706,000 in 1905-1906 to 12,102,-000 in 1915-1916, and its f.o.b. return increased from $9,936,000 to $27,-703,000. During this ten-year period, the portion of the total California crop shipped by the Exchange increased from 47 to 67 per cent. [13]

One of the major points of difference in the contract between the members of the Orange Growers Protective Union and that of the Fruit Growers' Exchange was the requirement for delivery of products. The Union's contract read:

It is expected that the stockholders will always give the preference to this Company by buying, selling, shipping and transacting their business through the said Corporation. But this provision is not compulsory, the stockholders being at liberty to exercise their own judgment and consult their own interests. [14]

The Exchange's contract read:

It shall be the duty of all members of this Corporation, and they hereby agree, to sell and market their citrus fruit through the agency

---

[11] MacCurdy, pp. 16-17.
[12] Cumberland, pp. 55-58.
[13] *Ibid.*, p. 187.
[14] MacCurdy, pp. 11-12. Reprinted by permission.

of or by means provided and directed or by the agency or agents selected and employed by this Corporation only, and no member shall be at liberty to sell, market, or consign his citrus fruits through or by any other agency than such as are directed and provided or selected and employed by this Corporation.

In case any member of this Corporation does otherwise sell, market, or consign his said citrus fruits, his voting power and interest in this Association is forfeited, and he shall immediately pay to the Treasurer of this Corporation the sum of Twenty-five (25) cents for each and every packed box of commercial weight so sold, marketed, or consigned during the remainder of such fiscal year as liquidated damages; it being impracticable and extremely difficult to fix the actual damages suffered by this Corporation. In default of such payment, the same may be recovered by action in any court having jurisdiction, in the name of this Corporation as plaintiff.[15]

A brief description of the pattern of the organization and operation of the California agencies is offered at this point because this pattern, quickly followed by one Pacific Coast commodity group after another, became the blueprint and body of doctrine for the farmers' marketing upheaval in the 1920's. The pattern is about as follows: A group of producers of a given commodity signed a mutual contract to pool their products for the purpose of marketing; they incorporated under state law and democratically elected a board of directors which set up the business organization and employed the management; the management, under the directing policies of the board, operated the sales agency—receiving, processing, packing, shipping, financing, advertising, and selling the products of the whole pool; each member was bound by contract to deliver his whole crop to the organization and was penalized by "liquidating damages" if he failed to do so; careful accounts were kept and after deducting costs of operation, the funds from net sales were prorated to members according to quality and quantity of products.[16]

The more than thirty years of experience of California citrus growers by 1920 constitutes a dramatic story, beginning with a chaotic market, almost universal discontent on the part of growers, protest mass meetings

---

[15] Powell, p. 60.
[16] *Ibid.*, chap. iv.

and futile resolutions and false starts; continuing with fifteen years of trial and error; and finally culminating in fifteen years of outstanding success. Its experiences were duplicated on the Pacific Coast—to some extent at least—by raisin growers, apple growers, poultry producers, pear growers, berry growers, walnut and almond growers, honey producers, bean growers, prune and apricot growers, fig and peach growers, rice growers, alfalfa growers, and a number of others. It was out of this background, and in the face of falling postwar farm commodity prices, that the great surge forward in cooperative marketing came in the 1920's.[17]

From what has been presented in this brief chapter on cooperative marketing, it should be apparent that by 1920 many American farmers had come to understand quite thoroughly the issues and processes involved in the price and market economy. Events during the next two decades proved to them that even powerfully organized cooperatives could not successfully cope with all of these issues. The 1920's and 1930's therefore saw them demanding assistance which they believed could come only by way of legislation. During the 1920's, what was then called "McNary-Haugenism" staged one of the outstanding farmers' legislative fights in all American history. Out of this struggle, the newly organized American Farm Bureau Federation developed as rapidly as did the Grange out of the Granger political fight in the 1870's. Giant commodity marketing associations, built on the California Fruit Growers' Exchange pattern, joined with general farm organizations in the battle. The Farmers' Holiday Association organized market strikes out of which considerable violence developed. The farm depressions of the 1920's and 1930's resulted from farm conditions very similar to those which, in the 1880's and 1890's, gave rise to the Populist party. The political attack in the latter period was by farm blocs, legislative pressure groups, and powerfully organized farmer publics. That type of attack has ever since been the operating technique of the Farmers' Movement in the United States.

———

[17] Steen's book, *Cooperative marketing: the golden rule in agriculture*, written in 1922 when the so-called Sapiro movement was in full tide, tells the story of the rise and experience of most of these organizations. In chap. xxvi, he attempts to list all the associations in existence in 1922. Since it is not the purpose of this treatise to present a detailed survey of the history of cooperative marketing associations, only the oldest and best known of the commodity associations have been described.

· 2 0 ·

CONCEPTS

AND CONCLUSIONS

The preceding chapters have presented information on the outstanding episodes—revolts, economic and political upheavals, and farmers' organization activities—in which American farmers participated between 1620 and 1920. Each of a number of these episodes has been called a farmers' movement by others—the Grange movement, the Greenback movement, the Farm Holiday movement, etc. The theory was stated in Chapter 1 that each episode has been but one link in a chain of events which together constitute the American Farmers' Movement. The purpose of all chapters presented between the first chapter and this, the last chapter, has been to present what might be called laboratory observations of this movement.

The task of conceptually threading one's way through such vast and diverse bodies of information as are available to one who would study a movement of more than three hundred years' duration would be less difficult if other studies had patterned the social behavior and structure of movements. But literally no such studies have been made. A number of books and articles have been written which describe "reform movements," or have used the word "movement" to describe one or another relatively ephemeral upheaval or one or another body of ideologies promoted for a considerable period of time. The author of one such book stated that

"... the student of society is not yet in a position to make any scientific generalizations from the study of such complex phenomena."[1] Another analyst, in a review of American college Ph.D. theses in this field, said that he found no common concepts of movements used.[2] Both Blumer and Heberle, however, have set their hands to the conceptualizing of movements, the first more or less as an intellectual enterprise, and the second as a basis for analyzing phenomena which he himself has studied.[3] Heberle's concepts will be referred to later in this chapter.

It would have been impossible to interpret the vast and diverse body of information available to one who would study a movement without the use of concepts with which to winnow that information and arrange it in orderly fashion. Some of the author's concepts and theories were stated in Chapter 1 to assist the reader to see *a movement* as he read the various stories and accounts presented in succeeding chapters. The fact, is however, that the author did not have these concepts or hold these theories until a number of years after he began assembling information on farmers' class organizations and farmer upheavals. They evolved as he assembled and attempted to interpret a much greater body of information than it has been possible or necessary to present in this book. They were not and could not be borrowed from others who had studied movements, because no such studies had been made. Since this was the case, the author deems it necessary to explain how these concepts were derived and used. He in fact has two purposes in mind in doing this: first, to provide the reader with the rationale by which information was ordered and interpreted; and second, to describe what might be called the natural history of a concept.

---

[1] Jerome Davis, *Contemporary social movements*, p. 871. New York: Appleton-Century-Crofts, Inc., 1930.

[2] Paul Meadows, "Theses on Social Movements," *Social Forces*, Vol. XXIV, May, 1946, pp. 408-412.

[3] Herbert Blumer, "Social Movements," chap. xxii in Robert E. Park, ed., *The outline of the principles of sociology*. New York: Barnes and Noble, 1939. Rudolph Heberle, "Observations on the Sociology of Social Movements," *American Sociological Review*, Vol. XIV, No. 3 (June, 1949), pp. 346-357.

THE NATURAL HISTORY OF THE CONCEPT,
A FARMERS' MOVEMENT

The study started from a research undertaking quite different from the one into which it developed. The first search was for an answer to the question: "Are American farmers a social class?" Using the extant (1914-1915) theories of social classes, this search was fruitless, as it would probably be today. It, however, led to a study of the behavior of organized farmer groups. There were three well-known, national, general farm organizations at that time—the Grange, the Farmers' Union, and the American Society of Equity, the latter two quite militant in their behavior and public expressions. For more than a decade, the Union had been the chief spokesman for the farmers of the cotton belt and the Equity the chief spokesman for the farmers of the wheat belt. Both, over that period, had been persistently attacking farmers' marketing problems. The knowledge of this fact, interpreted by Thorstein Veblen's emphasis on the revolutionary results of the evolution of "the price and market regime" in Western society, furnished the author the first germ of a concept of an American Farmers' Movement. The broad hypothesis was: **that agriculture had lagged in its adjustment to the evolving price and market economy, and that farmers, by organized efforts, were struggling to catch step with that economy.**

A careful study of Buck's outstanding monograph *The Granger Movement* (1913) and consideration of the information furnished in Barrett's *The Mission, History and Times of the Farmers' Union* (1909) lent validity to this hypothesis, as did Powell's *Cooperation in Agriculture* (1913). The Equity Cooperative Exchange began to be powerful in 1915, and the Nonpartisan League was organized that same year. Each of these was making a direct attack on the grain growers' marketing problems. All of these facts, plus the author's boyhood knowledge of Farmers' Alliance activities, provided further validity to the hypothesis. It was not, however, a hypothesis of a movement.

It was a study of John R. Commons' two-volume work *The History of Labour in the United States* (1921) which furnished the final component of the concept, "a Farmers' Movement." Commons' book was not a history of the American Labor Movement, but in the last paragraph of his Introduction he wrote: "Thus while each period or decade has its characteristic features, and each has called forth differences both in emphasis and methods of treatment, yet through them all may be seen the evolution, more or less clear, of the economic conditions and social and political philosophies, which, like streams from different sources, have formed the labour movement of the twentieth century." [4]

This statement seemed to say that a movement does not necessarily consist of a series of events which are rationally or even consciously connected, but may consist of the evolution of economic conditions and the development of social and political philosophies, and that its main stream may be derived from various sources and may flow through various channels. On the basis of these concepts, the author formulated the following hypothesis: that, just as the various and varying struggles of laborers arose out of, and have always revolved about, the issues of wages, hours, and working conditions, and just as all these struggles combined constitute the American labor movement, so the various and varying struggles of farmers arose out of, and have always revolved about, the issues of prices, markets, and credits, and all these struggles combined constitute the American Farmers' Movement.

THE USE AND USEFULNESS OF THE HYPOTHESIS

There is the possibility that the fairly early formulation of the theory or hypothesis just stated may have served to bias the author in the assembling, selection, analysis, and interpretation of the great and diverse body of information, the gathering, sifting, and classification of which constituted his research task from that time forward. Patented concepts, especially borrowed ones, can do that very thing. But its formulation and use served as a guide in two important and necessary research activities. It furnished a thread of meaning (which is the function of concepts) to an almost incomprehensible body of known facts, and it led to a meticulous search for missing links in chains of facts. Much, if not most, of the information on farmers' revolts and agrarian ideologies was assembled as expositions of single episodes or narrowly limited historic periods. Other types of information came from newspaper accounts, which portrayed

---

[4] Commons, *The history of labour in the United States,* Vol. I, p. 21. Reprinted by permission of The Macmillan Company.

events merely as current news but served to reveal prevailing farmer sentiment. Much came from the reading and hearing of farm organization resolutions, farm leaders' speeches, propaganda shibboleths and slogans. Insight was gained by searching out and reading the fugitive literature which appeared during periods of pronounced farmer upheavals. Some of these types of information, especially those which revealed what the farmers themselves said, thought, and felt, were believed to be more significant than what the historians said or the statistical records on economic trends revealed. Out of this vast, diverse, and uneven body of information, there was no alternative but to use the prescription, "Cut down as far as you dare the number of things you are talking about; as few as you may; as many as you must." [5] Only the use of concepts and hypotheses will drive one to follow this edict in tracing a movement over a long period of recorded history. It is, however, submitted that the detailed study of volumes of information with little more than a general frame of reference—and not borrowed categories, all too often called concepts—is the first step in formulating a working hypothesis.

In this study, it seemed necessary to document the existence of the movement itself before starting to wrestle with the problem of where to classify it among academically catalogued social phenomena. Only after this was done, by means of a working hypothesis, and after a great body of information on the movement itself had been assembled and studied, could the patterns of behavior and the social structure of the movement be validly seen.

The use of only a concrete focus of reference or working hypothesis, quite different from borrowing a set of categories of classification from someone else, which may not be concepts at all for the task at hand, almost inevitably leads to some modification of the original working hypothesis. Such modification was necessary in the analysis of the American Farmers' Movement in order to adequately encompass the increasing complexity of the American economy over the long period the movement has covered. Not only prices and markets but transportation, credits and banking, corporations, taxes, and other economic functions of government became necessary components of the expanding and proliferating economy

---

[5] G. C. Homans, *The human group,* pp. 16-17. New York: Harcourt, Brace and Co., 1950.

and culture of American society. American farmers have inveighed against "corporations" and "monopolies," against "the grain exchange and the stock exchange," "the harvester trust," "the jute and binder twine trusts," "railroad rates," "high taxes," "high government expenditures" and "too much government." All of these are part and parcel of what Beard, Commons, and others have called "commercial capitalism." A more adequate statement of the hypothesis therefore became: that the American Farmers' Movement grew out of and has been continued by the more or less organized efforts of farmers either to protect themselves against the impact of the evolving commercial-capitalist economy or to catch step with it.

PATTERNS OF THE AMERICAN FARMERS' MOVEMENT

It is doubtful that the existence of the American Farmers' Movement could have been visualized or its stages precisely identified had there not been recurrent farmer upheavals. The upheavals took many forms: violent revolts, giant parades, formal farmers' organizations, political parties, and others. All, however, dealt with the same set of basic issues. A pattern of issues was therefore found to be the most consistent factor in structuring the movement. A concomitant of this pattern of issues was a pattern of ideologies, philosophies, and sentiments. Like the pattern of issues, they are not easily isolated one from the other, and probably should not be.

The interpretations of the issues by farmers were quite often nothing more than that they were being robbed by the tobacco buyers and the British tobacco monopoly, at the time of the revolt of the Virginia and Maryland tobacco growers; or that they as debtors, at the time of Shays' Rebellion, were being robbed by the Boston merchants who were their creditors and were being unjustly treated by lawyers and the courts who were prosecuting them for nonpayment of debts. The dramatic episodes resulting from these convictions not only expressed but generated sentiments which became carriers of the movement from area to area. The shibboleths and slogans coined during dramatic episodes became something like norms of thought which gave loose structure to the continuing movement. The philosophies, which were the ideologies expressed by the agrarian intellectuals, were probably not at first rationally understood by the average farmer or his average local leader. Nevertheless, during Jefferson's political campaign, these so-called average people called their opponents "thieves on the farmers' backs," "the fiscal crew," "stock gamblers," etc. Intellectual and political leaders, on the other hand, expressed sympathy with the farmers' protests. Jefferson believed that Shays' rebels had some just complaints, and John Taylor wrote that "The masses have always been exploited by the ruling class," and ". . . within recent times, a new class, capitalist in character, has sprung up." Andrew Jackson said, in his veto of the recharter of the United States Bank, that farmers and laborers had a right to complain of their government when laws undertook to favor the "rich and potent." [6]

Gradually the ideologies of intellectual and political agrarian leaders became better understood by an ever-increasing number of farmers who, because of this understanding, took a larger part in seeing that political leaders who shared their points of view and sentiments were elected to public office. This type of action was apparent during the Jeffersonian period and was quite evident in the Jacksonian period. By the time large general farmers' organizations came into existence, and ever since, agrarian intellectuals, agricultural philosophers, many political leaders, the representatives of large farmers' organizations, and hundreds of thousands of farmers have shared something like a common body of ideologies, sentiments, and philosophies about the role of agriculture in our commercial economy. Out of this degree of unity, they now form farmer pressure groups, farm blocs in Congress and in state legislatures, and both guide and create public opinion to buttress the Farmers' Movement.

One must, however, agree with Heberle "that mere like sentiments and like actions which occur independently among a large number of people do not constitute a movement; nor does mere imitative mass-action." That "a sense of group and solidarity is required," as Heberle asserts, is not so clearly demonstrated in the American Farmers' Movement. It is doubtful if it has been, in all of its stages, "a collective ready for action" or that "the acting individuals" who have participated in it at all stages have been "aware of the fact that they had social sentiments and goals in common" or that they thought "of themselves as being united with each other in action for a common goal," as Heberle asserts. Its structuring has

---

[6] See chap. 3.

been more tenuous, at least until its later stages. Each episode in the movement has undoubtedly had "social sentiments" among its participants, who thought of themselves as being united with each other in action for a common goal, but it probably cannot be said that this "sense of group and solidarity" [7] carried over from episode to episode. Instead, we must conclude that the American Farmers' Movement has not had such a degree of group solidarity or structure.

It is almost certain that the sentiments about issues did carry over from one episode to the next, fluctuating in intensity with the intensity of the issues with which the episodes were concerned. Furthermore, the sentiments involved or developed by each episode were shared by others than those who actively participated in the overt behavior of the episode. Each farmers' upheaval apparently developed a pronounced broader public, which included participant nonfarmers whose sympathies buttressed the farmers' cause. If, therefore, one looks for some more tangible social structure in the early stages of the American Farmers' Movement than a pattern of issues and a congeries of ideologies and sentiments, he will not find it in any one type of social collective unless it be in the nebulous form of recurrent publics.

A public is undoubtedly the most ephemeral and formless social structure known. It is not an institution, has no stable and abiding membership, no specific core or definite periphery. The adherents of publics mobilize on one or the other side of arguments, philosophies, or prejudices about issues. Not just one but many types of collective behavior are used by publics to influence the resolution of the issues which for the moment have become the gauge of battle. All of the many farmer publics which have arisen during the course of the Farmers' Movement have developed on the same issues. In that sense, the movement can be said to consist of a chain of recurrent publics.

The steps by which the Virginia and Maryland tobacco farmers' upheaval, Shays' Rebellion, and the Granger Revolt evolved are not so easily visualized as are those in the development of more recent farmer publics, which were described in detail in newspapers and magazines or which have come under personal observation. Nevertheless, information from newspapers and fugitive literature published at the time of the earlier

---

[7] All quotations are from Heberle's article previously cited.

revolts make the tracing of these steps fairly easy. The rise of the Equity Cooperative Exchange public, the Nonpartisan League public, the Mc-Nary-Haugen public, the Sapiro Cooperative Marketing public, and the violent public associated with the Farm Holiday Association were all either observed personally by the author or were quite thoroughly documented by newspaper and magazine accounts.

Some of the techniques in the mobilization of these publics are well recorded by the stories of giant parades in the Grange and Alliance periods, by the florid oratory and literature which has been recorded for most periods of farmers' upheavals, and by books and pamphlets published by partisans of these publics. Previous chapters have given many citations on these. It is possible to document the steps and the timing with which peripheral segments of the population were drawn into these publics. Similarly, it is possible to identify the counterparts of these publics, that is, the organized efforts against them, or at least attempts to dilute them. Shays' rebels were told by some newspapers to make more of pearl ash and sell it to pay their debts. The Alliances and Populists were told to "raise more hogs and less hell." An actual countermovement called "Better Farming in North Dakota" was introduced to dilute the Nonpartisan League public.

The numerous types of activity and forms of organization used by farmers to develop and implement their various publics furnish a commentary on the futility of trying categorically to conceptualize their social forms. They used local meetings by the hundreds of thousands, staged mammoth parades, held mass meetings, organized secret societies, passed resolutions, organized economic enterprises, entered politics, and organized political parties. In the case of the Virginia-Maryland tobacco growers' revolt, Shays' Rebellion, the Whiskey Rebellion, the Kentucky and Tennessee Night Riders, and the Farmers' Holiday Association, they practiced direct action of a violent sort. Since 1870, they have operated principally through general farmers' organizations and cooperative marketing associations. It could hardly be said, however, that these organizations constitute the social structure of the Farmers' Movement, because politicians, columnists and editors, intellectuals, and government are not members of these organizations, but are parties to the publics which constitute the loose social structure of the movement.

For the period of the last seventy-five years, it is possible to know precisely the connecting links between episodic publics, and thus see at least the shadow of a continuous farmer public. The Farmers' Alliance in its Declaration of Purposes in 1880 actually copied phrases from the Grange declaration of purposes formulated in 1874. Newt Gresham, founder of the Farmers' Union, in 1902, had been a Farmers' Alliance organizer in the 1880's, and Barrett, in his "Biographical Sketches" of state and national Union leaders, mentions the Alliance membership of many of them, and even Grange membership of some of them.[8] It cannot be maintained, however, that the continuity of the Farmers' Movement was sustained solely or largely by these types of connecting links. There is little evidence that such links existed before the time when farmers' clubs and associations fed the Granger movement. Furthermore, it has been the author's observation over a period of thirty-five years that leaders of general farmers' organizations have relatively little knowledge of either the structure or tactics of earlier farmers' organizations.

Some may argue that the body of phenomena described in this book does not in fact constitute a movement. But there is need for some term and some concepts by the use of which to classify and make meaningful such phenomena. The concepts used here in an attempt to do this would seem to be useful also in analyzing the American Labor and Suffrage movements, and probably also in analyzing the Abolition and Prohibition movements. Such concepts separate "movements" from mere reform and utopian episodes and ideologies, and from other ideologies which are often called movements only because they gain an increasing number of adherents.

Our concept implies that a continuous, and probably a progressive, adaptation to economic and cultural situations is accomplished by a movement. It implies that upheavals not tending toward this end turn out to be unrelated and therefore episodic events. In the American Farmers' Movement, the expressed animus or sentiments of the farmers in all of the dramatic episodes which have marked its course were against the same situation or conditions; and their intellectual leaders, all through the long period, expressed ideologies and philosophies which buttressed the farmers' opinions and sentiments about these conditions. These, and the basic issues at stake, provided continuity to the movement. Its ideologies or

---

[8] Barrett, *The mission, history, and times of the Farmers' Union*, pp. 259-414.

philosophies, its arguments about and apparent understanding of the issues, and its organized attack on these issues have evolved in ways that warrant being characterized as progressive adaptations. Ideologies which were at one time little more than sentiments against other sectors of our society's economy and culture now rest forthrightly on attempts to attain "equality" or "parity" in the society's economy and culture. They had to be progressive adaptations because the evolution of this economy was greatly accelerated by the advent of the Industrial Revolution, and it was inevitable that American agriculture should become more and more deeply involved in and concerned about prices and markets, and in due time about finances and credits, taxes, and other functions of government.

The American Farmers' Movement has therefore continued and still continues. It is not so much a social structure as it is a body of ideologies and sentiments about a continuing set of issues. These were the issues of an evolving social order, society, or economy. The movement has been, and is most precisely observed in, the dramatic episodes marking its course, because they clearly reveal the issues about which it revolves and the ideologies and sentiments which constitute its norms. These ideologics and sentiments did not arise anew with each farmer upheaval; they have been in existence in all of the periods between episodes and are still in existence. They are the norms of the current powerful farmer public, which is sustained by farmers' organizations, farmer pressure groups, farm journalists, columnists and editors, congressmen and senators from rural areas, and government programs. All of these are still attempting to resolve the same issues with which the farmers of America have wrestled as they have become increasingly conscious of their increasing involvement in the commercial economy of modern society. In a highly static society, the issues would have to be attacked and resolved by revolution or not attacked at all. In a dynamic society, which assumes that change is inevitable, and encourages the masses to initiate change by democratic methods, the issues are attacked and their resolution attempted by means of movements. Today many of the adherents of the Farmers' Movement are highly intelligent about this inevitable involvement, but the issues still exist and the movement continues.

SELECTIVE BIBLIOGRAPHY

This is a highly selective bibliography, listed for the purpose of aiding teachers of college courses who may themselves want to do additional reading, or who may want to assign additional reading to their students. It therefore includes, chiefly, documents that are fairly easily obtainable. The exception to this is the inclusion of some fugitive books—that is, books printed by agencies and publishers that no longer exist—which are quite important for special periods in the Farmers' Movement.

Aiken, D. Wyatt, *The Grange: its origin, progress, and educational purposes.* United States Department of Agriculture, Special Report No. 55. Washington, D. C.: Government Printing Office, 1883.

Allen, E. A., *The life and public services of James Baird Weaver . . . [and] James G. Field.* People's Party Publishing Company, 1892.

Allen, Leonard L., *History of New York State Grange.* Watertown, New York: Hungerford-Holbrook Company, 1934.

American annual cyclopaedia and register of important events of the year, 1873-1908. New York: Appleton-Century-Crofts, Inc.

Arnett, A. M., *The Populist movement in Georgia.* New York: Columbia University Press, 1922.

Ashby, N. B., *The riddle of the sphinx.* Chicago: Mercantile Publishing and Advertising Company, 1892.

Atkeson, T. C., *Semi-centennial history of the Patrons of Husbandry.* New York: Orange Judd Publishing Company, 1916.

Bahmer, R. H., "The American Society of Equity," *Agricultural History,* XIV (January, 1940), 33-63.

Barr, Elizabeth N., "The Populist Uprising," in William Connelly, ed., *A standard history of Kansas and Kansans,* Vol. II. New York: Lewis Historical Publishing Company, 1918.

Barrett, C. S., *The mission, history, and times of the Farmers' Union.* Nashville, Tennessee: Marshall and Bruce Company, 1909.

———, *Uncle Reuben in Washington.* Washington, D. C.: Farmers' National Publishing Company, 1923.

Bemis, E. W., "The Discontent of the Farmer," *Journal of Political Economy,* I (March, 1893), 193-216.

Bidwell, Percy W., "The Agricultural Revolution in New England," *American Historical Review,* XXVI (July, 1921), 683-702.

Bland, T. W., *The Spartan band.* Washington, D. C.: R. H. Darby, 1879.

Bliss, Wm. D. P., ed., *The encyclopedia of social reform,* pp. 605-611. New York: Funk & Wagnalls Company, 1897.

Blood, F. G., *Handbook and history of the National Farmers' Alliance and Industrial Union.* Washington, D. C.: 1893.

Blumer, H., "Social Movements," chap. xxii in Park, R. E., *The outline of the principles of sociology.* New York: Barnes & Noble, Inc., 1939.

Bowers, Claude G., *Jefferson and Hamilton: the struggle for democracy in America.* Boston: Houghton Mifflin Company, 1925.

Boyle, J. E., "The Agrarian Movement in the Northwest," *American Economic Review,* September, 1918, p. 518.

Brackenridge, Hugh H., *Incidents of the insurrection in the western parts of Pennsylvania in the year 1794.* Philadelphia: printed by John McCulloch, 1795.

Brewton, W. W., *The life of Thomas E. Watson.* Atlanta, Georgia: published by the author, 1926.

Brinton, J. W., *Wheat and politics.* Minneapolis: Rand Tower, 1921.

Brooks, T. J., *Origin, history and principles of the Farmers' Educational and Cooperative Union of America.* Greenfield, Tennessee: National Union Print, 1908.

Bruce, A. A., *Non-partisan League,* 3rd edition. New York: The Macmillan Company, 1921.

Bryan, J. E., *The Farmers' Alliance: its origins, progress and purposes.* Fayetteville, Arkansas: 1891.

Bryan, Wm. J., *The first battle.* Chicago: W. B. Conkey Company, 1898.

Buck, S. J., *The agrarian crusade.* New Haven, Connecticut: Yale University Press, 1921.

———, "Agricultural Organization in Illinois, 1870-1880," *Illinois State Journal,* April, 1910, pp. 10-13.

———, *The Granger movement.* Cambridge, Massachusetts: Harvard University Press, 1913.

Butterfield, Kenyon L., "Farmers' Social Organizations," in L. H. Bailey, ed., *Encyclopedia of American agriculture,* Vol. IV, pp. 289-297. New York: The Macmillan Company, 1909.

Carnahan, James, "The Pennsylvania Insurrection of 1794," *New Jersey Historical Society Proceedings,* Vol. VI, pp. 115-152.

Carr, E. S., *The Patrons of Husbandry on the Pacific Coast.* San Francisco: A. L. Bancroft and Company, 1875.

Chamberlain, H. R., *The Farmers' Alliance; what it aims to accomplish.* New York: Minerva Publishing Company, 1891.

Clark, J. B., *Populism in Alabama.* Auburn, Alabama: Auburn Printing Company, 1927.

Cloud, D. C., *Monopolies and the people.* Davenport, Iowa: Day, Egbert and Fidlar, 1873.

Commons, John R., *et al*, *History of labor in the United States*. New York: The Macmillan Company, 1921.

Crane, L. E., *Newton Booth of California, his speeches and addresses*. New York: G. P. Putnam's Sons, 1894.

Crawford, J. B., *The credit mobilier of America*. Boston: C. W. Calkins & Co., 1880.

Cumberland, W. W., *Cooperative marketing*. Princeton, New Jersey: Princeton University Press, 1917.

Darrow, J. W., *Origin and early history of the order of Patrons of Industry in the United States*. Chatham, New York: Currier Print House, 1904.

Davenport, B. R., *The crime of caste in our country*. Philadelphia: Keystone Publishing Company, 1893.

Davis, A. C., *The Farmers' Educational and Cooperative Union of America*. Texarkana, Texas: *Texarkana Currier*, 1910.

Davis, Andrew M., *The Shays' Rebellion, a political aftermath*. Worcester, Massachusetts: American Antiquarian Society, 1911.

Davis, J., *Contemporary social movements*. New York: Appleton-Century-Crofts, Inc., 1930.

Delap, S. A., "The Populist party in North Carolina," *Historical papers*, Vol. XIV, pp. 40-74. Durham, North Carolina: Trinity College Historical Society, 1922.

Diggs, Annie L., "The Women in the Alliance Movement," *Arena*, VIII, (July, 1892), 161-179.

Donnelly, Ignatius, *The American people's money*. Chicago: Laird and Lee, 1895.

———, *Caesar's column*. Chicago: F. J. Schulte & Company, 1890.

Drayton, C. O., *Farmers must be cooperators*. Greenville, Illinois: Farmers' Equity Union, 1912.

Drew, F. M., "The Present Farmers' Movement," *Political Science Quarterly*, VI (June, 1891), 282-310.

Dunning, N. A., *The Farmers' Alliance history and agricultural digest*. Washington, D. C.: Alliance Publishing Company, 1891.

Emerich, C. E., "An Analysis of Agricultural Discontent in the United States," *Political Science Quarterly*, September, 1896; December, 1896; March, 1897.

Everitt, J. A., *The third power*. Indianapolis: published by the author, 1907.

Farmers' Educational and Cooperative Union of America, *Proceedings*.

Fine, N., *Labor and farmer parties in the United States, 1828-1928*. New York: Rand School of Social Science, 1928.

Fisher, C. B., *The Farmers' Union*. Studies in Economics and Sociology, No. 2. Lexington, Kentucky: University of Kentucky, 1920.

Flagg, W. C., "Historical Sketch of National Agricultural Organizations." *Proceedings of Fifth Annual Session of National Agricultural Congress.* Chicago: printed by Prairie Farmer Co., 1877.

Fossum, P. R., *The agrarian movement in North Dakota,* Johns Hopkins Studies in Historical and Political Science. Baltimore: Johns Hopkins Press, 1925.

Garvin, W. L., *History of the Grand State Farmers' Alliance of Texas.* Jacksboro, Texas: J. N. Rogers and Company, 1885.

———, and Daws, S. O., *History of the National Farmers' Alliance and Cooperative Union of America.* Jacksboro, Texas: J. N. Rogers and Company, 1887.

Gaston, H. E., *The Nonpartisan League.* New York: Harcourt, Brace and Company, 1920.

Gray, L. C., "Agricultural History," *William and Mary College Quarterly Historical Magazine,* January, 1928; August, 1930.

———, "The Market Surplus Problems of Colonial Tobacco," *Agricultural History,* January, 1928.

Hammond, M. B., *The cotton industry.* New York: The Macmillan Company, 1897.

Harvey, W. H., *Coin's financial school.* Chicago: Coin Publishing Company, 1894.

Haynes, F. E., *James Baird Weaver.* Iowa City: Iowa State Historical Society, 1919.

———, *Social politics in the United States.* Boston: Houghton Mifflin Company, 1924.

———, *Third party movements since the Civil War, with special reference to Iowa.* Iowa City: Iowa State Historical Society, 1916.

Heberle, R., "Observations on the Sociology of Social Movements," *American Sociological Review,* XIV (June, 1949), 346-357.

———, *Social movements.* New York: Appleton-Century-Crofts, Inc., 1951.

Hibbard, B. H., *Marketing agricultural products.* New York: Appleton-Century-Crofts, Inc., 1921.

Hicks, J. D., *The Populist revolt, a history of the Farmers' Alliance and the People's party.* Minneapolis: University of Minnesota, 1931.

History of the State Agricultural Society of South Carolina, 1839-1945. Columbia, South Carolina: R. L. Bryan Company, 1916.

Holland, Park, "Reminiscences of Shays' Rebellion," edited by H. G. Mitchell. *New England Magazine,* XXII (January, 1901), 538-542.

Holmes, George K., "Three Centuries of Tobacco," *Year Book of the United States Department of Agriculture, 1919,* pp. 151-175. Washington, D. C.: Government Printing Office, 1920.

Hunt, R. L., *A history of farmer movements in the Southwest, 1873-1925.* College Station, Texas: Texas A. and M. Press, 1935.

Jacobstein, Meyer, *The tobacco industry in the United States.* New York: Longmans, Green & Company, Inc., 1907.

Kelly, Oliver H., *Origin and progress of the order of Patrons of Husbandry in the United States: a history from 1866 to 1873.* Philadelphia: J. A. Wagenseller, 1875.

Knapp, J. G., *The rise of cooperative marketing.* Washington, D. C.: Farm Credit Administration, 1942.

Laidler, H. W., *Toward a Farmer-Labor party.* New York: League of Industrial Democracy, 1938.

Larrabee, Wm., *The railroad question.* Chicago: The Schulte Publishing Company, 1893.

Libby, O. G., "A study of the Greenback movement, 1876-1884," *Transactions of the Wisconsin Academy of Science, Arts, and Letters,* Vol. XII, pp. 530-543.

Loomis, C. P., "Activities of the North Carolina Farmers' Union," *North Carolina Historical Review,* Vol. VII (October, 1930).

————, "The Rise and Decline of the North Carolina Farmers' Union," *North Carolina Historical Review,* Vol. VII (September, 1929).

McCulloch-Williams, Martha, "The Tobacco War in Kentucky," *Review of Reviews,* XXXVII (February, 1908), 168-170.

McGrane, R. C., *The panic of 1837.* Chicago: The University of Chicago Press, 1924.

McKee, Thomas H., *The national conventions and platforms of all political parties, 1789-1905,* 6th edition. Baltimore: Friedenwald Company, 1906.

McMaster, John B., *A history of the people of the United States, from the Revolution to the Civil War.* New York: Appleton-Century-Crofts, Inc., 1883. Vols. I, II, and III.

McPherson, Edward, *The handbook of politics for 1874 and 1876.* Washington, D. C.: Solomons and Chapman, 1874-1876.

McVey, F. L., *The Populist movement.* New York: The Macmillan Company, 1896.

Martin, E. W., *History of the Grange movement; or the farmers' war against monopolies.* Philadelphia: National Publishing Company, 1873.

Meadows, P., "Theses on Social Movement," *Social Forces,* XXIV (May, 1946), 408-412.

Melton, L., *Plan and purpose of the Farmers' Equity Union.* Greenville, Illinois: Farmers' Equity Union, 1924.

Miller, J. G., *The black patch war.* Chapel Hill: University of North Carolina Press, 1936.

Minot, George R., *The history of the insurrection, in Massachusetts, in the year 1786.* Worcester, Massachusetts: printed by Isaac Thomas, 1788.

Morgan, W. S., *History of the Wheel and Alliance and the impending revolution.* Hardy, Arkansas: published by the author, 1889.

Nall, J. O., *The tobacco night riders of Kentucky and Tennessee, 1905-1909.* Louisville, Kentucky: The Standard Press, 1939.

National Economist. Official organ of the Southern Alliance, Washington, D. C.

National Greenback party, platform and address to the people and the clergy. Chicago: Blakely, Brown and March, printers, 1889.

Nixon, H. C., "The Populist Movement in Iowa," *Iowa Journal of History and Politics,* XXIV (January, 1926), 3-107.

Noblin, S., *Leonidas La Fayette Polk: agrarian crusader.* Chapel Hill: University of North Carolina Press, 1949.

Nonpartisan Leader. Official organ of Nonpartisan League, Fargo, North Dakota.

Nourse, E. G., and Knapp, J. G., *The cooperative marketing of livestock.* Washington, D. C.: The Brookings Institute, 1931.

Paine, A. E., *The Granger movement in Illinois.* The University Studies, Vol. I (September, 1904). Urbana, Illinois: University of Illinois, 1904.

Peffer, W. A., "The Mission of the Populist Party," *Review of Reviews,* XIV (September, 1896), 298-303.

———, "The Farmers' Defensive Movement," *Forum,* VIII (December, 1889), 464-473.

Periam, Jonathan, *The groundswell.* Cincinnati: Hannaford and Thompson, 1874.

Pierson, C. W., "The Rise of the Granger Movement," *Popular Science Monthly,* XXXII (December, 1887), 199-208.

Poe, Clarence, *How farmers cooperate and double profits.* New York: Orange Judd Publishing Company, 1916.

Powell, G. H., *Cooperation in agriculture.* New York: The Macmillan Company, 1913.

Prairie Farmer, issues of 1850-1860, Chicago, Illinois.

Proceedings of the National Grange from 1874 to 1951. National Grange, Washington, D. C.

Rice, S. A., *Farmers and workers in American politics.* New York: Columbia University Press, Vol. 113.

Rivers, G. R. R., *Captain Shays, a Populist of 1786.* Boston: Little, Brown & Company, 1897.

Robison, D. M., *Bob Taylor and the agrarian revolt in Tennessee.* Chapel Hill: University of North Carolina Press, 1935.

Russell, C. E., *The story of the Nonpartisan League.* New York: Harper & Brothers, 1920.

Saloutos, T., "The Decline of the Wisconsin Society of Equity," *Agricultural History,* XV (June, 1941).

———, "The Expansion and Decline of the Nonpartisan League in the Western Middle West, 1917-1921," *Agricultural History,* XX (October, 1946), 235-252.

———, "The Rise of the Equity Cooperative Exchange," *Mississippi Valley Historical Review,* XXXII (June, 1945).

———, "The Rise of the Nonpartisan League in North Dakota (1915-1917)," *Agricultural History,* XX (January, 1946), 43-61.

———, "The Wisconsin Society of Equity," *Agricultural History,* XIV (June, 1941), 78-90.

———, and Hicks, J. D., *Agricultural discontent in the Middle West, 1900-1939.* Madison, Wisconsin: University of Wisconsin Press, 1951.

Sanborn, J. B., *Congressional grants of land in aid of railways.* Bulletin of the University of Wisconsin, No. 30. Madison, Wisconsin: University of Wisconsin, 1899.

Schmidt, L. B., and Ross, E. D., *Readings in the economic history of American agriculture* (especially Part 3). New York: The Macmillan Company, 1925.

Scott, S. M., *The subtreasury plan and the land and loan system.* Topeka, Kansas: Hamilton Print Company, 1891.

Sheldon, W. D., *Populism in the Old Dominion.* Princeton, New Jersey: Princeton University Press, 1933.

Simkins, F. B., *The Tillman movement in South Carolina.* Durham, North Carolina: Duke University Press, 1926.

Smith, Stephe, *Grains for the Grangers.* San Francisco: Union Publishing Company, 1873.

Spearman, F. H., *The strategy of great railroads.* New York: Charles Scribner's Sons, 1904.

Steen, H., *Cooperative marketing: the golden rule in agriculture.* New York: Doubleday & Company, Inc., 1923.

Stewart, E. D., "The Populist Party in Indiana," *Indiana Magazine of History,* December, 1918; March, 1919.

Taylor, John, *An inquiry into the principles and policies of the Government of the United States.* Fredericksburg, Virginia: Green and Cady, 1814.

True, Rodney H., "Early days of the Albemarle Agricultural Society," *American Historical Association Annual Report, 1918.* Vol. I, pp. 243-259. Washington, D. C.: Government Printing Office, 1921.

Up-to-Date Farming. Files for 1901-1907. Indianapolis, Indiana.

Walker, C. Irvine, *History of the Agricultural Society of South Carolina.* Charleston, South Carolina: Agricultural Society of South Carolina, 1919.

Walker, C. S., "The Farmers' Movement." Annals, American Academy of Political and Social Science, IV (March, 1894), 790-798.

Warren, R. P., *Night rider.* Boston: Houghton Mifflin Company, 1939.

Wells, J. G., *The Grange illustrated, or Patrons' handbook.* New York: Grange Publishing Company, 1874.

White, H. K., *History of the Union Pacific Railway.* Chicago: The University of Chicago Press, 1898.

White, T., *Silver and gold.* Philadelphia: Publishers Union, 1895.

Wiest, Edward, *Agricultural organization in the United States.* Lexington, Kentucky: University of Kentucky, 1923.

Wiley, R. T., *The Whiskey Insurrection, a general view.* Elizabeth, Pennsylvania: Herald Print House, 1912.

Woodburn, J. A., *Political parties and party problems in the United States.* G. P. Putnam's Sons, 1900.

Wooddy, C. H., "Populism in Washington," *Washington Historical Quarterly,* XXI (April, 1930), 103-119.

Woodward, C. V., *Tom Watson, agrarian rebel.* New York: The Macmillan Company, 1938.

INDEX

This index lists both the participants in the Farmers' Movement and the commentators on it. The principal episodes, organizations, and publications of the first three hundred years of the Movement are given. In addition, the names of the principal authors who have contributed to this study are listed. When a person named has been prominently identified with the Movement in a particular state, the state name is shown. Because of the multiplicity of names in a work such as this, the author has been forced for lack of space to list only those authors who have been used most frequently as sources.